Edexcel Psychology for A Level Year 1 & AS

Cara Flanagan

Matt Jarvis

Rob Liddle

Julia Russell

Mandy Wood

Illuminate Publishing

Acknowledgements

The authors would like to express their appreciation to all of those people who have made this book possible and supported us during the long hours of work to produce this little gem.

At Illuminate Publishing we have the gorgeous and talented Rick Jackman who is a delight to work with – he is held in great esteem by all of us. The book is also managed by Clare Jackman, Peter Burton, Saskia Santos and Vikki Mann who each help make the company very special.

We write the text but then Nic Watson comes along and meticulously checks and cross-references all elements of the content. We are very grateful to her for her painstaking care and dedication to her work.

Our third big thanks go to the team who actually produce the printed book – Nigel Harriss is the master designer who makes our words look so elegant and appealing on the page. Sarah Clifford of Kamae Design had the job of implementing the design and has done a fabulous job of it.

Cara Flanagan is the lead author and would like to publicly thank her co-authors for keeping to a punishing schedule and managing to pull together as a team. Most particularly Cara would like to thank Julia and Mandy who have gone above and beyond authoring to craft a book full of gems of knowledge and exam advice. Until you have written a book it is difficult to appreciate what time and concentration goes into its organisation and production, and they have been the core element of this work.

In order to ensure that this resource offers high-quality support for the associated Pearson qualification, it has been through a review process by the awarding body. This process confirms that this resource fully covers the teaching and learning content of the specification or part of a specification at which it is aimed. It also confirms that it demonstrates an appropriate balance between the development of subject skills, knowledge and understanding, in addition to preparation for assessment.

Endorsement does not cover any guidance on assessment activities or processes (e.g. practice questions or advice on how to answer assessment questions), included in the resource nor does it prescribe any particular approach to the teaching or delivery of a related course.

While the publishers have made every attempt to ensure that advice on the qualification and its assessment is accurate, the official specification and associated assessment guidance materials are the only authoritative source of information and should always be referred to for definitive guidance.

Pearson examiners have not contributed to any sections in this resource relevant to examination papers for which they have responsibility.

Examiners will not use endorsed resources as a source of material for any assessment set by Pearson. Endorsement of a resource does not mean that the resource is required to achieve this Pearson qualification, nor does it mean that it is the only suitable material available to support the qualification, and any resource lists produced by the awarding body shall include this and other appropriate resources.

The authors

Cara has written many books for A level Psychology, and she speaks at and organises student conferences. In addition to books, she is senior editor of *Psychology Review*. In a previous life she was a teacher probably for more years than you have been alive and also an examiner for an equally long time. Her spare time (what there is of it) involves travelling with her husband and/or children (all now 25+). She lives in the Highlands of Scotland (despite being American by birth) and loves a long walk in the mountains and night in a bothy.

Julia has been teaching psychology for longer than a life sentence and still loves it. As well as being a Head of Psychology, she has two senior examiner roles in psychology and has authored scores of books and other resources for students and teachers. She lives in a barn on a farm and walks her mad dog whatever the weather.

Mandy has 20 years' experience of teaching psychology. She leads a thriving department, teaching A level and International Baccalaureate and runs popular workshops and training days for teachers. She did take a break for a few years and worked as a psychologist with gorgeous babies and children with Down syndrome. Mandy loves visiting her psychology friends in far-flung places and first got to know Cara on a trip to Auschwitz. When her addled brain is incapable of lucid thought, she likes to cook (Middle Eastern phase at the moment), chain-watch *Grey's Anatomy* and look at the sky. She also drinks tea, a lot of tea.

Matt is a Chartered Psychologist and Associate Fellow of the British Psychological Society. He teaches part-time, is an editor of *Psychology Review*, works as a freelance trainer and holds a Research Fellowship at Keele University. When not working (which is fairly rare) Matt likes walking in the Lake District, listening to anything by Maynard Keenan and watching anything by Joss Whedon.

Rob was an A level Psychology teacher for more than 20 years, before turning to writing. He ventured back into teaching again recently and would like to give a big shout out to his ex-colleagues at Winstanley College. In his spare moments, Rob likes nothing better than to pluck away skill-lessly at his guitar. He is enthusiastically looking forward to *Frozen 2* coming out, even though his granddaughters couldn't care less.

Published in 2018 by Illuminate Publishing Ltd, P.O. Box 1160, Cheltenham, Gloucestershire GL50 9RW

Orders: Please visit www.illuminatepublishing.com or email sales@illuminatepublishing.com

© Cara Flanagan, Matt Jarvis, Rob Liddle, Julia Russell, Mandy Wood

The moral rights of the authors have been asserted.

All rights reserved. No part of this book may be reprinted, reproduced or utilised in any form or by any electronic, mechanical, or other means, now known or hereafter invented, including photocopying and recording, or in any information storage and retrieval system, without permission in writing from the publishers.

British Library Cataloguing in Publication Data

A catalogue record for this book is available from the British Library

ISBN 978-1-911208-59-4

Printed by Cambrian Printers, Aberystwyth

05.18

The publisher's policy is to use papers that are natural, renewable and recyclable products made from wood grown in sustainable forests. The logging and manufacturing processes are expected to conform to the environmental regulations of the country of origin.

Every effort has been made to contact copyright holders of material produced in this book. Great care has been taken by the authors and publisher to ensure that either formal permission has been granted for the use of copyright material reproduced, or that copyright material has been used under the provision of fairdealing guidelines in the UK – specifically that it has been used sparingly, solely for the purpose of criticism and review, and has been properly acknowledged. If notified, the publisher will be pleased to rectify any errors or omissions at the earliest opportunity.

Editor: Nic Watson

Design: Nigel Harriss

Layout: Kamae Design

Contents

4	How to use this book	
6	Understanding the exam	Looking at different kinds of exam questions and how to answer them effectively.
20	Issues and debates	Topics that concern psychologists and are important for making the subject as valuable as it can be.
26	*Chapter 1* Social psychology	The term 'social' refers to other members of your own species. The behaviour of others influences what you do.
66	*Chapter 2* Cognitive psychology	'Cognition' is mental processes, such as thoughts and feelings, and these have a profound effect on your behaviour.
94	*Chapter 3* Biological psychology	Knowing about genes and connections between neurons helps understand our behaviour.
128	*Chapter 4* Learning theories	A group of early psychologists (called behaviourists) explained all new behaviour in terms of forming associations.
166	*Chapter 5* Research methods	Covers the methods used by psychologists to investigate behaviour, cognition and emotion and provide data to support their theories.
232	Index with glossary	
	References	A full set of references are available for download from the Illuminate Publishing website. Please visit www.illuminatepublishing.com/edexcelpsychreferences1

How to use this book

Chapters 1–4

Each chapter starts with a table of contents.

The bulk of the chapter consists of one spread for each subtopic – an example is shown on the right.

The chapters end with …

• Key question spread	Guidance on how to prepare and construct high quality answers.
• Practical investigation spread	Two ideas for practical investigations, with detailed advice.
• Revision summary	A neat pictorial representation reminding you what has been covered.
• Exam questions with student answers and comments	Sample answers from students with comments on what is good and bad.
• Multiple-choice questions	Four questions on each spread to test your knowledge.

Research methods

Almost all the research methods content for both year 1 and year 2 is covered in chapter 5.

The chapter follows the order of topics in the specification for social, cognitive and biological psychology and learning theories.

This chapter ends with:
- Revision summary
- Exam questions with student answers and comments
- Multiple-choice questions

A typical main spread

Each spread deals with one subtopic. There is an overview of all the spreads in the **revision summary** at the end of the chapter.

This is the bit in the **specification** that we are covering on this spread.

Key terms in the specification defined. Other terms on the spread can be found defined in the glossary at the end of the book (with the index).

Stretch and challenge yourself and enhance your understanding of the subtopic. This ends with a question to help you think more deeply.

Main descriptive content (AO1) We have usually divided this into four sections to help you structure your knowledge.

Think link to developmental psychology or individual differences.

The specification requires that students consider both of these links throughout each topic.

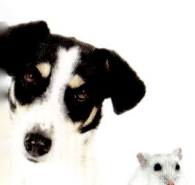

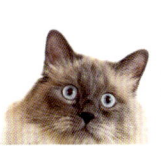

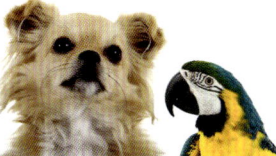

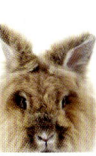

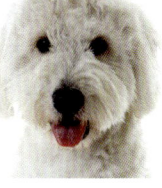

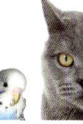

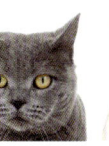

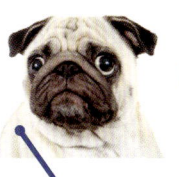

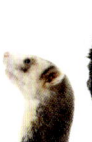

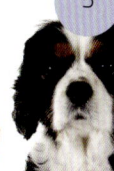

The evaluation (AO3)

There are always at least four points:

- One strength.
- One weakness.
- One practical application.
- One issue/debate.
- (Plus one competing argument.)

In an 8-mark question you may only need two of these including a competing argument – see exam advice on page 16.

Remember 'less is more'. What counts is well-developed and logical evaluation, containing logical chains of reasoning throughout.

To help you we have structured each evaluation point:

P – Identify the **Point** to be made.

E – **Elaborate** the point. Which can be done with an **Example**, or some **Evidence** or an **Explanation**.

T – End with a link back to the essay title and/or give a conclusion: '**This** suggests ...' '**Therefore** ...' 'This means ...'

What do we want?

PETS.

Where do we want them?

IN EXAM ANSWERS.

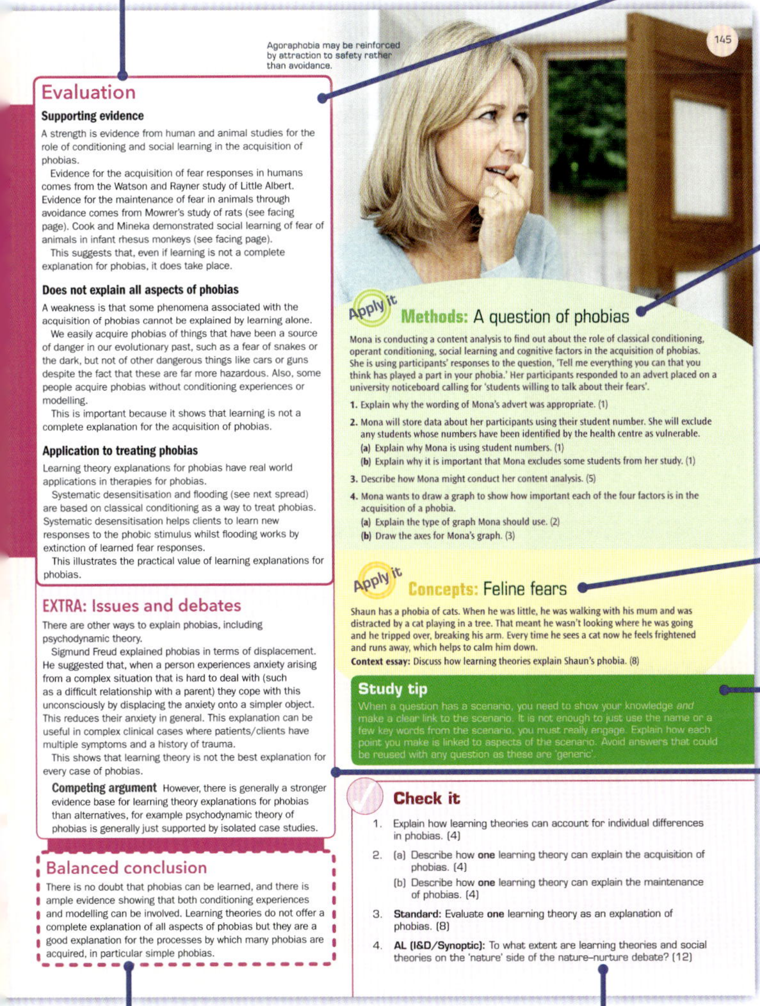

145

Agoraphobia may be reinforced by attraction to safety rather than avoidance.

Evaluation

Supporting evidence

A strength is evidence from human and animal studies for the role of conditioning and social learning in the acquisition of phobias.

Evidence for the acquisition of fear responses in humans comes from the Watson and Rayner study of Little Albert. Evidence for the maintenance of fear in animals through avoidance comes from Mowrer's study of rats (see facing page). Cook and Mineka demonstrated social learning of fear of animals in infant rhesus monkeys (see facing page).

This suggests that, even if learning is not a complete explanation for phobias, it does take place.

Does not explain all aspects of phobias

A weakness is that some phenomena associated with the acquisition of phobias cannot be explained by learning alone.

We easily acquire phobias of things that have been a source of danger in our evolutionary past, such as a fear of snakes or the dark, but not of other dangerous things like cars or guns despite the fact that these are far more hazardous. Also, some people acquire phobias without conditioning experiences or modelling.

This is important because it shows that learning is not a complete explanation for the acquisition of phobias.

Application to treating phobias

Learning theory explanations for phobias have real world applications in therapies for phobias.

Systematic desensitisation and flooding (see next spread) are based on classical conditioning as a way to treat phobias. Systematic desensitisation helps clients to learn new responses to the phobic stimulus whilst flooding works by extinction of learned fear responses.

This illustrates the practical value of learning explanations for phobias.

EXTRA: Issues and debates

There are other ways to explain phobias, including psychodynamic theory.

Sigmund Freud explained phobias in terms of displacement. He suggested that, when a person experiences anxiety arising from a complex situation that is hard to deal with (such as a difficult relationship with a parent) they cope with this unconsciously by displacing the anxiety onto a simpler object. This reduces their anxiety in general. This explanation can be useful in complex clinical cases where patients/clients have multiple symptoms and a history of trauma.

This shows that learning theory is not the best explanation for every case of phobias.

Competing argument However, there is generally a stronger evidence base for learning theory explanations for phobias than alternatives, for example psychodynamic theory of phobias is generally just supported by isolated case studies.

Balanced conclusion

There is no doubt that phobias can be learned, and there is ample evidence showing that both conditioning experiences and modelling can be involved. Learning theories do not offer a complete explanation of all aspects of phobias but they are a good explanation for the processes by which many phobias are acquired, in particular simple phobias.

Apply it **Methods:** A question of phobias

Mona is conducting a content analysis to find out about the role of classical conditioning, operant conditioning, social learning and cognitive factors in the acquisition of phobias. She is using participants' responses to the question, 'Tell me everything you can that you think has played a part in your phobia.' Her participants responded to an advert placed on a university noticeboard calling for 'students willing to talk about their fears'.

1. Explain why the wording of Mona's advert was appropriate. (1)
2. Mona will store data about her participants using their student number. She will exclude any students whose numbers have been identified by the health centre as vulnerable.
   (a) Explain why Mona is using student numbers. (1)
   (b) Explain why it is important that Mona excludes some students from her study. (1)
3. Describe how Mona might conduct her content analysis. (5)
4. Mona wants to draw a graph to show how important each of the four factors is in the acquisition of a phobia.
   (a) Explain the type of graph Mona should use. (2)
   (b) Draw the axes for Mona's graph. (3)

Apply it **Concepts:** Feline fears

Shaun has a phobia of cats. When he was little, he was walking with his mum and was distracted by a cat playing in a tree. That meant he wasn't looking where he was going and he tripped over, breaking his arm. Every time he sees a cat now he feels frightened and runs away, which helps to calm him down.

Context essay: Discuss how learning theories explain Shaun's phobia. (8)

Study tip

When a question has a scenario, you need to show your knowledge *and* make a clear link to the scenario. It is not enough to just use the name or a few key words from the scenario, you must really engage. Explain how each point you make is linked to aspects of the scenario. Avoid answers that could be reused with any question as these are 'generic'.

Check it

1. Explain how learning theories can account for individual differences in phobias. (4)
2. (a) Describe how **one** learning theory can explain the acquisition of phobias. (4)
   (b) Describe how **one** learning theory can explain the maintenance of phobias. (4)
3. **Standard:** Evaluate **one** learning theory as an explanation of phobias. (8)
4. **AL (I&D/Synoptic):** To what extent are learning theories and social theories on the 'nature' side of the nature–nurture debate? (12)

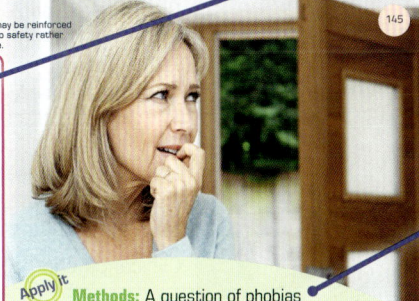

Apply it – methods (AO2)

An opportunity to practise your research methods knowledge applied to this subtopic.

This is important because research methods questions are scattered throughout your exams. These questions have a scenario and you must apply your knowledge of research methods. The more you practise the better you will get.

Apply it – concepts (AO2)

There are other scenario questions in the exam where your understanding of subtopics is assessed. These questions may be short (just a few marks) or may be essays. You can read advice about these on pages 10 and 11.

Study tip

Advice for you from experienced teachers and examiners.

An extra point of evaluation to help you link each subtopic to **issues and debates**.

Remember, there are always two aspects to giving good answers in exams.

First, you need to 'know your stuff'. This involves more than just memorising the information – you need to understand it and we explain all the ideas you will need clearly.

Second, you need to be able to use your knowledge to answer questions. This book will help you with that too. The layout makes the knowledge you need to use for different questions (such as describing, looking at strengths and weaknesses, etc) very clear and there are plenty of questions to give you practice.

You are expected to provide a **balanced conclusion** in most extended writing questions. We give you our thoughts on what you might include.

You can provide conclusions at the end of each evaluation point (as we have done) and that may help satisfy the criteria in some essays to include a conclusion (see page 13).

In this **Check it** box we have given a few example exam-style questions – we cannot hope to cover every possible question but just give a flavour of the kind of thing you might expect on this subtopic.

Questions 1 and 2 are SHORT ANSWER QUESTIONS.

Question 3 is a STANDARD ESSAY on the subtopic.

Question 4 is a special essay, e.g. METHODS, I&D, SYNOPTIC – these essay types are explained on pages 17 and 18.

DON'T FORGET

There are shorter chapters on understanding exams (pages 6–19) and issues and debates (pages 20–25).

And, at the end of the book, there is a glossary combined with the index.

Understanding the exam

Overview of the exam

AS level

Paper 1 **Social and cognitive psychology** 1½ hours 70 marks 50% of total qualification	Section A Social psychology	29 marks, mixed question types.
	Section B Cognitive psychology	29 marks, mixed question types.
	Section C Social and cognitive psychology	12 marks, ERQ covering both social and cognitive psychology.
Paper 2 **Biological psychology and learning theories** 1½ hours 70 marks 50% of total qualification	Section A Biological psychology	29 marks, mixed question types.
	Section B Learning theories	29 marks, mixed question types.
	Section C Biological psychology and learning theories	12 marks, ERQ covering both biological psychology and learning theories.

A level (AL)

Paper 1 **Foundations in psychology** 2 hours 90 marks 35% of total qualification	Section A Social psychology	70 marks, mixed question types.
	Section B Cognitive psychology	
	Section C Biological psychology	
	Section D Learning theories	
	Section E Issues and debates	20 marks, two ERQs.
Paper 2 **Applications of psychology** 2 hours 90 marks 35% of total qualification	Section A Clinical psychology	54 marks, mixed question types.
	Section B Choose one from three optional topics: • Criminological psychology • Child psychology • Health psychology	36 marks, mixed question types.
Paper 3 **Psychological skills** 2 hours 80 marks 30% of total qualification	Section A Research methods	24 marks, mixed question types.
	Section B Psychological and classic studies	24 marks, mixed question types on psychological studies and one ERQ on classic studies from Paper 1 and from Clinical psychology.
	Section C Issues and debates	32 marks, two ERQs.

Exam question styles

Both AS and AL contain similar question styles and these tend to fall into two main categories:

1. **Short answer questions (SAQs)** Marks range from 1 to 7 and are awarded for each 'creditworthy' idea.
2. **Extended response questions** (ERQs), often called 'essays'. Marks range from 8 to 20 and these questions always have an evaluative component. They are level-marked, meaning the examiner will compare your answer to sets of descriptors and choose the set which best describe your essay. This is explained on page 15.

Both SAQs and ERQs include the following types of question:

Application questions

These begin with a short description of a 'real life' situation or context. These are sometimes called 'scenario' questions. They may be SAQs (see page 10) or ERQs (see pages 17 and 19).

For example:

Karen is a regular at Millstones bookstore. She gets her 'loyalty card' stamped every time she makes a purchase. She gets a £10 voucher for every ten stamps.

Describe how Millstones could use **two** schedules of reinforcement to tempt customers to buy more books. (4)

Some questions look like application questions but are not. The 'stem' is just a prompt.

For example:

There are many research studies that have used animals within psychology.

Explain the practical issues of using animals in psychological research. (4)

Research methods questions

These obviously assess your knowledge of research methods and may appear anywhere in the exam. They may or may not begin with a scenario.

These are discussed on page 11.

For example:

Describe **one** key feature of the case study as a research method in cognitive psychology. (2)

Assess the usefulness of twin studies as a research method in biological psychology. (8)

Synoptic questions

These require you to draw on ideas from multiple areas of the specification. These are found in AS Papers 1 and 2 (Section C) and AL Papers 1 (Section E) and 3 (Sections B and C).

For example:

To what extent can the classic studies from social and cognitive psychology (Sherif et al. 1954/1961 and Baddeley et al. 1966b) be considered reliable? (12)

Assessment objectives

Your exam answers are assessed in terms of three skills:

AO1 Description This is explained on page 8–9.

Demonstrate knowledge and understanding of scientific ideas, processes, techniques and procedures.

AO2 Application This is explained on pages 10–11.

Apply knowledge and understanding of scientific ideas, processes, techniques and procedures: in a theoretical context, in a practical context, when handling qualitative data and when handling quantitative data.

AO3 Evaluation and analysis This is explained on pages 12–13.

Analyse, interpret and evaluate scientific information, ideas and evidence, including in relation to issues, to make judgements and reach conclusions and to develop and refine practical design and procedures.

Command words

In all exam questions there are command words (listed below) which tell you what you are required to do in the exam question. This list is provided by Edexcel.

Analyse	Break something down into its components/parts. Examine each part methodically and in detail in order to discover the meaning or essential features of a theme, topic or situation. Explore the relationship between the features and how each one contributes to the topic.
Assess	Give careful consideration to all the factors or events that apply and identify which are the most important or relevant. Make a judgement on the importance of something, and come to a conclusion where needed.
Calculate	Obtain a numerical answer, showing relevant working. If the answer has a unit, this must be included.
Compare	Looking for the similarities and differences of two (or more) things. This should not require the drawing of a conclusion. The answer must relate to both (or all) things mentioned in the question. The answer must include at least one similarity and one difference.
Complete	To fill in/write all the details asked for.
Convert	Express a quantity in alternative units.
Define	Provide a definition of something.
Describe	To give an account of something. Statements in the response need to be developed as they are often linked but do not need to include a justification or reason.
Determine	The answer must have an element that is quantitative from the stimulus provided, or must show how the answer can be reached quantitatively. To gain maximum marks there must be a quantitative element to the answer.
Discuss	Explore the issue/situation/problem/argument that is being presented within the question, articulating different or contrasting viewpoints.
Draw	Produce an output, either by freehand or using a ruler (e.g. graph).
Evaluate	Review information then bring it together to form a conclusion, drawing on evidence including strengths, weaknesses, alternative actions, relevant data or information. Come to a supported judgement of a subject's qualities and relation to its context.
Explain	An explanation that requires a justification/exemplification of a point. The answer must contain some element of reasoning/justification. This can include mathematical explanations.
Give	Generally involves the recall of one or more pieces of information; when used in relation to a context, it is used to determine a candidate's grasp of the factual information presented.
Identify	This requires some key information to be selected from a given stimulus/resource.
Interpret	Recognise a trend or pattern(s) within a given stimulus/resource.
Justify	Rationalise a decision or action.
Name	Synonymous with 'Give'.
Plot	Produce, or add detail to, a graph/chart by marking points accurately (e.g. line of best fit).
Predict	Articulate an expected result.
State	Synonymous with 'Give'.
Suggest	Make a proposal/propose an idea in written form.
To what extent	Review information, then bring it together to form a judgement conclusion, following the provision of a balanced and reasoned argument.

Understanding description (AO1)

8 Understanding the exam

In order to answer exam questions successfully you need to understand certain skills. We start by looking at *description skills*. What is it you have to do when you *describe* something?

Think of describing an orange. You might say – *it is round and orange* – which is true but that is a rather *limited* description.

A better description would include more *detail* – *The skin is a little squishy and pockmarked. The remains of the green stalk are set in a dimple. The inside is divided into segments of very juicy flesh.*

To do well at description you need to grasp this concept of *detail*.

Describing concepts

Short answer questions (SAQs) may concern concepts. One of the first concepts in this book is *obedience*.

This is what we have written:

Obedience – A form of social influence in which an individual follows a direct order. The person issuing the order is usually a figure of authority who has the power to punish when obedient behaviour is not forthcoming. There is usually the assumption that the person receiving the order is made to respond in a way they would not otherwise have done.

If you were asked to describe this concept for *1 mark* you might write:

Obedience is when a person follows a direct order from an authority figure.

This is a *basic* answer.

If you were asked to describe this concept for *2 marks* you might write:

Obedience is when a person follows a direct order from an authority figure. This usually entails doing something that they would not otherwise have chosen to do.

This answer provides two points. The number of points made should equal the number of marks available (see top of facing page).

Example questions

- Define what is meant by the term 'unconditioned response (UCR)'. (1)
- Give examples of information that might be stored as an episodic memory and as a semantic memory. (2)
- Explain the process of synaptic transmission. (3)

Describing research studies

SAQs may also relate to research studies. Each of the foundation topics requires you to know at least two studies in detail (a classic and a contemporary study). Some topics also include other studies (e.g. Milgram and Pavlov).

For these studies you need to know the aim, procedure, findings and conclusions in detail.

Aims One or two sentences should be sufficient to explain the study's main objectives.

Procedures This can include details about the research method, variables, design, sample, controls, ethical considerations, materials and, most importantly, what the participants actually had to do. You should prepare about six key points.

Findings You should identify about four key points and try to include exact figures for quantitative data. Knowing how the figures relate to each other is important, e.g. quoting two means (one for each condition of an experiment) would not necessarily gain you two marks as it is the *relationship* between the figures which is important. If you are asked to explain findings, state what the findings are and then say why this is important with regard to the hypothesis.

Conclusions Report the researcher's conclusions – not your conclusions. A conclusion is a statement about what the findings mean ('This shows that …') which is linked back to the aims and hypotheses.

Example questions

- Describe the aim of Sherif *et al.*'s Robbers Cave Experiment (1954/61). (2)
- Describe the procedure of **one** contemporary study from cognitive psychology. (5)
- Explain Raine *et al.*'s (1997) findings. (4)
- Describe the conclusion(s) of **one** contemporary study for the learning topic. (2)
- Describe **one** contemporary study from social psychology. (5)

Timing

In the AS exams there are 70 marks for each paper and you have 90 minutes. In the AL exams all three papers are 2 hours long and there are 90 marks available on Papers 1 and 2 and 80 marks available on Paper 3.

Dividing the time equally across the paper would give you 1 minute 20 seconds per mark which gives you 11 minutes for an 8-mark essay. Spending a bit longer on these will probably pay off – but not more than 15 minutes!

Start every question by circling the mark allocation in order to work out how long you can spend on the question. It's really important to keep an eye on the time, all the time. Writing too much on one question could jeopardise your chances of finishing the paper – and then you risk losing many marks.

Researcher's names

The convention, when referring to a study, is to give the first researcher's last name and the date of the study. If you can't remember the name but you do know the study, just get stuck in with what you do know, and try not to worry! However, knowing the name ensures that the reader knows which study you are describing – otherwise you might not perform so well because the reader can't tell which specific study you are referring to.

Research dates

Again if you know the date, great! But don't worry too much if you don't. The important thing is knowing how studies relate to each other over time.

A special note

Research studies can also be used when writing evaluation. In this situation, you will need to focus on findings/conclusions of the studies and show how they either support or refute the explanation you are discussing. You might also find research studies are helpful when you are asked to explain a scenario but in this case always make sure you have made clear links between aspects of the study and the scenario.

How much should I write?

Match the number of points you make to the number of marks available.

Check out this example of a mark scheme to get an idea of what this looks like in practice. Notice how you have to make quite a detailed point for each mark. Also be aware that this list is an example – any four accurate and relevant points in a similar amount of detail would be creditworthy.

> *Describe the multi-store model of memory. (4)*
>
> One mark for each point describing the multi-store model. For example:
> - Information primarily enters the system through a sensory experience and into the sensory register which is modality specific (1).
> - Information is then passed to short-term memory where it can be held for around 18–30 seconds before it decays (1).
> - If this data is rehearsed to maintain the information it can be transferred to long-term memory (1).
> - Long-term memory is said to have a potentially infinite capacity and duration (1).
>
> From AL Paper 1, June 2017, question 4

Describing theories

SAQs may require you to describe a theory (model or explanation). In this book we have generally identified four key features for every theory. If you can write something for each of these four features that should enable you to describe a theory well.

If the question is worth 2 marks then only write about two of the features. However, note that if the features are linked (for example, writing about capacity and duration in the context of the multi-store model), they only jointly count as one feature. There must be two *distinct* points.

If the question is worth 5 marks then you need to provide a bit of extra information for one of the features.

Example questions
- Describe **two** features of agency theory. (2)
- Describe how **one** human behaviour can be explained using evolution and/or natural selection. (2)
- Describe social learning theory as an explanation of human behaviour. (4)

Describing key questions

In each of the four foundation topics you need to prepare an answer on a key question.

If you are asked to *describe* your key question for 4 marks (an SAQ), you need to do just that. You do not need to apply any psychological theories or back your ideas up with research evidence, you simply need to describe the key question.

Let's imagine your key question is 'Should schools do more to educate pupils and parents about the possible effects of playing violent video games?'. In a 4-mark answer you could include information about:

- Why such games are popular and with whom. Maybe include some statistics to back this up such as the number of sales of a particular game.
- Why people are worried about this issue. You could relate to a high profile case in the news about a crime committed by someone who played a lot of violent video games.
- What will happen if this question goes unanswered. Might more crimes be committed? Could more people be injured/lose their lives?
- Why directly educating pupils and parents might be helpful and why this ought to be the school's responsibility.

Describing your practical investigation You may also be asked an AO1 question about this.

Creating a well organised response

On the right is chaos – the floor of a badly organised bedroom – where you have to search high and low to find things. Teachers often feel like this when reading student answers. Ordering the information in your answer logically requires a little thought before you get started but it could make a lot of difference. Each point should follow systematically from the last. Try to avoid randomly dumping everything you know onto the page as it makes it hard to find the marks, just like a messy bedroom!

Good description

Good description needs to be **accurate** and **thorough**. You should demonstrate your **understanding**. A creditworthy point will also be **clear** and **coherent** using appropriate **specialist terminology**.

What is meant by *accurate* and *thorough*?

Being correct. If you write something that is wrong, you can't expect to be credited for it. It is important that you write in plain and simple language in order to convey your knowledge and understanding precisely and concisely.

Your answers need to be thorough and specific. This does not always mean writing lots. Instead it means including the small pieces of information that really bring your answer into focus. For example:

> *Information is then passed to short-term memory which is very limited and information can be forgotten easily.*
>
> *Information is then passed to short-term memory where it can be held for around 18–30 seconds before it decays.*

The second answer is more detailed and thus more thorough but not much longer.

When describing findings try to include numerical information, for example compare these two answers:

> *By Stage 3, the number of friends drawn from the outgroup had increased significantly.*
>
> *By Stage 3, the number of friends drawn from the outgroup had increased from 6.4% to 36.4% for the Rattlers.*

What is meant by *understanding*?

It is important that you do understand what is written in this book and don't simply try to memorise it. One way to do this is to read what is in the textbook for each feature of, for example, a theory or study and then close the book and try to summarise it in one sentence. This makes you process the meaning.

What is meant by *clear* and *coherent*?

Clarity is achieved by writing short sentences that can be easily understood by someone else. Clarity is improved by coherence, where one sentence links obviously to the sentence that came before it.

What is meant by *specialist terminology*?

Take care to learn the meanings of the specialist words for any topic so you can use them effectively in your descriptions. This provides detail in your answers.

However, just dropping terms into your answers will not earn marks. Make sure you are using them correctly and explaining them when necessary.

Chaos.

Understanding application (AO2)

We will now move on to the second of the skills, *application*.

The trick of the application questions is that you are required to *apply* what you have learned about psychological concepts, studies and theories – to a **stem**, also known as the **context** or **scenario**.

Imagine the following scenario …

It is a dark night with a thin sliver of moon and ink black clouds. The wind is starting to get stronger. You walk home down a street with no lights and suddenly …

A scenario is a scene – it's context. You now have a chance to put your psychology into action. This kind of question is intended to be something that tests your real understanding of psychology.

You should become brilliant at this because we have provided lots and lots of practice throughout this book.

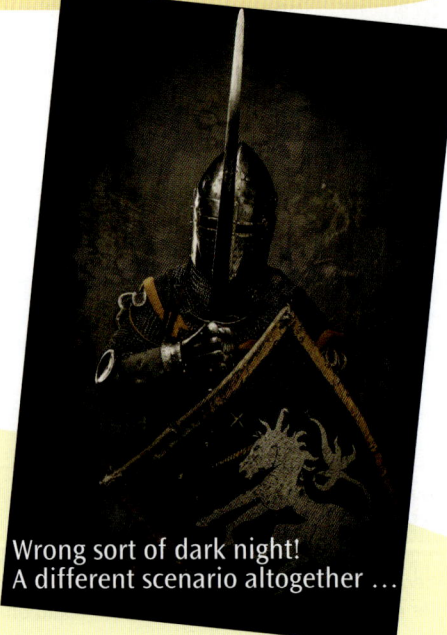

Wrong sort of dark night! A different scenario altogether …

 **Concepts:**

On every main spread of this book we have an **Apply it – concepts** box, with lots of examples of a scenario and a question (or questions).

In chapter 1 we discuss social identity theory (SIT).

> 'Donate not Hate' are a charity that help refugees. They have a web page where people can show their support and join the group at the click of a button. However, the page also attracts attention from people who are anti-refugees and leave nasty comments. Sometimes, the page supporters retaliate with equally aggressive comments.
>
> Using concepts from social identity theory, explain why tensions arise between groups of people in situations such as this. (4)

The context or 'scenario' above contains a number of 'hooks' or ideas that you might be able to relate to features of the theory. It provides you with a context for your answer.

You would need to make four points in answer to this question, because the question is worth 4 marks.

It is critical that *every* point combines material from the scenario with your understanding of social identity theory in order to gain credit.

Your first point might say something like…

As soon as people click to join the 'Donate not Hate' group-chat they are going through social categorisation, meaning they will now see other group members as part of their ingroup.

The point combines material from the scenario with features of SIT:

Scenario material: Focus on 'Donate not Hate', joining the web pages, refugees, donating aid, negative comments.

Features of SIT: Focus on ingroups and outgroups, social categorisation, social identification and social comparison, self-esteem, social selves etc.

Some scenarios are shorter.

For example, in chapter 4 we discuss phobias.

> Gladys has a phobia of pineapples.
>
> Describe how Gladys' phobia of pineapples could be treated using systematic desensitisation. (3)

Your first point might say something like…

Gladys' therapist will try to help her to relax when she sees a pineapple by teaching her breathing exercises or using aromatherapy.

The point combines material from the scenario with aspects of systematic desensitisation:

Scenario material: Focus on Gladys and treating her phobia of pineapples.

Features of systematic desensitisation: Focus on fear hierarchy, reciprocal inhibition, relaxation techniques, stages of classical conditioning.

You can read marked examples on page 162.

Explain questions

All questions that have the word 'explain' require justification (explain why) or exemplification (give an example).

Such questions may be AO1 or AO2 – but that is not important, what is important is that when you see the command word 'explain', you must add a justification or example. This is highlighted in yellow below.

Using a justification to turn a description into an explanation

Explain **one** weakness of classical conditioning as a theory of human learning. (3)

One weakness of classical conditioning is that much of the support for this theory comes from animal experiments. *This is a weakness because adults with classically conditioned fear responses, for example, can consciously control their fear using strategies such as positive self-talk ('this can't hurt me'). This suggests that classical conditioning is flawed as a theory of human learning as it does not take account of the role of cognition.*

Using an example to turn a description into an explanation

Explain **one** feature of social identity theory. (3)

Social identification occurs when an individual begins to adopt the beliefs, values and attitudes of the group that they see themselves as belonging to, that is the ingroup. They may also start to change their behaviour and appearance in line with group norms in order to gain acceptance from the group. *One example of this is when the Rattler boys in Sherif's Robbers Cave began swearing more, crying less and acting tough to fit in with the others as they started to bond as a group.*

 **Methods**

A minimum of 25% of your exam questions will assess skills in relation to research methods and most of these questions require you to apply your knowledge of research methods to a scenario. So we have provided lots of examples – on every main spread of this book we have an **Apply it – methods** box.

For example:

> Agnes was very interested by the comments on the 'Donate not Hate' web page and decided to attend a donation event where people were dropping off food and clothing to be taken overseas. She conducted semi-structured interviews with some of the supporters. She asked questions about their attitudes towards refugees and how they felt about people who are opposed to the campaign.
>
> Explain **one** way that Agnes might prepare for her semi-structured interviews. (2)

The description of the research study is the scenario. It again provides the context for your answer.

For example, when studying research methods you will learn about semi-structured interviews. You need to use that knowledge in the context of this research study.

Answering **Apply it – methods** is different from **Apply it – concepts**. This time there are two parts to a 2-mark answer:

- Identify: Suggest one idea about *how* Agnes might prepare for the interviews.
- Justify: Explain *why* she would do this.

For example:

IDENTIFY

> To prepare for the interviews Agnes might have searched through the 'Donate not Hate' web page comments thread to get ideas for the open and closed questions that she will use to guide the semi-structured interview. (This is the *how* bit.)

JUSTIFY

> This ensures her questions are relevant as they are based on actual comments from ingroup members rather than Agnes' preconceptions, meaning her data will be more valid.
> (This is the *why* bit.)

Notice that each time you have to link the scenario material to your knowledge of the specific area of psychology.

There are marked examples of research methods questions on pages 226–227.

What do students do wrong in research methods questions?

Ethics – Not elaborating sufficiently. Try to explain ethical considerations by linking them together, e.g. lack of informed consent is a problem because, without it, participants are at greater risk of psychological harm.

Graphs and tables – Dashing off graphs too quickly. If you are asked to draw a graph, the title should be well-detailed, including reference to your independent and dependent variables. Also take extra care with the scaling and labelling of your axes.

Arithmetic questions – Messy/non-existent workings. Show all your working with extreme care, as you get marks all the way through multistage calculations. If numbers make you flustered practise relaxation. Don't miss these easy marks.

Inferential tests – Not reporting the result correctly. When reporting the outcome of an inferential test, you must state the observed value you calculated and state the critical value (including the information you used to obtain the critical value). You must also state your conclusion, i.e. apply the result to the hypothesis. We have examples of this on pages 191, 193, 200 and 212.

There are many more comments throughout the research methods chapter.

Individual differences and developmental psychology

The specification requires that you think about how each topic relates to individual differences and developmental psychology, and you will be examined on these links.

Individual differences refers to the ways that one person differs from another, such as their personality or gender or age. Questions could include any command term:

- Describe how individual differences can affect obedience. (2)
- Explain **one** way in which memory can be affected by individual differences. (3)
- Learning theorists explain individual differences in a variety of ways. Evaluate **one or more** of these explanations using examples of individual differences in any one human behaviour. (8)

Developmental psychology is about how and why people change over the course of their lives.

- Describe **one** reason why a person's level of prejudice might change as they get older. (2)
- Using your knowledge of biological psychology, explain **two** reasons why levels of aggression might change over the life span. (4)
- To what extent are biological and learning theories able to account for developmental differences over time? (12)

Compare questions

The command term 'compare' needs some special attention, 'answers must include at least one similarity AND one difference', even in a 2-mark question.

For example:

Compare classical and operant conditioning as theories of learning. (2)

One thing these theories have in common is that they were both tested using animal experiments, for example Pavlov classically conditioned dogs to salivate to the sound of a bell and Skinner used operant conditioning to train rats to press a lever.

However, the theories differ in that classical conditioning focuses on what happens before the learned behaviour, e.g. the pairing of an unconditioned and a neutral stimulus whereas operant conditioning focuses on what happens after the behaviour, i.e. the consequences.

- The language of comparison is picked out in green. You could use words such as 'same' and 'likewise' for similarities, and 'in contrast,' and 'but' to indicate differences.
- Notice how each point includes BOTH the things you were asked to compare highlighted in orange.
- Finally, we have picked out the theme in purple – the basis of the similarity or difference. The key to answering compare questions is to identify themes.
- Comparison points can come from both descriptive and evaluative content, so theories could be compared with regard to research evidence, applications and issues and debates.

Understanding evaluation and analysis (AO3)

Let's get judgemental. Evaluation involves making judgements and drawing conclusions.

What is evaluation and analysis?

This is a very important question. If you don't know an answer to this question this could cost you a LOT of marks in the exam! Evaluation is about assessing the VALUE or worth of something, for example a study, a theory or a therapy.

Time to get judgemental

We evaluate in order to *make judgements* and *reach conclusions*.

It's a bit like being in court, trying to work out whether someone is innocent or guilty – you need to look at the evidence from both sides and think about where the evidence came from. This allows you to make **judgements** (for example, 'is it 'credible'?').

Once the court has heard all the evidence, the judge will pronounce his or her verdict. At the end of your essays, you need to give your final verdict or **conclusion** regarding the overall worth of the thing that you have been evaluating.

There are THREE key skills required when writing great evaluation. Each is identified in the mark scheme (on the next spread) so it is important to understand what they are and how to do them well.

AO3 skill 1: Chains of reasoning

Good evaluation/analysis will include several of these 'chains' depending on the mark allocation – the more marks, the more chains needed.

Imagine making a paperchain, the chain can be built up over several links. You start with three links – one at the start and one at the end, and at least one in-between. Your evaluative chains of reasoning will build up in just the same way. Building up your point gradually will help you to argue in a way which is clear and convincing!

Step 1: Identify the point Criticism can be positive or negative and there are many different types of criticism depending on what you are evaluating. You will see many different examples in this book. For example, if a theory is supported by evidence from a research study, this is a strength of the theory, whereas lack of research support is a weakness (limitation). When evaluating a study, high validity is a strength whereas low validity is a weakness. This first link in the chain is likely to start by saying something like, 'A strength of the theory is…'.

Step 2: Elaborate the point Your elaboration needs to be relevant, focused and specific. If you are evaluating a theory using a research study, focus on the findings of that study and try to be exact if you can. If you are evaluating a study, ensure that you use specific procedural details of that study. Being specific in this way will help you avoid writing what examiners call 'generic criticism'. Generic points are ones that could be rote learned and dropped in anywhere. Specific evidence-based points show that you really know what you are talking about and can make your argument convincing.

Step 3: Link back or provide a conclusion It's not over yet! This chain needs a final link – to make a truly effective point you need to explain why the information in step 2 is important. You will need to make links back to the theory or study that you are evaluating. If you are evaluating a theory, which particular keywords or features could be drawn out in your final point? If you are evaluating a study think carefully about what the study was actually about and ensure that the last point in your argument links back to that.

Chains of reasoning: Building your argument, point by point, will make it clear and convincing. Imagining the links in different colours might help you to remember that each link has a different job.

Look at any of the critical points (AO3) in this book. We have tried to create three link 'chains of reasoning' which follow these simple rules…

- **P** – Identify the **P**oint to be made.
- **E** – **E**laborate the point. Which can be done with an **E**xample, or some **E**vidence or an **E**xplanation.
- **T** – End with a link back or conclusion: '**T**his suggests …' '**T**herefore …' '**T**his means …'

Here's a chain of reasoning (PET) from page 31, using research evidence:

> **Immediacy less important than strength**
>
> A weakness of social impact theory is that the role of immediacy may not be a key ingredient in social impact.
>
> Charles Hofling *et al.* (1966) arranged for an unknown doctor to telephone 22 nurses and ask each of them to administer an overdose of a drug that was not on their ward list. A startling 95% of the nurses started to administer the drug (they were prevented from doing so). Although the doctor was not immediately present, the nurses obeyed without question.
>
> This challenges social impact theory because the source being absent should have reduced the effect but it didn't.

AO3 skill 2: Competing arguments

Remember the point of evaluation/analysis? It is to make judgements and draw conclusions. Think about the judge in court. He or she can only announce the verdict having considered both sides of the argument, for and against. In your evaluative essays, it's important that you present 'both sides'. So you might present a chain of reason that argues that a certain theory, study, therapy etc. is good or bad.

However, once you have done this, you can sometimes *inject a competing argument*. Competing means 'opposing'. For example, you might have presented a chain of reason that suggests that, 'on the one hand' study 'x' supports a theory 'y'. However, you could then argue that, 'on the other hand', the study might only be seen as weak support due to certain methodological flaws, such as low validity (and explain why).

In order to put this competing view across effectively, you will need to follow the PET rule outlined on the facing page. Be sure to always keep a steady eye on the essay title so that your final explain point is made explicitly relevant to the title.

You don't need competing arguments every time, but overall the essay should be 'balanced'.

For a 'super' essay, don't forget to 'inject' your evaluative essays with at least one competing (opposing) argument.

Signposting competing arguments

You don't have to keep saying 'on the one hand … on the other hand', in fact that could get rather weird! Try mixing it up a bit with phrases like…

- This said,
- In contrast,
- Alternatively,

Here's a chain of reason (PET) from page 41, with a competing argument:

The minimal group experiment

A strength of SIT is support from the minimal group experiment.

Tajfel (1970) worked with 15-year-old Bristol school boys. Ingroups and outgroups were created by telling each boy which other boys had behaved like them or not like them in a previous task (choosing which painting they liked). Later the boys were asked to allocate points to the other boys and were told these points would later be exchanged for cash. Tajfel found that more points were awarded to ingroup members than outgroup members. Boys even opted to maximise the difference in points awarded to the ingroup compared with the outgroup, even if this reduced the total final sum awarded to the ingroup!

This study shows how social categorisation is sufficient to trigger *ingroup favouritism* and discrimination against the outgroup.

Competing argument: Although this study appears to support SIT, the task of privately allocating points lacks mundane realism. In real life, we may be less discriminatory as there may be unpleasant social consequences of such actions. Discrimination is rarely this covert, meaning that the study lacks ecological validity.

AO3 skill 3: Conclusions

Conclusions should draw together the evidence and arguments in your essay. You should reach a judgement about whatever it is you have been considering, just like the judge reaching his or her verdict. You might consider what this study or theory contributed to the understanding of this area of psychology or how has it helped people in society to live happier, more functional or more productive lives.

Conclusions come in two forms:

1. **Mini conclusions** – These can come at the end of each evaluation point, as described on the facing page. The 'T' part (Therefore …, This shows that …) is a conclusion. Make sure these mini-conclusions are not *generic* (i.e. could fit anywhere), instead link them to the content of your chain of reasoning. These mini-conclusions are an invaluable part of your evaluation/analysis.

2. **End of essay conclusions** – Essays should end with a balanced conclusion. This must:
   - Not just summarise the points you have already made.
   - Not introduce any major new themes or pieces of evidence that have not been previously mentioned.

You should present a *balanced* verdict (mentioning both positive and negative points). You need to be fairly succinct – two or three sentences are plenty.

We have tried to give you ideas throughout this book about what a balanced conclusion might look like but your conclusions will depend upon what you have written in your essay – and on your views.

Writing conclusions can be tough – if your conclusion is too superficial, it won't receive much credit. Looking on the bright side, like all skills, practice makes perfect. So get practising!

You can't 'high five' without *two hands*! Remembering the simple phrase, '*On the one hand, on the other hand*' will help you to present competing arguments in your written work.

Using research studies in evaluation

On page 8 we noted that you may present information about a research study as part of your descriptive content – but you can also use research studies as evaluation.

If you do this then it is really only the findings/conclusion that will be creditworthy as AO3. You will also need to 'top and tail' the findings using the PET rules to create effective 'chains of reasoning'.

Any description of the procedure might be credited as description (AO1) but only if it is deemed relevant to the focus of the question.

Using applications as evaluation

Each of the main spreads in this book provides one evaluation point on how the subtopic has been applied – either applied to something practical which can be used to change people's lives or applied to understanding something theoretical.

Such applications are a central aim of psychology and therefore when a theory or study can be applied elsewhere that is considered a strength.

Using issues and debates as evaluation

The final flourish on our evaluation pages is an 'issues and debates' chain of reasoning, demonstrating how every subtopic can be used to build synoptic essays.

Although you can use these in any essay, they are primarily there to help you build a collection of points that can be made in your AL synoptic essays, which you learn about in our Year 2 book.

Essays (extended response questions)

Understanding the exam

Your AO1, AO2 and AO3 skills are assessed in SAQs but also in extended response questions (ERQs) – called 'essays' for short.

We will begin by looking at 8-mark essays and how they are assessed. There are two kinds of 8-mark questions:
- AO1 + AO3
- AO1 + AO2 scenario (context)

On page 18 we look at 12-mark essays and how they are assessed.

Essays are about description *and* evaluation

In this book we have given you a lot of description for each topic (the left-hand side of each spread). You need this descriptive content for SAQs.

You also need the descriptive content in essays – but a cut-down version of what we have covered in this book. You must 'cut it down' so you have time for the application/evaluation component of the essay (AO2 and AO3) – the chains of reasoning, competing arguments and balanced judgements (see mark schemes below).

Use description wisely. While a small chunk of your essay may be pure description (see plan on the next spread), much of your answer will be made from chains of reasoning which contain further description as relevant to the point you are making.

On the next two spreads we look at how to construct answers but we start here by explaining the levels-based mark scheme used to assess your answers.

AO1 and AO3: Evaluate and Assess questions

The grid below summarises the levels-based mark scheme used for such questions.

AO1 (4 marks)   AO3 (4 marks)   Candidates must demonstrate an equal emphasis on knowledge and understanding vs evaluation/conclusion in their answer.

Level	Mark	Description (AO1) Knowledge and understanding	Evaluation (AO3)	Chains of reasoning (AO3)	Competing arguments (AO3)	Conclusion (AO3)
0	0	No rewardable material.				
1	1–2	Isolated elements.	Limited attempt to address the question.	Limited supporting evidence.		Generic.
2	3–4	Mostly accurate.	Statements with some development.	Mostly accurate and relevant factual material.		Superficial.
3	5–6	Accurate.	Arguments developed but may be imbalanced.	Mostly coherent.	Grasp of competing arguments.	Arguments lead to a conclusion.
4	7–8	Accurate and thorough.	Well-developed and logical.	Logical throughout.	Demonstrates an awareness of competing arguments.	Balanced conclusion. (Nuanced).

AO1 and AO2: Discuss questions (have a scenario)

'Discuss' questions have a scenario. The levels-based mark scheme used for such questions is shown below.

Note that 'Discuss' essays do not require conclusions.

AO1 (4 marks)   AO2 (4 marks)   Candidates must demonstrate an equal emphasis on knowledge and understanding vs application in their answer.

Level	Mark	Description (AO1) Knowledge and understanding	Argument (AO2)	Chains of reasoning (AO2)	Competing arguments (AO2)	Application (scientific ideas, processes, techniques or procedures) (AO2)
0	0	No rewardable material.				
1	1–2	Isolated elements.	Little or no reference to relevant evidence from the context.			
2	3–4	Mostly accurate.	Partially developed.	Superficial.	Imbalanced.	Occasionally supported through the application of relevant evidence.
3	5–6	Accurate.	Arguments developed.	Mostly coherent.	Grasp of competing arguments but discussion may be imbalanced or contain superficial material.	Supported by applying relevant evidence from the context.
4	7–8	Accurate and thorough.	Well-developed and logical.	Logical.	Demonstrates a thorough awareness of competing arguments.	Supported by sustained application of relevant evidence from the context.

The mark schemes used in this book are <u>illustrative</u> of the levels-based mark schemes (LBMS) used by Edexcel. Always ask your teacher for up-to-date advice about the Edexcel mark schemes, as these may have been amended.

Unpacking the 'language of assessment'

The mark scheme on the facing page uses specific terms for assessment. But what do they mean? We have covered some of the terms already on previous spreads: chains of reasoning (page 12), competing arguments (page 13), balanced conclusions (page 13) and accurate/thorough description (page 8).

Here are a few more key explanations to help you produce top level answers.

Generic

This means that the same sentence or sentences could be used in many different essays by just changing a few words. This is especially an issue for conclusions as students like to write, 'This theory is good because it can be applied to everyday life but, on the other hand, the research evidence is weak.' Avoid being generic – if what you have written could apply just as well to a different theory or study, it is probably generic and worth little if any credit.

Superficial

This describes conclusions which lack depth or understanding. They may be true on the surface but do not reflect any meaningful understanding of the psychological research in this area.

Coherent

This describes an essay where the parts fit neatly together to create the whole argument. Incoherent work is muddled and fragmented, there are a series of ideas but they do not flow together which suggests the writer does not really understand the content. Coherence is a bit like writing a story.

Well-developed and logical

This links to the chains of reasoning. These should be structured so they have a beginning, middle and end. Each sentence has a specific purpose and should link clearly to the sentence before and the sentence afterwards. At the end the critical point should have a conclusion that explains how the whole chain relates to the topic of the essay.

Imbalanced

This describes an essay where the writer has not paid attention to matching the number of strengths to the number of weaknesses, or number of arguments for to those against.

Relevant

When you read the essay title it is important that you think carefully about the theories and studies in that specific area of the specification. Be selective, don't just chuck ideas in willy-nilly. The content of your essay must all be appropriate to the area of psychology identified in the essay title.

Nuanced

This only applies to 12-mark 'to what extent' questions and refers to having subtle shades of meaning, a multifaceted conclusion.

Preparation

Read our marked examples at the end of each chapter to get a feel for where students go wrong and what they do right.

And practise – select an exam question and prepare a small list of points. Maybe allow yourself 20 key words. Then sit down in a room on your own and set the timer for an appropriate number of minutes. You might even time the AO1 bit and then, when the buzzer goes off, time the AO3 bit and finally the conclusion.

It is absolutely essential to practise answering questions under timed conditions.

Ms Examiner (or it could be a Mr Examiner)
Spare a thought for the person marking your exams. She (or he) has to read hundreds of student answers. Make your answer stand out and make it easier for the examiner to mark. Use paragraphs, one for each evaluation point and signpost the chains of reasoning (One strength is ... Therefore I conclude ...). Underline important words and write as legibly as you can.

How essays are marked

In the mark schemes published by the exam board there are two distinct parts:

- **The indicative content** outlines the possible content. This is not *required* content. It is there to indicate what *might* be included.
- **The mark grid** which describes how each assessment objective will be evidenced e.g. Level 2 says 'Demonstrates mostly accurate knowledge and understanding. (AO1)'. The tables on the facing page are summary versions of the mark grids provided.

When an examiner decides how to reward an answer using a levels-based mark scheme, a 'best fit' approach should be used:

- Examiners should first decide which descriptor most closely matches the candidate answer and place it in that band.
- The mark awarded within the band according to each of the assessment objectives will be decided according to how securely all bullet points are displayed at that level.
- In cases of uneven performance, this will still apply. Candidates will be placed in the band that best describes their answer, and they will be awarded marks towards the top or bottom of that band depending on how securely they have evidenced bullet points in that, or other descriptors.

However ...

In an AO1 + AO3 question, an answer that has no conclusion may be limited to Level 1 because this important criterion is lacking.

On the other hand, if there have been mini-conclusions within each evaluation point, that may be sufficient to place the answer at a higher level.

Similarly, if an answer was all description this may limit the overall mark to Level 1 because the criteria of the upper levels have not been evidenced.

This means it is vital in an essay response that you supply evidence of all of the five main criteria.

Partial performance

Some questions ask for two things, for example:

> Christopher loves buying books online. He has a huge collection already but just can't stop himself.
>
> Evaluate **two** explanations for Christopher's behaviour relating to biological psychology and learning theories. (12)

If you only look at one topic, i.e. you explain Christopher's behaviour using biological factors but not learning theories, you have not answered the question fully and will be subjected to a 'partial performance' penalty.

8-mark essays

Understanding the exam — 16

This spread considers the different kinds of 8-mark questions and how you should answer them.

Both the AS and AL exams will contain several 8-markers of varying types (see facing page). Although there's no 'one size fits all' approach as such, there is some basic advice that will help you answer these 'mini' essays with confidence!

Planning your essay

Our advice, for an 8-mark essay, is to spend about 15 minutes and write about 350 words. That's around 20–25 words per minute. If you have average-sized handwriting, this should fit into the available space on the exam paper.

Beware – spending too much time on your essays may result in a poor mark overall – you may gain a slightly higher mark for the essays, but lose lots of marks on the SAQs.

Dividing up your time

There are two ways to approach essay writing – each has advantages and some topics are more suited to one approach rather than another:

The divided approach

80 words	Describe the theory or study.
230 words	Two or three chains of reasoning, including some competing arguments.
40 words	Balanced conclusion.

If you do all the description at the start of the essay you can keep track of how much you have done and ensure you focus on the chains of reasoning.

The sandwich approach

30 words	Describe one element of the theory or study.
80 words	Relevant chain of reasoning + competing argument.
200 words	Repeat once or twice (if time), not always with competing argument.
40 words	Balanced conclusion.

Your chains of reasoning must be related to the descriptive content. For this reason, it may be better to deal with smaller chunks of description, each then followed by a chain of reasoning.

In this book there are four subheadings in each AO1 section (almost all of the time). 80 words of AO1 means about 20 words for each subheading.

Be sure to use the PET approach in your chains of reasoning – and then your evaluations will contain some description and that will add to your AO1 credit.

How many evaluation points?

In this book we have provided four chains of reasoning for each topic. You don't have to use all of these ideas, especially in an 8-marker. But, as the mark allocations increase and the question becomes more challenging much of this material may be necessary!

At the end of each chapter in this book are some student answers to practice questions, including answers for essay questions.

Example answer

Evaluate agency theory as an explanation of obedience. [8]

Student answer

Milgram's (1974) agency theory says that in order for humans to live in groups, some people have to be subordinate and obey orders from people above them. He says we are generally in the autonomous state where we behave independently and take responsibility for our actions. When faced with an authority figure, we make the agentic shift, into the agentic state and then we will do what the authority figure says and believe they are responsible for anything that we do because they told us to do it.

One strength of agency theory is it's supported by Milgram's (1963) study. He found that 100% of participants would administer shocks up to 300 V to a confederate and 65% would go to 450 V. This is important because it shows that people are highly likely to obey orders even when they feel extremely anxious and don't want to do it. However, some people have questioned the internal validity of this study. For example, Perry (2013) says many participants questioned whether the shocks were real and there is film footage to back this up.

Agency theory also has some other problems. For example, some studies show that people aren't very obedient even when you think they would be. One example is the nurses study where nearly all of them would not give a patient Valium and most of them said they were responsible for what they do.

Finally, agency theory has been useful to society because Tarnow (2000) showed how it can be related to commercial airline pilots. He says first officers make the agentic shift when they work with the Captain and this means they don't tell the Captain if he or she makes a mistake and this can cause huge loss of life. Now pilots are trained to be more assertive as agentic state can cause avoidable human errors.

In conclusion, agency theory may look like it is supported by his well-controlled experiments, but his studies have many problems and his theory is over-simplified – people don't always make an agentic shift probably because of their personality traits and it would be good to know more about this.

Around 360 words

You could try to rewrite this essay using the sandwich plan.

Teacher comments

The student has started with a block of AO1. This is all accurate but there are some specialist terms missing. They could have used the terms 'hierarchies' and 'legitimate' for example. Using specialist terms is important as it adds to the accuracy.

It would be more thorough if moral strain had been mentioned as it is a key element of the agentic shift.

The first evaluation uses PET to ensure it is well-structured and logical. There is also a competing argument, although this could have been developed more fully to explain the quality of the support that Milgram's studies provide agency theory.

This second evaluation point feels as if the student has a list of points they want to get through and this has meant there are lots of points but they lack development. The student doesn't explain the point of the nurses study (or even identify the researcher's name) and has not given exact findings.

The third evaluation point is better as it uses the terminology of agency theory but the PET structure has not been clearly applied making the point less well-developed.

The conclusion is balanced but includes information about personality not previously mentioned.

This is a good Level 3 response (almost Level 4) as the AO1 is accurate but lacks some detail and clarity. The chains of reasoning are coherent but could be developed more fully. It is balanced with a strength and a competing argument, followed by a weakness and another strength. The conclusion is rather basic but is not entirely generic.

Types of 8-mark essay questions

All essays have a central focus – a theory, study or psychological concept from the specification. The command word and the way the essay is phrased tells you specific elements of the theory/study/concept that you must address.

STANDARD question: Evaluate or assess

The 'standard' essay question requires you to describe and evaluate one of the subtopics in the specification. There should be equal amounts of description and evaluation in your answer but remember that some of the description will be in the chains of reasoning. For example:

- Evaluate **one** contemporary study from cognitive psychology. (8)
- Assess the usefulness of systematic desensitisation as a therapy for people with phobias. (8)
- Pavlov conducted research on classical conditioning. Evaluate Pavlov's research into learning. (8)

> Note that this is not a scenario/context question, even though there is a stem.

CONTEXT question: Discuss

'Discuss' questions begin with a scenario (context). These should be treated in a similar way to SAQs with scenario – you must apply your whole discussion to the scenario.

The 'discuss' mark scheme on the previous spread shows how such questions are marked. You can see examples of such questions throughout the book in the Apply it concepts boxes. For example:

- Psychology students Annie and Frankie are performing in the whole school musical but there are so many lines, songs and dance moves to remember, they are worried they will never remember them all.

  Discuss how the multi-store model of memory could help the girls to remember everything they need to learn. You must make reference to the context in your answer. (8)

METHODS question

You may be asked to write an essay relating a topic or subtopic to a specific research method. For example:

- Evaluate the use of interviews as a research method in social psychology. (8)
- Assess the use of case studies in research on memory. (8)

To evaluate or assess you must think in terms of strengths and weaknesses or arguments for and against. You might also make comparisons with other research methods, which might be more or less useful for conducting research in the area highlighted in the question. Use at least one example to illustrate your answer and present a balanced conclusion at the end.

ISSUES AND DEBATES (I&D) question

AL exam questions may be on issues and debates. There are I&D questions for more than 8 marks (see next spread) but for an 8-mark I&D question the issue or debate is linked to one of the topics or subtopics you have studied. For example:

- With reference to biological psychology, assess the way in which psychology may be used for social control. (8)

KEY QUESTION question

8-mark key question essays will have the command term 'discuss' and require description and application. We have given detailed instructions about these essays towards the end of each topic chapter (see pages 56, 84, 118 and 156). Longer questions will use a different command term and will assess your evaluation skills as well as description and application.

PRACTICAL INVESTIGATION question

You might be asked about any of your four investigations. For example:

- Evaluate the procedure used to collect and analyse the qualitative data in the practical investigation you carried out when studying learning theories. (8)

For this question you would need to describe the aim of your investigation and then how you collected and analysed the data, followed by strengths and weaknesses of both the collection and analysis stages. Finally you would need to make a judgement about the overall merit of this investigation and the conclusions that you drew from it.

What do students do wrong in essays?

- **Students give too much description** – You need to portion up your time carefully, keep your eye on the clock and be self-disciplined. This said, it can also be easy to be too superficial in the description – make sure you include detail but don't go overboard leaving yourself short of time for your evaluation.
- **Students fail to make their evaluation effective** – Use the lead-in phrases such as 'A strength is …' or 'However …' to make it clear when you are presenting evaluation.
- **Evaluation points are under-developed, i.e. poorly explained** – Be obsessive about using PET when creating your chains. Many students think quantity is better, for example doing three instead of two evaluations but if you do that you will sacrifice quality and may not get beyond Level 1.
- **Students fail to answer the question** – Take time to plan your answer, focusing on what is truly relevant and creditworthy. If you just start writing your answer, you may forget the focus of the question – it really does pay to do some planning. It may also help, as you start each new paragraph, to go back to the title to remind yourself what the essay should be about.
- **Students do not use paragraphs** – Which makes the essay very difficult to read. Each new chain of reasoning needs a new paragraph.

> ATCHOO (BC)
> This mnemonic will help you remember all the ingredients for a great essay:
> **A**ccurate and **T**horough (AO1).
> **Ch**ains of reasoning.
> **O**n the one hand, **O**n the other hand – your competing arguments (AO3).
> And then … why do we sneeze? Bad Cold, which stands for **B**alanced **C**onclusion!

> The practical investigation for social psychology and for learning theories involves the collection of both qualitative and quantitative data. This means either of these might be the focus of an essay.

12-mark essays

Understanding the exam — 18

There are questions on AS and AL papers that combine two or more topics. These are called SYNOPTIC questions (*synoptic* means giving an overview).

12-mark essay questions can be
- AO1 + AO3
- AO1 + AO2 + AO3 scenario (context)

Types of 12-mark essay questions

In comparison with the 8-markers, you now have 50% more time for the 12-mark essays. This is about 20 minutes (including planning time) and about 500 words.

SYNOPTIC question

AS synoptic questions link two of the topics you have studied. For example:
- To what extent can the classic studies from biological psychology and the learning theories be considered ethical? (12)

SYNOPTIC + METHODS question

At AS the synoptic style can also be combined with research methods content. For example:
- Evaluate the use of laboratory experiments to further understanding in social and cognitive psychology. (12)

SYNOPTIC + CONTEXT question

At AS and AL a 12-mark synoptic question may have a scenario. For example:
- Noah and Richelle are in the same dance team. After rehearsal, they start discussing the other dancers' performances. It seems they both have very different ideas about how the rehearsal went.

  Evaluate **two** explanations for Noah and Richelle's differing points of view relating to social and cognitive psychology. (12)

SYNOPTIC + I&D question

At AL the synoptic style (two topics) is combined with I&D topics. For example:
- To what extent can research from cognitive and social psychology be considered scientific? (12)

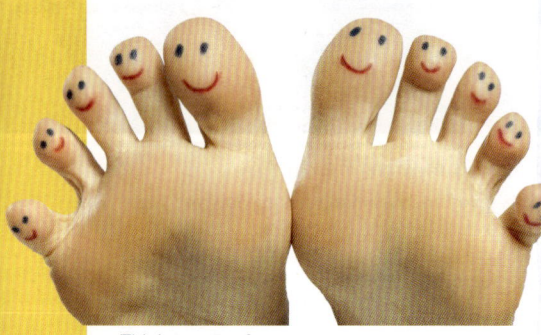

Think on your feet.
We have outlined a number of different kinds of essay on this page and the previous page but basically you need to be ready for any combination.

AO1 and AO3: Evaluate and To what extent

The levels-based mark scheme used for these 12-mark questions is similar to the one used for 8-mark evaluate/assess questions (see page 14) – except the marks for each level are different, as shown on the right.

Level	Mark
0	0
1	1–3
2	4–6
3	7–9
4	10–12

AO1 and AO2 and AO3: Evaluate questions (have a scenario)

'Evaluate' questions may also have a scenario and then they are marked differently from those with no scenario. The levels-based mark scheme used for such questions is shown below, and is different from the one used for 8-mark Discuss questions – because AO3 is now added and conclusions are expected.

AO1 (4 marks)   AO2 (4 marks)   AO3 (4 marks)   Candidates must demonstrate an equal emphasis between knowledge and understanding vs application vs evaluation/conclusion in their answer.

Level	Mark	Description (AO1) Knowledge and understanding	Line(s) of argument based on relevant evidence from the context (AO2)	Ability to integrate and synthesise relevant knowledge (AO2)	Chains of reasoning (AO3)	Competing arguments (AO3)	Conclusion (AO3)
0	0	No rewardable material.					
1	1–3	Isolated elements.	Little or no reference to relevant evidence from the context.		Limited supporting evidence.		Generic. Little or no attempt to address the question.
2	4–6	Mostly accurate.	Argument occasionally supported.		Some development in the form of mostly accurate and relevant factual material.		Superficial.
3	7–9	Accurate.	Argument supported.	Might demonstrate.	Mostly coherent.	Grasp of competing arguments but evaluation may be imbalanced.	Arguments lead to a conclusion.
4	10–12	Accurate and thorough.	Argument sustained.	Demonstrates.	Well-developed and logical throughout.	Demonstrates an awareness of competing arguments.	Balanced conclusion.

The mark schemes used in this book are <u>illustrative</u> of the levels-based mark schemes (LBMS) used by Edexcel. Always ask your teacher for up-to-date advice about the Edexcel mark schemes, as these may have been amended.

Example answer

> Christopher loves buying books online. He has a huge collection already but just can't stop himself. Evaluate **two** explanations of Christopher's behaviour relating to biological psychology and learning theories. [12]

Student answer

Dysfunction of the orbitofrontal cortex (OFC) could be responsible for Christopher's behaviour as this region controls rational thinking and self-control and his impulsive purchasing shows he is behaving irrationally – he might not be able to afford the books! OFC dysfunction has also been linked to a serotonin deficiency in this area. Furthermore, when Christopher buys a book it might activate the release of dopamine which stimulates his brain's reward centres making him feel elated. This could be addictive meaning that he wants to buy more and more books.

A strength of this explanation is that animal experiments support the idea that dopamine is involved with pleasure and is rewarding. For example, scientists have used lesioning to stop mice from releasing dopamine and this stopped them from self-administering cocaine, as there was no reward. This shows that dopamine release could be the reward that maintains Chris' behaviour.

However, this research may not be relevant to humans because mice brains are very different from human brains. Although they share much of the same neurochemistry sometimes drugs can have the opposite effects in mice as they do in humans meaning you should be very cautious when extrapolating from mice to humans.

Furthermore, much of the research linking specific brain regions to certain behaviours is only correlational so just because the OFC appears to be active during rational decision-making it doesn't mean that damage to this region causes irrational behaviour like impulsive buying.

Christopher's behaviour can also be explained using operant conditioning. For example, book-buying may have been stamped in through positive reinforcement, meaning he experiences a reward for buying books such as being complimented on his huge collection by his friends. Or he might experience negative reinforcement, for example, he feels stressed but when he is looking at Amazon he starts to feel more relaxed, so going onto this site is rewarding because it temporarily relieves stress.

This explanation is also supported by rodent research, for example Skinner rewarded rats with food to increase lever pushing. He found that a variable ratio reinforcement created the highest rate of lever pressing. This shows that Christopher might buy more books if the website uses unpredictable rewards like occasional vouchers and discounts.

However, operant conditioning has its weaknesses when applied to humans as Christopher may find buying books intrinsically rewarding rather than extrinsically, meaning that he just enjoys looking at the website and finding books that interest him. He might just like owning books because it makes him feel in control as he has a book on every topic.

Overall, I would say that both the biological and learning explanations have their downsides due to the evidence mainly being from animal studies. However, I conclude that the biological explanation is the best as it can be used to explain intrinsic motivation as buying books is rewarding due to the feelings of pleasure generated by the release of dopamine and this causes Christopher to keep adding more books to his collection.

Around 500 words

Teacher comments

This is a well-structured answer. In the first paragraph he has thought about the biological content he has studied and selected appropriate material relating to the OFC and the role of serotonin and dopamine, all of which is contextualised back to the scenario.

In paragraph 2 the student signals his evaluation with care using 'PET' chains of reasoning and injects a competing argument in paragraph 3 about problems of extrapolating research from animals to humans. This is reasonably well-developed with the link to the idea that drugs have the opposite effects in some cases. He has not linked this back to Christopher.

The student continues with a further paragraph of evaluation looking at the correlational nature of some brain research. This is contextualised to book-buying, but it is rather cursory and not a well-developed chain. This makes the argument for and against biological explanations a little imbalanced.

Operant conditioning is selected for the section on learning theory, which is a sensible choice and is contextualised well, demonstrating a good understanding of positive and negative reinforcement.

The student moves on to evaluation relating to animal research and links this to reinforcement schedules showing further AO1 knowledge which again is contextualised to Christopher.

To create balance a final competing argument is injected relating to the weaknesses of operant conditioning with reference to intrinsic rewards and feeling in control. As with the previous evaluation paragraphs this shows a reasonably well-structured chain of reasoning – point, explanation, conclusion.

The essay finishes with a conclusion considering the problems of both explanations before judging which is the better explanation. There is a good link between the way biological psychology explains intrinsic motivation, which had been presented as a weakness of operant conditioning.

This is a top level answer. There is a good range of accurate and detailed knowledge, though perhaps a bit short for learning theory. There are sustained links to the scenario throughout and the evaluation is generally well-developed and logical with explicit competing arguments. The conclusion follows well from the arguments presented and is balanced. 11 out of 12 marks.

Less is more

Don't try to cram in too much. Latané's law of diminishing returns is certainly true in essays written under exam conditions – often you pick up marks quickly in the first stages of the essay but the more you write, the fewer marks there are to gain and the more time you are potentially wasting, which could be used for other questions.

Writing fewer points in an essay can definitely lead to more marks, because it gives you time to develop your points fully. Think quality not quantity.

Maybe it is the dopamine release that keeps Christopher loving his books.

To summarise!

Exam questions may be SAQs:
- Identify
- Give
- Describe
- Explain
- Compare

ERQs may be 8 marks:
- Evaluate
- Assess
- Discuss (has a scenario)

ERQs may be 12 marks:
- Evaluate
- To what extent
- Evaluate (has a scenario)

ERQS may also be 16 or 20 marks – but these are AL essays which we discuss in our Year 2 book.

Issues and debates

What is Psychology?

Psychology is the science of human behaviour, including thoughts and emotions as well as actions.

Everyone offers explanations about why people (and animals) behave the way they do. We are all 'armchair psychologists'. Studying psychology aims to be scientific and therefore tests and criticises evidence systematically.

One of the features of any subject (such as biology or the study of literature) is that there are underlying questions that can be asked about any individual topic within that subject, and so it is with psychology.

You are required, as part of the Edexcel course in psychology, to focus on certain issues and debates and try to apply them to each topic you study.

Exam information

In the AS exam there are no extended writing questions (essays) on issues and debates. However:

1. You can use these topics as evaluation points (as we have done on the subtopic spreads), but you must ensure that your point is well contextualised — as we have illustrated here by looking at each issue/debate in relation to sleep.
2. Those of you who are going on to do the AL exam might start practising the issues and debates essays, and there are examples throughout this book of questions on issues and debates (I&D). You can also read about them in the exam section on pages 17 and 18.

Issues in psychology

An issue is a topic for discussion. Such issues often lead to discussions because people hold polarised opinions on these topics — that is why they have become issues. There are no simple answers but it is important for us to discuss these issues in relation to our studies of human behaviour.

- Ethical issues in research (animal and human).
- Practical issues in the design and implementation of research.
- Comparisons of ways of explaining behaviour using different themes.
- Cultural and gender issues in psychological research.
- An understanding of how psychological understanding has developed over time.
- The use of psychology in social control.
- The use of psychological knowledge in society.
- Issues related to socially-sensitive research.

Debates in psychology

Debates are also topics for discussion but, in comparison with issues, debates have two quite distinct 'sides', such as nature versus nurture. Psychologists consider the evidence for each side of the debate and weigh it up. No one side of the debate is likely to ever win and the answer may lie in intermediate possibilities between two extreme positions.

- Reductionism in the explanation of behaviour.
- Psychology as a science.
- The role of both nature and nurture in psychology.

Why do we dream?

Psychologists want to explain why people (and animals) behave as they do. They are always on the lookout for interesting things that people do. Just look in any newspaper or on social media – they are full of stories about people's behaviour.

What about dreams?

Let's start with Sigmund Freud

According to Freud in the early 19th century, dreams represent unfulfilled wishes but their contents are expressed symbolically. The real meaning of a dream (latent content) is transformed into something emotionally harmless (manifest content, the content you actually experience) that may be meaningless to anybody but a psychoanalyst trained to interpret these symbols.

For example, a penis may be represented by a snake or a gun, a vagina by a tunnel or a cave. In order to understand the meaning of dream symbols fully, however, Freud believed it was necessary to consider them in the context of a person's life. For example, a fish could represent a person's friend who is a fisherman or another friend who has a Piscean star sign. For this reason Freud did not support the idea of dream dictionaries.

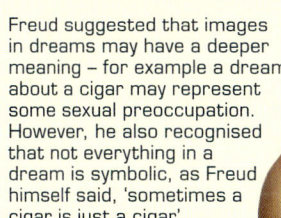

Freud suggested that images in dreams may have a deeper meaning – for example a dream about a cigar may represent some sexual preoccupation. However, he also recognised that not everything in a dream is symbolic, as Freud himself said, 'sometimes a cigar is just a cigar'.

A more scientific approach

In the 1950s Nathaniel Kleitman decided to study the unconsciousness of sleep (his work was sponsored by the company that produced Ovaltine, looking for ways to promote a remedy for sleeplessness).

Kleitman together with Eugene Aserinsky (1953) and later William Dement (1957) was the first to make the link between REM activity (rapid eye movements during sleep) and dreaming. They woke participants up when their brain waves (displayed on an EEG – see diagram below) showed REM sleep and found that participants were highly likely to report dreaming. However, they also found that dreams that were less vivid were recorded outside REM sleep and that sleepers, when awoken in REM sleep, did not always report dreaming.

Why REM sleep?

Knowing that dreaming happens during REM sleep doesn't tell us anything about what REM sleep is for. Susanne Diekelmann and Jan Born (2010) suggest that sleep is a great opportunity to sort out memories as the brain is 'offline'. Imagine trying to organise the contents of a hard drive if new entries kept being made as you were tidying files and folders.

When you are sleeping there is minimal new incoming sensory data or feedback from muscles, and this gives your brain time to identify which memories to strengthen. REM sleep alternates with non-dreaming (nREM) sleep and these alternating cycles are important to both cutting down connections that are not needed and building up those that are.

Dreams are basically a read-out of all the shuffling of memories that is going on.

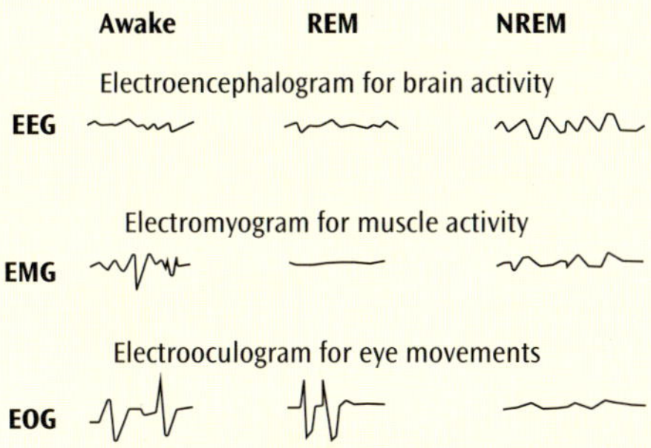

Freud may have had a point

More recent research has supported Freud's link between dreaming and wish fulfilment. Mark Solms (2000) used PET scans to identify the parts of the brain that are active during dreaming. The results showed that the rational part of the brain is indeed *inactive* during REM sleep, whereas the forebrain centres concerned with memory and motivation are very active. In Freud's language, the ego (rational and conscious thought) becomes suspended while the id (the more primitive, unconscious-'driven' part of the mind) is given free rein to process those unfulfilled wishes. Furthermore, evidence suggests that REM sleep is very important to emotional memories.

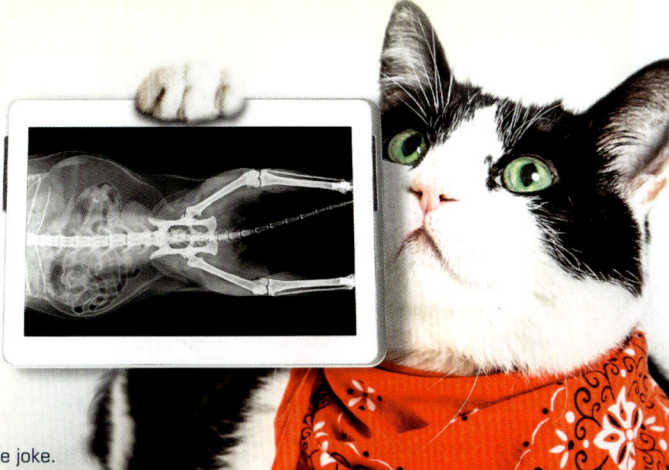

A PET scan, just a little joke.

Issues in psychology

Ethical issues in research (animal and human)

The issue: Making sure animals and humans in research are treated with respect

The way participants are treated in research is an issue for psychologists because we do not have the right to cause other people to experience psychological or physical distress. All professionals (lawyers, doctors, etc) are governed by a professional group, in the UK the British Psychological Society (BPS) helps psychologists to think about ethical issues by giving them guidelines to follow. For example, when conducting a research study psychologists must ensure that participants leave a study in the same physical and psychological state as at the start of the study.

Animals too need protecting. Many psychological studies involve the use of animals, who also experience pain and distress.

Why is it an issue?

Ethics raise issues because people have the right to privacy, confidentiality, safety, choices etc.

However, there is a second reason – the 'public face' of psychology. If participating in investigations conducted by psychologists is distressing, annoying or embarrassing, people could lose faith in psychology. People would be, for instance, less willing to consider therapies based on psychological ideas.

Animals need monitoring and protecting so that pain and distress are identified and avoided or reduced so that the animals do not suffer.

The issue in practice

Research on sleep and dreaming raises ethical issues because dreams are very personal.

Dement and Kleitman (see previous spread) asked participants about the content of their dreams. The participants may have felt uneasy telling a stranger about their dreams as dreams often reveal inner emotions and thoughts.

This means that researchers must be careful at the outset to consider how participants may feel and then they can take steps to avoid such psychological discomfort.

People may not wish to reveal the true content of their dreams but also don't want to let the researcher down – and this may create discomfort.

Practical issues in the design and implementation of research

The issue: Facts and fake news

It's possible to find evidence to support almost any claim, but is it *good* evidence? Psychologists want their body of knowledge to be trustworthy. As a consequence, studies have to be designed and conducted following careful procedures.

Why is it an issue?

Researchers set out with an aim for their research and must be sure the data they collect really is measuring what they were intending to study, rather than being affected by lying, guessing or external factors that should have been controlled. These are problems of *validity* – the genuineness of the research results.

Researchers also need to be certain that if they, or someone else, did the study again the results would be the same. If the results are different this would suggest there was something affecting the data collection making the results inconsistent. This is a *reliability* problem.

Finally, researchers must be sure that the results from the people they have tested would apply to other people, places and times. This is a problem of generalisability.

The issue in practice

Studies need to be designed and implemented to produce results with high validity, reliability and generalisability.

Dement and Kleitman's research, unlike Freud's, was valid as it measured observable data such as brain waves to identify dream sleep. Measures such as EEGs are also very reliable, whereas Freud's interpretations of dreams were unlikely to be the same as another researcher's interpretations. As Dement and Kleitman only used a restricted group of people (nine American adults) we cannot be sure that the results would apply widely.

This means that Dement and Kleitman's research was a well-designed scientific study, however it may lack generalisability.

Comparisons of ways of explaining behaviour using different themes

The issue: Which approach?

There are always different ways to look at a problem. In psychology this means considering different types of psychological explanations, for example ones based on interactions with other people (social psychology) or on brain structure (biological psychology).

Why is it an issue?

Each chapter in this book provides a different 'theme' or type of explanation. These explanations are often at odds with each other. For example, a 'cognitive' theme focuses on our thinking, our beliefs or how we deal with information. This will provide quite different reasons for a behaviour compared with a learning theory theme, which would consider how the factors in the environment affect how we act, by providing rewards and punishments.

The issue in practice

In dream research, there are two opposing themes: the Freudian explanation, based on hidden motives in our unconscious mind, and a biological explanation, based on the role of connections between neurons.

Freud said the dreams we recall are meaningless but useful in helping us to express inner conflicts safely. Biological explanations in contrast suggest that the content of our dreams is meaningless, they are just a byproduct of the brain's attempts to organise our memories. There is recent evidence for both ideas, suggesting they are both partially correct.

This suggests that different themes can share ideas as well as be conflicting. Our final understanding of dreaming may be a combination of the two. For example, REM seems to be especially important in the consolidation of emotional memories.

Cultural and gender issues in psychological research

The issue: Men, women and cultural groups

These issues arise because of *individual differences* – the extent to which people differ from each other in ways that are important to psychology. Boys and girls (men and women) certainly vary, and people in different cultures behave differently in some ways.

Why is it an issue?

The problem is whether psychological theories reflect genuine gender or cultural differences. If these differences are real, what causes them? For example, do gender/cultural differences reflect underlying biological differences or are the differences the product of society? This has important implications for how we treat men and women and people from different cultures.

On the other hand, we can ask whether psychological theories erroneously assume that everyone is the same. This is a problem because we may ignore some important differences. For example, a theory that proposes how memory works is largely based on research in the Western world. It may be that people in other cultures use their memories differently – but, if people from non-Western cultures are measured against Western theories, they may appear deficient.

The issue in practice

An issue with research on dreams is that men and women, and people from different cultures, may not experience the same dreams.

There are similarities between the genders, for example both men and women often dream about negative feelings such as sadness and anger (in about 80% of dreams) and this pattern exists in many cultures, for example dreaming about aggression instead of friendliness. However, women tend to have slightly more characters in their dreams than men but men's dreams include more male characters than female ones. There are cultural differences in attitudes about dreaming – some cultures dismiss them as unreal thus irrelevant in everyday life, whereas others see great relevance in the content of dreams.

This shows that gender and cultural issues are a problem for research on dreams because you can't generalise from a gender- or culturally-biased sample.

The use of psychology in social control

The issue: Use and misuse of psychology

Psychological knowledge enables people to change the behaviour (and the thoughts and emotions) of others. On the one hand this is a good thing because it can be used to help people, for example if they are experiencing psychological problems. On the other hand it can also be abused by people who wish to manipulate the behaviour of others for less positive reasons.

Why is it an issue?

The British Psychological Society states that their aim is to 'enhance the development and application of psychology for the greater public good'. Psychology can improve people's lives both by enriching their experiences and by helping them to overcome problems – such as using psychological therapies for mental disorders. However, techniques that are developed to produce change can also be used in more sinister ways, such as to persuade people to change their minds for political reasons or for financial gain.

The issue in practice

Sleep research has provided opportunities to control people's sleep in beneficial ways.

For example, drugs can be used to help people with insomnia (who sleep too little) and hypersomnia (who sleep too much). Conversely, sleep research can be used to know how to keep people awake and this has been used as a form of torture. Sleep is fundamental to our well-being, so being deprived of sleep is very distressing and damaging.

This illustrates the good that comes from psychological research but also the potential dangers.

The French drive on the wrong side of the road and speak a foreign language. Both these statements are only true from our perspective. *Ethnocentrism* is the term used to describe how we all see the world from our own perspective.

The idea that a British memory test may have no relevance in another culture (see text on left) may never have occurred to you – because we are all rooted in our own culture.

An understanding of how psychological understanding has developed over time

The issue: More than just history

Psychology must adjust its focus in response to current events. For example, the Holocaust led psychologists to investigate obedience.

Why is it an issue?

It is important to look at development over time for two reasons. First, when we view research conducted decades ago it is valuable to see it within the historical context because different social norms were operating which may explain the behaviours observed.

Second, when looking at today's psychology we should be reminded that it is not the end of the story. Psychologists always criticise research and in that way our knowledge improves over time.

It is not simply a story about who discovered what and when but is about making comparisons over time such as:

- How historical events influence the viewpoints held by psychologists.
- Whether the progression of knowledge within a topic is getting wider or narrower.
- Whether explanations have changed in terms of looking for environmental or genetic causes.
- How the methods psychologists have used to investigate ideas have changed.

The issue in practice

Explanations of dreaming, and the ways it is studied, have changed over time.

Freud's early beliefs suggested dreams were an expression of the unconscious. Although this now seems unlikely, psychologists still cannot agree on the function of dreaming. There may be many functions or none at all. The methods used to study dreaming have also changed, from Freud's case studies to more objective ways to understand the brain mechanisms involved in dreaming.

These changes enable psychologists to develop better explanations for why we dream based on more sophisticated sources of evidence.

Issues in psychology (continued)

The use of psychological knowledge in society

The issue: How to help?

Psychology has many practical applications. Each of the key questions suggested in the specification illustrate ways in which psychology can be used to explore, explain, predict and improve aspects of society.

Why is it an issue?

The issue is how we should make the best use of our psychological knowledge in society. Are there ways in which we can improve people's mental health or avoid people becoming mentally ill, help those with addictions, give advice about children to parents or schools, or help in the identification and rehabilitation of criminals? These are all uses of psychology that are explored in different areas of your course.

The issue in practice

Sleep research has led to many advances in the treatment of sleep disorders. For example, Freud used his explanation of dreaming to develop the first 'talking therapy' to help people with mental health problems. This led to the development of many other successful talking therapies.

Since Freud, an understanding of the stages of sleep has given insight into other disorders, such as narcolepsy, a condition in which the onset of dream sleep is so rapid that the individual falls instantly to the ground, wherever they are and whatever they are doing.

Therefore, for psychology to be useful in society, people must have faith in the research and practices of psychologists. This leads back to the importance of ethics. If psychology is not trusted as a discipline, people will not be prepared to benefit from what it has to offer.

Happy pilot – because psychologists worked on the design of his cockpit. Human factors research (ergonomics) employs psychologists to design instruments and equipment with human perceptual systems in mind.

The results of psychological research are widely published – and not always correctly. That doesn't mean psychologists should withhold their results but they need to monitor the public understanding of what their research means.

Issues related to socially-sensitive research

The issue: Considering the impact of research

There are areas of study in psychology that can provoke intense feelings within communities. Studies may generate findings or theories may make predictions that people find unpalatable.

For example, studies that conclude there are fundamental differences between genders or cultures may have the potential to offend or may defend the divide between groups of people.

Studies may appear to represent some people in a negative light, for example indicating that people who live in cities are less caring or more prejudiced. This may lead those groups of people to behave differently.

Why is it an issue?

As psychology aims to improve lives, the discipline must be careful not to do the opposite. That is not to say that certain research should not be done because that would mean psychologists would have to avoid all meaningful research.

What it does mean is that psychologists have a duty to make their research available in responsible ways. This means ensuring that research is valid, that the findings can be verified and that the impact of publication has been duly considered.

The issue in practice

Research on sleep has the potential to be socially sensitive. The negative effects of sleep deprivation are well documented, such as lack of concentration, performance and vigilance. Research showing these effects in critical situations such as for pilots or surgeons could potentially frighten people. Such research is obviously essential but the impact both on 'consumers' (passengers or patients) as well as on people's careers should be recognised and some effort made to limit negative effects, for example by proposing solutions.

The impact of such suffering on the public face of psychology means any research needs to be carefully justified and reported.

Debates in psychology

Issues and debates

Reductionism in the explanation of behaviour

The debate: Reductionism versus holism

There are two opposing sides to this debate (as in all debates). Reductionism says that cognitions, emotions and behaviour can best be understood by breaking explanations down to the smallest possible parts. Holism on the other hand says that cognitions, emotions and behaviour can best be explained by taking a wider perspective.

A reductionist view would say that we can best investigate and explain aspects of sleep and dreams by looking at the role of individual neurotransmitters such as serotonin on the sleep process or the regions of the brain that are involved, such as the *pons*.

A holistic view in contrast would argue that whole brain processes of dream production and the waking experience of recalling and understanding our dreams is more valuable and informative.

What are the arguments for reductionism?

The reductionist approach suggests that individual elements are simpler, therefore more understandable, so can be studied and explained more effectively. Reductionist research therefore tends to use laboratory studies where variables can be controlled and precise details can be explored.

What are the arguments for holism?

The holistic approach suggests that without considering the 'bigger picture' we cannot hope to understand the complex interactions within whole systems. This is especially true of humans because there is so much more interplay between their thinking and social behaviour than is the case for animals. Holistic research therefore tends to use more all-encompassing methods such as case studies and unstructured interviews.

The role of both nature and nurture in psychology

The debate: Nature versus nurture

This is the argument about the extent to which a behaviour can be explained by innate, genetic factors or by factors such as the environment and experience. This dichotomy is best illustrated by biological psychology and the learning theories.

- Biological psychology uses explanations from genetics, such as the innate structure of the brain and this illustrates the nature end of the debate. However, some biological factors are nurture and not nature, for example the use of drugs may alter the processes in your body and that is the result of experience (nurture).
- Learning theories focus on the effects of experiences and factors within the environment and thus illustrate the nurture end of the spectrum. For example operant conditioning explains learning in terms of consequences (such as rewards). However, the process of conditioning is innate (nature).

This illustrates how difficult it is, in practice, to separate nature and nurture. There is a continuum with some behaviours being more nature and some more nurture.

What are the arguments for nature?

Within the domain of sleep and dreams, the nature argument prevails, for example the role of neurotransmitters and brain areas in governing sleep, which are largely biologically determined.

Evidence for the nature approach comes from sources such as studies of twins reared apart (similarities may be genetic), cross-cultural studies (similarities may be genetic) and from direct studies of genes.

What are the arguments for nurture?

Some aspects of our sleep are responsive to the environment. For example, if you move to live close to a railway, you might be kept awake by the noise at first. People tend to adapt to such situations, this is 'nurture' at work. Conversely, stressful experiences in our lives may cause us to lose sleep so the root cause of this problem is environmental.

Evidence for the influence of nurture comes from sources such as longitudinal studies (changes over time may be due to experience, though they can also be due to maturation, i.e. nature). In addition, cross-cultural studies that demonstrate differences between communities support the nurture perspective as they demonstrate that the environment in which you grow up affects your development.

> In our Year 2 book we look at each of the issues and debates in greater depth.

A piece of buttered toast has a 'right side up' but there is no 'right' side in a debate – that's why they are debates. If there was a solution there would be no continuing debate. The importance of the debate is the discussion.

Psychology as a science

The debate: Is psychology a science or not?

Psychology is categorised as an A level science subject. However, not everyone agrees that psychology is a science. Many factors determine what is a science, and some are less apparent in psychology than other science subjects.

What are the arguments for psychology being a science?

Your experience with the course will show you that psychologists do a lot of experiments and that psychology is awash with scientific ideas such as controls, standardisation and inferential testing.

This last point is very important – science should be falsifiable, that is we should be able to demonstrate that the ideas being tested are *not* true. This is entirely possible in psychological research, such as identifying whether dreams occur in a particular stage of sleep. EEGs are reliable measures of sleep stages and studies can be rigorously controlled, even when participants are asleep!

What are the arguments for psychology not being a science?

Freud's approach is much less scientific. The main problem with his explanation of dreaming is that it cannot be falsified. There is no way to demonstrate with certainty whether his explanation of the meaning of a dream is correct or not.

Less scientific methods in psychology include those which are more subjective, such as thematic analysis, case studies and the use of unstructured interviews with open questions. In each case the problem lies in the lack of objectivity in the interpretation of the findings. This leads to questions over the validity and reliability of the findings.

Social psychology

Chapter 1

Contents

Obedience
28 Agency theory
30 Social impact theory
32 Milgram's baseline study
34 Milgram's variation studies

Factors affecting obedience and dissent
36 Individual differences (personality and gender)
38 Situation and culture

Prejudice
40 Social identity theory
42 Realistic conflict theory

Factors affecting prejudice (and discrimination)
44 Individual differences (personality)
46 Situation and culture

Methods – see pages 168-181 of Chapter 5

Studies
48 Classic study: Sherif et al. (1954/1961)
    Contemporary study, select one of:
50   Burger (2009)
52   Reicher and Haslam (2006)
54   Cohrs et al. (2012)

56 **Key questions for social psychology**

58 **Practical investigations for social psychology**

End of chapter
60 Revision summary
62 Practice questions, answers and feedback
64 Multiple-choice questions

Human beings are social animals and being part of a group can lead to many benefits to the individual members.

However, group membership can also encourage individuals to participate in behaviours that they may never have considered had they not been 'one of the gang'.

These young men may be harmless skaters but many gangs are involved with violence and organised crime.

Why do you think young people join gangs? What costs and benefits might there be?

Obedience: Agency theory

The specification says…
1.1.1 Theories of obedience, including agency theory.

Key terms

Obedience – A form of social influence in which an individual follows a direct order. The person issuing the order is usually a figure of authority who has the power to punish when obedient behaviour is not forthcoming. There is usually the assumption that the person receiving the order is made to respond in a way they would not otherwise have done.

Autonomous state – A mindset where we behave independently, make our own decisions about how to behave and take responsibility for the consequences of our actions.

Agentic state – A mindset which allows us to carry out orders from an authority figure, even if they conflict with our personal sense of right and wrong. We absolve ourselves of responsibility, believing that as we are acting on someone else's behalf, blame for any negative consequences ultimately lies with them.

Agentic shift – The switch between the autonomous and agentic state that occurs when we perceive someone to be a legitimate source of authority and allow them to control our behaviour.

Moral strain – A state of mental discomfort or anxiety experienced in the agentic state when a person's actions conflict with their personal morality.

Think Link
Individual differences

The role of socialisation

Agency theory suggests that we have an innate potential for obedience, which implies that everyone should be the same (no individual differences). However, obedience is shaped by experiences such as differing parenting styles and educational experiences. These experiences may explain individual differences in obedience rates.

The origins of obedience: Nature meets nurture

Stanley Milgram (1974) said that obedience to authority is necessary for the smooth running of society. Humans live in hierarchically organised social groups and in order for these groups to function successfully, *subordinate* individuals sometimes have to suppress their personal desires in order to carry out the wishes of their superiors. Milgram (1974) maintained that 'we are born with a potential for obedience, which then interacts with the influence of society to create the obedient man'.

Milgram suggested that we have two mindsets or states that enable us to operate on our own and with others – the autonomous and agentic states.

Autonomous state

In this state, our behaviour is 'self-directed'. We are at liberty to choose how to behave. We take greater responsibility for the consequences of our actions and, dependent upon the situation, we will be more likely to exercise our personal understanding of right and wrong to guide our choices. We operate in this state when we are on our own, with peers or with people who we perceive to be below us in the social hierarchy.

Making the agentic shift

When meeting others, we quickly judge whether the other person is higher or lower than us in the social hierarchy and the extent to which they have legitimate authority. Authority is legitimate when there is a consensus that a person has the right to give orders and to enforce obedience. When confronted with a legitimate authority figure, we change from our normal autonomous state to the agentic state. The change from one state to the other is called the agentic shift.

When we are in the agentic state, we become the 'agent' of the authority figure, meaning that we believe that we are *acting on their behalf* and that responsibility for our actions lies with them. We may follow the orders of the authority figure feeling that we have no choice but to obey and this may lead us to do things that we might not normally choose to do. Milgram believes that this agentic state is what leads people to commit acts of *destructive obedience*.

Moral strain

In this state, people may experience symptoms of anxiety, especially when obeying orders that result in harm and Milgram called this moral strain. For example, if we believe that harming people is wrong, yet we also know that our actions have resulted in harm, these two conflicting ideas lead to cognitive dissonance, a state of mental conflict that leads to moral strain. However, for the majority of people this strain is not sufficient to provoke defiance and Milgram explains that powerful *binding factors* ensure that the individual remains in the agentic state and does nothing that might jeopardise the status quo.

Lynndie England followed orders to 'break' the prisoners in Abu Ghraib. Milgram would say that she made the agentic shift when given instructions by her superior and that many people behave similarly, in the face of legitimate authority.

Can good people be turned evil?

In 2004, explicit photographs provided stark evidence of human rights abuses committed by US military personnel against Iraqi detainees in Abu Ghraib, a prison in Baghdad.

Some of the military personnel, such as Lynndie England (left), were tried in court for their offences. They blamed the chain of command saying that they were just following orders to 'be tough' and 'break' the prisoners. She is quoted as saying, 'We don't feel like we were doing things that we weren't supposed to, because we were told to do them' (CBS News 2004).

Psychologist Philip Zimbardo appeared as an expert witness, defending the actions of the soldiers and citing his own research (the Stanford Prison Experiment) and that of Stanley Milgram. He explained the power of the social situation in eliciting 'evil behaviour' from 'good people', not least due to our deeply ingrained predisposition to obey orders (Zimbardo 2007). His testimony was unpalatable for many who prefer to think that evil people commit evil acts.

You can find out more by watching Zimbardo's TED talk *The psychology of evil*. (tinyurl.com/p86ymd3)

What do you think the implications might have been for Lynndie England if she had refused to take part in the scenes shown in the photographs?

Evaluation

Supporting evidence

A strength of Milgram's agency theory is that it is supported by his 1963 study (described on page 32).

In this study he found that 100% of participants would administer a shock of 300 V to a confederate as a punishment for making a mistake on a word learning task and 65% would go right up to the final 450 V, beyond the shock labelled 'danger, extreme shock'.

This is important because it clearly supports Milgram's suggestion that in the face of legitimate authority people are highly likely to carry out orders, despite high levels of moral strain.

> **Competing argument** However, Gina Perry (2012) questioned the internal validity of this evidence saying that the participants saw through the deception. She examined recently released evidence from the Yale University archives of his study. This evidence reveals that many participants questioned whether the shocks were real. This new evidence shows that across all of Milgram's variation studies more than 60% of participants *disobeyed* the experimenter. This reinterpretation of Milgram's data leaves agency theory in question.

Agentic shift isn't inevitable

A weakness of the theory is that the agentic shift does not appear to be inevitable.

Steven Rank and Cardell Jacobson's (1977) study with nurses found that 16 out of 18 (89%) nurses failed to obey orders from a doctor who asked them to administer an overdose of the drug Valium.

This shows that despite the doctors being an obvious source of authority, the vast majority of the sample remained autonomous. This qualitative data demonstrates that the nurses *did* consider themselves responsible for their actions.

Application to the military

Milgram maintained that when *binding factors* outweigh moral strain, obedience follows. This principle has been applied in a variety of military strategies devised to ensure soldiers follow orders without question by reducing moral strain.

One example is the use of euphemisms such as 'collateral damage' (unintentional deaths of civilians in pursuit of a legitimate military target) and dehumanising language used to refer to the enemy.

This shows how an authority figure's communication can minimise moral strain, ensuring that soldiers remain in the agentic state, even when ordered to commit barbarous acts, including torture (Gibson and Haritos-Fatouros 1986).

EXTRA: Issues and debates

There are alternative ways to explain obedience, using a different theme/theory.

Steve Reicher et al. (2012) have used *social identity theory* (discussed later in this chapter) to explain obedience, using the concept of 'engaged followership'. According to them, people obey leaders who are seen to be part of their social group, therefore the followers identify with the leader. Disobedience occurs when the followers fail to identify with the leader.

This alternative theme/theory is important as it helps to explain when *and* why people disobey whereas agency theory doesn't.

Balanced conclusion

On balance, it would appear that while Milgram provided extensive well-controlled experiments to explore the phenomenon of destructive obedience, his theory is perhaps oversimplified and overstated. The agentic state is not inevitable and therefore it would be more beneficial to society to examine the factors that lead people to resist destructive obedience, allowing them to think more independently and take greater conscious control of their actions.

When we are in the agentic state we may feel 'bound' to the authority figure. However, Milgram (1974) remained positive saying, 'It may be that we are puppets – puppets controlled by the strings of society. But at least we are puppets with perception, with awareness. And perhaps our awareness is the first step to our liberation.'

 **Methods:** Fair play?

Adam and Miron asked 50 people if they believed they would act agentically or autonomously in different situations.

Table showing participants' responses about their behaviour in different situations.

	At work	In the car	Football match	At the shops	Mean
Agentic	40	45	20	25	
Autonomous	10	5	30	25	

1. (a) Calculate the mean number of people who believed they would behave agentically. (1)
   (b) Express this mean as a percentage of all the people questioned. (1)
2. Adam also asked some participants why they would act agentically in some situations and not others.
   (a) Would this question produce qualitative or quantitative data? (1)
   (b) Explain **one** advantage of this extra information. (2)
   (c) Explain **one** problem with this extra information. (2)

 **Concepts:** Naughty Lilly

Lilly is hiding from her mother because it's bedtime but she wants to play. Her mother finds Lilly behind the sofa and tells her to go to bed. Lilly says 'no' but her mother says she must come to bed, so reluctantly Lilly follows her.

1. Identify **two** pieces of evidence that suggest Lilly was in an autonomous state. (2)
2. Identify **one** piece of evidence that suggests Lilly was in an agentic state. (2)
3. Identify what caused Lilly to enter the agentic state. (1)

Study tip

Be very careful about 'circular definitions', i.e. avoid saying that agentic state means 'acting as an agent'. Never define one term by using the same term – explain what an agent is.

Check it

1. Identify **two** differences between the agentic and the autonomous states. (2)
2. Ruby and Mia are in the same class. Ruby does what her teacher tells her but Mia refuses. Explain the girls' behaviour using agency theory. (2)
3. **Standard:** Evaluate Milgram's agency theory as an explanation of obedience. (8)
4. **AL (I&D/Synoptic):** Evaluate the issue of reductionism in relation to the use of social and biological theories in explaining human behaviour. (12)

Obedience: Social impact theory

The specification says...
1.1.1 Theories of obedience, including social impact theory.

Key term

Social impact theory – An explanation of the extent to which other people's real or imagined presence can alter the way an individual thinks, feels or acts. The impact is determined by strength, immediacy and number of sources during any interaction.

Think Link
Individual differences

The subjectivity of strength

The usefulness of the formula I = f(SIN) relies upon the researcher inputting valid numbers in the place of the letters. The problem is that factors such as source strength are subjective to the target.

This explains why individuals may be 'impacted' to a lesser or greater degree in comparison with one another, dependent upon their personal perception.

For example, a government official's perceived strength may be dependent upon the political persuasion of the target and this may account for individual differences in the level of compliance that the official is able to elicit from others.

Study tip

The 'think links' can be used as evaluation, especially the individual differences ones because they point out that the concepts/conclusions only apply to some people.

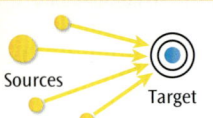 

Multiplication of impact
The source is depicted in yellow. The size of the yellow dot indicates the strength of the source. The closeness to the target (blue circle) indicates immediacy. The number of black rings around the target shows the amount of influence exerted – created by number, strength and immediacy of the source.

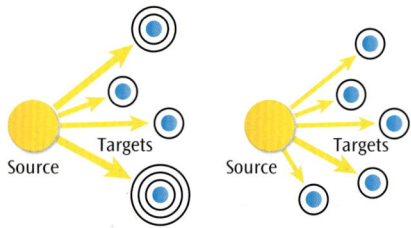

Division of impact
The source (yellow dot) has a reduced effect because its impact is now divided between several targets. The closer the target to the source, the less the influence because the targets impact on the source.

Social impact theory

Sources and targets

The term 'social impact' refers to the effect that real or imagined people can have on our behaviour – 'social' referring to the fact that the effect comes from other people. Bibb Latané (1981) developed social impact theory to describe how we behave within 'social forcefields', all impacting on each other through our ongoing interactions.

The person doing the influencing is the 'source' and the people who are influenced are the 'targets'. Latané produced a mathematical formula to represent his theory about how 'sources' impact 'targets', i.e. change the thoughts, feelings and actions of the target:

$$\text{Impact on the target} = f(SIN) \text{ [where SIN refers to the source(s)]}$$

Social impact is a function of strength (S) multiplied by immediacy (I) multiplied by the number of sources (N).

Strength, immediacy and number

The formula indicates how three key factors (strength, immediacy and number) predict how much the target will change their thoughts, feelings and actions.

- *Strength* (S) refers to the perceived power/authority of the source and the messages that they convey. For example, a strong source may have power over the target and/or they may communicate in an authoritative, intense or charismatic way. Strength can be affected by socio-economic status, age and the nature of any past or future relationship with the target.
- *Immediacy* (I) reflects the closeness of the source and the target in terms of space, but also time. Physical or psychological barriers to communication will affect immediacy.
- *Number* (N) relates to how many sources are present during the interaction, which determine the level of social impact.

Multiplicative and divisional effects

Latané used the phrase *multiplicative effect* to explain how increasing strength, immediacy and/or number of sources can significantly increase the social impact. The *light bulb analogy* explains this further – brightness is affected by:

- The 'strength' of the bulb (100 watts compared with 70 watts).
- How far away the light source is ('immediacy').
- The 'number' of bulbs.

Divisional effect explains the idea that social impact is reduced if there are more targets than there are sources – the impact is divided by the number of targets and therefore the impact on each person is reduced. This was represented by another formula:

$$\text{Impact on the target} = f(1/(SIN)) \text{ [where SIN refers to the target(s)]}$$

The law of diminishing returns

Latané made a specific point about number, saying that once the source group is bigger than three, each additional person has less of an influencing effect. Therefore, the difference of one extra person in a group that goes from two to three people is larger than the difference of adding an extra person to a group of 52 to make 53. Economists call this the *law of diminishing returns*. Latané didn't mean that a group of one hundred people would be less powerful than a group of three, but that adding the 100th person to a group of 99 changes the level of impact less than adding a third person to a group of two.

Social engineering

Latané used the term 'social engineering' to refer to planned efforts to change the way members of a society think, feel and behave. This may have positive effects, such as helping people to comply with orders from their doctor, for example to adopt a healthier lifestyle that will extend their life. Equally it could be used by malevolent leaders to persuade people to act maliciously.

In either case, success is enhanced if the source's message is strong, proximity between the source and the target is reduced and ideally there should be fewer targets present at any one time. However, Latané also suggested that if targets are strong, close to each other and numerous, impact from a source is reduced.

Using social impact theory, what would be the best way to change something in your school?

Evaluation

Obedience at the zoo

A strength of social impact theory is that it is supported by research evidence.

For example, Constantine Sedikides and Jeffrey Jackson (1990) conducted a field experiment at a New York zoo, where visitors were asked not to lean on a railing. The researchers manipulated the strength of the source by dressing a confederate either as a zoo keeper (58% obedience) or in a T-shirt and shorts (35% obedience). Obedience also declined when the visitors were further from the person making the request (61% when in the same room, 7% when in an adjacent room) – testing immediacy. Finally the divisional effect was also tested – obedience was greater in a smaller group of one or two visitors (fewer targets, 60%) compared with a group of five or six (more targets, 14%).

This study demonstrates the importance of strength, immediacy and number in social impact.

Competing argument As this was a field experiment, the researchers were not able to manipulate the number of people in each group, a threat to internal validity. For example, people who choose to go around in larger groups may have less obedient personalities (a confounding variable). Meaning it may not be group size alone that determined the level of defiance observed.

Immediacy less important than strength

A weakness of social impact theory is that the role of immediacy may not be a key ingredient in social impact.

Charles Hofling et al. (1966) arranged for an unknown doctor to telephone 22 nurses and ask each of them to administer an overdose of a drug that was not on their ward list. A startling 95% of the nurses started to administer the drug (they were prevented from doing so). Although the doctor was not immediately present, the nurses obeyed without question.

This challenges social impact theory because the source being absent should have reduced the effect but it didn't. Or at least it didn't appear to make a difference – we actually have no comparison with the source being present so we can't be certain about this.

Application to political influence

Social impact theory can be easily applied to understand how people enhance their social influence.

For example, political leaders may increase their influence by (1) adopting a strong and persuasive style of communication to connect with their target voters, (2) aiming to reach voters by talking face-to-face rather than through TV or radio broadcasts and (3) addressing smaller groups rather than larger crowds, where the divisional effect may reduce the impact of their messages.

This shows how psychological knowledge can be applied to society and how people's behaviour (e.g. voting) could be influenced through a strategic campaign.

EXTRA: Issues and debates

Social impact theory could be seen as reductionist.

It reduces the complexity of human thoughts, feelings and experiences to three numbers in order to predict outcomes. This is arguably a fruitless task as quantifying 'strength', in particular, is very tricky because it is subjective to the individual sources and targets involved.

This suggests that, in order for social impact theory to make accurate predictions, it may be necessary to gather qualitative data to better understand how the targets and sources perceive each other.

Balanced conclusion

Social impact theory is supported by research studies (such as Sedikides and Jackson), which demonstrate the importance of strength, immediacy and number in predicting obedience and other forms of social impact. However, the results of other research suggest that there isn't a simple formula that can be applied – in fact trying to do this is a rather reductionist approach to understanding human behaviour. It may not be possible to work out a universal equation.

The strength of a source can be affected by many things, wearing horns isn't usually one of them. However, if the cap fits ...

Apply it — Methods: SIN

Evie is exploring social impact theory. She can measure 'number' but is not so sure about 'strength' and 'immediacy'. She is studying the head in her school, teachers, prefects and students in different years, and using situations where people are standing together or various distances apart.

1. (a) Describe **two** methods she could use to measure strength numerically. (2)
   (b) Explain which of these methods would be more objective. (2)
   (c) Explain **one** problem with each of your suggested measures of strength. (2)
2. (a) Give **one** numerical measure of immediacy. (1)
   (b) Explain how the level of measurement of this method differs from the measures of strength. (1)

Apply it — Concepts: Junior Jake

Jake plays football for the school juniors. They are either coached by a senior school player, or senior school players, or by a teacher. Some days the coaches stay on the sidelines, or they move around among the players.

1. Use social impact theory to describe the effect of:
   (a) Strength in this situation. (2)
   (b) Immediacy in this situation. (2)
   (c) Number in this situation. (2)
2. Suggest **one** way that the targets could vary which would affect division of impact. (2)

Study tip

When evaluating social impact theory, you can create an evaluation point by making comparisons with agency theory. Be careful though – simply describing the other theory will not gain credit, you need to show how social impact theory is either better or worse.

Check it

1. Explain **two** ways in which the source can vary in terms of its impact according to social impact theory. (2)
2. Distinguish between 'multiplication of impact' and 'division of impact' according to social impact theory. (2)
3. **Standard:** Evaluate social impact theory. (8)
4. **AL (I&D/Synoptic):** To what extent are social and biological psychology on the 'nature' side of the nature–nurture debate? (12)

Obedience: Milgram's baseline study

The specification says...
1.1.2 Research into obedience, including Milgram's research into obedience.

Stanley Milgram (1933–1984)

Stanley Milgram was born in New York City to working-class Jewish immigrants. This meant that the events of the Holocaust were personally significant to him, especially in 1960 when Adolf Eichmann was caught and tried for war crimes. Eichmann had been in charge of the 'final solution' but excused his behaviour by saying 'he was just obeying orders'.

Milgram worked at the prestigious Yale University and carried out the obedience studies there. The work caused great controversy which affected his career.

Think Link
Individual differences

Personality and life experiences
Alan Elms (2009) found a positive correlation between the maximum shock delivered in the Milgram studies and participants' scores on the F-scale which measures the 'obedient personality' (see page 36). This suggests that behaviour in Milgram's study was influenced by individual differences.

An analysis of the post-study interviews also reveals that life experiences affected how people thought and felt whilst taking part. For example, a participant in a later study (Gretchen Brandt) dropped out at 210 V. She had grown up in Nazi Germany and explained 'perhaps we have seen too much pain' (Milgram 1974), suggesting that we all bring something of our past to new situations.

The impact of the differing prods
Milgram believed that his results showed that people were very obedient. However, a recent analysis by Alex Haslam et al. (2014) shows that participants only continued after the first three prods. All participants who were given prod 4 – 'You have no other choice, you *must* go on' – disobeyed. This challenges the conclusion that people are highly obedient to authority because, in fact, when participants were told they must blindly obey, they didn't.

Milgram himself suggested in his conclusions that obedience was related to identification with important scientific research ('The experiment requires that you continue'). People don't simply obey, they only obey if they identify with the authority figure.

What new conclusion(s) should be drawn about obedience to authority?

A behavioural study of obedience

Aim
Stanley Milgram (1963) aimed to understand the behaviour of those Germans who followed orders to kill over 10 million people in the Holocaust. There was a belief that the 'Germans were different', i.e. they were very obedient and Milgram wanted to explore this.

In order to do this he needed to develop a method to test obedience to legitimate authority even when the command required destructive behaviour. The test had to involve destructive behaviour because, if participants were asked to obey a neutral or constructive order, then there would be little reason *not* to obey.

Procedure
Milgram described his study as an experiment but it isn't because there is no independent variable – researchers use the term 'experiment' more carefully now.

He recruited a volunteer sample of 40 men, aged 20–50 years, from New Haven (in America) through the local newspaper and letters in the post. They varied from unskilled workers to professionals. The men were offered $4.50 for participation, a reasonable sum in those days.

On arrival, participants were told that they could drop out at any point and still keep the money. They were introduced to two men. One was the experimenter, a 'mild-mannered, likeable man' dressed in a grey technician's coat. He was a confederate of Milgram's and given the name Mr. Williams.

The second man, who was also a confederate, was introduced as the other participant and referred to as Mr. Wallace. Lots were drawn to decide whether the real participant would be the teacher or the learner, but participants were always the teacher.

The 'teacher' was told that his job was to give the 'learner' an electric shock for every mistake on a word recall task. The voltage supposedly increased 15 volts at a time but in fact the shocks were fake. Only one real shock (of 45 volts) was given to the teacher to make him believe that the machine was real. The learner was taken to a separate room and the teacher saw him being strapped into a chair and electrodes being attached to his wrists.

The participant teacher sat in front of the shock machine with 30 switches from 15 V to 450 V. Switches were labelled from 'slight shock' to 'danger; severe shock' and 'XXX'. The teacher communicated through an intercom but could not hear the learner, who gave his answers by pressing buttons. When the teacher delivered 300 V (intense shock), the learner was heard pounding on the wall. At 315 V more pounding was heard but from there on, no further sound was heard from him.

If the participant teacher protested, the experimenter used a series of standardised prompts ('verbal prods') to urge the participant to continue. The same prods were always used in the same order, starting with (1) 'Please continue' or 'Please go on', (2) 'The experiment requires that you continue', (3) 'It is absolutely essential that you continue', and (4) 'You have no other choice, you *must* go on'. If participants protested after the fourth prod, they were allowed to leave and the maximum shock delivered was recorded.

Milgram also collected a lot of film footage, including the participants' reactions and dialogue. Post-study interviews also provided further qualitative data.

Findings
Milgram found that 65% of his sample administered the full 450 V shock. A full 100% continued to 300 V although at this point 12.5% of the sample dropped out. Participants were observed to tremble, sweat, bite their lips and dig fingernails into their flesh. 35% exhibited nervous laughter. Three participants had full-blown uncontrollable seizures.

Conclusions
The findings showed that ordinary Americans are surprisingly obedient to legitimate authority. Milgram suggested that a number of factors may explain obedience such as the perceived competence and reputation of the researcher and the idea that participation was somehow advancing science.

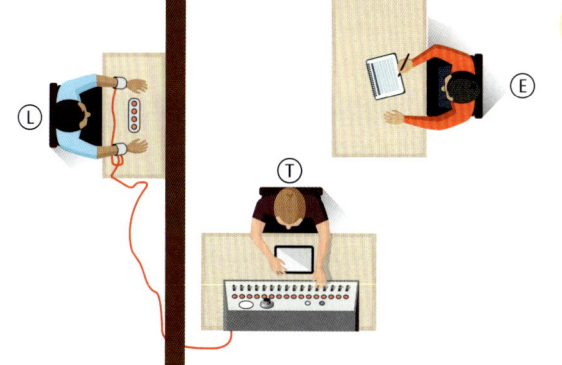

A diagram of the room set up showing the position of the experimenter (E), teacher (T) and learner (L) in a separate room. The shock generator is in front of the teacher. The teacher could not see or hear the learner. The learner communicated his answers by pressing buttons and the teacher had to work out whether the answer was right or wrong according to which light flashed on the signal board.

Evaluation

Standardised procedure
A strength of Milgram's procedure is that it was standardised, meaning that every participant had the exact same experience.

The two confederates were always played by the same actors, the number and timing of the learner's mistakes was the same for every participant and the experimenter's responses were supposedly tightly scripted, for example, the prods were always delivered in the same order and tone of voice.

This is important because it means that the study is replicable and has been tested, successfully – see Burger (2009) on page 50.

Competing argument Gina Perry (2012) (see previous spread) argues that there were occasions when the experimenter deviated from the script and in one instance, he allegedly gave as many as 20 prods before he allowed a participant to leave. This departure from the procedure suggests that Milgram's study may not be as standardised as he claimed.

The task didn't make sense
A weakness is that participants may only have obeyed because they did not believe that the shocks were real.

Martin Orne and Charles Holland (1968) argued that participants behaved the way they did because they didn't really believe in the set-up – participants guessed it wasn't real electric shocks but just went along with it anyway. Orne and Holland argued that the participants must have found it odd that the experimenter did not administer the learning task himself and that he showed so little concern for the learner. Again, Perry supports this, as previously unseen film footage shows participants expressing their suspicion regarding the authenticity of the shock machine.

This calls into question the internal validity of the findings of the study, as Milgram was not testing what he intended to test.

Application to pilot training
Milgram's findings have been applied to improve pilot training.

Eugen Tarnow (2000) describes how first officers often fail to monitor and challenge errors made by the captain due to his or her legitimate authority. Tarnow draws parallels between behaviour in the Milgram studies and in the commercial airplane cockpit, whereby first officers are often hesitant to question the captain even when his or her behaviour is putting others at risk. Tarnow believes that training first officers in how to challenge the authority of the pilot could prevent up to 20% of plane crashes.

This has led to training to improve cockpit behaviour and potentially save lives.

EXTRA: Issues and debates
Milgram's study raises ethical issues and for many people this is a major downfall in his research.

Diana Baumrind (1964) presented a scathing attack arguing that just because someone volunteers for a study does not take away the researcher's responsibilities towards them. Baumrind felt that the level of psychological harm was unacceptable. Milgram claimed to have debriefed his participants, which goes some way to mitigating the harm. However, Perry claims that some of Milgram's participants left the study believing the learner may have actually died.

These are critical issues as deception could lead the general public to lose faith in authority and could also jeopardise the reputation of psychological research.

Balanced conclusion
Milgram's study has probably created more debate than any other in psychology. The applications of his work, in terms of protecting people from following dangerous or unethical orders in business, medicine or the military for example have contributed positively to society. However, the study will also be remembered for Milgram's disregard for his participants' welfare. In addition, recent research has revealed evidence to suggest that the study may have had more worrying flaws than previously acknowledged.

 **Methods:** Unfair game!

Mr Singh organises a study similar to Milgram's. A confederate pretends to be a participant who is the 'loser' in a new computer game. The real participant, chosen by a fixed draw to be the 'winner' plays against the loser who he can see in the next room getting frustrated then upset, because he keeps losing. Each time the participant says, 'It's not fair, I want to stop', another confederate claiming to have written the new game uses Milgram-type prods to insist they continue.

1. Milgram's study was realistic because it was based at a prestigious university, the experimenter wore a technician's coat and used a realistic shock machine.
   (a) Describe **two** ways in which Mr Singh could make his study realistic. (2)
   (b) Explain why realism is essential to such studies. (2)
2. Milgram's study had 40 participants, and 65% were obedient and gave the 450 V shock.
   (a) Calculate the number of participants who were obedient and disobedient. (2)
   (b) If 12.5% of participants dropped out after 300 V, what fraction continued?

 **Concepts:** Disobedient swimmers

Ryan goes swimming but worries because people at the pool break the rules by jumping and diving in which is dangerous. When he tells them to stop, they usually ignore him.

1. How could Ryan change his appearance so that people would obey him? (1)
2. Ryan also worries about the authority that instructors have and fears that unfit swimmers might hurt themselves if they feel obliged to obey.
   (a) How would Milgram's findings explain this situation? (1)
   (b) Explain what would need to happen to help the unfit people. (2)
3. Explain why Ryan's ideas could be useful. (4)

Study tip
When you are evaluating a study always aim to have an even balance of strengths and weaknesses as the mark scheme is clear about the need for balance in your answer.

Check it

1. Explain the purpose of deception in Milgram's study. [4]
2. Describe **two** ways in which Milgram collected data in his original study. [2]
3. **Standard:** Evaluate Milgram's study of obedience. [8]
4. **AL (I&D):** Assess Milgram's study as an example of psychology as a science. [8]

Obedience: Milgram's variation studies

The specification says...

1.1.2 Research into obedience, including three of Milgram's variation studies: Rundown Office Block (Experiment 10), Telephonic instructions (Experiment 7), Ordinary man gives orders (Experiment 13) as they demonstrate situational factors that encourage dissent.

Key term

Situational factors – Features of the immediate physical and social environment which may influence a person's behaviour. The alternative is dispositional factors where behaviour is explained in terms of personality.

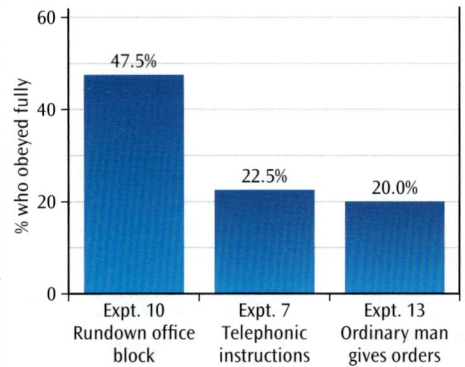

A bar chart to show the percentage of participants who administered the full 450 V in each of the three variation studies.

Think Link
Developmental psychology

Children and obedience

Psychological research has shown that the way people think about authority changes as they get older, presumably as a result of socialisation (learning social norms).

For example, Lawrence Kohlberg (1968) developed a stage theory in which he proposed that children aged 4–10 years have an unquestioning deference to authority. This changes with age until early adulthood when some people, but not all, develop a more universal sense of right and wrong and no longer defer to authority if they think the orders are wrong.

'That's right Mr Williams, everything is going just fine!' – do you always do the right thing, when no one is there to tell you off?

Further research into obedience

New baseline

Following his original study (see previous spread) Stanley Milgram set out to investigate the **situational factors** which might encourage or discourage dissent. To do this he created new standard procedures to establish a new baseline (Experiment 5).

This involved moving to a slightly more modest laboratory (in his own words, it wasn't as 'posh'!). The learner (Mr Wallace) also mentioned that he had 'a mild heart condition' before the study began. Once the study was underway, the participant teacher was able to hear the learner's responses, although in reality this was all pre-recorded. Despite the changes to the set-up, the results were the same – 65% of the participants were fully obedient. Each of the studies cited below used 40 male participants, as before.

Experiment 10: Rundown office block

Many of Milgram's participants said that the prestigious university setting led them to trust the integrity and competence of the 'experimenter'. To test the effect of the setting Milgram moved the study to a rundown building, in the downtown shopping district of Bridgeport, an industrial city near Yale University (which was located in New Haven, Connecticut).

Participants were told the study was being run by a private firm, conducting research for industry. The results of this study were that 47.5% of participants were fully obedient. Interview transcripts show that participants voiced their doubts about the legitimacy of the research and their fears for the learner's safety.

It appears that the prestigious context is an important situational factor that affects levels of obedience. The shabby setting reduced the legitimacy of the researcher. However, the link to 'scientific' research seemed to be enough to still encourage relatively high levels of obedience.

Experiment 7: Telephonic instructions

In this variation, the 'experimenter' gave orders over the telephone. Milgram states that only 9 out of 40 (22.5%) were fully obedient under these circumstances.

Participants also lied on the phone, saying they were raising the shock level when they weren't and often repeatedly administering the lowest shock on the machine. Participants seemed to find it easier to resist authority in this passive way than openly challenge the authority figure. When the researcher came back into the room, defiant participants became obedient again.

The physical presence of the authority figure appears to be an important situational factor that increases obedience and reduces dissent.

Experiment 13: Ordinary man gives orders

Milgram wanted to disentangle the question of whether people will obey an order due to the strength of the command itself or due to the status of the person giving the order. In this variation, the participant arrives with two confederates rather than one. One confederate is assigned the role of learner and the other confederate is assigned the role of recording times from a clock (acting as a confederate recorder). The real participant is the 'teacher'. The experimenter explains the task as usual and the teacher observes 'Mr. Wallace' being strapped into the chair.

At this point, the experimenter receives a fake phone call calling him away. Apparently flustered, he asks the participant teacher and the confederate recorder to get the learner to learn all the word pairs. Once he has gone, the confederate recorder enthusiastically suggests administering shocks that increase by 15 V every time the learner makes a mistake and insists that they follow this procedure.

In this variation, 80% of participants refused to continue when an 'ordinary man' gave orders to shock the learner. This shows that orders must come from a legitimate source to be effective and this is an important situational factor that can encourage dissent.

Experiment 13a: What Milgram did next

As in Experiment 13, in 13a there is a participant teacher and a confederate recorder, and no experimenter present. If the participant teacher refused the confederate recorder's directions, the confederate recorder would become angry. He said he would administer the shocks himself and that the participant teacher should record the duration of the shocks.

This situation unleashed heroic behaviour, in stark contrast to the more usual deferential politeness shown to the 'experimenter'. Nearly all participants protested against this, some unplugged the shock machine, four physically restrained the confederate who was supposedly delivering the shocks and one threw him across the room. However, one participant broke the mould, he seemed to admire the confederate and described him as 'strong and capable'.

Why do you think this person felt and acted differently from all the others?

Evaluation

Experiment 10: Rundown office block
A strength of this variation was the fact that Milgram collected not only quantitative data but also qualitative data in the form of audio recordings of the dialogue between the participants and the researcher.

Andre Modigliani and François Rochat (1995) conducted a re-analysis of the interview transcripts of 36 of the 40 participants in this variation and found that the earlier in the procedure that the participant challenged the experimenter, the more likely they were to be fully defiant.

This qualitative data allowed Modigliani and Rochat to gain a deeper insight into different types of resistance and use what they had learned to explain the 'ordinariness of goodness' displayed by people who defied the authorities and rescued potential victims during the Holocaust.

Experiment 7: Telephonic instructions
A strength of this variation is that subsequent research has replicated this finding, demonstrating high external validity.

For example, on page 31 we outlined a study by Sedikides and Jackson (1990) conducted at a New York zoo. This study also demonstrated that when the authority figure is no longer present, obedience drops significantly – once the people had moved onto a new area of the birdhouse it was like the request had never been made. The people leaned on the rail just as much as they did in the baseline condition, when no request was made at all!

This shows that Milgram's results on physical proximity generalise well to other more naturalistic situations.

Experiment 13: Ordinary man gives orders
A weakness is that variation 13 possibly lacks internal validity.

Milgram, himself, explains that the withdrawal of the experimenter from the laboratory was awkward. Although the aim of this variation was to see what happens when the orders come from someone who has no legitimate authority, this was almost impossible to achieve. Milgram says there were many traces of so-called 'derived authority' as it was the experimenter who had initially described the study and the idea of administering shocks.

This suggests that obedience may be even lower in situations where the person giving orders is completely unrelated to any authority figure or institutional context.

EXTRA: Issues and debates
Milgram faced many practical issues in the design and implementation of his research.

For example, about 900 participants took part in this series of studies which were conducted over many months. This may have resulted in participants being exposed to people who had already participated who may have discussed the fact that the shocks were not real.

This could have jeopardised the validity of future results as 'contaminated' participants may have acted in accordance with what they thought was expected of them rather than showing natural behaviour.

Balanced conclusion
The variations of the original baseline study show insights into the factors that reduce or increase obedience, most particularly that people obey not necessarily because they are obedient people but because features of the situation demand more or less obedience. While these ingenious experiments reveal important situational factors which affect obedience, the potential benefits to society may be overshadowed by concerns about the validity of his procedures.

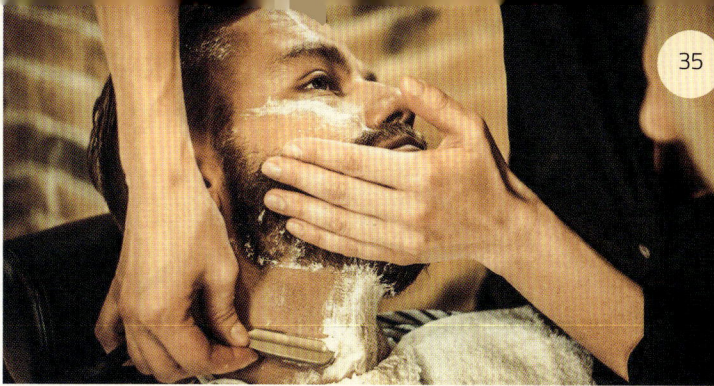

Context is an important situational factor which affects whether people obey orders. For example, you might obey orders from a barber to expose your throat to a man with a razor blade but in a shoe shop you would react with horror. On the other hand, in a shoe shop you would obey orders to take off your shoes but maybe not if you were in a barber shop.

Apply it — Methods: Wearing a uniform
A study tested children's understanding of authority figures by telling stories (with pictures) about three men who saw a crime. The children were first told which man was a policeman. They were then told that each man changed their clothing – to a police uniform, other uniform or ordinary clothes. An explanation was given (e.g. they changed because they were in a play). Finally the children were asked 'Who is allowed to arrest people?' (Durkin and Jeffery 2000).

1. Scores out of 4 for correctly identifying the actual policeman were: 5-year-olds = 1.46, 7-year-olds = 2.68, 9-year-olds = 2.59.
   (a) Draw these results on a graph. Label the axes. (3)
   (b) Explain what the results show about socialisation. (3)
2. Incorrectly choosing the non-policeman in a police uniform accounted for 94% of the children's errors. Choosing the man in another uniform was another error.
   (a) Explain each of these **two** findings. (4)
   (b) The children's explanations for their choices were also recorded. Explain how this data could be analysed using thematic analysis. (4)

Apply it — Concepts: Classroom variations
A school has staffing and rooming problems. The head is deciding how to cover classes. Three possible strategies are:
- One teacher watches three classes over video links.
- Some classes are moved to rented houses nearby.
- Lunchtime supervision staff are used to cover lessons.

Context essay: Using evidence from Milgram's variations, discuss how the strategies might affect the children's obedience in comparison with a normal classroom situation. (8)

Study tip
When you are evaluating Milgram's variation studies, much of the standard evaluation for the baseline study (see previous spread) still applies as the procedures were so similar. However, you should try to use at least one evaluation point which is specific to the variation in question.

Check it
1. State **two** differences between Milgram's original study and the 'telephonic instructions' variation. (2)
2. Give **two** weaknesses of Milgram's 'ordinary man' variation. (2)
3. **Standard:** Evaluate any **one** of Milgram's variation studies. (8)
4. **AL (I&D/Synoptic):** To what extent do theories from social psychology and the learning theories favour nurture more than nature? (12)

Factors affecting obedience and dissent: Individual differences

The specification says...
1.1.3 Factors affecting obedience and dissent/resistance to obedience, including individual differences (personality and gender).

Key terms
Dissent – Having opinions that differ from those held by others. In relation to obedience it means refusing to carry out orders (disobedience).

Resistance – The ability of people to withstand the social pressure to conform to the majority or to obey authority. This ability to withstand social pressure is influenced by both situational and dispositional (personality) factors.

Personality – An individual's characteristic, coherent and relatively stable set of behaviours, attitudes, interests and capabilities. These characteristics are useful for predicting future behaviour, e.g. we have expectations that a kind person will behave in a kind fashion. Personality is a means of distinguishing between people. It is an individual difference.

Gender – A person's sense of their maleness or femaleness, including attitudes and behaviour of that gender.

Heroes of the Rwandan genocide
In 1994 the African country of Rwanda was devastated by genocide. An estimated one million people were killed in just 100 days, at the hands of ordinary townsfolk who began attacking their neighbours. There were some who risked their own lives to protect others. For example, Paul Rusesabagina protected more than a thousand people in his workplace (his story is portrayed in the film *Hotel Rwanda*). Similarly Sister Félicité Niyitegeka provided refuge for 43 Tutsis in her workplace, defying Hutu orders. When she was captured, she was told she would be spared as she was also a Hutu, but she said she would rather die with the Tutsis she had sheltered (Svoboda 2017).

How might gender and personality have affected the ability of such individuals to resist orders?

Think Link
Developmental psychology

Gender differences
Experiences in childhood may be responsible for the differences between males and females with regard to obedience. Social learning theory (covered in chapter 4) explains that boys and girls are rewarded for different kinds of behaviour. For example, boys are more likely to be rewarded for being dominant and independent than girls.

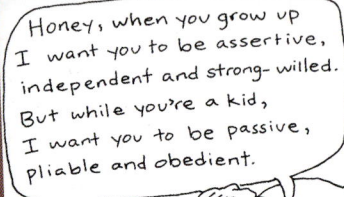

Personality factors
Stanley Milgram demonstrated the power of situational factors in eliciting obedience, yet he also said, 'I am certain that there is a complex personality basis to obedience and disobedience, but I know we have not found it' (Milgram 1974).

The authoritarian personality
Theodor Adorno *et al.* (1950) explained the high levels of obedience (and prejudice) in terms of a person's disposition and called this the *authoritarian personality*. Adorno believed that a harsh style of parenting leads children to develop personality traits such as toughness, destructiveness and cynicism, all of which he termed 'authoritarianism'. He measured this trait using the F-scale (F for fascism).

Adorno believed this parenting style was rife in Germany in the first part of the 20th century meaning that many adult Germans had personalities that were submissive to authority but harsh to those seen as subordinate to themselves. A more permissive style of parenting, centred around unconditional love might mean that children grow into adults who score low on the F-scale and are more likely to show resistance and defy what they perceive to be destructive orders.

Internal and external locus of control (LOC)
Julian Rotter (1966) proposed the idea that some people tend towards an internal locus of control (LOC), meaning they take greater responsibility for their actions as they believe they are in control of what they do and what happens to them. By contrast other people tend towards an external LOC. They take less responsibility for their actions and feel that what happens to them is governed by other people and by chance factors.

'Internals' are more likely to show dissent and defy orders, whereas 'externals' are more likely to be obedient. Frederick Miller (1975) demonstrated this in a study where a high or low status experimenter told participants to grasp live electric wires. Externals obeyed the high status experimenter more than the low status experimenter, while internals were unaffected by status.

Gender
There is evidence that males and females do indeed differ with regard to obedience, however there is a lack of agreement over which gender is most obedient.

Women are more obedient than men
Charles Sheridan and Richard King's (1972) participants were ordered to give real electric shocks to a live puppy. They found that a staggering 100% of female participants were fully obedient, compared with only 54% of the males. This said, the ladies showed grave distress, sobbing their way through the study! It is worth noting that the males in this study were more defiant when asked to shock a puppy than the male participants in Milgram's study who were asked to shock a human being.

Men are more obedient than women
Wesley Kilham and Leon Mann (1974) replicated Milgram's study in Australia and found an unusually low obedience rate of just 28%. In terms of gender 40% of males were fully obedient, whereas this was true of just 16% of the females.

Moral reasoning
Carol Gilligan (1982) suggested that moral decision-making is guided by differing principles in men and women. The 'ethic of justice' is the principle more commonly seen in males and this pertains to values of equality and fairness and requires a detached outlook to avoid bias. In contrast, Gilligan claimed that females use the 'ethic of care' to guide their decision-making. This principle relates to interpersonal relationships and nurturing and supporting those in need.

In terms of destructive obedience, one might expect males to be more obedient due to their feelings of obligation to an authority figure, whereas females may be less obedient due to their desire to support the person being harmed. In Milgram's study, males may be more swayed by the apparent scientific goals of the research, which was supposedly for 'the greater good' whereas females may have been more concerned about the learner.

Evaluation

Support for authoritarianism

A strength of the authoritarian personality is research support.

Alan Elms and Stanley Milgram (1966) used the F-scale with participants from Milgram's studies, testing 20 fully obedient participants and 20 who were not. Obedient participants scored higher on the F-scale and also reported other characteristics of the authoritarian personality, such as less closeness to their fathers.

These findings suggest that obedience is related to the personality characteristic of authoritarianism.

Competing argument We cannot claim that there is a causal relationship between childhood experiences and authoritarianism/obedience because these are correlations. Other factors may be involved, for example both obedience and authoritarian personality may be caused by a lower level of education (Hyman and Sheatsley 1954).

Internal locus of control does not predict defiance

A weakness of the LOC explanation comes from Grete Schurz (1985).

In a task similar to Milgram's original study, Austrian participants were instructed to give painful doses of ultrasound to a female student. Those participants who were fully obedient did not differ significantly from those participants who resisted in terms of their scores on a questionnaire measuring locus of control.

This suggests that personality may have little impact on obedience.

Application to the world of work

This research can be applied to the field of human resources (HR).

Some jobs require higher (or lower) levels of obedience. For example, organisations that require employees to follow procedures may prefer people who are obedient. To select suitable applicants the HR department might use a scale assessing LOC.

The use of personality tests as part of the recruitment process may result in more successful matching of people and jobs, leading to greater productivity and job satisfaction.

Evaluation

Support for Gilligan

A strength of Gilligan's explanation is support from qualitative research (Gilligan and Attanucci 1988).

Male and female participants were interviewed about real-life moral dilemmas and, although most participants used both the ethic of justice and care in their moral reasoning, overall men favoured a justice orientation and women favoured a care orientation. These gender differences were highly significant.

This suggests that there are quite important gender differences in moral orientations which may well affect decision-making in situations relating to destructive obedience.

There may be no difference

A weakness is that many studies find no gender differences.

Thomas Blass (1999) summarised the findings of nine Milgram-style studies that included both male and female participants. In all but one case there was no significant difference in the observed levels of obedience between men and women.

This suggests that gender does not affect obedience.

EXTRA: Issues and debates

The issue of gender is relevant here. Milgram's original research was androcentric as he only studied men.

Carol Gilligan raised awareness that women may see the world differently from men and behave differently as a consequence. This said, research has found no consistent gender difference.

This shows that, whilst it is important to combat androcentrism, it is also important that psychologists do not overlook the similarities between men and women.

Balanced conclusion

Although some of the research indicates a role for personality and gender in determining obedience, the picture is a mixed one and there is little to suggest a causal relationship between personality and/or gender and obedience.

Adorno et al. measured authoritarian personality using the F-scale. F stands for 'fascism' which is a form of government which expects unquestioning support and obedience.

Apply it Methods: Musician Max

Max plays music in various bands and always goes to rehearsals, unlike some band members who ignore instructions to attend. Max wonders if they are different from him in terms of personality. He asks everyone to complete a questionnaire to assess their locus of control (LOC).

1. Write a closed question Max could use to test LOC. (1)
2. Write an open question Max could use to test LOC. (1)
3. From the closed questions, Max calculates a total score for internal locus for each participant.
   (a) Explain which measure of central tendency would be best to use with Max's data. (1)
   (b) (i) Write a directional (one-tailed) alternate hypothesis for Max's study. (2)
       (iii) Max finds that the 'attenders' have a lower internal locus of control than 'non-attenders'. Explain this in relation to your hypothesis. (2)

Apply it Concepts: Ask the parents

Paige works in a boarding school. She is aware that some of the children are more obedient than others, even when they first arrive. She wonders if this is the influence of their parents. After a discussion with the head teacher, Paige posts a questionnaire on the school website for parents to fill in.

1. Explain the topics Paige might ask about, using the authoritarian personality as a guide. (4)
2. Describe the relationship Paige expects between the children's behaviour and their experience at home. (2)
3. Describe **one** alternative reason for differences in the children's obedience. (3)

Study tip

If you are given an application question about obedience/defiance and asked to explain why someone has resisted authority, be sure to use specific personality traits as outlined on this spread.

Check it

1. (a) Define 'dissent'. (1)
   (b) Explain **one** factor other than personality that may affect obedience. (3)
2. Explain **two** weaknesses of personality as an explanation of resistance. (2)
3. **Standard:** Assess the influence of gender and other individual differences on disobedience. (8)
4. **AS (Synoptic):** To what extent are individual differences explained by social and biological theories of human behaviour? (12)

Factors affecting obedience and dissent: Situation and culture

The specification says...
1.1.3 Factors affecting obedience and dissent/resistance to obedience, including situation and culture.

Key terms

Situation – Features of the immediate physical and social environment which may influence a person's behaviour. The alternative is dispositional factors where behaviour is explained in terms of personality.

Culture – The ideas, customs and social behaviour of a particular group of people or society. Note that the term 'culture' does not describe the group of people – it refers to their shared practices and beliefs.

Think Link
Developmental psychology
Socialisation

'Socialisation' refers to the way in which people acquire the beliefs, values and attitudes of their culture. We are socialised by parents, teachers, peers, religion and the media. Through these sources we learn about our culture and how to behave in order to fit in and be accepted. The need to belong is an important drive for human beings and therefore learning the social and cultural norms of our community are a critical part of our development.

Gupta's findings (see Stretch and challenge on right) could not have been predicted using Hofstede's cultural dimensions, suggesting that the impact of culture on obedience is likely to be complex and may involve interactions between culture, gender, situation and other factors such as education and religiosity.

Situation

Both social impact theory (page 30) and Stanley Milgram's obedience research (pages 32–35) demonstrate how factors in the situation may increase or decrease obedience.

Legitimacy
Reducing the perceived legitimacy of the authority figure, through altering his or her mode of dress for example, can reduce obedience. Similarly, reducing the prestige or status of the venue (as in Milgram's rundown office) also leads to reductions in obedience.

Proximity
When the distance between the authority figure and participant is increased, obedience reduces, as in the telephonic instruction variation. Bibb Latané (1981) used the term *immediacy* in social impact theory to refer to closeness of the target in terms of space and also time. Physical or psychological barriers to communication will affect immediacy – these are sometimes called 'buffers'. In one of Milgram's variations (experiment 3), the learner was in the same room as the teacher. In this variation, removing the physical buffers (the wall between learner and teacher) led to obedience falling to just 40%.

Behaviour of others
Exposure to role models who are disobedient decreases obedience – in one of Milgram's variations (two peers rebel, experiment 17) there were two further teachers (confederates) who refused to carry on. In this experiment obedience dropped to 10% illustrating how the presence of others may affect obedience.

Culture

Geert Hofstede (2011) has identified six dimensions, which allow for comparison between countries with regard to their cultural values. Two of the dimensions are particularly interesting with regard to possible links to obedience.

Individualism–collectivism
Individualist cultures value personal autonomy and self-reliance whereas collectivist cultures value loyalty to the group, interdependence and cooperation in pursuit of group goals. In brief, individualism is about 'I', whereas collectivism is about 'we'.

Consequently we might expect that people from more individualist cultures (such as the US and Northern Europe) may be less obedient due to the value placed on self-determination and independence compared with those from more collectivist cultures (such as China and Brazil), where obligation and sense of duty may override the desire to rebel.

Power distance index (PDI)
PDI refers to how accepting people are of hierarchical order and inequality in society. In high PDI cultures 'subordinates expect to be told what to do and the ideal boss is a benevolent autocrat' (Hofstede 2017).

We might expect that identification with the values of such a culture would lead a person to be highly obedient while people from nations low on this dimension might be more likely to show resistance or dissent.

All individualism–collectivism and PDI scores cited here come from a wonderful website that you might enjoy using when working on any topic that involves cultural differences. See tinyurl.com/y959tzgh

Stretch & Challenge
Unexpected findings and interaction effects

A Milgram replication conducted in India returned a surprising result – despite a high power distance score of 77% (Hofstede 2017) the study found a distinctly low rate of obedience of just 42.5% (Gupta 1983).

There was also an interesting gender result – the females were considerably less obedient than males. However, Vaidehi Rajagopalan et al. (1992) reports that, although Indian women may be expected to be submissive in some situations, when it comes to family and the household, Indian women have the authority. Mothers are held in high regard, can be relatively independent and make all the important family decisions. They can also demand absolute obedience from their children (Rao and Rao 1985).

What do these studies tell us about factors affecting obedience and dissent?

Evaluation

Supporting evidence

A strength is that there is much evidence that shows how legitimacy, proximity and the behaviour of others affect obedience.

For example, Wim Meeus and Quinten Raaijmakers (1995) asked their participants to deliver increasingly unkind insults to a confederate who was applying for a job. More than 90% delivered all 15 insults in the baseline condition compared with 36% when the experimenter left the room and 16% when they had witnessed two rebellious stooges as in Milgram's experiment 17.

This suggests that it is possible to reduce obedience significantly through adjusting aspects of a situation.

Competing argument However, in all of Milgram's variations there were individual differences – some people refused to continue to higher shock levels despite the situational pressures to obey. This shows that personality (as discussed on the previous spread) must be a key part of any explanation.

Application to rule-breaking

Research on situational factors and obedience has been applied to improve compliance with countryside rules.

In the countryside there is no one to enforce the rules (as in Milgram's experimenter absent condition) and therefore some people disobey, threatening wildlife and increasing risk of forest fires for example. James Gramann et al. (1995) found that if information was provided about the reasons behind the rules, this increased the likelihood that participants felt they would obey. Such signs provide *immediacy*, even when there is no authority figure there and they provide *strength* as they indicate the power that could potentially be brought to bear.

This is an important application of the work on situational factors and obedience which may help protect sites of natural beauty.

Evaluation

Cultural dimensions do correlate with obedience

A strength of cultural explanations is a close relationship between obedience and Hofstede's cultural dimension, PDI.

For example, Wesley Kilham and Leon Mann (1974) found a strikingly low level of obedience of 28% in Australia, which scores very low for power distance (36%) while a very recent replication in Poland by Dariusz Doliński et al. (2017) found a very high level of obedience of 90% as one might expect in a country with a much higher power distance score of 68%.

This suggests that Hofstede's power distance dimension is useful in predicting obedience.

Cultures don't differ

A weakness with cultural explanations is that, in general, most nations around the world return similarly high levels of obedience.

For example, Thomas Blass (2012) calculated the average obedience rate for eight non-US Milgram replications (see graph above) finding an overall percentage of 66% compared with an average of 61% for the US replications. Although there is some variation both within the US studies and across the world, Blass draws attention to these very similar averages.

This finding is important as Blass concludes that perhaps obedience is in fact a universal social behaviour and culture therefore doesn't affect obedience much.

EXTRA: Issues and debates

Cross-cultural studies can be helpful in assessing the extent to which behaviours are seen as being caused by nature or nurture.

For example, if obedience levels were high the world over, despite exposure to differing cultural norms, one might regard obedience as biological, a product of genes as opposed to experience. However, if obedience levels vary broadly from culture to culture, one might consider nurture to play the more important role.

This is important because understanding the origins of destructive obedience is necessary in order to determine how to prevent future atrocities.

Balanced conclusion

It would appear that the impact of situational factors on obedience is well supported by the evidence from Milgram but also by more recent studies with increased ecological validity (e.g. Meeus and Raaijmakers). However, the role of culture is less clear. Blass' analysis does suggest universality but collectivist cultures may be under-represented. In addition procedural differences between studies make comparison difficult.

A bar chart to show the percentage of fully obedient participants in Milgram replications from around the world.

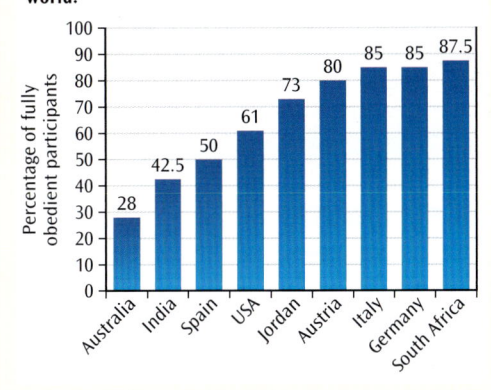

Country	%
Australia	28
India	42.5
Spain	50
USA	61
Jordan	73
Austria	80
Italy	85
Germany	85
South Africa	87.5

Blass (2012) observed that rates of obedience are strikingly high in most tested nations – though not all of them.

Apply it — Methods: Testing

Karen and Khan are using a questionnaire in three languages (English and two others) to test culture and obedience. Karen is testing a culture she believes will be highly obedient and Khan is testing a culture he believes will show dissent.

1. Some differences they find may be caused by practical issues in the study.
   (a) Explain **one** reason why the findings for the other cultures may differ from those of the English participants. (2)
   (b) Explain **one** reason why the findings might differ between the two non-English cultures. (2)
2. Khan suggests that an interview might have been a better method for this study.
   Explain **one** advantage and **one** disadvantage of using an interview for this study. (4)

Apply it — Concepts: Obey me

Greg is supervising car parking at an outdoor event and doesn't want people to disobey him.

Context essay: Discuss strategies that Greg could use to help him. (8)

Study tip

Remember you can sometimes use ideas about *obedience* to answer questions on disobedience/dissent by talking about what makes people obedient.

Check it

1. Explain why **two** cultures may differ in terms of dissent. (4)
2. Describe the effect of **two** situational factors on disobedience. (4)
3. **Standard:** Assess the influence of culture on disobedience/dissent. (8)
4. **AL (I&D/Synoptic):** Evaluate research into social and biological psychology in terms of social sensitivity. (12)

Prejudice: Social identity theory

The specification says...
1.1.4 Explanations and research into prejudice, including social identity theory (Tajfel and Turner, 1979, 1986).

Key terms

Prejudice – Literally, a pre-judgement. There are three key components. A for affect as it is experienced as an emotion. B for the resulting behaviour, which is *discrimination*. C for cognitive because prejudice is a biased belief held about an individual or group prior to direct experience of that person/people. Such attitudes are often based on stereotypes and/or group characteristics. Individual attributes are ignored.

Social identity theory – The view that your behaviour is motivated by your social identity. A person's self-image has two components: personal identity and social identity. Personal identity is based on your characteristics and achievements. Social identity is determined by the various groups of people to which you belong, your 'ingroups'.

Think Link
Developmental psychology

Prejudice across the life span

Prejudices towards different social groups develop over time. Across the course of our lives we are exposed to differing social groups, meaning that as our ingroup changes so will the people who are categorised as the outgroup. This may mean that we exhibit prejudices towards different outgroups at different points in our lives.

Ingroup identity may also increase during development if self-esteem is damaged – for example, adolescents often feel uncertain about their identity and self-esteem. A way to repair lowered self-esteem is to identify more strongly with a popular and admired ingroup.

A byproduct of these fluctuations in social identification may be increased levels of prejudice, stemming from social comparison with the outgroup.

Social identity theory (SIT)

The self and the group

According to Henri Tajfel and John Turner (1979, 1986) our *self-concept* (sense of who we are) is made up of many social identities. These identities are linked to the social groups to which we belong. Tajfel and Turner's social identity theory suggests that humans have a strong desire to 'belong' and that we derive self-esteem through group membership and the acceptance of others. Much of our social behaviour is driven by the motivation to maintain a positive sense of self as a valued member of 'the group'.

Social categorisation

The *ingroup* is the group to which we see ourselves as belonging and the *outgroup* comprises anyone who is not part of the ingroup. *Social categorisation* refers to the separation of individuals into one of these two groups: 'like me' and 'us' (ingroup) or 'not like me' and 'them' (outgroup).

Tajfel and Turner (1979) argue that categorisation is a basic characteristic of human thought and as such we have little control over this automatic sorting process. They argue that mere existence of an outgroup is enough to bring about prejudice and discrimination between 'them' and 'us'.

Social identification

Social identification involves the individual adopting the beliefs, values and attitudes of the groups to which they see themselves belonging. They will also alter their behaviour to fit with the norms of the group(s), i.e. the typical behaviours and attitudes of the ingroup.

In addition to the more obvious outward changes in behaviour and appearance, identification includes a shift in a person's thinking and involves a change to his or her self-concept as a new social identity is formed. Once this process has occurred, *social comparison* may follow.

Social comparison

An individual may boost his or her self-esteem through making comparisons between the ingroup and outgroup. Self-esteem is the value attached to your self-concept – high self-esteem means you feel good about yourself.

Since the outcomes of these comparisons affect our self-esteem, the comparisons may not be objective. For example, we may perceive the ingroup as superior, exaggerating their successes and attributing such successes to innate ability (disposition). Whereas the outgroup are seen as inferior and their achievements are denigrated and seen as being caused by external factors (situational).

If ingroup members are seen as better, then we too, as an ingroup member, must also be better. We are therefore motivated to perceive our ingroup in a positive light and this can be enhanced further through seeing the outgroup in unfavourable terms.

The desire to see the ingroup as different and better is known as the *quest for positive distinctiveness*. Differences between groups are emphasised and similarities minimised. These cognitive processes may lead to discrimination between ingroup and outgroup members, meaning not only do we think about outgroup members differently, we also may treat them differently.

Stretch & Challenge

War, identity and self-esteem

Steve Carlton-Ford *et al*. (2008) researched the link between self-esteem and social identity in a study about the impact of the 2003 war in Iraq on a thousand randomly selected teenagers in Baghdad. Although conflicts such as this can often be related to decreases in psychological well-being, this study looked at how threats to social identity, especially in times of conflict, can be associated with increases in self-esteem. Their survey found that teenagers who perceived the highest level of national threat had the highest levels of self-esteem.

Using concepts from SIT, how would you explain why self-esteem increased? Would this always be the outcome of a conflict situation?

Portsmouth Pompey has got the very best fans – maybe a touch of ingroup favouritism as one of our authors counts herself as one of them.

Evaluation

The minimal group experiment

A strength of SIT is support from the minimal group experiment.

Tajfel (1970) worked with 15-year-old Bristol school boys. Ingroups and outgroups were created by telling each boy which other boys had behaved like them or not like them in a previous task (choosing which painting they liked). Later the boys were asked to allocate points to the other boys and were told these points would be exchanged for cash. Tajfel found that more points were awarded to ingroup members than outgroup members. Boys even opted to maximise the difference in points awarded to the ingroup compared with the outgroup, even if this reduced the total final sum awarded to the ingroup!

This study shows how social categorisation is sufficient to trigger *ingroup favouritism* and discrimination against the outgroup.

Competing argument Although this study appears to support SIT, the task of privately allocating points lacks mundane realism. In real life, we may be less discriminatory as there may be unpleasant social consequences of such actions. Discrimination is rarely this covert, meaning that the study lacks ecological validity.

Ethnocentrism

A weakness of SIT is that research evidence suggests that it may only explain intergroup behaviour in Western societies.

Margaret Wetherell (1982) conducted a replication of Tajfel's experiment using eight-year-old schoolchildren in New Zealand. She found that indigenous Polynesian children were significantly more generous in their allocation of points to outgroup members than their white New Zealand classmates.

This suggests that SIT may be ethnocentric because it fails to predict the behaviour of people from more collectivist backgrounds. It may also not apply to people who belong to minority groups.

Application to reducing prejudice

SIT provides testable suggestions about how prejudice can be reduced through efforts to increase self-esteem.

Steven Fein and Steven Spencer (1997) gave students a sense of high or low self-esteem (using false feedback on an intelligence test). Students who now had low self-esteem later rated Jewish applicants for a job less favourably than an Italian candidate but this was not true of those with high self-esteem. In a second study, self-esteem was increased by asking the students to write about something they valued. This had the effect of reducing anti-Jewish prejudice.

This suggests that prejudice in society could be decreased by implementing policies which target low self-esteem.

EXTRA: Issues and debates

The debate around the development of psychological knowledge over time is relevant to our understanding of SIT.

Researchers have studied brain activity whilst showing people pictures of outgroups in society, such as people who are homeless. Emotional centres in the brain, such as the *insula* (involved in the disgust response) seem to be more active when viewing outgroup members compared with other control images (Harris and Fiske 2006). Jay Van Bavel and colleagues (2008) took this a step further. They replicated Tajfel's minimal group experiment and then used fMRI to monitor brain activity whilst viewing images of in- and outgroup members, finding that the *orbitofrontal cortex* (OFC) was more active when viewing ingroup members than outgroup members.

This study reveals that our perception of in- and outgroup members is mediated by an assortment of differing brain regions. The studies show how social, cognitive and biological topics can combine to develop psychological knowledge over time.

Balanced conclusion

The idea that prejudice stems from social identity and levels of self-esteem is useful in explaining group processes such as in- and outgroup behaviour. SIT also offers useful implications for reducing prejudice, for example by increasing self-esteem. However, support for SIT is undermined by the fact that the minimal group experiments have low mundane realism.

Tajfel (1970) asked his participants to choose between two paintings by the famous artists, Wassily Kandinsky (right) and Paul Klee (below) in order to create his minimal groups.

Apply it — Methods: The scarf

Caz is testing social identity theory by watching people on her university campus one winter. She asks her friend Jan to pretend to slip on the ice in a public square. Jan wears identical clothes each time except for her scarf. Sometimes it is the scarf representing Caz's university, sometimes an obviously different one of another rival university in competition with Jan and Caz's university.

1. Explain why it is important that Jan wears identical clothes in this study. (2)
2. Explain why always using the same place for the test could be a problem. (2)
3. (a) Explain **two** ethical issues raised by this study. (2)
   (b) Describe how to solve **one** of the ethical issues that you identified in (a). (2)
4. Suggest how Caz could record a measure of prejudice in her experiment. (2)

Apply it — Concepts: Nike boys

At Hal's school the boys all have to wear uniform. The only way they can express themselves is through their trainers for PE: the boys wear either Nike or Reebok. On the bus home at night, the Nike boys gang up on the Reebok boys, calling them nasty names, stealing their stuff and trying to throw their bags out of the bus windows.

(a) Explain the situation above using social identity theory. (4)
(b) Give **two** strengths of the theory that you described in part (a). (2)

Study tip

You could also use studies such as Sherif *et al.* (page 48) and Reicher and Haslam (page 52) to support SIT as they provide a good contrast to Tajfel.

Check it

1. Describe social identity theory. (4)
2. With reference to research evidence, give **one** weakness of social identity theory. (2)
3. **Standard:** Evaluate social identity theory as an explanation of prejudice. (8)
4. **AS (Methods/Synoptic):** Evaluate the use of experiments to study social and cognitive psychology. (12)

Prejudice: Realistic conflict theory

The specification says...

1.1.5 Explanations and research into prejudice, including realistic conflict theory (Sherif 1966).

Key terms

Realistic conflict theory – An explanation of prejudice which sees competition for limited resources as a key determinant of intergroup relations.

Stretch Challenge

Prejudice towards unrelated outgroups

RCT states that intergroup competition increases prejudicial attitudes towards outgroup members, but this begs an interesting question – does a sense of competition in general predispose people towards more hostile attitudes to unrelated outgroups?

Kai Sassenberg and colleagues (2007) investigated just this question. They primed East German participants to have either a competitive or cooperative 'mindset' by getting them to complete a general knowledge test in pairs. In the competition condition they were told that the person who scored top would get extra money, whereas in the cooperation condition they were told they would only get extra money if both people scored 20/20.

Sassenberg et al. found that participants in the competitive condition later showed more prejudicial attitudes towards an unrelated outgroup (West Germans) than those in the cooperative condition. West Germans were chosen due to the pre-existing prejudice between East and West Germany and it is interesting to see that those in the cooperative condition subsequently demonstrated less prejudice.

Why do you think competition leads to an increase in prejudice in situations like this? Does this help to support RCT or not?

The tabloid press have consistently reinforced the impression that migrants and refugees are a threat to the indigenous population with regards to competition for housing, jobs, education and healthcare. As RCT would predict, there has been an increase in racially-motivated hate crime.

Realistic conflict theory (RCT)

Realistic conflict theory (RCT) is a situational theory of prejudice proposed by Muzafer Sherif (1966), developed as an explanation of his famous Robbers Cave study (see page 48).

Intergroup competition

Sherif suggested that the key to prejudice is *competition* in any form, be it for political power or to be crowned as victors in a local pub quiz. He suggested that when two or more groups are striving for the same goal, prejudice and hostility will intensify.

In competitive sport, for example, two local teams might have to compete against each other for a place in the regional finals. In this instance, as both teams strive to achieve the top spot in the regionals, an increase in animosity between players and fans would be expected.

Negative interdependence

Negative interdependence occurs in situations where two groups of people are both seeking to achieve a goal that is important for both of them, yet only one group can reach that goal. This means there is a real 'conflict of interests'. The 'negative' aspect relates to the fact that each group will act to obstruct the other group's achievement. The 'interdependent' aspect relates to the fact that one group's win is contingent upon the other group's loss.

In situations of negative interdependence, intergroup relations will deteriorate. Interactions with members of the opposing group will become antagonistic and hostile, while interactions between members of one's own group will become increasingly cooperative. There will also be an increase in solidarity within each group. Whether a person is perceived to be a collaborator or a competitor will become of prime importance in determining whether they are to be treated favourably or with suspicion and hostility.

Limited resources

The struggle between the groups may be for scarce material or physical resources, such as food and territory. It might also be for symbolic resources, such as political power, prestige and authority.

Situations involving competition for physical and finite resources, such as a specific strip of land, often lead to the highest levels of prejudice and discrimination and can result in the fiercest of conflicts. However, if some form of compromise is possible or when the commodity is more subjective, levels of prejudice and discrimination are much lower.

Positive interdependence and superordinate goals

Sherif argued that prejudice that has arisen through intergroup conflict can be reduced through groups working cooperatively to accomplish a common goal. However, the key factor is that the two groups must be interdependent – *positive interdependence* (as opposed to negative interdependence) occurs in situations where neither group can reach its goals unless the other group also reaches theirs.

Sherif used the term *superordinate goals* to describe goals which can only be achieved through intergroup cooperation. The introduction of such goals can be instrumental in reducing prejudice, leading to increasingly favourable perceptions of the opposing group and harmonious intergroup interactions. For example, if two groups of students in the same year fell out at school, a task could be created to decorate their year group common room – one group might decorate the room while the others collected money to pay for the new decorations. The key is that the task could not be completed unless both groups contributed, i.e. they were interdependent.

Think Link
Developmental psychology

Changing times

RCT is helpful in explaining why the nature of group relations changes over time. For example, two groups might coexist in relative peace until there is some sort of competition whether that be a food shortage, economic downturn or struggle for political control.

This means that an individual's behaviour might change over time dependent upon the socio-cultural, political and economic climate. People who at one point in their lives were relaxed and stoic may become antagonistic and bigoted, for example.

Evaluation

The Robbers Cave experiment

A strength of RCT is that it is supported by Sherif et al.'s (1961) study.

In stage 2 of the Robbers Cave experiment, the researchers created intergroup competition in the form of a sporting tournament where only one group could win and there were prizes for the winners and nothing for the losers. This was a situation of negative interdependence and the outcome was an escalation of violence and increased prejudice (evidenced by the fact very few outgroup boys were named as friends).

These findings demonstrate that competition does lead to intergroup hostility and prejudice as the theory suggests.

Competing argument Although this is a field experiment and arguably has good ecological validity due to the naturalistic setting, the original paper tells how the boys needed some serious provocation in order to trigger any explicit display of prejudice or discrimination. The experimenters had to secretly raid one group's cabin to make it appear that the other group had attacked them. Thus intergroup competition did not lead to hostility.

Competition may not be necessary

A weakness is that externally imposed competition between groups is not necessary to create prejudice.

Tajfel's (1970) minimal group experiment (described on the previous spread) showed that prejudice, or at least discrimination, can arise from the simple act of perceiving someone as 'not like me', in this case on the basis of a very trivial task of estimating the number of dots.

This study shows that boys will treat others differently on the basis of information about group membership alone, suggesting that prejudice may be less about competition and more about our own knowledge of who we are and our self-worth (i.e. if boys like me deserve more points, this means I too deserve more points because I am a worthy person), which can be assessed through comparison with others.

Application to reducing prejudice

The theory has been successfully applied to reduce prejudice and discrimination in society.

RCT proposes that intergroup relations can be enhanced through the introduction of superordinate goals, which require in- and outgroup members to work cooperatively to achieve a goal that would be unobtainable without joint effort.

This is a major strength of the theory as prejudice and discrimination are arguably two of the most important problems facing the modern world. The survival of our planet may hinge on diverse groups of people working together for the greater good as in the Paris Agreement on climate change.

EXTRA: Issues and debates

One debate that applies to RCT is the question of whether psychology is a science.

For a theory to be considered scientific it must be falsifiable, i.e. it should be possible to demonstrate that the claims of the theory are wrong. RCT produces testable hypotheses, for example 'Levels of prejudice are greater before rival groups engage in a superordinate task than afterwards'. Such a hypothesis allows disproof.

This shows that RCT is a scientific theory, adding credibility to this explanation of prejudice and indeed the claims that it makes about how prejudice might be reduced.

Balanced conclusion

RCT is a useful theory as it highlights the fact that individuals and groups do not interact within a socioeconomic vacuum – real competition for limited resources including social power is an important trigger for prejudice. However, Tajfel's research clearly demonstrates that outgroup status alone is enough to provoke differential treatment even in the absence of any realistic conflict for limited resources.

While competition can breed contempt, RCT tends to ignore some of the positive aspects of competition such as enhanced ingroup solidarity.

Apply it — Methods: Disputes

Robin is investigating realistic conflict theory in college by looking at disputes over who can use the printers in the sixth form common room and who wins subject prizes and house points.

1. When testing realistic conflict theory it is important to be able to measure whether conflict is realistic.
   (a) Explain **one** problem with measuring realistic conflict theory in the college scenario. (2)
   (b) Describe **one** way to measure realistic conflict theory in the college scenario that avoids this problem. (1)

2. Conflict could be measured qualitatively or quantitatively.
   (a) Describe **one** quantitative measure of **one** of the behaviours above. (2)
   (b) Describe **one** qualitative measure of disobedience/dissent for **one** of the behaviours above. (2)

Apply it — Concepts: Situation in Snorston

Outside the chip shop and pub in Snorston is a big stone bus shelter. It is warmish, dry and within earshot of music from the pub. And it is the only decent place for the local teenagers to eat chips. One group, who get called the 'bussies', tends to take possession of the bus shelter each night. The 'coldies' have to eat their chips in the rain.

(a) Explain the situation in Snorston using realistic conflict theory. (4)
(b) Explain **two** weaknesses of the theory that you described in part (a). (4)

Study tip

Always focus on the findings when you are using a study as evaluation of a theory and make clear links between the study and key features of the theory. Also, if the study is weak then the theory it supposedly supports is weakened too. Get those weaknesses (or strengths) as competing arguments and link them back to the theory to gain credit!

Check it

1. Describe realistic conflict theory. (4)
2. Explain **one** strength of realistic conflict theory. (2)
3. **Standard:** Assess realistic conflict theory as an explanation of prejudice. (8)
4. **AS (Methods/Synoptic) and AL (I&D/Synoptic):** Evaluate research into social and cognitive psychology in terms of the ethical issues they raise. (12)

Factors affecting prejudice (and discrimination): Individual differences

The specification says...
1.1.5 Factors affecting prejudice (and discrimination), including individual differences (personality).

Key terms

Discrimination – Literally means 'to distinguish between two things'. It is the behaviour that results from prejudiced attitudes so that a person behaves differently towards a particular group of people because of their negative attitudes.

Individual differences – The characteristics that vary from one person to another. People vary in terms of their intelligence, emotional type, resilience and so on – two key individual differences are personality and gender.

Think Link
Developmental psychology

Modelling
Research suggests that the degree of social dominance a person exhibits correlates significantly more strongly with their father's level of SDO (+.40) than their mother's (+.13) (Altemeyer 2004). This can be explained in terms of identification with role models – children learn attitudes and behaviours from important people around them, and parents are important role models. Furthermore people are more likely to model male behaviours when the behaviour is sex-typed (Bandura et al. 1961) – and males are more likely to have an SDO than females. This fits in very well with Altemeyer's finding.
This argument is based on Albert Bandura's social learning theory which is discussed in Chapter 4 on Learning theories (see page 138).

Personality

Personality is a key example of *individual differences* between people.

The authoritarian personality

Theodor Adorno et al.'s (1950) authoritarian personality was described earlier in this chapter (see page 36) as an explanation for obedience – but it also explains prejudice and *discrimination*. An overly harsh parenting style is claimed to create a personality type that is both highly obedient and also highly prone to display prejudice. Harsh parents expect absolute loyalty and extremely high standards of achievement. They offer conditional love – the child only receives love if they behave correctly.

Children identify with their parents but the children with authoritarian parents also feel hostile towards their parents' conditional love. The child cannot express such feelings due to fear of punishment, therefore they have to *displace* their anger on to something else. This is called *scapegoating* – selecting someone on whom to vent your anger. In the case of people with an authoritarian personality, their feelings of hostility are displaced onto those who are socially inferior (i.e. members of the outgroup).

Allport's authoritarian personality

Gordon Allport (1954) also discussed the authoritarian personality and compared this to more 'generalised tolerant types' who have a sense of inner security and confidence stemming from unconditional parental acceptance. This parenting style leads to an empathic and accepting orientation towards others, a more liberal ideological outlook and the ability to think in shades of grey. By contrast, authoritarians think in rigid 'black and white' categories and require 'cognitive closure', meaning they prefer to find solutions, as opposed to generating further questions.

Unlike Adorno, Allport believed people with authoritarian personalities are not necessarily prejudiced, however they may be particularly receptive to political arguments which target their inner fears and insecurities.

Right wing authoritarianism (RWA)

Bob Altemeyer (1988) focused on just three of Adorno's nine original authoritarian traits: authoritarian submission, aggression and conventionalism. He felt that these were the only three that were not heavily correlated with any of the other six traits and therefore deserved further attention. People high in RWA tend to hold prejudiced attitudes towards various groups, including women and those who identify as LGBT.

Altemeyer's ideas differ from Adorno because he says RWA is not a product of early parental experiences but develops as a consequence of social learning. He says that when children are socialised to believe that the world is a dangerous and threatening place, RWA may result. This theory therefore is not about feelings of personal inadequacy – for Altemeyer, RWA stems from a learned set of beliefs about the world.

RWA develops as a reaction to fear and uncertainty. People high in RWA seek security through preserving existing social order, they are suspicious and overtly hostile towards anyone who defies the norm or seems 'different'. They also tend to be highly conscientious but closed to new experiences.

Social dominance orientation (SDO)

Felicia Pratto et al. (1994) developed the concept of SDO to describe people who are motivated to seek out ingroup power, dominance and superiority. They prefer hierarchical versus equal distribution of power.

The SDO worldview is different from the RWA one – people with an SDO see the world as a 'competitive jungle' where people have to be ruthless and fight for their share of limited resources and power. Like RWA this worldview is transmitted via role models, as part of the socialisation process.

SDO is positively correlated with key personality characteristics such as tough-mindedness and correlates negatively with agreeableness and empathy. It is more common in men and is thought to develop through exposure to social situations involving high levels of inequality and competition (Sibley et al. 2007).

Duckitt's dual process model explains how personality (and context) plus worldview combine with RWA/SDO to create right-wing attitudes.
Diagram adapted from Duckitt and Sibley (2010)

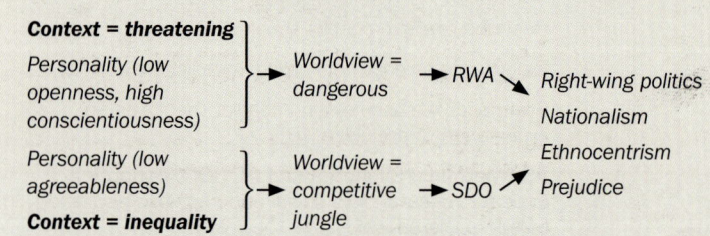

Context = threatening
Personality (low openness, high conscientiousness)
→ Worldview = dangerous → RWA → Right-wing politics, Nationalism, Ethnocentrism, Prejudice

Personality (low agreeableness)
Context = inequality
→ Worldview = competitive jungle → SDO

Duckitt's dual process motivational (DPM) model

John Duckitt (2005) created a model to explain prejudice that combines the concepts of RWA and SDO. He suggests that these dimensions develop when people with specific personality profiles (e.g. low openness) are exposed to certain worldviews (e.g. the world is dangerous). This model was tested by Christopher Cohrs et al. (2012), one of the contemporary studies for this topic (see page 54).

How do you think people acquire their 'worldviews' and why do you think these might be hard to change once they become established?

Evaluation

Supporting evidence

A strength is that the relationship between personality and prejudice is supported by much research evidence.

For example, Cohrs et al. (2012) found that RWA (+.48) and SDO (+.28) were both positively correlated with generalised prejudice ($p < 0.001$). RWA was negatively correlated with openness to experience (−.22) while SDO was negatively correlated with agreeableness (−.40).

This suggests that levels of prejudice can be accurately predicted from people's personality traits.

Competing argument It may be wrong to think that RWA and SDO are consistent over time – both dimensions interact with social factors, making prejudice much harder to predict in the real world. For example, when Shana Levin (1996) primed Jewish participants to think about their social identity within Israel, she found that Ashkenazi Jews showed higher SDO scores in comparison with others types of Jew. However, differences in SDO disappeared when the Jewish groups were primed to think about the relationship between Israel and Palestine. This shows the malleability of SDO and that SDO scores can be an effect of prejudice as well as a cause (Kteily et al. 2011).

Conflicting evidence

A weakness of the individual differences approach to prejudice is that it ignores the role of social norms and situational factors.

Winnifred Louis et al. (2003) note that RWA and SDO scales do not include items which are heavily affected by social attitudes or norms, meaning the role of these factors is ignored in the research. For example, the majority of people (72%) in their Australian study strongly disagreed with the statement, 'The white race is the best race' but agreed with the exclusion of asylum seekers.

This suggests it is important to understand the social as well as the individual factors in order to address the consequences for prejudice effectively.

Application to reducing prejudice

Research on individual differences may provide suggestions for how prejudice could be reduced.

Both Allport and Altemeyer highlight that prejudice may be learned through exposure to specific worldviews and prejudicial rhetoric. This suggests that greater regulation of media sources (such as social media sites that promote prejudiced views) may be beneficial. Furthermore, strategies that challenge the view of the world as dangerous, threatening and competitive (such as international exchanges and school twinning projects) may help to combat RWA and SDO.

These suggestions demonstrate the importance of thinking about the root causes of prejudice as a way to combat it.

EXTRA: Issues and debates

This research may be considered as socially sensitive.

Much of the research in this area has treated right-wing attitudes as abnormal, polarising the right and the left yet further. Gordon Allport's claims regarding thinking styles are especially harmful and could be taken to mean that those with right-wing views are less capable of critical thinking. Given the fact that Democrats currently outnumber Republicans 12:1 in American psychology departments (Duarte et al. 2015), publication bias could certainly be responsible for the weight of literature focusing on RWA as opposed to left wing authoritarianism (LWA).

This suggests that psychologists must be careful to ensure their research is not used to denigrate people who hold certain views.

Balanced conclusion

There is much empirical support for the idea that certain personalities are more prone towards generalised prejudice than others. However, there is a risk that such profiles suggest rather simple answers to complex issues. This said, ignoring the influence of individual differences (and the sources that create them) may be damaging to progress towards the reduction of prejudice and discrimination.

"Grampa didn't like the internet until he found sites that confirm his biases."

Apply it Methods: Muddled Mary

Mary is planning a questionnaire study using a stratified sample but is rather muddled. Her aim is to find out about prejudice towards disability.

1. Mary needs help writing her questionnaire.
   (a) Write **one** open question that is relevant to her aim. (1)
   (b) Write **one** ranked scale question that is relevant to her aim. (1)

2. Mary also needs help to collect her sample. Write a list of instructions that Mary could use to collect a stratified sample from the population of her local town. (3)

3. Mary is uncertain how to make her study ethical.
   (a) Describe **two** ethical guidelines that are important for Mary to follow in her study. (2)
   (b) Explain why **one** of these guidelines is specifically important for Mary to follow in her study. (2)

Apply it Concepts: Prejudiced people

Carl and Anna have different personalities. Carl seems to hold prejudiced beliefs about many different groups and Anna cannot understand why. To her everyone is equal. She often sees Carl being discriminatory and doesn't understand why.

(a) Explain the differences in behaviour between Carl and Anna. (4)
(b) Give **one** piece of evidence to support your answer to part (a). (3)

Study tip

If a question asks about '*Personality factors* affecting prejudice' you can use the personality dimensions covered here. If the question says '*Factors* affecting prejudice', that also includes situation and culture, covered next.

Check it

1. (a) Describe **two** examples of individual differences in personality that are important in prejudice. [4]
   (b) Explain how these **two** individual differences result in prejudice and discrimination. [4]
2. Distinguish between 'prejudice' and 'discrimination'. [2]
3. **Standard:** Assess whether individual differences between people are the only factors that affect prejudice. [8]
4. **AL (I&D/Synoptic):** Sometimes we like people as soon as we meet them and don't really know why.
   To what extent can themes from social and cognitive psychology explain this behaviour? [12]

Factors affecting prejudice (and discrimination): Situation and culture

The specification says...

1.1.5 Factors affecting prejudice (and discrimination), including situation and culture.

Key terms

Situation and culture – see page 38.

Think Link
Developmental psychology
Exposure to cultural norms

The longer a person has been exposed to a specific set of cultural norms, the greater the likelihood that the person's behaviour will be affected by those norms. This suggests that the influence of situation and culture on prejudice is developmental and explains why a person's prejudicial attitudes and discriminatory behaviour may change over time.

The amount of prejudice shown by an individual will also be affected by the extent to which a person identifies with the prevailing ingroups/culture. For example, you may be living in a certain culture but remain relatively unaffected by its norms and values if you continue to identify with your 'home-culture'.

Exposure to a demagogue or rabble-rouser may be all it takes to turn feelings of inner conflict into expressions of prejudice and discrimination.

Body-bag journalism

Patrick Colm Hogan (2001) argues that mood can affect levels of prejudice and discrimination and this idea extends to the collective mood of a nation. He uses the term *body-bag journalism* to describe the proliferation of sensationalist stories about crime and disasters, which feed cynicism and fear, fueling negative mood and increased hostility and disdain directed towards outgroups.

How could you test Hogan's idea about media consumption, as a situational factor that increases prejudice?

Situation

Social norms

Social norms are part of the situation. They refer to the unwritten rules about what is socially acceptable and desirable within specific social groups. A part of social identity theory (page 40) is that people follow the norms created by their ingroup because violations may lead to rejection. They wish to avoid rejections because group belonging is a strong motivator due to its link with self-esteem. Therefore, such norms can act as powerful situational influences.

Hadley Cantril (1941) suggested that this group identity, and thus socialisation by the group, is central to the formation of prejudiced views. Individuals become increasingly prejudiced as they internalise a group's 'frame of reference'.

Many studies have shown that the expression of prejudice and discrimination are influenced by social norms. For example, Ralph Minard (1952) noted the difference in relations between white and black coal miners in the US. Below ground (when individuals identified with being a miner) they were friendly and worked well together whereas above ground (when they identified with their white and black social groups) they held negative views towards each other.

Competition and resource stress

Realistic conflict theory (page 42) highlighted the importance of competition in escalating prejudice. When groups are in competition for limited resources the result is prejudice. This competition between groups is a situational factor.

Victoria Esses and colleagues (2001) use the term *resource stress* to describe the problem that occurs when people believe that commodities, such as jobs and money, are limited. Prejudice arises if and when the ingroup perceive themselves to be in direct competition for scarce resources with some other salient group – in this study the other group were immigrants.

This is heightened if the situation is seen as 'zero-sum', meaning provision for the other group (immigrants) will come at a cost to the indigenous population. At this point the ingroup try to demonstrate the outgroup's lack of 'worthiness' due to the perceived threat they pose.

Culture

The norm of intolerance

John Baldwin (2017) states that all cultures are ethnocentric to some extent, i.e. they believe their own culture is superior to others. However, some cultures are more prejudiced than others.

In some cultures, the norm is to be more accepting of diversity and tolerant of difference though often prejudice and discrimination still exist in more subtle and covert ways. Baldwin refers to these behaviours as *micro-aggressions* and describes *benevolent intolerance* whereby ingroups behave differently towards outgroups and justify this as a kindly attempt to support people with a perceived lower status, for example, giving money to a homeless person but not wanting a homeless shelter to be built on your street.

In other cultures the outward expression of prejudice towards certain outgroups may be accepted and even encouraged. One example is the very high levels of prejudice and discrimination shown by the white population in South Africa. Between 1948 and 1994, racial segregation known as apartheid was legal and led to gross discrimination of the black majority. The system was abolished in 1994 but prejudice and discrimination are still overt and widespread.

The norm of fairness

Some cultures are more concerned with fairness than competition and this should lead to reduced levels of prejudice and discrimination. For example, Margaret Wetherell (1982) replicated Tajfel's minimal group experiment (see page 41) in a New Zealand school. She used school records to determine the ethnic origin of her eight-year-old participants and found the immigrant Polynesian children were more generous (fairer) in their allocation of points to outgroup members than the Caucasian (white) classmates.

Such cultural differences may reflect the individualist–collectivist continuum discussed on page 38. New Zealand is an individualist culture (scoring 79/100 on Hofstede's continuum) whereas Fiji (very close to Polynesia) scores just 14/100. We might expect collectivist cultures to be more focused on sharing and cooperation, thus reducing their level of discrimination.

Evaluation

Supporting evidence

A strength of using situational factors to explain prejudice is research support.

A Swedish study conducted by Nazar Akrami et al. (2009) experimentally manipulated social norms – some participants heard a confederate express scepticism that anyone could agree with the statement: 'Discrimination of women is no longer a problem in Sweden'. Mean levels of sexism were significantly lower for a group who had heard this statement compared to a control group who had not heard the statement. Furthermore, participants who read a short article predicting a bleak social and economic future for Sweden expressed more prejudiced attitudes than a control group.

This shows that prejudice can be affected by situational factors such as perceived social norms and social threat.

Competing argument Although the mean levels of prejudice differed between the experimental and control groups, Akrami et al. also report that personality variables (e.g. RWA and SDO) had an influence. The rank order of the participants' individual levels of prejudice were related to personality, demonstrating that both situational factors and individual differences are important determinants of prejudice.

Application to reduction of prejudice

One strength of the work on situational factors is that it provides ideas about how to combat prejudice.

Esses et al. (2001) suggest targeting the zero-sum beliefs that lead to prejudice against immigrants for example. In their experimental study they found this to be an effective strategy although reactance in participants who were high in SDO (social dominance orientation) created even more negative attitudes showing that a more indirect approach may be necessary to address prejudice in some people.

This is critical research if we are to move successfully towards a 'truly harmonious global village' as described by Esses.

Evaluation

Pressure to be prejudiced

A strength of the argument that cultural norms affect prejudice is that it is supported by research evidence.

For example, Christopher Orpen (1971) notes that F-scale scores were not significantly correlated with prejudice in a group of white South African participants. However, measures of social conformity, susceptibility to cultural pressure and adherence to culturally-approved norms showed significant correlations with prejudice towards black South Africans.

This suggests that conformity to cultural norms may be a critical determinant of intolerant attitudes towards specific outgroups.

Competing argument One problem with this evidence is that the participants were 16-year-old schoolchildren. Young people may have a stronger desire to fit in with their social group.

EXTRA: Issues and debates

The studies discussed on this spread raise a variety of practical issues relating to cross-cultural research.

In such research it is not possible to randomly allocate participants to groups and this hampers internal validity. Furthermore, if the same experimenter works with two separate cultural groups of participants, it is likely that one group of participants will be from the same culture as the experimenter and one not.

This means that there are likely to be many confounding variables.

Balanced conclusion

There is evidence that social and cultural norms have a considerable influence on levels of prejudice, such as the cultural dimension of individualism–collectivism (e.g. Wetherall 1982). However, research suggests that individual differences exist with regard to the extent to which people feel compelled to behave in line with cultural values (e.g. Orpen 1971) and personality factors may override these situational and cultural influences at times.

Research based on the minimal group experiment found that Polynesian immigrants to New Zealand (a collectivist background) were more generous to an outgroup than Caucasian children from New Zealand (individualist perspective) – suggesting that cultural orientation affects prejudice (see Wetherell study on facing page).

Apply it — Methods: In-group helping

Josh is accessing newspapers from two cultures via the internet. One culture is individualist, the other collectivist. Using thematic analysis, he finds examples of helpfulness and who these acts are directed towards. When coding the articles, Josh first identifies whether the helpfulness is between two people of the same or different cultural groups, then he uses codes to identify themes in helping.

1. Describe a theme for **one** helping behaviour that Josh could record. (2)
2. Explain why using only **one** newspaper from each culture could be problematic in Josh's study. (2)
3. Describe how Josh could present his final results. (3)

Apply it — Concepts: Cheese-rolling

Two villages, Round Red and White Ball, have an annual cheese-rolling competition. Villagers dress up in traditional clothes and sing village songs to support their cheese-rollers. The winners get a 'Speediest Sphere' plaque for their village and investment in the village cheese industry, which employs most of the villagers.

1. (a) Identify **two** sources of competition between social groups that arise from the cheese-rolling event. (2)
   (b) Use **two** different theories to explain the effects of each source of competition on prejudice in the villages. (6)
   (c) Explain **two** strengths and **two** weaknesses of one of the theories that you identified in part (b). (4)
2. A psychologist has observed the villagers and believes that the Round Reds are far more prejudiced than the White Balls.
   Explain **two** reasons that could account for this difference. (6)

Study tip

It is useful to know, and to be able to use, terms that are relevant to situational and cultural factors, such as ethnocentrism.

Check it

1. Explain **one** situational factor that affects prejudice. [4]
2. Describe **one** example showing how cultural factors affect prejudice. [4]
3. **Standard:** Assess the influence of cultural factors on prejudice and discrimination. [8]
4. **AL (I&D/Synoptic):** Different areas of psychology present different problems for research, such as taking gender and culture into account.
   To what extent does research from social and cognitive psychology take gender and culture into account? [12]

Classic study: Sherif et al. (1954/1961)

The specification says...

1.3.1 Classic study: Sherif et al. (1954/1961) Intergroup conflict and cooperation: The Robbers Cave experiment.

Cave sign at Robbers Cave State Park.

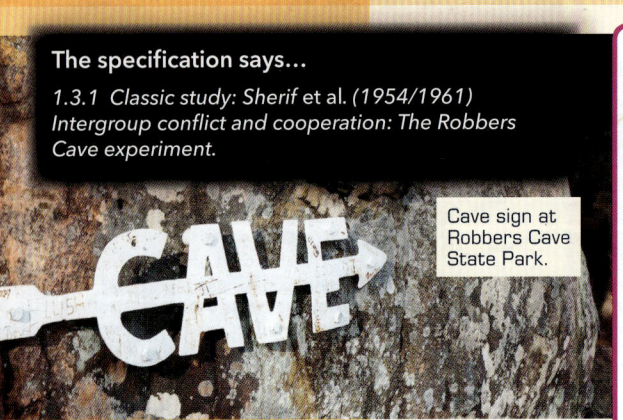

Muzafer Sherif wasn't just a pioneering social psychologist, he was a political activist who lived with ideological unrest and war throughout his early years in Turkey. He completed his Masters degree in the US and in 1932 he visited Berlin and witnessed the rise of the Nazi Party. In 1944, back in Turkey, his anti-Fascist beliefs resulted in a short spell in prison.

He finally fled his home country for good, however life in the US was not without problems as he was on the FBI list of Communist sympathisers during the 1950s. Eventually, his name was cleared but the impact on him personally, politically and professionally was significant. He lived into his 80s before he died of a heart attack in 1988.

Carolyn and Muzafer Sherif

Stretch & Challenge

The only way is Ethics!

Sherif et al.'s study raises a number of ethical issues. The boys were not aware that they were being observed and therefore could not give their informed consent or withdraw from the study and the researcher purposefully created situations which could expose them to physical and psychological harm.

To what extent can these violations of ethical standards be justified?

Think Link
Individual differences

Group competitiveness

Tyerman and Spencer's study (see facing page) shows that intergroup behaviour can be affected by individual differences. The four patrols at their Scout camp responded very differently to the introduction of intergroup competition. Two patrols were keen to compete, one was unenthusiastic and the other, indifferent.

This suggests that the personalities of group members may underpin a group's engagement in competition and this in turn will affect relationships within and between groups.

The Robbers Cave experiment

Aims

Muzafer Sherif, O.J. Harvey, Jack White, William Hood and Carolyn Sherif (1954/1961) set up a summer camp at Robbers Cave State Park aiming to explore how competition and frustration of a group's goals can lead to unfavourable stereotyping and prejudiced attitudes towards an outgroup, and encourage ingroup solidarity and cooperation.

Procedure

This was a field experiment. The independent variable was whether the atmosphere at the camp was one of competition or cooperation. There were many dependent variables, such as number of friends identified in the outgroup. The sample was 22 middle-class, Protestant, 11-year-old boys from Oklahoma, USA. They were all socially and emotionally well-adjusted. None of the boys knew each other prior to the camp.

The boys were divided into two groups ensuring that each group comprised boys with equivalent abilities, e.g. IQ, sporting prowess. The parents and the children's doctors gave consent for full participation in all activities but the boys were unaware they were being observed. The parents paid a small fee for the camp and were asked not to visit. The two groups arrived on separate days and were delivered to different locations, each with its own bunkhouse, hide-out and swimming places.

A vast amount of qualitative and quantitative data was collected over the three-week study using a wide variety of methods including covert observation and recordings, ranked scales to measure the boys' beliefs about each other and questionnaires asking them, for example, to estimate how long a tug of war contest had lasted.

The camp had three stages:

- **Stage 1: Group formation** – The boys took part in non-competitive activities so they would bond within their group ('The Rattlers' or 'The Eagles'). Activities included canoeing, tent pitching and building campfires. Two Eagles went home towards the end of the week due to homesickness.
- **Stage 2: Friction** – Each group learned of the other group's existence. The researchers then created a tournament with prizes of medals and a trophy for the winners. Contests included tug of war, baseball and tent pitching. Extra points were awarded for cabin inspections, comedy sketches and a treasure hunt.
- **Stage 3: Reducing friction** – Initial tasks involved increased social contact, e.g. eating or watching a movie together. Later superordinate goals were introduced – tasks that required intergroup cooperation, e.g. mending a broken water supply and starting a broken-down truck.

Findings

- **Stage 1:** The groups called themselves 'The Rattlers' and 'The Eagles', leaders were established and differing social norms became apparent – the Rattlers were tough and swore a lot whereas the Eagles cried more when injured and were anti-swearing.
- **Stage 2:** On discovering each other, both groups wanted to challenge the other to a baseball contest and hostility developed rapidly. There was name-calling, fights and scuffles, they raided and trashed each other's cabins, took each other's possessions and one group burnt the other's flag. Ranked scales showed more ingroup members were seen as brave, tough and friendly than outgroup members who were more likely to be seen as sneaky, smart Alecs or stinkers. Only 6.4% of Rattlers' friends were Eagles and 7.5% of Eagles' friends were Rattlers.
- **Stage 3:** Social contact and superordinate tasks initially did little to reduce friction. Soon after fixing the water supply, the groups were hurling insults again but after getting the truck going, the boys made dinner together and hostility was greatly reduced. The boys entertained each other round the campfire on the last night and left the camp as friends on the same bus. Outgroup friendships had increased – 36.4% of Rattlers' friends were now Eagles and 23.2% of Eagles' friends were Rattlers.

Conclusions

Intergroup competition leads to increased ingroup favouritism and solidarity but also to outgroup hostility.

Increased social contact is not enough to reduce prejudice but a series of superordinate goals can reduce prejudice effectively.

The conclusions from this study led Sherif to develop realistic conflict theory, discussed on page 42.

Evaluation

Selection and allocation of the children
A strength of the study is that Sherif et al.'s careful matching of the two groups improved the internal validity of the study.

The researchers spent over 300 hours observing, interviewing and testing potential participants until they found the final 22, who they then carefully allocated across the two groups to ensure an even match of personalities, skills and interests.

This ensured that the results could not be explained as due to pre-existing differences between the two groups of boys and really were dependent on the situations which were created.

Competing argument The two boys who went home due to homesickness were both Eagles. Therefore, the careful matching process disintegrated once the study started, as one group had 11 boys and the other had nine. This would have given the Rattlers an unfair advantage and also the Eagles may have become friendlier towards each other having been exposed to the two children who were initially upset and returned home. This meant that the two groups were not equivalent, reducing the internal validity of the study.

Failed replication
A weakness of this study is that subsequent research by Andrew Tyerman and Christopher Spencer (1983) failed to replicate the findings.

As a Sea Scout leader, Tyerman decided to study his sea scout troop of 30 boys. They each belonged to one of four patrols and knew each other well. At their annual two-week camp Tyerman observed that ingroup solidarity within each patrol did not increase. In fact it decreased a little and the different patrols interacted well as a troop rather than becoming hostile during a competition phase.

This suggests that competition may only elicit prejudice from people who do not already know each other well.

Application to reducing prejudice
This study can be applied to reducing prejudice in society, using the idea of superordinate goals.

For example, Elliot Aronson and Diane Bridgeman (1979) used Sherif et al.'s idea about superordinate goals to develop the *jigsaw classroom*, an intervention for tackling racial prejudice in American schools. Students had to work together and each take responsibility for a different part of a group project. The end result was increased liking and empathy for outgroup members and improved academic performance for black minority students.

This shows that Sherif's study led to interventions which have helped students from ethnic minorities to reach their academic potential at school rather than being held back by discrimination from their peers.

EXTRA: Issues and debates
Sherif et al.'s study is affected by cultural and gender issues.

The participants were all male and American and children. Biological and social differences between males and females may have primed the boys to behave in a more competitive manner than girls would. Being American, an individualist culture which values competition, may also mean the participants were more aggressive. In addition, adults may have been less impressionable.

This means that the conclusion that levels of prejudice are affected by competition and cooperation may not be true universally, and interventions for reducing prejudice such as the jigsaw classroom (see above) which is based on the conclusions of this study, may also be less effective with some groups.

Balanced conclusion
Sherif et al.'s focus on competition may be a particularly important contribution to helping predict if, and when, groups who have co-existed in relative peace, may become prejudicial and hostile towards one another. While his study has some obvious limitations in terms of the sample and the relatively short duration of the study, the application to fostering cooperation as a means to reduce prejudice has had a useful impact.

A series of superordinate goals forced the Robbers Cave boys to cooperate and they then enjoyed a final campfire together as one unified group. However, these boys had only been competing for one week and were all from very similar backgrounds. It may be much more difficult to overcome long-standing prejudice in the 'real world'.

Apply it — Methods: Hector's house
Hector is planning a replication of Sherif et al.'s Robbers Cave study using girls in a huge house.

1. (a) Describe **one** way that Hector could obtain a random sample of girls from a large town. (2)
   (b) Hector intends to follow similar procedures to Sherif et al. Explain **one** reason why the sample may in fact end up being biased. (2)
2. Hector needs to interview the children's parents. He believes that researcher effects may be a problem when conducting these interviews. Explain **one** way in which researcher effects could arise from the interview. (2)
3. Explain the risk management procedure that Hector should use when setting up his study. (4)
4. (a) Define **three** behaviours that Hector could observe that indicate competition or frustration in the girls. (3)
   (b) Draw a frequency chart to collect data about the three behaviours you defined in (a). (1)

Apply it — Concepts: Bean bag wars
Mr Walker is a primary school teacher. His school has just merged with another school and moved to brand new buildings. His class consists of ten children from one school and ten from the other. After a week the children are still not integrating and are fighting over resources.

1. Use the findings of Sherif et al.'s study to explain why the children might be fighting. (4)
2. Use the findings of Sherif et al.'s study to explain how the fighting could be reduced. (4)
3. Explain **two** differences between the situation in the school and the situation in Sherif et al.'s study. (4)

Study tip
You may be asked to compare classic studies. Comparing the aims, findings and conclusions will help you to weigh up the contributions of each study to wider society. Comparing procedures will help consider the methodological and ethical merits of the studies.

Check it
1. The study by Sherif et al. (1954/61) had several stages. Describe the procedure of the stage intended to produce competition between the boys. (4)
2. It has been claimed that the findings of Sherif et al. (1954/61) are not generalisable. Justify this claim. (3)
3. **Standard:** Assess the findings from the classic study by Sherif et al. (1954/61). (8)
4. **AL (I&D):** Evaluate the practical issues in the design and implementation of Sherif et al.'s (1954/61) Robbers Cave study. (12)

Contemporary study: Burger (2009)

The specification says...

1.3.2 One contemporary study: Burger (2009)
Replicating Milgram: Would people still obey today?

Jerry Burger works at Santa Clara, a private Jesuit university, in California. The Jesuits founded their first school in 1548 and the main principles of the Jesuit education system is to care for the 'whole person', to value each individual's humanity and to create an environment which will equip students to change the world for the better.

Burger's students describe him as 'a fantastic teacher, who brings the material to life and helps you relate it to how people behave in the real world' and he is known for his amusing anecdotes!

Think Link
Individual differences

Personality and obedience

Burger found that the personality trait *desire for personal control* was linked to disobedience but *empathic concern* was not.

However, he did find a significant negative correlation between empathic concern and 'first prod' score, meaning that the higher the empathic concern, the lower the voltage at which the 'teacher' first expressed a wish to stop – i.e. empathic concern may not have been linked to full disobedience but the 'teacher' was thinking about it.

Drama meets psychology

Burger's study has been criticised for lacking 'the drama' of Milgram's original experiments (Elms 2009) – in other words participants didn't feel as deeply involved in the experience and therefore weren't acting as they would in everyday life.

Alex Haslam's et al. (2015) replication overcomes this objection without breaching ethical guidelines. Professional actors trained in 'immersive digital reality' worked with a director to create fictional characters. They were told that their characters had volunteered for a psychology experiment. No further information was provided until they reached 'the lab' where they were briefed by 'the experimenter', just like in the real study. They then had to improvise their way through the experiment, which followed the same standardised procedure as the original. Afterwards the researchers interviewed them extensively about their experiences.

Burger and Haslam have both tried to find ethical ways of replicating Milgram's study. Which study do you feel has greater validity?

Would people still obey today?

Aim

Jerry Burger's (2009) aim was to see whether Stanley Milgram's findings were era-bound. Burger also wanted to see whether obedience is affected by gender as well as the personality traits *empathic concern* and *desire for personal control*.

Procedure

This was a laboratory experiment using an independent measures design. The volunteer sample consisted of 70 adults (29 men and 41 women) aged 20 to 81 (mean age 42.9), 60% had university degrees, 55% were white Caucasian, 4% Black Afro-American. The sample was obtained by distributing flyers at libraries, farmer's markets, coffee shops and community centres and advertisements were placed in local newspapers and online.

The study basically replicated Milgram's Experiment 5 (described on page 34) but Burger employed six ethical safeguards to protect his participants:

- To avoid high levels of anxiety Burger stopped the shocks at 150 V. He argued that 79% of those participants in Milgram's study who gave the 150 V shock continued to 450 V. Therefore, he could predict at the 150 V level how many participants would have continued and had no need to subject them to the increasing distress.
- A two-step screening process excluded volunteers who might have a negative reaction to the experience.
- Participants were given three reminders (twice in writing) of the right to withdraw.
- A real but very mild 15 V shock was given to the participants at the start compared with Milgram's 45 V shock.
- Participants were debriefed almost immediately after the study ended. They met the actor who played the 'learner' and were told that the shocks were not real.
- A clinical psychologist supervised all trials and was told to end the trial immediately if anyone appeared excessively distressed.

Self-report questionnaires were used to measure:

1. *Empathic concern* – The tendency to experience feelings of sympathy and compassion for unfortunate others.
2. *Desire for personal control* – How motivated a person is to see themselves in control of the events in their lives.

The researcher recorded the final shock administered and terminated the trial either when the participant refused to continue, after hearing all four prods (almost word-for-word the same as those used by Milgram) or when they had administered the 150 V shock.

Findings

The obedience rate was only slightly lower than Milgram found 45 years earlier – 70% pressed the 150 V button compared with 82.5% in Milgram's Experiment 5.

There was no significant difference in the obedience rates of men and women, although women were slightly more likely than men to press the 150 V switch (men 66.7%, women 72.7%).

There was no significant difference in the empathic concern scores between the defiant (19.25) and obedient participants (19.20), however the defiant participants did have significantly higher desire for personal control scores, (106.92) than obedient participants (98.24).

Conclusions

The findings show that Milgram's findings are not era-bound nor are they androcentric. Lack of empathy does not seem to be a valid explanation for the high obedience rates as both defiant and obedient participants had very similar scores for this trait. However, desire for personal control does seem to determine the likelihood of defiance.

(Note the article actually covers two investigations but we have focused on just one of them in order to highlight the ethical issues investigated.)

Evaluation

Strong internal validity

A strength is that none of Burger's participants had knowledge of Milgram's research, enhancing the study's internal validity.

All participants were asked whether they took any psychology classes. Anyone who had taken two or more classes was excluded. Five people admitted their awareness of the Milgram study at this stage and also dropped out.

This suggests that demand characteristics would not be a problem.

Poor generalisability

A weakness of Burger's finding is that the sample is not representative of the target population.

Although the rigorous pre-study screening was excellent ethically, 38% of volunteers were deselected in order to exclude anyone who might have found the study particularly distressing.

This is important because the people in the final sample may have been more psychologically robust than many people in the general population. This may have led to lower levels of obedience and reduces the generalisability of the findings.

Competing argument A recent Milgram replication by Jean-Léon Beauvois et al. (2012) is arguably more representative of the wider population because they did not exclude any participants (except volunteers with health problems requiring medication). It was also conducted in a different country (France). Their results (80% full obedience shocking to 460 V) confirm what Burger found and suggest the conclusions may be generalisable after all.

Limited application

Alan Elms (2009) claims that Burger's research tells us little about real-world obedience and thus lacks application.

The fact that participants were stopped before they suffered any real tension or dissonance about what they were doing meant that the situation lost its potency. The conversations in Milgram's studies between the participant and the experimenter post-150 V perhaps provided some of the most illuminating findings, however Burger was of course unable to explore this.

This seriously reduces the meaningfulness of the study in helping us to understand obedience in real-world situations today.

EXTRA: Issues and debates

A strength of Burger's work is that it has reawakened debate around ethical decision-making in modern psychology.

Milgram's research caused uproar at the time, however Burger's meticulous safeguards have also prompted discussion. Ludy Benjamin and Jeffrey Simpson (2009) argue that ethical standards are now so stringent that only very tame studies can be conducted which is seen as detrimental to progress in this field.

This suggests that some psychologists feel the rights of participants are being given more weight in ethical decision-making than the wider benefits of research to society.

Balanced conclusion

Burger's study showcases the fact that obedience research can be conducted without violating ethical guidelines. But the 150 V solution means the study was unable to explore some of the interesting aspects of Milgram's study, for example the interactions between the teacher and the experimenter as the learner's distress became increasingly evident. This limits the applicability of the work. However, Burger's study has certainly inspired the next generation of obedience researchers to come up with increasingly ingenious solutions to the ethical issues presented by obedience research.

Not all the recent replications seem quite so ethical! Researcher Jean-Léon Beauvois wondered whether our 'fascination with TV' would lead people to obey a game show host to 'inflict cruel acts on others'. Participants believed they were contestants in a pilot episode of a real television gameshow, involving obeying orders from the host to deliver electric shocks to another contestant, played by an actor.

Apply it — Methods: Slaves to authority

Sarah designs a study on obedience. She tells prospective participants she is giving auditions for a film about torturing slaves and wants to see how they respond to a painful shock. She says there are other parts they can audition for if they don't want to join in. She pairs up apparent cast members as master and slave, ordering the 'master' to give increasingly strong electric shocks to the 'slave', who is a confederate. The participant (the 'master') thinks the shocks which go up to 150 V are real.

1. Which roles in this study are equivalent to the learner and teacher in Burger's study? (2)
2. Describe **two** ways in which this study is less ethical than Burger's study. (4)
3. Explain **one** problem with the validity of this study. (2)
4. Explain **one** problem with generalisability in this study. (2)

Apply it — Concepts: Marcel the meany

In Marcel's study participants are told the research is investigating a new procedure for increasing resilience. One person (a confederate) has to ask for personal advice and the participant must insult him. The confederate gets progressively more upset and ultimately ends up crying.

1. Explain how the nature of this obedience act differs from Burger's study. (2)
2. Explain **either** why the participants may be more obedient than Burger found **or** less obedient. (3)
3. Marcel also tested a 'modelled refusal' condition in which a second confederate played the part of another participant. Explain what the results are likely to be. (4)

Study tip

If you find yourself writing an Issues and debates essay about 'ethics' you could focus on Burger's procedure and additional ethical safeguards.

You might also use this study in an evaluation of agency theory, but here the focus should be on the findings.

Check it

1. Explain **two** features of the procedure used in your contemporary study from social psychology that make it more ethical than Milgram's study. (4)
2. Explain **one** strength and **one** weakness of your chosen contemporary study from social psychology. You must not use ethics in your answer. (4)
3. **Standard:** Assess your chosen contemporary study from social psychology in terms of generalisability. (8)
4. **AS (Methods/Synoptic):** Evaluate the procedures of your chosen contemporary studies from social psychology and cognitive psychology with reference to validity and reliability. (12)

Contemporary study: Reicher and Haslam (2006)

The specification says…
1.3.3 One contemporary study: Reicher and Haslam (2006) Rethinking the psychology of tyranny.

Steve Reicher and **Alex Haslam** head psychology departments at opposite ends of the world – St Andrews in Scotland and the University of Queensland in Australia, respectively. How did they come to work together? Alex explains: 'Steve and I have known each other (and been friends) for about 20 years. We have always worked on similar issues (leadership, group dynamics) and always from a similar perspective (the social identity perspective), due in large part to the fact that we had the same PhD supervisor, John Turner.'
[2017, personal communication]

Professors Steve Reicher (left) and Alex Haslam (right)

Think Link
Individual differences

Personality and situation
The prisoners and guards were matched on personality traits associated with tyranny such as right wing authoritarianism (RWA) and social dominance orientation (SDO) (see page 44) to try to control the impact of individual differences. However, three of the most forceful personalities ended up as guards and it could be argued that this accounts for the findings of this study.

The Stanford Prison experiment (SPE)
Philip Zimbardo conducted the original prison study (published as Haney et al. 1973), upon which Reicher and Haslam based their replication. In the SPE 21 'normal' male college students were randomly allocated to play the role of prisoner ($n = 11$) or guard ($n = 10$). Over the course of what was planned to be a 14-day study, the guards grew increasingly brutal while the prisoners became submissive and subdued. In just five days, the guards had created a tyrannical regime that led to the mental collapse of five of the prisoners, who had to be released. On day 6, Zimbardo terminated the study for ethical reasons.

Reicher and Haslam wanted to further investigate the relationship between dominant and subordinate groups, rejecting Zimbardo's explanation that brutality and tyranny were inevitable. Haslam and Reicher believed that social identification would enable subordinates to join together to challenge prevailing inequalities and overthrow tyranny.

Can a replication of a study which caused such grave psychological harm be justified?

Rethinking the psychology of tyranny

Aim
Steve Reicher and Alex Haslam (2006) set out to explain antisocial group behaviour in terms of social identity theory (see page 40). They wished to explore factors which lead subordinates (in a prison) to collectively challenge an unequal social system involving the arbitrary use of power by one group over another (i.e. tyranny).

Procedure
A mock prison was created and filmed by the BBC. The volunteer sample of 15 socially and ethnically diverse males were screened for psychological and medical issues, and recruited via national newspapers and leaflets. They were randomly allocated to two groups: guards ($n = 5$) and prisoners ($n = 10$), which were matched for racism, social dominance and authoritarianism.

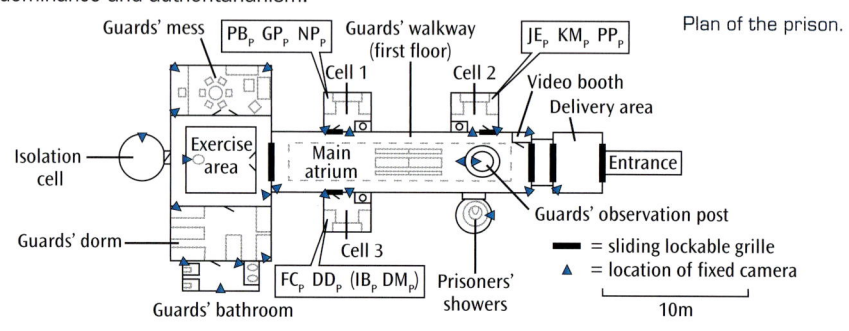

Plan of the prison.

This was a case study of one group. It was experimental because of the planned interventions, i.e. independent variables, which were:

1. *Permeability* Prisoners were told they might be promoted to the role of guard (groups were permeable). On day 3, one prisoner was promoted but then roles were fixed (groups became *impermeable*).
2. *Legitimacy* Initially prisoners felt the system was fair because roles were determined by personality. On day 3 they were told it was random, creating a sense of unfairness (lack of legitimacy).
3. *Cognitive alternatives* (i.e. choices) On day 4, prisoner 10 (a trade unionist) was introduced to challenge inequality and create insecurity through suggesting alternatives to the current regime.

The dependent variables were social identification, right wing authoritarianism (RWA), compliance with rules, depression and self-efficacy. These were measured using daily ranked scales. Stress was measured with daily saliva swabs to monitor cortisol levels.

The study was filmed at Elstree Studios in London and broadcast on the BBC. The guards were told to create the prison rules but to respect the prisoners' basic rights. The prisoners' heads were shaved and they wore numbered orange uniforms. The guards had better accommodation and food to deepen the inequality between the groups.

Findings
Phase 1: Rejecting inequality Social identification scores (measured using ranked scales) increased for prisoners when the situation became impermeable but decreased for guards.

By day 5 the prisoners were challenging the guards. On day 6 some of the prisoners broke out of their cells and occupied the guards' quarters.

Phase 2: Embracing inequality Participants set up a new social structure but within a day two ex-prisoners had violated communal rules so this broke down. A new regime with harsher rules was set up. This was judged unethical and the study was stopped after eight days.

In general, RWA increased over the study. However, participants who became guards after the 'revolution' showed a small decrease in RWA, whereas participants who chose to be prisoners showed an increase in RWA.

Conclusions
Subordinate group members will challenge inequality when they identify with their own group and when permeability and legitimacy of the dominant group are low. This supports social identity theory as an explanation for how tyranny can be challenged.

Evaluation

The use of quantitative data
A strength of the study is that it used ranked scales to collect quantitative data from the prisoners and the guards.

For example, measures of social identification and authoritarianism were used before and after the promotion of one of the guards, meaning that the researchers could calculate the statistical significance of any differences that were found.

This is a strength of the study because this type of data does not require any form of interpretation, unlike qualitative data.

Competing argument Although ranked scales have their advantages, self-reports can lack validity as participants may find it hard to reflect on their own state of mind and some people are less self-aware than others. This means the data may simply have reflected what they thought the researchers wanted to hear.

Observer effects
A weakness of the study is that the participants were aware that their behaviour was being filmed and broadcast on the BBC and therefore they may not have acted naturally.

For example, the guards may have wanted to come across as more egalitarian and not exercised as much force as they would have done had they not been concerned about how the audience might view them.

This suggests that the data may lack validity and had the guards behaved more forcefully in the early days the reactions of the prisoners may have been different and more in line with Zimbardo's original study.

Application to improving prison conditions
This study can provide useful insights that can be applied to improving prison conditions.

Prisons are becoming increasingly unmanageable places. The reasons for this are complex, yet this study demonstrates that lack of group identification in the dominant group may signal a lack of legitimacy leading to resistance and collective action in the subordinate group.

This suggests that strategies to raise morale, including increases in funding and training of guards, may be beneficial in controlling collective resistance which can result in violent disorder.

EXTRA: Issues and debates
This study clearly demonstrates how psychological knowledge may be used in society.

The notion of permeability may prevent outgroups in society from uniting against inequality. As long as members of these groups believe that one day they might be able to leave behind their subordinate status, they will continue to accept the status quo. Similarly, so long as the dominant group is able to maintain some sense of legitimacy, this too will prevent civic unrest. However, globalisation and social media mean that cognitive alternatives may be more readily available to oppressed outgroups than ever before, leading to the potential for collective action.

This study is therefore important in terms of helping to explain and predict social and political unrest.

Balanced conclusion
This study has many strengths due to the huge range of qualitative and quantitative data collected. However, the fact that participants were constantly filmed means the findings lack some credibility. This aside, the study provides a compelling contrast to Zimbardo's prediction that tyranny is the inevitable outcome of conflict between dominant and subordinate groups. This new account provides insight into group processes that may be integral to predicting uprisings which may endanger members of society.

Prisoners and guards in the BBC experiment.
The prisoners were allocated to lockable three-person cells off a central atrium. This was separated from the guards' quarters by a lockable steel mesh fence. There were facilities throughout for video and audio recording.

Apply it — Methods: Ojas observes
Ojas has decided to watch the documentaries produced of Reicher and Haslam's study and analyse the data himself.

1. Define **one** behaviour that Ojas could record from **each** of the following categories: social identification, compliance with rules, depression and self-efficacy. (4)
2. Ojas has traced one of the participants and wants to interview him. He cannot decide whether an unstructured or semi-structured interview would be best.
   (a) Explain **one** reason for Ojas choosing an unstructured interview. (2)
   (b) Explain **one** reason for Ojas choosing a semi-structured interview. (2)
   (c) Explain **one** way Ojas could analyse the qualitative data that he collects from the interviews. (4)

Apply it — Concepts: Shiny Shoes
Karol and Jim work for Shiny Shoes, a company with a tyrannical boss. They and other workers have been told that there is a chance of several promotions to the management team, who have many privileges. Jim is promoted and then everyone is told that no further promotions will happen.

Use Reicher and Haslam's findings to explain:
(a) How initial failure of the management team to form a common group identity would affect their ability to maintain order in the company. (1)
(b) (i) How the potential for promotion would affect the groups. (1)
   (ii) The effect on group structures of being told that no further promotions would be made. (1)
(c) The effect if workers were told that the management team were chosen based on their taste in music. (2)
(d) The probable effect if a worker from a modern, egalitarian company joined Shiny Shoes. (2)

Study tip
Drawing a cartoon strip or storyboard can be a helpful way of memorising the complicated procedures and findings of your classic and contemporary studies.

Check it
1. Describe how the results were analysed in your chosen contemporary study from social psychology. (4)
2. Explain **one** ethical improvement you could make to the procedure of this study. (2)
3. **Standard:** Assess your chosen contemporary study from social psychology in terms of generalisability. (8)
4. **AS (Methods/Synoptic):** Evaluate the procedure of your chosen contemporary studies from social psychology and cognitive psychology with reference to validity and reliability. (12)

Contemporary study: Cohrs et al. (2012)

Chapter 1 Social psychology

The specification says...
1.3.4 One contemporary study: Cohrs et al. (2012) Individual differences in ideological attitudes and prejudice: evidence from peer report data.

Christopher Cohrs is Professor of Psychology at Philipps University in Germany and says he aims to better understand the social psychological processes that lead to social justice and peace on one hand and to prejudice and violence in and between societies on the other. He is dedicated to understanding contemporary social issues and combines qualitative and quantitative methods in his research.

His message to students of psychology is: 'Be sceptical and critical of advice that you receive and question why that kind of advice is given to you and try to focus on things you are really interested in and passionate about.'

Think Link
Developmental psychology

Parenting, personality and prejudice

Bob Altemeyer (1988), who developed the concept of RWA, speculated that parents and other role models may be responsible for the development of the worldviews which underpin the development of ideological attitudes such as RWA. For example, overly-protective parental warnings and/or strict codes of moral conduct which seek to protect children could lead the child to believe that the world is a dangerous threatening place.

Furthermore, it has been shown that permissive parenting (non-punitive and undemanding, where the parent explains and discusses family rules, rather than enforcing them) is negatively correlated with RWA.

Choosing a friend to complete a peer report of your personality and attitudes – hmmm, will they write good things or bad things?

Individual differences and prejudice

Aim
Christopher Cohrs, Nicole Kämpfe-Hargrave and Rainer Riemann (2012) aimed to build on previous research investigating John Duckitt's (2005) dual process model of prejudice (see page 44) by using both self and peer report, to investigate concerns that self-reported data may lack validity. They predicted that:

1. *Right wing authoritarianism* (RWA) would correlate positively with high conscientious and low openness.
2. *Social dominance orientation* (SDO) would correlate negatively with agreeableness.
3. Both RWA and SDO will correlate positively with generalised prejudice.

Procedure
The study consists of two separate investigations. We will focus on investigation 1, however we have made reference to investigation 2 in the evaluation section on the facing page.

An opportunity sample of 193 people (125 women and 64 men plus four who didn't specify gender), aged 18–67 years (mean age 34) from diverse social backgrounds were gathered from a region of East Germany. The peers (recruited by each participant and also from East Germany) knew the target person 'well' or 'very well'. There was an even split of male and female peer raters aged 13–73 (mean age 34).

Participants completed self-reports which measured 'The Big Five' personality dimensions (openness to experience, conscientiousness, extraversion, agreeableness and neuroticism = OCEAN). Ranked scales were used, for example from 1–7 ('not true at all' to 'completely true'). RWA was measured using a 12-item questionnaire while SDO was measured using a shortened version of the original scale, translated into German (Pratto *et al.* 1994). Generalised prejudice was measured using questionnaires about attitudes towards homosexuality, foreigners and people with disabilities.

Participants were asked to give a separate set of the questionnaires to one of their peers (a friend/acquaintance). The forms ensured anonymity by using unique codes so they could be matched up on completion. Respondents were asked to answer spontaneously and honestly. Only responses from heterosexual, able-bodied, German nationals were analysed because people from any of the target groups (e.g. disabled) might understandably not express prejudices.

All participants received a personality profile and €12 for their time.

Findings
There are a large number of findings but here are some example correlations based on the peer reported data:

	RWA		SDO
Openness	–.22 ($p < 0.05$)	Agreeableness	–.40 ($p < 0.001$)
Generalised prejudice	+.48 ($p < 0.001$)	Generalised prejudice	+.28 ($p < 0.001$)

Conclusions
The data collected shows that specific personality traits are highly predictive of RWA and SDO which are in turn predictive of levels of generalised prejudice.

Based on the peer-reported data, the researchers concluded that the findings of previous research were valid, in the main, and not simply the product of social desirability bias resulting from the use of self-reports.

Stretch & Challenge

Left-wingers are equally inflexible

RWA is associated with rigid and inflexible views but it would be wrong to think that people with left-wing views are necessarily any less prone to this way of thinking. The term *partisan bias* refers to selective perception, interpretation and recall of information that confirms our political beliefs. Peter Ditto *et al.* (2017) conducted a meta-analysis including 41 experiments on the topic with over 12,000 participants and found that both liberals and conservatives were equally at risk of partisan bias.

Why do you think there is more psychological research into right wing authoritarianism compared with research into people with left wing authoritarianism?

People who view the world as a 'dangerous and threatening place' seek cohesion, security and stability to reduce their anxiety. This means some people may be more wary of visiting unknown places than others. Who knew your personality could dictate your holiday destination?

Evaluation

The use of quantitative data

A strength of this study was the use of questionnaires with closed questions.

This style of questionnaire makes it easy to analyse the data and examine many different correlations between each personality trait and RWA/SDO. Having a questionnaire with objective items means it would also be relatively easy to replicate the study with a different sample of people and even do it online to gain a large sample. For example, for comparison it might be good to investigate the relationship between personality and RWA/SDO in people from non-European countries or more collectivist cultures.

This means that wider conclusions can be drawn about the origins of prejudiced behaviour.

Peer reports may be biased

A weakness of this study is that peer reports may be subject to the same biases as self-reports, and therefore also lack validity.

For example, peers may be just as motivated as the individuals themselves to view their friends/acquaintances in a positive light.

This means that the data about personality, ideological attitudes and prejudice may lack validity, rendering the resulting correlations rather meaningless.

Competing argument Cohrs *et al.* were aware of this potential issue and therefore in their second study, they used two peers for each participant and combined the data in order to improve validity. However, it is still the case, that both peers may be biased, as the participants chose which peers to ask to complete the questionnaires, meaning these people may have been more likely to share a favourable view of the participant.

Application to reducing prejudice

The link between the development of certain worldviews and future levels of prejudice can be applied to reducing prejudice.

If prejudice is related to an individual's worldview, then the development of alternative worldviews could reduce prejudice. For example, the 'RWA mindset' is based on the world as a dangerous and threatening place and the 'SDO mindset' sees the world as a competitive jungle.

This means that social policies which combat these worldviews should also be helpful in reducing prejudice, leading to a fairer and more just society.

EXTRA: Issues and debates

One issue which is relevant here is the use of psychology in social control.

The media manipulate our worldviews through selective reporting of the news, readily creating outgroups and underlining the perception that the world is dangerous and competitive. As the Cohrs *et al.* study suggests, these narratives play straight into the hands of certain personality types who are already predisposed to prejudice, polarising and reinforcing viewpoints and potentially impacting on voting behaviour.

This demonstrates that some people's personalities may make them more vulnerable or receptive to this than others. This should be acknowledged by the media and lead them to behave more responsibly.

Balanced conclusion

This study has served to check the validity of existing data using peer- as well as self-reports. It appears that prejudice is indeed related to personality. This understanding is important because it shows that some people are more at risk of becoming prejudiced than others when exposed to, for example, exaggerated news broadcasts that emphasise how dangerous the world is. This study is not without limitations (for example the biased selection of peers), however one positive outcome is support for the idea that prejudice could be reduced by tackling worldviews.

Apply it — Methods: Structured interviewing

Bertha has decided to replicate the Cohrs *et al.* study using structured interviews instead of questionnaires.

1. Explain **one** strength and **one** weakness of structured interviewing compared to using questionnaires. (4)
2. Bertha uses opportunity sampling to obtain her sample.
   Explain **one** advantage and **one** disadvantage of opportunity sampling compared to the sampling method used by Cohrs *et al.* (4)
3. Bertha is going to interview each participant and someone who knows them well but is not a friend or family member, e.g. a colleague or neighbour.
   Explain **one** advantage and **one** disadvantage of this compared to self and peer assessments. (4)
4. Bertha collects quantitative data from many questions in her interview. She wants to use a measure of dispersion.
   Identify **two** measures of dispersion and explain which is the most useful. (2)

Apply it — Concepts: Prejudice in the home

Logan is concerned that the elderly people in the care home where he works are displaying some very prejudiced views.

1. Explain how Logan could use personality testing to find out which residents are most likely to hold prejudiced views. (4)
2. Some residents express fears about being mugged and worry about being hurt in terrorist attacks. Use the findings of Cohrs *et al.* to explain this perspective. (4)
3. Other residents feel that their grandchildren are fighting an impossible battle to find jobs or housing. Use the findings of Cohrs *et al.* to explain this perspective. (4)

Study tip

You need to know the strengths and weaknesses of the research methods used in psychological research and these can be used as a basis for creating evaluation points. Be sure, when writing evaluation points, that you create chains of reasoning that are specific to the study you are evaluating and not, for example, about questionnaires in general.

Check it

1. Explain the sampling method used in your chosen contemporary study for the social approach. (2)
2. Describe **two** findings of your contemporary study. (2)
3. **Standard:** Assess your chosen contemporary study from social psychology in terms of generalisability. (8)
4. **AS (Methods/Synoptic):** Evaluate the procedure of your chosen contemporary studies from social psychology and cognitive psychology with reference to validity and reliability. (12)

Key questions for social psychology

Chapter 1 Social psychology

On this page we have presented a full answer to one of the key questions in the specification and added comments to draw your attention to specific features.

The specification says...

1.4.1 One key question of relevance to today's society, discussed as a contemporary issue for society rather than an academic argument.

1.4.2 Concepts, theories and/or research (as appropriate to the chosen key question) drawn from social psychology as used in this qualification.

Suitable examples

- How can knowledge of social psychology be used to reduce prejudice in situations such as crowd behaviour or rioting?
- How can social psychology be used to explain heroism?

(Note that these are examples and therefore no exam question will specifically ask you about one of these.)

Example 1

Discuss the key question you have studied using concepts, theories and/or research from social psychology. (8)

State your key question: How can knowledge of social psychology be used to reduce prejudice in situations such as crowd behaviour or rioting?

In some ethnically diverse communities in London, the relationship with the police has become highly strained. This has led to riots, which have added to the prejudice towards the police. Social identity theory (SIT) suggests that rioters see the police as the outgroup, and they may categorise anyone in a police uniform as a target. The unity of the crowd may bring a sense of belonging, pride and self-esteem, from joining together as an ingroup with a shared identity. On the other hand, Sherif et al. (1954/1961) might argue that the mere presence of an outgroup (the police) is not the cause of the animosity. The uniform signifies a group with whom there is competition, in this case people may feel they are competing for justice or freedom of speech. (130 words)

In 2017, riots broke out in East London following the death of Rashan Charles, who was stopped by the police. Following a peaceful protest, a group of masked rioters broke shop windows, attacked a lorry and started fires. Social comparison suggests that the rioters may see their actions as acceptable as they view their group as superior to the police, as defenders of justice, in comparison with the police, who are seen as inferior due to their alleged racism. SIT assumes that prejudice is inevitable, however Sherif suggests that working together on superordinate goals, e.g. music or sports projects, could bring the police and young people together. The groups may find common ground and men and women who also happen to be police officers may be seen as people rather than 'the police', potentially improving future relations. (138 words)

Riots have many costs to society. They divide communities, leave residents fearful and cause financial costs to homeowners and businesses. This underlines the importance of researching evidence-based solutions. One suggestion has been to put more police officers onto our streets. However, social impact theory (Latané 1981) suggests that impact is not just about numbers. Police impact could be enhanced through increasing the strength and immediacy of officers, through strategies to improve the overall image of the police in the local area. This said, many rioters are not actually members of the local community. They may simply enjoy being part of any unrest and the opportunity to be aggressive. Their behaviour may be biological rather than social in origin. This suggests that social solutions may be limited in their effectiveness. (129 words)

In conclusion, reduction of prejudice may rely on strategies to bring disparate groups together, reducing the need for unity through shared opposition to the police. However, an analysis of rioting behaviour from cognitive and behaviourist perspectives may also be necessary. (40 words)

Total = 437 words

The key to key questions

Key questions may be worth anything between 1 and 12 marks for AS level and up to 20 marks for A level. On this spread we focus on 8-mark questions – but you can add more paragraphs to turn this into a 12- or 16- or 20-mark answer.

A 'key question' essay needs to combine a description of the key question with application of concepts, theories and research evidence from the social topic. We think the secret lies in using **black**/**blue**/**green** paragraphs.

When answering an 8-mark exam question, first state your key question and then write three paragraphs structured as follows:

- **Black:** Describe one aspect of your key question and explain why it is important in contemporary society.
- **Blue:** Link to relevant psychological concepts and theories.
- **Green:** Support your blue ideas with relevant research evidence or introduce competing arguments (from other research evidence or comparisons with other topics in psychology). Be sure to LINK BACK to the key question.

End with a balanced conclusion.

Each paragraph should be 100–140 words.

There is more advice on key questions on pages 9 and 17.

Identical police uniforms make these officers appear as one homogeneous group, giving the impression that all members share identical beliefs, values and attitudes. This could lead to stereotyping of the outgroup.

Identify groups who might come into conflict, leading to prejudice.

Integrating psychological theory: Notice how theoretical terminology is blended with terms from the key question about rioting.

Make it contemporary: A specific example of a recent riot to show that this is a contemporary issue.

Here comes a competing argument: Alternative evidence is introduced but in context, e.g. the source of the competition for the London rioters is highlighted – justice and freedom of speech.

Outline the costs to individuals and society of leaving this key question unanswered.

Use material from other topics: Once you have studied other topics/approaches in your psychology course you may want to introduce competing arguments.

The big finish: A balanced judgement is sometimes required by the command term and always a useful way to end your response. See how we finish using terms from the original key question.

Example 2

Discuss the key question you have studied using concepts, theories and/or research from social psychology. (8)

State your key question: How can social psychology be used to explain heroism?

Paragraph 1

Describe: What does heroism mean? Are heroes special or could we all be heroes? Briefly describe a recent incident involving an act of heroism.

Link: Use social identity theory to think about how the 'hero' might categorise the people he or she helped and anyone else involved such as an attacker. Think: in- and outgroups.

Support/challenge: Not everyone shows heroic behaviour. Relate this to personality differences such as desire for personal control or empathic concern.

Paragraph 2

Describe: Add more detail to your example, for example, did your hero go against orders from an authority figure? If so, outline who said what, to whom and how your hero behaved.

Link: Could you bring in legitimate authority, agentic shift and autonomous state? Don't forget to elaborate your ideas fully and link each point to details from your example.

Support/challenge: Support your idea with evidence from research that you have studied during the topic, such as Burger (2009).

Paragraph 3

Describe: Outline why your key question is relevant to contemporary society. What costs and/or benefits are there of labelling people as heroes? The use of the term 'hero' implies a villain may be lurking somewhere…!

Link: What are the implications of the media, for example, applying the term 'hero'? How does this encourage people to think about groups of people in society relating to in- or outgroup status? In Tajfel and Turner's opinion (1979) what is the inevitable outcome of social categorisation?

Support/challenge: Argue that social categorisation does not always lead to negative outcomes and back this up with reference to either the scientific flaws of research (such as Tajfel 1970) or look at cross-cultural research (such as Wetherell 1982).

Finish with a balanced judgement. Do social psychological concepts really explain acts of heroism or are these acts linked more to individual differences?

On this page we have provided a scaffold to help you prepare your own answer.

Remember that these are simply suggested answers. Use these suggestions to help you think about how you could structure your own response.

The key question on the left is about heroes. One example of heroism comes from a terror attack at Borough Market in London in 2017 – the flowers above were laid as a tribute to those who lost their lives. On a June night three terrorists jumped out of a van and indiscriminately started stabbing people in the market. Ordinary people like Florin Moraru became heroes, risking their lives to protect strangers. Florin left the bakery where he worked, grabbed a crate and hit one of the attackers with it. He then sheltered twenty terrified people in the bakery, while searching for a weapon to continue defending them. People shouted to him not to go into the street and the police were shouting 'get back' but Florin disregarded this.

Try your own

You don't have to do the key question in the specification.

Here is a different one that you might try: *Can social psychology explain 'hazing' rituals including the behaviour of the person being initiated and the people doing the initiating?*

'Hazing' (initiation ceremony) refers to rituals used when someone joins a group and may involve getting people to do unpleasant things. There are many areas of social psychology that are easily applied to this topic including social identity theory, agency theory and social impact theory.

Think about why the person being initiated is prepared to go to such great lengths to join the group, why those doing the initiating participate in acts which are cruel and humiliating, why some people may be more vulnerable to hazing than others.

Here are some links to kick-start your research:

- Read the story of a university band member who died following a hazing ritual, tinyurl.com/y724cj2p
- Look up infographics on hazing using your chosen search engine. Here is one: tinyurl.com/yav35t4h

You will find plenty of information about hazing very easily but be sure to stick to the social psychology in this topic when you discuss the phenomena otherwise you will not gain credit.

Study tip

When writing the blue and green sections be sure to contextualise every sentence with clear links to the information provided in the black section. Answers to key questions are all about application and you will not gain any credit for simply regurgitating chunks of theory or studies with no attempt to link to information from the description section.

Check it

1. Key questions relate to issues of relevance to modern society.
   (a) State your key question for social psychology. [1]
   (b) Explain why this question is relevant to today's society. [2]
   (c) Use **one** theory, concept or study to explain **one** way in which social psychology has helped to understand, explain or improve society in relation to this question. [2]
2. (a) State your key question for social psychology. [1]
   (b) Using theories, concepts and/or research from social psychology, explain why it is important to society that psychology answers this question. [4]
3. **Standard:** Discuss your key question using theories, concepts and/or research from social psychology. [8]
4. **AL (I&D/Synoptic):** Evaluate the usefulness to society of the psychological knowledge from your key questions in social and cognitive psychology. [12]

Practical investigations for social psychology

Practical investigation example from the specification.

The specification says...

1.5.1 One practical research exercise to gather data relevant to topics covered in social psychology. This practical research exercise must adhere to ethical principles in both content and intention.

In conducting the practical research exercise, students must:

- Design and conduct a questionnaire to gather both qualitative and quantitative data to look for a difference in the data. (See pages 168-169 for advice)
- Consider questionnaire construction, sampling decisions and ethical issues. (See pages 170-171 and 176-177)
- Collect and present an analysis of quantitative data using measures of central tendency, measures of dispersion (including range and standard deviation as appropriate), bar graph and frequency table. (See pages 172-173)
- Collect and present an analysis of qualitative data using thematic analysis. (See pages 175 and 213)
- Consider strengths and weaknesses of the questionnaire and possible improvements. (See pages 169 and 180)
- Write up the procedure, results and discussion section of a report. (See page 181)

Ethical principles

Ethical principles are discussed in detail in chapter 5, on pages 176–177. We strongly suggest that you complete this checklist before collecting data.

1. Participants know participation is voluntary. ☐
2. Participants know what to expect, i.e. the task(s) they will be doing. ☐
3. Participants know they can withdraw at any time. ☐
4. Participants' responses will be anonymous. ☐
5. I minimised the risk of distress to participants. ☐
6. I have avoided collecting any sensitive data. ☐
7. I considered all other ethical issues. ☐
8. I have not done anything that would bring my school/teacher/psychology into disrepute. ☐
9. My teacher has approved my plan. ☐

A questionnaire to see if males or females perceive themselves to be more obedient

Design considerations

This study looks at differences between males and females, so the independent variable (IV) is gender (male or female) and, therefore it has to have an independent groups design. The dependent variable is obedience, which is measured using a questionnaire.

Prepare materials

You should construct a questionnaire that collects quantitative data using closed questions *and* qualitative data using open questions.

You might wish to create some scenarios such as, 'You have an exam in ten minutes, how likely would you be to obey a year 10 student who tells you to go and see the headmaster?' Participants could indicate their level of agreement on a scale from 1 to 7, where 1 is strongly disagree and 7 is strongly agree. Include several questions and add up the scores for each participant to create an overall obedience score.

Qualitative data can be collected through open questions such as asking, after each scenario, 'Why would you behave in this way?'

Don't forget to ask participants to indicate whether they are male or female! But there is no need for any further identification.

Sampling decisions

You do not need an equal number of males and females (although you need enough of each gender to make a comparison). Opportunity or volunteer sampling is fine but stratified sampling might ensure better gender representation.

Special ethical concerns

Most people would probably prefer not to be classified as highly obedient, as they might infer that this is somehow a bad thing. Therefore, it is important to think about how you will protect your participants from harm to their self-esteem. For example, you could design a debriefing sheet explaining the benefits of being obedient. You should also think about how you will maintain your participants' anonymity. You could ask them to put their questionnaires into a 'postbox' or you could use a website such as 'SurveyMonkey' which will keep all the results anonymous for you.

Analyse your data

Use this investigation as an opportunity to practise your descriptive statistical skills, following the guidance in the specification box top left. You could create a frequency table for the 'headmaster' question where you tally how many males and females circle each number on the scale in order to identify the modal score. If you have given each participant an overall obedience score, you could work out the mean and standard deviation for males and females and plot these on a bar chart. (It is always good to practise calculating standard deviations using the formula on the exam papers.)

To analyse the qualitative data you use thematic analysis (see pages 175 and 213) and produce conclusions. The practical investigation on page 159 also provides a useful account of how to do this and on the facing page there is another example. You could convert the qualitative data to quantitative by counting up the number of times each theme arises for the males and then for the females.

Write the report

Write a detailed account of your procedures, which might include some example questions but the questionnaire itself belongs in the appendix. Remember to include specific details, such as how you actually collected the data, e.g. did everyone complete the questionnaire at the same time using pen and paper or was it online? Also in the appendix include the standardised instructions that were given to the participants and outline how you followed ethical guidelines.

The results section includes your tables, graphs and four technically accurate and well-detailed sentences to describe the findings of both parts of your analysis, i.e. four × qualitative and four × quantitative.

The discussion section includes strengths, weaknesses and improvements that you could make to the procedure and the questionnaire itself.

An investigation into ingroup and outgroup attitudes

Design considerations

We are going to look at ingroup and outgroup behaviours by selecting two ingroups – football fans and rugby fans. This will be your independent variable (IV). This will allow you to look at ingroup favouritism and outgroup bias. You might, for example, expect the football lovers to display more negative views about rugby and more positive views about football than the rugby lovers and vice versa. These views are your dependent variable (DV).

To avoid demand characteristics, you need to leave it until the end of the questionnaire to ask, for example whether the participants are rugby or football fans – or neither.

Prepare materials

You need to collect both quantitative and qualitative data in this study.

For quantitative data you should ask closed questions. You might ask people to agree or disagree with various statements (such as 'rugby fans are less aggressive than football fans'). Add up the responses for each group (rugby fans and football fans) so that you can compare the scores.

For qualitative data you should ask open questions. For example, 'How would you describe the behaviour of [insert your nearest club here] football fans following a match?'

Sampling decisions

Some ideas about sampling are provided on the facing page and the same advice applies here. You should be wary about recruiting participants at football/rugby matches or training sessions as you may have a biased sample. That said, it's fine to have a few problems with generalisability, for example, as exam questions may ask about potential improvements.

Special ethical concerns

This questionnaire is ultimately about a form of prejudice and even if the topic of attitudes about sports seems more benign than questions about racial prejudices, respect and sensitivity still need to be uppermost in your mind. All the usual rules apply here: you need a written statement that explains roughly how long the survey might take, the fact that participants have the right to withdraw at any point and an explanation of how you will ensure their confidentiality. Participants need to be reminded not to write their names on the questionnaire if they are filling it in by hand.

Analyse your data

It is important that you check that you are calculating appropriate measures of central tendency and dispersion (as listed in the specification on the facing page).

Your procedure section should include detailed information about how you analysed your quantitative and qualitative data as you might be asked this in the exam. For the qualitative data you should:

1. Include the raw data and your identification of the emergent themes, as shown in Example 1 on the right.
2. You should then group data together to illustrate the different themes and this will enable you to draw conclusions about your findings, as shown in Example 2 on the right.

Write the report

See facing page for advice.

Other ideas

Ingroup favouritism and outgroup hostility amongst Apple and Android users. Do Apple users have more favourable opinions of other Apple users than of Android users and vice versa?

Cross-cultural differences in ageism. Do people from different countries round the world have different opinions of elderly people in their communities?

Practical investigation example from the specification.

Apply it — Methods: Dan's group

Students in Dan's group are collecting data on ingroups and outgroups. Each student plans to use closed questions asking members of staff in an office if they mainly talk to, eat with and spend time outside work with people from their own department or not. They will also ask staff to explain their feelings towards people within their department and from other departments in the workplace.

1. Write **one** closed question that Dan's group could use. (1)
2. Explain how the **two** questions at the end differ from the closed questions. (2)
3. Dan decides to include questions about shopping, sports and family. Explain how this could improve validity. (2)
4. How could the students check the reliability of their interpretation of the responses to a qualitative question? (2)

Example 1: Qualitative data collected from three different participants. Colours have been used to identify emergent themes. For example, red identifies the mention of winning or losing.

Participant details	**Question:** How would you describe the behaviour of Aggroville footballs fans following a match?
Participant 1 Not a sports fan.	Well, put it this way, if they have lost they can get pretty aggro. They are very noisy and when they are in the pubs afterwards, they always seem to be fighting. I wouldn't want to be on a train after a match. They are often really drunk.
Participant 2 Loves football but can't often make it to matches.	Well, Aggroville fans tend to show a lot of camaraderie to each other, they are good lads, they love a bit of a knees-up, you know, obviously it depends on whether we win or not. Sometimes if it's a loss, you know, people just go home and have a quiet night, but yeah if there's a win, it's celebration time. I've never seen any violence or anything.
Participant 3 Identifies as a rugby fan.	My opinion would be that, well I wouldn't want to stereotype but essentially football fans… they don't always go to matches for the love of sport shall we say, it's the pack mentality, they're just there for the booze and to cause trouble a lot of the time.

Example 2: Examples are collected for each theme.

Emergent theme	Not a sports fan	Football fans	Rugby fans
Whether they win or lose	'if they have lost'	'depends on whether we win or not', 'if it's a loss', 'if there's a win'	
Aggressive	'they can get pretty aggro', 'always seem to be fighting'	'I've never seen any violence or anything'	'it's the pack mentality', 'to cause trouble a lot of the time'

Check it

1. You conducted a practical investigation in social psychology.
   (a) State the aim of a practical investigation you conducted collecting qualitative data. (2)
   (b) Describe how you analysed your qualitative data. (4)
2. Explain **two** improvements you could have made to your practical investigation in social psychology. (4)
3. **Standard:** Evaluate your practical investigation in social psychology. (8)
4. **AL (I&D/Synoptic):** To what extent were the procedures of your practical investigations for social psychology and learning theories scientific? (12)

Revision summary

Obedience

Theories | *Milgram's studies* | *Factors affecting obedience and dissent*

Agency theory

The origins of obedience: Nature meets nurture
Humans live in hierarchical groups and obedience aids social harmony.

Autonomous state
We choose how to behave and take more responsibility for our actions.

Making the agentic shift
Acting on behalf of another, usually this person has authority over us.

Moral strain
Anxiety caused by carrying out orders that conflict with our sense of what is 'right or wrong'.

Evaluation

Supporting evidence
100% of Milgram's (1963) participants pressed the 300 V switch and 65% went to 450 V.
However, Perry (2012) argues at least 60% were disobedient, if you discount the people who saw through the deception.

Agentic shift isn't inevitable
Rank and Jacobson (1977) found that 89% of nurses remain autonomous and disobeyed orders.

Application to the military
Military leaders decrease moral strain and increase obedience by using terms like 'collateral damage'.

EXTRA: Issues and debates
Alternative theory is explaining obedience as 'engaged followership' (Reicher et al. 2012).

Social impact theory

Sources and targets
Latané (1981) described social force fields. The 'target' is impacted by the 'source'.

Strength, immediacy and number
Impact is determined by the strength (S), immediacy (I) and number of sources (N).

Multiplicative and divisional effects
Increasing S, I and/or N of sources increases impact of source. Increasing S, I and/or N of targets decreases impact of source.

The law of diminishing returns
Once the source group is bigger than three, each additional person has less of an influencing effect.

Evaluation

Obedience at the zoo
Sedikides and Jackson (1990) found that S, I and N affected whether zoo-goers obeyed orders.
However, group size was not controlled which threatens internal validity.

Immediacy less important than strength
Hofling et al. (1966) found that 95% of nurses obeyed despite the source not being present.

Application to political influence
Could help political leaders gain greater influence over voters.

EXTRA: Issues and debates
Reductionist because 'strength' is subjective and dynamic not just represented by a single number.

Milgram's baseline study

Behavioural study of obedience (1963)

Aim
To understand Holocaust behaviour and test obedience to destructive orders.

Procedure
Experimenter instructs 'teacher' to give increasing shocks to 'learner' in a memory experiment.

Findings
All participants gave a shock of 300 V and 65% went up to 450 V.

Conclusions
Ordinary Americans are surprisingly obedient to legitimate authority.

Evaluation

Standardised procedure
Many variables were controlled, e.g. the number and timing of the learner's mistakes.
However, the experimenter deviated from the script, giving 20 prods in one case (Perry 2012).

The task didn't make sense
Orne and Holland (1968) suggest participants may have known the shocks were fake.

Application to pilot training
Commercial airlines now teach first officers to challenge the captain's authority (Tarnow 2000).

EXTRA: Issues and debates
Ethical issue, Baumrind (1964) criticised Milgram's excessive psychological harm and deception.

Milgram's variation studies

New baseline
Experiment 5, learner has 'a heart condition' and participants can hear his reactions, 65% fully obedient.

Experiment 10: Rundown office block
Obedience dropped to 47.5% in rundown building in Bridgeport.

Experiment 7: Telephonic instructions
Obedience dropped to 22.5% when orders were given by phone from a different room.

Experiment 13: Ordinary man gives orders
Obedience dropped to 20% when the person giving orders was just another participant (low status).

Evaluation

AO3 Experiment 10
Qualitative data analysed by Modigliani and Rochat (1995) gave deeper insight into those who were defiant.

AO3 Experiment 7
Sedikides and Jackson's zoo study shows obedience does drop when authority not present, thus high external validity.

AO3 Experiment 13
Internal validity was poor as there was still a sense of 'derived authority'.

EXTRA: Issues and debates
Practical issues, validity affected by people talking to each other about their experiences.

Personality

The authoritarian personality
Harsh parenting leads to submissiveness to authority and high levels of obedience (Adorno et al. 1950).

Internal and external locus of control (LOC)
Miller (1975) showed that externals were more likely to obey dangerous orders than internals.

Evaluation

Support for authoritarianism
Fully obedient participants score higher on F-scale than defiant participants (Elms and Milgram 1966).
However, this does not show a causal link between authoritarianism and obedience.

Internal locus of control does not predict defiance
In Austria, no difference in LOC between obedient and defiant participants (Schurz 1985).

Application to the world of work
Personality tests could help matching people to jobs requiring high/low levels of obedience.

Gender

Women are more obedient than men
Asked to deliver shocks to a puppy, 100% full obedience in females, 54% males (Sheridan and King 1972).

Men are more obedient than women
Milgram replication found 16% full obedience in females, 40% males (Kilham and Mann 1974).

Moral reasoning
Males use an 'ethic of justice' whereas females inclined to an 'ethic of care' (Gilligan 1982).

Evaluation

Support for Gilligan
Gilligan and Attanucci (1988) analysed real-life dilemmas and found predicted gender differences.

There may be no difference
Blass (1999) found that 8 out of 9 studies returned no significant gender difference in obedience.

EXTRA: Issues and debates
Gender bias, Milgram's original research was androcentric but balanced by more recent studies.

Situation

Legitimacy
Reducing authority figure's perceived legitimacy reduces obedience, e.g. dress code.

Proximity
Increased distance between authority figure and participant decreases obedience.

Behaviour of others
Witnessing disobedience in others increases defiance.

AO3 Evaluation

Supporting evidence
Meeus and Raaijmakers (1995) found obedience drops when 'experimenter absent' (36%) and 'two peers rebel' (16%).
However, personality is also important.

Application to rule-breaking
Changing wording of countryside rules increases the strength of the message (Gramann et al. 1995).

Culture

Individualism–collectivism
Hofstede (2011) identified six dimensions for cultural comparisons.
Individualist values may make people less obedient than those from collectivist cultures.

Power distance index (PDI)
High PDI may make people more obedient than those from low PDI cultures.

Evaluation

Cultural dimensions do correlate with obedience
Australia (low PDI 36/100), 28% fully obedient. Poland (higher PDI 68/100), 90% fully obedient.

Cultures don't differ
On average US obedience similar to rest of world, obedience may be universal (Blass 2012).

EXTRA: Issues and debates
Obedience may be more nature than nurture as it is fairly to very high the world over.

Prejudice

Theories

Social identity theory

The self and the group
Our social identity and self-esteem derive from our ingroup (Tajfel and Turner 1979, 1986).

Social categorisation
People place themselves in groups which creates in- and outgroups, and prejudice.

Social identification
Individual changes their behaviour and thinking to fit with group norms.

Social comparison
Self-esteem is boosted by perceiving ingroup as superior and outgroup as inferior.

Evaluation

The minimal group experiment
Boys tried to maximise the difference between in- and outgroup profits (Tajfel 1970).
However, privately allocating points lacks mundane realism.

Ethnocentrism
Polynesian children discriminated less against outgroup than white classmates (Wetherell 1982).

Application to reducing prejudice
Interventions to increase self-esteem may help to reduce prejudice (Fein and Spencer 1997).

EXTRA: Issues and debates
Development of knowledge using fMRI, OFC differences (Van Bavel et al. 2008).

Realistic conflict theory

Intergroup competition
Two or more groups competing for same goal, prejudice and hostility intensify (Sherif 1966).

Negative interdependence
Outgroup hostility and ingroup solidarity arises in contests where only one group can win.

Limited resources
Competition may be for physical resources (e.g. food) or symbolic resources (e.g. power).

Positive interdependence and superordinate goals
When groups work together to accomplish a common goal this can reduce prejudice.

Evaluation

The Robbers Cave experiment
Sherif et al.'s (1961) study showed prejudice escalated when boys were competing to win.
However, researchers secretly raided one cabin so prejudice not just due to competition.

Competition may not be necessary
Prejudice can arise without competition for limited resources (minimal group experiment).

Application to reducing prejudice
Superordinate goals help reduce prejudice by groups working cooperatively on shared goals.

EXTRA: Issues and debates
RCT illustrates the process of science as falsifiable hypotheses derived from RCT.

Factors affecting prejudice (and discrimination)

Personality

The authoritarian personality
Harsh parenting creates hostility, displaced onto inferior outgroups (Adorno et al. 1950).

Allport's authoritarian personality
Authoritarians are rigid 'black and white' thinkers, who prefer 'cognitive closure'.

Right wing authoritarianism (RWA)
See world as dangerous, closed to new experiences (Altemeyer 1988).

Social dominance orientation (SDO)
See the world as a competitive jungle, tough-minded, lacking in empathy (Pratto et al. 1994).

Evaluation

Supporting evidence
RWA/SDO predict generalised prejudice and relate to openness/agreeableness (Cohrs et al. 2012).
However, RWA/SDO may not be consistent over time (Levin 1996).

Conflicting evidence
Most participants were anti-asylum seekers, not predicted by RWA/SDO (Louis et al. 2003).

Application to reducing prejudice
Regulation of social media pages that promote prejudices, combat certain worldviews.

EXTRA: Issues and debates
Treating right-wing attitudes as abnormal increases prejudice and is socially sensitive.

Situation

Social norms
Identification with group norms (social identity theory).

Competition and resource stress
Competition escalates prejudice (realistic conflict theory), may be resource stress between groups (Esses et al. 2001).

Evaluation

Supporting evidence
Akrami et al. (2009) changed social norms, changed views.
However, RWA and SDO also influenced prejudice.

Application to reduction of prejudice
Immigration, challenging zero-sum beliefs (Esses et al. 2001).

Culture

The norm of intolerance
Even tolerant cultures show micro-aggressions (Baldwin 2017).

The norm of fairness
Fairness linked to collectivist values (Wetherell 1982).

Evaluation

Pressure to be prejudiced
Susceptibility to cultural pressure predicted prejudice towards black South Africans (Orpen 1971).
However, the participants were 16-year-old schoolchildren.

EXTRA: Issues and debates
Practical issues, e.g. mismatch between ethnicity of the researcher and some of the participants.

Classic study

Sherif et al. (1954/61)

The Robbers Cave experiment

Aims
To explore how competition can increase outgroup hostility and increase ingroup solidarity.

Procedure
Boys divided into Rattlers and Eagles. Stage 1: group formation, stage 2: friction (created through competition), stage 3: reducing friction.

Findings
Prejudice (e.g. more friendships with ingroup), relations improved following superordinate goals.

Conclusions
Competition increased ingroup favouritism and outgroup hostility. Prejudice not decreased just through contact.

Evaluation

Selection and allocation of children
Careful matching of the two groups, internal validity.
However, matching spoiled when two Eagles left camp.

Failed replication
Tyerman and Spencer (1983) replicated with Sea Scouts, patrols interacted well together even when in competition.

Application to reducing prejudice
Aronson and Bridgeman's (1979) 'jigsaw classroom' used superordinate goals to reduce racial prejudice in schools.

EXTRA: Issues and debates
Cultural and gender issues, used male American children.

Contemporary studies

Burger (2009)

Would people still obey today?

Aims
Confirm previous findings, assess gender role.

Procedure
Replication of Milgram using 150 V solution and other additional ethical safeguards.

Findings
70% pressed 150 V compared to Milgram's 82.5%. No gender difference.

Conclusions
Milgram study not era-bound/androcentric.

Evaluation

Strong internal validity
Checked for prior knowledge of psychology, so unlikely to have seen through the set up.

Poor generalisability
Pre-study screening excluded 38%, thus sample may have been unrepresentative.
However, 80% obedience in study with less rigorous screening (Beauvois et al. 2012).

Limited application
Less tension, so less representative.

EXTRA: Issues and debates
Burger's attention to ethical issues was meticulous, but maybe studies too tame now.

Reicher and Haslam (2006)

Rethinking the psychology of tyranny

Aim
Do subordinates collectively overthrow tyranny?

Procedure
Five guards, 10 prisoners, changed permeability, legitimacy and cognitive alternatives.

Findings
Increased social identification meant tyranny challenged, guards' RWA decreased.

Conclusions
Supports social identity theory because identification key in challenge to tyranny.

Evaluation

The use of quantitative data
Quantitative measures e.g. social identification, allows comparisons.
However, self-reports may lack validity.

Observer effects
Participants aware of filming, lower validity.

Application to improving prison conditions
Raise guards' morale to control collective resistance.

EXTRA: Issues and debates
Use of psychological knowledge, study helps predict social and political unrest.

Cohrs et al. (2012)

Individual differences and prejudice

Aims
Test the 'dual process' model (Duckitt 2005).

Procedure
Tested OCEAN, RWA, SDO and generalised prejudice, using self and peer reports.

Findings
Negative correlations between openness and RWA, and agreeableness and SDO.

Conclusions
Certain personality traits are predictive of RWA and SDO and generalised prejudice.

Evaluation

The use of quantitative data
Closed questions (quantitative data) make data analysis easier and more objective.

Peer reports may be as biased
May lack validity because friends are motivated to see each other in positive terms.
However in study 2, two peer reports were used.

Application to reducing prejudice
Combat worldviews (i.e. RWA and SDO).

EXTRA: Issues and debates
Social control, attitudes easily moulded by the media, who should behave responsibly.

Practice questions, answers and feedback

On this spread we look at some typical student answers to questions. The comments provided indicate what is good and bad in each answer. Learning how to produce effective question answers is a SKILL. Read pages 6–19 for guidance.

Question 1: Psychology has been used to explain key questions of relevance to today's society. Describe the key question that you studied as part of the social psychology topic on your course. [4]

Sam's answer

The key question that we looked at in social psychology was about hazing. Hazing is when people do dangerous or humiliating things in order to be accepted into a group like a 'frat house' in an American university or a sports team. These have often hit the headlines as there have been cases where people have died or committed suicide after hazing.

Sam has correctly identified the topic of his key question, but has not actually stated it as a question. Sam has defined what hazing is (briefly) and added a sentence about the outcomes of hazing but, as we don't know the actual question, he might only gain 1 mark at best.

Ella's answer

The key question from social was 'How can social psychology be used to explain heroism?' Heroism involves putting yourself at risk to protect others and this may be a one-off act or an ongoing commitment to helping others. One example was when a shopkeeper confronted an armed terrorist during an attack in London and barricaded customers into his shop despite bystanders and the police shouting at him to get back. This is an important question for society because not following orders from police could jeopardise people's safety.

Ella's answer is very good. She has stated the question clearly, explained what heroism means, given an example and linked this back to the key question. There is enough for the full 4 marks.

Larina's answer

Our key question was 'How can social psychology explain and reduce prejudice in situations such as rioting?' Social identity theory says rioters see the police as an outgroup and other protesters as their ingroup while realistic conflict theory says hostility increases when the police and rioters feel like they are in competition. For example, the rioters may feel like they are fighting for people's rights and that the police symbolise the unfair system they are fighting against.

Larina has not engaged with the command term 'describe', instead she has given a good answer to the command term 'explain' by applying social psychological theories to help understand the question. She should have given details about what rioting involves and why it is a problem for society. This answer might only gain 1 mark.

Question 2: As part of your specification you were required to learn about Sherif et al. (1954/1961). Describe this classic study from social psychology. [5]

Sam's answer

The aim of the Robbers Cave study was to create frustration through a competition, where the winning team would win penknives as their prize. Sherif et al. wanted to see how this situation would affect group relations between two gangs of 11-year-old schoolboys. There were a variety of contests including tug of war, baseball and tent pitching and they were observed for three weeks. The researchers used questionnaires to find out how the boys felt about each other and who they were friends with. The groups developed their own social norms, e.g. the Rattlers swore and acted tough. Competition led to physical and verbal abuse and the boys rarely made friends outside their own group.

Sam has managed to cover a lot of ground in his answer, all of which is accurate. He has mentioned the aim of the study, a variety of procedural details and given information about findings. He has missed the conclusions but this still constitutes a full answer (worth 4 marks). That said, it would have been nice to see some exact findings, e.g. the percentages of friends chosen from the outgroup.

Ella's answer

Sherif et al. set up a field experiment at a summer camp with 22 schoolboys aged 11 from Oklahoma. The researchers manipulated the situation by secretly raiding one of the cabins and creating a sports tournament with prizes. The two groups were matched on IQ and sporting ability. Data was collected by observation, tape recordings and using questionnaires about boys' attitudes towards boys in their own group and in the other group. There were three stages of the camp group formation when the groups were allowed to bond, friction when there were contests like treasure hunts, baseball and tug of war and then reducing friction where they worked together to start the broken-down truck and mend the water supply.

Ella has a detailed knowledge of this study. However, she has sadly made a fatal error! She has only described the procedure of the study and thus would only receive 2 marks. This is critical – in a question asking you to describe a study you need to cover at least three of aim, procedure, findings and conclusions. You need to practise précising your classic and contemporary studies as the procedures are often very lengthy and you don't want to spend precious exam time deciding what to put in and what to leave out – prepare the 'Goldilocks' version in advance (not too short and not too long).

Larina's answer

The study was about the prejudice and conflict that arises when groups are fighting for the same goal. The researchers created a camp and the children were not allowed to see their parents and the parents were told they must not visit. Two boys became homesick and went home leaving 9 boys in one group and 11 in the other. This was a weakness because Sherif had carefully matched the two groups and he should have had a waiting list of reserves. They had to pitch tents and do activities like canoeing and swimming. This meant the study was very much like an ordinary camp meaning the boys were acting naturally as they had no idea the researchers were watching them and this means the study was high in ecological validity.

Larina seems to know a few key details but unfortunately not ones of central importance and therefore does not give a decent overview of the whole study. More importantly she has spent time evaluating the study which is not creditworthy in a 'describe' question. At best this answer would receive 1 mark.

Question 3: Assess the impact of culture on obedience. (8)

Ella's answer

There are many studies of obedience in different countries, for example Kilham and Mann found that 16% of women and 40% of men were fully obedient in Australia and in Jordan 73% were fully obedient. Gupta found that Indian students were not so obedient as they only got an obedience rate of 42.5% but people in Poland were very obedient indeed as they scored 90% when Burger's study was replicated.

All these different percentages show that obedience does differ round the world, however there have not been many studies in some areas of the world like South America and this is a problem.

Also, there are weaknesses with all these studies as Milgram's study has many flaws like it was not generalisable as it was only done on American men and it lacked validity as Gina Perry showed that the experimenter did not always stick to the script. It lacked ecological validity as most people have never been in a situation where they have to cause another person physical pain and a lot of people may have seen through the set-up. It was also highly unethical.

Overall, the studies of cultural difference show that in most countries you get very high obedience so obedience is probably nature not nurture and this supports agency theory because mostly people will be highly obedient because it aids survival and human beings are social animals and years ago it was essential to toe the line or you would be rejected from your group.

249 words

Ella starts by describing a large number of accurate findings. However, she has not thought about how to formulate her argument. She might have explained why one might expect to see high rates in some countries compared with others rather just stating that there are differences.

In the second paragraph she makes a weak link to the question but she is merely talking in terms of countries not cultural differences. She does mention the lack of studies in some areas of the world but this point is underdeveloped and she could have linked this with collectivism.

The third paragraph is problematic as she has merely evaluated Milgram's study without telling us what he found out about culture in the first place. She has already shown that his study *is* generalisable as she has cited a variety of studies on different populations. Overall this is an imbalanced list of four weaknesses, none of which are linked to the essay title.

She does remember to end with a conclusion but this does not really follow from the evidence provided in the rest of the essay. At the very end she mentions agency theory and it does feel like she is just chucking in everything she knows about obedience.

This is a level 2 response. There is a range of accurate findings but rather superficial evaluation and a failure to make links between the descriptive and evaluative content. Therefore, 3 rather than 4 marks.

Larina's answer

Obedience means following direct orders from an authority figure and some people believe that this is affected by a person's culture, meaning the beliefs and values that they have been brought up with.

Lots of Milgram replications have been conducted in different countries to try and find out whether culture affects obedience and there are a few suggestions about why some cultures might be more or less obedient. For example, individualist cultures value independence and self-reliance so you might expect them to be less obedient as people don't want to look like they are just doing as they are told without thinking for themselves but people from collectivist cultures might be more obedient because they put the group ahead of the individual and have a strong sense of obligation to their family.

Also, in some countries people are very accepting of the fact that some people have more power than others, whereas in other countries, people don't like that and are happy to rebel and try and change things to make them fairer for everyone. This is called the Power Distance Index (PDI) and could affect how obedient people are.

One strength of the idea that culture does affect obedience is that there is quite a wide variation between countries. For example, in a study conducted in Australia they got a very low rate of only 28% of people who were fully obedient compared with 65% in America. Also, these figures were in line with the cultural values of the countries as Australia is very individualist, also Australia has a relatively low PDI and their obedience rate also fits in with this. So it looks like culture does affect obedience. Furthermore, in another study conducted in Poland they got a very high rate of 90% and this also fits with their cultural values because Poland is more collectivist and has a higher PDI score than Australia.

On the other hand there is evidence that suggests that cultural values do not affect obedience that much as Jordan (which is a collectivist country) and America (a highly individualist country) have similar rates of obedience. Also many countries have very high rates of obedience despite different cultural values.

Overall it's hard to assess the impact of culture on obedience because there are procedural differences between the studies making it hard to compare them and draw conclusions. However, overall it does seem that Hofstede's PDI dimension is quite a good indicator of obedience.

409 words

Larina has done really well to write 400 words in the time given for such an essay. 350 words is more realistic and it is likely that other answers on the paper would suffer because she overspent time here.

In the first paragraph she defines culture. This would have been better if she had tied it to a point she was making because it would have helped the essay to flow better whereas currently it feels rather fragmented.

Paragraph 2 is a clear outline of cultural differences – it could be more succinct and would be better if supported by actual evidence though she does discuss the individualism–collectivism dimension.

The descriptive content of the essay continues in paragraph 3 demonstrating specific knowledge of the Power Distance Index (PDI) but she hasn't explained how this is linked to culture.

Larina has given a good balance of description versus evaluation. She frames her first evaluation point well and develops her argument coherently, referring to accurate knowledge about obedience rates in different countries – though she might have given specific reference to the studies. Then she neatly links this paragraph back to the question.

In the penultimate paragraph she has ensured that she has a competing argument where she looks at evidence against the effect of culture on obedience although this is not presented effectively – and is more just a weakness than a competing argument.

Her conclusion relates directly to the question although it would have been nice to see her explain why procedural differences make it hard to draw comparisons.

This essay would score in level 3, possibly at the top (6 marks). Larina writes a lot but actually does not say that much. For example, paragraph 2 would have been improved if it had been linked to specific findings – as it is there are no details of what the levels of obedience were. The chains of reasoning could have been developed more fully. Both of these improvements would make this a top-class essay.

Multiple-choice questions

Obedience: Agency theory

1. The agentic shift occurs when:
(a) Subordinate tells us what to do.
(b) Subordinate disobeys orders.
(c) We follow orders from an authority figure.

2. In an autonomous state a person:
(a) Feels no choice but to obey.
(b) Behaves independently.
(c) Experiences moral strain.

3. In an agentic state a person:
(a) Experiences cognitive dissonance.
(b) Uses own sense of right and wrong to guide their behaviour.
(c) Takes responsibility for the consequences of their actions.

4. Percentage of autonomous nurses in Rank and Jacobson's study:
(a) 19%
(b) 49%
(c) 89%

Obedience: Social impact theory

1. When the target is stronger than the source, social impact will be:
(a) Increased.
(b) Decreased.
(c) Cancelled out.

2. If the source is strong, near to the target and there are more sources than targets this will result in the:
(a) Divisional effect.
(b) Multiplicative effect.
(c) Cumulative effect.

3. The law of diminishing returns says:
(a) Targets reduce the impact of a source by increasing numbers.
(b) When sources and targets are very far away from each other there is no social impact.
(c) The extra impact of additional sources is gradually reduced the more sources are added.

4. In Sedikides and Jackson's study, which factors affected social impact most?
(a) Decreasing strength of source.
(b) Decreasing immediacy of sources and targets.
(c) Increasing the number of targets to 5 or 6 from 1 or 2.

Obedience: Milgram's baseline study

1. What shock was given to participants to suggest it was real?
(a) 15 V
(b) 30 V
(c) 45 V

2. The measured variable in this study was the:
(a) Type of prods used.
(b) Level of shock given to learner.
(c) Presence of the experimenter.

3. Learner pounds on the wall at:
(a) 150 V
(b) 270 V
(c) 300 V

4. Attacked Milgram's ethics:
(a) Alan Elms.
(b) Gina Perry.
(c) Diana Baumrind.

Obedience: Milgram's variation studies

1. When the study moved to Bridgeport, the obedience rate was:
(a) 52%
(b) 48%
(c) 36%

2. When orders were given over the phone, Milgram also observed:
(a) Tension rates went up as people were confused.
(b) People administered lower shocks than they should have.
(c) The learner felt more at ease and got more answers correct.

3. In experiment 13 orders were given by:
(a) A phone call.
(b) A confederate.
(c) A man in guard's uniform.

4. Percentage of people who obeyed up to 450 V in Experiment 13:
(a) 10%
(b) 15%
(c) 20%

Factors affecting obedience and dissent: Individual differences

1. Elms and Milgram found that people with high F-scale scores:
(a) Blamed themselves for when carrying out destructive orders.
(b) Resisted orders from authority.
(c) Were highly obedient.

2. When asked to obey, people with an internal locus of control are likely:
(a) To show high levels of moral strain.
(b) To remain in an autonomous state.
(c) To believe that other people govern what happens to them.

3. Sheridan and King found that women were:
(a) Much less obedient than men.
(b) Much more obedient than men.
(c) Similar to men in obedience.

4. Carol Gilligan suggested men make decisions based on an ethic of:
(a) Justice.
(b) Care.
(c) Logic.

Factors affecting obedience and dissent: Situation and culture

1. Individualist cultures value:
(a) Self-reliance and autonomy.
(b) Sense of duty and obligation.
(c) Preservation of tradition.

2. Levels of obedience were found to be very low in a study conducted in:
(a) Austria.
(b) Australia.
(c) Italy.

3. Doliński found the obedience rate in Poland was:
(a) 42%
(b) 66%
(c) 90%

4. PDI stands for:
(a) Power distance index.
(b) Power dimension index.
(c) Pulse distance index.

Prejudice: Social identity theory

1. Tajfel and Turner believe that prejudice can result from:
(a) Competition between rival groups.
(b) The mere existence of an outgroup.
(c) Evolutionary forces which make people aggressive.

2. The outcome of social identification is:
(a) Categorising oneself as a member of the ingroup.
(b) Adherence to the social norms of your ingroup.
(c) Behaving in a discriminatory manner towards members of the outgroup.

3. Tajfel and Turner believe that group membership has the effect of:
(a) Increasing self-esteem.
(b) Sharing limited resources.
(c) Forging new friendships.

4. In a replication of the minimal group experiments, Wetherell found:
(a) White New Zealanders were less discriminatory than Tajfel's British sample.
(b) Polynesian New Zealanders were more discriminatory than white new Zealanders.
(c) White New Zealanders were more discriminatory than Polynesian New Zealanders.

Prejudice: Realistic conflict theory

1. The fiercest conflicts result from competition for resources which are:
(a) Finite and abstract.
(b) Infinite and abstract.
(c) Finite and physical.

2. Sherif et al. created hostility by:
(a) Holding a tournament where only one group could win.
(b) Making one group think the other group trashed their cabin.
(c) Both (a) and (b).

3. Prejudice can be reduced using superordinate goals to promote:
(a) Collectivist activities.
(b) Positive interdependence.
(c) Cooperative fusing.

4. Competition can lead to decline in intergroup relations, but it can also:
   (a) Lead to increased ingroup solidarity.
   (b) Make ingroup members more antagonistic towards each other.
   (c) Lead to reduced productivity of ingroup members.

Factors affecting prejudice (and discrimination): Individual differences

1. RWA is linked to the view that the world is:
   (a) A competitive jungle.
   (b) Dangerous and threatening.
   (c) A playground to be explored.
2. People with high RWA scores:
   (a) Have a fear of the unknown.
   (b) Experience feelings of superiority over others.
   (c) Enjoy new experiences.
3. Social dominance is positively correlated with the trait of:
   (a) Agreeableness.
   (b) Tough-mindedness.
   (c) Empathy.
4. Prejudice research may be biased, as US university departments tend to be dominated by:
   (a) Democrats 12:1
   (b) Republicans 12:1
   (c) Democrats 1:12

Factors affecting prejudice (and discrimination): Situation and culture

1. Esses says, when resources are limited, we experience:
   (a) Moral strain.
   (b) Contest fatigue.
   (c) Resource stress.
2. Baldwin used the term *micro-aggression* to describe discriminatory acts which are:
   (a) Subtle and covert.
   (b) Mild but explicit.
   (c) Indirect and ambiguous.
3. Orpen found that prejudice is correlated with:
   (a) Susceptibility to cultural pressure.
   (b) Right wing authoritarianism.
   (c) Conscientiousness.
4. Akrami et al.'s participants were less likely to express sexist attitudes if they:
   (a) Heard a confederate disagree with a statement that denied sexism was a problem.
   (b) Saw positive images of women before taking the survey.
   (c) Read a newspaper story about equality between the sexes.

Classic study: Sherif et al. (1954/1961)

1. In the tournament in stage 2 of the study, which activity was included?
   (a) Tent-pitching.
   (b) Table tennis.
   (c) Diving.
2. In stage 1 group norms were established, for example:
   (a) The Eagles were known for being tough and swearing.
   (b) The Eagles cried more and were anti-swearing.
   (c) The Rattlers were more religious and anti-swearing.
3. At the end of stage 2, the boys' friendship patterns were assessed:
   (a) Eagles chose more outgroup friends than Rattlers did.
   (b) Eagles chose friends from both groups equally.
   (c) Rattlers did not choose any friends from the outgroup.
4. At the end of stage 3, friendship patterns were assessed again and:
   (a) 36.4% of Rattlers' friends were Eagles.
   (b) 36.4% of Eagles' friends were Rattlers.
   (c) 23.2% of Rattlers' friends were Eagles.

Contemporary study: Burger (2009)

1. At what voltage did Burger terminate the study?
   (a) 150 V
   (b) 300 V
   (c) 450 V
2. How many participants were fully obedient in Burger's study?
   (a) 65%
   (b) 70%
   (c) 82%
3. Burger considered obedience in males and females and found:
   (a) A significant difference between men and women.
   (b) Women were marginally more obedient than men.
   (c) Men were significantly less obedient than women.
4. Burger looked at 'desire for personal control' and found:
   (a) No significant difference between obedient and defiant participants.
   (b) Defiant participants scored significantly higher on this trait than obedient participants.
   (c) The difference between defiant and obedient participants was only significant in men.

Contemporary study: Reicher and Haslam (2006)

1. How many participants were there in the study?
   (a) 15
   (b) 30
   (c) 40
2. Reicher and Haslam measured stress levels using:
   (a) Saliva swabs for cortisol levels.
   (b) Galvanic skin response.
   (c) Ranked scale from 1 to 7.
3. Social identification increased amongst the prisoners when:
   (a) Guards started squabbling amongst themselves.
   (b) Groups seen as impermeable.
   (c) Egalitarian system introduced.
4. The fact that the participants knew they were being watched decreases:
   (a) Ethics.
   (b) Reliability.
   (c) Validity.

Contemporary study: Cohrs et al. (2012)

1. The participants were all from:
   (a) East Germany.
   (b) Southern France.
   (c) Northern Italy.
2. Which sampling method did Cohrs et al. use for the initial sample (not the peers)?
   (a) Volunteer.
   (b) Opportunity.
   (c) Stratified.
3. Which personality trait was negatively correlated with RWA?
   (a) Extroversion.
   (b) Openness.
   (c) Agreeableness.
4. Generalised prejudice was measured using questions about:
   (a) People with mental health problems.
   (b) Travellers.
   (c) People with disabilities.

MCQ answers

Obedience: Agency theory 1C, 2B, 3A, 4C
Obedience: Social impact theory 1B, 2B, 3C, 4B
Obedience: Milgram's baseline study 1C, 2B, 3C, 4C
Obedience: Milgram's variation studies 1B, 2B, 3B, 4C
Factors affecting obedience and dissent: Individual differences 1C, 2B, 3B, 4A
Factors affecting obedience and dissent: Situation and culture 1A, 2B, 3C, 4A
Prejudice: Social identity theory 1B, 2B, 3A, 4C
Prejudice: Realistic conflict theory 1C, 2C, 3B, 4A
Factors affecting prejudice (and discrimination): Individual differences 1B, 2A, 3B, 4A
Factors affecting prejudice (and discrimination): Situation and culture 1C, 2A, 3A, 4A
Classic study: Sherif et al. (1954/1961) 1A, 2B, 3A, 4A
Contemporary study: Burger (2009) 1A, 2B, 3B, 4B
Contemporary study: Reicher and Haslam (2006) 1A, 2A, 3B, 4C
Contemporary study: Cohrs et al. (2012) 1A, 2B, 3B, 4C

Cognitive psychology

Chapter 2

Contents

Memory
68	The working memory model
70	The multi-store model of memory
72	Explanation of long-term memory
74	Reconstructive memory

Methods – see pages 182-197 of Chapter 5

Studies
76	Classic study: Baddeley (1966b)
	Contemporary study, select one of:
78	Schmolck *et al.* (2002)
80	Steyvers and Hemmer (2012)
82	Sebastián and Hernández-Gil (2012)

84	**Key questions for cognitive psychology**
86	**Practical investigations for cognitive psychology**

End of chapter
88	Revision summary
90	Practice questions, answers and feedback
92	Multiple-choice questions

Can you trust your memory?

Most people feel their memory is very reliable. They say, 'I am absolutely certain I was wearing that hat last week.' But is memory accurate?

Try this bit of research. Look carefully at the list of words below and try to remember them:

bed, duvet, pillow, blanket, cosy, lamp, PJs, snore, sheet, dark, night, tired, warm, onesie, dream

Now do something completely different for ten minutes, and then write down all the words you can remember (without looking at this page of course!).

When you have written down the words, read the explanation on page 93.

Memory: The working memory model

The specification says...
2.1.1 The working memory model (Baddeley and Hitch 1974).

Key term

Working memory model – A representation of short-term memory (STM). It suggests that STM is a dynamic processor of different types of information using different subunits coordinated by a central decision-making system.

You may prefer to read about the multi-store model (next spread) first as historically it was the precursor to the WMM.

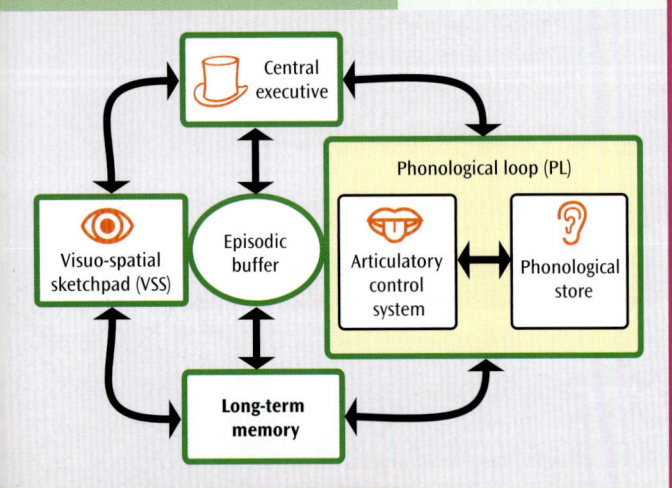

Think Link
Individual differences

Central executive function

Working memory has been linked to many cognitive functions that differ between individuals.

For example, a positive correlation has been found between the capacity of working memory and reading comprehension. People with greater working memory capacity are also better at mental arithmetic, spelling, note-taking and giving directions. They also score higher on intelligence tests (Baddeley 2003).

Recent research has tried to identify the underlying processes that link these functions, with attention focused on the role of the central executive.

The working memory model

Alan Baddeley and Graham Hitch's (1974) working memory model (WMM) is an explanation of how short-term memory (aka working memory) is organised and how it functions. The model is concerned with the 'mental space' that is active when we temporarily store and manipulate information, for example when tackling a maths problem, playing chess or understanding language, etc.

The model consists of four main components, a central control system assisted by three 'slave' subsystems. Each component is *qualitatively* different, especially in terms of *capacity* and *encoding*.

Central executive

The *central executive* (CE) is essentially an attentional process that has a 'supervisory' role. It focuses, divides and switches our limited attention. It monitors incoming data, makes decisions and allocates slave subsystems to tasks. The CE has a very limited processing capacity and does not store information, even very briefly.

Phonological loop

One of the slave subsystems is the *phonological loop* (PL). It deals with auditory information, i.e. sounds, including the sounds of language (so encoding is acoustic). It also preserves the order in which the information arrives. The PL is subdivided into:

- The *phonological store*, which stores auditory information (e.g. the words you hear).
- The *articulatory process*, which allows *maintenance rehearsal* (repeating sounds or words in a 'loop' to keep them in the phonological store while they are needed). The capacity of this 'loop' is believed to be two seconds' worth of what you can say.

Visuo-spatial sketchpad

The second slave subsystem is the *visuo-spatial sketchpad* (VSS). It can temporarily store visual and/or spatial information when required. For example, if someone asks you for directions you can visualise the route in your VSS. This subsystem also has a limited capacity, which according to Baddeley (2003) is about three or four objects. Robert Logie (1995) subdivided the VSS into:

- The *visual cache*, which stores visual data (e.g. images).
- The *inner scribe*, which records the arrangement of objects in the visual field. It is a process that allows you to rehearse visual/spatial information, to maintain it in the visual cache.

Episodic buffer

The third slave subsystem is the *episodic buffer*. This was added to the model in 2000. It is a temporary store that integrates the acoustic, visual and spatial information processed by other subsystems. It also maintains a sense of time sequencing, basically recording events (episodes) that are happening. It has a limited capacity of about four chunks (Baddeley 2012). It combines information from the other subsystems with long-term memory and links to wider cognitive processes such as perception.

VSS and PL in action

Stretch & Challenge

This activity (based on Pearson *et al.* 1999) uses your visuo-spatial sketchpad and phonological loop. Picture in your mind the capital letters J and D, side-by-side, the same size and colour. Now mentally manipulate these letters to form an umbrella. You can change their size and orientation but not the letters themselves – they have to be capital J and capital D. You can colour them in if you wish.

Let's try that again with different elements. Imagine a square, a triangle and the capital letter H. Try and arrange these into an object – your choice this time.

One more go. How about an oval, a triangle, capital letter K and lower case letter b? And a question mark. Have you noticed how quickly it becomes difficult (and eventually impossible) to mentally hold onto that much information?

What does this tell us about working memory? Does the central executive have a role as well?

Evaluation

Support from laboratory experiments

A strength is that dual-task performance studies have supported the predictions of the WMM.

Baddeley et al. (1975) found that when participants performed a visual and verbal task together (dual-task performance), performance on each was no worse than when they carried them out separately. On the other hand, when they performed two visual tasks, performance on both declined considerably (the same is true when two verbal tasks are performed together). This is because both visual tasks compete for the same slave subsystem whereas, when doing a verbal and visual task together, there is no competition.

This supports the WMM because it shows there must be separate slave subsystems (VSS and PL) that process visual and verbal input.

Lack of clarity over the central executive

A weakness is that the central executive is an unsatisfactory component and doesn't really explain anything.

Baddeley (2003) recognised this when he wrote, 'The central executive is the most important but least understood component of working memory.' The central executive needs to be more clearly specified than just being simply 'attention'. Some researchers (including Baddeley) suspect it consists of separate subcomponents (for example, a conscious 'supervisory' attentional process and an unconscious, automatic process).

This means that working memory has not been fully explained.

Application to understanding amnesia

The WMM has been applied to understanding more about the nature of a clinical memory disorder called amnesia.

Tim Shallice and Elizabeth Warrington (1970) conducted a case study of 'patient KF' who experienced amnesia after a brain injury. He had poor short-term memory for auditory (sound) information, but could process visual information relatively normally. For example, his immediate recall of words and digits was much better when he read them (visual) than when they were read out to him (sound). KF's phonological loop had been damaged, but his visuo-spatial sketchpad was intact.

This means that amnesia is not necessarily a 'global' disorder that affects all memory functioning. Its exact nature can be explained by the WMM.

Competing argument Brain-injured patients like KF are unique individuals who are not necessarily typical of the wider population. So case studies are difficult to replicate, and we cannot be sure the findings are valid. This doesn't means that we should dismiss evidence from clinical studies of amnesia, but we should be cautious in generalising their findings.

EXTRA: Issues and debates

There are ethical issues associated with case studies of people with amnesia.

A major issue is confidentiality. Researchers must not report case studies in a way that identifies the participant/patient. They should also keep data provided by the participant safe and not reveal it without the participant's consent. There are also issues concerning whether someone with a severe memory deficit can ever provide true consent if they cannot recall doing so.

Therefore, case studies use initials and avoid names to maintain the patient's confidentiality (hence 'KF'). In extreme cases, a legally-appointed guardian can take decisions of consent on their behalf.

Balanced conclusion

The WMM has proven highly successful at explaining the findings of a wide range of studies and contributed to our understanding of cognitive functions and dysfunctions (e.g. learning difficulties). However, more work is needed to better clarify some key components such as the central executive – looking especially at whether it is made up of different subcomponents.

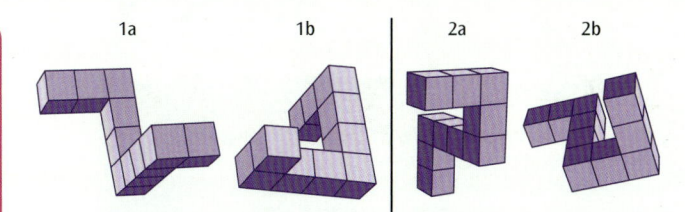

Mental rotation test – are figures 1a and 1b the same except for their orientation? What about 2a and 2b? Doing this test is an example of the visuo-spatial sketchpad (VSS) in action. You have to mentally create and manipulate this image in your VSS to work out the answer.

Apply it Methods: Testing the WMM

A psychologist is studying a patient with amnesia, testing their performance on a visual and an auditory task requiring them to remember as many items as possible. The results are in the table below.

Table showing results from performance tests.

| Visual task | 3 | 6 | 1 | 4 | 2 |
| Auditory task | 9 | 7 | 6 | 9 | 8 |

1. Calculate the mean and the median number of items remembered for each task. (4)
2. Identify the experimental design used in this study. (1)
3. Explain the results of this study in relation to the working memory model. (2)

Apply it Concepts: Football podcast

Ahmed is cycling home from school with his older sister along a quiet lane. He is listening to a podcast of a football match with his headphones round his neck so he can still hear other noises around him. Each time the commentator describes the ball being kicked across the field from left to right or back again, Ahmed swerves across the road.

When they get home, Ahmed is still listening to the podcast as his sister tells him off – she thought his cycling was dangerous and he might have been hurt. While she is talking he loses track of the football commentary.

Context essay: Discuss how the working memory model can explain Ahmed's experiences. You must make reference to the context in your answer. (8)

Study tip

'Précis' is a French word which means a 'summary' – précising is an important skill that you should practise. We have given you quite a bit of AO1 (descriptive) information about the working memory model on this spread. Why not try creating a précis of around 100 words, to help you answer any short answer question about this theory?

Check it

1. According to the working memory model it is possible to do two memory tasks simultaneously.
   Explain how this is possible. (3)
2. Explain **one** difference in encoding and **one** other difference between two parts of the working memory model. (4)
3. **Standard:** Evaluate the working memory model of memory. (8)
4. **AS (Methods/Synoptic):** Evaluate the use of laboratory experiments to study cognitive theories and social theories. (12)

Memory: The multi-store model of memory

Chapter 2 — Cognitive psychology

The specification says...
2.1.2 The multi-store model of memory (Atkinson and Shiffrin 1968), including short- and long-term memory, and ideas about information processing, encoding, storage and retrieval, capacity and duration.

Key terms

Multi-store model – A representation of how memory works in terms of three stores. It also describes how information is transferred from one store to another, how it is remembered and how it is forgotten.

Short-term memory (STM) – The limited-capacity memory store. Encoding is mainly acoustic (sounds), capacity is between 5 and 9 items, duration is between about 18 and 30 seconds.

Long-term memory (LTM) – The permanent memory store. Coding is mainly semantic (meaning), it has unlimited capacity and can store memories for up to a lifetime.

Information processing – The mind works like a computer in that it processes (manages) information in terms of input, storage and retrieval.

Encoding – The format in which information is stored in the various memory stores.

Storage – The process of holding information in memory.

Retrieval – The process of transferring information from LTM to STM, recalling information.

Capacity – The amount of information that can be held in a memory store.

Duration – The length of time information can be held in memory.

Think Link
Developmental psychology

Dyslexia
Children with dyslexia tend to perform poorly on tests of memory span. On average they remember fewer digits or words than children who do not have dyslexia. This suggests that dyslexia may involve a problem with the capacity of STM. Unsurprisingly this has a negative impact on children's ability to learn, specifically in relation to reading which is heavily reliant on STM functioning.

The case of HM
Case studies of people with memory disorders have given us useful evidence about the MSM. One of them has become especially well-known – the case of a man referred to as HM (discussed in detail on page 197). HM's specific form of amnesia (clinical memory loss) was explained by the MSM. His LTM was tested many times but never improved with practice. But he performed well on tests of immediate memory span, a measure of STM. The fact that one of HM's memory stores was damaged but the other was relatively intact strongly suggests that his STM and LTM were independent of each other. This was the organisation of memory proposed by the MSM.

> Studies of amnesia have also been used to show that there is more than one short-term memory store. Can you explain how?

The multi-store model (MSM)

Richard Atkinson and Richard Shiffrin's (1968, 1971) multi-store model describes how information gets into the memory system (encoding) through storage (in working memory/short-term memory), how it remains there (long-term memory) and how it gets out again (retrieval).

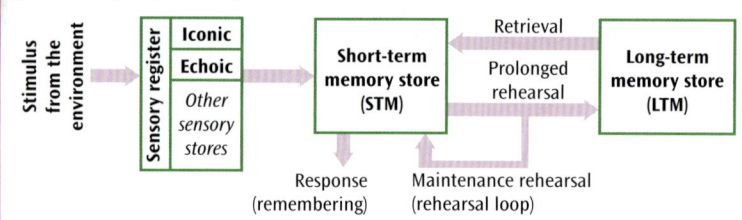

The MSM, showing the flow of information through the system.

The sensory register (SR)
All stimuli from the environment pass into the sensory register. So this part of memory is not one store but several, one for each of our five senses. Encoding in each store depends on the sense. For example, in the *iconic store* it is visual, in the *echoic store* it is acoustic (sound). There are other stores for touch, taste and smell.

Material in sensory registers lasts only very briefly – the duration is less than half a second. The sensory registers have a high capacity, for example over one hundred million cells in one eye, each storing data. However, very little of what goes into the sensory register passes further into the memory system. But it will if you pay attention to it. So the key process at this point in the system is *attention*.

Short-term memory store (STM)
Information we attend to passes into STM. This is a temporary store, basically equivalent to working memory (see previous spread). It has a limited capacity because it can only contain a certain number of 'things' before forgetting occurs. George Miller (1956) noted that in everyday life, things often appear in sevens: seven notes on the musical scale, seven days of the week, seven deadly sins. He suggested that the span (or capacity) of STM is between five and nine items, on average. He called this 'the magic number 7 plus or minus 2'.

Alan Baddeley (1966a) discovered that information is encoded acoustically in STM, i.e. how it sounds. He found that when people recall words from a list immediately, any mistakes are acoustic (e.g. substituting a word with another that sounds the same).

Lloyd and Margaret Peterson (1959) found that the duration of STM is between 18 and 30 seconds. So most information is forgotten quickly, but the duration of STM can be extended by *maintenance rehearsal*. This occurs when we repeat (rehearse) material to ourselves over and over again. We keep the information in STM as long as we rehearse it. If we rehearse it long enough, it passes into long-term memory (LTM). So, the key process here is *rehearsal*.

Long-term memory store (LTM)
LTM is the potentially permanent memory store for material that has been rehearsed for a prolonged time. Its capacity is practically unlimited. Baddeley (1966b, the classic study on page 76) found that LTM encoding is semantic, i.e. what information means. As for duration, Harry Bahrick et al. (1975) found that many of their participants were able to recognise the names and faces of school classmates almost 50 years on.

When you want to recall material stored in LTM, it has to be transferred back into STM. According to the MSM model none are recalled directly from LTM.

Information processing
The information processing approach suggests that information flows through the human cognitive system in a sequence of stages including input, storage and retrieval.

If this sounds like how a computer works, that is not accidental. Cognitive psychologists use computer models in which the mind is compared to a computer (the 'computer analogy') by suggesting that there are similarities in the way information is processed. The MSM model uses the concepts of a central processing unit (the brain), encoding (to turn information into a useable format) and stores (to hold information).

Evaluation

Supporting research evidence

A strength is that the MSM is supported by research studies that show STM and LTM are qualitatively different.

For example, Baddeley (1966a, b) found that we tend to mix up words that *sound* similar when we are using our STM. But we mix up words that have similar *meanings* when we use our LTM. So, encoding in STM is acoustic, but in LTM it is semantic. Further support comes from the studies of capacity and duration by Miller, Bahrick et al. and the Petersons (see facing page).

This shows that STM and LTM are different in terms of encoding, capacity and duration and supports the MSM view that these two memory stores are separate and independent.

Competing argument Not all psychologists accept that STM and LTM are separate stores. It is often more difficult than suggested by the MSM to identify in everyday life where one store ends and the other begins. Some researchers suggest that STM and LTM are 'integrated'. For example, Guillermo Campitelli (2015) argues that STM is the part of LTM that we are currently focusing our attention on.

More than one type of STM

A weakness is that the MSM states there is only one type of STM store. But evidence from people with a clinical condition called amnesia shows that this cannot be true.

Tim Shallice and Elizabeth Warrington (1970) studied a patient known as KF. His short-term memory for digits was very poor when they were read out loud to him. But his recall was much better when he was able to read the digits himself. Further studies showed that there could even be a short-term store for nonverbal sounds (such as noises).

This shows the MSM is not a complete explanation of memory because there must be separate stores for visual and auditory information. There are also several types of LTM, discussed on the next spread.

Application to improving memory

The MSM has been applied to ways of improving memory.

For example, research has shown that the limited capacity of STM can be increased through a process called 'chunking'. There are 15 letters in this list: C A R D O G L I T P E N B U Y. This is over double the average capacity of STM. But perhaps you spotted that the letters are organised: CAR DOG LIT PEN BUY. By putting them into bigger 'chunks' (words in this case), the number of items to be stored is five, well within most people's STM capacity.

This shows how knowledge of the memory system, as represented in the multi-store model, can be applied to practical ways of improving memory.

EXTRA: Issues and debates

The MSM is a good illustration of how the content and methods of psychology change and develop over time.

The MSM was created to account for research findings current at the time. When tested further, some aspects of the model were supported and some were not. But the model soon outlived its usefulness because it could not explain all of the research findings, so was replaced by the working memory model. In addition, evidence initially came from highly quantitative laboratory experiments. Researchers also realised that more everyday examples of memory needed to be studied, and returned to some of the earlier studies by Frederic Bartlett (1932) – see page 74.

This shows how knowledge changes direction over time, combining older and newer research to gradually reach a deeper and more complete understanding of behaviour.

Balanced conclusion

The MSM was a useful model of the memory system in its day. It encapsulated many research findings describing the nature of memory stores and the processes that connect them. However, further research established that the model was oversimplified – for example, there is more than one type of STM and LTM, and more than one type of rehearsal. The MSM eventually gave way to the working memory model, which was able to accommodate these findings more successfully.

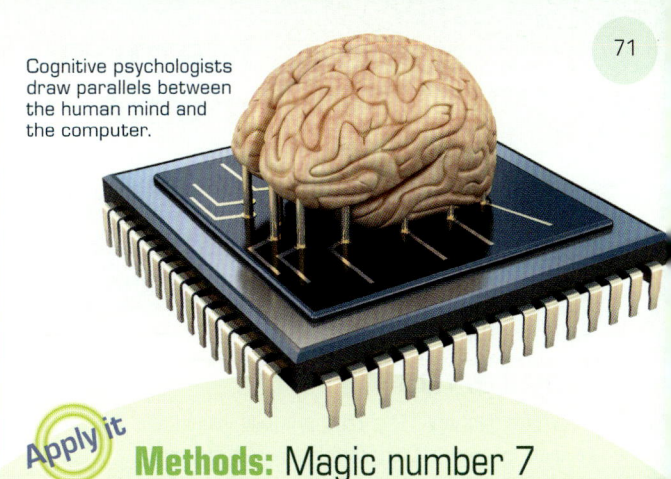

Cognitive psychologists draw parallels between the human mind and the computer.

Apply it — Methods: Magic number 7

Amelia and James are investigating whether Miller's 'magic number seven' applies to memory for pictures as well as words. They are presenting two groups of participants with different stimuli, either a box of 21 objects or a list of the names of the same 21 objects.

Both groups have two minutes to study the stimuli before they are taken away. They are immediately asked to write a list, in any order, of all the stimuli they can remember. Amelia deals with the 'objects' group and James deals with the 'words' group.

1. State a fully operationalised non-directional (two-tailed) hypothesis for Amelia and James' study. (2)
2. This study used an independent groups design. Explain why this was a good choice in this situation. (2)
3. Amelia and James decided to debrief each of the participants individually after the study. Explain **one** ethical advantage of individual debriefing. (2)

Apply it — Concepts: Red car, green car

Hector is walking to school. He sees cars passing him, but even seconds later he cannot remember any of them.

On the way home, Hector pays attention and starts a list of cars in his head: red Vauxhall, green VW, cream mini, etc. Soon he finds that although he can remember the first few cars, he can't remember many more. When he gets home he can still recall the red Vauxhall, the green VW and the cream mini but the only other cars he can remember are the last few before he reached his house.

Context essay: Discuss how the multi-store model of memory can explain Hector's experience. You must make reference to the context in your answer. (8)

Study tip

For the MSM you need to know several things about each memory store. To help you learn this, construct a summary table, listing the three stores and the various features (encoding, retrieval, capacity and duration). Fill in this table twice (either on different copies or in different colours). Do it once to give a description of each aspect and again to consider the evidence.

Check it

1. Compare short-term memory and long-term memory in terms of encoding and duration. (4)
2. Explain the difference in capacity of the two memory stores in the multi-store model. (2)
3. **Standard:** Evaluate the multi-store model of memory. (8)
4. **AS (Synoptic):** To what extent are individual differences important to social and cognitive theories of human behaviour? (12)

Memory: Explanation of long-term memory

The specification says...
2.1.3 Explanation of long-term memory – episodic and semantic (Tulving 1972).

Key terms

Long-term memory (LTM) – See previous spread.

Episodic memory – A long-term memory system for personal events. It includes memory of when the events occurred (time-stamped) and of the people, objects, places and behaviours involved. Memories from this store have to be retrieved consciously and with effort.

Semantic memory – A long-term memory system for our knowledge of the world. This includes facts and our knowledge of what words and concepts mean. These memories usually need to be recalled deliberately.

Think Link
Developmental psychology

Alzheimer's disease

Episodic and semantic memory systems are disrupted in Alzheimer's disease, a form of dementia. Both research and the personal experiences of people living with Alzheimer's suggest that episodic memory is affected first. This may be because the hippocampus – which plays a central role in episodic memory – is damaged early in the disease.

Later on, patients begin to lose the ability to use knowledge stored in semantic memory (e.g. they find it hard to name objects). Again this is probably because the disease now affects the brain areas closely involved in semantic memory (the frontal lobes).

Episodic or semantic? Or procedural?

Episodic and semantic memory

Endel Tulving (1972) was one of the first cognitive psychologists to realise that the multi-store model's view of long-term memory (LTM) was too simplistic and inflexible. He proposed that there are in fact at least two LTM systems, containing quite different types of information. He called them episodic memory and semantic memory.

Episodic memory

Episodic memory refers to our ability to recall events (episodes) from our lives. This has been likened to a diary, a record of daily happenings. Episodic memories are 'autobiographical' because you have personally experienced the events. Some examples are: your most recent visit to the dentist, a gig you went to last week, the psychology class you had yesterday, the breakfast you had this morning, and so on.

Key features of episodic memory

These memories are much more complex than you might think. First, they are *time-stamped* – in other words you remember when they happened, recently or last week or this morning. So as well as storing the events, we also store information about how they relate to each other in time.

Second, your memory of a single episode includes several elements (people and places, objects and behaviours) all of them interwoven to produce a single memory.

Third, episodic memory allows us to 'time travel'. We can think back to past events and relive them, because episodic memories have a subjective quality that no other memories have. When we remember a past event, we may not recall the exact details, but we are immediately aware that it is part of our personal experience (and not a dream, for example). Tulving (1985) called this form of awareness *autonoetic consciousness*.

Semantic memory

This stores our knowledge of the world, including facts, but in the broadest possible sense. Semantic memory has been likened to a combination of an encyclopaedia and a dictionary. So it includes knowledge of such things as: applying to university, the taste of an orange, Donald Trump's hair and the meaning of words.

Key features of semantic memory

This last example is very important, because semantic memory is necessary for us to use language. It stores your organised knowledge of language and contains an impressive number and range of concepts such as 'Donald Trump', 'hair' and 'normal'. Semantic memory allows us to mentally represent things (objects, people, places, etc.) that are not present. According to Tulving, semantic memory is less vulnerable to distortion and forgetting than episodic memory.

Semantic memories are not time-stamped, we don't usually remember when we first learned about Donald Trump, for example. Semantic knowledge is less personal and more about facts we all share. However, as the brief list above demonstrates, semantic memory is about much more than 'facts'. It contains an immense collection of material which, given its nature, is constantly being added to.

Stretch Challenge

Procedural memory

Tulving (1985) identified a third type of long-term memory. This is our memory for actions, or skills, or basically how we do things. We recall these memories without conscious awareness or a great deal of effort. A good example is driving a car. Our ability to do this (eventually, after much practice) depends on *procedural memory*. We change gear without having to recall how. We indicate left or right at a junction without even realising we've done so. These are the sorts of skills we might even find quite hard to explain to someone else. If you try to describe what you are doing as you drive the car, the task may well become more difficult.

So the third kind of memory, procedural memory, allows us to learn (e.g. store associations between stimuli, the basis of classical conditioning) and to respond to the environment.

Some psychologists believe LTM can be divided into declarative and non-declarative. Find out what these terms mean and explain how the three types of LTM on this spread fit into that distinction.

Evaluation

Clinical evidence

A strength is that the distinction between episodic and semantic memories is supported by evidence from the case study of HM.

HM's episodic memory was severely impaired as a result of brain damage (see previous spread). He had difficulty recalling events from his past, but his semantic memory was relatively unaffected (e.g. he still understood the meanings of words). So HM could not recall stroking a dog half an hour earlier and could not remember having owned a dog in the past. But he did not need to have the concept of 'dog' explained to him.

This supports Tulving's view that there are different memory stores in LTM. In HM's case one store was damaged and the other wasn't.

Competing argument A major weakness of clinical studies is that they lack control of variables. These studies involve people who have experienced brain damage, which is usually unexpected. This means the researcher has no knowledge of the patient's memory before the damage. Without this, it is difficult to judge exactly how much worse it is now. This lack of control reduces the validity of clinical studies and limits what they can tell us about types of LTM.

Overlapping types of LTM

Some psychologists do not accept that episodic and semantic memories are entirely different forms of LTM.

Tulving (2002) came to view episodic memory as a 'specialised subcategory' of semantic memory. In his research into amnesia, Tulving showed that it is possible to have a fully functioning semantic memory with a damaged episodic memory. Some people with amnesia *know* that past events have happened to them (semantic), but cannot re-experience them (episodic). However, it is not possible to have a fully functioning episodic memory alongside a damaged semantic memory.

This shows that the relationship between types of LTM is more complex than Tulving originally believed.

Application to improving memory

An understanding of the episodic/semantic distinction has given rise to real-life applications.

Sylvie Belleville *et al.* (2006) worked with older people who had a mild memory impairment. The participants undertook a training programme to improve their episodic memories. Compared with a control group, these participants performed better on a test of episodic memory after the training. The fact that it is possible to improve one type of LTM rather than another argues in favour of there being different types.

This is a benefit of identifying different types of LTM because it can be used to help people with specific memory problems to lead more normal lives in old age.

EXTRA: Issues and debates

The distinction between episodic and semantic memories is related to socially sensitive research.

A good example is research into Alzheimer's disease (see Think link box on facing page). Such research risks creating a negative perception of people with Alzheimer's as deficient, helpless, 'mindless' and a burden on family and society. This perception threatens the dignity of patients, as do some of the procedures used in memory research.

This does not mean that psychologists should avoid conducting research into memory deficits in Alzheimer's. But they should be sensitive to the social issues that such research raises.

Balanced conclusion

There is overwhelming evidence for at least two forms of LTM. The evidence comes from a variety of sources, including clinical studies of people with amnesia and Alzheimer's. However, clinical studies also raise some doubts about the exact nature of LTM. For instance, a more complex view is that semantic and episodic memories may be stored together, with episodic being an 'offshoot' or subsystem of semantic. Conclusions about LTM are somewhat limited because of the methodological weaknesses of clinical studies (e.g. lack of control).

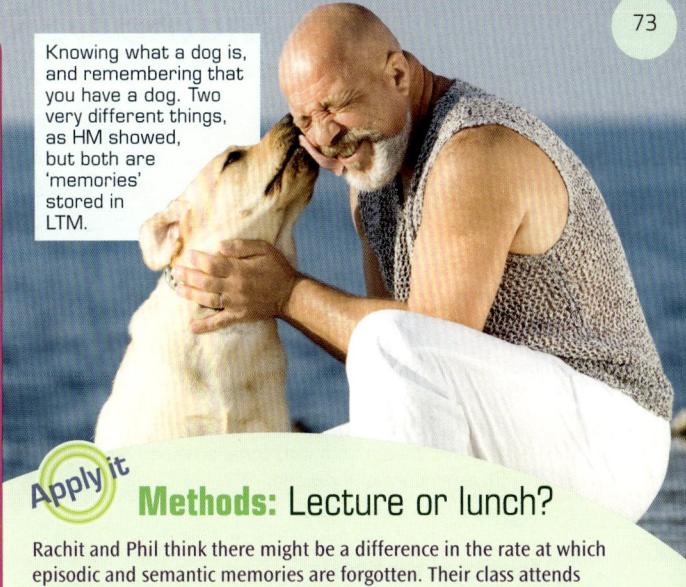

Knowing what a dog is, and remembering that you have a dog. Two very different things, as HM showed, but both are 'memories' stored in LTM.

Apply it — Methods: Lecture or lunch?

Rachit and Phil think there might be a difference in the rate at which episodic and semantic memories are forgotten. Their class attends a lecture in a local city and the next day Rachit and Phil give their classmates a questionnaire. Some of the questions are about facts they learned from the lecture and others are about the experiences the class had in the city at lunchtime.

1. (a) Write **one** closed question that Rachit and Phil could use in their study. (1)
   (b) Write **one** open question that Rachit and Phil could use in their study. (1)
2. Some of the data that Rachit and Phil collect will be quantitative. Define the term 'quantitative data'. (1)
3. State a fully operationalised null hypothesis for Rachit and Phil's study. (2)

Apply it — Concepts: Eloise's memory

Eloise is 99 and is thinking about the past. She wonders what happened to her friends from university. She can remember the things they did together, the fun, food and panicking! She studied psychology, and in 1937 she had been one of the first students to take the course at Cambridge. She can still remember some of the ideas she had to learn, and her great-granddaughter, who is studying psychology now, has recently told her about some new theories, which Eloise finds fascinating.

Context essay: Discuss whether theories of memory can explain Eloise's recollections. (12)

Study tip

Tulving recognised that there were similarities as well as differences between episodic and semantic memory. Draw a table to help you understand the ways that these two memory systems are similar and different. Give each comparison point a 'heading', for example, the 'type of information they store', 'how long the memory lasts', etc.

Check it

1. Define the terms 'episodic memory' and 'semantic memory' as used by Tulving (1972). (2)
2. As we grow older, both our episodic and our semantic memories change. Describe **one** way in which either episodic memory or semantic memory develops. (2)
3. **Standard:** Evaluate Tulving's concepts of episodic and semantic memory. (8)
4. **AL (I&D/Synoptic):** To what extent have cognitive and biological psychology developed over time? (12)

Memory: Reconstructive memory

Chapter 2 Cognitive psychology

The specification says...
2.1.4 Reconstructive memory (Bartlett 1932), including schema theory.

Key terms

Reconstructive memory – Fragments of stored information are reassembled during recall. The gaps are filled in by our expectations and beliefs so that we can produce a 'story' that makes sense.

Schema – A mental framework of beliefs and expectations that influence cognitive processing. We are born with some schemas but they develop in complexity with experience of the world.

Stretch Challenge

The War of the Ghosts
Read this story and then close the book and write down as much as you can remember.

One night two young men from Egulac went down the river to hunt seals, and while they were there it became foggy and calm. Then they heard war-cries, and they thought: 'Maybe this is a war-party.' They escaped to the shore and hid behind a log. Now canoes came up, and they heard the noise of paddles, and saw one canoe coming up to them. There were five men in the canoe, and they said:

'What do you think? We wish to take you along. We are going up the river to make war on the people.'

One of the young men said: 'I have no arrows.'

'Arrows are in the canoe,' they said.

'I will not go along. I might be killed. My relatives do not know where I have gone. But you,' he said, turning to the other, 'may go with them.'

So one of the young men went, but the other returned home.

And the warriors went up on the river to a town on the other side of Kalama. The people came down to the water, and they began to fight, and many were killed. But presently the young man heard one of the warriors say: 'Quick, let us go home: that Indian has been hit.' Now he thought: 'Oh, they are ghosts.' He did not feel sick, but they said he had been shot.

So the canoes went back to Egulac, and the young man went ashore to his house, and made a fire. And he told everybody and said: 'Behold I accompanied the ghosts, and we went to fight. Many of our fellows were killed, and many of those who attacked us were killed. They said I was hit and I did not feel sick.'

He told it all and then became quiet. When the sun rose he fell down. Something black came out of his mouth. His face became contorted. The people jumped up and cried.

He was dead.

Compare your remembered account with the story. What are the differences? What do the kind of differences tell us about memory processes?

Reconstructive memory

Reproduction versus reconstruction

Can you accurately recall events from your past? Many people strongly believe they can. Psychologists once also thought that memory is simply an act of reproduction – we store information about an event and recall it later without altering the record in any way. Sir Frederic Charles Bartlett (1932) challenged this view, by arguing that memories are not reproductions but *reconstructions*, hence reconstructive memory.

He saw memory as an active process in which we store fragments of information. When we need to recall something we build (reconstruct) these fragments into a meaningful whole. The result is that some elements are missing, some are distorted, and memory is not a completely accurate record of what happened.

The 'War of the Ghosts' study

Bartlett demonstrated reconstructive memory in a famous study. He showed his British participants a story, the *War of the Ghosts*, a folk tale from a very different culture (Native American), so it would have been unfamiliar. He showed participants the story on the left and asked them to reproduce it 15 minutes later. Then Bartlett showed the new version to another person and asked them to recall it a short time later, and repeated this chain with further participants – a technique called *serial reproduction*.

He found that the story was transformed over time. For example, it became shorter through omissions (unfamiliar details were left out). Also, phrases were altered to match the participants' own culture (Bartlett called these *rationalisations*, e.g. 'canoe' frequently became 'boat').

These reconstructions were not random – they had the effect of making the story more conventional, coherent and meaningful to the participants. Bartlett explained reconstructive memory in terms of his schema theory.

Schema theory

Bartlett believed that what we remember is governed by our schemas. A schema is a mental structure in memory, a 'package' containing all our stored knowledge of aspects of the world (e.g. people, situations, objects, actions, events, abstract concepts, etc.). For example, imagine everyone in your class was asked to write ten words relating to a bank robbery – these would represent their schema. There would be similarities and differences.

When we come across new knowledge or experiences (e.g. an unfamiliar situation), the relevant schema is activated. We assume that the situation matches the knowledge already contained in the schema. This allows us to process information about the world efficiently, by making some 'guesses' about what the situation is probably like.

For example, if I tell you I went to a gig last night, you will probably make several assumptions about what happened even before I begin to tell you the details – tickets were involved, most likely a band, perhaps crowdsurfing in a mosh pit. But what if I told you there were violins, a conductor, cocktails and lots of sitting down? Perhaps this would change your 'gig' schema.

Schemas and memory

Schemas influence memory in two main ways – what you encode/store and what you retrieve. New knowledge that conflicts with an existing schema could easily fail to be encoded in the first place. It just doesn't fit in with what you expect, so you don't notice it or it doesn't 'register' in memory. Later, when you try to recall a memory, you might recall only those elements that fit in with the relevant schema. Other elements that don't fit are either forgotten altogether or are recalled in a distorted form.

This is what happened in Bartlett's War of the Ghosts study. The 'foreign' nature of the story meant that large parts of it simply didn't match the British participants' view of the world (their schemas). Whenever this happened, memories became distorted, unfamiliar details were left out, and familiar details were elaborated to fill the gaps.

Evaluation

Realistic theory and research

A strength is that the theory of reconstructive memory is based on research that is more realistic than a lot of memory research.

Before (and after) Bartlett's work, psychologists investigated memory using artificial materials to be learned (e.g. nonsense syllables such as RIZ and KUY). These are 'artificial' because we rarely use our memories to deal with such things.

This means the social origins of memory are obscured in such artificial research. But Bartlett's findings and the theory based on them are more relevant to real-life memory processes.

Competing argument However, Bartlett's research did not use rigorously controlled methods and lacked objectivity. For example, instructions were not standardised, so the participants' experiences of the procedure were inconsistent, making it hard to compare reproductions. This means the evidence underlying reconstructive memory lacks reliability and validity (although better-controlled studies conducted since have been supportive).

Some memories are accurate

A weakness is that it is wrong to suggest that all memories are inaccurate or affected by schemas.

Other studies have shown that memory can be very accurate. For example, in situations that are personally important or distinctive, we do remember considerable and accurate detail. There are examples of this in the War of the Ghosts – participants often recalled the phrase 'Something black came out of his mouth' because it was quite unusual.

This shows that people may not always actively reconstruct memories, or when they do these reconstructions can be highly accurate and relatively unaffected by expectations or beliefs.

Application to eyewitness testimony

This theory can be used to explain problems with eyewitness testimony (EWT) – as well as earwitness testimony.

EWT is often used in court trials to give an accurate picture of what actually happened when a crime was committed. For example, an eyewitness might swear on oath that they had seen a particular person at the crime scene whereas later evidence challenged this. Bartlett's research showed that memory can be affected by our schemas, which include expectations of what 'should' happen. Research on EWT (e.g. Loftus and Palmer 1974) has subsequently shown that people do not always recall what they see or hear accurately.

The consequence is that no convictions are now based on EWT alone as it is not trustworthy – an important application of research.

EXTRA: Issues and debates

Schema theory has contributed to the nature–nurture debate.

It focuses on the role of experience in forming schemas which in turn influence memory encoding and retrieval. This puts nurture at the centre of our understanding of how memory works. This is in sharp contrast with theories of memory that emphasise underlying brain functions and dysfunctions (e.g. what clinical studies of amnesia tell us about types of long-term memory).

Thus schema theory provides a welcome balance to nature-linked theories, giving us a more rounded picture of human memory.

Balanced conclusion

Bartlett's schema theory and his research into reconstructive memory drew attention to a problematic feature of human memory – that it is often inaccurate and influenced by our existing beliefs and expectations (and by extension, stereotypes and prejudices). However, it is an overstatement to argue that memory is always reconstructive or inherently unreliable when Bartlett's own research methodology was questionable and other studies demonstrate how accurate memory can be.

Think Link
Individual differences

Differing experiences, differing schemas

Schemas are built from our experiences of the world, and everyone's experiences differ. This is why the contents of schemas are not identical from one person to another – we all have different knowledge, expectations and beliefs derived from experience.

For example, imagine you are unfortunate enough to witness a crime such as an armed robbery. Your recollection of what happened could differ substantially from another eyewitness' account. This is because you have different schemas for what 'should' have happened or what you expected to happen.

Apply it Methods: Eva's strange story

Eva and Josh are investigating *repeated reproductions*, another method that Bartlett used in his investigations. They have two groups of people who have read a bizarre story that Eva made up. It is deliberately hard to understand so the participants will lack a schema to interpret it. In one group, the participants individually recall the story to Josh at weekly intervals over a five-week period. Over the same five weeks, the other group only recall the story to Josh twice.

1. Identify the experimental design used in Eva and Josh's experiment. (1)
2. Eva and Josh disagree about how to produce a recall score. Eva wants to count the number of words that are the same in the original and final versions of the story. Josh wants to read the final version and give an overall rating for how similar he thinks it is to the original.
   (a) Explain whose idea, Eva's or Josh's, would be more objective. (1)
   (b) Identify the level of measurement of Eva's scoring system. (1)

Apply it Concepts: Jade's recall

Jade was at college and thought she saw someone stealing a purse from another student's bag. She tells her friend, Anya, who tells their teacher. When the teacher asks Jade to tell her what happened, the story Jade tells is different from what actually happened and from the story she originally told Anya.

Context essay: Discuss how reconstructive memory theory can explain the changes in the reports. You must make reference to the context in your answer. (8)

Check it

1. Bartlett found people were not entirely accurate when asked to recall. Explain why recall can be inaccurate, using the ideas of reconstructive memory and schema theory. (4)
2. Explain **two** weaknesses of Bartlett's reconstructive memory theory. (4)
3. **Standard:** Evaluate reconstructive memory theory. (8)
4. **AS (Synoptic) and AL (I&D/Synoptic):** Evaluate research into cognitive and social psychology in terms of the ethical issues they raise. (12)

Classic study: Baddeley (1966b)

The specification says...
2.3.1 Classic study: Baddeley (1966b) Working memory model: The influence of acoustic and semantic similarity on long-term memory for word sequences.

Alan Baddeley CBE FRS is one of the world's foremost cognitive psychologists. This is what he had to say: 'This study is part of a series of experiments that eventually led to the concept of working memory. The whole series began with an attempt to measure the quality of telephone lines by requiring people to remember what they heard, assuming that noisy lines would lead to poorer memory. It did not but purely incidentally showed that short-term memory for sequences of words is disrupted when words are similar to each other in sound, but is little affected by similarity of meaning. The experiments [in this study] describe the next step, showing that exactly the opposite is true for long-term memory, which relies more on meaning than sound presenting evidence for two separate systems.'

Graphs showing the results of experiment 1, with the effects of the acoustic lists on the left and the semantic lists on the right.

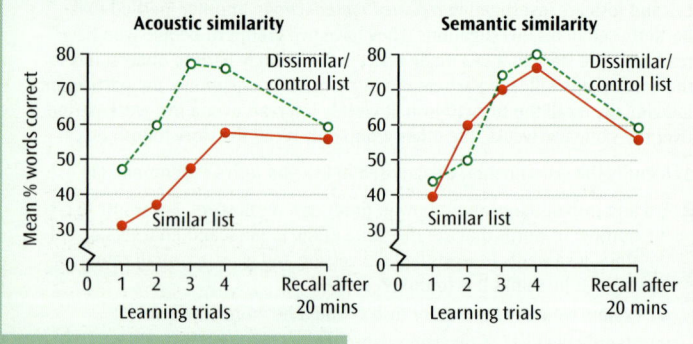

Acoustic and semantic similarity in LTM

Aim
Alan Baddeley (1966a) conducted a study where he showed that recall of *acoustically* similar words from short-term memory (STM) was poor. However, STM was not affected by *semantically* similar words. In the study we are considering here (Baddeley 1966b) he aimed to apply the same procedures to find out if a similar pattern of results existed for long-term memory (LTM).

Procedure
This was a laboratory experiment using an independent groups design with four conditions of the independent variable. All 75 of the participants were young servicemen (i.e. from the Army, etc.). A hearing test was given before the procedure, and three participants were excluded from the study.

The materials were four lists of ten words each:
- List A – Acoustically similar words (they all sounded similar, e.g. man, can, mad, map).
- List B – Acoustically dissimilar words (all sounded different, a control list: e.g. pit, few, cow, pen).
- List C – Semantically similar words (all had similar meanings; e.g. great, huge, large, big).
- List D – Semantically dissimilar words (all different meanings, another control list; e.g. good, safe, thin, deep).

Four separate groups of participants learned one list each. The numbers of participants recalling each list were: 18 for list A, 17 for list B, 20 for list C, 20 for list D.

Each list was presented aloud on tape, one word every three seconds. Participants had 40 seconds to write down as many of the ten words that they could recall, in the order they heard them in. This procedure was carried out four times (these were the learning trials).

Each participant then spent 20 minutes on an unrelated task (recalling sequences of 8 digits). After this time, they again had to recall the ten words in the correct order. This was an unexpected test – the participants were not told about it in advance.

Findings
Each participant's performance was measured by the number of words they recalled in the correct position in the list. Differences in performance on the four lists were compared using the Mann–Whitney U test.

On the learning trials (STM), recall of the acoustically similar list (A) was consistently lower than for the acoustically dissimilar control list (B). But on the recall test after 20 minutes (LTM), there was no significant forgetting of words in the acoustically similar list, although there was in the acoustically dissimilar control list. These findings are shown in the graphs on the left.

There were no significant differences in recall of the two semantic lists (C and D) on the learning trials. This was also true of the recall test – there was a significant amount of forgetting, but of both the semantically similar and dissimilar lists.

Conclusions
The conclusions are not what we would expect given the aims. This is because the findings were, in Baddeley's words, 'puzzling'. Performance on the acoustically similar list (List A) was the only list to show no forgetting in LTM, suggesting that encoding in LTM is acoustic rather than semantic, contradicting several earlier studies.

Because the result was so unexpected, this was not the end of the study. Baddeley reasoned that some aspect of the procedure meant that the semantic nature of encoding in LTM was being 'hidden'. In other words, the procedure used in this experiment was not a true test of LTM, which was being influenced by material stored in STM. This led him to carry out two more experiments to clarify the precise nature of LTM encoding (see Stretch and challenge, left).

Stretch Challenge

The other two experiments
Baddeley's study was actually three experiments. You only need to learn about one, so experiment 1 is described on the right in detail.

In experiment 2, new groups of participants ('housewives') learned two of the original lists (A and C). But this time, the participants carried out the interference task after each learning trial. Now there was an effect on LTM of semantic similarity. This confirmed Baddeley's suspicion that STM was operating in experiment 1.

However, experiment 2 did not include all the appropriate control groups, so Baddeley conducted experiment 3. This time he also presented the words visually rather than auditorily. Having devised a procedure which completely eliminated the role of STM, the effect of semantic similarity on LTM was clear. Baddeley was able to conclude that LTM uses semantic coding extensively.

Baddeley's study evolved because he identified flaws in his procedures. Do you think this is a strength or a weakness of the study? Explain your answer.

Evaluation

High internal validity
A strength of all three of Baddeley's experiments is that they used well-controlled procedures.

For example, lists A and B and lists C and D were matched with each other in terms of how frequently the words appear in English (i.e. Baddeley only used words of equal frequency). This meant that the results could not be explained by participants being able to remember more familiar (i.e. frequent) words.

This degree of control is a strength of the study because it avoids potential confounding variables that would lower internal validity. This makes the relationship of cause-and-effect between IV and DV much clearer.

Competing argument A limitation specific to experiment 1 is that an important confounding variable was *not* controlled. The procedure did not rule out STM as an influence on later recall from LTM because the participants could still rehearse the words between learning trials. This is why Baddeley went on to conduct two further experiments – he realised that experiment 1 could not fully test his hypothesis.

Low external validity
A limitation of Baddeley's experiments is that they were so tightly controlled that they were artificial and unlike real life.

For example, in real life STM and LTM probably do interact in the way that occurred in experiment 1. But Baddeley saw this as a confounding variable that needed to be eliminated. It was only when Baddeley increased control over the procedure (i.e. experiments 2 and 3) that semantic encoding in LTM became obvious.

Therefore, encoding in the study may not resemble encoding in real life. This suggests that the study may exaggerate the role of semantic encoding in LTM.

Application to learning to learn
Understanding that encoding in LTM is mostly semantic can help to improve long-term recall of information.

This is useful for students revising for exams. Rather than just repeating material (rehearsal), students are better advised to think about the information, to reorganise it (e.g. use mind maps/spider diagrams) and try to relate it to things they already know about. These strategies allow you to process the meaning of the material, which matches the form of encoding in LTM.

This is a strength because it shows that Baddeley's study has validity in terms of being applicable to real-life situations.

EXTRA: Issues and debates
Laboratory experiments like Baddeley's illustrate the role of reductionism in psychology.

Reductionism asserts that behaviour such as memory recall can be studied in terms of the simplest cognitive processes divorced from the social context of the real world. This is a limited approach because it views humans as little more than fairly complicated machines and fails to take into account the richness and complexity of the influences on memory.

This is a weakness because reductionism ignores the interactions between cognitive processes and real-world social factors which are more valid explanations of how LTM works.

Balanced conclusion
Baddeley's study used controlled scientific procedures which meant he could conclude that encoding operates differently in STM and LTM. However, the findings have limited generalisability to real life because of the artificial nature of the laboratory-based procedures and tasks. Despite this, the study was an important stepping stone to a deeper understanding of memory because it highlighted the separation of STM and LTM. This allowed Baddeley to focus on STM in his working memory model.

Think Link
Individual differences

Encoding and brain activity

Brenda Kirchhoff (2009) points out that people use different encoding strategies in memory (e.g. semantic, acoustic, visual) that reflect differences in brain activity when information is encoded. This suggests that there may be individual differences in the importance of acoustic encoding in STM and semantic encoding in LTM.

This also highlights the limitations of a reductionist approach which assumes that basic cognitive processes operate in the same ways in all individuals (see Issues and debates, below left).

Apply it
Methods: Odd recall

Jim is testing the effect of semantic similarity on LTM recall. To do this participants learn a list of numbers that are either all odd or all even. Participants are later asked to recall the list but in the interval between learning and recall they listen to another list of numbers that is also either odd or even. In the 'semantic interference' task the two lists are alike, e.g. both are odd numbers. In the control task they are different, e.g. the first list is odd but the second is even.

1. Identify the independent variable in Jim's study. (1)
2. Jim had 20 participants in the semantic interference task and 19 in the control task. Identify the experimental design Jim used. (1)
3. Jim conducted a Mann–Whitney *U* test and found an observed value of 7.
   (a) Explain whether Jim should accept his null hypothesis. (2) (See critical values table on page 193.)
   (b) Jim excluded some participants because they studied maths. Justify Jim's decision. (1)

Apply it
Concepts: Fast French

Zara is testing herself on her French homework. She has to learn to say some words and remember what they mean. Some have similar meanings, such as *gros* (means 'big') and *lourd* (means 'heavy'). Others sound similar in French such as *trois* (three) and *toit* (roof). Sometimes she tests herself straight after practising and sometimes she practises, waits for an hour, then tests herself.

Using the results of Baddeley (1966b) explain when Zara is likely to make different kinds of mistakes. (4)

Study tip
For A level you need to be able to apply the issues and debates to all topics. Consider how you could link this study to issues of gender, ethics, reliability, validity and generalisability.

Check it
1. Baddeley (1966b) excluded participants with poor hearing in some of his experiments.
   Explain why it was important to do this. (2)
2. Explain **two** weaknesses of the classic study by Baddeley (1966b). (4)
3. **Standard:** Assess the findings from the classic study by Baddeley (1966b). (8)
4. **AS (Synoptic):** As part of your AS Psychology specification you were required to learn about the classic studies by Sherif *et al.* (1954/61) and Baddeley (1966b).
   To what extent were the studies by Sherif *et al.* (1954/61) and Baddeley (1966b) valid and objective? (12)

Contemporary study: Schmolck et al. (2002)

The specification says...
2.3.2 One contemporary study: Schmolck et al. (2002) Semantic knowledge in patient HM and other patients with bilateral medial and lateral temporal lobe lesions.

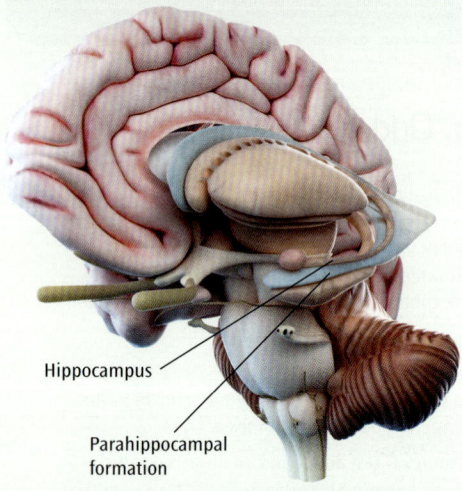

Semantic knowledge (i.e. memory) in patients with brain lesions

Aim
Heike Schmolck, Elizabeth Kensinger, Suzanne Corkin and Larry Squire studied the effects of brain damage on semantic knowledge (i.e. memory). They specifically wanted to find out if there was:
- A link between damage to the *lateral temporal cortex* of the brain and performance on tests of semantic memory in people with amnesia.
- Anything unique about the performance of patient HM (see page 197 for details of his case study).

Procedure
This was a difference study making comparisons between pre-existing groups of participants (thus it is not a 'true' experiment, it's called a *quasi-experiment*). It compared test performances between brain-injured amnesic patients and healthy control participants. Thus the (non-manipulated) independent variable was type of brain damage. There were various dependent variables, all testing semantic memory.

The researchers studied six amnesic patients (five male, one female).
- Three patients had large lesions to the *medial temporal lobe* (MTL+ patients), and some damage to the *anterolateral temporal cortex*.
- Two patients had damage limited to the *hippocampus* (HF patients).
- The patient HM had hippocampal and some MTL damage.

The damage in all patients was bilateral (both *hemispheres*).
There were eight control participants, healthy male volunteers matched with some of the patients on age and education.

Each participant completed nine main tests of semantic memory, on three to five occasions (see box on the right). Most tests were scored by percentage of correct responses. Some participants also completed four additional tests of semantic memory.

Findings
Pointing/naming tests: HF patients and control participants made almost no errors, but MTL+ patients showed significant impairments. HM performed close to the controls on three tests; he was impaired on item 4.

Yes/no test: HF patients performed at the same level as controls. MTL+ patients showed significant impairments. HM performed no worse than the poorest control participant.

Categorising tests: The controls produced more examples (mean 128.8) than HF patients (112) and MTL+ patients (75.7). HM performed poorly. All participants performed well on the category sorting test.

Definitions tests: MTL+ patients gave definitions of lower quality than controls (e.g. less detail). They also gave fewer correct statements and more incorrect statements than controls and HF patients. HM performed similarly to the MTL+ group (i.e. significantly impaired).

Overall: HF patients performed better than the other groups. For HM and the MTL+ patients, there was a strong positive correlation between overall performance and the extent of damage to the *lateral temporal cortex*.

Conclusions
This study confirms previous studies of semantic dementia showing a link between impaired semantic memory and damage to the *anterolateral temporal cortex*.

This study also indicates that the structures of the *parahippocampal cortex* are not involved in semantic memory impairments. However, there is a lack of clarity on this finding. This is because MTL+ patients all had damage in this area linked to the severity of their semantic memory impairments. Yet, although HM showed similar impairments, his *parahippocampal cortex* was mostly undamaged.

HM's performance on most tests was in line with control participants but significantly impaired when he named items from their descriptions (item 4), produced examples from categories and provided definitions. The researchers concluded that this pattern of results indicated similar damage to that in the MTL+ group (i.e. *medial temporal lobe* damage).

Semantic memory tests

There were line drawings of 24 living items and 24 non-living items including: foreign land animals, water creatures, birds, electrical household items, non-electrical household items, vehicles.

The tests involved the following tasks:
1. Point at the picture from its name.
2. Point at the picture from its description.
3. Name the item in the picture.
4. Name the item from its description.
5. Semantic features: answer eight yes/no questions about 24 items.
6. Category fluency: name examples from each category.
7. Category sort: sort pictures into categories.
8. Define an item from its name.
9. Define an item from its picture.

Hippocampus

Parahippocampal formation

The major structures of the medial temporal lobe. These were damaged to varying degrees in the participants in this study.

Think Link
Individual differences

Brain damage and cognitive impairment
The patients in this study differed in the type and extent of their brain injuries. These individual differences were reflected in the degree of amnesia and thus performance on tests of semantic memory. The findings show that even subtle differences in brain injury can have consequences for behaviour, in this case impairments to semantic memory.

Stretch Challenge

HM's uniqueness
HM differed from the other patients in several ways. For instance, the researchers noted that he had a monotone voice and made many grammatical errors. The MTL+ patients did not show these traits even though they had more extensive medial and lateral lesions. This suggests that HM's language-related deficits were not related to his temporal lobe damage.

Explain how the researchers came to this conclusion.

Evaluation

Convergence of evidence

A strength is that the findings of this study support – and are supported by – research into several other aspects of amnesia and brain injury.

Schmolck et al. identify four additional sources of evidence. Each piece of evidence uses different methodologies, the strengths of each one compensating for the limitations of the others. The findings from these sources converge to the same conclusion – that the *anterolateral/lateral temporal cortex* has a central role in semantic memory.

This is a strength because it increases the validity of the conclusions the researchers drew from their results.

Competing argument However, this is partly undermined by a major limitation of the research. This study compares brain-injured participants and controls and is based on case studies of individual patients. By definition these brain injuries are relatively rare. This is reflected in the small sample sizes in the study – just three MTL+ and two HF patients. Also, we don't know about the cognitive functioning of patients before they experienced an unexpected brain injury, making valid comparisons impossible. This makes it difficult to generalise conclusions to the wider population.

Problems with matching

A weakness is not all of the participants were matched.

The researchers matched MTL+ patients and control participants on age and education, but the HF patients were not matched. As they were younger and more educated than the controls, this could explain their better performance.

This means the performance of the HF patients may have been exaggerated. As the HF patients had damage to the hippocampal brain areas, this failure to match could minimise the role of this brain structure in semantic memory.

Application to amnesic patients

Studying amnesic patients with brain injuries has valuable real-life applications.

For example, such research provides a detailed 'map' for neurosurgeons to use when removing a brain tumour so they can avoid areas involved in crucial cognitive functions.

Therefore, this research has value beyond the theoretical understanding of semantic memory that it provides.

EXTRA: Issues and debates

This research is reductionist.

It locates semantic memory in one area of the brain, but overlooks the possibility that other areas (and the connections between them) are also involved. For example, Alex Martin and Linda Chao (2001) suggest that semantic memory may be organised by several areas and structures widely distributed throughout the brain (a holistic interpretation).

The fact there are extensive individual differences in semantic memory in patients with broadly similar brain injuries reinforces this argument (see individual differences on facing page).

Balanced conclusion

This study has made a key contribution to a growing body of research stressing the importance of the medial temporal lobes and lateral temporal lobe cortex in processing semantic memory. However, it is difficult for differences studies to establish that damage to specific brain areas is the cause of an impairment, for example because the cognitive functioning of patients before they suffered an unexpected brain injury is by definition unknown, making valid comparisons impossible.

Heike Schmolck was born in Germany but now lives and works in the United States. She is a medical doctor working in Des Moines, Iowa and specialises in neurology, diagnosing and treating disorders of the nervous system (especially amnesia and Alzheimer's disease).

She has published many academic papers, and worked on this study with the legendary Professor Suzanne Corkin, who spent decades studying the famous Patient HM (Henry Molaison), well known to psychology students the world over.

Apply it Methods: Dr Singh's semantics

Dr Singh wants to investigate semantic memory loss in patients with Alzheimer's disease. He chooses six patients and six control participants and uses task 5 on the facing page (Semantic features: answer eight yes/no questions about 24 items).

Table showing results of task 5 for the Alzheimer's and control participants as a score out of 192.

Alzheimer's patients	186	161	153	170	176	182
Control participants	190	190	192	188	192	192

1. Suggest **two** variables that Dr Singh should use to match his Alzheimer's and control participants. (2)
2. Calculate the percentage score of the first control participant. Give your answer to **one** decimal place. (1)
3. Calculate the mean for the control participants. Show your working and give your answer to **two** significant figures. (1)
4. Explain the conclusion that Dr Singh is most likely to draw from these results. (2)

Apply it Concepts: Dr McSoley's surgery

Dr McSoley is deciding how best to treat a patient with epilepsy. She wants to avoid damaging his semantic memory.

Using your knowledge of Schmolck et al. (2002), write a letter to Dr McSoley giving her advice about how to avoid any damage. (3)

Study tip

If you discuss the strengths/weaknesses of the methodology of a study (such as the sample or the range of measures used) don't be generic. You must ensure that your point is specific to the study. One way to do this is to illustrate your point with an example from this study.

Check it

1. (a) Describe the sample used in your chosen contemporary study from the cognitive approach. [1]
   (b) Explain why this sample was chosen. [1]
2. Explain how the results were analysed in your chosen contemporary study from the cognitive approach. [3]
3. **Standard:** Assess your chosen contemporary study from the cognitive approach. [8]
4. **AS (Synoptic):** Evaluate the procedures of your chosen contemporary studies from social psychology and cognitive psychology with reference to objectivity and generalisability. [12]

Contemporary study: Steyvers and Hemmer (2012)

The specification says...

2.3.3 One contemporary study: Steyvers and Hemmer (2012) Reconstruction from memory in naturalistic environments.

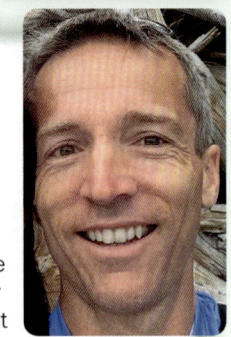

Mark Steyvers gained his undergraduate degree in Psychology from the University of Amsterdam before moving to the United States where he is now Professor of Psychology in the Department of Cognitive Science, University of California, Irvine. He supervised Pernille Hemmer's PhD, and the research paper covered on this spread came out of that collaboration. Professor Steyver's most recent research interests are in the field of 'cognitive science', especially where human judgement/memory and machine learning meet.

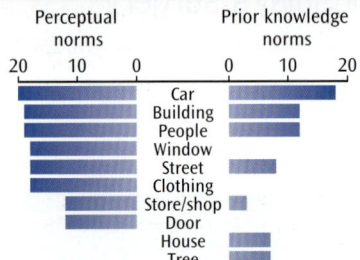

Images (such as the urban scene on the left) were presented randomly on one computer screen and responses were recorded on another screen.

The bars below left show the frequency distribution of objects seen by the 'perception' group. The numbers represent the number of participants who saw the object (e.g. 20 out of 25 saw a car). The bars on the right show the frequency distribution for the 'prior knowledge' group, of objects they expected to see in an 'urban scene' (e.g. 18 out of 22 participants expected to see a car).

Perceptual norms | Prior knowledge norms
20 10 0 | 0 10 20
Car
Building
People
Window
Street
Clothing
Store/shop
Door
House
Tree

Think Link
Individual differences

Eyewitness accuracy

People differ in the extent of their 'prior knowledge' of a situation, and this is a reflection of their experience. To take one example from this study, some people have more experience of 'urban settings' than others, which leads to individual differences in what they expect to see in such a scene.

This means that in an ecologically valid setting, a recall strategy of guessing based on prior knowledge will be more successful (i.e. accurate) for people with greater knowledge (and therefore experience) of that setting. This could explain why eyewitnesses differ in the accuracy of their recall of an event such as a robbery.

Reconstruction from memory in naturalistic environments

Aim

Mark Steyvers and Pernille Hemmer aimed to measure the contributions of episodic and semantic memories to recall of objects in naturalistic scenes. They did this by experimentally assessing prior knowledge (held in semantic memory) and testing recall of information from realistic, ecologically valid materials.

Procedure

The study was a laboratory experiment using an independent groups design. In total 96 students took part in this study: the 'prior knowledge' group ($n = 22$), the 'perception group' ($n = 25$) and the 'memory experiment' group ($n = 49$).

Phase 1 assessed prior knowledge (held in semantic memory). The first group of students ('prior knowledge' group) were asked to list all the objects they would expect to find in five 'scenes': kitchen, office, dining room, hotel room, urban scene. The objects themselves were either 'expected' or 'unexpected'.

The researchers then selected five images for each of the five scenes. The 'perception group' were shown each image and asked to name all the objects in the image (i.e. what they *actually could see*). The process is explained on the left.

Phase 2 was a memory experiment using two of the images from each scene type (so 10 in total). The 'memory experiment' group of participants saw each image for either a short (2 seconds) or long (10 seconds) duration. The participants carried out a short distractor task after each scene and then listed all the objects they could recall seeing in any order (free recall).

Findings

All the findings are from the final 'memory experiment' group.

Analysis of errors The error rate for high probability (expected) objects was 9% and was 18% for low probability (unexpected) objects. When stimuli are representative of the environment, recall for high probability items is more accurate.

Steyvers and Hemmer also looked at 'false memory' errors (i.e. recalling objects that were not present). The rate in this study was 19%, compared with 30% in earlier studies. The lower figure again reflects the greater accuracy of recall when scenes are representative of the environment.

The mean number of responses provided by the participants was 7.75 items in the 2-second condition and 10.05 items in the 10-second condition.

Contribution of prior knowledge The researchers looked at the number of correct responses as a function of 'output position' (the order in which items were recalled). They found that the first item guessed in the prior knowledge phase led to 85% accuracy in the memory experiment (phase 2), decreasing to 55% after 16 items. This represents the contribution of semantic memory. Actual correct recall in the memory experiment was over 80%. The 'gap' in accuracy between prior knowledge and actual recall represents the contribution of episodic memory.

Conclusions

Prior knowledge (semantic memory) makes a greater contribution to recall (and episodic memory a surprisingly smaller one) than earlier research suggests. People's general knowledge about what they expect to see in a naturalistic situation can make their episodic recall of objects significantly more accurate. These guesses are 'adaptive' because they allow us to save limited cognitive resources – we can make 'educated guesses' about items that are likely to be present and focus our attention on remembering/recalling items that are novel or unusual. This is why people are capable of recalling both expected and unexpected items from a scene.

Steyvers and Hemmer also concluded that many researchers do not consider ecological validity in their research design because greater realism may reduce experimental control. On the other hand, too much control risks making the study of memory sterile and leading to wrong conclusions about how memory works in natural settings.

Evaluation

High external validity

A strength of this study was that it investigated memory in an ecologically valid way.

The materials the researchers used were of naturalistic settings rather than artificial stimuli. They studied memory as an active reconstructive process rather than as a passive reproductive one. They studied recall as a combination of semantic and episodic memories, recognising that it makes no sense to isolate them as they both contribute to accuracy of recall in real life.

This means that the study had a high degree of realism.

Excessive experimental control

A weakness, which Steyvers and Hemmer themselves acknowledged, was the procedure could be considered too controlled, especially given their aim of enhancing ecological validity.

For instance, the procedure was carried out in laboratory conditions and was not a real-life situation, and they used photographs of scenes instead of real settings. They also presented some images for just two seconds, which is an experimental manipulation very unlike real life.

Therefore, the study was not as ecologically valid as the researchers wished.

Competing argument However, the procedure was undoubtedly more ecologically valid than the majority of studies in memory research. The researchers argue that ecological validity exists on a spectrum 'from nonsense syllables to natural observation'. The challenge for memory research is to strike a balance between control and realism, and this study represents a significant step in that direction.

Application to eyewitness testimony

The findings of this study can be applied to improving the accuracy of eyewitness testimony.

The use of prior knowledge should not be discounted but encouraged when eyewitnesses (e.g. to a crime) recall what they have seen. For example, strategies could be developed to help eyewitnesses to make 'educated guesses' using prior knowledge of familiar situations.

This could lead the criminal justice system to treat eyewitness evidence more positively than it has in recent decades.

EXTRA: Issues and debates

This study is a good illustration of cultural issues in psychological research.

Prior expectations are heavily influenced by culture because they are based on our knowledge and experiences of our environment. The study was rooted in one culture – the participants were American university students. Expectations of what might be found in an 'urban scene' or a 'kitchen' will vary considerably across cultures (e.g. between American and Japanese students). Culture in this sense does not just refer to countries – expectations probably differ from one subcultural group to another within the same country.

This means that the findings of the study – which the researchers believe are ecologically valid – are generalisable only to a limited extent.

Balanced conclusion

Steyvers and Hemmer tried to maintain a tricky balance. They wanted to make their research more ecologically valid than what had come before. But they also did not want to sacrifice experimental control completely to achieve this aim. So they conducted a laboratory experiment using ecologically valid stimulus materials. This could be considered a somewhat limited view of ecological validity. On the other hand, they produced counter-intuitive findings about the accuracy of recall when materials are radically different from those used in previous research.

Stretch Challenge

Trivial, pointless research

Many research studies into memory have something in common that stands out like a 'sore thumb' – the materials they use are often extremely contrived and artificial. This goes back to a tradition in memory research begun by Herman Ebbinghaus in the 1880s. The outcome of this approach was, as Steyvers and Hemmer put it, psychologists knew a lot about how memory works in the 'constrained' conditions of the lab. But is that enough?

Ulric Neisser (1978) was one of the first to point out that the failure to consider real life had led cognitive psychology into a crisis of irrelevance – it was ignoring all the important questions about memory, the ones that really matter to people in their everyday lives. He argued it was time for memory research to leave the lab and get into the real world.

> What do you think are some of the important questions about memory?

Apply it Methods: Tina's test

Tina is planning an ecologically valid test of memory for her class. She recorded a long list of items that could be found in a classroom and is testing her class by playing them a recording of the list while they are blindfolded. The students then recall as many items as they can.

1. Explain **one** reason why this test may have high ecological validity. (2)
2. (a) Explain **one** reason why this test may not have high ecological validity. (1)
   (b) Identify **one** improvement to Tina's study to make it more ecologically valid. (1)
3. Describe **one** control group that Tina could include in her study. Justify your decision. (2)

Apply it Concepts: Aid for memories

Inma teaches English to Spanish students in London. She is developing a new teaching style based on the findings of Steyvers and Hemmer (2012). She needs to know what will help her students increase their language knowledge – give them building blocks for their memories, or make their learning personal, so that they can recall the contexts in which they learned new words.

1. (a) Design an ecologically valid measure that Inma could use to assess her students. (2)
   (b) Use the findings of the contemporary study by Steyvers and Hemmer (2012) to explain which strategy would best aid her students' memories. (4)

Study tip

You can use the ideas from this study to help you to decide on the ecological validity, or not, of the other studies you are learning about. Be sure you can define ecological validity too.

Check it

1. State **two** fully operationalised variables from your chosen contemporary study from the cognitive approach. (2)
2. Suggest **one** way in which your chosen contemporary study from the cognitive approach can explain individual differences in memory. (3)
3. **Standard:** Assess your chosen contemporary study from the cognitive approach. (8)
4. **AS (Synoptic):** Evaluate the procedure of your chosen contemporary study from social psychology and cognitive psychology with reference to objectivity and generalisability. (12)

Contemporary study: Sebastián and Hernández-Gil (2012)

The specification says...

2.3.4 One contemporary study: Sebastián and Hernández-Gil (2012) Developmental pattern of digit span in Spanish population.

María Victoria Sebastián is Professor of Psychology at the Complutense University of Madrid, but she received her PhD from the University of Leicester after studying in the UK for many years. Her research interests are memory in elderly people, including forms of dementia such as Alzheimer's disease and frontotemporal dementia.

Think Link
Developmental psychology

Phonological loop capacity

Sebastián and Hernández-Gil showed that the capacity of the phonological loop component of working memory increases with age – it is a developmental process operating gradually throughout childhood up to adolescence (and perhaps into young adulthood).

This developmental course changes in old age when loop capacity reduces to resemble that of older children. This is a consequence of ageing rather than of, for example, dementia.

Word length effect

Alan Baddeley et al. (1975) showed that the capacity of the phonological loop in working memory depends on word length. We are generally able to recall more short words than long ones from lists of words. This is because it takes longer to rehearse the longer words.

The crucial factor influencing this process is the time it takes to pronounce the word (the articulation rate). This means the capacity of the phonological loop is limited not by the amount of storage space but by time. In Baddeley et al.'s study, participants were able to recall as many words as they could pronounce in about 2 seconds. You can test this for yourself very easily. Try saying out loud as many digits as you can in 2 seconds – this should roughly be your digit span.

Studying digit span in speakers of various languages has been a popular way to test the phonological loop. An impressive quantity of research confirms a close relationship between recall and reading speed/pronunciation time in many languages. There is even evidence of a 'sign length effect' – deaf users of American Sign Language have poorer recall for signs that take longer to produce (Wilson and Emmorey 1998).

How would you test the mean digit span of users of British Sign Language?

Developmental pattern of digit span

Aims

María Victoria Sebastián and Laura Hernández-Gil investigated the development of the *phonological loop* component of working memory (Baddeley and Hitch 1974, see page 68). They aimed to do this by using verbal digit span as their measure of loop capacity. They wanted to confirm the finding of studies with Anglo-Saxon (e.g. English) participants that digit span increases with age then levels off at 15 years.

They also aimed to compare Spanish schoolchildren with Anglo-Saxon elderly adults and people with dementia tested in an earlier study (Sebastián and Hernández-Gil 2010).

Procedure

This was an experiment conducted in field settings (schools). The independent variable was year of schooling (and year group) and the dependent variable was mean verbal digit span. The researchers also made comparisons between schoolchildren, elderly adults and people with dementia.

The participants were 575 children from pre-, primary and secondary schools (public and private) in Madrid. All were born in Spain. They were selected from all 13 years of the Spanish education system (aged 5–17 years). No child had repeated a year and none presented with hearing disorders, reading or writing difficulties or any other cognitive impairment. The children were tested individually during break times.

The materials used consisted of sequences of random digits that gradually increased by one in length each time. They were read aloud to each participant. The task began with three sequences of three digits and then three sequences of four digits each and so on. The participants listened to each sequence and then were asked to repeat them in order. Each child completed a practice sequence at the start. Digit span was defined as the longest sequence the child could recall, two times out of the three presented, in order and without error.

Findings

The results showed a clear increase in digit span with age. The youngest age group (5 years) had a significantly lower average digit span (mean = 3.76) than the other age groups. Digit span increased significantly and smoothly up to 11 years (mean = 5.28). The rate of increase then slowed and stabilised up to 17 years (mean = 5.91).

The researchers compared these findings to data from the earlier study with Anglo-Saxon elderly participants. Digit span in a group of healthy elderly people was significantly higher than for 5- and 6-year-old children (but no different from that of older children). The pattern of findings for a group of people with dementia (Alzheimer's disease) was similar to the healthy elderly people.

In contrast, in the previously-studied group of nine patients with *frontal variant frontotemporal dementia* (fvFTD), mean digit span was not significantly different from that of the 5- and 6-year-old children.

Conclusions

Both the current study and previous research with Anglo-Saxon elderly participants show that digit span increases with age up to adolescence. However, in Spanish children the increase continues until at least 17 years, whereas in English children it levels out at 15 years (e.g. Gathercole and Alloway 2008). Also, the average digit span was lower for Spanish children compared with English children.

The researchers explain these differences in terms of the word length effect (see Stretch and challenge, left). Because it takes more time to rehearse longer words, more information is likely to be lost. The word length effect applies in this case because Spanish words for digits are longer than their English equivalents. Most Spanish digit words are two syllables (e.g. cuatro, cinco, ocho), whereas most English ones are one syllable (e.g. four, five, eight).

Furthermore, the word length effect occurs because we rehearse words subvocally, but we don't begin to do this until about 7 years of age. This means there should be no difference in digit span between Spanish and English children younger than 7 years. This and other studies (e.g. Engle and Marshall 1983) confirm this.

The comparison of dementia groups, healthy elderly people and schoolchildren suggests that the capacity of the phonological loop component in working memory is affected more by age than by dementia.

Evaluation

Control of variables

A strength is that the researchers used several standardised procedures.

For example, the digits were read aloud at a constant rate of one per second for every participant. These procedures ensured that the experience of the study did not vary greatly from one participant to another. This means the outcomes could not be attributed to differences in how the procedure was conducted.

The use of standardised procedures helped to control potentially confounding variables and therefore contributed to a reasonable degree of internal validity.

Competing argument However, the procedure lacked control in some areas. For instance, the researchers report that the children 'did not present…impairments…' This means the children were not directly tested, and the researchers relied upon the children or their parents to divulge any hearing, reading or other cognitive impairments. Given that any such impairments could influence performance on the digit span task, this may have seriously undermined the validity of the study.

Small sample size

A weakness of this study was that one of the samples used in the comparison study was small.

There were only nine participants with fvFTD. Small sample sizes have an impact on the findings of the study because they reduce the power of statistical tests. This makes a Type I error more likely, in which a statistically significant result is found when none really exists. So the findings relating to this dementia group may only have arisen because the sample was so small – they might not be real effects.

Therefore, the study may not have enough statistical power to reject the null hypothesis, making the conclusions regarding the phonological loop in old age questionable.

Application to understanding cognitive abilities

Although recalling sequences of digits may not be how we use working memory in real life, digit span has been applied to understanding specific cognitive abilities.

For instance, people with a longer digit span are also better readers and have higher general intelligence (Gignac and Weiss 2015). Conversely, short digit span is associated with specific learning disorders such as dyslexia (Giofrè et al. 2016).

Therefore, digit span can be used to explain people's crucial real-life cognitive skills.

EXTRA: Issues and debates

A key issue in psychology is cultural influences.

This study revealed a cultural difference in children's digit span (shorter for Spanish than for English children). Other research supports the view that digit span is linked to culture. For instance, MeowLan Chan and John Elliott (2011) found that Chinese-speaking children had longer digit spans than Malay-speaking children, because words for digits are shorter in Chinese than in Malay. However, these findings do not suggest that working memory is culturally determined. The apparent cultural differences arise from structural differences between languages (and consequently how they are processed by the brain).

Therefore, this study supports cultural similarities rather than differences.

Balanced conclusion

Sebastián and Hernández-Gil's study demonstrates developmental changes in the capacity of the phonological loop, increasing up to adolescence and decreasing in old age. However, the limited number of fvFTD participants means the study may not be powerful enough to support its conclusions about the effect of age (rather than dementia) on loop capacity. Therefore, the studies (this and the researchers' previous one) should be replicated to establish the validity of the findings.

There are consistent differences in digit span between children of different cultures. But are these due to culture or the structure of languages?

Apply it — Methods: Memory aids

Nadia is investigating a computer game which claims to improve working memory by increasing digit span. She tests seven participants' verbal digit span, asks them to play the game for at least half an hour every day for a week and retests them.

1. (a) Name the experimental design that Nadia is using. Explain your answer. (2)
   (b) Which inferential test should Nadia use? (1)
   (c) Nadia only has seven participants. Is she more at risk of making a Type I or a Type II error? Justify your answer. (2)

2. Nadia only tells her participants to 'Play the game for at least half an hour every day for a week.'
   Suggest how Nadia could improve her instructions to the participants so there is better reliability in terms of the game-playing aspect of the procedure. (2)

Apply it — Concepts: Patients' memories

Gavin works with people with cognitive impairments. He is planning to use verbal digit span as an indicator of cognitive decline in his early-onset Alzheimer's patients. He tests each patient on the first occasion that he meets them, and at regular intervals thereafter.

1. Write a simple explanation for a patient to read that would tell them:
   (a) What will happen in the test. (2)
   (b) What the test measures. (2)

2. Explain why it is important in terms of ethics that the patients understand this. (2)

Study tip

To give full details of the procedure of a study, make sure you include details of the sampling process, such as where the participants were from and their ages.

Check it

1. Describe what was measured in your chosen contemporary study from cognitive psychology. (2)
2. (a) Explain **one** feature of the procedure that helped to ensure that this measure was reliable. (2)
   (b) Suggest **one** potential problem with data collection in this study. (2)
3. **Standard:** Assess your chosen contemporary study from the cognitive approach. (8)
4. **AS (Synoptic):** Evaluate the procedure of your chosen contemporary study from social psychology and cognitive psychology with reference to objectivity and generalisability. (12)

Key questions for cognitive psychology

The specification says...

2.4.1 One key question of relevance to today's society, discussed as a contemporary issue for society rather than an academic argument.

2.4.2 Concepts, theories and/or research (as appropriate to the chosen key question) drawn from cognitive psychology as used in this specification.

Suitable examples

- How can psychologists' understanding of memory help patients with dementia?
- How can knowledge of working memory be used to inform the treatment of dyslexia?

Note that these are examples and therefore no exam question will specifically ask you about one of these.

The key to key questions

Key questions may be worth anything between 1 and 12 marks for AS level and up to 20 marks for A level. On this spread we focus on 8-mark questions – but you can add more paragraphs to turn this into a 12- or 16- or 20-mark answer.

A 'key question' essay needs to combine a *description* of the key question with application of concepts, theories and research evidence from the cognitive topic. We think the secret lies in using **black**/blue/green paragraphs.

When answering an 8-mark exam question, first state your key question and then write three paragraphs structured as follows:

- **Black:** Describe one aspect of your key question and explain why it is important in contemporary society.
- Blue: Link to relevant psychological concepts and theories.
- Green: Support your blue ideas with relevant research evidence or introduce competing arguments (from other research evidence or comparisons with other topics in psychology). Be sure to LINK BACK to the key question.

End with a balanced conclusion.

Each paragraph should be 100–140 words.

There is more advice on key questions on pages 9 and 17.

The lack of 1:1 correspondence between letters and their sounds in English makes reading difficult for children with dyslexia as it makes the job of the phonological loop harder.

Example 1

Discuss the key question for society you have studied using concepts, theories and/or research from cognitive psychology. (8)

State your key question: How can knowledge of working memory be used to inform the treatment of dyslexia?

Dyslexia affects 10% of the population, making writing and reading hard. Unrelated to intelligence, it can nevertheless make coping at school or work difficult. Individuals with dyslexia would benefit from improved treatment as would society. One problem is linking letters to sounds (phonics). In the working memory model the phonological loop (PL) makes this link. A shorter PL span than normal (two seconds of speech) would explain why children with dyslexia can muddle up similar letter sounds. Smith-Spark and colleagues (2003) found that adult participants with dyslexia had poor verbal memory, compared to controls. English children learn to read slowly because letter-sound links are inconsistent (e.g. go/do). Goswami (2003) observed that in languages with consistent spellings, such as German, dyslexics learn more quickly, supporting the role of the PL. Children with dyslexia therefore need specific teaching in phonics. (139 words)

Dyslexia leads to other problems such as with following instructions, so children with dyslexia may also need help with organisation and sequencing. Working memory issues in dyslexia may therefore extend beyond the PL to the visuo-spatial sketchpad (VSS). Smith-Spark and Fisk (2007) tested VSS span in dyslexic adults using a computerised visual block test (the Corsi test). This showed that the dyslexics had a significantly shorter visuo-spatial span than controls. Therefore, to help children with dyslexia, systematic, sequential information is needed, e.g. simplifying complex ideas by providing lists or visual maps to aid the VSS. (95 words)

Finally, evidence suggests there may be central executive (CE) impairments in dyslexia. Some evidence for CE problems comes from day-to-day experiences, such as getting distracted. Swanson and Sachse-Lee (2001) tested children with reading disabilities. Those with the lowest central executive function were also poor on a range of tasks including memory and sentence listening tests. This suggests that support for people with dyslexia could assist overall information processing. For example, Shaywitz and Shaywitz (2004) described a systematic intervention for dyslexia, teaching phonemic awareness that built up into reading and writing. Not only did reading improve but brain activity changed too. One year after the intervention the dyslexic participants still showed greater activation in left hemisphere brain areas associated with automatic, fluent reading compared with dyslexic controls who had not experienced the intervention. (132 words)

Help for children with dyslexia is currently based on overcoming PL problems, for example with letter-sound links. However, newer evidence suggests that help with VSS and CE functions would also be beneficial for people with dyslexia. (36 words)

Total = 402 words

On this page we have presented a full answer to one of the key questions in the specification and added comments to draw your attention to specific features.

Describe the contemporary problem of dyslexia, and the advantages of helping.

Integrate concepts: Use ideas from the working memory model to provide possible explanations of the problems of dyslexia.

Detail: You are explaining an application, so you don't have to describe the whole model first.

Support your point with evidence about how ideas from working memory are useful and link this back to the key question.

Include competing arguments: Use your knowledge of the working memory model to counter your argument for the role of the PL, e.g. with roles for the VSS or central executive.

And now a different argument: Alternative ideas are introduced but in context, in this case a link to biological psychology as well as cognition.

Balanced judgement: This doesn't have to be lengthy but it could reflect alternative views.

On this page we have provided a scaffold to help you prepare your own answer.

Remember that these are simply suggested answers. Use these suggestions to help you think about how you could structure your own response.

Example 2

Discuss the key question for society you have studied using concepts, theories and/or research from cognitive psychology. (8)

State your key question: How can psychologists' understanding of memory help patients with dementia?

Paragraph 1

Describe: Introduce the key question by describing memory loss in dementia.

Link: Explain one cognitive factor, for example the loss of episodic memories first.

Support/challenge: Evaluate your explanation, for example use evidence about the types of episodic memories lost or the role of the hippocampus in these memories.

Paragraph 2

Describe: Consider the impact on society, for example why is it important that we try to combat the memory problems related to dementia?

Link: Explain why those memories are important, how they are formed or how they might be preserved through cognitive strategies.

Support/challenge: You could evaluate by considering the effectiveness of cognitive strategies or by contradicting the cognitive viewpoint with a biological reason for dementia.

Paragraph 3

Describe: Extend the description of cognitive losses in dementia to include the loss of semantic memories as well.

Link: Focus on the loss of specific knowledge, using examples such as forgetting words.

Support/challenge: By considering the biological changes caused by the disease you can both support and contradict the argument. For support you can say how semantic memories are stored in the frontal lobes, which are damaged later. As a counterargument you can consider how complete an explanation of dementia cognitive deficits alone would be.

Finish with a balanced judgement, for example looking at whether cognitive explanations alone are sufficient or whether we need to consider biological factors as well, especially to give a full understanding versus an immediate impact on society.

Forgotten your password? Forgotten the answer to your 'memorable question'? Think how your knowledge of working memory might help

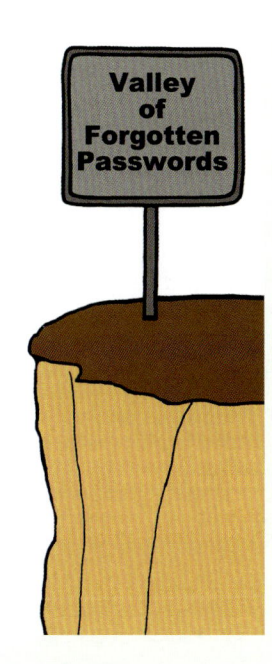

Try your own

You don't have to do the key question in the specification.

Here is a different one that you might try: *How can cognitive psychology help with everyday memory such as remembering passwords?*

- You could approach this question by considering how the working memory model and multi-store model would suggest people learn passwords. By verbal repetition? Learning no more than seven characters at once? In chunks? By visualising them?
- Another approach would be to consider whether the passwords could be made into episodic memories with personal links and whether this would improve recall or whether they should be semantic memories.
- Finally, you could suggest employing a strategy based on reconstructive memory, where individuals do not have to recall the password in its entirety but merely rebuild it accurately as they reconstruct their memory. How could cues be provided to help them to do this effectively?

Study tip

We have focused on 8-mark key question essays. However, it's worth thinking about the fact that all 'key questions' are about the *use of psychological knowledge in society* which is one of the eleven 'Issues and debates' which you need to know about for Section E of A level Paper 1. These essays can be 12-markers requiring evaluation and conclusions. Be ready to be flexible with everything that you learn.

Check it

1. State your key question for cognitive psychology and explain how psychology can help to resolve the issues it raises. (4)

2. You will have studied a key question from cognitive psychology.
   (a) Explain why your key question for cognitive psychology is relevant to today's society. (2)
   (b) Explain **one** way in which concepts, theories and/or research drawn from cognitive psychology can answer your key question from cognitive psychology. (4)

3. **Standard:** You will have studied a key question for cognitive psychology.

   Discuss whether cognitive psychology can help or has helped to resolve this key question. (8)

4. **AL (I&D/Synoptic):** Evaluate the usefulness to society of the psychological knowledge from your key questions in social and cognitive psychology. (12)

Chapter 2 Cognitive psychology

Practical investigations for cognitive psychology

Practical investigation example from the specification.

The specification says…

2.5.1 One practical research exercise to gather data relevant to topics covered in cognitive psychology. This practical research exercise must adhere to ethical principles in both content and intention.

In conducting the practical research exercise, students must:

- Design and conduct a laboratory experiment to gather quantitative data and include descriptive statistics as analysis and a non-parametric test of difference. (See pages 172-173, 191 and 192-193 for advice)
- Make design decisions when planning and conducting their experiment, including experimental design, sampling decisions, operationalisation, control, ethical considerations, hypothesis construction, experimenter effects and demand characteristics. (See pages 170, 176-177, 182, 184-187)
- Collect, present and comment on data gathered, including using measures of central tendency (mean, median, mode as appropriate); measures of dispersion (including range and standard deviation as appropriate); bar graph, histogram, frequency graph as relevant; normal distribution if appropriate; and draw conclusions. (See pages 172-173 and 195)
- Use a Mann-Whitney U or Wilcoxon non-parametric test of difference to test significance (as appropriate), including level of significance and critical/observed values. (See pages 190-191 and 192-193)
- Consider strengths and weaknesses of the experiment, and possible improvements. (See pages 186-189)
- Write up the procedure, results and discussion section of a report. (See page 181)

Ethical principles

Ethical principles are discussed in detail in chapter 5, on pages 176–177. We strongly suggest that you complete this checklist before collecting data.

1. Participants know participation is voluntary. ☐
2. Participants know what to expect, i.e. the task(s) they will be doing. ☐
3. Participants know they can withdraw at any time. ☐
4. Participants' responses will be anonymous. ☐
5. I minimised the risk of distress to participants. ☐
6. I have avoided collecting any sensitive data. ☐
7. I considered all other ethical issues. ☐
8. I have not done anything that would bring my school/teacher/psychology into disrepute. ☐
9. My teacher has approved my plan. ☐

Dual task experiment to investigate components of working memory

Design considerations

This practical is a laboratory experiment to investigate dual-task performance (based on Hitch and Baddeley 1976). It uses an independent groups design with two groups of participants. You would like each participant to perform two tasks – a reasoning task and a verbal task.

All of your participants carry out the first task, a reasoning task that uses the central executive (see the next section for details). Participants carry out the second verbal task simultaneously with the first task, either:

- Group 1 – Repeating the word 'the' over and over again (involves just the phonological loop).
- Group 2 – Saying out loud any random digits (involves both the central executive and the phonological loop).

Therefore, the independent variable is the nature of the verbal task. The dependent variable is measured by timing how long it takes to complete the first task.

Write an alternate hypothesis that includes operationalised variables, decide whether it should be directional or non-directional and explain why. Finally, think about any potential confounding variables – what factors could affect performance on the task, and how can you control the procedure to counteract these?

Preparing materials

For the reasoning task, participants are shown two letters and a statement of the relationship between them. For example, you might show them the letters 'AB' and the statement 'B is followed by A'. The participant indicates whether the statement is true or false.

You need to devise ten such pairs and statements. Write them in a table with a column for participants to circle their responses, as shown on the right.

AB	B is followed by A	True or false
BA	A follows B	True or false
BA	B is followed by A	True or false

You will also have to time how long it takes for participants to complete the task – they should try to be as fast as possible but without making mistakes. You will probably want to write down some instructions that you can read to your participants to make the procedure clear.

You will be testing participants individually on a task that requires concentration so it would be better to run the tests somewhere quiet.

Sampling decisions

There are no special requirements for your sample so you can use opportunity or volunteer sampling.

Special ethical concerns

Apart from the usual considerations of consent, confidentiality and so on, you need to think about protection from psychological harm. Some participants might feel they are being evaluated, or worried that they have a poor memory. You should prepare a debriefing script that includes reassurances on these points.

Analysing your data

You are analysing the differences between the two groups in the time taken to complete the reasoning task. Calculate measures of central tendency and dispersion, present the results in a table and draw a suitable graph.

You should also carry out an inferential statistical test to see if any difference between the two groups is significant. The appropriate test is the Mann–Whitney U test. Follow the instructions on pages 192–193 to calculate this test, choose an appropriate significance level and explain whether the outcome is significant or not.

Write the report

There are three sections of a report you can write up. See facing page for details.

An experiment to look at acoustic similarity of words and the effect on short-term memory

Design considerations

This practical investigates a difference in short-term recall of lists of acoustically similar and dissimilar words. It is an experiment using a repeated measures design. The independent variable is the nature of the word list, acoustically similar and acoustically dissimilar. The dependent variable is the number of words correctly recalled from each list.

Think about the potentially confounding variables that you need to control. Standardising your procedures will help, so consider how you will do this. For example, how long will you give participants to hear and recall the lists? You will read out the words, so what speed should you read at? As you are investigating recall from short-term memory, how long should there be between hearing the lists and recalling them? How will you control for order effects?

Write some standardised instructions so the participants are clear about what they need to do. Construct an appropriate alternate hypothesis (directional or non-directional).

Preparing materials

You need to create two lists of words – acoustically similar (they sound similar, such as pat, pan, pin) and acoustically dissimilar (they sound different, such as pat, tic, mob).

Again, consider how the materials could be standardised. For example, the two lists should be equivalent in every way apart from acoustic similarity/dissimilarity (for example, the length of each word and familiarity).

Sampling decisions and special ethical concerns

See facing page.

Analysing your data

As in the previous practical, you are analysing differences between the two conditions, this time in the number of words correctly recalled. You can again calculate measures of central tendency and dispersion, present results in a suitable table and draw up a graph.

This time you will calculate a different inferential test because the design of the experiment is repeated measures. The appropriate test is Wilcoxon. See the instructions on page 191 and make sure you follow the whole process, including choosing the significance level, finding the critical value and so on.

Write the report

The procedure should describe in detail steps you took to carry out the experiment, including how you controlled potentially confounding variables and used standardised procedures. A reader should be able to replicate what you did on the basis of this section.

In the results section, present your table(s) of descriptive statistics, graphs, and the process you followed to calculate the statistical test (and the outcome). Do not present any raw data or the calculations themselves (they go into an appendix at the back of the report, which is not necessary for this practical).

Finally, the discussion section should include an explanation of the conclusions you can draw from your results (i.e. what they tell us about short-term memory, how they relate to Baddeley's original findings). Explain some strengths and weaknesses of the study and suggest improvements.

Practical investigation example from the specification.

When creating lists of words, try not to make them too long – use a short-ish list and uniformly short words.

Other ideas

You could carry out studies to test hypotheses in relation to the multi-store model. For example:

Capacity of short-term memory – Use digit span to compare the capacity of STM in younger (under 10) and older people (over 20 but under 40). Ask participants to repeat sequences of digits, increasing the length of the sequence each time (e.g. 5279, 48027, 716938, etc.). Instructions for this are on page 82. Is there a difference in digit span related to age?

Duration of long-term memory – Use real-life materials to find out the duration of LTM. For example, present participants with photographs of people and test their recognition after a period of time (e.g. a month). This is a repeated measures design.

Apply it Methods: Ambiguity

Olly is testing schema theory using an ambiguous passage to assess the effect of schema on recall. He is using people who are or are not musical. The passage could be interpreted in two ways, as being about a music rehearsal or about playing cards.

1. Write a directional (one-tailed) hypothesis for Olly's experiment. (2)
2. Explain **two** controls that Olly should employ. (4)
3. (a) Identify the inferential test that Olly should use. Justify your choice. (2)
   (b) Identify the **three** pieces of information Olly will need to find the critical value for his statistical test. (3)

(Note: This is based on an actual study and you can read the passage on page 10 here: tinyurl.com/y8q5uwek.)

Study tip

When you describe aspects of your practical investigation, such as controls or measures of central tendency, be sure you refer to your actual practical work rather than giving generic answers. For example, be specific about what your controls were by giving examples.

Check it

1. You will have conducted an experiment for your practical investigation in cognitive psychology.
   (a) Explain how you operationalised your independent variable. (2)
   (b) Describe **two** ways in which you standardised your procedure, other than by using standardised instructions. (2)
2. (a) State the null hypothesis from your practical investigation in cognitive psychology. (2)
   (b) Explain how you decided whether to accept or reject this hypothesis. (4)
3. **Standard:** Evaluate your practical investigation in cognitive psychology. (8)
4. **AS (Synoptic):** To what extent could the procedure of your practical investigations for cognitive psychology and social psychology have been improved? (12)

Revision summary

Chapter 2 Cognitive psychology

Memory

The working memory model

Central executive
Attentional process with supervisory role. Allocates subsystems to tasks, limited capacity, no storage.

Phonological loop
Processes auditory information (acoustic). Storage in phonological store, articulatory process allows maintenance rehearsal.

Visuo-spatial sketchpad
Stores visual/spatial information, limited capacity. Storage in visual cache, inner scribe for rehearsal.

Episodic buffer
Integrates information processed by other subsystems. Maintains time sequencing, limited capacity, LTM interface.

Evaluation

Support from laboratory experiments
Dual-task performance studies (Baddeley et al. 1975) – poor performance on two tasks using same subsystem.

Lack of clarity over central executive
CE vague and least understood component. Perhaps has separate subcomponents but unclear.

Application to understanding amnesia
Shallice and Warrington (1970) studied patient KF, poor STM for sounds but visual was normal. PL damaged but VSS OK.
However KF was unique, not typical of population, so caution in generalising findings.

EXTRA: Issues and debates
Ethical issues in amnesia research (can patients consent?), need for confidentiality (e.g. initials not names).

The multi-store model (MSM)

Sensory register (SR)
One store for each sense (e.g. iconic for visual). High capacity, very brief duration, requires attention.

Short-term memory (STM)
Temporary store (a working memory). Limited capacity (7±2), acoustic encoding, duration 18–30 seconds, extended by maintenance rehearsal.

Long-term memory (LTM)
Permanent store for rehearsed material. Unlimited capacity, semantic encoding, lifetime duration.

Information processing
Computer analogy describes memory in terms of input, storage, retrieval. Information is encoded, stored and processed by the CPU (brain) encoding.

Evaluation

Supporting research evidence
STM/LTM separate, different capacities (Miller 1956), durations (Peterson and Peterson 1959, Bahrick et al. 1975), encoding (Baddeley 1966b).
However STM and LTM not obviously separate in everyday life, more integrated (e.g. Campitelli 2015).

More than one type of STM
Clinical studies (amnesia, e.g. KF) suggest more than one STM store (e.g. visual and auditory).

Application to improving memory
Knowledge of memory has practical uses (e.g. increase STM capacity through chunking).

EXTRA: Issues and debates
Memory models illustrate development over time – MSM could not explain all findings (including everyday memory), so replaced by working memory.

Explanation of long-term memory

Episodic memory
Contains events from our lives (i.e. diary), autobiographical.

Key features of episodic memory
Time-stamped (stores how memories relate). One memory, several elements. Allows 'time travel' (autonoetic consciousness).

Semantic memory
Contains knowledge of world (facts, word meanings), acts like an encyclopaedia + dictionary.

Key features of semantic memory
Organised into concepts, mentally represents things not present. Not time-stamped, less personal.

Evaluation

Clinical evidence
HM's episodic memory was impaired but semantic memory unaffected, provides evidence for different LTM stores.
However lack of control in such studies because cannot compare memory after damage to before, reduces validity of clinical studies.

Overlapping types of LTM
Episodic memory is a specialised subcategory of semantic (Tulving 2002) relationship between types is complex.

Application to improving memory
Training programme to improve episodic memory in older people (Belleville et al. 2006).

EXTRA: Issues and debates
Socially sensitive research, e.g. risks creating negative perception of people with Alzheimer's (helpless burdens, etc.).

Reconstructive memory

Reproduction versus reconstruction
Bartlett (1932) suggested that memory is active, a meaningful reconstruction from fragments and therefore has inaccuracies.

The 'War of the Ghosts' study
Unfamiliar story transformed over time – became shorter, there were rationalisations, and became more meaningful (to fit schemas).

Schema theory
Mental structure, 'package' of knowledge. Unfamiliar situation activates schema, makes processing efficient ('guesses').

Schemas and memory
New knowledge conflicting with schema not encoded. Recall later only what matches schema.

Evaluation

Realistic theory and research
Not artificial materials (e.g. nonsense syllables). Bartlett uncovered social origins of memory.
However his methods lacked control and objectivity (e.g. no standardised procedures), reduced reliability and validity.

Some memories are accurate
Not all memories reconstructed inaccurately or affected by schemas (e.g. if personally important).

Application to eyewitness testimony
Recall of crime affected by schemas (expectations of what 'should' happen), therefore may be inaccurate.

EXTRA: Issues and debates
Illustrates nature-nurture debate – experiences form schemas (nurture), contrast with theories emphasising brain dysfunctions (nature).

Classic study

Baddeley (1966b)
Acoustic and semantic similarity in LTM

Aim
Is recall from LTM affected by semantically or acoustically similar words?

Procedure
Lab experiment, four lists recalled after 20 minutes – acoustically/semantically similar/dissimilar words.

Findings
LTM recall – forgetting of acoustically dissimilar list. No effect for semantic lists.

Conclusions
'Puzzling' results suggested LTM encoding was acoustic. But not a true test of LTM, so more experiments conducted.

Evaluation

High internal validity
Well-controlled procedures (matched lists) avoids confounding variables and demonstrates cause-and-effect.
However a confounding variable not controlled in experiment 1 was the influence of STM on LTM, therefore conducted more experiments.

Low external validity
Treated the STM/LTM interaction as confounding, making the task artificial and unlike real-life encoding.

Application to learning to learn
Improves long-term recall. Revision – Semantic strategies (e.g. reorganisation) not just repetition.

EXTRA: Issues and debates
Illustrates reductionism because simplest cognitive processes studied which were divorced from social context, humans viewed as machines.

Contemporary studies

Schmolck et al. (2002)
Semantic knowledge in patients with brain lesions

Aim
Is there a link between lateral temporal cortex damage and semantic knowledge/memory? Was there anything unique about HM's performance?

Procedure
Difference study comparing MTL+ patients, HF patients, HM and healthy volunteers on 9 tests.

Findings
HF and controls showed similar performance. MTL+ patients significantly impaired. HM mixed.

Conclusions
Link between impaired semantic knowledge and anterolateral temporal cortex damage. Results suggest HM had similar damage as MTL+ group.

Evaluation

Convergence of evidence
Additional evidence with different methods supports role of anterolateral/lateral temporal cortex, increases validity.
However brain injuries rare (small samples) so no knowledge of memory before, this makes valid comparisons impossible.

Problems with matching
HF patients not matched – younger/more educated than controls, means their performance was exaggerated which minimised role of hippocampal areas.

Application to amnesic patients
Provides 'map' for neurosurgeons to be able to avoid important cognitive areas when doing operations.

EXTRA: Issues and debates
A reductionist approach, locating semantic memory in one area of brain. Widespread distribution of semantic memory is a more holistic view.

Steyvers and Hemmer (2012)
Reconstruction from memory in naturalistic environments

Aim
Study effect of prior knowledge (semantic memory) on episodic recall of realistic scenes.

Procedure
Lab experiment. Phase 1 assessed prior knowledge (images). Phase 2 tested recall of scenes.

Findings
Analysis of errors – 9% error for expected objects, 18% for unexpected. Contribution of prior knowledge – correct recall over 80%.

Conclusions
Semantic memory greater and episodic memory smaller contribution to recall in naturalistic situations compared with previous research.

Evaluation

High external validity
Ecologically valid, naturalistic situations not artificial because did not separate episodic and semantic.

Excessive experimental control
Too controlled (e.g. lab conditions, photographs, quick presentation), reduces ecological validity.
However this was still more ecologically valid than most studies, trying to strike balance between control and realism.

Application to eyewitness testimony
Encourage use of prior knowledge (e.g. make educated guesses), leads to a more positive view of testimony.

EXTRA: Issues and debates
Cultural issues because the study was in one culture, but expectations vary widely across cultures. Therefore, limited generalisability of findings.

Sebastián and Hernández-Gil (2012)
Developmental pattern of digit span

Aims
To investigate the development of the phonological loop through digit span – in Spanish children, Anglo-Saxon children and Anglo-Saxon elderly/dementia.

Procedure
Field experiment, Spanish children (5–17 years) recalled increasing digit sequences, and compared with other groups.

Findings
Digit span increased with age. Healthy elderly people and those with dementia different from 5/6-year-olds; people with fvFTD were the same as 5/6-year-olds.

Conclusions
Spanish digit span lower than Anglo-Saxon due to word length effect. Loop capacity affected by age not dementia.

Evaluation

Control of variables
Standardised procedures (e.g. same rate of digits). Controls confounding variables and increases internal validity.
However the study lacked some control, e.g. children not tested for cognitive impairments, which would affect digit span performance.

Small sample size
fvFTD 9 participants – Type I error more likely with few participants. Low statistical power leads to uncertain conclusion.

Application to understanding cognitive abilities
Longer digit span linked with higher intelligence/better reading, shorter span may explain dyslexia.

EXTRA: Issues and debates
Cultural issues involved because digit span differences in study not due to culture but to structure of languages (e.g. Chan and Elliott 2011), thus cultural similarities.

# Chapter 2 Cognitive psychology

Practice questions, answers and feedback

On this spread we look at some typical student answers to questions. The comments provided indicate what is good and bad in each answer. Learning how to produce effective question answers is a SKILL. Read pages 6–19 for guidance.

Question 1: Give **one** example of an episodic memory and **one** example of a semantic memory. [2]

Sam's answer
Episodic memory is about doing things like playing the piano, sometimes you don't have to think about it much, once you have rehearsed it just comes back to you. However, you might also remember how nervous you were waiting for your first piano exam. Semantic memory is when you know that two famous composers are Chopin and Mozart.

Sam's answer is rather muddled. He says episodic memory is about doing things and the rest of the sentence sounds more like procedural memory. The middle sentence about 'your first piano exam' is an accurate example of episodic memory but it's hard to credit as Sam has muddled two examples together, one which is right and another which is wrong. His example of semantic memory is concise and accurate. Overall 1 mark.

Ella's answer
Episodic memory means remembering events from your past and semantic memory means remembering facts about the world.

Ella has unfortunately misinterpreted the question. She has given accurate but brief descriptions of the two types of memory but not given an example of either, so no marks.

Larina's answer
Episodic memory is about remembering things that have happened to you like remembering that you were wearing a red jumper the day your baby sister was born. Semantic memory tends to be more about facts and knowledge about the world, for example 'London is the capital of England'.

Larina certainly knows the difference between episodic and semantic memory. She gives accurate examples of both episodic and semantic memory. As the command term is 'give' and is asking for examples, Larina has wasted a bit of time here, unnecessarily describing the types of memory. However, clearly full marks.

Question 2: Compare the use of **two** different research methods used to investigate memory. [4]

Sam's answer
Two methods which are used to research memory are experiments and case studies. Experiments involve changing the independent variable to see how it affects the dependent variable, for example Baddeley changed whether words sounded alike or not and recorded what could be remembered whereas case studies are about collecting lots of information which can be qualitative and quantitative about one person or small group, e.g. HM had part of his temporal lobe removed to treat his epilepsy and was unable to form new memories.

Sam has a basic understanding of two appropriate research methods but he has not engaged with the command term at all – he has given a description of each method and with an accurate example that relates to memory, as required in the question. But he has not compared the methods. He has linked the two descriptions together with the word 'whereas' and this gives him 1 mark, but that is not sufficient for any more marks. Without the 'whereas' he would get zero.

Ella's answer:
Two methods from cognitive psychology are laboratory experiments and case studies. One similarity between these methods is that both of them can be used to collect quantitative data. For example, Baddeley did an experiment looking at recall of acoustically similar or dissimilar words and there was a case study on amnesia patient HM's working memory which was tested to see how long he could remember information measured in seconds. However, one difference between these two methods is that experiments tend to be more generalisable because they have more participants (e.g. Baddeley had 75 participants) meaning that averages can be calculated whereas case studies lack generalisability because they are only conducted on one person who might be unique and not comparable to others for various reasons. For example, HM might have had brain damage to other areas of his brain due to his original accident as well as the section of brain that was removed in the operation, and this might explain his memory problems.

This is an excellent answer although Ella may have gone over the time a little on this response which may have knock-on effects on her other answers on this exam paper. It pays to practise writing more succinct answers. She has focused on the question and given one similarity and one difference just as the command term 'compare' requires. Although it is possible to gain credit for giving more examples in less detail, Ella's approach ensures that each point is really effective. Quality is more important than quantity. An accurate and thorough answer worth the full 4 marks.

Larina's answer
Baddeley's study on short-term memory used a laboratory experiment and this means the study has good reliability as he used a standardised procedure which can be replicated. This is a strength of laboratory experiments compared with case studies where they sometimes collect data using techniques like semi-structured interviews which can't be replicated. Another difference between case studies and experiments is that experiments tend to collect quantitative, primary data like the number of mistakes a person makes when recalling words whereas case studies often collect qualitative data, meaning the psychologists might make notes while watching the person doing some sort of task. Case studies also sometimes use secondary data from medical records and this doesn't tend to happen in a laboratory experiment.

Larina starts by talking about a study as an example of a laboratory experiment. Whilst this question requires a focus on cognitive psychology, the question needs to start by looking at the methods. The main problem with Larina's answer is that she has provided only differences and no similarities – for 4 marks you must include both. You will only gain a maximum of 2 marks with just differences. Larina throws a lot of ideas in which wastes time that could have been spent planning the answer more carefully in order to meet the needs of the command term. This answer is worth 2 out of 4 marks because there are no similarities.

Question 3: Psychology students Annie and Frankie are performing in the whole school musical but there are so many lines, instructions, songs and dance moves to recall, they are worried they will never remember them all.

Discuss how the multi-store model of memory could help the girls remember everything they need to learn. You must make reference to the context in your answer. (8)

Sam's answer

The multi-store model has three stores: sensory register, short-term memory and long-term memory. The sensory register has a very short duration of about half a second. Although the capacity is great not much will transfer to short-term memory unless we pay attention to it. Short-term memory has a limited capacity of 7 items plus or minus 2 and information is stored acoustically. Without rehearsal new information will only last for about 18–30 seconds. Rehearsal allows for transfer to LTM which has infinite capacity, the duration is limitless and information is coded semantically.

The two girls need to think about the model carefully to help them remember their lines and dance moves. They need to pay attention to the director and dance teacher. They need to keep on repeating the lines and practise the dances frequently and learn new material in groups of seven and no more. They need to make links between what they need to learn and what they already know and make sure that they code the information in different ways. They will find that, if they think about the place where they originally learn the materials, this might help them to remember it better. They need to try not to get nervous as stress stops you from remembering things so they should practise techniques to help them relax, like breathing exercises or meditation.

One weakness of the multi-store model is that it is oversimplified as it shows only one type of STM and one type of LTM. Research evidence shows that amnesia patients can sometimes have problems with episodic memory but semantic memory is unaffected. This is important because if MSM has flaws it might not be the best theory to help Annie and Frankie.

Overall the multi-store model can be somewhat helpful if it is applied to everyday situations like this one but Annie and Frankie need to also think about other models such as the working memory model and reconstructive memory theory.

328 words

Sam has opted to put all his AO1 descriptive knowledge into a block before attempting to apply it to the scenario. This is not necessarily the best approach because he has got distracted by describing the model in detail instead of applying it. It is better to try and link individual concepts from the model to parts of the scenario one at a time.

When Sam does start applying his knowledge to the scenario, his ideas lack development – he just gives one sentence for each idea. He never explains why these ideas might be helpful or how.

Sam also injects two ideas which are not relevant to the multi-store model – the place where learning took place and stress are both linked to memory but not to the multi-store model.

In the penultimate paragraph Sam wastes more time on an unnecessary evaluation point. Although he has structured it well using PET, he doesn't actually need strengths and weaknesses in this essay as the command term 'discuss' assesses only AO1+AO2.

Finally, Sam attempts a conclusion but again this is not required for an 8-mark 'discuss' question.

If you look at the amount of relevant content in this essay, you are left with very little and therefore the mark comes out as level 2, probably at the lower end.

Ella's answer

Annie and Frankie should be confident about their ability to memorise everything they need to know because the multi-store model suggests that the capacity of long-term memory is limitless and the duration is years and potentially a lifetime! They just need to find ways to encode all the information so it can travel through the sensory register and the short-term memory in order to be stored and retrieved at future rehearsals and of course in the final performance.

First of all they need to think about the fact that information from the outside world can only pass from the sensory register into the short-term memory if they are paying attention. This means that when they are learning their lines, they need to put their phones away and make a conscious effort to listen to each other carefully.

Another way they can improve their ability to remember this information is to think about the fact that short-term memory has a limited capacity. When the girls are learning a new dance, their teacher might shout out the names of all the steps individually which would be really hard to remember. However, if she breaks the dance into blocks of seven steps at a time it will be easier for them. This is because Miller says STM has a capacity of 7 plus or minus 2. However, capacity can be increased by chunking items together. So instead of trying to remember the names of each individual step, they could break the dance into chunks and give each chunk a name.

Furthermore the girls should think about Atkinson and Shiffrin's comments on 'rehearsal' which is necessary to move information from STM to LTM. When they are learning songs or sections of the script, they need to go over these plenty of times to aid the transfer to long-term memory.

LTM is coded semantically, so items are stored according to their meaning. The girls need to ask questions and do some research to help them understand the meaning otherwise it will be hard to retrieve the information at the next rehearsal. When it comes to learning new dance moves they could think about the patterns they are making and give the moves names like 'the snake' or 'the curly wurly' as coding the information semantically will again make it more memorable.

386 words

Overall Ella has done a great job in the time allowed. She has clearly thought about everything she knows about the multi-store model and then systematically applied each concept to something from the scenario.

In the first paragraph she has given a rather general introduction to the model which is perhaps a bit of a waste of time. There isn't much detail here.

In the second paragraph she links her knowledge of the model with examples and suggests a way the girls can alter their behaviour that is related to the multi-store model, as required in the question.

This continues in the next three paragraphs ensuring that she has covered each of the three stores and the two control processes (attention and rehearsal). She refers to capacity, duration and coding and uses key terms encoding, storage and retrieval. Doubtless this was no accident, suggesting she spent time planning her answer.

Ella has engaged well with the context and thought about what it might be like to be involved in a musical. She refers to the dance teacher and rehearsals neither of which are mentioned explicitly in the scenario. This is fine as long as your inventions are implied in the description. Don't go too wild though, otherwise your answer will stray too far from the information you have been given and will not be creditworthy.

This essay is likely to score level 4, at the lower end. The main criticism is a lack of depth in some areas, for example what was the meaning behind the song lyrics. This was not strongly linked to the scenario and therefore needed greater explanation.

Multiple-choice questions

Memory: The working memory model

1. The component with a supervisory role is the:
   (a) Visuo-spatial sketchpad.
   (b) Central executive.
   (c) Phonological loop.

2. The phonological loop is divided into the phonological store and the:
   (a) Episodic buffer.
   (b) Inner scribe.
   (c) Articulatory process.

3. The subsystem that interfaces with long-term memory is the:
   (a) Central executive.
   (b) Visuo-spatial sketchpad.
   (c) Episodic buffer.

4. KF had damage to his:
   (a) Phonological loop.
   (b) Visual cache.
   (c) Central executive.

Memory: The multi-store model of memory

1. According to Miller, the capacity of short-term memory is, on average:
   (a) 7 plus or minus 2 items.
   (b) Between 7 and 9 items.
   (c) 5 items.

2. Information is transferred from STM to LTM by:
   (a) Attention.
   (b) Rehearsal.
   (c) Chance.

3. Encoding in LTM is mostly:
   (a) Acoustic.
   (b) Semantic.
   (c) Visual.

4. Capacity of STM can be increased through:
   (a) Clunking.
   (b) Dunking.
   (c) Chunking.

Memory: Explanation of long-term memory

1. Episodic memories:
   (a) Include knowledge of what words mean.
   (b) Allow us to mentally 'time travel'.
   (c) Are likely to be short-term.

2. Semantic memories:
   (a) Include facts we all share.
   (b) Are time-stamped.
   (c) Are autobiographical.

3. HM:
   (a) Had a poor episodic memory.
   (b) Could not recall concepts.
   (c) Could not understand what words meant.

4. According to Tulving, _____ consciousness is a feature of episodic memory.
   (a) Automatic.
   (b) Noetic.
   (c) Autonoetic.

Memory: Reconstructive memory

1. Bartlett saw memory as:
   (a) Active.
   (b) Reproductive.
   (c) Extremely accurate.

2. Over time, reproductions of the *War of the Ghosts*:
   (a) Stayed unchanged in meaning.
   (b) Were very accurate.
   (c) Became shorter.

3. Schemas:
   (a) Are physical parts of the brain.
   (b) Have no influence on recall.
   (c) Are 'packages' of knowledge in memory.

4. Bartlett's research used:
   (a) Word lists.
   (b) Nonsense syllables.
   (c) Folk tales.

Classic study: Baddeley (1966b)

1. A pair of semantically similar words in the study was:
   (a) Safe and thin.
   (b) Great and huge.
   (c) Map and mad.

2. In experiment 1, there was no long-term forgetting of the:
   (a) Acoustically similar words.
   (b) Acoustically dissimilar words.
   (c) Semantically similar words.

3. Because the finding of experiment 1 was surprising, Baddeley:
   (a) Abandoned his theory of LTM encoding.
   (b) Conducted further experiments.
   (c) Accepted his hypothesis.

4. Baddeley's study had:
   (a) Low internal validity.
   (b) High external validity.
   (c) Low external validity.

Contemporary study: Schmolck *et al.* (2002)

1. The independent variable in this study was:
   (a) Type of brain damage.
   (b) Semantic knowledge.
   (c) Gender.

2. HM's brain damage was in the:
   (a) Prefrontal cortex.
   (b) Limbic system.
   (c) Medial temporal lobes.

3. The best overall performance came from:
   (a) The HF patients.
   (b) HM.
   (c) The MTL+ patients.

4. A methodological weakness of the study was:
   (a) The HF patients were older than the MTL patients.
   (b) The HF patients were not matched.
   (c) There was no control group.

Contemporary study: Steyvers and Hemmer (2012)

1. The design of this experiment was:
   (a) Repeated measures.
   (b) Matched pairs.
   (c) Independent groups.

2. The 'false memory' error rate was:
   (a) 9%.
   (b) 19%.
   (c) 30%.

3. Participants were able to recall:
   (a) Unexpected objects only.
   (b) Both expected and unexpected objects.
   (c) Expected objects only.

4. The study had:
   (a) Low internal validity.
   (b) High ecological validity.
   (c) Little control of variables.

Contemporary study: Sebastián and Hernández-Gil (2012)

1. The study investigated which component of working memory?
   (a) Phonological loop.
   (b) Central executive.
   (c) Visuo-spatial sketchpad.

2. The digit span of 5-year-olds was similar to that of:
   (a) People with Alzheimer's disease.
   (b) Healthy elderly people.
   (c) People with fvFTD.

3. Differences between Spanish and English children are due to:
   (a) The word length effect.
   (b) Intelligence.
   (c) Age.

4. A small sample size increases:
   (a) The chances of a Type I error.
   (b) The chances of a Type II error.
   (c) External validity.

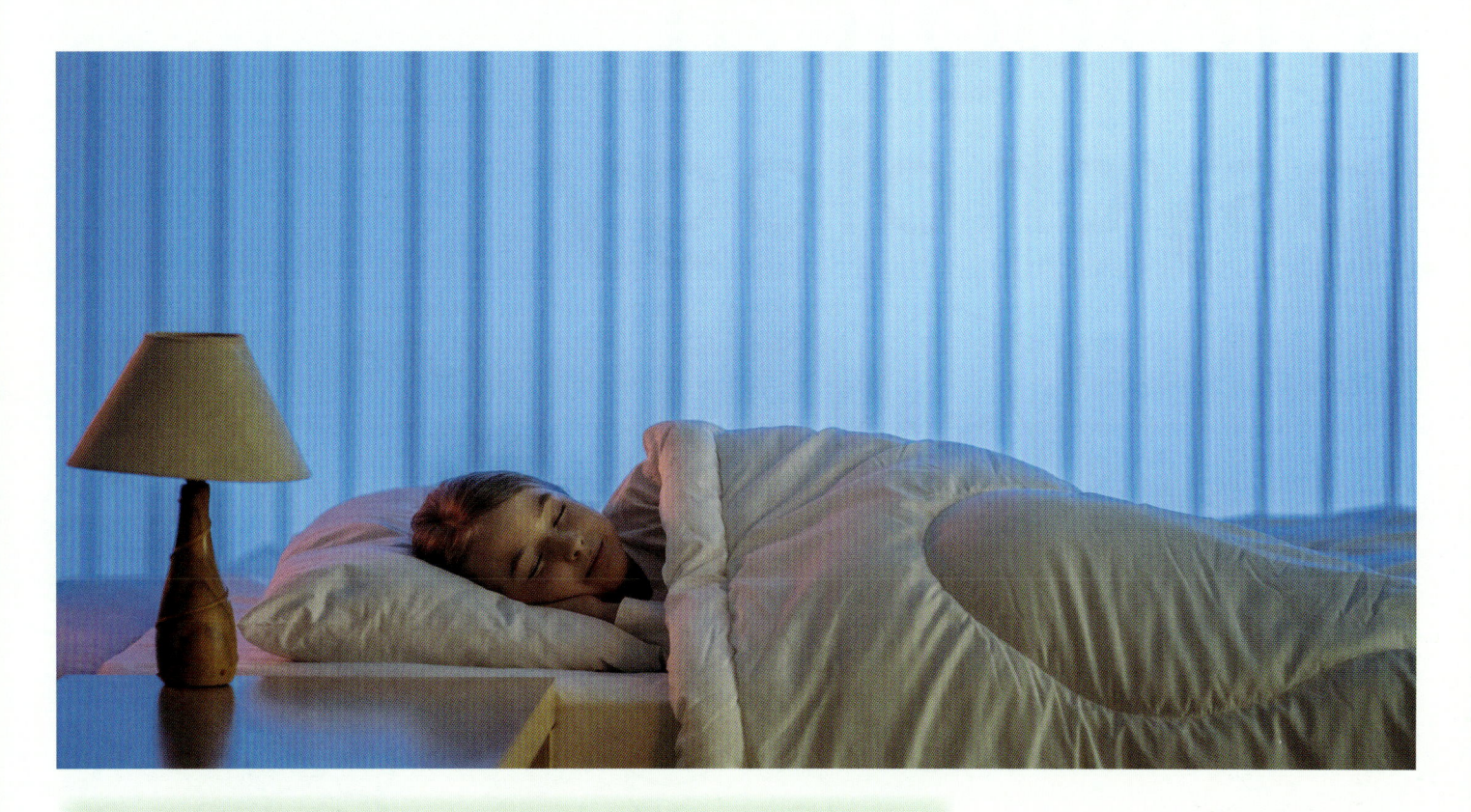

Explanation from page 67

Which words did you remember?

Did you say 'sleep' by any chance? It wasn't on the first list.

Can you explain why your memory was 'fooled'?

Can you trust your memory? Can your friends trust theirs?

MCQ answers

Memory: The working memory model 1B 2C 3C 4A
Memory: The multi-store model of memory 1A 2B 3B 4C
Memory: Explanation of long-term memory 1B 2A 3A 4C
Memory: Reconstructive memory 1A 2C 3C 4C
Classic study: Baddeley (1966) 1B 2A 3B 4C
Contemporary study: Schmolck et al. (2002) 1A 2C 3A 4B
Contemporary study: Steyvers and Hemmer (2012) 1C 2B 3B 4B
Contemporary study: Sebastián and Hernández-Gil (2012) 1A 2C 3A 4A

Biological psychology

Chapter 3

Brain myths

There are lots of myths about the brain that many people believe. For example, there's the one that says we only use about 10% of our brainpower. But scientific research shows that there is no evidence for this statement. In fact, we all use most of our brains most of the time.

Another common myth rests on the (undisputed) fact that our brains are divided into two halves (or 'hemispheres'), left and right. The myth goes that these hemispheres are completely different – that the left is scientific, rational, logical and keen on detail, whereas the right is wacky, creative, artistic and sees the 'big picture'.

You can test whether you are a left- or right-brained person with the spinning dancer test.

Which way is the dancer spinning?

You need to see it in motion (e.g. tinyurl.com/nlme4hd)

If she appears to you to be spinning clockwise, then your right hemisphere is dominant and you are a creative person (whether you know it or not). But if you reckon she's spinning anticlockwise, your left hemisphere is dominant and you are a rational and logical type.

The thing is… there is no evidence that the spinning dancer has anything to do with your left and right hemispheres. It's true that the hemispheres do have different functions, and one is a bit more dominant than the other. But the idea that you can be a 'right-brain person' or a 'left-brain person' is just another brain myth.

What this shows is that it's always a good idea to look at claims about the brain with a bit of scepticism.

Contents

96	The central nervous system and human behaviour
98	Neurons, synaptic transmission and neurotransmitters
100	Effect of recreational drugs
102	The structure of the brain and aggression
104	Evolution, natural selection and aggression
106	Freud's psychodynamic explanation of aggression
108	Role of hormones in human behaviour

Methods - see pages 198-205 of Chapter 5

Studies

110	Classic study: Raine *et al*. (1997)
	Contemporary study, select one of:
112	Li *et al*. (2013)
114	Brendgen *et al*. (2005)
116	Van den Oever *et al*. (2008)
118	**Key questions for biological psychology**
120	**Practical investigations for biological psychology**

End of chapter

122	Revision summary
124	Practice questions, answers and feedback
126	Multiple-choice questions

The central nervous system and human behaviour

Chapter 3 Biological psychology

The specification says...
3.1.1 The central nervous system (CNS) in human behaviour.

Key term

Central nervous system – Consists of the brain and the spinal cord and is the origin of all complex commands and decisions.

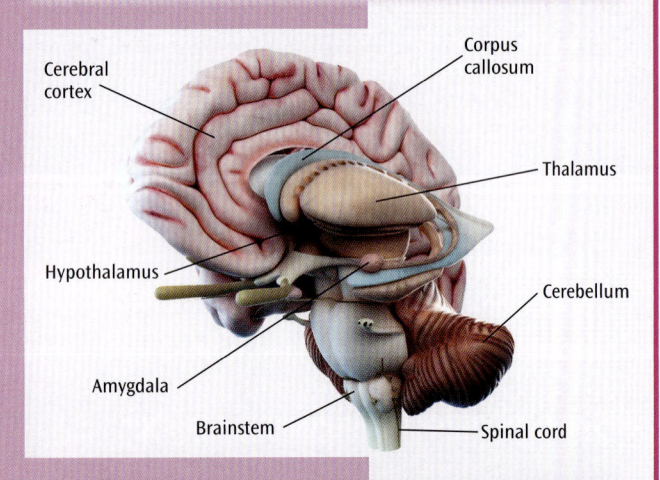

[Diagram of brain with labels: Cerebral cortex, Corpus callosum, Thalamus, Hypothalamus, Cerebellum, Amygdala, Brainstem, Spinal cord]

Think Link
Developmental psychology

Handedness

You would think that the structure and functioning of the brain are identical for every human. Not so. There are in fact some quite significant differences between people.

For instance people differ in terms of something psychologists call *handedness*. Most people are right-handed. Control of their language functions resides in the left hemisphere. The parts of the left hemisphere associated with movement are more developed than the equivalent areas of the right hemisphere. In right-handed people, the differences between left and right hemispheres are quite marked.

For the 13% of the population who are left-handed, however, the same rule doesn't apply. Lateralisation in left-handers is often, as you would expect, the reverse of right-handers. However, many left-handers' brains are more symmetrical and balanced than right-handers', with fewer differences between the hemispheres.

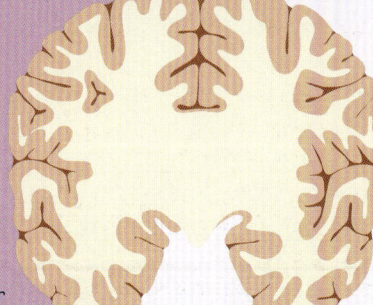

[Diagram of cortex cross-section]
The cortex is the thin layer of neurons that lies over the brain. Higher order thinking takes place in this layer of neurons.

The central nervous system (CNS)

The nervous system is a specialised and complex network of cells in the human body. It is our primary internal communication system and has two main functions:
- It collects, processes and responds to information in the environment.
- It coordinates the working of different organs and cells in the body.

The nervous system is divided into two main subsystems – the central nervous system (CNS) and the *peripheral nervous system* (PNS). The focus in this chapter is on the CNS, which is made up of the spinal cord and the brain.

The spinal cord

The spinal cord is a tube-like extension of the brain, connected to the brain via the brain stem. It is responsible for reflex actions such as pulling your hand away from a hot plate. It passes messages to and from the brain, linking it to the peripheral nervous system.

The brain

The brain is the source of our conscious awareness and where decision-making takes place. It is divided into two near-symmetrical hemispheres, which are connected by a group of structures, the main one being the *corpus callosum*. The brain's control of the body is generally *contralateral* – the left hemisphere controls activity on the right side of the body, the right hemisphere controls activity on the left side.

The outer layer of the brain, the *cerebral cortex* (or just 'cortex'), is highly developed in humans and is what distinguishes our mental functioning from that of other animals. It is about 3 mm thick and – like a tea cosy – covers the 'inner' parts of the brain. For this reason, the various areas and parts of the brain are often divided into *cortical* (belonging to the cortex) and *subcortical* (below the cortex).

Subcortical structures

Thalamus This is the brain's relay station. It receives information from various senses (e.g. hearing, sight, touch, but not smell which takes a more direct route to the brain) and passes it on to the appropriate areas of the cerebral cortex for higher-level processing. But the thalamus is also more active than this, because it carries out some initial processing of its own. Therefore, it acts as a 'gate' or filter of information. It is thought to play a role in sleep, wakefulness and obsessive compulsive disorder (OCD).

Hypothalamus Sitting below ('hypo') the thalamus, this structure's involvement in a variety of behaviours is well out of proportion to its tiny size (about the tip of your finger). The hypothalamus controls motivational behaviours such as hunger, thirst and sex. It has a key role in the body's stress response through its control of 'fight or flight' (i.e. fighting an aggressor or fleeing). It maintains balance in many bodily functions such as temperature (homeostasis). It also regulates the activity of the endocrine system (hormones) via its connection with the pituitary gland (see page 108) and even secretes hormones of its own.

Limbic system This consists of several structures such as the amygdala, which plays a large role in regulating emotional responses (e.g. aggression, see page 102). It also has a role in memory and learning. The limbic system is highly interconnected with areas of the cortex, integrating cortical and subcortical parts of the brain.

Cerebellum The word cerebellum means 'little brain'. Like the 'big brain' it has two hemispheres and is highly convoluted (wrinkled). The cerebellum's primary role is to coordinate posture, balance and movement. It does this by receiving and integrating information from the spinal cord and other areas such as the *motor cortex* (see facing page). Despite being only about 10% of the brain's entire weight, the cerebellum contains almost 50% of its neurons.

Corpus callosum This dense collection of nerve cells physically connects the two hemispheres below the cerebral cortex. It allows communication between the hemispheres by passing signals back and forth. This is critical given the brain's contralateral control of the body, because it integrates the activities of both sides of the body.

Lateralisation and localisation

The two hemispheres of the human brain are (with some exceptions) structurally identical. But in terms of what they do, the picture is very different. The two hemispheres have different functions (for example, language is associated with the left hemisphere) – this is known as *lateralisation*.

Within each hemisphere, certain areas are responsible for specific functions and behaviours – this is called *localisation*. For example, not only are language functions lateralised (usually) in the left hemisphere, they are localised to specific areas within this hemisphere (see below).

The cerebral cortex

The cerebral cortex of both hemispheres is subdivided into four lobes each named after the bones beneath which they lie (so there are eight lobes in total, four in each hemisphere). As predicted by localisation theory, each lobe is associated with different functions.

The most striking feature of the cerebral cortex is its wrinkliness. It looks like a giant walnut with many *convolutions* – ridges called *gyri* (singular, *gyrus*) and 'valleys' called *sulci* (singular, *sulcus*). The convolutions have a valuable purpose – they increase the cortex's surface area, giving it more processing power. The surface area of the cortex is roughly that of four sheets of A4 paper.

Frontal lobes Unsurprisingly located right at the front of the brain, the frontal lobes make up about 40% of the cerebral cortex in humans. They control high-level cognitive functions such as thinking, planning, problem-solving and decision-making. They also contain the *motor cortex*, a long strip of neurons that runs down alongside the central sulcus of both hemispheres. Each motor cortex controls voluntary movements on the opposite side of the body (contralateral). The left frontal lobe also includes *Broca's area* (see below).

Parietal lobes These are found on the other side of the central sulcus, further back in the brain. Directly alongside this sulcus lies the *somatosensory cortex*, which processes sensory information from the skin (e.g. touch, temperature, pressure), again in a contralateral manner. The area of somatosensory cortex devoted to a particular body part reflects that part's sensitivity to touch. For instance, neurons processing sensory information from the face and hands take up over half of the area of the somatosensory cortex.

Temporal lobes These lie beneath the lateral sulcus of each hemisphere. Each lobe contains an *auditory cortex* which deals with sound information coming mainly from the opposite ear. They process the location, volume and pitch of sounds, and therefore have a role in understanding language. The left temporal lobe is also the location of *Wernicke's area* (see below).

Occipital lobes Located at the back of the brain, each lobe contains a primary *visual cortex* (sometimes called V1) and several secondary areas (V2, V3, etc.). Everything we see to the right of our field of vision (from both the left and right eye) is initially processed by the left visual cortex before being shared (via the corpus callosum) with the right visual cortex (and vice versa).

Language areas of the brain

Broca's area Pierre Paul Broca, a surgeon working in the 1860s, identified a small area in the left frontal lobe responsible for speech production. Damage to this area causes Broca's aphasia, the main feature of which is slow, laborious speech lacking in fluency.

Wernicke's area Around the same time as Broca, Karl Wernicke was describing patients who had difficulty understanding language, producing fluent but meaningless speech (Wernicke's aphasia). He located the main area of damage in the left temporal lobe.

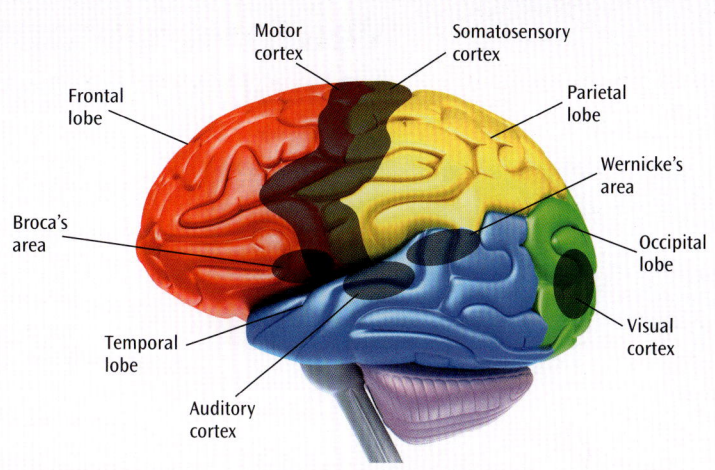

The four lobes of the left hemisphere plus key regions of the cerebral cortex.

Apply it Methods: Right brain, left brain

Stefan Knecht *et al.* (2000) tested participants' handedness and measured the 'right dominance' of their language processing. The results are summarised in the scatter diagram.

1. (a) Describe the relationship shown in the scatter diagram. (2)
   (b) Describe the conclusion that could be drawn from the scatter diagram. (1)
2. The sample consisted of approximately 320 participants. The ratio of females:males was 6:4. Calculate the number of males and females. Give your answers to **two** significant figures. (2)

Scatter diagram showing relationship between right language dominance and handedness.

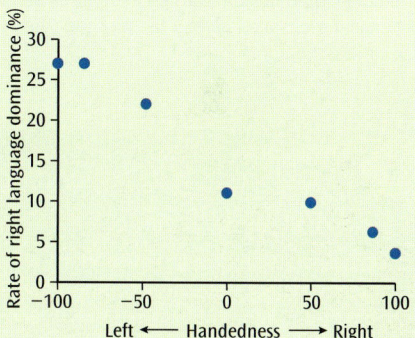

Apply it Concepts: One-sided strokes

It is known that when right-handed people have a stroke it is more likely that their speech will be affected if the damage is on the left side of the brain. However, for at least some left-handed people, a stroke affecting the right side of their brain is more likely to cause speech problems.

Explain these findings using your understanding of the structure and function of the CNS. (5)

Study tip

You will be using the names and locations of the lobes and other areas of the brain throughout this chapter – so get a good grasp of them now. Make some nice models of the brain to help you remember them.

Also, be sure you can distinguish these from other structures you have learned (such as the hippocampus, hypothalamus and limbic system).

Check it

1. Name and describe **one** structure in the brain. (2)
2. Describe how the central nervous system (CNS) controls any **one** named human behaviour. (5)
3. **Standard:** Discuss how differences in a person's central nervous system (CNS) might account for their individual differences. (8)
4. **AS (Synoptic):** To what extent can the theme of biological psychology explain individual differences in behaviour rather than learning theories? (12)

Neurons, synaptic transmission and neurotransmitters

Chapter 3 — Biological psychology

The specification says…
3.1.1 Neurotransmitters in human behaviour including the structure and role of the neuron, the function of neurotransmitters and synaptic transmission.

Key terms

Neuron – The basic building block of the nervous system. Neurons are nerve cells that process and transmit messages through electrical and chemical signals.

Neurotransmitters – Brain chemicals released from synaptic vesicles. Neurotransmitters relay signals from one neuron to another across a synapse. Neurotransmitters can be broadly divided into those that perform an excitatory function and those that perform an inhibitory function.

Synaptic transmission – The process by which neighbouring neurons communicate with each other by sending chemical messages across the tiny gap (the synapse) that separates neurons.

Think Link
Developmental psychology

Development of the brain

Cognitive abilities develop in tandem with the central nervous system. More primitive brain structures, such as the brain stem, are relatively highly developed at birth. This makes sense, because the brain stem regulates bodily functions that are essential for survival (such as breathing).

The parts of the brain involved in more advanced mental functions take longer to develop. For example, the frontal areas of the cerebral cortex continue to develop and grow into adolescence. Children become capable of more sophisticated and 'adult-like' ways of thinking as the cortex changes (e.g. as myelination of axons progresses).

Stretch & Challenge

Increasing connectivity

We are born with (just about) all the neurons we will ever possess, but the connections (synapses) between them change in childhood and beyond. *Synaptogenesis* is the process by which new synapses are formed between neurons, as axons and dendrites of neurons grow towards each other to form networks. This begins before birth in *exuberant synaptogenesis*, during which up to a million new synapses are created each second by the time of birth (Greenough et al. 1987). The process continues postnatally.

Synaptogenesis contributes to greater complexity in the brain. More synapses create more neurotransmitter activity.

What are the benefits to the brain of synaptogenesis?

The neuron

Structure of the neuron

A neuron is a nerve cell, the basic unit of the nervous system. Of the roughly 100 billion neurons in the human nervous system, about 80% are located in the brain. Neurons allow the nervous system to fulfil its communication function by transmitting signals electrically and chemically.

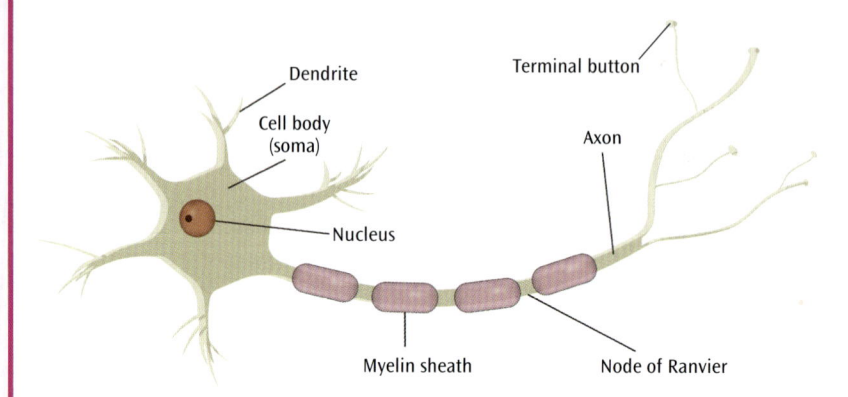

Neurons vary in size from less than a millimetre up to a metre long, but all share the same basic structure.

The *cell body* (soma) includes a *nucleus* containing the genetic material of the cell. Branch-like structures called *dendrites* stick out from the cell body. These carry impulses from neighbouring neurons towards the cell body.

The *axon* is a tube-like structure that carries the impulses away from the cell body down the length of the neuron. In many neurons, the axon is covered by a fatty layer called the *myelin sheath*. This is formed from special cells (called glial cells in the CNS) which wrap themselves around the axon.

The myelin sheath both protects the axon and speeds up electrical transmission of the impulse. Gaps in the myelin sheath – called *nodes of Ranvier* – allow this increase in speed by forcing the impulses to 'jump' across the gaps along the length of the axon.

Finally at the end of the axon are *terminal buttons*. These are not physically connected to the next neuron in the chain, but are involved in communication across a gap known as a *synapse*.

Types of neuron

There are three main types of neuron.

- *Sensory neurons* carry messages from sensory receptors (e.g. touch- and temperature-sensitive receptors in the skin) along nerves in the peripheral nervous system (PNS) to the central nervous system (CNS). They have long dendrites and short axons.
- *Motor neurons* carry messages from the CNS, along nerves in the PNS, to effectors in the body (e.g. muscles and glands). They have short dendrites and long axons.
- *Relay neurons* connect sensory and motor neurons together, and also connect to other relay neurons. They have short dendrites and short axons and are only found in the CNS.

Functions of the neuron

When a neuron is in a resting state, the inside of the cell is negatively charged relative to the outside. When a neuron is sufficiently activated by a stimulus, the inside of the cell becomes positively charged for a split second. This rapid switch from negative to positive charge is called *depolarisation* and it creates an electrical impulse (*action potential*, AP) that travels down the axon towards the terminal buttons of the neuron. This is sometimes called 'firing' an action potential.

The AP is generated once depolarisation reaches a certain threshold. It is always the same intensity, regardless of the size of the stimulus that originally generated it. If the threshold is not reached, there is no AP. Therefore, an action potential is an all-or-nothing event. Most myelinated neurons are capable of conducting up to 500 action potentials a second.

Synapses and neurotransmitters

Synaptic transmission

Neurons communicate with each other within groups known as *neural networks*. They do not physically touch, but are separated by a tiny gap called a *synaptic cleft*. So although signals within neurons are transmitted electrically, signals between neurons have to be transmitted chemically across the synapse. Therefore, synaptic transmission is a chemical process using biochemical substances called neurotransmitters. When the AP reaches the end of the neuron (the presynaptic terminal button) it triggers the release of neurotransmitter from tiny sacs called *synaptic vesicles*.

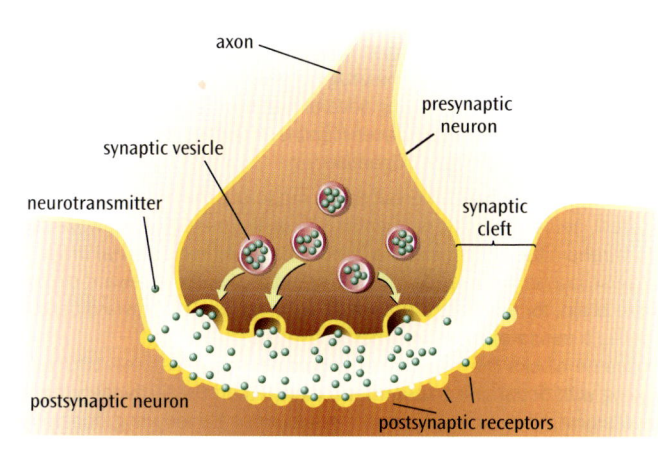

Neurotransmitters are chemicals that diffuse across the synapse to the next neuron in the chain. When the neurotransmitter molecules cross the gap, they fit into matching receptor sites on the postsynaptic neuron. There are different receptors for different neurotransmitters. The chemical signal carried by the neurotransmitters is converted back into an electrical signal in the postsynaptic neuron, which may fire another AP.

Neurotransmitter molecules that remain in the synapse are reabsorbed into the presynaptic neuron, usually being broken down first. This process is called *reuptake* and means the neurotransmitters can be used again.

Functions of neurotransmitters

Several dozen neurotransmitters have been identified in the human brain (as well as in the spinal cord and in some glands). Each neurotransmitter has its own specific molecular structure and fits perfectly into a specific type of postsynaptic receptor (like a key in a lock).

Neurotransmitters have specific functions. For instance, *acetylcholine* (ACh) is found where a motor neuron meets a muscle and upon its release will cause the muscle to contract.

Excitation and inhibition

Neurotransmitters fall into two main categories depending on their effect on neighbouring neurons. This can be either *excitatory* or *inhibitory*. For instance, the neurotransmitter *serotonin* causes inhibition in the postsynaptic neuron making the neuron more negatively charged and less likely to fire. In contrast, *dopamine* causes excitation of the postsynaptic neuron by increasing its positive charge and making it more likely to fire.

Summation

A postsynaptic neuron can receive inhibitory or excitatory inputs from the neural network. Firing depends on *summation* or 'adding together' of signals over time (temporal summation) or 'space' (spatial summation).

The excitatory and inhibitory influences are summed – if the net effect on the postsynaptic neuron is inhibitory then it is less likely to fire. If the net effect is excitatory the postsynaptic neuron is more likely to fire and, momentarily, the inside of the postsynaptic neuron becomes positively charged, depolarisation takes place and the action potential travels down the dendrite towards the cell body and then along the axon.

Gratuitous cute cat picture. Many behaviours are influenced by the activity of neurotransmitters at synapses, including sleep (even in cats), aggression and sexual behaviour. But neurotransmission can malfunction and contribute to behaviours often described as 'abnormal'. For instance, reuptake may be disrupted, leaving excessive quantities of neurotransmitter in the synapse. Receptors become less sensitive in an attempt to lessen the effects of neurotransmitter over-availability (this is called downregulation).

Apply it — Methods: Fatter and faster

Gemma is investigating the relationship between the diameter of motor neuron axons and the speed of their action potentials. The graph on the right shows her results.

Graph showing relationship between axon diameter and speed of action potentials.

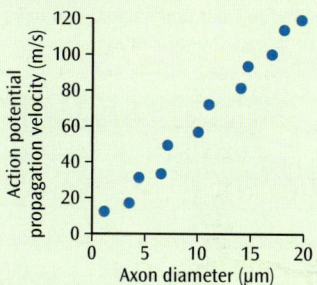

1. (a) Name the type of graph Gemma has used and explain why she has chosen it. (1)
   (b) State the relationship shown in Gemma's results. (1)
   (c) Explain what Gemma can conclude about the variables in her study from the graph. (2)
2. Using the graph, estimate the speed (velocity) associated with a diameter of 10 μm. (1)
3. (a) State the level of measurement of both variables. (1)
   (b) State the statistical test that Gemma should use. Justify your answer. (2)

Apply it — Concepts: Neil's diamonds

Neil is a participant in a study on vision in which tiny diamond flashes of light are changed until he notices them. There are three conditions: increasing the diameter of the light, increasing the brightness of the light or increasing the frequency of the flashes. In all cases there is a point at which Neil first notices the light changing (the 'threshold').

1. Explain why Neil does not see the lights at first, but then can at some point. (3)
2. Two common neurotransmitters in the retina are glutamate, which is excitatory and GABA, which is inhibitory. Explain the difference between these two types of neurotransmitter. (2)

Study tip

When answering a question on this topic, it often helps to add a diagram to express yourself clearly. But remember, a diagram is only a diagram, not an explanation, especially when you are describing processes such as synaptic transmission.

Check it

1. Define the term 'neurotransmitter' with an example. (2)
2. Describe the structure of a neuron. (4)
3. **Standard:** Evaluate the way in which biological psychology is able to explain individual differences between people (8)
4. **AS (Context):** Zhara is explaining how neurons work. She says to imagine lots of uprooted trees all lying in a line with the branches of each one nearly touching the roots of the next. There are some birds on the roots of each tree and sometimes they hop onto the branches of the next tree one by one, and sometimes all together. This makes the branches quiver.

   Discuss the accuracy of Zhara's explanation of how neurons work, using correct psychological terms. (8)

Chapter 3 Biological psychology
Effect of recreational drugs

The specification says...
3.1.2 The effect of recreational drugs on the transmission process in the central nervous system.

Key term
Recreational drugs – Drugs are biochemicals that have specific effects on the functioning of the body's systems. Drugs may be used for physiological purposes (e.g. antibiotics used to kill viruses) or for psychological purposes (e.g. antidepressants). Drugs for psychological treatments are called 'psychoactive' and affect transmission in the central nervous system (CNS), altering an individual's mental processes. A distinction is made between using such drugs for medical purposes (as in the case of antidepressants used to treat depression) and using drugs for enjoyment or leisure purposes (i.e. recreation).

Think Link
Individual differences
Genes and drug responses
It is well known that individuals vary widely in their responses to recreational drugs. This has most often been attributed to social and psychological factors, such as personality, motivation or peer group influences.

Genetic influences are also involved. Genes affect how sensitive or responsive an individual's nervous system is to recreational drugs, including the impact on CNS transmission (Bardo *et al.* 2013).

Dopamine has a central role in the effects of all recreational drugs. Drugs such as cocaine (see text) stimulate ❶ the *ventral tegmental area* (VTA) and ❷ the *nucleus accumbens* directly to produce more dopamine. The effect is enhanced because the VTA also stimulates the nucleus accumbens. The result is increased dopamine release into ❸ the *frontal cortex*.

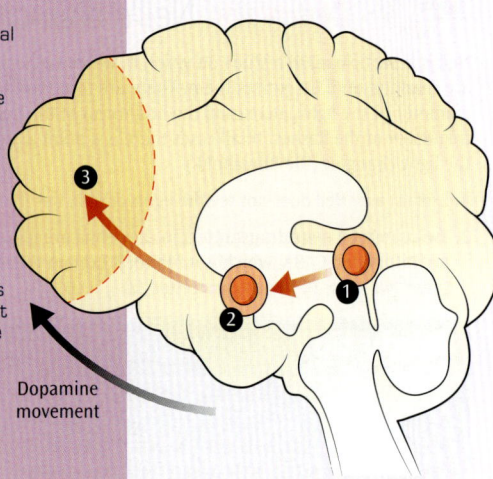

Dopamine movement

Ecstasy and serotonin
Most drugs also have additional effects on other aspects of neurotransmission. For example, MDMA (or 'ecstasy') is a CNS stimulant that blocks reuptake of *serotonin* at the synapse. But it also causes neurons to hugely increase their output of serotonin in the first place. These neurons are part of the brain's serotonin pathway that originates in the brainstem but spreads out into almost every other region, including the *frontal lobe* involved in higher-level processes. The activity of MDMA creates a 'double whammy' of serotonin enhancement – greater quantities are produced and made available in the synapse for binding to postsynaptic receptors.

Do you think MDMA is an agonist or antagonist drug? Explain your answer.

Recreational drugs and neurotransmission
Recreational drugs include stimulants, sedatives, hallucinogens and opioids. Each kind of drug 'operates' in a particular way, increasing or decreasing specific neurotransmitters at the synapse. We will focus on cocaine (a stimulant) and heroin (an opioid).

Cocaine
Cocaine has a stimulant effect on the central nervous system (CNS), especially on the neurons of the brain's main reward system (the *mesocorticolimbic pathway* which connects subcortical emotional brain centres with frontal areas). The drug achieves its effects by altering synaptic transmission involving several neurotransmitters, such as *noradrenaline*, *serotonin* and *acetylcholine*. However, its most profound impact is on the activity of *dopamine*.

The role of dopamine Different drugs moderate the effects of different neurotransmitters such as serotonin and GABA. However, the neurotransmitter dopamine is a special case. All recreational drugs increase dopamine release (directly or indirectly) in the reward centres of the brain, for example the *nucleus accumbens*. This 'reward centre' creates a sense of pleasure when activated.

Cocaine blocks the reuptake of dopamine (see pages 99–100) by binding with dopamine transporter molecules on the terminal buttons of the presynaptic neuron. These are responsible for recycling dopamine back into the neuron that produced it. As cocaine prevents this process, the synapse is flooded with surplus quantities of dopamine, all available for binding with postsynaptic receptors. This is probably the main cause of the euphoric 'high' associated with cocaine use.

Long-term effects After repeated cocaine use, dopamine receptors become *downregulated*. That is, fewer receptors are active – some are damaged and shut down, and the quantity of dopamine produced declines. This explains withdrawal, craving for the drug and the higher doses needed to get the same effects (tolerance).

Heroin
Heroin ('diacetylmorphine') has depressant effects on the CNS. It slows down CNS activity, including the activity of neurons involved in pain. This is why opiates are valued as analgesics (painkillers).

Heroin is usually injected intravenously and, once it reaches the brain, most of it is processed into a closely-related opioid called *morphine*. Morphine binds with a specific opioid receptor at the synapse (the μ (mu) receptor) found in the *cerebral cortex*, *limbic system* and *hypothalamus*.

The reason why such receptors exist for heroin/morphine is that the CNS has its own opioid system. *Endorphins* and *enkephalins* are produced by the body as natural painkillers, a system that heroin readily taps into. It binds with the receptors of the natural opioid system to massively enhance the natural response.

Agonist and antagonist Heroin is an *agonist* drug because it mimics the action of another natural biochemical. *Naloxone* is an *antagonist* that blocks opiate receptors (see facing page).

Long-term effects The long-term effects of repeated heroin use on neural transmission include downregulation. Regular use of heroin over time means that opioid receptors on postsynaptic neurons are constantly binding with morphine molecules, which desensitises them to the effects of the drug. This is the basis of tolerance.

You will have noticed that each of the drugs discussed above works in a different way. Some directly increase or decrease the amount of neurotransmitter produced by a neuron, others prevent reuptake of a neurotransmitter. Some block receptor sites to prevent the neurotransmitter from binding (antagonists), others mimic or increase the neurotransmitter's effects, for example by occupying and stimulating the postsynaptic receptor sites (agonists).

Choose a recreational drug that does not feature on this spread (e.g. LSD, cannabis, nicotine, 'legal highs'). Research how this drug affects transmission within the CNS.

Evaluation

Research supporting the role of dopamine

A strength is that the explanations are supported with research using non-human animals.

For instance, one commonly-used procedure involves deliberately damaging (lesioning) the *mesocorticolimbic pathway* in mice brains (Weinshenker and Schroeder 2007). This means neurons are unable to produce levels of dopamine normally associated with reward. When this is done the mice then fail to self-administer cocaine intravenously. This does not occur when the lesions are performed in other parts of the mouse brain.

This finding supports the view that cocaine's effects are due to the activity of dopamine in the brain's reward system.

Validity of non-human animal studies

A weakness is problems with using mainly non-human animal studies to understand drug effects on human CNS transmission.

The basic transmission processes in mammals are similar. But some differences arise because the human brain is more complex than the rat brain. For example, isolating the effects of just one neurotransmitter greatly oversimplifies the process. It is very unlikely that the complexity of recreational drugs effects on transmission can be explained by just one mode of action of a drug. The interactions of dopamine with other neurotransmitter systems (e.g. noradrenaline, serotonin, GABA) are not well understood.

This means that extrapolation from non-human animals to humans is risky and should be undertaken only very cautiously.

Competing argument Evidence of drug effects on CNS transmission comes from studies of humans as well. For example, Nora Volkow *et al.* (1997) used PET scans to track the activity of dopamine transporters during a cocaine-induced 'high'. They found that the extent to which cocaine occupied dopamine transporters correlated positively with the course of the subjective experience. In other words, subjective experience intensified as more dopamine transporters were occupied by cocaine and declined as they became less active. This supports the view that evidence from animal models is valid, as human studies produce similar results.

Application to better treatments for addiction

As our knowledge of drug effects on CNS transmission grows, more treatments for addiction become available.

For example, once heroin was identified as an agonist that binds to opiate receptors, other drugs were developed with a reverse mode of action. *Naloxone* is an antagonist drug that blocks opiate receptors and prevents heroin (more precisely morphine) from occupying them. Naloxone does not produce the rewarding euphoria associated with heroin use, so it can help manage the withdrawal process and reduce symptoms.

This is a treatment that developed from greater knowledge of the transmission effects of drugs.

EXTRA: Issues and debates

Research into recreational drugs is one example of how psychological knowledge can be used within society.

For example, a clearer understanding of how recreational drugs affect CNS functioning may lead to better treatments for addiction and help to discover more effective methods of preventing it. A controversial perspective is suggested by Celia Morgan *et al.* (2013) – that recreational drugs may have potential benefits (e.g. the pain-reducing effects of cannabis).

This highlights the valuable contribution that psychological research can make to addressing social issues, with benefits for individuals and wider society.

Balanced conclusion

Psychologists have learned a great deal about the neurology of recreational drugs, enough to establish the biological basis of addiction. However, the overall picture is one of highly complex interacting neurotransmission systems being affected by recreational drugs in ways that are not yet fully understood.

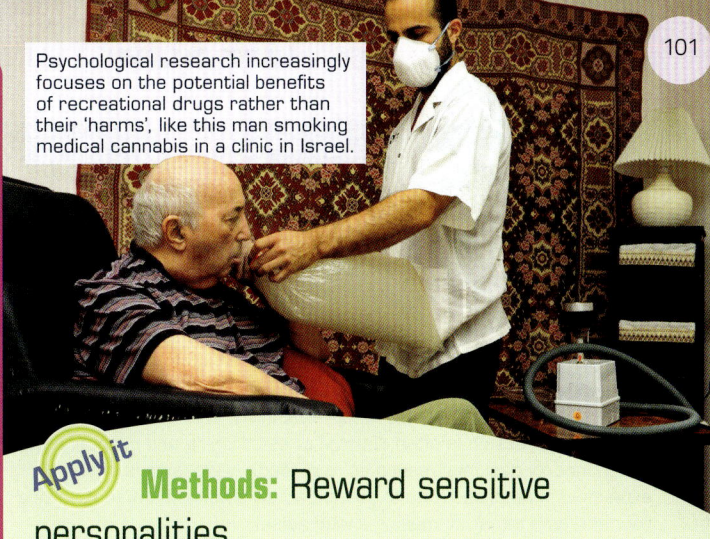

Psychological research increasingly focuses on the potential benefits of recreational drugs rather than their 'harms', like this man smoking medical cannabis in a clinic in Israel.

Apply it — Methods: Reward sensitive personalities

Dan is looking at personality and drug effects. He is measuring a personality trait called 'reward sensitivity' and subjective ratings of euphoria. He finds that the higher an individual's reward sensitivity score, the greater the effects of the drug *zapamine* on euphoria.

1. Name Dan's research method. (1)
2. Dan concludes that the findings show that some individuals respond more strongly to the immediate effects of *zapamine*.
   Explain why Dan cannot say that people's personalities determine the way that they respond to the drug. (2)
3. Dan also says that the findings suggest that some people are more likely to end up abusing *zapamine*.
   Explain why he could draw this conclusion from the findings. (2)

Apply it — Concepts: Snorine

Alysha has found a new drug and called it 'snorine' because it makes laboratory rats sleep. Snorine attaches to receptors for a neurotransmitter which makes us feel awake. She believes that snorine is an antagonist.

1. Explain why Alysha thinks the new drug is an antagonist. (2)
2. Explain what an agonist drug which attached to the same receptors would do. (2)
3. An enzyme normally breaks down the neurotransmitter in the synapse. Explain the possible effect of a drug that stopped the enzyme from working. (2)

Study tip

When writing about the effect of recreational drugs on the transmission process, focus on what they do at the synapse. Do not drift away from the question and describe how a drug changes a person's emotions or behaviour (such as feeling euphoric or losing balance). This information may be relevant depending on the wording of the question but the focus should be on neurotransmission.

Check it

1. Explain what is meant by a 'recreational drug'. (2)
2. Explain **one** similarity and **one** difference between the way that neurotransmitters and recreational drugs affect the transmission process in the central nervous system. (4)
3. **Standard:** Evaluate how similar the action of recreational drugs on the nervous system is to the normal functioning of the nervous system. (8)
4. **AL (I&D):** To what extent can psychological knowledge about recreational drugs be useful in society? (8)

The structure of the brain and aggression

Chapter 3 Biological psychology

The specification says...
3.1.3 The structure of the brain, different brain areas (e.g. prefrontal cortex) and brain functioning as an explanation of aggression as a human behaviour.

Key term

Aggression – Behaviour that is intended to cause injury. In humans this could be psychological as well as physical injury. In animals (including humans), aggression is often directed at establishing and maintaining dominance, or acquiring resources (e.g. food). Aggression is often expressed in ritualised form to prevent actual physical harm (e.g. raising your arm as a threat, or making a loud noise).

Think Link
Developmental psychology

Different rates of development

The two crucial brain areas/structures involved in control of aggression develop at different rates. The amygdala begins to develop relatively early, meaning a child rapidly becomes sensitive to environmental threats. But the prefrontal cortex, involved in control of impulsive behaviour in social contexts, does not mature until several years later (probably not until adolescence). The combination of rapid amygdala development and slower prefrontal cortex maturation is a 'double whammy' contributing to aggressive behaviour in childhood.

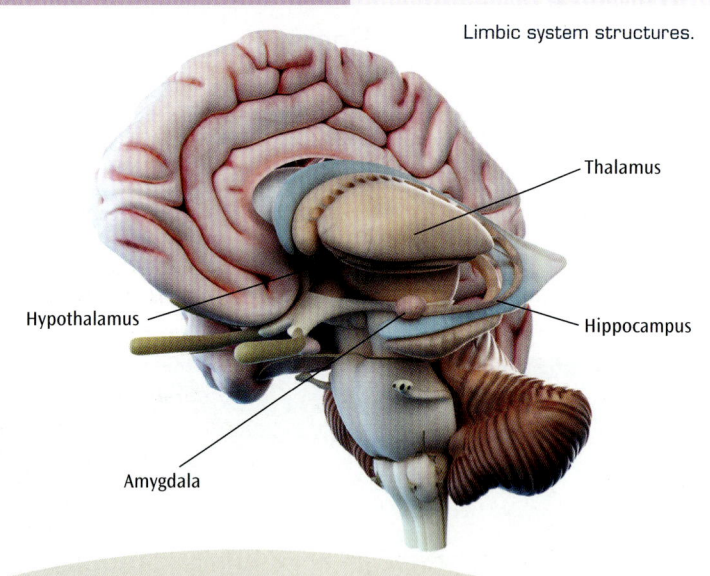

Limbic system structures.

- Thalamus
- Hypothalamus
- Hippocampus
- Amygdala

Stretch Challenge: The missing link

What is the underlying neural mechanism that explains the link between the amygdala and aggression?

Yu Gao *et al.* (2010) highlighted the amygdala's role in fear conditioning (you will learn about conditioning in chapter 4, see page 144). We learn throughout childhood that we should generally avoid behaving aggressively for fear of being punished. Most of us can detect the cues (e.g. angry facial expressions) that signal aggression may be likely. But some people with dysfunctions of the amygdala cannot process such cues. This disrupts normal fear conditioning and so these individuals appear to be 'fearless' and unusually aggressive.

Why is it beneficial to understand the brain mechanism underlying a behaviour?

Aggression and the brain

Brain structure: Role of the limbic system

Buried deep inside the brain is a collection of structures known as the *limbic system*. The first attempt to link limbic structures to emotional behaviours such as aggression was by James Papez (1937), later revised by Paul MacLean (1952). They identified the limbic system as comprising a number of structures (see diagram below left).

The key structure involved in aggression is the *amygdala*. This has a central role in how an organism assesses and responds to environmental threats and challenges. The reactivity of the amygdala in humans is proven to be an important predictor of aggressive behaviour.

For example, Emil Coccaro *et al.* (2007) studied people with intermittent explosive disorder (IED), a major feature of which is a tendency to outbursts of extreme reactive aggression (i.e. 'hot-blooded', impulsive). The participants' brains were scanned by fMRI while they viewed images of faces. IED participants showed high levels of amygdala activity when viewing images of angry faces, a response not found in non-IED controls.

This evidence of an association between amygdala reactivity and aggression is especially meaningful because an angry facial expression is an ecologically valid sign of threat (i.e. it exists in the real world).

Brain structure: Role of the prefrontal cortex

More recent research indicates that the amygdala does not operate in isolation in determining aggression. It appears to function in tandem with the *orbitofrontal cortex* (OFC). The OFC is a region of the *prefrontal cortex* just above the eye sockets (the orbits). It plays an important role in higher cognitive functions such as rational thinking and decision-making. It is thought to be involved in self-control, impulse regulation and inhibition of aggressive behaviours. In patients with psychiatric disorders that feature aggression, activity in the OFC is reduced, which disrupts its impulse-control function (Coccaro *et al.* 2007).

Adrian Raine *et al.* (1997) used PET scans to study murderers whose crimes included an overwhelming element of reactive aggression. They found greater glucose metabolism (a measure of activity) in the amygdala, but abnormally low metabolism in the prefrontal cortex (including the OFC), compared with a group of matched controls. We will be looking at this classic study in greater detail on page 110 of this chapter.

Brain function: Role of serotonin

Serotonin (as discussed on page 99) is a neurotransmitter with widespread inhibitory effects on transmission between neurons in the brain – it slows down and dampens neuronal activity. Normal levels of serotonin in the OFC are associated with a reasonable degree of behavioural self-control. Decreased serotonin may well disturb this link, reducing self-control and leading to more impulsive behaviours including aggression (Denson *et al.* 2012).

Matti Virkkunen *et al.* (1994) compared levels of a serotonin breakdown product (a metabolite called 5-HIAA) in the cerebrospinal fluid of violent impulsive and violent non-impulsive offenders. The levels were significantly lower in the impulsive offenders, who also suffered from more sleep irregularities. This is a particularly interesting finding because serotonin helps to regulate sleep patterns. Disturbance of sleep strongly implies some disruption of serotonin functioning.

Brain function: Role of dopamine

Dopamine is a neurotransmitter that has inhibitory effects in some areas of the brain and excitatory effects in others. It is involved in regulating motivated behaviour and our experience of reward.

Dopamine's main influence on aggression comes through its interaction with serotonin. According to Dongju Seo *et al.* (2008), serotonin underactivity (hypofunction) stimulates dopamine overactivity (hyperfunction) and both are linked with impulsivity and aggression. So serotonin hypofunction is the primary cause of impulsive aggression and dopamine hyperfunction makes an additional contribution.

Evaluation

Support from longitudinal research
A strength is some powerful research evidence for the role of the amygdala in aggression.

Dustin Pardini et al. (2014) identified 56 males who had been part of a study 20 years earlier, when they were 6 or 7 years old. Over the 20 years these men had consistently behaved aggressively, including being involved in serious criminal violence. Using fMRI brain scans, the researchers found a strong negative correlation between levels of aggression and amygdala volumes. The finding is particularly significant because it could not be explained by potential confounding variables (e.g. race, age, substance abuse) or by earlier levels of aggression, because these were all controlled in the study.

This is strong support for the influence of the amygdala, especially as it shows the explanation has predictive validity.

Correlational research
A weakness is that the research into neural influences on aggression is often correlational.

Typically, a study will find links between high levels of aggression and a brain function, dysfunction or structure, perhaps by using fMRI scans. There are good ethical reasons for conducting correlational research because experimental research would have to make people be aggressive. One alternative is to conduct animal studies, which raises other practical and ethical issues.

This means it is impossible to establish whether a particular structure or function/dysfunction is a cause or effect of aggressive behaviour, or whether a third variable is involved.

Competing argument Some researchers have attempted to overcome this problem by using drugs known to increase serotonin activity. For example, participants given *paroxetine* gave fewer and less intense electric shocks to others (Berman et al. 2009). This is evidence of a link between serotonin and aggression that goes beyond the usual correlational findings.

Application to understanding aggression
There are potential practical benefits to understanding neural influences on aggression.

For example, one goal of research is to discover a drug that affects the brain's serotonin system, reducing aggressive behaviour with minimal side effects. A category of serotonin agonist drugs called *serenics* (e.g. eltoprazine) has been found to have significant anti-aggressive effects in animals and humans (Verhoeven and Tuinier 2007).

This may be invaluable given that human aggression is at the root of so many personal, social and economic costs.

EXTRA: Issues and debates
A narrow focus on biological factors is reductionist.

The truth is that amygdala dysfunction (or serotonin hypofunction) is not an inevitable cause of aggression. Whether or not aggression occurs depends on many interacting risk factors, including social, psychological and environmental ones. These interact with a biological (e.g. genetic) predisposition to behave aggressively (called a diathesis). But the diathesis is not enough on its own to trigger aggression.

The problem with any reductionist explanation is that it rarely reflects the true complexity underlying the causes of aggression.

Balanced conclusion
There is good evidence for the role of brain structures in aggression, such as the amygdala. However, conclusions from such research are limited because we cannot be certain that brain structures actually cause aggression and also because other factors interact significantly in determining aggressive behaviour. This means that at best we can only conclude that brain structures contribute to aggression – control of aggression may be better served by looking at many factors all at once.

Spreading rumours about someone is an indirect form of aggressive behaviour often favoured by girls.

Apply it Methods: Fahim's fMRI
Fahim is using fMRI to monitor changing amygdala activity while 12 participants play an aggressive video game. Subjective aggression level is assessed by measuring how hard the participants hit a button that lights up and says, 'How do you feel?' every 60 seconds.

1. Identify the **two** co-variables in Fahim's study. (2)
2. Write a null hypothesis for Fahim's study. (2)
3. (a) Explain how Fahim could collect a stratified sample for his study. (2)
   (b) Explain **one** strength and **one** weakness of the stratified sampling technique in Fahim's study. (4)
4. Fahim conducts a Spearman test. His observed value of *rho* is .48 and he is using a significance level of $p \leq 0.05$. (See critical values table on page 200.)
   Explain whether Fahim should accept his null hypothesis. (2)

Apply it Concepts: Layla's life
Layla is aggressive and also shows other unusual behaviour patterns. Give different biological explanations for each of these patterns:

1. Layla gets into a rage if something goes wrong, rather than just getting a bit cross or calmly sorting it out. (2)
2. Layla sometimes gets confused and can't seem to make up her mind. Making choices in complex situations seems very difficult for Layla. (2)
3. As a child, Layla found it hard to understand what other people were thinking and she often took big risks. (2)
4. As Layla has got older, she has developed sleep problems. (2)

Study tip
When you are evaluating or assessing explanations/theories, remember to stick to evaluation points that are relevant to the explanations/theories – don't be tempted to stray into mentioning reliability or validity (which relate to studies not theories).

Check it
1. Explain the role of **one** brain area in aggression. [4]
2. Describe how brain function can explain aggression. [4]
3. **Standard:** Assess the usefulness of biological psychology in explaining individual differences in aggression. [8]
4. **AL (I&D/Synoptic):** Some people say biological and cognitive explanations of human behaviour are reductionist.
   To what extent would you consider this statement to be true? [12]

Evolution, natural selection and aggression

The specification says...
3.1.4 *The role of evolution and natural selection to explain human behaviour, including aggression.*

Key terms

Evolution – The changes in inherited characteristics in a biological population over successive generations.

Natural selection – The major process that explains evolution whereby inherited traits that enhance an animal's reproductive success are passed on to the next generation and thus 'selected', whereas animals without such traits are less successful at reproduction and their traits are not selected.

Sexual selection – An evolutionary explanation of partner preference. Attributes or behaviours that increase reproductive success are passed on and may become exaggerated over succeeding generations of offspring.

Think Link
Developmental psychology

Development and survival

The role of evolution in some aspects of development is obvious. It governs behaviours present at birth which enhance survival. For example, reflex blinking when an object approaches really fast helps survival by protecting the eyes.

Evolution also plays a part in the way we acquire behaviours during development. For example, in chapter 4 you will read about the role evolution has in our tendency to more readily learn to be afraid of things that were risky for our distant ancestors (page 145).

Evolution of bullying

Bullying is unquestionably an aggressive behaviour but has traditionally been viewed as maladaptive (e.g. the result of poor social skills). However, our evolutionary ancestors may have used bullying as an adaptive strategy to increase their chances of survival by promoting their own health and creating opportunities for reproduction.

Tony Volk et al. (2012) argue that the characteristics associated with bullying behaviour are attractive to the opposite sex. This behaviour would be naturally selected in males because bullying-associated characteristics are related to greater reproductive success.

Female bullying more often takes place within a relationship and is a method of controlling a partner – women use bullying behaviour to secure their partner's fidelity.

Give examples of bullying behaviours in males and females and explain how they might be associated with reproductive success.

The role of evolution to explain human behaviour

Evolution by natural selection

Evolution happens because genetic differences between organisms create variation. Such variation arises because genes from parents are combined and also due to spontaneous mutations (changes) in genes. Minor differences between individuals don't matter much when things are going well, but when life is hard those individuals who possess characteristics that help them to stay alive and reproduce are the ones who pass their genes on to the next generation. Individuals who cannot survive or fail to reproduce are not represented in future generations. Note that reproduction is the key – if an individual doesn't reproduce successfully the characteristics are not passed on.

The process of natural selection After many generations of small differences, there are individuals who are different from their predecessors. The process by which this occurs is **natural selection** – the 'choosing', done by the environment, of individuals who can survive and reproduce successfully. This idea, proposed by Charles Darwin (1859), is often called the 'survival of the fittest'. Fittest in this context refers to the characteristics that best match ('fit') the demands of the environment.

Natural selection, although Darwin didn't know it, is due to the survival of *genes*. Natural selection happens when there is competition for scarce resources (including reproductive mates). The genes which are most useful (because they produce characteristics which aid survival and reproduction) are retained in the population and over time become more frequent. The outcome of selection is adaptation – the (average) survivors are better suited to life in the current environment than the (average) predecessors.

Sexual selection

The influence of evolution acting on the success of reproduction (rather than survival) is called **sexual selection**. Sexual selection explains why some characteristics that might appear disadvantageous actually confer a survival advantage because the characteristics are attractive to potential mates. The classic example is the peacock's tail. This appears to be a huge handicap that threatens the male bird's survival – it is heavy, difficult to manoeuvre and is a highly visible target for predators. The advantage for the male is that his tail is attractive to females, because it is a sign of his genetic *fitness* – he carries such a burden and yet still manages to survive.

Other characteristics (especially behavioural ones) are adaptive because they provide an advantage over competitors for reproductive rights. For example, it pays for a male to be aggressive because it allows him to fend off potential reproductive rivals. The aggressive characteristics that allowed the animal to reproduce in the first place are passed on to offspring if they are genetically-determined and the genes that gave rise to the characteristics remain in the population.

Evolution and aggression

In human evolution, being able to protect yourself and your possessions (including partner and offspring) would all have enhanced survival and reproduction so would have been modified by natural selection.

Guarding your partner Mate retention strategies are the often aggressive behaviours men use to retain their partners and prevent them from 'straying'. According to Margo Wilson and Martin Daly (1996) direct guarding involves male vigilance over a partner's behaviour, for example checking who they've been seeing, coming home from work early, keeping tabs on their whereabouts, etc.

Guarding your offspring For example, human parents will direct aggressive acts against other people (or animals) that threaten their children. This aggression is adaptive because each child is a valuable genetic commodity. Aggression is a way for parents to protect their 'investment', increasing the offspring's reproductive chances later in life. Eric Steiner (2016) points out that protecting offspring is one of the very few situations in which females behave just as aggressively as males.

According to sexual selection theory, outward signs of success in a male may be attractive to females because choosing him as a partner is likely to enhance her reproductive success.

Evaluation

Explains gender differences

A strength of evolutionary theory is that it can explain why males are more aggressive than females.

Females who are cooperative are likely to be naturally selected because cooperation helps them protect themselves and their offspring as a group. Therefore, reduced aggression is selected in females. In contrast males who are aggressive are more likely to be naturally selected because they make better hunters. Evidence from studies of chimpanzees supports this pattern of gender differences (e.g. Manson and Wrangham 1991).

This is a strength because it explains gender differences in aggression today, and increases the validity of the theory.

Competing argument However, any evolutionary explanation is uncertain because it is impossible to test evolution directly. This is why most research is correlational, for example finding associations between mate retention behaviours and aggression. This method does not allow us to draw cause-and-effect conclusions. Because variables are just measured and not manipulated, correlational research can never rule out the effects of other factors on aggressive behaviour.

Cannot explain cultural differences

A weakness in evolutionary theory is there are differences between cultures in aggressive behaviour.

For example, amongst the !Kung San people of the Kalahari aggression is discouraged from childhood and is therefore rare. In contrast the Yanomami of Venezuela and Brazil have been described as 'the fierce people' – aggression appears to be an accepted behaviour to gain status in their structured society (Wolfgang and Ferracuti 1967).

These differences in aggression are not universal and suggest that innately determined behaviour can be outweighed by cultural norms.

Application to reproductive behaviour

Evolutionary theory can help us understand human relationships as it predicts that we should choose partners who will enhance our reproductive success.

David Buss (1989) found that, across 33 countries, males preferred younger, more attractive and chaste women, presumably because this enhances their reproductive success because such women are more likely to be fertile. Females preferred older, wealthier and ambitious or hard-working men, which is likely to enhance their reproductive success because their children are well-supported.

This supports evolutionary theory because it shows that the predictions from the theory are upheld by evidence.

EXTRA: Issues and debates

The use of fossils as evidence for evolution illustrates psychology as a science.

Sandrine Ladevèze et al. (2011) reported a fossil find of a group of extinct marsupials which showed that the males were much bigger than the females. This size difference demonstrated the existence of male–male competition (also called *intra-sexual selection*). This is because bigger males had an advantage in an aggressive competition for reproductive rights, and were more likely to be reproductively successful, passing on the genes that made them bigger to the next generation of males.

This shows how an objective scientific approach makes studying the evolution of aggressive behaviour possible.

Balanced conclusion

While there is no doubt that adaptive behaviours evolve, and that this affects human behaviour, finding objective evidence is difficult. However, what makes humans special is their complex behaviour and this means it is difficult to disentangle the effects of natural selection and *cultural* evolution – i.e. the extent to which the behaviours 'passed on' from generation to generation are the product of *social* rather than biological influences.

Apply it Methods: Evolutionary sat-nav

Cross-cultural studies can demonstrate the evolutionary roots of a behaviour. In one study men and women in the USA and Hungary were compared in terms of their preferred way-finding strategies.

Table showing mean cross-cultural preference ratings for different way-finding strategies.

Way-finding strategy	Nationality	Mean preference rating for men	Mean preference rating for women
Using landmarks	American	29.32	25.23
	Hungarian	28.83	25.78
Using routes	American	21.22	23.78
	Hungarian	21.65	22.07

1. The researchers used a questionnaire to test participants' preferences for using route-based and landmark-based wayfinding strategies. Write a closed question that could be used to assess preference for using landmarks. (1)
2. The gender differences were significant at $p \leq 0.001$.
   (a) Explain what is meant by a significance level of $p \leq 0.001$. (1)
   (b) Explain whether you would be more likely to make a Type I or a Type II error at $p \leq 0.001$ than at $p \leq 0.01$. (2)
3. (a) Explain how **one** result above could support evolution. (2)
   (b) Explain how this result may not support evolution. (2)

Apply it Concepts: Book brawls

Cali watches other students in the library. They often build a 'wall' around themselves with piles of books and bags. If someone walks by and picks up a book from their pile, some of the students get possessive and aggressive.

Use evolutionary theory to explain the behaviour that Cali sees in the library. (5)

Study tip

The explanation of evolution in psychology is exactly the same as you may have learned in science, except that here we are applying it to behaviours rather than structures.

Check it

1. Explain what is meant by 'natural selection'. (2)
2. Many animals protect their offspring. Use evolution to explain this behaviour. (2)
3. **Standard:** Evaluate evolution as an explanation for aggression in humans. (8)
4. **AS (Synoptic):** Developmental psychologists are interested in the ways in which we change over the life span.

   Evaluate ways in which biological psychology and the learning theories might explain developmental differences. (12)

Freud's psychodynamic explanation of aggression

The specification says...

3.1.5 Biological explanation of aggression as an alternative to Freud's psychodynamic explanation, referring to the different parts of the personality (id, ego, superego), the importance of the unconscious, and catharsis.

Sigismund Schlomo Freud (1856–1939)

Key terms

Unconscious – The part of the mind that we are unaware of but which continues to direct much of our behaviour.

Id – The part of the personality driven by the pleasure principle, which functions only in the unconscious and is made up of selfish aggressive instincts that demand immediate gratification.

Ego – The 'reality check' that balances the conflicting demands of the id and the superego.

Superego – The moralistic part of the personality which represents the ideal self – how we ought to be.

Catharsis – The process of releasing pent-up psychic energy.

Think Link
Individual differences

Personality and aggression

Freud argued that we develop in childhood through a series of stages which each present several psychological challenges. Some people deal with these challenges more successfully than others, and if we fail to overcome a challenge, we become 'fixated' or stuck in one stage, which affects our adult personality.

For example, in their first year of life children pass through the oral stage. Fixation here can result in being verbally aggressive. This means we all grow up to have different personalities. So individual differences in aggressive behaviour can be explained by the varying degrees of success we have in negotiating the stages of childhood development.

Freud's explanation of aggression

The unconscious and aggression

For Sigmund Freud, the **unconscious** is the part of the mind containing thoughts, memories and desires of which we are unaware. He described it using the metaphor of an iceberg – the unconscious is the largest part, below the surface of the water and hidden from view. But the unconscious is far from being a passive and static storage container where nothing happens. It is an active processor of its contents, requiring a lot of psychic energy to keep them unconscious.

One of the key influences of the unconscious is its role as the origin of powerful aggressive instincts. Even if we are not thinking aggressive thoughts (i.e. ones that we are conscious of), our behaviour may still be influenced by aggressive urges that are 'hidden' in the unconscious.

Personality and aggression

According to Freud's tripartite theory, personality is made up of three components.

The id and the pleasure principle The **id** exists from birth and is the most primitive element, contained entirely in the unconscious mind. It is the origin of the energy that motivates all of our behaviour, including aggression. It contains instincts, impulses and drives that are socially unacceptable, including aggressive drives. The id obeys the *pleasure principle* – it demands the immediate gratification of its desires, with no consideration of other factors, such as social reality. This makes aggression unavoidable and inevitable. As we cannot eradicate it, we should instead direct it. This is the role of the ego.

The ego and the reality principle The **ego** is the logical, rational and mostly conscious part of personality that begins developing shortly after birth. It follows the *reality principle* – it is the interface between the unrealistic desires of the id and social reality (e.g. the expectations other people have of us). So the ego does not fulfil the id's aggressive urges directly (e.g. by punching someone who annoys you). Instead, it satisfies the id by fulfilling its urges indirectly and symbolically (e.g. by fantasising about violence). The ego has no moral sense – it does not 'judge' the id, but tries to control and direct its urges.

The superego The **superego** fulfils the 'moral' role and emerges later in development, around the age of about 5 or 6 years. It represents our conscience and moral sense of right and wrong, as well as the ideal image we have of ourselves and would like to live up to. Because aggression is destructive, the superego opposes the id's aggressive drive through guilt and shame when we fail to meet the highest moral standards. The superego is just as irrational and punishing in its demands as the id.

Catharsis and aggression

Aggression is an instinctive drive that can be satisfied, according to Freud, by **catharsis** – expressing aggression (e.g. venting anger) releases psychic energy, reduces the aggressive drive and makes further aggression less likely (hence phrases in everyday language such as 'letting off steam').

Preventing catharsis creates a build-up of energy which will eventually produce a destructive aggressive outburst directed either inwards (e.g. self-harm, suicide) or outwards (e.g. a violent assault) – an undesirable outcome.

Freud believed that direct expression of the impulse in aggressive behaviour was most beneficial. However, catharsis can be achieved in a variety of indirect ways, for example:

- *Displacement* is where aggression towards one person (e.g. your boss or 'the government') is redirected against a less powerful and more available substitute (e.g. a younger sibling, an animal or even an object such as a pillow).
- Observing others behaving aggressively (e.g. in violent films).

Stretch Challenge
Eros and Thanatos

Freud originally believed that aggression was not inevitable because governing all behaviour is the life instinct (which, drawing upon Greek mythology, he called *Eros*). So he believed that our natural tendency is towards enhancing and sustaining life (especially our own), and aggression only occurs when Eros is blocked or frustrated.

However, Freud became pessimistic after the horrors of the First World War, which could hardly be explained in terms of the thwarting of the life instinct. He then introduced his opposing drive, an anti-*Eros* force, the death instinct (which he called *Thanatos*).

Thanatos is directed towards annihilation, a state of 'non-being'. It is an instinctive drive to destroy life, including your own. Eros and Thanatos are constantly locked together in a powerful conflict. To prevent the death instinct threatening the self, psychological mechanisms (e.g. displacement) try to direct it outwards. This protects your own self, but unfortunately leads indirectly to acts of aggression against others.

Explain how Thanatos might relate to the roles of the id and the ego in aggression.

Evaluation

Explains different types of aggression

A strength of Freud's theory is that it can explain the traditional distinction between 'hot-blooded' and 'cold-blooded' aggression.

Hot-blooded aggression is impulsive, angry and has no purpose other than its own satisfaction. This is the domain of the id. It represents a failure of the ego's normal function of redirecting the id's aggressive impulses. Cold-blooded aggression is deliberate, 'rational' and instrumental (i.e. it has a purpose). It is the outcome of the ego's successful control of id impulses.

This matches the reality of the behaviour and gives us confidence in the validity of the theory.

Aggression is not cathartic

A weakness is that 'letting off steam' may lead to more aggression rather than less.

Brad Bushman (2002) made 600 college students angry by getting a confederate to criticise an essay each had written. One group of randomly-allocated students was then allowed to vent their anger by hitting a punchbag while thinking about the confederate. Bushman found that these students blasted the confederate with the loudest and longest noises in a subsequent task compared with control participants who did not vent anger.

This is the opposite of the finding predicted by Freud's theory. According to Bushman, '…venting to reduce anger is like using gasoline to put out a fire – it only feeds the flame'.

Competing argument However, there is evidence that expressing anger can be cathartic. Jennifer Graham et al. (2008) suggest we should *rant* rather than vent. Ranting (especially in writing) involves consideration of the reasons why one is angry. Venting is uncontrolled expression of anger, but ranting allows the individual to gain control over their feelings and avoid aggressive behaviour.

Application to reducing aggression

Catharsis can be used practically to prevent a build-up of destructive aggressive energy.

People can build into their lives harmless ways of expressing anger. These are based on Freudian concepts such as displacement, for example hitting an object rather than a person. More formally, catharsis could feature in therapy. In Freudian psychoanalysis, catharsis can be achieved just by bringing unconscious and 'forgotten' memories into the conscious mind.

This means that Freud's theory offers a practical solution to reduce aggressive behaviour with potential benefits for individuals and wider society.

EXTRA: Issues and debates

Freud's theory and biological explanations can be compared in terms of their similarities.

Both Freud and the biological approach share the view that aggression is instinctive and therefore innate. For Freud, this takes the form of an unconscious impulse originating in the id. In the biological approach, aggression is linked to brain structures and functions and hormonal activities that are mostly genetic in nature. The evolutionary approach to aggression highlights its crucial survival function. Freud suggests that directing aggression away from the self towards others promotes self-preservation (see Eros and Thanatos in the Stretch and challenge on the facing page).

This shows that two very different approaches to explaining a behaviour can nevertheless share some of the same assumptions, increasing the validity of the view (in this case) that aggression has a survival function.

Balanced conclusion

There are some strengths of Freud's approach, in its ability to explain types of aggression and its application of catharsis. However, Freud's concepts of id, catharsis, etc. are not accepted within a scientific, biological approach to understanding aggression. Freud's theory is also untestable because these concepts are so vague they are impossible to measure. This breaches a central requirement of science, which fundamentally underpins the biological approach.

The benefits of catharsis or 'letting off steam' to reduce aggression are strongly disputed.

Apply it Methods: The id and the superego

Lotty believes that there will be a correlation between the strength of the id and the weakness of the superego. She thinks that greedier people, with a more selfish id, are less helpful (they have a poor social conscience).

1. Explain the type of correlation Lotty expects. (1)
2. (a) Describe **one** way to operationalise 'greediness'. (1)
   (b) Describe **one** way to operationalise 'helpfulness'. (1)
3. Write a null hypothesis for Lotty's study. (1)
4. Lotty obtains a numerical score on each variable, greediness and helpfulness, for 30 participants.
   Identify which statistical test Lotty should use for her correlation. (1)

Apply it Concepts: Noisy neighbours

Gregory is 74. He wants to punch his neighbours – their children are screaming again. Instead he slams cupboard doors as he makes his tea. Waiting for the kettle to boil an idea pops into his head. He could play his radio loudly all night. That would serve them right. Suddenly, Gregory feels terrible, thinking back to raising his own family and the flimsy bedsit walls – it must have been just as bad for his neighbours.

1. Describe the **three** parts of the personality according to Freud. (3)
2. Explain how **two** of the parts of the personality relate to the context above. (2)
3. Explain how catharsis relates to the context above. (2)

Study tip

You might be asked to compare Freud's theory of aggression with any of the biological explanations of aggression. Remember, the command term *compare* always requires at least one similarity and one difference.

Check it

1. Describe how Freudian theory can account for aggressive behaviour. (5)
2. Two 14-year-old girls, Flis and Liv, have just moved into the same street. Flis is much more aggressive than Liv.
   Explain how ideas from the biological psychology topic could account for this difference in the girls' development. (6)
3. **Standard:** Assess Freudian theory as an explanation of aggression. (8)
4. **AS (Synoptic/Context):** Carl and Jess are both aggressive. Carl's dad is violent and Carl hits other children to get sweets. Jess always looks sad but Carl doesn't know why. He thinks something happened to her when she was young.
   Evaluate Freud's psychodynamic explanation and learning theory explanations of Carl and Jess' behaviour. (12)

Role of hormones in human behaviour

The specification says...

3.1.6 The role of hormones (e.g. testosterone) to explain human behaviour such as aggression.

Key term

Hormones – Chemical substances that circulate in the bloodstream and only affect target organs. They are produced by glands in large quantities but disappear quickly. Their effects are very powerful and widespread in the body.

The *endocrine system* works together with the nervous system to control vital bodily functions. It consists of several glands located throughout the body, as illustrated below. The key gland is the *pituitary*, located beneath the *hypothalamus* in the brain (although it is not structurally part of the brain). The pituitary is often called the 'master gland', because it controls the activities of all the other glands of the endocrine system.

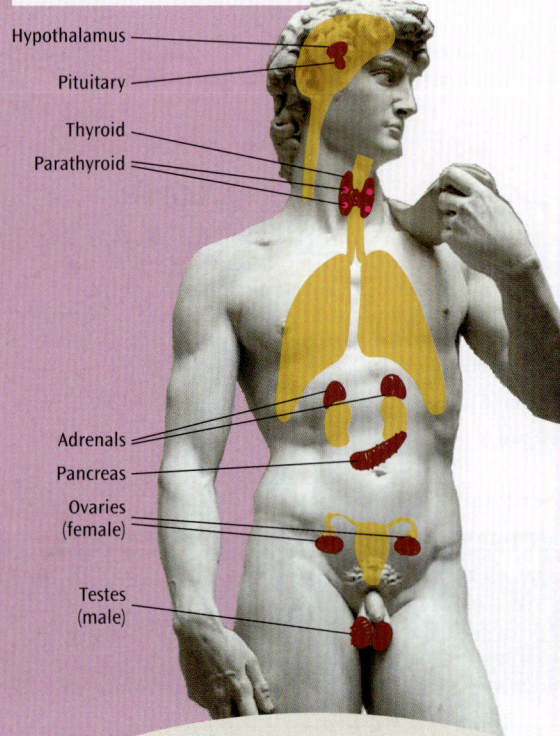

- Hypothalamus
- Pituitary
- Thyroid
- Parathyroid
- Adrenals
- Pancreas
- Ovaries (female)
- Testes (male)

Stretch & Challenge

Hormones and empathy

Empathy is the ability to understand the world from another person's point of view. It is at the root of behaviours such as social support – if you can empathise with, say, someone who is depressed, you are more likely to help them.

Levels of the hormone *oxytocin* (secreted by the pituitary gland) are closely associated with empathy. For example, a study by Katie Daughters et al. (2016) showed that people with endocrine system disorders that reduce oxytocin (e.g. cranial diabetes insipidus) also have low levels of empathy compared with healthy controls.

Can you think of any real-life applications of this research?

Hormones and aggression

Research with humans and other animals has found that several **hormones** directly or indirectly regulate aggressive behaviour.

Hormones

Endocrine glands manufacture a variety of hormones and secrete them directly into the bloodstream. Hormones are biochemical messengers. They are transported around the body and affect any cells that have receptors for particular hormones, including target organs and other glands. Hormones act much more slowly than the nervous system but have widespread and powerful effects.

Each hormone affects certain target organs or cells. For example, the *adrenal glands* secrete the hormones *adrenaline* and *noradrenaline*, which affect cells in organs throughout the body (e.g. the heart). They have a crucial role in the fight-or-flight response to perceived stressors (e.g. by increasing heart rate), helping to fuel the aggressive response that may be needed to respond to a threat.

Role of testosterone

When seeking an explanation for aggression, psychologists have focused on the male sex hormone *testosterone* because of the common observation that males are generally more aggressive than females. This hormone also has a role in regulating social behaviour through its influence on areas of the brain implicated in aggression.

Animal studies (e.g. Giammanco et al. 2005) have demonstrated that experimental increases in testosterone are related to more aggressive behaviour in the males of several species. The converse is also true, with reductions in aggression accompanying decreases in testosterone as a result of castration (removal of testicles).

Some evidence for a similar association in humans comes from studies of prison populations (for example violent offenders). Mairead Dolan et al. (2001) found a positive correlation between testosterone levels and aggressive behaviours in a sample of 60 male offenders in UK maximum security hospitals. These men mostly had personality disorders (such as *psychopathy*) and histories of impulsively violent behaviour.

Dual-hormone hypothesis

Hormonal causes of aggression are much more complex than the role of a single hormone implies. One theory highlights the role of a second hormone – cortisol – secreted by the adrenal glands to protect the body against the effects of stress. This suggests there is an interaction between the systems responsible for regulating aggression and the stress response.

Justin Carré and Pranjal Mehta (2011) claim that high levels of testosterone lead to aggressive behaviour only when levels of cortisol are low. When cortisol is high, testosterone's influence on aggression is blocked. A study by Arne Popma et al. (2007) of adolescent males found exactly this association in relation to direct physical aggression.

So according to the dual-hormone hypothesis, the combined activity of testosterone and cortisol may be a better predictor of human aggression than either hormone alone.

Female aggression

Although testosterone levels in females are (on average) lower than in males, female aggressive behaviour may still be enhanced by this hormone. There is some evidence for this view (see Evaluation on facing page).

However, Christoph Eisenegger et al. (2011) found that women given a dose of testosterone behaved more generously and sociably in a lab-based negotiating game. The testosterone–aggression link in females appears to be more complex than it is in males, suggesting that non-biological factors (e.g. related to gender roles) may be important.

Think Link
Developmental psychology

Prenatal influences

The primary influence of testosterone on aggression may occur not in childhood, adolescence or adulthood but prenatally. Embryos that eventually develop to become males are exposed to higher levels of testosterone in the womb than those that become females. It is thought that exposure to testosterone has profound effects on brain development, and this may at least partly explain postnatal differences in aggressive behaviour between the sexes. This is further evidence of the causal link between hormones and behaviour.

Depo-Provera is a brand name of *medroxyprogesterone acetate*, and is most commonly used as a contraceptive injection. It has also been used to reduce aggressive and sexual behaviour in male sex offenders because of its anti-testosterone properties.

Evaluation

Research support

A strength is evidence of testosterone effects in females.

James Dabbs and Marian Hargrove (1997) measured testosterone in the saliva of 87 female inmates of a maximum security prison. They found that the degree of criminal violence used by these women was positively correlated with testosterone level. Testosterone also correlated with the extent of the women's aggressive dominance within the prison.

The aggression–testosterone link so often found in male prisoners was replicated in this study of females, increasing the validity of the association.

Competing argument Many studies of hormonal influences on human aggression are correlational, including the one above. This is a sensible methodology to use for ethical and practical reasons, however we cannot establish a causal relationship. For instance, elevated testosterone may be the outcome of aggression, or both may be the result of changes in another hormone.

Measuring testosterone

A weakness is that it is difficult to determine testosterone levels.

This is partly because the concept of 'testosterone level' is more complex than it might at first appear. Psychologists distinguish between *baseline* and *fluctuating* testosterone. Baseline is a person's 'usual' level of testosterone and is relatively stable across days, weeks and even months. But testosterone also fluctuates from one social encounter to another. Justin Carré et al. (2011) argue that baseline testosterone plays a less important role in human aggression than it does in animals. However, baseline is often used in human research (e.g. violent prisoners).

This means that the baseline measure used in many studies may not provide a valid indicator of testosterone level in relation to aggression.

Application to controlling aggression

Understanding the effects of hormones on aggression could lead to real practical benefits.

For example, if aggression is chemically controlled it should be possible to manufacture a drug that influences the hormonal mechanism and reduces aggressive behaviour, preferably without widespread effects on bodily systems and behaviours. For example, Barry Maletzky et al. 2006 found that a testosterone-lowering drug called *Depo-Provera* reduced levels of sexually aggressive behaviour in some offenders.

As there is a close link between aggression and some serious crimes, anti-testosterone drugs may have positive consequences for individuals, communities and whole societies.

EXTRA: Issues and debates

This area of research illustrates the issue of reductionism.

Explaining a behaviour in terms of basic biological units such as hormones means we may lose sight of the 'bigger picture'. We have already seen that the effects of one hormone (testosterone) can be modified by another (cortisol) in response to stressful events.

This demonstrates that the extent to which hormones influence aggression very much depends on how we perceive the social context (which is a psychological factor).

Balanced conclusion

There is certainly a range of evidence to support the link between high testosterone and aggression (even if there are methodological issues). But the popular view of the testosterone-fuelled rampaging male (usually) is too simplistic. Rather than causing aggression directly, testosterone interacts with other hormones and the nervous system to *predispose* the individual to aggressive behaviour. Whether or not aggression occurs depends on additional psychological and environmental factors.

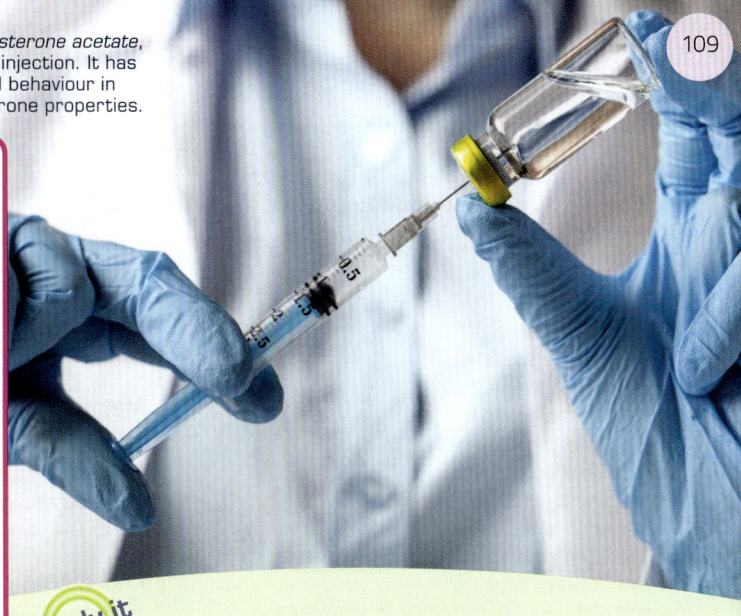

Apply it Methods: Shout to shoot

Jill is conducting a laboratory experiment to study whether levels of cortisol affect aggression. She records participants' cortisol level at the start of a violent game and uses the number of opponents they 'kill' as the measurement of aggression during the game. Jill divides the participants into 'high', 'medium' and 'low' cortisol levels and works out an average aggression score for each group.

1. Describe the independent variable (IV). (2)
2. Describe the dependent variable (DV). (2)
3. Explain **one** participant variable that should be controlled in this experiment. (2)
4. (a) Explain **one** other variable that should be controlled in this experiment. (2)
   (b) Describe how this variable could be controlled. (1)
5. Write a non-directional (two-tailed) hypothesis for this experiment. (2)

Apply it Concepts: Not-so-friendly neighbours

Carl and Liam are both 15 years old and are neighbours. Carl is more aggressive than Liam.

1. Explain how differences in hormones could account for the difference in the behaviour of Carl and Liam. (5)
2. Explain **one** way in which Carl's behaviour could be managed. (2)
3. Hailey lives next door to Liam and is also 15.
   Explain why Hailey may differ in her aggression level compared with either Carl or Liam. Use a different reason from the one you used in question 1. (2)

Study tip

You can use other explanations of aggression, such as evolution or the brain, as 'competing arguments', i.e. to provide alternative explanations when evaluating the role of hormones.

Check it

1. Describe the role of hormones in the human body. (4)
2. Describe how **one** named hormone can explain **one** named human behaviour. (4)
3. **Standard:** Assess how far hormones can explain developmental differences in aggression. (8)
4. **AL (I&D/Synoptic):** To what extent are biological psychology and learning theories on the 'nature' side of the nature–nurture debate? (12)

… Chapter 3 Biological psychology

Classic study: Raine et al. (1997)

The specification says…
3.3.1 Raine et al. (1997) Brain abnormalities in murderers indicated by positron emission tomography.

Adrian Raine started out as an airline accountant with British Airways, but then did a degree in psychology. His first job was as a prison psychologist in top-security prisons in England. Then, in 1987, he emigrated to the US were he is now Professor of Criminology, Psychology and Psychiatry at the University of Pennsylvania.

He has been involved in the Mauritius Child Health project which, in contrast to this study, identified the importance of environmental factors.

Think Link
Individual differences

Brain structure and function
Brain scan studies measure the average activity of brain areas across many people. This technique can obscure some important individual differences in brain structure and function. There are lots of characteristics (other than whether someone is a murderer or not) that differ between people and can influence (or are influenced by) brain function. There is some evidence for this in the study because Raine et al. found that past experiences of head injury had an effect on the activity of some brain areas.

Stretch & Challenge

Double dissociations
One of the study's findings was a powerful phenomenon called a *double dissociation*. The researchers found evidence linking violence with dysfunctions of specific brain areas. These areas were well-known through previous research (e.g. the amygdala, frontal cortex, hippocampus, etc.). Murderers and non-murderers differed significantly in brain activity in these areas.

But Raine et al. also found no significant differences between murderers and non-murderers in the activity of other areas of the brain. These areas were not linked with violence in previous research (e.g. the caudate, putamen, etc.).

This is a classic double dissociation, two complementary findings that support each other. In this case, brain areas linked to violence did differ between the two groups, PLUS brain areas *not* linked to violence did *not* differ between the groups.

Explain why a double dissociation is especially strong evidence of a link between aggression and the brain.

Brain abnormalities in murderers

Aim
Adrian Raine, Monte Buchsbaum and Lori LaCasse (1997) wanted to use brain scanning technology to identify brain impairments in people charged with murder who had pleaded not guilty by reason of insanity (NGRI). The researchers hypothesised that brain scans would show dysfunctions in areas linked in previous research to violence – the *prefrontal cortex*, *angular gyrus*, *amygdala*, *hippocampus*, *thalamus* and *corpus callosum*.

Method
The study looked at differences between two groups – 41 murderers and 41 non-murderers. The independent variable was murderer or non-murderer. Participants are not assigned to these conditions and therefore this is not a true experiment. A matched pairs design was used. The dependent variable was glucose metabolism (i.e. activity) in specific brain areas.

Procedure
The experimental group consisted of 39 men and two women charged with murder or manslaughter in California, USA. Some had been referred to the University of California, Irvine to be assessed for a defence of not guilty by reason of insanity (NGRI). The participants were free from all medication in the two weeks up to their brain scan, as confirmed by urine tests.

The murderers were matched on sex, age and ethnicity with a control group of non-murderers. The control participants had a physical examination and a psychiatric interview. None of them were taking medication and none had a history of psychiatric illness (except for six control participants diagnosed with schizophrenia and who thus were also matched on this characteristic).

Each participant underwent a PET scan of their brain. They were injected with a radioactive tracer to 'light up' brain metabolism on the scanner. Each then completed a continuous performance task (CPT) which involved identifying targets on a screen and pressing a button during a 32-minute period after the injection. The purpose of the task was to encourage uptake of the radioactive tracer in the areas of the brain that the researchers wished to investigate.

The PET scan was conducted immediately after the 32-minute period. The scan took 10 images ('slices') through the brain at 10 mm intervals.

Findings
Cortical regions Murderers had significantly lower glucose metabolism (i.e. less activity) than controls in the following cortical regions: lateral and medial *prefrontal areas*, left *angular gyrus*, and left and right *superior parietal areas*. Murderers showed higher metabolism than controls in the *occipital lobe*, a brain area not previously linked to violence.

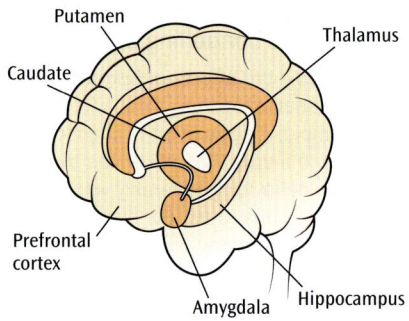

The subcortical areas of the brain lie in the centre of the brain surrounded by the cortex.

Subcortical regions Murderers had lower glucose metabolism than controls in the following subcortical regions – *corpus callosum*, left *amygdala*, and left *medial temporal lobe* (including the *hippocampus*) as indicated in previous research. Murderers had greater activity in the right *amygdala*, the right *medial temporal lobe* and the right *thalamus* (not previously implicated in violent behaviour).

Conclusions
The hypothesis was supported. The findings showed that murderers pleading NGRI have different brain activity from people who are not violent offenders. The murderers had impaired functioning in areas of the brain previously identified as involved with violent behaviour.

The researchers concluded that dysfunctions of a single brain area *cannot* explain violent behaviour *per se*, and certainly not in a simplistic cause-and-effect manner. The most likely explanation is that networks of interacting brain areas are functionally impaired. These impairments create a predisposition to violence that is only expressed in behaviour when social, environmental and psychological conditions are 'right'.

Raine et al. also concluded that we should be very cautious in interpreting the findings because there are other brain areas known to be involved in violence that they were unable to scan. They acknowledge that their study cannot give us a complete explanation of the neurophysiology of violence for this reason. However, the study is valuable because it provides useful preliminary evidence and signposts several directions for future research.

Evaluation

Experimental control

A strength is that there was a high degree of control in the study.

For example, participants were matched across the experimental and control groups on three potentially confounding variables. Standardised procedures were also used to control other variables (e.g. the same CPT was used with all participants for a standard 32 minutes). The PET scans followed the same well-established protocol so that the experience of the procedure would have been identical for all participants.

This means the study had high internal validity as potentially confounding variables were controlled.

Competing argument A key element was not controlled – the participants were not randomly allocated to the experimental or control groups. Matching was used to partly overcome this limitation, but the matching was not thorough. Failure to match on some variables may have confounded some of the results. For example, Raine et al. acknowledged that a history of head injury (in 23 murderers) may have explained differences in corpus callosum activity between the two groups.

Inappropriate PET scanning technique

A weakness is that the PET scanning technique may have given misleading results.

The technique scanned the brain in 10 mm slices relative to what is known as the *canthomeatal line*. This is an imaginary line from the outer corner (canthus) of the eye to the middle of the ear. This line is known to vary significantly between individuals (e.g. different sizes and positions of ears), which makes it hard to locate precisely the different brain areas under study.

This is a limitation because it reduces the internal validity of the study and casts some doubt on the accuracy of the findings.

Application to understanding biological evidence

One potential application is to be cautious about biological evidence.

On the face of it this research appears to suggest that particular brain structures can be identified that cause aggression and thus aggression can be 'treated' by changing biological structures through medication or surgery. However, Raine et al. take great pains to argue that their findings do not show that such treatment would be justified because the brain structures offer only a partial explanation.

Therefore, this research is important in identifying what biological evidence does and does not tell us.

EXTRA: Issues and debates

Raine et al.'s research is highly socially sensitive.

This is because it has serious implications for how society responds to aggressive criminal behaviour and deals with issues of crime and punishment. It provokes deep concerns about the nature of criminal responsibility and even free will. For instance, the research raises the possibility that murderers may not be entirely responsible for their crimes because a brain dysfunction (which they have no control over) contributes to their behaviour.

Raine's area of research (which he calls neurocriminology) raises profound ethical questions because its ultimate goal is to reliably predict who is likely to commit violent crimes.

Balanced conclusion

The researchers are very moderate in their claims for their findings – they acknowledge the methodological limitations of their study and resist the temptation to attribute violent behaviour to biological factors alone. Even so, it is clear from the findings that brain dysfunctions play a potentially key role in violence (at least in specific groups). This means that the research has some potentially useful practical applications, but they do raise very serious ethical concerns.

Should we use findings from studies such as this one to design a better system of criminal justice? What are the ethical issues involved in identifying potentially aggressive criminals from their patterns of brain activity?

Apply it — Methods: Raine's bar charts

Some data from Raine et al.'s study is shown in the table below.

Table giving mean rates of glucose metabolism in controls and murderers in the left and right hemispheres.

	Controls	Murderers
Left	1.12	1.09
Right	1.14	1.11

1. (a) Plot a bar chart of this data. (3)
   (b) Explain **one** conclusion from this data. (1)

2. Raine et al. also calculated standard deviations.
   (a) Explain what a standard deviation of this data would show. (1)
   (b) State why a standard deviation is so informative as a measure. (1)

Apply it — Concepts: Oliver's view

Oliver is preparing for a debate on psychology in society. He is arguing that violent criminals should have the right to defence based on their brain differences and if sentenced should receive biological treatments in prison to enable them to apply for early release.

1. (a) What evidence from Raine et al. supports Oliver's view that criminals should not be 'blamed' for their wrongdoing? (2)
   (b) Raine et al. say that brain structures offer only a partial explanation. Suggest **two** other important factors. (2)

2. Suggest **two** weaknesses of the study that undermine Oliver's view. (4)

Study tip

When learning your classic or contemporary study, you need to know about five clear points of procedural detail. These must focus on a range of details.

Check it

1. (a) Use your knowledge of brain scanning techniques to explain the choice of technique used in the classic study by Raine et al. (1997). (2)
   (b) Explain the findings of Raine et al.'s (1997) study. (4)

2. Use the classic study by Raine et al. (1997) to explain how individual differences in aggression can arise. (4)

3. **Standard:** Evaluate the classic study from biological psychology by Raine et al. (8)

4. **AS (Synoptic):** Evaluate the classic study from biological psychology by Raine et al. in terms of reliability and generalisability. (8)

Contemporary study: Li *et al.* (2013)

The specification says...

3.3.2 One contemporary study: Li et al. (2013) Abnormal function of the posterior cingulate cortex in heroin addicted users during resting-state and drug-cue stimulation task.

Think Link
Individual differences
Handedness
There are significant differences in brain structure and function between individuals. For example, the left brain hemisphere is functionally dominant in most of us (see page 96). This is especially true for right-handed people, but less so for left-handers. So studies of brain function have to control 'handedness' to prevent hemispheric lateralisation becoming a confounding variable. Li *et al.* did this by selecting only right-handed people as participants.

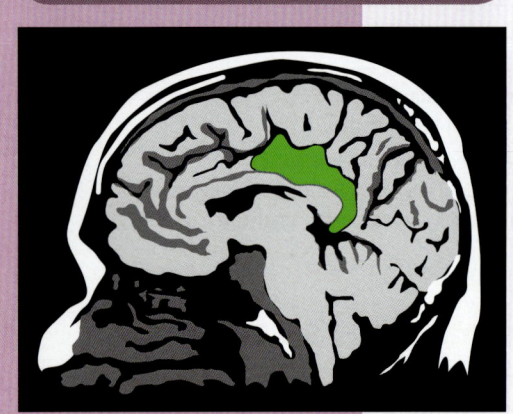

The posterior cingulate cortex (in green).

The PCC and DMN
Neurobiologists disagree strongly over the role of the PCC but it seems likely that it is an important part of the brain's *default mode network* (DMN). This is a highly integrated collection of brain structures and regions that are involved in attention, episodic memory and emotional processing. It is active by 'default' when our minds are 'free-wheeling', i.e. wandering or daydreaming.

The DMN appears to regulate our ability to focus attention internally, i.e. away from the outside world. This has led some researchers to argue that the PCC, via its key role in the DMN, may be where our sense of self is represented in the brain and may even be the seat of our conscious awareness (although there is intense debate about this).

If this is the function of the PCC, how do you think it might operate in heroin addicts responding to heroin-related cues?

Abnormal brain function in heroin addicted users

Aim
Qiang Li *et al.* (2013) sought to investigate the involvement of a brain structure called the *posterior cingulate cortex* (PCC) in heroin dependence. They aimed to show that:

- The PCC is activated in a task that involves drug-related cues.
- This activation is abnormally stronger in heroin addicts than in healthy controls, and is therefore a sign of brain dysfunction in addiction.

Procedure
This study compared the difference between two existing groups using a repeated measures design (this was not a true experiment). The experimental group of participants consisted of 14 male heroin users recruited from a drug rehabilitation centre in the city of Xi'an, China. All were in the 'detoxifying stage', i.e. they were withdrawing from heroin use. They were non-cocaine using, right-handed and aged 25–47 years (mean 35). They had previously used heroin for 19–182 months. All were required to be heroin-free (negative urine test). None had current or past psychiatric illness, neurological disease or head trauma.

A control group of 15 participants was also recruited who had no history of drug dependence, head injury or psychiatric disorders. All participants smoked.

The independent variable was experimental group (heroin-user) versus control participants. One dependent variable (DV) was the activity of reward-related brain areas (e.g. PCC) in a resting-state fMRI scan. Another DV was a self-report measure of subjective craving.

Each participant underwent three brain scans:

- **Scan 1:** Each participant first had a structural MRI scan to identify standard anatomical areas.
- **Scan 2:** A five-minute resting-state fMRI scan was performed. It was taken as the participant relaxed and fixated their gaze on a point (a 'cross-hair') in the centre of a screen.
- **Scan 3:** The cue-reactivity trial involved a second fMRI scan of 490 seconds, during which 48 images were shown to test cue-reactivity – 24 were related to heroin (e.g. syringes) and 24 were neutral. Each image was shown for 2 seconds in a pseudorandom order, with a gap of 4–12 seconds (average 8) between each. Before and after the cue-reactivity run, a self-report on a 0–10 scale was used to assess craving (0 = no craving).

All participants gave written consent and approval was obtained from the Ethics Committee at Tangdu Hospital.

Findings
Craving scores The heroin users had significantly higher subjective craving scores than the controls after (but not before) cue-induced craving (at $p \leq 0.004$) and their average scores rose from 2.23 to 3.21.

Brain activation in cue-induced task The researchers found stronger functional connectivity (i.e. joint activity) between the PCC and *insula*, and between the PCC and *dorsal striatum*, in heroin users compared with control participants. In the control participants, there was no brain region that showed more connectivity with the PCC.

Graphs showing a significant positive correlation between strength of connectivity and duration of heroin use in both the PCC-insula ($r = +.60$) and PCC-striatum ($r = +.58$).

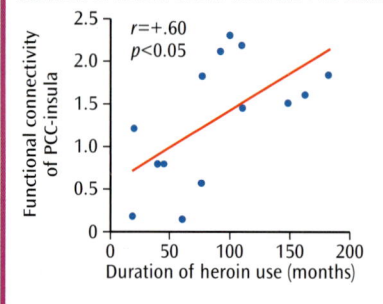

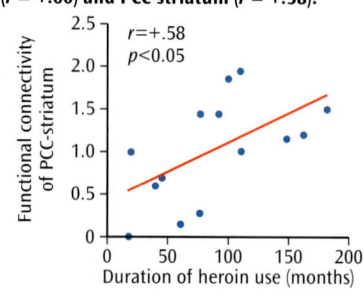

Conclusions
The findings show that drug-related cues are powerful predictors of reward for heroin addicts, and that the PCC is linked to neural circuits involved in drug cravings. This neural dysfunction affects the individual's ability to process external stimuli, especially those related to drug-taking.

The significant positive correlation between length of dependence and strength of functional connectivity shows that the neural connections between the PCC and the dorsal striatum and insula are closely related to chronic heroin dependence.

Evaluation

Standardisation
A strength is that the study featured a high degree of standardisation of procedures.

For instance, each participant saw the same heroin-related and neutral images, which were all presented for 2 seconds. The fMRI scans followed the same protocols (e.g. the resting-state scan always took 5 minutes to complete). This meant the experience of the procedure was identical for every participant.

Therefore, the researchers controlled potentially confounding variables, so the study had greater internal validity.

Competing argument However, some of the procedures were clearly inadequate. For example, sample sizes were small (e.g. just 14 heroin users). This increased the possibility of making a Type I statistical error, i.e. finding a significant result when none existed. The differences in brain activation between users and controls may not have been genuine.

Confounding variable
A weakness is that the influence of nicotine was a potentially confounding variable in this study.

All of the participants, including the controls, were smokers. The researchers claim they accounted for this by showing there was no significant difference between the two groups in scores on a test of nicotine dependence. However, this ignores the potential influence of an interaction between nicotine and heroin, which would have occurred in the user group but not in the control group. There is evidence that nicotine and heroin do interact biochemically (e.g. Kohut 2017).

This would make it a confounding variable because it was a systematic difference between the two groups.

Application to diagnosis
Li *et al.*'s findings could lead to improvements in diagnosing brain damage in heroin addicts.

The researchers found that abnormal functional connectivity involving the PCC was associated with the extent of a user's heroin dependence. If this finding proves to be reliable (e.g. by being replicated), functional connectivity could therefore be used as a biomarker (a biological indicator) of brain damage in addicts.

This means that fMRI scans similar to those used in the study could establish the severity of brain damage in heroin users, which could be the first step to providing a treatment or at least preventing further damage.

EXTRA: Issues and debates
The study illustrates practical issues in the design and implementation of biopsychology research.

fMRI scanning is highly complex – there is much more involved than simply taking a scan and then reading the resulting image. For example, as the researchers themselves explain, software is used to filter the data and 'smooth out' the image. This is done partly to compensate for movements caused by breathing. Li *et al.* acknowledged that there were limitations to the scanning process that made their images difficult to interpret.

This suggests that there are practical difficulties in conducting fMRI scans which make findings hard to explain and leads to conclusions that are speculative rather than definite.

Balanced conclusion
There has been an explosion of research into the functions of the PCC, and this study makes a valuable contribution by investigating a possible link with heroin addiction. However, this was a comparison study (with a correlational element), which did not fully control potentially confounding variables. Therefore, the researchers have not yet shown that long-term heroin use is a cause of abnormal functional connectivity in neural circuits involving the PCC.

The study presented 24 images of heroin-related cues (such as syringes) for 2 seconds each. There were also 24 'neutral' images.

Apply it Methods: Cues to relapse
A recent study used fMRI to detect heroin-cue reactivity. The experimental group (heroin-users on methadone therapy) and non-user controls were tested for craving. They were followed up to monitor relapse.

1. Follow-up data was used to divide the experimental participants into 'relapsers' and 'non-relapsers' on the basis of self-report and urine tests. Explain why **two** measures were used to assess relapse. (1)
2. The experimental group had higher craving scores after the cue-reactivity test than the control group. Of the experimental group, the relapsers had higher craving scores than the non-relapsers. Explain how this finding could be useful in the treatment of heroin users. (2)
3. A total of 69 participants were scanned but only 20 controls and 44 users (including 23 relapsers) completed the study. Show your working for all parts below.
   (a) How many participants were dropped from the study? (1)
   (b) What was the ratio of control to user participants? (2)
   (c) What percentage of the user participants were relapsers? Give your answer to **two** significant figures. (2)

Apply it Concepts: Drug rehab centre
Steph manages a drug rehab centre. She wants to find out which patients are most in need of help and which patients need to stay the longest. She must justify her decisions.

1. Explain how Steph could benefit from using fMRI scans to aid her decision-making. (1)
2. Steph wants to convince her boss that fMRIs would be useful and plans to base her arguments on Li *et al.*'s study. Write a short note that Steph could use. (2)
3. Steph's boss is not keen on the idea. Describe **two** weaknesses that he might suggest. (2)

Study tip
Feel free to disagree with our balanced conclusion – it is a suggested conclusion but you may wish to draw your own on the basis of the evidence presented. There is no right answer.

Check it
1. Explain **two** weaknesses of your chosen contemporary study for the biological approach. (4)
2. Describe how the method of your chosen contemporary study allowed the researchers to answer the question(s) posed by their aim. (2)
3. **Standard:** Evaluate **one** contemporary study from the biological approach. (8)
4. **AL (I&D/Synoptic):** Many contemporary psychologists believe that psychology should be a science.
   To what extent can the procedures of your chosen contemporary studies from biological psychology and cognitive psychology be considered scientific? (12)

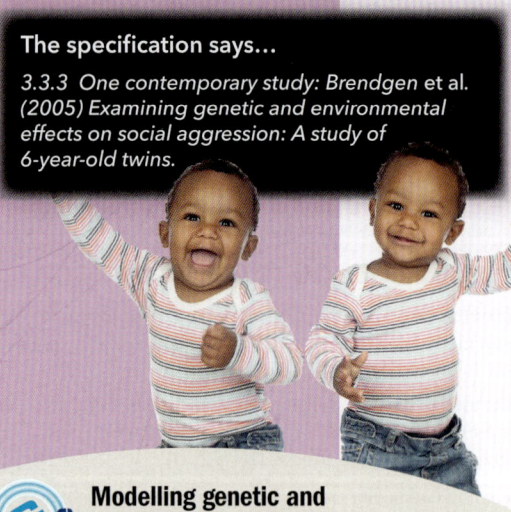

Contemporary study: Brendgen et al. (2005)

The specification says...
3.3.3 One contemporary study: Brendgen et al. (2005) Examining genetic and environmental effects on social aggression: A study of 6-year-old twins.

Twin study of social aggression

Aims
Mara Brendgen et al. investigated aggression in MZ (monozygotic, identical) and DZ (dizygotic, non-identical) twins to discover:

- The extent to which social and physical aggression are explained by genetic and environmental influences (shared and non-shared).
- Whether the overlap between social and physical aggression is explained by the direct effect of one type of aggression on the other.

Procedure
The researchers used a twin study design to calculate correlations between MZ and DZ twins, who were rated for socially and physically aggressive behaviour. 234 pairs of twins were selected from the longitudinal Quebec Newborn Twin Study (QNTS). The QNTS collected data from twins regularly, beginning at 5 months. At 72 months (6 years) the data reported in the article was collected. There were 44 pairs of male MZ twins, 50 female MZ pairs, 41 male DZ pairs and 32 female DZ pairs plus 67 mixed-sex DZ pairs not used in the final analysis.

Teacher ratings Kindergarten teachers rated the social and physical aggression of each child on a three-point scale ('never', 'sometimes', 'often') in response to items such as 'says bad things or spreads nasty rumours about others' (social) and 'hits, bites or kicks others' (physical).

Peer ratings The levels of the twins' social and physical aggression were also rated by their classmates. First, a research assistant checked that each child could recognise everyone in their class. Each classmate was given a booklet of photographs of all the children in their class and asked to nominate the three children on one page who best matched a description of behaviour, then to do the same for the next page, and so on. There were two descriptions for social aggression: 'tells others not to play with a child' and 'tells mean secrets about another child'. And there were two descriptions for physical aggression: 'gets into fights' and 'hits, bites or kicks others'.

Findings
The relative contributions of genetic and environmental influences (shared and non-shared) to ratings of social and physical aggression are summarised in the table below. It shows the proportion of variation in ratings accounted for by each factor.

Table showing teacher and peer ratings of aggression.

Aggression	Teacher ratings Genetic	Teacher ratings Shared Env	Teacher ratings Non-shared Env	Peer ratings Genetic	Peer ratings Shared Env	Peer ratings Non-shared Env
Social	20%	20%	60%	23%	23%	54%
Physical	63%	0%	37%	54%	0%	46%

The findings included:

- Only 20% (teacher ratings) to 23% (peer ratings) of social aggression was explained by genetic factors.
- Physical aggression was mostly explained by heritable (genetic) factors and partly by non-shared environmental influences. In contrast social aggression was mostly explained by non-shared environmental factors.
- A moderate but significant correlation between social and physical aggression, explained mostly by overlapping genetic influences.
- Statistical testing showed that high physical aggression led to high social aggression, but the opposite was not true (for teacher and peer ratings).

Conclusions
The data suggests that genetic characteristics predispose some children to aggressive behaviour in general (e.g. poor self-control, irritable temperament).

However, further analysis in the form of 'modelling' (see Stretch and challenge on the left) indicated that the specific form the aggression takes is more influenced by environmental factors (e.g. parental behaviours), which are different for social and physical aggression.

The directional relationship between social and physical aggression is explained by developmental processes (see 'Think link' on the left).

Stretch & Challenge

Modelling genetic and environmental effects

Researchers try to make sense of twin study data by creating a statistical model.

One influence is genes (given the label 'A'). Because MZ twins are genetically identical, we expect their behaviour to be more similar than the behaviour of DZ twins, if the behaviour is heritable. Another influence is shared environmental factors ('C'), which are experienced by both twins in a pair (if parents treat them similarly). The third influence ('E') is non-shared environmental factors, which are unique to each twin as an individual (e.g. having their own friends).

Following the labels, a common model of these influences is called the *ACE model*. The aim of complex statistical analysis is to see if the data collected in a study best matches (or 'fits') the ACE model. If it does, then all three influences contribute to the behaviour (most likely to differing extents). However, the data might fit another model more closely (e.g. the AE model, in which case shared environmental influences would not contribute).

Give examples of how genetic, shared environmental and non-shared environmental influences could contribute to aggression.

Think Link
Individual differences

Social versus physical aggression

The study shows that children's early aggressiveness is physical and genetically influenced. But children quickly learn that this is socially unacceptable, so they move on to less risky social methods of manipulative aggression.

The findings suggest that this transformation from physical to social aggression begins to take place at a very early age (i.e. six years in this study).

Evaluation

Multiple data sources
A strength of the study is that the researchers used ratings of aggression from two sources.

Each twin was rated by both their teachers and other children. It is common for research to use teacher ratings, but this was the first study of social aggression to collect data from both sources.

The two sets of ratings were essentially the same, which provides some reassurance that they are a valid and reliable measure of aggressive behaviour.

Potentially invalid assumptions
A weakness of this and all twin studies is that they are based on the equal environments assumption.

This assumption states that MZ and DZ twins experience similar treatment to the same extent (i.e. environmental influences are shared equally for both). However, this assumption may well be wrong. For example, it is likely that many parents of DZ twins behave more aggressively towards one child than the other because the twins are dissimilar but this is much less true for MZ twins who are more similar.

There are many ways in which this assumption may be violated, seriously undermining the validity of the twin study method.

Competing argument Many of the ways in which MZ similarity occurs are irrelevant to the behaviour being investigated (e.g. being dressed in the same clothes or not doesn't affect amount of aggression expressed). Eske Derks et al. (2006) conducted a study of aggression in adolescent twins, and used statistical methods to show that the assumption was not violated. So there is some evidence to show that the equal environments assumption is, after all, reasonably valid.

Application to reducing aggression
This study could lead to effective interventions to reduce aggression.

Given the progression of aggressive behaviour highlighted in this study, interventions should focus on preventing or reducing physical aggression in the early years. Brendgen et al. also suggest that future studies could identify the factors that smooth or block the 'path' from physical to social aggression.

Intervention based on this research could disrupt the transformation of physical aggression into social aggression, ultimately reducing both types.

EXTRA: Issues and debates
The study highlights how both nature and nurture are powerful influences on different types of aggression at different stages in development.

However, psychologists have long accepted that nature and nurture interact so intimately that attempting to separate them is profoundly unenlightening. In fact a criticism that could be directed at this study is that it did not consider the interactions between genes and environment (G×E interactions, as researchers call them).

Instead, the statistical analysis in the study was based on treating the two influences as independent, which is far from current thinking on the contributions of nature and nurture to behaviour.

Balanced conclusion
The study makes a useful contribution by modelling the relative influences of genes and environment on physical and social aggression in children. However, a statistical model only gives us figures indicating the size of these influences, it does not tell us exactly what the specific influences are. Given the complexity of the interacting genetic and environmental influences, it may not be possible to tease them apart.

Dr. Mara Brendgen is a Professor of Psychology at the Université du Québec à Montréal. Using a genetically informed longitudinal twin design, her research focuses on the interplay between individual, family-related, and peer-related risk and protective factors in the development of externalising and internalising problems in children and adolescents.

Apply it — Methods: Correlate, correlate

1. Describe what correlation between co-twins shows. (1)
2. If a characteristic is largely genetically controlled, explain whether you would expect MZ or DZ twins to have a higher correlation for that characteristic. (2)
3. Brendgen et al. used correlations in different ways.
   (a) In the preliminary analysis, teacher ratings for social and physical aggression were +.43 and +.41 respectively. For peer ratings they were +.33 and +.25. Who rated the two kinds of aggression as more similar, the teachers or the peers? (1)
   (b) To test internal reliability, items on the physical aggression scale for teachers were correlated, giving a value of +.89. For the social aggression scale, the value was +.82. Which had better reliability? (1)

Apply it — Concepts: Shared and non-shared

Jason is a sixth-former at a school that has a lot of twins. He asks permission to send letters to parents of all the twins to ask about their home life. He asks many questions such as, 'Describe how you discipline each of your twins.' and 'Is one twin more aggressive than the other? Y/N' and 'Do the twins have the same friends? Y/N'. He knows from school records whether each twin pair is MZ or DZ.

1. Explain what Jason could discover about shared and non-shared environments. (2)
2. Explain why knowing about the twin type matters. (1)

Study tip
Consider all your classic and contemporary studies in terms of developmental and individual differences. This study contains several useful ideas to help you illustrate these themes in biological psychology.

Check it

1. (a) Describe the aim(s) of **one** contemporary study that you have learned about as part of the biological psychology topic. (2)
   (b) Explain how the study tested this aim. (4)
2. Explain **two** strengths of your chosen contemporary study in terms of reliability. (2)
3. **Standard:** Evaluate **one** contemporary study you have learned about as part of the biological psychology topic. (8)
4. **AL (I&D/Synoptic):** Many contemporary psychologists believe that psychology should be a science.
   To what extent can the procedures of your chosen contemporary studies from biological psychology and cognitive psychology be considered scientific? (12)

Contemporary study: Van den Oever et al. (2008)

The specification says...

3.3.4 One contemporary study: Van den Oever et al. (2008) Prefrontal cortex AMPA receptor plasticity is crucial for cue-induced relapse for heroin-seeking.

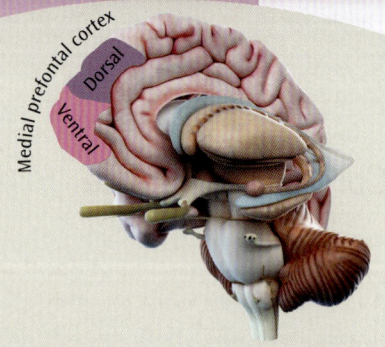

Stretch & Challenge

The AMPA receptor and plasticity

The AMPA receptor is at the heart of our story. It is a postsynaptic receptor in the central nervous system (CNS) that binds to the neurotransmitter *glutamate*. It is made up of four distinct subunits, given the labels GluR1 to GluR4. (AMPA stands for α-amino-3-hydroxy-5 methylisoxazole-4-propionic acid.)

Glutamate generally has excitatory effects in the CNS, i.e. it makes transmission of action potentials more likely. AMPA receptors are linked to critical brain functions, such as learning and memory.

Research has often demonstrated the synaptic plasticity of AMPA receptors. This 'plasticity' means that they can adapt to new situations. For instance, the number of AMPA receptors on the postsynaptic neuron can increase (upregulation) in order to speed up the response to a stimulus. The process can also be disrupted via a reduction in the number of receptors (downregulation). Research has shown that this downregulation can be caused by abuse of recreational drugs (such as heroin).

Explain how heroin-related cues in the study might cause downregulation of AMPA receptors.

Think Link
Individual differences

Relapse

Human (and rat) heroin addicts relapse at different rates, and some addicts do not relapse at all. This could be explained by individual differences in the ratios of the various subunits described above. Some individuals' AMPA receptors have a greater proportion of one subunit (e.g. GluR3) than of others. This is almost certainly due to genetic differences (because the expression of each subunit is controlled by separate genes).

Heroin addiction relapse and the AMPA receptor

Aims

Heroin addicts learn to associate certain cues (e.g. a syringe) with the rewarding effects of the drug. After a period of abstinence, users may relapse when exposed once again to heroin-associated cues. Earlier research indicated that the *medial prefrontal cortex* (mPFC) of the brain is involved in cue-induced relapse. Michel Van den Oever et al. (2008) wanted to use recent technology to investigate:

- The effects of cue exposure on one type of receptor in the mPFC – the AMPA receptor, as well as its subunits, especially the GluR2 subunit.
- The effects of cues on heroin-seeking behaviour when the activity of AMPA receptors was blocked.

Procedure

Heroin self-administration training Male Wistar rats each had a catheter surgically implanted in their jugular vein (travels from head to the heart) to deliver heroin.

The rats were trained to self-administer heroin in response to cues. This involved operant conditioning – the rats were in a *Skinner box* (see page 134). Each time they poked their nose into an active 'hole' indicated by cues (a red light above the hole, a yellow light within it and a high-frequency sound) they received a two-second delivery of heroin. Training involved a three-hour session every day, and lasted for 15 days. A control group was trained to self-administer a sugar (sucrose) solution using the same procedure.

Extinction sessions The experimental rats were divided into two groups: an extinction group and an abstention group. Over a three-week period, the extinction group spent 15 further days, 60 minutes per day, in the Skinner box but received no reward when presented with a cue. The abstention group had no time in the Skinner box and no self-administration of heroin for 21 days (and no exposure to cues).

Injection Before the relapse test, some rats were injected in the mPFC with a synthetic peptide (TAT-GluR2$_{3Y}$) to block activity of the AMPA receptors (and the GluR2 subunit). Some rats were injected in the dorsal (back) mPFC and some in the ventral (front) mPFC.

Relapse testing Half of the rats from each of the injection groups were relapse-tested in Skinner boxes with the red cue light above the active hole turned on, but without heroin self-administration. A rat was considered to have relapsed if it nose-poked the active hole in response to the cues.

Immediately after the relapse test, all the rats were decapitated and their brains were frozen. The mPFC of each brain was dissected.

Findings

The researchers identified 417 proteins in total in the dissected mPFCs. The quantities of just six of these changed significantly after exposure to the cues in the relapse test, compared with the control rats (not exposed to cues). There was rapid downregulation (reduction) of GluR2 (10% less) and GluR3 (15% less), plus downregulation of other receptor subunits. The level of subunit GluR1 was unaffected by cue exposure. The overall picture was one of depressed synaptic activity in the mPFC after re-exposure to heroin-related cues.

The injected rats showed reduced synaptic activity in the GluR2 AMPA receptor subunit, but only when injected in the ventral mPFC (this was again compared with a control group, and measured immediately after the relapse test). These rats also demonstrated reduced heroin-seeking behaviour in response to cues (i.e. reduced relapse). These findings were not repeated in the sucrose-infused rats (i.e. the effect was specific to heroin-seeking).

Conclusions

Combined with other research into heroin and cocaine addiction relapse, this study illustrates the importance of the ventral mPFC (and other regions) in controlling cue-related relapse. It also demonstrates the central role of glutamate neurotransmitter systems in both heroin-seeking behaviour specifically and addiction-related motivational behaviour generally.

The researchers showed that heroin-related cues cause a reduction in the numbers (downregulation) of the GluR2 subunit of the AMPA receptor in particular. This is associated with relapse into heroin-seeking behaviour. Preventing downregulation of the GluR2 reduced the likelihood of relapse, suggesting a new target for treatment of heroin addiction.

Evaluation

Experimental control

A strength of the study is that the researchers used several standardised procedures throughout the various stages.

For example, self-administration training, extinction training and relapse testing were all carried out in controlled ways that were identical for each rat. Established protocols were used to dissect mPFCs and to identify AMPA receptor subunits in samples. Identical treatment of the rats within each group meant the findings could not be attributed to differences in how the procedures were carried out.

Using standardised procedures and protocols meant that potentially confounding variables were controlled, giving the study a high degree of internal validity.

Use of non-human animals

A limitation is that the study used rats in order to draw conclusions about human behaviour.

The researchers used a non-human animal to model the human brain's response to drug-related cues. This is limited because relapse measured in this study does not represent the whole process of relapse in humans. For instance, humans exposed to drug-related cues experience 'cravings', which are usually measured through subjective self-reports (i.e. the user tells you).

It is difficult to independently assess cravings in rats, except to argue that they must exist because the rats relapse. This is a circular argument that lacks validity.

Competing argument Although we should be cautious in interpreting animal models, they are undoubtedly crucial in furthering our understanding of heroin's effects on the CNS. Heroin has rewarding effects on the human brain and is readily self-administered by rats – it is a powerful reinforcer in both species, with similar effects on motivation. Drug-related cues reinstate heroin-seeking behaviour in humans and rats in predictable ways. Therefore, animal models are reliable and valid explanations of human addiction and relapse.

Application to treatment

The findings could help in the search for a treatment.

Addiction is usually marked by a cycle of use, withdrawal and relapse. Relapse indicates a failed attempt to stop taking the drug, and is often triggered by environmental cues. The researchers identify (albeit in an animal model) the AMPA receptor as a target for intervention, by inhibiting its activity.

As this research helps us to understand the neurobiological basis of cue-induced relapse, it could lead to the development of an effective treatment for heroin addiction.

EXTRA: Issues and debates

This study is relevant to the issue of reductionism in science.

The researchers reduce the complex behaviour of drug-taking relapse into the activity of a specific synaptic receptor in a limited area of the brain. This means that they do not consider relevant psychological factors, such as how individuals interpret heroin-related cues. This is inevitable in a study using non-human animals, but the researchers still conclude that their findings could lead to a new treatment for heroin addiction in humans.

A reductionist approach risks oversimplifying the causes of heroin addiction by failing to take into account the interactions between biological, social and psychological factors.

Balanced conclusion

This study makes a valuable contribution to our understanding of how drug-related cues interact with synaptic plasticity to cause relapse into heroin-seeking. It also shows how this process can be modified, with implications for a potential treatment to prevent relapse. However, a non-human animal model is used so the findings should be extrapolated very carefully to human addiction and relapse.

Michel Van den Oever gained a degree in Medical Biology and his PhD in Neuroscience from the Free University of Amsterdam. He carried out postdoctoral research in Canada at the Hospital for Sick Children in Toronto.

Michel returned to Amsterdam and now heads the Memory Circuits research team at the Center for Neurogenomics and Cognitive Research at the VU University Amsterdam, The Netherlands. His research focuses on the encoding of memories related to drugs of abuse and fear in the brain.

Apply it — Methods: Rat research

Dr Ryan is concerned about two new drugs that have appeared on the streets. Both seem to lead rapidly to addiction and users find it hard to stop taking them completely. He plans to compare extinction rates as a measure of addiction as well as relapse rates.

1. First Dr Ryan trains two groups of rats, each group learning to administer one of the two drugs.
   (a) What is the purpose of this step? (1)
   (b) He then puts the rats through an extinction process to measure how addicted they are.
   Explain how the level of addiction could be measured during this process. (2)

2. Dr Ryan will use a Skinner Box to measure relapse after a period of abstinence.
   Explain **one** way that he could operationalise relapse. (2)

Apply it — Concepts: Respond then relapse

Van den Oever et al. plotted the frequency of nose-pokes against the session number for all groups during the period of self-administration.

1. (a) Explain why 'nose-poking' was a measure of relapse. (1)
   (b) Explain how the variation in nose-poking by different rats illustrates individual differences in relapse. (2)

2. Explain **one** similarity and **one** difference between relapse in animals and humans. (4)

Study tip

You must know the reference for your chosen contemporary study by name. Could you choose it from a list?

Check it

1. Explain **one** reason for the choice of participants in your contemporary study in biological psychology. (2)
2. Explain how the conclusion follows from the aim in your contemporary study in biological psychology. (4)
3. **Standard:** Assess the validity of the procedure of **one** contemporary study from biological psychology. (8)
4. **AL (I&D/Synoptic):** Many contemporary psychologists believe that psychology should be a science.
   To what extent can the procedures of your chosen contemporary studies from biological psychology and cognitive psychology be considered scientific? (12)

Key questions for biological psychology

The specification says...

3.4.1 One key question of relevance to today's society, discussed as a contemporary issue for society rather than as an academic argument.

3.4.2 Concepts, theories and/or research (as appropriate to the chosen key question) drawn from biological psychology as used in this specification.

Suitable examples

- How effective is drug therapy for treating addictions? For example, methadone to treat heroin addiction.
- What are the implications for society if aggression is found to be caused by nature not nurture?

(Note that these are examples and therefore no exam question will specifically ask you about one of these.)

The key to key questions

Key questions may be worth anything between 1 and 12 marks for AS level and up to 20 marks for A level. On this spread we focus on 8-mark questions – but you can add more paragraphs to turn this into a 12- or 16- or 20-mark answer.

A 'key question' essay needs to combine a *description* of the key question with application of concepts, theories and research evidence from the biological topic. We think the secret lies in using black/blue/green paragraphs.

When answering an 8-mark exam question, first state your key question and then write three paragraphs structured as follows:

- **Black:** Describe one aspect of your key question and explain why it is important in contemporary society.
- **Blue:** Link to relevant psychological concepts and theories.
- **Green:** Support your blue ideas with relevant research evidence or introduce competing arguments (from other research evidence or comparisons with other topics in psychology). Be sure to LINK BACK to the key question.

End with a balanced conclusion.

Each paragraph should be 100–140 words.

There is more advice on key questions on pages 9 and 17.

Pie chart showing how much money drug-related crime costs based on data from a UK Government document (Singleton *et al.* 2006).

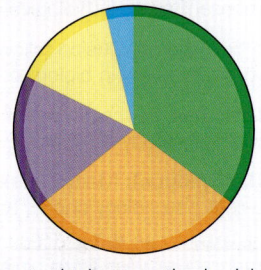

Total cost £13.9 bn
- Fraud £4.866 bn
- Burglary £4.07 bn
- Robbery £2.467 bn
- Shoplifting £1.917 bn
- Drug arrests £0.535 bn

You will enhance your answer to the key question by doing some further research.

Example 1

Discuss the key question for society you have studied using concepts, theories and/or research from biological psychology. (8)

State your key question: How effective is drug therapy for treating heroin addiction? For example, methadone to treat heroin addiction.

An NTASM (2009) report suggests that £13.9 billion is spent annually on the crime and health costs of the abuse of drugs such as heroin and cocaine. Individuals may be victims of drug-related violence or crimes such as burglary (three-quarters of heroin and crack users report using crime to fund their habit) or exposed to health risks (such as from discarded needles). In methadone therapy users minimise symptoms of heroin withdrawal by taking methadone, a long-acting oral opioid. It has an agonistic effect at the same receptors as heroin and the endorphin neurotransmitters, so helps to prevent relapse. Van den Brink and Haasen (2006) reviewed a number of studies and concluded that methadone does reduce heroin use. However, as methadone is an opioid drug it can also be abused, for example, for its sedative effects. Methadone programmes may therefore replace one addiction with another. (144 words)

Drug users tend to increase their drug use over time due to tolerance, so their problems worsen. Methadone therapy combats this. It helps the user because methadone doses can be reduced more easily than heroin doses, breaking their dependence. This works because methadone combats withdrawal without producing the euphoria that heroin does. However, Li *et al.* (2013) looked at brain scans of activity in relation to drug-related cues. They found that areas of the limbic system and prefrontal cortex still responded to these cues even in patients on methadone, suggesting craving does still arise. This explains why many patients don't reduce their methadone dose. (104 words)

As methadone therapy is provided in pharmacies, health advice and psychological support can also be given to users, and they are motivated to attend. This is important as methadone withdrawal produces side effects as doses are reduced. This could dissuade users from continuing the programme. Other drugs, such as clonidine, can be used to reduce side effects. Therefore, users need extra support because they are fighting the effects of methadone withdrawal which can only be partially reduced. The dopamine reward system which so powerfully motivates heroin use can trigger relapse. Additional drugs and social support from staff and new non-user friends can help to avert this. (106 words)

On balance, although the biological theory behind methadone therapy suggests it should be a perfect solution to heroin abuse, in practice, both biological and other factors, including cognitive and social ones, can limit or enhance its success. (37 words)

Total = 391 words

On this page we have presented a full answer to one of the key questions in the specification and added comments to draw your attention to specific features.

- **Describe the contemporary problem** of heroin addiction.

- **Integrate concepts:** Use ideas about neurotransmitters and the brain as well as drug action to explain methadone therapy.

- **Dates:** Don't feel you always have to cite dates.

- **Support your point** with evidence about the effect of drugs.

- **Include competing arguments:** Use your knowledge of drug effects, such as sedation.

- Include psychological concepts wherever you can, such as 'withdrawal', 'side effects' and 'clonidine'.

- **And now a competing argument:** Alternative ideas are introduced but in context, e.g. the role of social factors in helping to combat relapse.

- **Balanced judgement:** This doesn't have to be lengthy but it should reflect opposing views.

On this page we have provided a scaffold to help you prepare your own answer.

Remember that these are simply suggested answers. Use such suggestions to help you think about how you could structure your own response.

Example 2

Discuss the key question for society you have studied using concepts, theories and/or research from biological psychology. (8)

State your key question: What are the implications for society if aggression is found to be caused by nature not nurture?

Paragraph 1

Describe: Introduce the key question by describing the idea of biological influences on aggression versus environmental influences.

Link: Explain one biological influence, for example evolution or genetics.

Support/challenge: Evaluate your explanation, for example use twin and adoption studies to consider whether genetic influences can ever be studied in isolation.

Paragraph 2

Describe: Consider the impact on society, for example if aggression is controlled by hormones, what might society be obliged to do?

Link: Explain why boys have higher testosterone levels and make a suggestion, such as whether we should be giving more support to boys than girls in terms of anger management.

Support/challenge: You could evaluate by considering whether a biological reason for aggression (men have more testosterone so they are inevitably more aggressive) provides an 'excuse' for it. How might that impact on legal decisions?

Paragraph 3

Describe: Identify decisions based on biological causes and how these might affect individuals in today's society, such as the impact on suspects, people on trial or victims of aggression.

Link: Explain the role of brain areas in aggression and how brain scanning evidence might be used to attempt to claim innocence in violent crimes.

Support/challenge: Use the classic study by Raine *et al.* (1997), which can be used both as evidence of 'nature' and used to cast doubts on what biological evidence tells us that is practical or useful in society.

Finish with a balanced judgement, for example looking at whether cognitive explanations alone are sufficient or whether we need to consider biological factors as well, especially to give a full understanding versus an immediate impact on society.

The reward system that helped us to survive by encouraging us to eat fatty sugary foods is now threatening our survival through obesity.

Try your own

You don't have to do the key question in the specification.

Here is a different one that you might try: *Is addiction inevitable in Western society, for example to recreational drugs, eating or exercise?*

You could approach this question by considering how natural selection could explain the behaviours listed. In what way is addiction an adaptive behaviour? How does this make addiction inevitable? How might an eating addiction or running addiction be adaptive?

Each of the articles listed below will help you to see how the behaviour may have evolved and also how it has become maladaptive in modern society.

[Note that you could also consider the involvement of brain areas and neurotransmitters in the various addictions.]

- *Addiction to drugs* (see tinyurl.com/ya7wgvtz) In many modern societies, drug addiction is a health and welfare problem. With the availability of treatments such as methadone, why is this so? You already know about the action of recreational drugs on the brain, and the same mechanism seems to underlie other addictive behaviours. This article considers how addictive behaviours could ever be 'adaptive'.

- *Eating addiction* (see tinyurl.com/y9tzwz7u) It is claimed that there are now more obese people than starving ones. Why is obesity such a problem in societies in developed countries? This website will help you to think about the importance of a strong motivation to eat high-fat foods, especially in winter months.

- *Addiction to running* (see tinyurl.com/y79n4ra7) Even though people in modern society seem so busy, they often still find time to go jogging. Some suffer damage to their legs as a consequence. This website will help you to think about the importance of a motivation to run to hunt for food that is strong enough to keep you running even when you are exhausted.

Study tip

Each point you make using a theory, concept or research should be linked to the key question to show how it is relevant to society. You also need to follow a clear structure in each paragraph, so that you achieve a balance between description and discussion.

Check it

1. You will have studied a key question from biological psychology that is of relevance to issues in modern society. State it below: Explain why your key question for biological psychology is relevant to today's society. (2)

2. State your key question for biological psychology and explain how psychology can help to resolve the issues it raises. (4)

3. **Standard:** Discuss your key question using theories, concepts and/or research from biological psychology. (8)

4. **AL (I&D/Synoptic):** Evaluate the usefulness to society of the psychological knowledge from your key questions in biological and cognitive psychology. (12)

Practical investigations for biological psychology

The specification says...

3.5.1 *One practical research exercise to gather data relevant to topics covered in biological psychology. This practical research exercise must adhere to ethical principles in both content and intention.*

In conducting the practical research exercise, students must:

- *Design and conduct a correlational study. (See page 198 for advice)*
- *Link their research to aggression or attitudes to drug use.*
- *Include inferential statistical testing (Spearman's rho) and explain the significance of the result and the use of levels of significance. (See page 200)*
- *Use descriptive statistics (strength/direction) to explain the relationship. (See page 198)*
- *Produce an abstract of the research method and a discussion section that includes conclusions. (See pages 181 and 220)*
- *Include research question/hypothesis, research method, sampling, ethical considerations, data-collection tools, data analysis, results, discussion. (See pages 170 and 176)*
- *Consider strengths and weaknesses of the correlational study and possible improvements. (See page 198)*

Ethical principles

Ethical principles are discussed in detail in chapter 5, on pages 176–177. We strongly suggest that you complete this checklist before collecting data.

1. Participants know participation is voluntary.	☐
2. Participants know what to expect, i.e. the task(s) they will be doing.	☐
3. Participants know they can withdraw at any time.	☐
4. Participants' responses will be anonymous.	☐
5. I minimised the risk of distress to participants.	☐
6. I have avoided collecting any sensitive data.	☐
7. I considered all other ethical issues.	☐
8. I have not done anything that would bring my school/teacher/psychology into disrepute.	☐
9. My teacher has approved my plan.	☐

A correlation to see if there is a relationship between height and a self-rating of aggressive tendencies

Design considerations

The measured co-variables in this investigation are self-reported aggression and height. Aggression can be measured using a scale or questionnaire (see below).

Aggression is notoriously hard to operationalise, but you must settle on a definition you can work with (e.g. physical aggression, aggressive feelings, social aggression such as swearing and unpleasant comments, etc.). Write an alternate hypothesis, taking into account whether it should be directional or non-directional.

Preparing materials

Design a highly-structured questionnaire/scale that will collect quantitative data by using closed questions. You need to write some questions/items that can measure your operationalised definition of self-reported aggression.

One way to do this is to devise a series of 'scenarios'. Here's an example: 'You are standing in a queue and someone treads on your foot without apologising.' This could be followed by a question such as: 'How likely are you to be physically aggressive in this situation?' You can provide a ranked scale for your participants to respond to, such as a 7-point scale where 1 is very likely (or strongly agree, etc.) to 7 very unlikely (strongly disagree, etc.).

Try to write several items and add up the scores for each participant to produce an overall aggressive-tendency score. You will also need a measure of each participant's height.

Sampling decisions

An important issue in sampling for this practical is gender representation. This is because males are generally (but not always) taller and more aggressive than females, so gender is a potentially confounding variable. Opportunity or volunteer sampling are suitable for this practical but to ensure a better gender balance you might prefer to use stratified sampling.

Special ethical concerns

Most people are likely to be very sensitive to any suggestion that they may be aggressive. So think carefully about how to word your scale/questionnaire to avoid damaging your participants' self-esteem or invading their privacy. Debriefing will be crucial to this.

It is important to reassure participants that their responses are not 'abnormal' or indicate unusual behaviour. Avoid implying that tall or short people are unusually aggressive. You could produce a debriefing sheet to address these concerns, and be prepared to answer any questions participants might have.

Analysing your data

You must provide some analysis of data. As this is a correlation it is important to do an initial analysis using a scatter diagram, thus 'sense-checking' the data. Then you should use Spearman's test to analyse the correlation for significance (follow the instructions on page 200).

Write the report

For this practical you are required to write a report on the research question/hypothesis, research method, sampling, ethical considerations, data-collection tools, data analysis, results, discussion (conclusions). Details about writing the report are given on page 181.

You are also required to write an abstract. This is the last thing to write and is usually a summary of the aims, research method, results and discussion (including conclusions) in about 150 words (see page 220). However, the specification says you do not need to include the aims.

A correlation into age and attitudes to drug use

Practical investigation example from the specification.

You are likely to focus on the use of recreational drugs as that is what you have studied in this course.

Design considerations

The study requires two pieces of data for each participant – their age and a quantitative measure of their attitude to (recreational) drug use. The first major consideration is how to measure attitudes. This is best done by way of a self-report method (i.e. questionnaire or interview). This time you might consider collecting some qualitative data to allow participants to express their views more freely (and then convert this to quantitative data) and/or you could use ranked scales to measure attitudes.

Write an alternate hypothesis – with operationalised variables – and decide whether it should be directional or non-directional.

Preparing materials

You can collect qualitative data using open questions in an unstructured interview. You need to think about effective questions. Just asking, 'What is your attitude to recreational drug use?' is probably too open. You could break down this question to cover different aspects of drug use and people's attitudes.

Ranked scales might have a variety of statements about drug use and participants are asked to rate their agreement/disagreement on a scale of 1 to 5 or 1 to 7.

Apart from asking participants to indicate their age (or age bracket), there is no need to collect any identifying information.

Sampling decisions

As you are looking for a correlation between age and attitude, make sure you select people from as wide a range of ages as you can, not just 'young' and 'old' people. Note that all participants must be 16 or over.

Opportunity and volunteer sampling are unlikely to achieve this, so think about using stratified sampling.

Furthermore, you might think of other 'strata' other than age that might influence attitudes towards drug use. Obviously you cannot hope to select a sample that is representative of all groups, but you might want to focus on one or two potentially confounding variables (e.g. gender).

Special ethical concerns

You will be investigating a very sensitive issue. Most people would consider their attitude to drug use a private matter and find questioning about it unwelcome. As drug use is sometimes thought of as a 'moral' issue, many people are sensitive to any indication that they are being judged. So keep questions respectful, not overly prying and make sure participants do not have their self-esteem lowered. Avoid any questioning about the participants' own use of drugs – this is an unacceptable invasion of privacy.

Keeping responses anonymous helps – how will you do this? Debriefing also has an important role to play. At the very least you should produce a debriefing sheet.

Analysing your data

You can use thematic analysis to analyse your qualitative data (see pages 59, 159, 175 and 213) and generate some conclusions based on this. However, you do need to derive a quantitative 'score' from qualitative data. Choose a few of your identified themes and count the number of times it appears for each participant.

You can then add this to your quantitative data and calculate a total score. Analyse your data using an inferential statistical test for correlation, as on the facing page.

Write the report

See facing page.

Perhaps age-related attitudes to drugs depend on which drug you're talking about?

Other ideas

Parents' and childrens' attitudes towards whether aggression is innate. We would expect there to be a positive correlation although, if there is, we cannot conclude whether it is caused by nature or nurture.

Superego strength: Beliefs and behaviours should correlate. You could measure beliefs with questions about attitudes (e.g. towards animal cruelty – take care to avoid sensitive topics such as homelessness) and measure behaviour using scenario-based questions (e.g. whether someone does give money to such charities).

Apply it — Methods: Squash or give?

Taz has conducted a practical investigation with 12 participants using a video game which includes different activities that score equal numbers of points. The player either gives presents of flowers and cakes to others or viciously squashes flowers and cakes.

1. Taz worked out each participant's 'aggression' score by subtracting the 'present-giving' score.
   Write a directional alternate hypothesis for Taz. (2)
2. Taz used a questionnaire to give each participant a score for 'ambitiousness'.
   (a) Write **one** ranked scale question for Taz to use in his questionnaire. (1)
   (b) Write **one** open question and explain how Taz could use it to obtain qualitative data. (2)
3. Taz correlated the aggression and ambitiousness scores. His value of *rho* was +.5. Explain whether he should accept his directional alternate hypothesis. (2) (See critical values table on page 200.)

Study tip

In any practical investigation collecting quantitative data, ensure you have memorised example data to use in exam questions, such as the totals, percentages, means, medians, modes, or, as in this case, the statistical analysis of your own data.

Check it

1. You will have conducted a practical investigation for biological psychology.
   (a) Describe how you measured the variables in your investigation. (4)
   (b) Explain **one** improvement to the way one of these variables was measured. (2)
2. Describe the results of the Spearman's test you used to analyse your results. (3)
3. **Standard:** Evaluate your practical investigation for biological psychology. (8)
4. **AS (Practicals/Synoptic):** To what extent could the procedures of your practical investigations for biological and social psychology have been improved? (12)

Revision summary

Chapter 3 Biological psychology

The nervous system

The central nervous system (CNS)

The spinal cord
Links peripheral nervous system (PNS) to CNS via brainstem, responsible for reflex actions.

The brain
Conscious awareness, two hemispheres, contralateral control of body, cerebral cortex is the top layer (3 mm thick).

Subcortical structures
Thalamus – Relay station, receives and passes on sensory information, acts as a gate/filter.
Hypothalamus – Controls motivational behaviours, stress response, homeostasis, endocrine system and produces some hormones.
Limbic system – Memory and learning, interconnected with cortex. Includes amygdala (emotional processing).
Cerebellum – Two hemispheres, control balance and coordination, integrate information from spinal cord and brain.
Corpus callosum – Connects two hemispheres, integrates activity of both sides of brain and body.

Lateralisation and localisation
Two hemispheres have different functions (lateralisation). Specific brain areas have specific functions (localisation).

The cerebral cortex
Higher cognitive processing. Four lobes per hemisphere, convoluted surface (sulci and gyri).
Frontal lobes, cognitive functions (e.g. thinking), e.g. motor cortex controlling voluntary movements.
Parietal lobes e.g. somatosensory cortex processing sensory information from skin.
Temporal lobes e.g. auditory cortex processing sound information, role in understanding language.
Occipital lobes e.g. visual cortex for processing of visual information.

Language areas of the brain
Broca's area – Left frontal lobe, speech production. Damage causes Broca's aphasia, dysfluent speech.
Wernicke's area – Left temporal lobe, language understanding. Damage causes Wernicke's aphasia, meaningless speech.

Neurons

Structure of the neuron
Cell body, dendrites, axon with myelin sheath, nodes of Ranvier, terminal buttons.

Types of neuron
Sensory – Receptors to CNS, long dendrites, short axons.
Motor – CNS to effectors, short dendrites, long axons.
Relay – Connects sensory, motor and other relay neurons, short axons.

Functions of the neuron
Cell depolarises, carries action potential (all-or-nothing) down axon to terminal buttons.

Synapses and neurotransmitters

Synaptic transmission
Neurons separated by gap (synaptic cleft), communication is chemical (neurotransmitters bind with postsynaptic receptors).

Functions of neurotransmitters
Neurotransmitters fit receptors like key-and-lock, e.g. acetylcholine involved in muscle contractions.

Excitation and inhibition
Excitatory (e.g. dopamine) makes next neuron more likely to fire.
Inhibitory (e.g. serotonin) makes it less likely.

Summation
Excitatory and inhibitory inputs summed (added), neuron firing depends on net effect.

Effects of recreational drugs

Cocaine
Stimulant effect on mesocorticolimbic (reward) pathway, alters dopamine transmission.

The role of dopamine
Cocaine blocks dopamine reuptake, leaving surplus dopamine in synapse and creating euphoria.

Long-term effects
Dopamine receptors downregulated (fewer active), less dopamine, explains tolerance and withdrawal.

Heroin
CNS depressant, binds with μ (mu) receptor in body's natural opioid system (e.g. endorphins).

Agonist and antagonist
Heroin mimics action of natural painkiller (agonist). Naloxone blocks opiate receptors (antagonist).

Long-term effects
Opioid receptors downregulated, system becomes less sensitive to heroin (tolerance).

Evaluation

Research supporting the role of dopamine
Lesions to mesocorticolimbic pathway in mice (Weinshenker and Schroeder 2007), less self-administered cocaine, highlights role.

Validity of non-human animal studies
Human brain more complex (e.g. interactions of dopamine with other neurotransmitters).
However human studies are also supportive (e.g. Volkow et al. 1997), confirm validity of animal models.

Application to better treatments for addiction
Antagonist drugs developed to prevent heroin binding, but without euphoric effects.

EXTRA: Issues and debates
Illustrates psychological knowledge and society, potential benefits (Morgan et al. 2013) addressing social issues.

Aggression

The structure of the brain and aggression

Brain structure

Role of the limbic system
Link with emotional behaviour, amygdala reactivity linked to processing angry faces (Coccaro et al. 2007).

Role of the prefrontal cortex
OFC activity lower in aggressive people, who show disrupted self-control and more impulsive behaviour (e.g. Raine et al. 1997).

Brain function

Role of serotonin
Decreased serotonin in OFC means less self-control and more impulsive behaviour (Denson et al. 2012).

Role of dopamine
Serotonin underactivity stimulates dopamine overactivity, both involved in aggression (Seo et al. 2008).

Evaluation

Support from longitudinal research
Strong negative correlation between aggression and amygdala volume (Pardini et al. 2014).

Correlational research
Links between brain function and aggression, but cannot establish cause and effect.
However participants given drug known to increase serotonin activity are less aggressive (Berman 2009).

Application to understanding aggression
Leads to drug treatments, e.g. serenics are serotonin agonists with anti-aggressive effects.

EXTRA: Issues and debates
Reductionist explanation, aggression linked to amygdala dysfunction ignores interacting social and psychological factors.

Evolution, natural selection and aggression

Evolution by natural selection
Evolution – Genes for characteristics that allow an individual to reproduce are passed on.
Natural selection – Environmental pressures select individuals who can survive and reproduce successfully.

Sexual selection
Apparently disadvantageous traits selected because attractive to mates (e.g. peacock's tail), sign of genetic fitness.

Evolution and aggression
Guarding your partner – Mate retention strategies (Wilson and Daly 1996) - males prevent females straying.
Guarding your offspring – Parents use aggression to protect genetic investment in children, female aggression.

Evaluation

Explains gender differences
Cooperation in females protects offspring, aggression in males provides food (e.g. Manson and Wrangham 1991).
However cannot test evolution directly, so research correlational and other influences may be important.

Cannot explain cultural differences
!Kung San no aggression, Yanomami very aggressive. Not universal, so not innate.

Application to reproductive behaviour
Explains why partners selected to enhance reproductive success e.g. men select younger women (Buss 1989).

EXTRA: Issues and debates
Psychology as science shown in use of marsupial fossils as objective evidence of sexual selection (Ladevèze et al. 2011).

Classic study

Raine et al. (1997)
Brain abnormalities in murderers

Aim
To investigate whether murderers have dysfunctions in areas of the brain linked in previous research to violence.

Method
Matched pairs design to compare 41 murderers and 41 non-murderers.

Procedure
PET scan after performing task (identifying targets), produced 10 brain images in 10 mm 'slices'.

Findings
Murderers had lower glucose metabolism in areas previously linked to violence:
- Cortical, e.g. lateral and prefrontal areas.
- Subcortical, e.g. corpus callosum, left amygdala.

Conclusions
Murderers have different brain activity from non-murderers, but not a simple cause-and-effect.

Evaluation

Experimental control
Good control (e.g. matching, standardised procedures) avoids confounding variables.
However participants not randomly allocated to conditions and matching not thorough, confounding variables (e.g. head injury).

Inappropriate PET scanning technique
Images taken relative to canthomeatal line – varies between individuals, reduces internal validity.

Application to understanding biological evidence
Findings may not justify 'treating' aggression by changing biological structures because this is only a partial explanation.

EXTRA: Issues and debates
Socially sensitive research, has implications for criminal responsibility and nature of free will.

Contemporary studies

Li et al. (2013)
Abnormal brain function in heroin-addicted users

Aim
Is PCC activated more strongly in heroin addicts, and a sign of brain impairment?

Procedure
14 heroin users and 15 controls, fMRI scans while viewing drug-related images (cues) and neutral images.

Findings
Strong joint activity between PCC/insula and PCC/dorsal striatum in heroin users.

Conclusions
Cues are powerful predictors of reward for heroin addicts. PCC linked to dysfunctional neural circuits.

Evaluation

Standardisation
Several standardised procedures used (e.g. same images, fMRI protocols), controls confounding variables.
However some procedures inadequate, e.g. small sample sizes, so Type I error more likely, no genuine differences.

Confounding variable
Participants all smokers, so nicotine interacted with heroin in addicts but not controls.

Application to diagnosis
PCC dysfunction is a biomarker of brain damage in addicts, and can be a first step towards treatment.

EXTRA: Issues and debates
Illustrates practical issues, fMRI scans are complex and hard to interpret, speculative conclusions.

Brendgen et al. (2005)
Twin study on social aggression

Aims
To find whether social and physical aggression can be explained by genetic and/or environmental factors.

Procedure
234 pairs of MZ and DZ twins rated for social and physical aggression by teachers and peers.

Findings
Physical aggression mostly due to genetic influences, social mostly to non-shared environmental influences.

Conclusions
Genes predispose some children to aggression, but specific form depends on environment.

Evaluation

Multiple data sources
Ratings from two sources (teachers, peers) provide valid and reliable measure of aggression.

Potentially invalid assumptions
Equal environments assumption may be wrong – MZ twins treated more similarly than DZs.
However many MZ similarities are not relevant to study (e.g. same clothes), so assumption may not have been violated (Derks et al. 2006).

Application to reducing aggression
Prevent aggression early to disrupt progression of physical into social – reduces both.

EXTRA: Issues and debates
Nature and nurture interact closely but study did not consider gene–environment interactions, which makes it limited.

Van den Oever et al. (2008)
Heroin addiction relapse and the AMPA receptor

Aims
To investigate effects of drug-related cues on AMPA receptor, and on heroin-seeking when receptor blocked.

Procedure
Rats trained to self-administer heroin, injected with AMPA blocker and then given a relapse test, brain dissected.

Findings
Downregulation of GluR2, depressed mPFC activity after relapse test. Blocking worked in ventral mPFC only.

Conclusions
Ventral mPFC controls cue-related relapse. Preventing downregulation of GluR2 reduced relapse.

Evaluation

Experimental control
Several standardised procedures – avoided confounding variables, high internal validity.

Use of non-human animals
Limited model of human brain's response to cues (e.g. can't measure 'cravings' in rats).
However animal models crucial – heroin is a powerful reinforcer and cue effects predictable in rats and humans.

Application to treatment
Inhibit activity of AMPA receptor to reduce cue-related relapse – potential target for treatment.

EXTRA: Issues and debates
Reductionism – relapse reduced to specific receptor, ignoring psychological factors, oversimplified.

Freud's explanation of aggression

The unconscious and aggression
The unconscious (iceberg metaphor) is hidden but is an active processor, origin of aggressive thoughts, instincts, etc.

Personality and aggression
Id and pleasure principle – Primitive, unconscious, origin of aggressive energy. Demands immediate gratification of desires.
Ego and reality principle – Rational, mostly conscious, directs id impulses in realistic ways.
Superego – Moral role, conscience, ideal self-image. Opposes id urges with guilt and shame.

Catharsis and aggression
Expressing aggression reduces drive. Can be indirect (e.g. displacement).

Evaluation

Explains different types of aggression
Hot-blooded (impulsive) = failure of ego to control id. Cold-blooded (logical) = success of ego.

Aggression is not cathartic
Venting increases aggression rather than decreasing (e.g. Bushman 2002).
However ranting rather than venting can be cathartic, control over anger (Graham et al. 2008).

Application to reducing aggression
Harmless ways to vent in everyday life (displacement) and also in therapy.

EXTRA: Issues and debates
Compare similarities between Freud and biological approach, both see aggression as instinctive/innate/useful for survival.

Role of hormones in aggression

Hormones
Produced in endocrine glands, travels in bloodstream to target cells/organs, widespread effects.

Role of testosterone
Increased levels linked with aggression in male animals and humans (e.g. Dolan et al. 2001).

Dual-hormone hypothesis
Aggression occurs in interaction between high testosterone and low cortisol (Carré and Mehta 2011).

Female aggression
Testosterone linked with both high and low aggression, and also greater sociability (e.g. Eisenegger et al. 2011).

Evaluation

Research support
Aggression–testosterone link found in females as well as males (Dabbs and Hargrove 1997).
However research is correlational, elevated testosterone may be outcome of aggression not cause.

Measuring testosterone
Hard to measure because levels fluctuate and not reflected by baseline measures (Carré et al. 2011), invalidates findings.

Application to controlling aggression
Anti-testosterone drugs used to reduce aggression in male offenders (e.g. Depo-Provera).

EXTRA: Issues and debates
Reductionist approach, focusing on hormones means we lose sight of 'bigger picture', e.g. social context.

– Chapter 3 Biological psychology

Practice questions, answers and feedback

On this spread we look at some typical student answers to questions. The comments provided indicate what is good and bad in each answer. Learning how to produce effective question answers is a SKILL. Read pages 6–19 for guidance.

Question 1: As part of your psychology specification, you were required to carry out a practical investigation when studying biological psychology. Explain **one** improvement that you could have made to the procedure of your practical. (2)

NB. This question would probably appear as part of a series of questions on your practical investigation, including a question about what your practical actually involved.

Sam's answer
We should have done a pilot study to trial our aggression questionnaire as our participants sometimes wrote comments instead of ticking the boxes. The pilot study would have helped to identify any confusing questions or ones where we had not given a broad enough array of answer choices. This would improve the validity by making the data more accurate.

This is a super answer from Sam and worth full marks. He has given an appropriate improvement and explained why this was necessary in a well-developed first sentence. He has then said why the pilot study would have helped improve the study and how.

Ella's answer
One problem with our study was the fact that when we were measuring height it was not easy to get an accurate reading using the metre stick. This meant that our data would not have been valid as we might have recorded their height incorrectly.

Ella's answer does not actually match the question so would be awarded no marks. When thinking about improvements, you may want to mention the weakness first but the marks are for the improvement and Ella just described the weakness. Allowing time for reading through your answers will help you avoid problems like this.

Larina's answer
We could have asked the school nurse if we could use the height measuring device in her room.

Larina has given an improvement that relates to the problem that Ella outlined above but she has not given sufficient elaboration. Larina needs to remember that the command term 'explain' requires her to give a justification as to why this change to the procedure will improve her study. She might just scrape 1 mark for this answer.

Question 2: Explain the process of synaptic transmission. (3)

Sam's answer
I am going to use cocaine as an example to talk about synaptic transmission. Cocaine can make people feel euphoric because it stops dopamine being reabsorbed to the presynaptic cell causing an excess of dopamine. This means there is more dopamine left in the synapse, which increases transmission. The excess dopamine can damage the receptors and dopamine production can slow down, making people tolerant of cocaine and so they need more and more of it to get the same effect.

Sam remembers that the command term 'explain' needs a bit more thought than 'describe', for instance by using an example. But unfortunately his example has taken over his whole answer and we learn more about cocaine than we do about synaptic transmission. He needs to think carefully about what the question is asking him and match his answer more carefully to the question asked. No marks for this answer.

Ella's answer
Two neurons communicate at a synapse. This is where one neuron ends and another begins. Information has to get across this very very small gap. Chemical messengers are released into the little gap between the cells and this causes the message to be passed on in the next cell. The molecules are the lock and the sites are the key. Sometimes people can have too much or not enough neurotransmission and this can cause problems like addiction and mental disorders.

Although Ella starts off well, her answer overall is quite weak, suggesting she might not have understood this area very well. She has missed some key stages of the process and does not use relevant terminology. She has also got the 'lock and key' analogy the wrong way round. Her answer is a good length and she attempts to use an example but unfortunately her example just further underlines the fact that she really doesn't understand synaptic transmission. An answer worth 1 mark only.

Larina's answer
When an action potential reaches the presynaptic terminal, it triggers neurotransmitter molecules to be released into the synapse. When they reach the other side, they bind to receptors on the postsynaptic neuron and the signal continues on its way. Following transmission, leftover molecules are recycled back into the presynaptic cell but sometimes this can go wrong. For example, cocaine blocks the reuptake of dopamine meaning the synapse is flooded with too much dopamine and this can lead to feelings of elation, which make cocaine addictive.

Great answer from Larina, she uses plenty of specialist terminology effectively demonstrating her detailed knowledge and understanding. She has also engaged well with the command term 'explain', as she has used an example to help the reader understand more about this process. The example links to her knowledge of recreational drugs but, unlike Sam, she has not made this the focus of her answer. There is definitely enough for the full 3 marks.

Question 3: Assess the role of hormones in explaining human aggression. (8)

Sam's answer

Hormones travel through the blood and send messages round the body about how to react in various situations. For example, adrenaline is released following exposure to a threat. This prepares us for fight or flight, meaning we are preparing ourselves to attack or run away. It is not clear however, why in some circumstances we attack or become aggressive and in others we flee, suggesting aggression is dictated by other factors as well as adrenaline. More commonly, human aggression has been linked to testosterone because males are generally more aggressive than females and testosterone is known to regulate social behaviour linked to aggression.

One strength of the testosterone hypothesis is that Dolan et al. found a positive correlation between testosterone levels and aggressive behaviour in a sample of 60 male offenders in UK maximum security hospitals. This suggests that high levels of testosterone may be a cause of aggression.

On the other hand, as this research was correlational, it's possible that aggressive behaviour causes testosterone levels to increase rather than vice versa. However, animal experiments permit researchers to show that testosterone does cause aggression because the hormone can be manipulated – increasing testosterone does lead to increased aggression (Giammanco et al.). Animal experiments allow for a level of control that would not be ethical or practical with humans.

Other research focuses on cortisol, a stress hormone. When cortisol is low, high testosterone leads to aggression but when cortisol is high, high testosterone does not lead to increased aggression. This idea is supported by Popma et al. who used saliva swabs to measure hormone levels and self-reports to measure aggression. The results were exactly as expected demonstrating that the link between aggression and testosterone is not as straightforward as the animal research suggests.

Whilst there seems to be some evidence for the role of hormones in aggression, aggression can also be affected by observation of aggressive role models or exposure to competition for limited resources.

Therefore, I conclude that the most important evidence comes from studies of the interaction between different hormones in humans, as social and cognitive factors can affect stress in humans and cortisol levels seem important in mediating the effect of testosterone on aggression. However, social and cognitive factors affect the stress hormone, cortisol and therefore aggression is not merely controlled by hormones.

384 words

Sam starts with an accurate description of how the hormone adrenaline is related to aggression.

There is some evaluation starting with the sentence 'It is not clear ...' and this serves as his first effort to meet the command term 'Assess'. This argument was not very well-developed, however.

Sam then goes into a little more description linked to testosterone.

Next comes a chunk of well-developed chains of reasoning with a nice balance of competing arguments showing good understanding of the relevance of these arguments to the overall argument. Notice how the material used here (Dolan et al.) is actually given as description in this textbook but here it has been presented as evaluation – it is all about how you use material.

Sam then racks up some more AO1 credit with the link between testosterone and cortisol and shows off his accurate (and detailed) knowledge of research studies in this area.

Note that Sam has not included dates in his answer. It is a nice touch of detail but by no means required and certainly something you should not stress about.

Sam concludes his essay with a thoughtful consideration of which piece of evidence he finds most compelling and this shows good engagement with the command term 'assess'.

This essay should achieve a mark within the top level, and probably full marks.

Larina's answer

The endocrine system is a set of glands in the body that secrete hormones which control many bodily functions and behaviours. This system is slower than the nervous system but the effects last longer. So how do hormones link with aggression? One of the main hormones that has been studied is testosterone. This can be measured objectively by collecting saliva so you can see how high a person's testosterone is and then see if they are an aggressive type of person or not.

Studies of both male and female violent offenders have shown that there is a link. This research is correlational though. Other research has also been done on animals. For example, animals can be castrated so they then have no testosterone in their bodies and they become much less aggressive.

Chemical castration is used to treat sex offenders but research on testosterone and aggression shows it could also be useful for very aggressive people as well and this is a benefit of this research for society.

Some researchers also think cortisol is important in aggression in humans. This is a stress hormone. A study on young males showed that high levels of cortisol can make people very aggressive. This is because they are stressed and frustrated. The problem with this study though was that they only measured stress using questionnaires and therefore the young men may have said that they were feeling aggressive but they might not have actually acted aggressively, and vice versa they might not feel aggressive but if they were in a real-life situation where someone was rude to them they might act aggressively. This shows that self-reported aggression might not be very accurate.

Overall, the correlational studies on humans and the experiments on animals show that aggression is linked to testosterone and therefore lowering testosterone is a sensible option for helping to make society a safer place.

313 words

Larina's essay starts with some descriptive knowledge which is generally relevant, although she could have saved time by cutting to the chase and talking about aggression a bit earlier.

Larina then states a possible way of researching the link between testosterone and aggression, although this is rather underdeveloped.

Next, she introduces research on violent offenders but there is no detail. Furthermore, she has failed to frame this up effectively as evaluation. She seems to have forgotten the advice about developing chains of reasoning, one link at a time.

In the fourth paragraph, Larina introduces cortisol. The study she mentions is actually more complicated than this as it showed that when testosterone levels were high this only increased aggression when cortisol levels were *low*. On the plus side she has tried to develop some of her points by giving an analysis of problems within the study, such as the use of self-reports although she does not use appropriate terminology, such as validity.

Larina has not named researchers in her essay and while this is not strictly necessary it does make it hard to know which studies she is talking about.

She finishes with a fairly basic conclusion.

This essay would probably score top of level 2.

Chapter 3 Biological psychology — Multiple-choice questions

The central nervous system and human behaviour

1. The two hemispheres of the brain are connected by the:
   (a) Hypothalamus.
   (b) Corpus callosum.
   (c) Hippocampus.

2. Our emotional responses are regulated mostly by the:
   (a) Occipital lobe.
   (b) Limbic system.
   (c) Spinal cord.

3. Different functions of the two brain hemispheres are referred to as:
   (a) Lamination.
   (b) Localisation.
   (c) Lateralisation.

4. The somatosensory cortex is located in the:
   (a) Parietal lobe.
   (b) Frontal lobe.
   (c) Temporal lobe.

Neurons, synaptic transmission and neurotransmitters

1. The part of a neuron that carries the electrical impulse away from the cell body is the:
   (a) Axon.
   (b) Terminal button.
   (c) Nucleus.

2. There are three main types of neuron – motor, sensory and:
   (a) Cortical.
   (b) Synaptic.
   (c) Relay.

3. Neurotransmitters are released from:
   (a) Postsynaptic receptors.
   (b) Dendrites.
   (c) Vesicles.

4. What is generally the effect of serotonin in the CNS?
   (a) Inhibitory.
   (b) Excitatory.
   (c) Summatory.

Effect of recreational drugs

1. Drugs that mimic a neurotransmitter's effects are called:
   (a) Antagonists.
   (b) Recreational.
   (c) Agonists.

2. Most recreational drugs increase release of:
   (a) Serotonin.
   (b) Dopamine.
   (c) Endorphins.

3. Heroin withdrawal, craving and tolerance are explained by:
   (a) Receptor downregulation.
   (b) Receptor upregulation.
   (c) Neurotransmitter reuptake.

4. Drug research with mice has involved damaging the:
   (a) Mesocorticolimbic reward circuit.
   (b) Hippocampus.
   (c) Cerebellum.

The structure of the brain and aggression

1. Which of the following is part of the limbic system?
   (a) Corpus callosum.
   (b) Amygdala.
   (c) Frontal cortex.

2. Which part of the brain is involved in self-control and inhibition of aggression?
   (a) Motor cortex.
   (b) Orbitofrontal cortex.
   (c) Somatosensory cortex.

3. Impulsive aggression is linked with:
   (a) Normal serotonin function and dopamine hypofunction.
   (b) Serotonin hyperfunction and normal dopamine function.
   (c) Serotonin hypofunction and dopamine hyperfunction.

4. Amygdala dysfunction is best described as:
   (a) The direct cause of aggression.
   (b) Not linked to aggression.
   (c) Interacting with non-biological factors to cause aggression.

Evolution, natural selection and aggression

1. 'Survival of the fittest' refers to the:
   (a) Match between traits and environment.
   (b) Strongest animal being most successful.
   (c) Amount of time spent in the gym.

2. The peacock's tail is a good example of:
   (a) Natural selection.
   (b) Guarding territory.
   (c) Sexual selection.

3. Females can behave as aggressively as males in guarding:
   (a) Offspring.
   (b) Territory.
   (c) Partner.

4. Evolutionary theory is supported because there are:
   (a) Cultural differences in aggression.
   (b) Gender differences in aggression.
   (c) Lots of laboratory experiments.

Freud's psychodynamic explanation of aggression

1. According to Freud, the unconscious mind:
   (a) Is like the bit of an iceberg above the waterline.
   (b) Is relatively unimportant in influencing behaviour.
   (c) Contains thoughts and memories we are unaware of.

2. The ego:
   (a) Is mostly unconscious.
   (b) Redirects aggressive impulses in socially acceptable ways.
   (c) Punishes the id for its aggressive urges.

3. According to Bushman, venting anger:
   (a) Reduces the aggressive drive.
   (b) Has no effect on aggression.
   (c) Leads to more aggression.

4. Freud's theory and the biological approach:
   (a) Disagree that aggression is useful for survival.
   (b) Agree that the contents of the unconscious play a role in aggression.
   (c) Agree that aggression is partly innate.

Role of hormones in human behaviour

1. The key gland of the endocrine system is the:
(a) Pituitary gland.
(b) Adrenal gland.
(c) Thyroid.

2. The main hormonal influence on aggression is:
(a) Elevated testosterone.
(b) Low levels of adrenaline.
(c) Oestrogen.

3. The role of cortisol is emphasised by the:
(a) Twin hormone theory.
(b) Cortisol–aggression theory.
(c) Dual-hormone hypothesis.

4. Dabbs and Hargrove studied aggression in:
(a) Male prisoners.
(b) Female prisoners.
(c) Sportsmen and sportswomen.

Classic study: Raine et al. (1997)

1. The design of this study was:
(a) Matched pairs.
(b) Repeated measures.
(c) Independent groups.

2. The murderers and controls were matched on sex, age and:
(a) Handedness and history of head injury.
(b) Ethnicity and schizophrenia diagnosis.
(c) Ethnicity and handedness.

3. The researchers concluded that brain dysfunction:
(a) Causes aggression.
(b) Is impossible to study in violent offenders.
(c) Interacts with non-biological factors.

4. The canthomeatal line is:
(a) Part of the London Underground.
(b) In the same position in everyone.
(c) Used to guide a PET scan.

Contemporary study: Li et al. (2013)

1. The researchers used what kind of brain scans?
(a) CAT.
(b) PET.
(c) fMRI.

2. Each participant was shown:
(a) 48 images.
(b) 24 images.
(c) 4 to 12 images.

3. The researchers found a functional link between the PCC and the:
(a) Dorsal striatum.
(b) Hypothalamus.
(c) Prefrontal cortex.

4. The small sample size:
(a) Increased the chance of a Type I error.
(b) Was a strength of the study.
(c) Had no effect on the conclusions.

Contemporary study: Brendgen et al. (2005)

1. Data was collected when the children were:
(a) 24 months old.
(b) 48 months old.
(c) 72 months old.

2. The contribution of genetic factors to teacher ratings of physical aggression was:
(a) 63%.
(b) 24%.
(c) 0%.

3. Social aggression was mostly explained by:
(a) Genetics.
(b) Shared environment.
(c) Non-shared environment.

4. The findings are only valid if the _____ assumption is true.
(a) Equal genes.
(b) Equal environments.
(c) Unique environments.

Contemporary study: Van den Oever et al. (2008)

1. Nose-poking behaviour in some rats was removed through a process of:
(a) Excitation.
(b) Extinction.
(c) Extraction.

2. The study highlights the importance of the neurotransmitter:
(a) GABA.
(b) Dopamine.
(c) Glutamate.

3. The key subunit of the AMPA receptor targeted by the injection was:
(a) GluR1.
(b) GluR2.
(c) GluR3.

4. In this study there were many:
(a) Confounding variables.
(b) Human participants.
(c) Standardised procedures.

"Every time he lectures about serotonin, he puts me to sleep."

MCQ answers
The central nervous system and human behaviour 1B 2B 3C 4A
Neurons, synaptic transmission and neurotransmitters 1A 2C 3C 4A
Effect of recreational drugs 1C 2B 3A 4A
The structure of the brain and aggression 1B 2B 3C 4C
Evolution, natural selection and aggression 1A 2C 3A 4B
Freud's psychodynamic explanation of aggression 1C 2B 3C 4C
Role of hormones in human behaviour 1A 2A 3C 4B
Classic study: Raine et al. (1997) 1A 2B 3C 4C
Contemporary study: Li et al. (2013) 1C 2A 3A 4A
Contemporary study: Brendgen et al. (2005) 1C 2A 3C 4B
Contemporary study: Van den Oever et al. (2008) 1B 2C 3B 4C

Learning theories

Chapter 4

Contents

Classical conditioning
130 The main features
132 Pavlov (1927)

Operant conditioning
134 The main features
136 Reinforcement and behaviour modification

Social learning theory
138 The main features
140 Bandura et al. (1961)
142 Bandura et al. (1963, 1965)

Phobias
144 Learning theory explanations
146 Treatments based on learning theories

Methods – see pages 206–215 of Chapter 5

Studies
148 Classic study: Watson and Rayner (1920)
Contemporary study, select one of:
150 Becker et al. (2002)
152 Bastian et al. (2011)
154 Capafóns et al. (1998)

156 Key questions for learning theories

158 Practical investigations for learning theories

End of chapter
160 Revision summary
162 Practice questions, answers and feedback
164 Multiple-choice questions

I help the rat to run the maze.
I am the punishment and reward.
I show you how you should behave.
I give you fear and take it away.
What am I?

Chapter 4 Learning theories

Classical conditioning

The specification says...

4.1.1 *The main features of classical conditioning, including: unconditioned stimulus (UCS); unconditioned response (UCR); conditioned stimulus (CS); neutral stimulus (NS); conditioned response (CR); extinction, spontaneous recovery and stimulus generalisation.*

Key terms

Classical conditioning – Learning by association. It occurs when a neutral stimulus is repeatedly paired with an unconditioned stimulus. The neutral stimulus eventually produces the same response as the unconditioned stimulus.

Unconditioned stimulus (UCS) – A stimulus that produces a response without any learning taking place.

Unconditioned response (UCR) – An unlearned response to an unconditioned stimulus.

Neutral stimulus (NS) – A stimulus that does not produce the target response. It becomes a conditioned stimulus after being paired with the unconditioned stimulus.

Conditioned stimulus (CS) – A stimulus that only produces the target response *after* it has been paired with the UCS.

Conditioned response (CR) – The response elicited by the CS, i.e. a new association has been learned so that the NS/CS produces the UCR which is now called the CR.

Extinction – When the CS and UCS have not been paired for a while and the CS ceases to elicit the CR.

Spontaneous recovery – An extinct response activates again so that the CS once again elicits the CR.

Stimulus generalisation – When an individual who has acquired a conditioned response to one stimulus begins to respond to similar stimuli in the same way.

When chocolate wrappers are paired with chocolate they can become conditioned stimuli and trigger the same salivation response as chocolate itself.

The main features

Classical conditioning is the simplest form of associative learning, i.e. learning that takes place when we come to associate two stimuli with one another. Classical conditioning was discovered by Ivan Pavlov in the 19th century. Pavlov did not use the term 'classical' himself but it is now used to distinguish this form of learning from more recently discovered forms.

The process of classical conditioning

Classical conditioning takes place when two stimuli are repeatedly paired together – an unconditioned (not learned) stimulus (UCS) and a new neutral stimulus (NS). The NS eventually produces the same response as that produced by the UCS. We can think of this as taking place in three phases:

- *Before conditioning* – UCS triggers a reflex response such as salivation, anxiety or sexual arousal. This is called the unconditioned response (UCR). An unrelated NS does not produce this response.
- *During conditioning* – The UCS and the NS are experienced *contiguously*, i.e. close together in time. This is called *pairing*. The effect of pairing is greatest when the NS occurs just before the UCS. Usually pairing has to take place many times for conditioning to occur.
- *After conditioning* – Following pairing, the NS produces the same response as the UCS. The NS is now a conditioned stimulus (CS) and the response to it is called a conditioned response (CR).

An example of classical conditioning is learning to salivate in response to a chocolate wrapper. The wrapper is a NS until it is paired with chocolate, an UCS. After pairing, the wrapper becomes a CS and elicits a CR (salivation).

Extinction

When a CS is experienced without the UCS over a period of time the CR is *extinguished*, i.e. the CS ceases to elicit the CR, effectively making it extinct. This extinction of responses has survival value because it means that our learning is flexible – we can for example learn to stop fearing something that has been conditioned as a fear stimulus but which poses little danger.

Spontaneous recovery

Sometimes extinct responses reappear, even without new pairings with the UCS. Generally such responses are weaker than the original ones. This phenomenon is called spontaneous recovery.

Imagine you were conditioned to salivate at the sight of chocolate wrappers and then went through a period of having chocolate unwrapped for you and not seeing wrappers. You might see wrappers and not respond to them but you would not have completely unlearned the salivation response. One day you might dribble a bit on seeing a wrapper.

Stimulus generalisation

Sometimes we become conditioned to respond to one stimulus but we find ourselves exhibiting the same response to other similar stimuli. This is called stimulus generalisation. To return to our chocolate wrapper example, once conditioned to salivate at one wrapper we might also find ourselves drooling at the sight of other wrappers, particularly those similar in appearance.

Stretch & Challenge

Doing it without a brain

Decerebration is a procedure in which laboratory animals have most of their cerebral cortex surgically removed. Jau-Shin Lou and James Bloedel (1988) found that decerebrated ferrets could still be conditioned to avoid hitting an obstacle as they moved around.

What does this tell us about classical conditioning?

Think Link
Developmental psychology

Explains our tastes

Classical conditioning plays a role in our development because it accounts for some of our responses. Our tastes in everything from chocolate to music can be partially explained by the associations we form during our development. For example, if we come to associate a particular song or style of music (the NS) with happy parties (party = UCS leading to fun = UCR) in our teens that may form part of our long-term behavioural repertoire.

Evaluation

Research evidence

A strength of classical conditioning is that it is supported by many studies conducted on both humans and animals.

Ivan Pavlov demonstrated classical conditioning of salivation responses in his studies of dogs (see next spread). John Watson and Rosalie Rayner (1920) demonstrated that a fear response could be conditioned in a human baby (see page 148). A recent review by Mirte Brom *et al*. (2014) concluded that human sexual responses can be largely explained by classical conditioning.

This is important because it means there is firm evidence supporting the existence of classical conditioning in human and animal learning.

Competing argument However, some of Pavlov's details of classical conditioning are open to question. For example, Pavlov believed that the essential factor linking NS to UCS was *contiguity* – the two stimuli occurring close together in time. Robert Rescorla (1968) found evidence that contiguity is in fact less important than *contingency* – the extent to which the NS reliably predicts the UCS.

An incomplete explanation of learning

A weakness of classical conditioning is that it can only explain how a limited range of behaviours can be acquired.

Classical conditioning only explains the acquisition of simple reflex responses like salivation, anxiety and sexual arousal. It cannot account for more complex chains of learned behaviour. For example, classical conditioning could explain how we come to fear dogs but not the maintenance of this fear over time or the behaviours we learn in order to avoid encountering dogs.

Therefore, classical conditioning is only a partial explanation for learning of behaviour.

Application to aversion therapy

Classical conditioning has therapeutic applications such as systematic desensitisation and flooding (see page 146).

Another example of a therapy based on classical conditioning is aversion therapy. This is used, for example, to treat people who have an unwanted behaviour such as experiencing sexual arousal to a photograph of a young child. A painful electric shock (UCS) is paired with the child's photograph (NS). The shock produces an UCR response of discomfort. The NS will become a CS and also produce a sensation of discomfort.

This shows that classical conditioning is useful to psychologists as well as being of theoretical interest.

EXTRA: Issues and debates

Classical conditioning is an example of good science because it is falsifiable.

Classical conditioning generates testable predictions and is therefore falsifiable. According to scientific philosophers such as Karl Popper this makes classical conditioning good science. The fact that Rescorla was able to test and challenge the importance of contiguity is an example of classical conditioning's falsifiability.

This is important because falsifiability is widely believed to be a hallmark of good science.

Balanced conclusion

There is ample evidence to show that both humans and animals can acquire simple behavioural responses by classical conditioning. Therefore, its existence is not controversial. However, it only explains the acquisition of a small range of simple behaviours and is therefore only a partial explanation of learning.

---

① **Before conditioning**
Flashbulb → Person blinks
UCS (unconditioned stimulus) UCR (unconditioned response)
UCS automatically produces UCR.

② Camera → Person does not blink
NS (neutral stimulus) Interest, no blinking
NS doesn't produce blinking.

③ **During conditioning**
Flashbulb and camera → Person blinks
UCR
UCS paired with NS (neutral stimulus)

④ **After conditioning**
Camera → Person blinks
CS (conditioned stimulus) CR (conditioned response)
NS (camera) is now the CS. It produces a CR, blinking, which is like the UCR produced by the flashbulb.

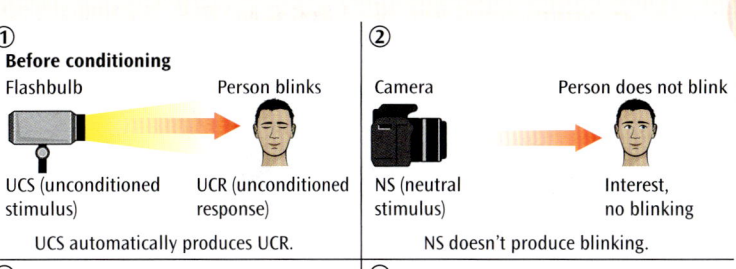

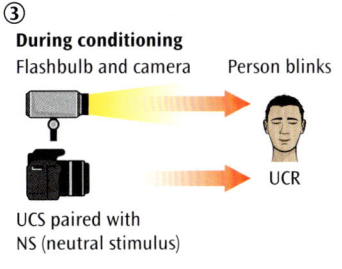

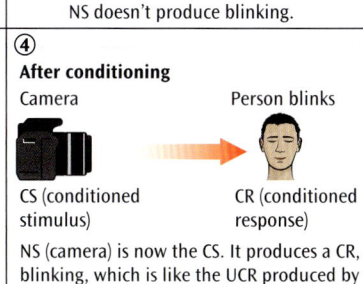

The process of conditioning a response, in this case to a camera.

Apply it — Methods: Squirrels

Chloe has conducted an observation of squirrels in the park, spending two hours watching them. She has recorded the frequency of three different behaviours the squirrels can display either on the ground or in the trees. These are standing up on two feet, resting on all four feet and running. Her results are shown in the table below.

Table showing squirrel observations.

Behavioural category		Standing	Resting	Running
Squirrel location	Ground	17	24	15
	Trees	20	4	14

1. Explain **one** conclusion that Chloe could draw from the results in the table above. (2)
2. Chloe has conducted a chi-squared test and found an observed value of 11.54.
   (a) Justify Chloe's choice of statistical test. (2)
   (b) Calculate degrees of freedom (*df*) for Chloe's data. (1)
   (c) Explain whether Chloe should accept her alternate hypothesis. (2)

Apply it — Concepts: The pet mouse

Jeff wears a blue school uniform and his sister has a yellow one. When Jeff feeds his pet mouse the mouse jumps around. Jeff's mum notices that, when she wears her blue jumper, the mouse also does a special jump when it sees her. Jeff goes on a school trip for two weeks and his little sister feeds the mouse. When Jeff returns his mouse no longer jumps round the cage when he feeds it, but a week later the mouse has started jumping again. Using classical conditioning, explain the behaviour of Jeff's mouse. (4)

Study tip

Remember that the *response* stays the same throughout the process of classical conditioning. The response elicited by the UCS is the same response that is later elicited by the CS.

Check it

1. Explain the process of classical conditioning. (6)
2. Pablo salivates when he hears the ice cream van.
   (a) Explain how Pablo could have acquired this behaviour. (3)
   (b) Explain how extinction and spontaneous recovery might occur in Pablo. (2)
3. **Standard:** Evaluate classical conditioning as an explanation of human behaviour. (8)
4. **AS (Context/Synoptic):** Friends Alexa and Barnie are about to have their first driving lessons. Alexa is very nervous but Barnie is excited.
   Evaluate explanations for their individual differences using learning theories and biological psychology. You must refer to the context in your answer. (12)

Classical conditioning: Pavlov (1927)

The specification says...
4.1.2 Pavlov (1927) experiment with salivation in dogs.

Stretch & Challenge

Pavlov the physiologist
Pavlov identified himself primarily as a physiologist and was extremely critical of psychologists, who he considered to be poor scientists! Throughout his work he was primarily interested in the functioning of the nervous system as opposed to the mind.

One of Pavlov's methods for learning about the physiological basis of conditioned reflexes was to cut through nerves to see which destroyed nerves would lead to the failure of the reflex. For example, he found that severing nerves from the ear to the brain or from the spinal cord to the salivary glands would abolish a salivation reflex conditioned to a sound. He also found that damage to the *cerebral cortex* would abolish the conditioned reflex. This was the foundation of our understanding of how reflexes work and the neural mechanisms underlying conditioning.

Pavlov proposed that the complexity of human eating behaviour, including all the social conventions surrounding it, could be explained by a complex series of conditioned reflexes. Do you agree, and why?

The process of conditioning in Pavlov's dogs.

Before conditioning
Food (UCS) → Salivation (UCR)
Bell (NS) → No response

During conditioning
Bell (NS) paired with food (UCS) → Salivation (UCR)

After conditioning
Bell (CS) → Salivation (CR)

Study tip
The specification refers to 'Pavlov (1927) experiment', therefore you are very likely to come across questions phrased in this way. In fact Pavlov's 1927 book describes several years of experimental studies. Don't be put off by this however – just make sure you can outline aims, method/procedure, findings and conclusions as we have done here.

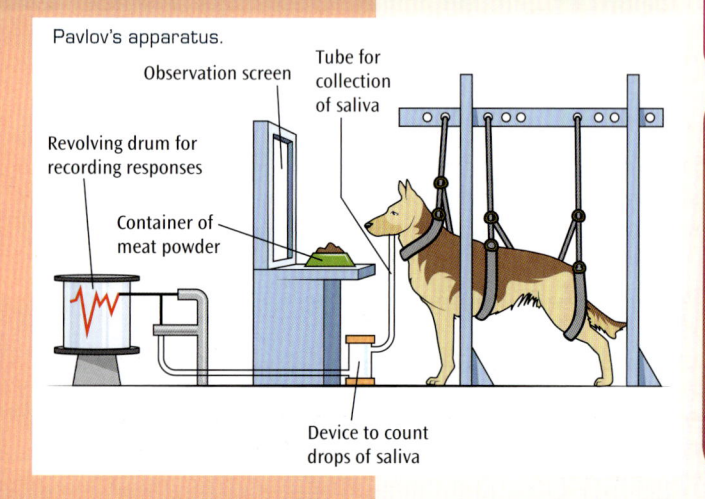

Pavlov's apparatus.
- Observation screen
- Tube for collection of saliva
- Revolving drum for recording responses
- Container of meat powder
- Device to count drops of saliva

Experiment with salivation in dogs

Aims
Ivan Pavlov's initial aim was to learn about the salivation reflex, however he noted that salivation in dogs occurred not only in response to food but to stimuli that typically occurred close in time to the presentation of food. Pavlov's broad aim then shifted towards exploring conditioned reflexes – what we now call *classically conditioned responses*. In particular Pavlov was interested in:
- Explaining the role of conditioned reflexes in the eating behaviour of dogs.
- Exploring how salivation becomes associated with new stimuli apparently unrelated to food and the properties of this association.

Procedure
Pavlov's best-known method was an experimental procedure involving collecting saliva from the salivary glands of an immobilised dog. This was done in a laboratory so the production of saliva could be easily observed and measured either by volume or number of drops in a cannula. Salivation was the dependent variable. The procedure took place in a soundproof chamber in order to minimise the effects of extraneous variables such as noise.

Pavlov established a baseline by measuring salivation in response to the neutral stimulus (NS), for example a metronome or a buzzer. Then he would pair the NS with the unconditioned stimulus (UCS) of food, usually around 20 times.

Pavlov varied the presentation so that the NS was presented before (forward conditioning) or after the UCS (backward conditioning).

Further variations in the procedure were used to investigate extinction and spontaneous recovery of salivation, for example the NS (e.g. metronome), now a conditioned stimulus (CS), was presented several times without the UCS which produced extinction.

Findings
An NS, such as the sound of a metronome or buzzer, did not initially elicit a salivation response, whereas the UCS of food elicited immediate salivation.

After forward pairings of NS and UCS, the NS typically did elicit salivation after it was presented for a few seconds. In one trial Pavlov recorded that salivation commenced nine seconds after the metronome sound, with 45 drops of saliva being collected.

No salivation was recorded in response to the NS in backwards pairing.

Pavlov noted that the salivation reflex only became associated with an NS if the dog was alert and undistracted.

Extinction of salivation could be seen as the salivary volume declined after repeated presentation of the CS *without* the UCS. The salivary response to the CS spontaneously recovered on some occasions.

Conclusion
A link is likely to be made in the brain between a UCS and an NS that occurs just before the UCS. Pavlov called this *signalisation* which has survival value in preparing an organism for events. For example, a dog can learn to salivate when it hears a buzzer so that it is prepared to eat by the time food is presented.

Think Link
Developmental psychology

Continuous development
There is a tension in developmental psychology between learning theories and stage theories. Learning theory, including the development of conditioned responses, predicts that behaviours can be acquired at any time during our lifespan and largely remain. This is at odds with stage theories of development which are very popular in psychology (such as Freud's psychosexual stages described on page 106). Stage theories predict that development goes in steps – particular behaviours can only be acquired when you reach a certain age and may be specific to an age/stage.

Evaluation

Some good experimental controls
A strength is that the design of the study had some clever features that reduced the impact of extraneous variables and therefore enhanced the internal validity of the study.

Pavlov's studies took place within a soundproof chamber to reduce the possibility of external sounds distracting the dogs or providing additional stimuli. The collection of saliva externally in a cannula helped prevent any loss of saliva and therefore invalid measurement of salivation. Neutral stimuli were carefully chosen and tested to ensure they did not already elicit a salivation response.

These controls make it more likely that salivation in response to the conditioned stimulus was due to conditioning rather than to extraneous variables.

Generalisability to humans
A weakness of Pavlov's work is that it was conducted on dogs, and there is a problem generalising the results of animal studies to humans.

It is always unclear how well the findings of animal studies will generalise to humans because humans have structurally different brains from other species, and may therefore respond differently. In particular humans have a larger cerebral cortex than other species and this permits greater complex cognitive processing, including conscious choice.

This is important because Pavlov (and others) believed his findings would generalise to humans and that may not be entirely true.

Competing argument In fact, studies like Little Albert (Watson and Rayner 1920, described on page 148) show that classical conditioning does take place in humans. Although humans can consciously try to overcome conditioned reflexes, this is very difficult.

Application to eating problems
Pavlov's study has clinical applications in helping understand problem eating behaviours.

Obesity can be partially understood in terms of conditioned responses very like those displayed by Pavlov's dogs. For example, Anita Jansen et al. (2003) suggest that overweight children have acquired very strong associations between cues that predict the arrival of food and the salivation response. Overeating follows exposure to these cues.

This application of Pavlov's research demonstrates its significance in developing therapies such as systematic desensitisation (see page 146).

EXTRA: Issues and debates
Pavlov's research is an example of how psychological knowledge can be used in society.

In health promotion, Pavlov's techniques can be used to create conditioned responses that encourage healthy behaviours and discourage unhealthy ones. An example is the use of distressing images such as cancerous lungs on cigarette packaging. This creates an association between the UCS of distressing image and the NS of cigarettes, causing cigarettes to elicit a CR of disgust and horror. However, there have been more controversial uses of knowledge from Pavlov's research in society, including the use of aversion therapy (see previous spread) to discourage homosexuality.

Thus Pavlov's research has both uses and abuses.

Balanced conclusion
Pavlov deserves great credit for discovering classical conditioning and for systematically exploring it, uncovering phenomena like extinction and spontaneous recovery. His procedures were well controlled and his conclusions largely supported by later research. His work has important applications – though some are controversial and it should be remembered that it only explains one aspect of learning.

Ivan Pavlov (1849–1936) was a Russian physiologist. He initially trained for the priesthood before studying medicine at St Petersburg University. After graduating in 1879 Pavlov worked in physiology research and was invited to lead the Russian Institute of Experimental Medicine. This was where he conducted his famous experiment in the 1900s (which is described on this spread). Pavlov was awarded the Nobel Prize in 1904 for his work on digestion, including conditioned reflexes.

Apply it — Methods: Pair wise
Fiona is a teacher whose class works in pairs. She sometimes gives her students sweets from a tin. Before one lesson, she asks one student from each pair to discreetly tally how many times their partner swallows. She tells the students to do this for five minutes at the beginning of the lesson and for another five minutes when she noisily puts the sweet tin on her desk.

1. (a) Who are the participants in this observation? (1)
   (b) Fiona believes this is a non-participant, overt observation. Explain whether she is correct. (2)
   (c) Explain **one** ethical issue raised in Fiona's study. (2)
2. Fiona asks the class to identify weaknesses of the study.
   (a) One student suggests that the way swallowing was counted was a problem. Explain how this might affect the validity of the data collected. (2)
   (b) Explain how the use of counting might affect the reliability of the data collected. (2)
   (c) Another student suggests there were some uncontrolled variables. Identify **one** uncontrolled variable in this study. (1)
   (d) Explain how this variable could be controlled. (2)

Apply it — Concepts: The sound of flushing
Sally is using a school shower when she hears a toilet flush. The water in the shower suddenly gets boiling hot and she cries out in pain and leaps to safety. Sally tests the water before getting back in to finish her shower, only to hear another flush.

1. (a) If Sally has been classically conditioned, what would she do next? (1)
   (b) Explain your answer using the terms CR, CS, NS, UCR, UCS. (5)
2. **Context essay:** Assess whether the findings of Pavlov's studies can be applied to Sally's situation. (8)

Study tip
Keep revisiting the taxonomy of command terms on page 7. It is easy to forget the difference between terms such as 'assess' and 'evaluate'. In the 8-mark assess question above, you need to carefully consider evidence for and against the usefulness of animal studies, such as Pavlov's, and make a judgement at the end.

Check it
1. Describe the conclusions of Pavlov's study using appropriate psychological terms. (5)
2. (a) Describe how Pavlov (1927) collected data from the dogs he used in his study. (3)
   (b) Explain **two** variables that were controlled by Pavlov's use of this apparatus. (2)
3. **Standard:** Evaluate Pavlov's (1927) research on classical conditioning. (8)
4. **AL (I&D):** To what extent do Pavlov's study and Bandura et al.'s (1961) study demonstrate the 'scientific status of psychology'? (12)

Operant conditioning

Chapter 4 Learning theories

The specification says...

4.1.3 The main features of operant conditioning including: types of reinforcement and punishment (positive and negative).

Properties of reinforcement, including primary and secondary reinforcement.

Key terms

Operant conditioning – Learning that occurs when a behaviour is followed by an event, and the nature of this event increases or decreases the probability of the behaviour being repeated.

Reinforcement – Takes place when a behaviour is followed by an event and this increases the probability of that behaviour being repeated.

Positive reinforcement – Occurs when something nice is introduced to the individual following a behaviour, increasing the probability of that behaviour being repeated.

Negative reinforcement – Occurs when something unpleasant is removed from the individual following a behaviour, increasing the probability of that behaviour being repeated.

Punishment – Takes place when an event follows a behaviour and this decreases the probability that the behaviour will be repeated.

Primary reinforcement – Takes place when the thing that acts as a reinforcer has biological significance, such as food.

Secondary reinforcement – Takes place when the thing that acts as a reinforcer has become associated with something of biological significance, such as money which is associated with being able to buy food.

Positive punishment – Occurs when something unpleasant is introduced to the individual following a behaviour, decreasing the probability of that behaviour being repeated.

Negative punishment – Occurs when something nice is removed from an individual following a behaviour, decreasing the probability of that behaviour being repeated.

An example of an operant chamber (aka a Skinner box).

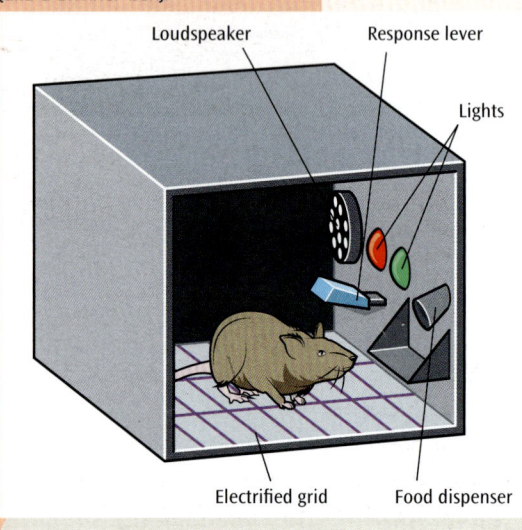

Loudspeaker — Response lever — Lights — Electrified grid — Food dispenser

The main features

Like classical conditioning, operant conditioning results in a link forming between a behaviour and an event. In this case the behaviour is an act that the individual produces and the event is the consequence of that behaviour. The consequence can lead to an increase or decrease in the probability of the behaviour being repeated.

The Skinner box

Much of our understanding of operant conditioning comes from the work of Burrhus Frederic Skinner (1948), an American whose ideas dominated psychology in the 1940s and 1950s. He carried out much of his research on animals using what has become known as an *operant chamber* or *Skinner box*. This contained a supply of food pellets that could be released as reinforcers when the animal learned to do something, for example to operate a lever. Some operant chambers also contained electrified floors which could be used to punish behaviour. Using reinforcement and punishment, Skinner and colleagues could train the animals to learn target behaviours.

Reinforcement

A behaviour is said to be reinforced when an event that follows it increases the probability of the behaviour being repeated. Normally this is a pleasant consequence, but remember that anything that makes the behaviour more likely is reinforcement – this means that escaping from something unpleasant is also reinforcing. The event that leads to the increased likelihood of the behaviour being repeated is called a *reinforcer*.

- **Positive reinforcement** takes place when something pleasant is introduced following a behaviour. This might be something tangible such as food or money, or something less tangible but also nice, such as a smile or praise.
- **Negative reinforcement** takes place when something unpleasant, such as pain, is removed following a behaviour.

Primary and secondary reinforcement

Some reinforcers are rewarding because they have biological significance. Thus food, drink, shelter and sex are all primary reinforcers.

However, money or an impressive job title can be just as powerful as reinforcers. This is because they have become associated with primary reinforcers – money buys us food, a cool job makes us more sexually attractive, etc. Rewards like money or job title that have become associated with primary reinforcers are known as secondary reinforcers.

Punishment

Punishment takes place when an event following a behaviour makes its repetition *less* likely. The event that leads to the decrease in likelihood of repeating the behaviour is called a *punisher*.

- **Positive punishment** takes place when something unpleasant or *aversive* is introduced following a behaviour. An example of a positive punisher is a slap.
- **Negative punishment** takes place when something nice is removed. An example of a negative punisher is being fined or grounded.

Some punishers are deliberately introduced by people in order to change someone's behaviour. For example, in the criminal justice system we use negative punishers like prison sentences that deprive people of freedom and labels (such as 'offender') that take away social status. In some societies positive punishers such as floggings are used.

Other punishers are naturally occurring, the first time we touch something hot like a stove we get burnt so we learn not to touch it again. In operant conditioning terms the pain is just as much a punisher as something done to deliberately punish us.

Stretch Challenge: An ideal society

Skinner pictured an ideal future society in his book *Walden Two* (1948) where all aspects of human behaviour are regulated by a complex system of reinforcement. He believed that society could escape the need for punishment-based systems but also that individuals should sacrifice their freedom for the greater good. Skinner was trying to apply his experiences of conditioning animals in operant chambers to build a better human society.

What problems can you see with Skinner's idea?

Evaluation

Research evidence

A strength of operant conditioning is that it is supported by many studies conducted on both humans and animals.

Skinner and many others conducted hundreds of laboratory experiments demonstrating operant conditioning in animals. There are consistent findings regarding the ability to modify behaviour using reinforcement and punishment. In addition, modern brain studies have revealed brain systems (neural correlates) that relate to reinforcement in humans (Chase et al. 2015).

This means there is a firm evidence base supporting the existence of operant conditioning in both human and animal learning.

An incomplete explanation of learning

A weakness of operant conditioning is that it can only explain how existing behaviours are strengthened or weakened, not where behaviours originate.

Although operant conditioning can explain a much wider range of behaviours than classical conditioning, including complex chains of behaviour, it is still incomplete as an explanation of the acquisition of all new behaviour. It cannot account for the learning of new behaviours which the animal has never performed before.

This shows that operant conditioning is only a partial explanation for learning of behaviour.

Application to education and childcare

Operant conditioning has many practical applications, for example in education and childcare.

Systems of reinforcement are used in a range of places, including schools, nurseries and other settings involving children. For example, giving a child a star for good work encourages them to repeat their good work. Parents often use star charts or food treats to reinforce desirable behaviour.

This shows that operant conditioning is of use in the real world as well as being of theoretical interest.

EXTRA: Issues and debates

Operant conditioning lends itself to social control.

Reward and punishment are the major ways in which societies regulate the behaviour of their citizens. One of Skinner's aims was to use reinforcement effectively in order to create a society in which everyone's liberty was tightly controlled (see Stretch and challenge on facing page). This raises important issues of respect for individual liberty.

This is important because as a society we place great value on individual liberty. Operant conditioning is open to abuse because it is a powerful tool that can be used to restrict individual liberty.

Competing argument Although operant conditioning techniques are open to abuse, a degree of social control is necessary for any large groups of people to live together. An understanding of operant conditioning allows behaviour to be regulated using more reinforcement and less punishment.

Balanced conclusion

See conclusion on the next spread.

Parenting skills training programmes aim to shift parents from using punishment in order to regulate children's behaviour to using reinforcement instead.

Reinforcement | **Punishment**

Apply it Methods: Moving the ball

Zach is testing rats in a Skinner box. There is a ball in the box which has a sensor inside. This sensor automatically records when the rats move the ball. The rats are fed a pellet each time they move the ball. Each rat spends two hours a day in the box during a period of one week.

1. Zach's study is a covert observation.
   Give **one** advantage of covert observation in this study. (1)
2. The number of ball-pushes per minute is an example of time sampling. Zach wants to use a measure of central tendency to compare the typical number of ball-pushes a rat performs in the first five minutes of the first session compared to the last five minutes of each session.
   (a) Explain which measure of central tendency Zach should use. (2)
   (b) Explain why time sampling is more useful to Zach than event sampling. (2)

Apply it Concepts: Dog treats

Sophie wants to teach her dog, Spot, to jump over a log. This means she has to stop him from just running around the side of the log. She has a bag of treats in her pocket. She tries not to shout as he doesn't like that.
Explain how Sophie could use operant conditioning to train Spot. (6)

Think Link
Developmental psychology

Making behaviour fit social conventions

Operant conditioning, like classical conditioning, takes place throughout our development. It is important in our social development as people around us constantly reinforce and punish our behaviour, often in order to make our behaviour more conventional. The school system uses a blend of reinforcers – everything from house points to a smiling teacher to make our behaviour more conventional.

Schools also use punishers, such as detentions, to shape behaviour. This regulation of our behaviour continues in adulthood where the legal system uses the threat of punishment to regulate us.

Check it

1. Explain the difference between reinforcement and punishment. (2)
2. Compare primary and secondary reinforcers. (2)
3. **Standard:** Evaluate the theory of operant conditioning. (8)
4. **AL (I&D/Synoptic):** To what extent can social psychology and learning theories explain social control of children by parents and/or teachers? (12)

Operant conditioning: Reinforcement and behaviour modification

The specification says…
4.1.4 Properties of reinforcement, including schedules of reinforcement.
4.1.5 Behaviour modification, including 'shaping' behaviour.

Key terms
Reinforcement schedule – A plan of how often and when reinforcement will be provided, i.e. vary or keep constant the ratio of behaviour to reinforcer and the time interval between reinforcements.

Behaviour modification – The use of operant conditioning techniques to change the frequency of desired behaviours, for example in therapeutic settings.

Shaping – A process of modifying behaviour by reinforcing successive approximations to a desired behaviour.

Think Link
Individual differences
Reinforcement and behavioural addiction
Individual differences in behaviour include patterns of behaviour that can be regarded as abnormal. Some abnormal behaviours can be explained by reinforcement schedules experienced by some people rather than others. For example, one person might develop an alcohol or gambling addiction because he or she is exposed to a variable ratio reinforcement schedule, whereas someone else might not have such reinforcements.

Stretch & Challenge
Lovaas therapy
Ivar Lovaas pioneered the use of behaviour modification (including shaping) to treat children with autism spectrum disorder. Lovaas therapy is a very intensive system of reinforcement and punishment that takes up most of a child's waking hours for a period of months or years. It is done in the child's home environment and makes use of a single trained practitioner, often a parent.

Punishment, for example painful shocks, is used to discourage self-injurious behaviour. Desirable behaviours are reinforced using whatever reinforcers work for the individual child. Language is developed using shaping, reinforcement only being maintained where utterances continue to approximate to intended sounds and, later, words.

What ethical issues do you think Lovaas therapy might raise?

Step 1: Give the pigeon food when it turns towards the button.
Step 2: Only give the pigeon food if it walks towards the button, not for just turning towards it.
Step 3: Give the pigeon food when it raises its head to the height of the button, but not when it just walks towards the button.
Step 4: Give the pigeon food when it taps the button with its beak but not if it just raises its head to the button.

An example of shaping.

Schedules of reinforcement

Continuous and partial reinforcement
A behaviour is said to be *continuously* reinforced when the reinforcer always follows a behaviour. For example, we might pay a child every time they do the washing up. Continuous reinforcement leads to rapid change in behaviour but the effects tend not to last. This is why children paid regularly for household tasks do not usually stick to them for long!

The alternative to continuous reinforcement is *partial* reinforcement. Here, reinforcement is irregular. In a reinforcement schedule we can vary either the *ratio* of behaviour to reinforcement or the *interval* between the reinforcements. In either case this can be *fixed* (consistent) or *variable* (ranges around a mean time).

Partial schedules are written as F (for fixed) or V (for variable) with a number indicating the ratio or interval. FI3 is a fixed interval of 3: three time units must pass before another response can be rewarded. For example, a rat on FI3 would wait 3 minutes after pressing the bar before it can receive another reward.

Fixed and variable *ratio* reinforcement schedules
- *Fixed ratio reinforcement* schedule – A reinforcer is given after a *specified* number of behaviours, for example we pay a child every seventh time they do the washing up.
- *Variable ratio reinforcement* schedule – A reinforcer is given after an *unpredictable* number of behaviours that varies around a mean value. A child on a variable ratio of 3 (VR3) may therefore get paid after one, three or five instances of doing the washing up (1 + 3 + 5 = 9 divided by 3 gives mean of 3). Variable ratio schedules lead to behaviour change that is difficult to extinguish (i.e. stop).

Fixed and variable *interval* reinforcement schedules
- *Fixed interval reinforcement* schedule – The time between reinforcers is kept constant. For example, paying a child at the end of the time interval if he has washed up one or more times during that interval.
- *Variable interval reinforcement* schedule – The time between reinforcers is varied around a mean length of time. As with fixed interval, only one behaviour per time period is needed for reinforcement. So a child is again paid at the end of the time period if he washes up one or more times during the interval – but this interval varies in length. Variable interval schedules tend to result in the most consistent behaviour.

Behaviour modification

Modifying behaviour
In the loosest sense, any use of operant conditioning to modify behaviour can be called behaviour modification. A stricter definition is as a form of therapy in which reinforcement is systematically used to increase the number of instances of desired behaviour.

An example of behaviour modification is in sport psychology where reinforcement is used to improve technique and reduce dangerous behaviour. Cassie Ford et al. (2017) assessed head-impact (a measure of risk of injury) using helmet sensors in American footballers and used individual mentoring to provide reinforcement to the high-risk players. Mean impact intensity dropped by 3.9% overall and by 4.7% on the top-of-head (particularly dangerous). This behaviour modification thus improved safety.

Shaping
Shaping is used to encourage complex behaviours. This is done by reinforcing successive approximations of the behaviour. In other words you start by reinforcing behaviour vaguely like what you are seeking, but only continue the reinforcement each time the behaviour becomes a step closer to the target behaviour.

Shaping occurs as children acquire language. When babies start to babble they are initially reinforced by adult attention and praise, but this only continues if the child goes on to produce recognisable words – and, later, sequences of words.

Evaluation

Research evidence

A strength of reinforcement schedules is that they are supported by many studies conducted on both humans and animals.

Hundreds of laboratory and field experiments have compared the effects of different partial reinforcement schedules on animal and human learning, with results consistently showing the properties of partial reinforcement schedules. For example, Gary Latham and Dennis Dossett (1978) found that mountain beaver trappers responded better to variable ratio pay in which they received $4 for a trapped animal if they also correctly guessed the colour of a marble than fixed ratio pay in which they received $1 per animal.

This means that there is a firm evidence base supporting the properties of partial reinforcement in both human and non-human animal learning.

Fails to take account of intrinsic motivation

A weakness is that understanding the properties of reinforcement does not provide a complete account of human motivation.

Humans are motivated by a range of factors. Reinforcement properties provide a detailed account of extrinsic motivation – the effect of 'outside' factors – when someone else offers us a reward. However, our behaviour is also a result of intrinsic ('inside') motives. At work for example we can be just as motivated by interest and enjoyment (intrinsic) as by extrinsic rewards, however well they are scheduled.

This shows that reinforcement properties only provide a partial explanation for human behaviour.

Application to treating inappropriate behaviour

Behaviour modification lends itself well to forms of treatment.

Behaviour modification systems have been used to treat a range of mental health problems, ranging from schizophrenia to autism spectrum disorder (ASD). For example, Lovaas therapy involves intensive reinforcement including shaping, in order to normalise some aspects of behaviour in children with ASD.

This shows that behaviour modification is of practical benefit to clients.

EXTRA: Issues and debates

Behaviour modification techniques give therapists the power to determine the future behaviour of their clients.

This is an ethical issue because this power is open to abuse. For example, behaviour modification could be used to condition a client to follow whatever behaviours the therapist considers normal. These might include wearing a suit and going to church. These things might conflict with the beliefs and preferences of the individual.

This is important because clients in behavioural therapy have the human right of individual liberty within the bounds of law.

Competing argument Although behaviour modification techniques are open to abuse they are not inherently abusive. In most cases therapist and client can agree on what behaviours they are working towards. Where this is not possible because of the client's cognitive or communication abilities, therapists need to give careful consideration to ethical issues.

Balanced conclusion

The existence of operant conditioning is not in question, and Skinner's account of reinforcement is largely supported. However, operant conditioning is not, as Skinner believed, a complete explanation for human behaviour. It does not, for example, explain the role of intrinsic motives in behaviour. Whilst operant conditioning has powerful applications it also gives rise to serious ethical issues.

Examples of reinforcement ratios.

Fixed-ratio schedule	Variable-ratio schedule
Trick-or-treating: Receiving one sweet per house.	Gambling machine: Pays out on average every 50th go.
Fixed-interval schedule	Variable-interval schedule
Getting paid £8 per hour for every hour worked.	A fish bites on average once every 15 minutes.

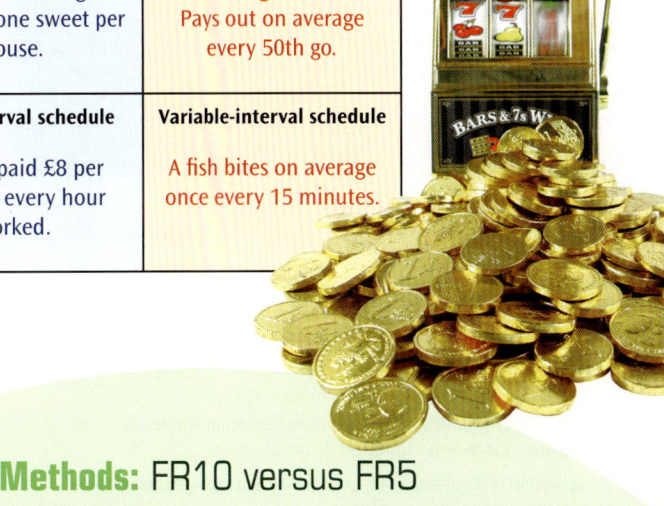

Apply it Methods: FR10 versus FR5

Zoe is using pigeons in Skinner boxes to test the effect of different fixed ratio (FR) reinforcement schedules on learning to peck a disc. The pigeons are rewarded with seeds to encourage learning and, to ensure they are motivated to learn, Zoe makes sure they are hungry before testing.

She wants to know whether FR10 is better than FR5, i.e. whether reinforcement given to every tenth behaviour is better than reinforcement given to every fifth behaviour.

1. Explain **one** advantage of Zoe using a Skinner box to measure the pigeon's behaviour. (2)
2. Zoe suspects that her study may raise ethical issues with her use of animals. Explain **two** ethical issues relating to the Animals (Scientific Procedures) Act (1986) or to the Home Office Regulations for the use of animals. (6)
3. Zoe's study is an experiment.
   (a) State how the independent variable has been operationalised. (1)
   (b) State how the dependent variable has been operationalised. (1)

Apply it Concepts: Seeking a quiet life

Bob looks after his grandchildren every afternoon. He wants the children to sit quietly and not disturb him. When they are noisy he growls scarily at them, or he turns the television off. He gives them sweets at the end of each day if they have been quiet. Sometimes he worries that the children don't 'do' very much and perhaps he ought to teach them some new skills, such as using a yoyo or doing a handstand.

Context essay: Discuss how operant conditioning could be helping Bob to keep his grandchildren quiet. (8)

Study tip

A common mistake is to muddle up the ethical issues for people and for non-human animals. Make sure that you know the difference.

Check it

1. (a) Using **one** example, explain what is meant by 'behaviour modification'. (3)
   (b) Explain **two** weaknesses of behaviour modification. (4)
2. Describe how the owner of a new cat could train it to go through a cat flap using shaping. (3)
3. **Standard:** Evaluate behaviour modification as a technique for altering human behaviour. (8)
4. **AL (I&D/Synoptic):** Learning theories and social theories have practical applications such as prejudice reduction and therapies. Evaluate the ethical issues raised by practical applications of learning theories and social theories. (12)

Social learning theory

The specification says...

4.1.6 The main features of social learning theory, including: observation, imitation, modelling and vicarious reinforcement.

4.1.7 Social learning 'stages' of attention, retention, reproduction and motivation (reinforcement).

Key terms

Social learning theory (SLT) – A way of explaining behaviour that includes both direct and indirect reinforcement, combining learning theory with the role of cognitive factors.

Modelling – From the observer's perspective modelling is imitating the behaviour of a role model. From the role model's perspective, modelling is the demonstration of a specific behaviour that may be imitated by an observer.

Observation – To observe is to watch or listen to behaviour in others.

Imitation – Copying behaviour previously observed in others. In SLT imitation is a selective process and only models with key characteristics are likely to be imitated.

Vicarious reinforcement – 'Reinforcement' refers to a consequence of behaviour that increases the likelihood of that behaviour being repeated. In the case of *vicarious* reinforcement, it is not directly experienced but occurs through observing someone else being reinforced for a behaviour. This is a key factor in imitation.

Attention – The cognitive process of focusing on a stimulus. In SLT the stimulus is the modelled behaviour.

Retention – The cognitive process of storing the modelled behaviour in memory.

Reproduction – The recall and enactment of the modelled behaviour in response to appropriate circumstances.

Motivation – The force that drives a person to enact the behaviour. In SLT this is the result of vicarious reinforcement.

Think Link
Individual differences

Personality

One aspect of personality is aggressiveness. Social learning theory is a powerful explanation for individual differences in social behaviour like aggressiveness because this is at least partly the result of imitating models. For example, domestic violence tends to run in families because children imitate the aggression of the adults in the family.

Chickens selectively imitate high-status flock members.

The main features

Earlier learning theorists like John B. Watson and Burrhus Skinner struggled to explain why learning sometimes took place in the absence of reinforcement, and why merely witnessing the behaviour of another individual was sometimes enough for a new behaviour to be learned.

In the 1960s Albert Bandura proposed social learning theory (SLT), the view that behaviour can be learned by imitating others (it is 'social' because of the role of others). Critically, unlike the early learning theorists, he believed that this kind of learning requires some quite sophisticated *cognitive* processing.

Modelling

To model behaviour is to demonstrate it. In social learning theory modelling takes place when one individual displays a particular social behaviour in the presence of another. The individual demonstrating the behaviour is called the *model*.

However, not all models demonstrating social behaviours are imitated. Models are most likely to be imitated if they are the same sex and age as the observer, and are likeable, conventionally attractive and appear to have high social status. This is because in such circumstances the observer identifies with the model (i.e. admires and wishes to become like them) and therefore imitates their behaviour.

Observation and imitation

Whilst one individual models behaviour another has to respond to this demonstration in order for learning to take place. Observation is an active process in which the observer chooses to focus their attention on the modelled behaviour and watch it.

Imitation is copying observed behaviour. In social learning theory imitation is the most important mechanism of learning. Once behaviour has been observed and stored it can be reproduced whenever the situation is appropriate.

Vicarious reinforcement

Recall that reinforcement is any consequence of a behaviour that increases the probability of that behaviour being repeated. Direct reinforcement takes place when the individual carries out a behaviour and a pleasant consequence follows. Vicarious reinforcement is experienced when an observer witnesses the model being rewarded in some way for the behaviour.

Stages of social learning

Bandura (1977) suggested that four cognitive processes mediate whether observation of a model will lead to imitation of the behaviour.

1. Attention to the behaviour of the model.
2. Retention of the observed behaviour, i.e. storage in memory. This is the main *cognitive* element of SLT.
3. Reproduction of the behaviour in an appropriate situation.
4. Motivation to repeat the behaviour because of vicarious reinforcement.

For example, a child may learn to punch others when angry. Social learning of this behaviour would mean the child (1) needs to pay attention to a model demonstrating the angry behaviour, (2) remembers the angry behaviour, (3) reproduces the angry behaviour when a similar situation arises and (4) is motivated to repeat by having seen the model rewarded in some way for their punch, for example getting a round of applause from friends.

Stretch & Challenge

Social learning in non-human species

Studies have found that SLT explains the acquisition of behaviours in a range of species, not just humans. For example, in one study chickens were taught to peck a particular pad to obtain food. The 'educated' chickens were then returned to their own flocks. The flock members were more likely to imitate an 'educated' chicken if it was a high-status member of the flock rather than a low-status chicken, even when hungry (Nicol and Pope 1999).

Can you think of a human parallel in which high-status people are more likely to be imitated than low-status individuals?

This is Chucky, a character from the film *Child's Play 3*. It has been suggested that the violence in this film was imitated by the 10-year-old boys who abducted and tortured James Bulger in Liverpool, 1993.

Evaluation

Research evidence for SLT

A strength of SLT is that it is supported by a number of studies, conducted on both humans and animals.

Bandura's studies (see pages 140–143) showed that children would imitate an aggressive model who demonstrated aggression against an inflatable doll, especially if the model was the same sex and was rewarded for doing so. Christine Nicol and Stuart Pope (see Stretch and challenge on facing page) showed that chickens would selectively imitate high-status same-sex models in pecking a pad for food.

This evidence is important because it supports Bandura's claims that behaviour can be acquired by observation and imitation and that the likelihood of imitation is affected by vicarious reinforcement and the characteristics of the model.

Research evidence against SLT

A weakness of SLT is evidence that genetic factors are important as well as environmental influences.

Kenneth Kendler *et al.* (2015) showed that identical twins are more similar in their levels of aggression than non-identical twins. This strongly suggests that individual differences in social behaviour like aggressiveness are genetically influenced and not simply a product of different experiences of modelling.

Therefore, SLT is not a complete explanation for the acquisition of behaviour.

Competing argument Bandura did not entirely ignore biological factors. He claimed that behaviours are not solely determined by social learning – it is the way it is expressed that is learned not the actual urge to be aggressive.

Application to violent behaviour

A further strength of SLT is that it explains the alleged effect of media violence on aggression, in particular in children.

There is concern that children may imitate aggressive behaviour modelled in violent television, film and video games. For example, some commentators blamed the James Bulger murder on one of the killers allegedly having watched *Child's Play 3*. SLT is useful because it helps us understand and predict when this might occur, for example when the aggressor is attractive and has high status and when they are seen to be reinforced for their aggression.

This application of SLT is important as it demonstrates the significant contribution of this theory in shaping society's thoughts about what behaviours are modelled in the media, the consequences of this behaviour and who models it.

EXTRA: Issues and debates

SLT is fairly reductionist, though less so than other learning theories.

Social behaviour has multiple influences, including genetic predispositions, social and cultural contexts as well as modelling. SLT focuses very much on modelling and ignores a host of other important factors. However, SLT is less reductionist than classical or operant conditioning because it takes account of cognitive processes that mediate whether modelled behaviour is imitated. Moreover, Bandura did acknowledge the biological roots of aggression.

Therefore, SLT can never be a complete explanation for the acquisition of social behaviour.

Balanced conclusion

On balance, it seems that SLT is a sound theory because it is testable and supported by a range of human and animal studies. Certainly it was a major step forward from earlier learning theories because it took account of the role of cognitive processes in mediating learning. That said, SLT does not appear to be a complete explanation of the acquisition of social behaviour because it fails to take sufficient account of factors other than modelling.

Apply it Methods: Copycat kids

Callie and Megan are planning an observational study on how children in younger years at school copy the behaviour of older children. Some behaviours that are copied include how the older children wear their ties, style their hair and carry their rucksacks on one shoulder.

1. (a) Write operational definitions for any **two** behaviours that Callie and Megan could observe. You can use the examples from the scenario. (4)
   (b) Describe how the study could be carried out using overt non-participant observation. (3)
2. Callie is concerned about reliability in the study.
   (a) Explain how she could test whether she and Megan are reliable observers. (2)
   (b) Explain **one** way that Callie could improve their reliability if necessary. (2)
3. Megan thinks they should collect both quantitative and qualitative data. Explain why this would be beneficial. (3)

Apply it Concepts: See it, do it

Hollie sits with Jess in school. One day Hollie plaits Jess' hair in an impressively complicated way. Hollie explains that she's watched her mum doing it for years on her sister's hair and her sister is always so pleased that she gives her mum a big hug.

1. What is the behaviour being imitated? (1)
2. According to SLT, who is the 'model'? (1)
3. Relate the four key processes (or 'stages') of social learning to this situation. (4)
4. Explain how social learning is a better explanation of Hollie's behaviour than operant conditioning. (4)

Study tip

If you are asked to apply SLT to a scenario be really careful about simply gallivanting through the terminology and expecting to pick up marks. Terms like attention, retention, reproduction and motivation may seem self-explanatory but your job is to actually explain them fully.

Check it

1. Define what is meant by 'modelling' in social learning theory. (2)
2. Compare direct reinforcement and vicarious reinforcement. (2)
3. **Standard:** Evaluate social learning theory. (8)
4. **AS (Synoptic):** 'Learning theories explain development better than biological psychology.'
   To what extent do you agree with this statement? (12)

Social learning theory: Bandura et al. (1961)

The specification says...
4.1.8 Bandura et al. (1961) original Bobo doll experiments.

In the top picture an adult models aggression towards the doll and in the bottom picture a children is imitating this.

Transmission of aggression through imitation

Aims
Albert Bandura together with Dorothea and Sheila Ross aimed to see whether aggressive behaviour could be acquired through observation of aggressive models. More specifically the researchers were interested in whether children were more likely to aggress having observed aggression, whether they selectively imitated same-sex models and whether boys were more prone overall to acquiring aggressive behaviour.

Procedure
The study was a laboratory experiment using a matched pairs design. 36 boys and 36 girls aged 3–6 years were selected from the Stanford University nursery in California. The dependent variable was the level of aggression the children displayed. There were a number of independent variables: modelling of aggression, sex of model and same/different sex model and observer.

Aggressiveness (a potential confounding variable) was controlled by ensuring that each group contained equally aggressive children. Ratings of the children were determined beforehand by an experimenter who knew the children well and one of the children's teachers, and used to match the children.

The children were placed in threes (three boys or three girls so that gender was also controlled) and randomly allocated to one of the three conditions:

- *Aggression group*: Observed an aggressive adult model (male or female) punching, kicking and shouting at a large inflatable 'Bobo' doll.
- *Non-aggression group*: Non-aggressive model assembling mechanical toys.
- *Control group*: No model was present while the children were playing.

Step 1 The children were brought into a room with an observation window and allowed to play with toys (with or without a model present).

Step 2 The children were then taken to another room where all the children were deliberately frustrated by being shown shiny new toys and told they were for other children. (If they weren't frustrated they would not have the 'urge' to be aggressive later.)

Step 3 Finally, the children were taken into a playroom containing a range of toys including an inflatable Bobo doll. Their behaviour was observed through a one-way mirror by the male model (i.e. covert). A second observer was present for half of the participants to determine inter-rater reliability.

Behaviours were categorised as:

- Imitative aggression, e.g. sitting on Bobo and behaving aggressively or saying 'Pow' (actions of the model).
- Partially imitative, e.g. using a mallet aggressively on toys other than Bobo.
- Non-imitative aggression, e.g. punching Bobo doll, saying hostile things not said by the model.

Findings
Children who had witnessed the aggressive model were likely to completely or partially imitate the aggression. On the other hand children who had observed non-aggressive behaviour or those who had not observed an adult at all displayed much less aggression (none in 70% of cases). Children in the aggression group were also *slightly* more likely to engage in non-imitative aggression.

Boys were more likely to imitate aggression shown by a same-sex model than an opposite-sex model and more likely overall to imitate physical aggression though not verbal aggression.

Conclusion
Social behaviour such as aggression can be acquired by imitation of models. Imitation is more likely when the modelled behaviour is gender-typical (e.g. physical aggression in males) and when the model and observer are of the same gender.

Bar chart showing overall comparison of aggression following modelled aggression and control conditions.

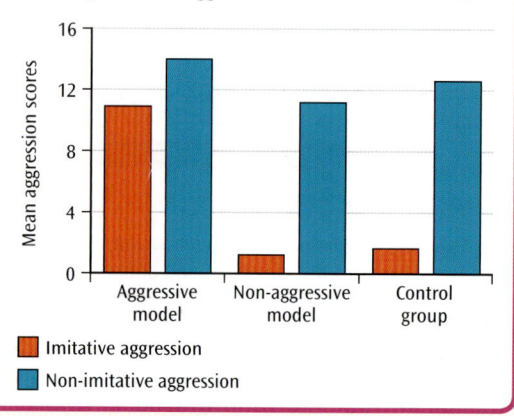

Stretch & Challenge

Social learning of prosocial behaviour
Inspired by Bandura et al.'s experiment on the social learning of aggression, some psychologists have attempted to design observations of more positive social behaviour in order to influence children to be more prosocial (i.e. nice to people).

Based on Bandura et al.'s study, how might they go about this? How could you use Bandura et al.'s findings to make a programme as effective as possible?

Think Link
Developmental psychology

Developing social behaviour
Observational learning like that demonstrated in Bandura et al.'s study can explain the acquisition of aggressive behaviour. Clinical psychologists and other professionals such as social workers have studied and applied Bandura et al.'s work on modelling of aggression to understand the impact of witnessing aggression on development. The risks to boys' development as a result of witnessing violence by adult models are now well understood; boys are particularly likely to imitate physical aggression modelled by adult males.

Evaluation

Clever experimental design

A strength is that the design of the experiment had several clever features that reduced the impact of extraneous variables and therefore enhanced the internal validity of the study.

Children taking part in each condition were matched for aggression, reducing the impact of individual differences in aggression, a potential extraneous participant variable. The non-aggressive conditions allowed researchers to control for spontaneous aggression. Observing the children one at a time controlled for conformity effects.

This is important because the degree of control in the experimental design means that we can be reasonably sure that the observed aggression was the result of imitation of the aggressive model.

Artificial environment

A weakness of the study is that it was conducted under artificial conditions.

The experiment was conducted in a laboratory and the situation in which aggression was measured – playing with a doll – is quite different from the typical situation in which the children might have displayed aggressive behaviour towards a person.

This means that the experimental procedure lacks external validity – we cannot be sure to what extent the results can be generalised to settings outside the laboratory.

Application to learning aggressive behaviour

The findings from this study can be applied to explaining how children can acquire aggressive behaviour from adult models such as parents.

As a result of Bandura *et al.*'s study, psychologists and social workers now have a better understanding of the risks to children's development posed by violent parents even when that violence is not directed towards the children themselves. In particular the study suggests that boys are especially at risk of imitating physical aggression modelled by adult males such as their fathers. This in turn has important implications in policy around custody and parental contact where fathers have a history of violence.

This application of Bandura's *et al.*'s research demonstrates its significance in shaping our thoughts and social policy when it comes to the risks of exposing children to violent adult models.

EXTRA: Issues and debates

Bandura *et al.*'s study raises a number of ethical issues.

There was a degree of distress involved when the children were deliberately frustrated in order to increase the likelihood of aggression. In addition there was no real opportunity for the children to withdraw from the study or be withdrawn by their parents – this is important where distress is involved.

Therefore, there is an argument for saying that Bandura *et al.*'s procedure should not have been carried out for ethical reasons.

> **Competing argument** It could be argued that Bandura *et al.*'s study is not unethical because the distress was mild and short-lived. In addition, the frustration (being deprived of toys) was no more than they would experience in their everyday lives.

Balanced conclusion

This study had a very good level of experimental control and the researchers built in some clever design features. It is also a good example of a study with important policy implications, such as the effects of parental violence on children's behaviour. Like all laboratory experiments however, Bandura *et al.*'s study is artificial and *may* not generalise entirely to everyday life.

Albert Bandura was born in 1925 in the province of Alberta, Canada. He came from a poor immigrant family and was educated in a school with poor facilities so the students were largely self taught. Through this he learned independence, 'The content of most textbooks is perishable, but the tools of self-directedness serve one well over time.' (tinyurl.com/ydgvnwqa). He went on to study psychology at the Universities of British Columbia and of Iowa. In 1953 Bandura accepted a teaching position at Stanford University, USA where he continued to work and teach into his 90s.

Apply it — Methods: Piotr's and Todd's play study

Todd and Piotr work in a nursery school and are planning to observe the children's behaviour. They have permission from the nursery owners and the children's parents and are planning to ask each child if it's okay to watch them play.

1. Explain why they asked the children and their parents if it was okay to watch the children play. (2)
2. Todd wants to time how long each child plays and rate their enjoyment on a 5-point scale.
   (a) Identify the levels of measurement for the **two** methods of data collection used by Todd. (2)
   (b) Piotr wants to collect qualitative data. Describe **one** way he could do this. (2)
   (c) Explain **one** strength and **one** weakness of Todd's methods of data collection compared to Piotr's. (4)
3. To compare how often younger and older nursery children play and sleep during the day, Todd and Piotr will do a chi-squared test.
   (a) Draw a two by two contingency table that Todd and Piotr could use for their results. (1)
   (b) Explain why they chose a chi-squared test. (2)
   (c) Calculate the degrees of freedom (*df*) for these results. Show your workings. (2)

Apply it — Concepts: Playing Zing!

A reception class teacher is worried because older children in the playground are playing a game using sticks as magic weapons and shouting special words like 'Zing!' and 'Shroo!'. The teacher is concerned that the boys and girls in her class will start to behave aggressively in the playground too.

Explain, using your knowledge of Bandura *et al.*'s (1961) study, what effects the older children could have on the younger ones. (5)

Study tip

You may be asked about Bandura *et al.*'s classic research or about his later social learning theory. Be very clear what the question is asking – you will pick up very few marks if you write about the theory when a question asks about the study and vice versa.

Check it

1. Describe the procedure of Bandura *et al.* (1961) from the point at which the children enter the last room for the test of delayed imitation. [4]
2. Explain **two** practical strengths of the design and implementation of Bandura *et al.*'s (1961) study. [4]
3. **Standard:** Assess the findings of Bandura *et al.* (1961). [8]
4. **AL (I&D/Synoptic):** Evaluate ways in which learning theories and biological psychology have been used for social control. [12]

Social learning theory: Bandura et al. (1963, 1965)

The specification says...

4.1.8 Bandura et al. (1963) original Bobo doll experiments.

4.1.9 Bandura (1965) Bobo doll experiment with vicarious reinforcement.

Think Link
Individual differences

Wider social influences

We have already established that individuals differ as a result of the behaviour of role models. The variations on Bandura et al.'s original study tell us a little more about these influences. The 1963 study shows that individual differences can be influenced not only by role models in our real social environments but also those we encounter on TV and in film.

The 1965 study tells us the importance of how society at large responds to modelled behaviour. In particular, the influence of undesirable modelled behaviour can be reduced by punishing the model.

Stretch Challenge

Sophisticated processing

Bandura was not the first to study imitation and the effect of reinforcement. What is key about Bandura's (1965) study is that it shows how children acquire novel behaviour as a result of observing the consequences of that behaviour for the model. Children were not only less likely to imitate specific acts when the model was punished but were also less likely to initiate new forms of aggression.

This is important because it shows that a sophisticated analysis of the observed behaviour is taking place. The observer is not simply responding to the stimulus of seeing the reinforcement or punishment but they are also understanding the social significance of the behaviour. Thus a child in Bandura's (1965) experiment learns not simply to imitate the model with the mallet but that aggression in general is an appropriate response to frustration.

What does the child learn when they see the model being punished?

Graph showing findings from Bandura (1965).

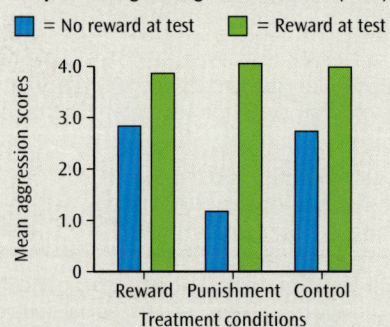

■ = No reward at test   ■ = Reward at test

(Bar graph: Mean aggression scores by Treatment conditions — Reward, Punishment, Control)

Film-mediated aggressive models (1963)

Aims

Albert Bandura and his co-researchers aimed to investigate whether a filmed model would have the same effect as a live model on children's aggression. A secondary aim was to investigate whether cartoon aggression would have a similar impact to realistic filmed aggression.

Procedure

This was a laboratory experiment using an independent groups design. 48 boys and 48 girls aged 39–52 months were selected from the Stanford University nursery. The independent variable was the model (live, filmed or cartoon). The dependent variable was the level of aggression the children displayed.

The children were randomly allocated to one of four conditions.

1. *Live aggression condition* – Watched an adult aggress towards a Bobo doll.
2. *Filmed realistic aggression* – Watched the same behaviour displayed on a screen.
3. *Cartoon aggression condition* – Watched on TV a model dressed as a black cartoon cat perform the same aggressive behaviours towards a Bobo doll as in the other conditions.
4. *Control group* – Did not watch aggression.

Afterwards the procedures were the same as the original study (see previous spread) – the children were frustrated and then observed in a playroom.

Findings

The three experimental groups all displayed increased aggression. The mean total number of aggressive acts was 83 (live), 92 (filmed realistic) and 99 (cartoon).

The differences between the three experimental conditions were not significant, however they did differ significantly from the control condition, which had a mean total aggression score of 54.

Conclusion

Exposure to live or filmed aggression increases the likelihood of aggression in response to frustration, even if the aggression is modelled by a cartoon figure.

Influence of models' reinforcement (1965)

Aim

The aim was to consider whether reinforcement and punishment of an aggressive model would influence the aggression displayed by observers (children) in response to frustration.

Procedure

The procedure was the same, this time with 33 boys and 33 girls aged 42–71 months from the same nursery school as before. The independent variable was the observed consequence for the model. The dependent variable was aggression in the children.

The children were randomly allocated to one of three conditions, all of which involved watching a film of an adult aggressing towards a Bobo doll.

1. *Model-rewarded condition* – Children saw a second adult praise the model for their aggression and give them a drink and chocolate.
2. *Model-punished condition* – Second adult scolded the model and spanked them with a rolled up magazine.
3. *No-consequence condition* – Model was neither reinforced nor punished.

Afterwards the children were, as before, deliberately frustrated and then taken into a playroom. There was a key difference in the procedure this time – all three groups were later offered attractive rewards to aggress towards the doll.

Findings

Children in the model-punished condition were significantly less aggressive than the other two groups. However, introducing the promise of a reward wiped out the difference, increasing the scores significantly for all the groups.

Conclusion

Vicarious punishment reduces imitated aggression. However, the promise of reinforcement is a more powerful influence on aggression.

Evaluation

Control of extraneous variables
A strength of both experiments is the controls used to reduce the impact of extraneous variables.

Children taking part in each condition were matched for aggression, reducing the impact of individual differences in aggression, a potential extraneous participant variable. The non-aggressive conditions allowed researchers to control for spontaneous aggression. Observing the children one at a time controlled for the possibility that a child may imitate the behaviour of another child.

This means that we can be reasonably sure that the observed aggression was the result of imitation of the aggressive model, enhancing the internal validity of the study.

Competing argument However, Bandura's research only showed short-term effects, and also aggression was only shown towards a doll. Therefore, there is some concern that, despite the clever design, the findings don't necessarily explain aggressive behaviour in everyday life.

Risk of demand characteristics
A weakness of both the studies is that elements of the procedure could have cued children as to how they were expected to behave.

Grant Noble (1975) reports that one child arriving at the laboratory for the experiment said, 'Look Mummy, there's the doll we have to hit.' This suggests that the children may have believed that they were expected to aggress towards the doll – why else would the adult have modelled aggression towards the doll then left them with one?

This means that the experimental procedures may lack validity – we cannot be sure to what extent the results reflect learning and to what extent they are affected by demand characteristics.

Application to the Sabido method
A further strength of SLT is that it has informed the development of the Sabido method.

Albert Bandura and Miguel Sabido (Bandura 2017) pioneered the use of telenovelas (like a soap opera) to tackle specific social problems in countries all over the world. Viewers identify with the popular characters who become role models. Research has shown that these serials have been highly effective in prompting behavioural change, for example increasing contraception use or the take-up of literacy classes.

This demonstrates the significant contribution of SLT in promoting behaviours which are of benefit to individuals and also to wider society.

EXTRA: Issues and debates
Bandura's work is socially sensitive because it has implications for parenting practice – this is always a sensitive issue.

Bandura's studies appear to show that parents who allow children to watch aggression on television and in films – even in cartoon form – are putting them at risk of acquiring aggressive behaviour themselves. As violence is a feature of much entertainment this means that most of us have put our children at risk!

This is important because no one wants to think they are a bad parent, and Bandura's research suggests that, at least in one respect, most of us are.

Balanced conclusion
In many ways Bandura's studies provide us with a model of how psychology should be done. His experimental design is impeccable, and his findings inform both a theoretical understanding of aggression and social learning, and also have potentially important real-world applications. However, Bandura's findings only show short-term effects, even if we accept that the results are the consequence of social learning rather than demand characteristics. Therefore, his conclusions about the acquisition of aggression may be flawed.

There is concern that combat sports might model aggression.

Apply it — Methods: Copyrats
Nathan is investigating whether a rat can learn by watching another rat and whether it is more likely to demonstrate this learning if it sees the 'model' rat being rewarded.

1. In stage 1, Nathan puts a model rat in a glass box containing the lever and lets a learner rat watch the 'model' for five minutes. Nathan records how long each learner rat spends watching the model and how many times the model pulls the lever.
   Explain why it is important that Nathan records **one** of these behaviours. (1)

2. In stage 2, Nathan puts each learner rat into the glass box for five minutes and records how many times it pulls the lever. He does the same with a group of control rats.
   Explain how the control group will have been treated. (1)

3. Finally, Nathan repeats stages 1 and 2 with different rats but this time when the model pulls the lever it receives food, and the learner rat can see the model eating the food.
   Nathan will conduct a 2 × 2 chi-squared test on the total number of lever pulls by four groups of rats. Draw a suitable table for Nathan to use for his data. (2)

4. Nathan's study is a structured observation. Explain **one** strength and **one** weakness of using a structured observation in Nathan's study. (4)

5. Pulling levers is not a behaviour rats would do 'accidentally', like pushing a bar. Explain why this is important to Nathan's study. (1)

6. Explain **one** reason why Nathan's results would apply to people and **one** reason why they would not. (4)

Apply it — Concepts: Clack-a-clown
AggApps is a software company producing violent gaming apps for adults. They have a new children's game involving lots of ways to knock clowns' heads off to score points.

Context essay: Discuss how Bandura et al.'s studies could help the app developers to find ways to make the children play aggressively. (8)

Check it
1. (a) State **two** differences between the methods used by Bandura et al. (1961) and Bandura et al. (1963). (2)
   (b) State **two** differences between the results of Bandura et al. (1961) and Bandura et al. (1963). (2)
2. Explain **one** weakness of Bandura (1965). (2)
3. **Standard:** Evaluate the study by Bandura (1965). (8)
4. **AL (I&D/Synoptic):** Psychologists studying learning theories and social psychology are concerned with the use of psychological knowledge within society.
   Evaluate the usefulness to society of the research by Bandura et al. and Milgram. (12)

Chapter 4 Learning theories

Phobias: Learning theory explanations

The specification says...
4.1.10 How learning theories explain the acquisition and maintenance of phobias.

Key terms

Learning theories – A collective term for explanations based on conditioning (classical and operant). This also includes social learning theory.

Acquisition – The process of *acquiring* (getting or developing) something, in this case a phobia. We tend to use the term 'acquisition' in psychology because it is theoretically neutral. This is preferable to saying 'learning' because learning is actually an explanation for acquisition, not a synonym.

Maintenance – The processing of *maintaining* something (keeping it going). If a phobia is acquired by classical conditioning we would expect it to decline over time unless some other process maintains it.

Stretch & Challenge

A modern model of learning phobias

Stanley Rachman (1998) proposed a newer model of phobia acquisition based (mostly) on learning theory and incorporating both classical conditioning and social learning. According to Rachman there are three pathways to acquiring a phobia:

1. Through classical conditioning.
2. Through social learning.
3. Through informational learning, i.e. finding out frightening facts about the phobic stimulus.

This is a more complete explanation for the acquisition of phobias than traditional classical conditioning or social learning alone because it incorporates both processes and accounts for cases where no modelling or exposure has taken place.

What aspect of phobias might the two-process model explain better than Rachman's model?

Explaining the acquisition of phobias

The two-process model

Hobart Mowrer (1960) proposed the two-process model, based on learning theory, to explain both the acquisition and maintenance of phobias. This states that phobias can be acquired (i.e. developed in the first place) by a process of classical conditioning, and are then maintained through operant conditioning.

Acquisition of phobias by classical conditioning

Classical conditioning of a phobia involves learning to associate one stimulus with another stimulus. One stimulus initially creates no fear (called a neutral stimulus, NS) and the other stimulus is one that already triggers a fear response (known as an unconditioned stimulus, UCS). Through association the NS becomes a conditioned stimulus (CS) producing a conditioned response (CR) of fear. This process of learning a fear response was demonstrated by John B. Watson and Rosalie Rayner (1920) in their classic study of Little Albert (described later in this chapter, see page 148).

Examples of unconditioned fear stimuli include loud noises as well as painful bites and stings. If a wasp stings you then the painful sting (UCS) is paired with the sight and sound of wasps which initially are neutral but become a CS and provoke a CR of fear.

Maintenance by operant conditioning

Responses acquired by classical conditioning tend to decline over time. This is called extinction. However, phobias are persistent. Mowrer explained this as the result of operant conditioning.

Operant conditioning takes place when behaviour is reinforced (i.e. rewarded) or punished. Reinforcement (positive or negative) increases the frequency of a behaviour. Negative reinforcement takes place when a behaviour is rewarded by the removal of something unpleasant like anxiety.

Mowrer demonstrated this by conditioning a rat to develop an avoidance response to a shock – the rat was placed in a cage where shocks were delivered. The rat could escape the shock by jumping over a barrier. Escape was negatively reinforcing and in this way the avoidance response was learned.

When someone with a conditioned phobia responds by avoiding the fear-provoking stimulus, their anxiety lessens and this provides negative reinforcement for the avoidance behaviour. Mowrer says this avoidance and its negative reinforcement is what maintains phobias.

Social learning of phobias

Michael Cook and Susan Mineka (1989) suggested another mechanism for the acquisition of phobias – observational learning. They demonstrated that infant rhesus monkeys who watched adult monkeys displaying fear of fear-relevant stimuli such as toy snakes and crocodiles acquired fear of those toys.

Humans may similarly acquire phobias by imitating the fear responses modelled by others such as parents. This might be one reason why there are gender differences in phobias (Kay and Morrison 2004) – men (fathers) traditionally display less visible fear than women, and so sons are less likely to acquire phobias than daughters.

To the nyctophobic night is terrifying. This fear can be maintained by avoiding going out at night.

Think Link
Individual differences

Avoidance behaviour

Just as Mowrer's rats learned to jump a barrier to escape the anxiety of anticipating a painful shock, people all develop distinctive individual patterns of behaviour through avoidance learning. This might be straightforward – such as avoiding going in the attic to reduce the anxiety associated with the huge and horrible spiders that populate this location.

Avoidance behaviour can thus affect individual differences in behaviour. It may also be *affected* by individual differences. Jeffrey Gray's (1970) *reinforcement sensitivity theory* suggests that some individual differences in personality can be explained by how sensitive individuals are to learning by reinforcement. Some of us may thus acquire avoidance behaviour more easily than others.

Agoraphobia may be reinforced by attraction to safety rather than avoidance.

Evaluation

Supporting evidence

A strength is evidence from human and animal studies for the role of conditioning and social learning in the acquisition of phobias.

Evidence for the acquisition of fear responses in humans comes from the Watson and Rayner study of Little Albert. Evidence for the maintenance of fear in animals through avoidance comes from Mowrer's study of rats (see facing page). Cook and Mineka demonstrated social learning of fear of animals in infant rhesus monkeys (see facing page).

This suggests that, even if learning is not a complete explanation for phobias, it does take place.

Does not explain all aspects of phobias

A weakness is that some phenomena associated with the acquisition of phobias cannot be explained by learning alone.

We easily acquire phobias of things that have been a source of danger in our evolutionary past, such as a fear of snakes or the dark, but not of other dangerous things like cars or guns despite the fact that these are far more hazardous. Also, some people acquire phobias without conditioning experiences or modelling.

This is important because it shows that learning is not a complete explanation for the acquisition of phobias.

Application to treating phobias

Learning theory explanations for phobias have real world applications in therapies for phobias.

Systematic desensitisation and flooding (see next spread) are based on classical conditioning as a way to treat phobias. Systematic desensitisation helps clients to learn new responses to the phobic stimulus whilst flooding works by extinction of learned fear responses.

This illustrates the practical value of learning explanations for phobias.

EXTRA: Issues and debates

There are other ways to explain phobias, including psychodynamic theory.

Sigmund Freud explained phobias in terms of displacement. He suggested that, when a person experiences anxiety arising from a complex situation that is hard to deal with (such as a difficult relationship with a parent) they cope with this unconsciously by displacing the anxiety onto a simpler object. This reduces their anxiety in general. This explanation can be useful in complex clinical cases where patients/clients have multiple symptoms and a history of trauma.

This shows that learning theory is not the best explanation for every case of phobias.

Competing argument However, there is generally a stronger evidence base for learning theory explanations for phobias than alternatives, for example psychodynamic theory of phobias is generally just supported by isolated case studies.

Balanced conclusion

There is no doubt that phobias can be learned, and there is ample evidence showing that both conditioning experiences and modelling can be involved. Learning theories do not offer a complete explanation of all aspects of phobias but they are a good explanation for the processes by which many phobias are acquired, in particular simple phobias.

Apply it Methods: A question of phobias

Mona is conducting a content analysis to find out about the role of classical conditioning, operant conditioning, social learning and cognitive factors in the acquisition of phobias. She is using participants' responses to the question, 'Tell me everything you can that you think has played a part in your phobia.' Her participants responded to an advert placed on a university noticeboard calling for 'students willing to talk about their fears'.

1. Explain why the wording of Mona's advert was appropriate. (1)
2. Mona will store data about her participants using their student number. She will exclude any students whose numbers have been identified by the health centre as vulnerable.
   (a) Explain why Mona is using student numbers. (1)
   (b) Explain why it is important that Mona excludes some students from her study. (1)
3. Describe how Mona might conduct her content analysis. (5)
4. Mona wants to draw a graph to show how important each of the four factors is in the acquisition of a phobia.
   (a) Explain the type of graph Mona should use. (2)
   (b) Draw the axes for Mona's graph. (3)

Apply it Concepts: Feline fears

Shaun has a phobia of cats. When he was little, he was walking with his mum and was distracted by a cat playing in a tree. That meant he wasn't looking where he was going and he tripped over, breaking his arm. Every time he sees a cat now he feels frightened and runs away, which helps to calm him down.

Context essay: Discuss how learning theories explain Shaun's phobia. (8)

Study tip

When a question has a scenario, you need to show your knowledge *and* make a clear link to the scenario. It is not enough to just use the name or a few key words from the scenario, you must really engage. Explain how each point you make is linked to aspects of the scenario. Avoid answers that could be reused with any question as these are 'generic'.

Check it

1. Explain how learning theories can account for individual differences in phobias. (4)
2. (a) Describe how **one** learning theory can explain the acquisition of phobias. (4)
   (b) Describe how **one** learning theory can explain the maintenance of phobias. (4)
3. **Standard:** Evaluate **one** learning theory as an explanation of phobias. (8)
4. **AL (I&D/Synoptic):** To what extent are learning theories and social theories on the 'nature' side of the nature–nurture debate? (12)

Phobias: Treatments based on learning theories

The specification says...
4.1.11 Treatments for phobias based on theories of learning, including systematic desensitisation and one other.

Key terms

Systematic desensitisation (SD) – A behavioural therapy designed to reduce an unwanted response, such as anxiety, to a stimulus. SD involves drawing up a hierarchy of anxiety-provoking situations related to a phobic stimulus, teaching a client to relax, and then exposing them to phobic situations. The client works their way through the hierarchy whilst maintaining relaxation.

Flooding – A behavioural therapy in which a phobic client is exposed to an extreme form of a phobic stimulus in order to reduce anxiety triggered by that stimulus. This takes place across a small number of long therapy sessions.

Think Link
Individual differences

Choosing SD or flooding

There is evidence to support the general idea that client individual differences are important in understanding effective treatments for mental health problems (APA 2006). Most clients given the choice of flooding or desensitisation opt for the latter. People are also more likely to drop out of flooding. However, some clients do choose flooding and many do complete it.

An understanding of the individual differences underlying choice and perseverance in flooding would help psychologists to target the best treatment to the individual. It may be that some clients are more motivated and therefore more willing to tolerate the trauma of flooding. It may also be that some clients are more resilient to the trauma of flooding as a function of their personality.

The exposure in systematic desensitisation is now sometimes carried out using virtual reality.

Systematic desensitisation (SD)

Systematic desensitisation is a behavioural therapy designed to gradually reduce phobic anxiety through the principle of classical conditioning. Essentially a new response to the phobic stimulus is learned (the phobic stimulus is paired with the response of relaxation instead of anxiety). This learning of a different response is called *counterconditioning*.

Success is further enhanced because it is impossible to be afraid and relaxed at the same time, so one emotion prevents the other. This is called *reciprocal inhibition*. There are three processes involved in SD, as outlined below.

The anxiety hierarchy

This is constructed by the client and therapist. A list of situations related to the phobic stimulus that provoke anxiety is arranged in order from least to most frightening. For example, an arachnophobic might identify seeing a picture of a small spider as low on their anxiety hierarchy and holding a tarantula at the top of the hierarchy.

Relaxation

The therapist teaches the client to relax as deeply as possible. This might involve breathing exercises or, alternatively, the client might learn mental imagery techniques. Clients can be taught to imagine themselves in relaxing situations (such as imagining lying on a beach) or they might learn meditation. Alternatively relaxation can be achieved using drugs such as Valium.

Exposure

Finally the client is exposed to the phobic stimulus while in a relaxed state. This takes place across several sessions, starting at the bottom of the anxiety hierarchy. When the client can stay relaxed in the presence of the lower levels of the phobic stimulus they move up the hierarchy. Treatment is successful when the client can stay relaxed in situations high on the anxiety hierarchy.

Flooding

Flooding also involves exposing phobic clients to their phobic stimulus but without a gradual build-up in an anxiety hierarchy. Instead, flooding involves immediate exposure to a very frightening situation. So an arachnophobic receiving flooding treatment might have a large spider crawl over them for an extended period. Flooding sessions are typically longer than SD sessions, one session often lasting two to three hours. Sometimes only one long session is needed to cure a phobia.

How flooding works

Flooding stops phobic responses very quickly. This may be because, without the option of avoidance behaviour, the client quickly learns that the phobic stimulus is harmless. In classical conditioning terms this process is called *extinction*. A learned response is extinguished when the conditioned stimulus (e.g. a dog) is encountered without the unconditioned stimulus (e.g. being bitten). The result is that the conditioned stimulus no longer produces the conditioned response (fear). In some cases the client may achieve relaxation in the presence of the phobic stimulus simply because they become exhausted by their own fear response!

Ethical safeguards

Flooding is not unethical *per se* but it is an unpleasant experience so it is important that clients give fully informed consent to this traumatic procedure and that they are fully prepared before the flooding session. A client would normally be given the choice of SD or flooding.

Stretch & Challenge
Systematic desensitisation in virtual reality

Exposure to the phobic stimulus in SD is often done in real-life settings but for some phobias this is impractical. For example, a psychologist treating a client who is afraid of flying cannot be expected to have weekly treatment sessions involving going to an airport and, in later sessions, going on an aeroplane flight. For cases like this an alternative approach is to expose the client to the phobic stimulus in *virtual reality* (VR). Studies have found VR exposure to be effective and it is often more convenient than real-life exposure.

Can you think of another phobia for which VR might be particularly useful?

Evaluation of systematic desensitisation

It is effective
A strength is that research shows that SD is effective in the treatment of specific phobias.

For example, Lisa Gilroy et al. (2003) compared clients receiving SD for spider phobia with a control group. At both three months and 33 months after the treatment the SD group were less fearful than the control group.

This shows that SD is helpful in reducing the anxiety in phobias.

Not suitable for all cases
A weakness of SD is that, although SD is acceptable to most clients, it may not be effective in all cases.

For example, clients with multiple phobias or other symptoms linked to a history of trauma (e.g. childhood abuse) may benefit from different therapies that allow them to explore their experiences or alter thought patterns as well as changing behavioural symptoms. SD really only tackles behavioural symptoms

Therefore, for a minority of clients, SD is probably not the most appropriate or successful way to treat a phobia.

EXTRA: Issues and debates
SD is more sophisticated than earlier versions of the therapy and thus shows development over time.

The original form of SD just involved gradually increased exposure to a feared item and was called 'exposure therapy'. SD introduced the element of relaxation making it more effective because there are two separate elements – the unlearning of one response and learning a new association. Modern SD has become more sophisticated still by incorporating virtual reality.

This is important because it shows how flawed methods are actually an important part of the development of, for example, a good therapy, because successive methods build on previous ones.

Evaluation of flooding

Cost-effective
A strength is that flooding is quicker and as effective as alternatives.

Studies comparing flooding to cognitive therapies (such as Ougrin 2011) have found that flooding is highly effective and quicker than alternatives.

This quick effect means that clients are free from their symptoms as soon as possible and this makes the treatment cheaper.

May not be effective for all phobias
A weakness is that flooding may not be effective for social phobias.

This may be because social phobias have cognitive aspects. For example, a person with a social phobia does not simply experience an anxiety response but thinks unpleasant thoughts about the social situation.

This means that flooding cannot be the sole treatment on offer for phobias because it only tackles behavioural responses.

EXTRA: Issues and debates
Flooding raises potentially serious ethical issues.

This is because flooding involves trauma. It is a very unpleasant experience because it involves extended exposure to an extreme form of the phobic stimulus.

This is a limitation of flooding because time and money are sometimes wasted preparing clients only to have them refuse to start or complete treatment.

Competing argument Although flooding is an unpleasant experience it is only done with the consent of the client. The trauma of the experience must be balanced against the improvement in clients' quality of life if treatment is successful.

Balanced conclusion
If you can bear it, flooding is quicker and probably more effective than SD. However, most people find the idea of flooding distressing and opt for SD given the choice.

Relaxation is an important and pleasant aspect of SD.

Apply it Methods: Theo's therapy work

Theo is on work experience at a doctors' practice near his university. He cannot watch sessions or see clients' individual records, but has been given the total number of effective treatments for the last 50 clients who visited the practice. The table below summarises this data.

Table showing success rates for each therapy.

	Males	Females
Systematic desensitisation	24	22
Flooding	16	17

1. Calculate Theo's chi-squared value. Show your workings. (4)
2. (a) Theo had a non-directional (two-tailed) hypothesis. Justify whether he should accept this hypothesis. (2) (See page 212 for the critical values table.)
   (b) Explain what these results show. (2)
3. Explain the importance of hypothesis testing for psychology in general. (2)
4. The doctors' practice ensured that Theo's research was ethical. Explain **two** ways in which this could be done. (2)
5. Explain whether Theo's study had good ecological validity. (3)

Apply it Concepts: It's hard to decide

Erin has a phobia of birds and has been avoiding therapy for years as she is so frightened about what might happen. She even finds discussing therapy difficult. However, she has promised herself she will do something but cannot decide which therapy to choose.

Context essay: Discuss which therapy, systematic desensitisation or flooding, would be best for Erin. (8)

Study tip
If you choose the study by Capafóns et al. (page 154) as your contemporary study, you can use that study as an evaluation point but it will not be sufficient in an analytical essay. You will need several other points too.

Check it

1. (a) Describe the process of systematic desensitisation. (3)
   (b) Explain how systematic desensitisation could be used with a person with a phobia of rats. (3)
2. Compare systematic desensitisation and flooding as therapies for phobias. (6)
3. **Standard:** Evaluate **one** treatment for phobias **other than** systematic desensitisation. (8)
4. **AL (I&D/Synoptic):** Evaluate research into learning theories and cognitive theories in terms of ethical issues. (12)

Classic study: Watson and Rayner (1920)

Chapter 4 Learning theories

The specification says...
4.3.1 Classic study: Watson and Rayner (1920) Little Albert: Conditioned emotional reactions.

Stretch & Challenge

Gulf War syndrome
Gulf War syndrome is a collection of symptoms ranging from pain and weakness to depression and confusion, widely reported in service personnel following the first Gulf War of 1990–91. The Gulf War was characterised by distinctive smells from burning oil and pesticides. Eamonn Ferguson and Helen Cassaday (2002) have suggested that the syndrome may be explained by classical conditioning. The UCS is noxious chemicals from the burning oil wells which produce an immune response (UCR). (An immune response is the body's response to invading bacteria etc.) The smells associated with the chemicals is a NS.

Based on the Little Albert case, explain how a conditioned response to smells could account for Gulf War syndrome.

The process of Little Albert's conditioning.

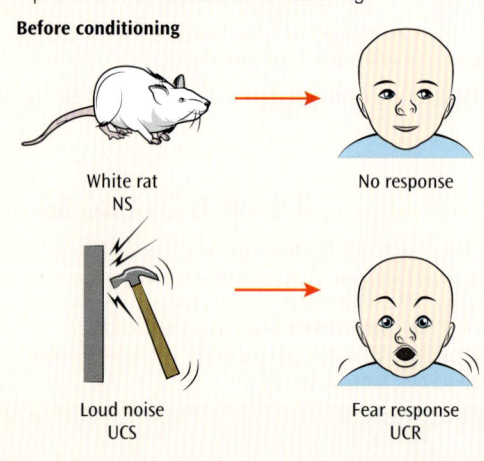

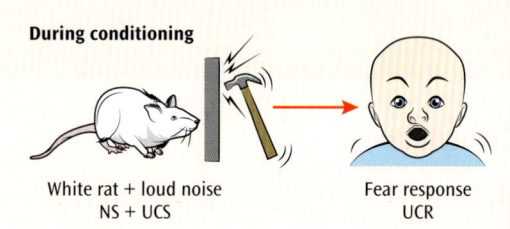

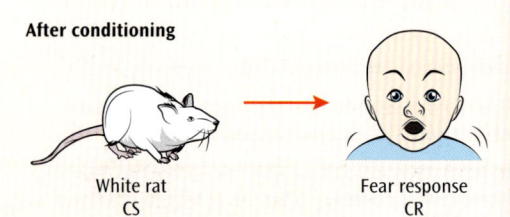

Before conditioning
- White rat (NS) → No response
- Loud noise (UCS) → Fear response (UCR)

During conditioning
- White rat + loud noise (NS + UCS) → Fear response (UCR)

After conditioning
- White rat (CS) → Fear response (CR)

Little Albert: Conditioned emotional reactions

Aim
John B. Watson and Rosalie Rayner's general aim was to demonstrate that simple emotional responses such as fear can be acquired through a process of *classical conditioning*.

Procedure
In this study there was only one condition and one participant. This is technically therefore an $n = 1$ *pre*-experiment, not a true experiment. This is not a case study because that involves a more complex study of many aspects of one individual. The participant was a healthy baby boy, nine months old at the start of the study. He was known as Little Albert.

The dependent variable was the fear response. The independent variable was the pairing of a loud noise (an *unconditioned stimulus*) with the sight of a rat (a *neutral stimulus*).

To test Albert's baseline emotional responses to a range of objects he was presented one at a time with a white rat, a rabbit, a dog, a monkey, various masks, cotton wool and a set of wooden blocks. He showed no fear response to any of these. Albert's response to a loud noise was then tested by striking a hammer upon a suspended steel bar. The conditioning began two months later. The researchers filmed each session.

Session 1 When Albert was 11 months and 3 days old he was taken to a 'lab' (it was a well-lit room where photographs were normally developed). A white rat was presented to him. When he reached towards the rat, the bar was struck loudly just behind his head.

Session 2 A week later Albert returned again. He was exposed five times to the paired sight of the rat and the loud noise behind his head. From this point he was tested with the blocks, to which he showed no fear. This is key to showing that he wasn't just getting more scared generally.

Session 3 A further five days later Albert returned and his responses to the rat and a range of other objects were assessed. The other objects included wooden blocks, a rabbit, a dog, a seal fur coat, cotton wool and John Watson's hair.

Session 4 Five days after that Albert was taken to a new environment – a lecture room with four people present. He was placed on a table and once again assessed for responses to the various objects.

Session 5 Albert was tested again one month later, when he was 12 months and 21 days old. The final tests involved a Santa Claus mask, fur coat, the rat, the rabbit, the dog and the blocks.

Findings
At baseline testing Albert displayed no fear of any of the objects but he did respond to the loud noise (he was startled and his lips trembled). This was the unconditioned response. In session 1 he again reacted to the noise (he cried). By session 2 he was more cautious towards the rat, not reaching out and pulling away when the rat nuzzled him. After further conditioning he began to cry and tried to rapidly crawl away.

In session 3 Albert reacted to the white furry objects (the rat and the rabbit) with fear (he cried – a conditioned response). He displayed mild fear towards the dog and none to the other objects.

Sessions 4 and 5 revealed that Albert's fear reactions to white furry objects remained but became less extreme when he was in a different environment and after time.

Conclusion
It is relatively easy to condition an emotional response to a neutral stimulus. In this study just two sessions pairing an unconditioned fear stimulus (the loud noise) and a neutral stimulus (the rat) were enough to produce a fear response (conditioned response) towards rats and similar objects, an example of *stimulus generalisation*.

Think Link
Individual differences

Extreme fear
Classical conditioning is a convincing explanation for the development of reflex responses during development. We all develop a range of conditioned responses in childhood and these explain some of our adult characteristics. An example is our phobias, irrational fears of stimuli that are not dangerous enough to warrant such a response. If for example we are bitten, clawed or growled at by an animal in childhood that animal is likely to become a conditioned stimulus, triggering a fear response when we encounter similar animals. This is just like what happened to little Albert.

Evaluation

Some good experimental controls

A strength is that the design of the study had some clever features that reduced the impact of extraneous variables and therefore enhanced the internal validity of the study.

Examples of the careful design include the fact that Little Albert was carefully selected for his emotional stability, making his individual characteristics less likely to affect results. In addition the procedure took place in a well-controlled room to prevent the influence of other stimuli and also responses to wooden blocks were checked to ensure the reaction to the phobic objects was not simply a general increase in anxiety.

This is important because the controls used in the experimental design make it more likely that changes in Albert's behaviour were due to conditioning rather than extraneous variables.

Competing argument Some aspects of the design were not well-controlled. For example, the rabbit was suddenly placed in front of Albert and a reluctant dog was pushed towards him. These actions might have triggered fear responses rather than the animals themselves.

Poor generalisability

A weakness of the study is that it used only one participant, who may have been unusual, although he was described as rarely being afraid or crying.

All n = 1 studies have problems of generalisability because the individual studied may not be representative of the population. In Albert's case this is a particular problem because we are not certain of his identity so we have no way of knowing how representative a child he was.

Therefore, the results might have been affected by participant variables.

Application to acquiring phobias

Watson and Rayner's study has clinical applications in helping understand how we can acquire phobias.

As a result of studies of classical conditioning in humans, psychologists now have a good understanding of how phobias and related symptoms (such as anxiety, arousal) can be acquired. This has led to the development of effective therapies (described on the previous spread).

This application of Watson and Rayner's research demonstrates its significance in shaping clinical practice.

EXTRA: Issues and debates

Watson and Rayner's study raises ethical issues.

There was a degree of distress involved when Albert was deliberately alarmed by the loud noise, specifically made to be unpleasant, to condition an avoidance response. Such an experience was beyond what you would normally expose a child to.

Therefore, there is a strong argument for saying that this study should not have been carried out for ethical reasons.

Balanced conclusion

The Little Albert study is of great historical importance as one of the very first studies of classical conditioning in humans. However, due to the lack of a control condition and the sample size there are serious problems of validity. It is to the researchers' credit that they filmed the procedure. However, a look at the film shows some serious flaws in their methods, for example presenting the dog and rabbit in frightening ways, perhaps to ensure they got to record a fear response.

John B Watson (1878–1958) was an influential but controversial figure in psychology. He established the behaviourist movement, which went on to dominate American psychology for the first half of the 20th century. He conducted his best-known research at Johns Hopkins University but was sacked for having an affair with Rosalie Rayner, his postgraduate student. They married and Watson left research to work as a New York city advertising executive. Watson and Rayner wrote a popular childcare guide, *Psychological Care of Infant and Child*, in which they advised parents to use behaviourist principles in child-rearing and that parental affection was detrimental to independence.

Apply it Methods: Scaredy-cats

Dr Flynn wonders whether animals can learn classically conditioned fears and, if so, whether different species vary in their learning speed. He is counting the number of trials it takes 10 rabbits and 10 cats to become afraid of a flash of green light that is associated with a loud noise.

1. Name the experimental design that Dr Flynn is using in his experiment. (1)
2. One possible confounding variable in Dr Flynn's study is that colour vision may differ between cats and rabbits. Explain what the problem would be if this were the case. (2)
3. Write an operationalised, non-directional (two-tailed) alternate hypothesis for Dr Flynn's experiment. (2)
4. (a) Explain which statistical test Dr Flynn should use to analyse his data. (3)
   (b) Dr Flynn is concerned about making a Type I error when analysing his findings. Explain Dr Flynn's concern. (2)

Apply it Concepts: Safety first

Olivia and Lilly live in a house with an open fire. They are worried that their young daughter Anna might burn herself. Lilly has a radical idea. They should classically condition Anna to be afraid of the fire, so that she keeps away from it.

1. Use the five terms NS, UCS, CS, UCR and CR to explain how this idea would work. (5)
2. Explain what problem might arise if the learned response generalises. (1)
3. Explain **one** problem, other than generalisation, of using classical conditioning to prevent Anna burning herself. (2)

Study tip

When evaluating studies your strengths and weaknesses cannot be 'generic', i.e. they cannot be written in general terms such that they could apply to many different studies. If the same point could be placed in the context of a different study and make sense then it is generic. Your evaluation points must contain specific information about the study that you are evaluating, so they cannot be placed elsewhere.

Check it

1. Explain why it was important that Watson and Rayner tested Little Albert with:
   (a) The blocks. (1)
   (b) **One** other object apart from the white rat. (1)
2. Describe **two** strengths of Watson and Rayner's procedure. (4)
3. **Standard:** Evaluate the classic study by Watson and Rayner (1920). (8)
4. **AS (Synoptic):** To what extent are the classic studies from the learning theories and biological psychology (Watson and Rayner 1920 and Raine *et al.* 1997) objective and generalisable? (12)

Contemporary study: Becker et al. (2002)

The specification says...
4.3.2 One contemporary study, for example: Becker et al. (2002) Eating behaviours and attitudes following prolonged exposure to television among ethnic Fijian adolescent girls.

Impossibly thin role models like this may have a serious effect on girls' body image, self-esteem and eating behaviour.

Bulimia nervosa (BN)
BN is a mental disorder characterised by bingeing and purging behaviours. Bingeing involves eating an excessive amount of food within a short period of time. After bingeing an individual with BN is likely to purge her/himself to compensate for the overindulgence and in order to prevent weight gain. This is achieved by self-induced vomiting or by misuse of laxatives or other medications.

Think Link
Individual differences

Body image
We all have a mental representation of our body, including our basic shape. This is called our *body image*. Given the importance placed on body shape by the mass media, it is not surprising that our body image is closely linked to our perceptions of our attractiveness and our self-esteem.

The problem for many of us is that the body shapes promoted as attractive in the media are impossibly thin for women and impossibly muscular for men. If we judge ourselves against these we are doomed to see ourselves as unattractive. In some vulnerable individuals this may lead to eating difficulties – an individual difference.

Eating behaviours following prolonged exposure to television

Aim
Anne Becker, Rebecca Burwell, Stephen Gilman, David Herzog and Paul Hamburg (2002) investigated social learning in the context of eating behaviour. Their specific aim was to investigate the impact of Western attitudes on the eating behaviours and related attitudes of teenage girls. Prior to 1995 there was no television in the country of Fiji, a collection of 300 islands in the South Pacific. The researchers were interested in the effect that the ideas communicated through television programmes would have on body satisfaction and eating disorders (such as the bingeing and purging behaviours typical of bulimia nervosa). This is a form of *social learning*.

Procedure
This study looked at the difference in attitudes before and after the introduction of television, using an independent measures design. (It was not a true experiment because the independent variable was not manipulated by the researcher.) The independent variable was exposure to Western television – one group of teenage girls were questioned just when television was introduced to Fiji in 1995. A different group of teenage girls were questioned three years later in 1998.

The dependent variables were eating behaviour, measured by a standard questionnaire called the EAT-26 and general attitudes to eating and body image, measured by semi-structured interview. The EAT-26 questionnaire gathered quantitative data and the interviews gathered qualitative data.

The initial sample consisted of 63 ethnic Fijian girls with a mean age of 17 and the second sample was 65 ethnic Fijian girls of the same age. All were still at school when the study was conducted.

Participants were interviewed and completed the EAT-26 questionnaires individually in their own homes. A translator was present in each case to prevent any difficulty in communicating across the cultural divide. Participants' height and weight were also measured. The 1998 group was asked additional questions:

- Have you ever tried to change your diet in order to change your weight?
- Do parents or family ever say you should eat more?
- How important is it to you that you like your weight?
- Do you ever think you should eat less?

Girls who scored over the threshold for dysfunctional eating based on the EAT-26 were given further interviews – these were recorded and transcribed.

Findings
Weight did not differ between the two groups of girls, with BMIs (body mass index – a measure of body fat based on height and weight) of 24.5 and 24.9 respectively. Television viewing did increase however, with 41% in 1995 and 71% in 1998 having a TV at home.

Scores of dysfunctional eating also increased, with 29.2% of girls scoring over the threshold of 20 on the EAT-26 in 1998, up from 12.7% in 1995. 11.3% reported purging in 1998, as opposed to none in 1995. In 1998, 74% said they felt too large or fat and 69% had dieted – the latter is important as dieting is alien to Fijian culture. Interviews also suggested that the girls considered TV characters to be role models.

Conclusion
Women in Western television programmes became role models for the Fijian girls, leading them to desire much thinner bodies than was the previous norm in Fiji. This led to a rise in dysfunctional eating attitudes and behaviour and a decline in body image. This is an example of the harm caused by rapid social change linked to importing elements of Western culture to indigenous populations.

Stretch & Challenge

The irony: TV also makes us fatter
Television watching is associated with poor body image, as we compare ourselves to our impossibly thin/muscly role models. Ironically, watching TV also appears to lead to weight gain and takes us further from the impossible ideal portrayed on TV. Jane Wardle (2014) found that families who eat in front of a screen consume significantly more calories than those who eat at a table.

In another study of the effect of different types of TV programme, Jamie Bodenlos and Bernadette Wormuth (2013) found that, even when food preference is controlled for, watching cooking shows leads to consuming more food, compared to nature shows.

Explain how watching TV can be said to have a 'double whammy' effect on our body type and body image.

Evaluation

Reliable measurements

A strength of this study is the use of reliable procedures to measure eating attitudes and behaviour.

Studies have generally shown good reliability for the EAT-26, the main measure of eating behaviour used in this study. For example, Juan Rivas et al. (2010) found good internal reliability – a correlation of +.9 for each item and the overall result (where +1.0 is perfect reliability).

This means that differences between the 1995 and 1998 groups were likely to be due to real changes over time and not simply the unreliability of the measures.

Competing argument Although reliability of the EAT-26 is good, there are issues with its validity. For example, we would expect that scores on the EAT-26 would predict eating disorders but that was not the case in a sample of Brazilian women (Nunes et al. 2005).

Poor generalisability

A weakness of the study is that it involved an unrepresentative sample therefore findings may not generalise.

There is a problem of generalising findings from Fiji to other populations. This is because Fiji traditionally has quite distinctive attitudes to body type – for example, high BMIs are traditionally considered attractive. The clash between Fijian cultural norms and those portrayed on American TV were much greater than is the case in most countries.

Therefore, the results might have been affected by culture and may tell us little about the effect of TV on body image in other countries.

Application to treating eating disorders

Becker et al.'s findings have applications for tackling eating disorders.

This study shows that modelling in the mass media may have a negative impact on body image and eating behaviour. This can be applied to advice for TV programming and advertising – understanding the value of 'larger size' models. It can also be applied to treatments for eating disorders because, if behaviours and attitudes can be learned through modelling, they can be unlearned in a similar way.

This application of Becker et al.'s research demonstrates its significance in both avoiding and treating eating disorders.

EXTRA: Issues and debates

This study raises the issue of reductionism because it looks only at the role of media modelling in eating behaviour.

Eating behaviour is affected by many influences, such as genes and upbringing. Because the study looked at different groups in 1995 and 1998, it is not possible to eliminate genetic and family differences between the groups as causes of the differences between the 1995 and 1998 results. There are also many important cultural influences on eating attitudes, and it may be that wider cultural change in Fiji – of which the introduction of TV is a symptom – accounted for the changes between 1995 and 1998.

This means that it is misleading to draw a simple conclusion that social learning is the explanation of eating behaviours and attitudes.

Balanced conclusion

The Becker et al. study has some methodological strengths and applications, and is generally of interest to psychologists focused on social learning. However, there are also fairly serious methodological limitations and, although results *suggest* a role for the media, there are other possible reasons for the findings, such as other simultaneous social changes.

Anne Becker is a Professor of Global Health and Social Medicine, based at Harvard University. As both a psychiatrist and an anthropologist, she is eminently qualified to carry out research into the clinical impact of cultural change in indigenous populations such as Fiji.

Professor Becker founded the Eating Disorders Clinical and Research programme at Massachusetts General Hospital and won a 2013 Award for Excellence from the National Eating Disorders Association and a 2014 Award for Exceptional Mentorship of Women.

Apply it Methods: Smart models?

Iona is comparing the body images of 8-year-old children who do and do not have access to a smartphone/tablet to investigate exposure to internet models. She is using a questionnaire with closed questions and also asking participants to do some descriptive writing about 'somebody beautiful/handsome who dazzles the world'. Iona will use thematic analysis to summarise the answers.

1. (a) The closed questions will collect quantitative data. Write **one** suitable question Iona could use. (1)
   (b) State **one** theme that Iona could look for in the thematic analysis. (1)
2. Iona is expecting that access to the internet will make children's body image worse. Write a directional (one-tailed) experimental hypothesis for Iona's study. (2)
3. Iona is concerned that even children without access to mobile devices may still be able to access the internet easily and frequently.
   Explain why this is a potential problem in Iona's experiment. (2)

Apply it Concepts: Sarah's website

Sarah is 13 years old and has created a website for other girls her age about TV programmes and movies. She wants to use this as an opportunity to show girls that most women are not super-skinny and makes sure that she uses pictures of women within a normal weight range.

1. (a) Identify the models used by Sarah on her website. (1)
   (b) Identify the behaviour being modelled. (1)
2. Explain **one** example of vicarious reinforcement from the context above. (2)
3. Explain what Sarah would hope to find if she compared body image of young girls before and after spending six weeks following her website. (2)

Study tip

Be prepared for questions of any size – 2 marks, 4 marks, etc., all of which may ask for a description of a study. You need to practise different length answers so you can adapt to the particular question you are asked.

Check it

1. (a) Describe the aims of **one** contemporary study that you have learned about as part of the learning theories topic. (2)
   (b) Explain how the study tested this aim. (4)
2. Explain **one** problem with your chosen contemporary study in terms of its internal validity. (2)
3. **Standard:** Evaluate **one** contemporary study that you have learned about as part of the learning theories topic. (8)
4. **AS (Synoptic):** To what extent are your chosen contemporary studies from the learning theories and biological topics valid and reliable? (12)

Contemporary study: Bastian et al. (2011)

The specification says...
4.3.3 One contemporary study, for example: Bastian et al. (2011).

Brock Bastian is Associate Professor at the University of Melbourne, Australia. He commented on his research for us: 'We were most interested in the self-dehumanising effects of playing these games, but I did realise after publishing the research, and being called most names under the sun on video gaming chat sites, that it was not well-received by the gaming community. Our key reason for doing the research was to show that how we act, even in online environments, can have implications for our self-perception, but I guess for those who enjoy playing violent games being told they were dehumanising themselves was not something they wanted to hear.'

Think Link
Individual differences

Dehumanisation

An important part of our humanity is our capacity to see ourselves and others as unique, emotional beings. The tendency to see people as less than human underlies some of the most horrific human behaviours such as racism and genocide (Haslam 2006).

Anything that encourages individuals' tendency for dehumanisation is therefore deeply worrying to psychologists. Although this study does not demonstrate a direct link between violent games and antisocial behaviour it does suggest negative effects on the attitudes of players. It may thus give us an insight into the origins of individual differences in dehumanisation.

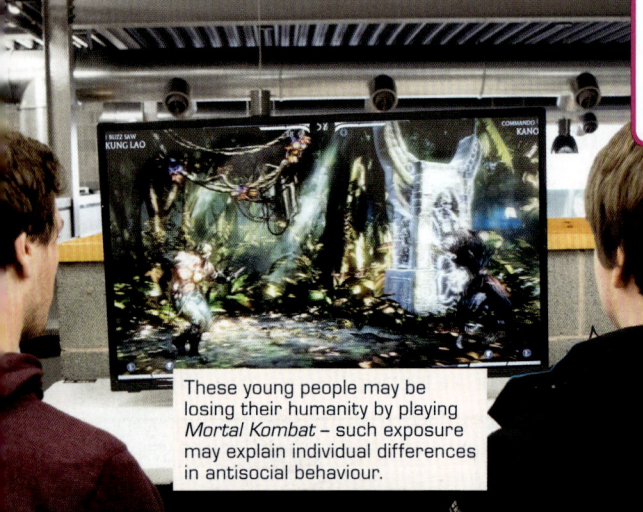

These young people may be losing their humanity by playing *Mortal Kombat* – such exposure may explain individual differences in antisocial behaviour.

Cyber-dehumanisation

Aim
Brock Bastian, Jolanda Jetten and Helena Radke (2011) investigated the link between violent video games and dehumanised attitudes. The aim of study 1 was to demonstrate that playing a violent game against another player would cause a dehumanised view of both the self and the other player. Study 2 aimed to eliminate the influence of possible confounding variables that had affected study 1, such as the nature of the game and individual differences in self-esteem and mood.

Procedure
Study 1 was a laboratory experiment, using an independent groups design. There were 106 participants, aged 17–34, 74 female, 32 male. They were randomly allocated to either experimental or control groups.

Participants in each group played in pairs on an X-Box. In the experimental violent group they played *Mortal Kombat* (a violent game) against another person. In the control group they played *Top Spin Tennis* (a non-violent game).

The independent variable was thus the violent/non-violent nature of the game. The main dependent variable (DV) was *humanness* (the extent to which we see ourselves and others as having human uniqueness, emotion and agency), assessed by means of an 8-item scale. Additional DVs included ratings of enjoyment, excitement and frustration.

Study 2 was also a laboratory experiment using an independent groups design, with 38 participants. This time in the violent group, participant pairs played together against computer avatars in *Call of Duty*. Unlike *Mortal Kombat*, *Call of Duty* involves all human characters. This helps eliminate the possibility that dehumanisation of avatars is due to their non-human status.

Humanness was again measured but this time self-esteem and mood were also measured so that they could be eliminated as confounding variables. Humanness of the avatars was also measured.

Findings
There were no consistent differences between violent and non-violent games. *Mortal Kombat*, but not *Call of Duty*, was rated more enjoyable than *Top Spin Tennis*. *Call of Duty*, but not *Mortal Kombat*, was also rated as more frustrating.

Self and other humanness ratings were significantly lower after playing both the violent games than the non-violent *Top Spin Tennis*. Controlling for self-esteem and mood in study 2 did not eliminate this effect.

In study 2 the avatars in the violent game were rated as low in humanness, however the co-players were not.

Graph showing self-rated humanity after playing violent and non-violent games.

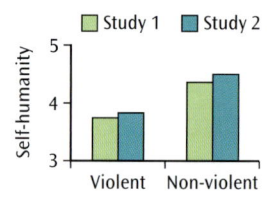

Conclusion
Playing violent video games leads to a tendency to see both the self and opponents as less human, i.e. less as unique, emotional beings. However, co-aggressors are not dehumanised in this way.

The dehumanisation effect cannot be explained away by individual characteristics of the participants or the characteristics of the particular game because controlling for self-esteem and mood made no difference and because the effect was the same for the two violent games.

Stretch & Challenge
Bandura on dehumanisation

Albert Bandura has incorporated the idea of dehumanisation into his theory, now called *social cognitive theory* rather than *social learning theory*. Briefly, Bandura (2001) explains how the social-cognitive human requires mechanisms of self-regulation in order to maintain moral judgement, but that we can use mechanisms such as dehumanisation in order to bypass our self-regulation mechanisms. Bandura uses the phrase *moral disengagers* for those who employ strategies such as dehumanisation.

Explain how engaging in dehumanisation through violent video games might lead to moral disengagement. What might be the consequences as a generation grows up playing violent games?

Dehumanisation leads to genocide where a group of people are killed because they belong to a particular ethnic group. This image is of Armenians massacred by the Ottoman Empire in 1918. There is a discussion of genocide on page 36 in chapter 1.

Evaluation

Good internal validity
A strength of the study is the use of laboratory experimental procedures that maintained good internal validity.

Because the studies were both conducted under controlled conditions this meant that extraneous variables such as temperature and lighting could all be kept constant. This is important because levels of enagagement with the videos might have differed, for example, if some participants were hotter they might have felt more aggressive. Controlled conditions meant that participants in each of the groups are likely to have had the same experiences as one another apart from the independent variable – the different games they played.

This means that differences between the effects of violent and non-violent games are very likely to be due to the games and not to other variables.

Competing argument The independent measures design means that participant variables may become confounding factors. The fact that participants were randomly allocated supposedly controlled for this but there may have been important individual differences (although an effort was made to control these in study 2).

Poor external validity
A weakness of the study is that the measure of humanness may not predict real-life dehumanisation.

Dehumanisation is judged to happen in real-life situations when people see other *real* people as less-than-human in the context of a real-life situation. In this study a scale was used to measure humanness – the answers given by participants may not reflect their feelings in a real-life situation. In addition the humanness measure was administered immediately after playing the video games, and therefore only reflects very short-term attitude changes.

Therefore, the apparent effects of the video games may not generalise to how people think and feel in real-life settings.

Application to parenting
Bastian *et al.*'s findings have applications for parenting.

The findings of this study suggest that playing violent video games leads to dehumanisation. Parents may want to bear this in mind in regulating the time children spend gaming and the nature of the games they allow their children to play. There is also a therapeutic application in advising parents of children with antisocial problems (such as bullies) of the effects of gaming.

This application of Bastian *et al.*'s research demonstrates its significance in shaping parenting and therapeutic practice.

EXTRA: Issues and debates
This study has implications for the nature–nurture debate in psychology as it concerns the impact of an environmental variable.

The study appears to show that violent gaming (nurture) can be a factor in the development of dehumanisation. It is particularly interesting because it suggests that only violent gaming has this effect, not gaming *per se*.

This is relevant to the nature–nurture debate because it suggests that we are predisposed to become dehumanised in response to images of violence, perhaps as an evolutionary mechanism to prepare us for conflict (nature).

Balanced conclusion
The Bastian *et al.* study is potentially very important as it suggests that a very common and 'normal' pastime – violent gaming – may leave people vulnerable to dehumanisation. This is very worrying given that dehumanisation is associated with extremely destructive human behaviours. However, this study demonstrates only short-term dehumanisation effects in artificial settings. Further research is urgently needed to see whether violent games impact in the long term on dehumanisation in real-life settings.

Apply it Methods: P is for prosocial
Dr Khan is testing the effects of video games on young children. He uses simple games:
- Game P is prosocial, the child player is part of a gang of animals that help injured animals in a forest.
- Game V is violent, the child becomes part of a gang who are trying to blow up trees to find treasure.
- Game N is neutral, the child is trying to build a tree house faster than any other player.

1. Explain the role of Game N. (2)
2. Identify **one** variable controlled in all three games. (1)
3. (a) Explain why an independent groups design would be the best design for this study. (2)
   (b) Explain **one** weakness of using this experimental design in this study. (2)
4. Dr Khan records the total number of aggressive noises each child makes, then calculates the median number of aggressive acts in each condition.
   (a) Explain **one** advantage of using the median. (1)
   (b) Sketch and label the axes for a bar chart that Dr Khan could use to display this data. (3)

Apply it Concepts: Mr Miller's monsters
The children in Mr Miller's school are becoming more aggressive. He wants to reduce this by persuading parents to limit their child's access to violent games for six months.

1. (a) Write a letter to parents from Mr Miller explaining why he plans to recommend this. You must refer to Bastian *et al.* (2011) in your answer. (6)
   (b) Write a reply to Mr Miller from a parent who doesn't believe this will make any difference. You must base your answer on criticisms of Bastian *et al.* (2011). (6)

Study tip
To give yourself flexibility, try to find different types of strengths and weaknesses of your chosen study, such as ones relating to reliability, different types of validity and ethics.

Check it
1. (a) Describe the sample of **one** contemporary study that you have learned about as part of the learning theories topic. (2)
   (b) Explain how this sample was collected. (2)
2. Use learning theory to explain the findings of your chosen contemporary study. (6)
3. **Standard:** Evaluate **one** contemporary study that you have learned about as part of the learning theories topic. (8)
4. **AS (Synoptic):** To what extent are your chosen contemporary studies from the learning theories and biological topics valid and reliable? (12)

Contemporary study: Capafóns et al. (1998)

The specification says...
4.3.4 One contemporary study, for example: Capafóns et al. (1998) Systematic desensitisation in the treatment of the fear of flying.

Juan Capafóns is Professor of Psychology at the University of La Laguna in Tenerife. His current research is on the abusive use of and addiction to mobile phones in adolescents in the Canaries. He defines mobile addiction as using a mobile for more than three hours per day and sending more than 10 messages per minute.

Systematic desensitisation for fear of flying

Aims

Systematic desensitisation (SD) is described on page 146. Juan Capafóns, Carmen Sosa and Pedro Avero (1998) aimed to assess the effectiveness of SD in the treatment of fear of flying. A secondary aim was to see whether fear of flying reduced spontaneously without treatment. More generally the researchers aimed to demonstate that SD remains comparable in effectiveness with newer therapies.

Procedure

The study was experimental using an independent groups design. A control group had their fear of flying assessed at two time points without treatment whilst an experimental group were assessed, treated then assessed again. (Note that, for ethical reasons, the 'no-treatment group' did later receive treatment, i.e. they were a waiting control group.) The independent variable was treatment/no treatment and the dependent variable was fear of flying, measured in a number of ways including the *Fear of Flying Scale* and the *Scales of Expectations of Danger and Anxiety*. In addition physiological measurements of muscle tension and heart rate were recorded in response to a videotape of flying.

41 adults with a fear of flying took part. There were 24 females and 17 males. Treatment and non-treatment groups were matched for sex, age and anxiety levels. Age differed slightly, with a mean of 29.65 for the treatment group and 34.05 for the control group.

Each participant was assessed for fear of flying individually on two occasions, one for completing anxiety scales and the other for the physiological measurements. For this second session measurements were taken while they watched a film of a flight, sitting in an armchair exactly 1.8 metres from the screen.

Each participant in the treatment condition had 12–15 one-hour treatment sessions (two per week). Each participant created their own desensitisation hierarchy with a minimal increase in anxiety between the elements. They were exposed to the experience of flying using a blend of their own imagination, videos of flight situations and, towards the end of the programme, real situations. Participants were also taught breathing techniques, progressive muscle relaxation and visualisation techniques to aid relaxation.

Findings

In the no-treatment control group there were no significant differences on any of the measures of anxiety from the first to second assessments. Neither were there any significant differences between anxiety in the first assessment between control and treatment groups.

There were highly significant reductions in reported anxiety and all physiological measures except body temperature in the treatment condition from before to after treatment. 90% of participants in the treatment condition had a significant reduction in symptoms.

Conclusion

These results indicate that SD is a highly effective treatment for fear of flying, with a success rate of 90%. There was no evidence of spontaneous recovery without any treatment.

Stretch Challenge

Desensitisation vs CBT

Capafóns et al. were keen to demonstrate the effectiveness of systematic desensitisation (SD) as a treatment for fear of flying in the light of the development of newer models of psychological therapy such as CBT. So how does their favoured treatment fare when compared to CBT? In a study by Merel Krijn et al. (2007) the two therapies were directly compared, along with a third treatment approach which involved reading self-help manuals.

CBT and SD had very similar success rates, both being superior to the self-help manuals. However, CBT led to greater symptom reduction than SD.

Explain the implications of these results for the Capafóns et al. study, given that one of the study's aims was to demonstrate the continued relevance of systematic desensitisation.

Clients with a fear of flying experience anxiety with all sorts of imagery linked to flying (such as a photograph of a plane), as well as flying itself.

Think Link
Individual differences

Exposure and anxiety

We all have anxieties, and one of the ways in which we all differ as individuals is the nature and extent of these anxieties. Approximately 13% of people experience a serious fear of flying at some point in their lives (Schindler et al. 2016) and around 1.3% suffer from it at any one time (Wardenaar et al. 2017).

Fear of flying can be disabling to those whose work involves travel and affects many people's ability to enjoy holidays. It is comforting to know that 90% of people with a fear of flying can be treated by SD.

Evaluation

Good range of anxiety measures

A strength of the study is the use of several measures of anxiety, including psychological and physiological ones.

The psychometric tests used in the study had previously been shown to be valid and reliable, for example the *Fear of Flying Scale* had better than +.85 test–retest scores (Sosa *et al*. 1995). In addition several physiological measures (such as heart rate) were taken, providing objective and reliable data. Measures were taken under controlled conditions.

This allows us to be as sure as possible that we have valid anxiety measures for each participant.

Short-term measures of improvement

A weakness of the study is that the measures of anxiety were only taken shortly after the treatment.

Although anxiety was measured thoroughly before and after treatment, we have no idea from the results of this study how long the benefits of treatment lasted. A criticism of behavioural treatments in general has been that their effects may not last as long as those of alternatives.

This is important because it means that the results may give us a falsely positive impression of the effectiveness of systematic desensitisation for fear of flying.

Competing argument Other studies since this one have shown longer-term effectiveness for SD for fear of flying. For example, one study found treatment effects were maintained a year later (Botella *et al*. 2004).

Application to treating fear of flying

Capafóns *et al*.'s findings have applications for clinical psychologists in choosing a treatment for fear of flying.

Clinical psychologists are committed to evidence-based practice. This means that they have an obligation to provide treatments that are known to work. Studies like this one by Capafóns *et al*. can be used to show what elements of the therapy may be useful, such as using imagination and watching videos rather than having to actually experience flying.

This application demonstrates the significance of this study in dealing with anxiety conditions such as fear of flying.

EXTRA: Issues and debates

This study has implications for the use of psychological knowledge in society.

The study shows that SD is an effective treatment for fear of flying. This suggests that as a matter of policy clinical psychologists should consider its use as one of the therapies they deliver. This in turn suggests that SD should be recommended and funded in public health care systems like the NHS. It also supports the teaching of systematic desensitisation in clinical psychology training.

This is important as it is an example of the use of evidence-based practice in applied psychology.

Balanced conclusion

In most respects the Capafóns *et al*. study is a very standard outcome study. The use of treatment and no-treatment groups and the measurement of symptom severity at two points in time is how all research of this type is done. The distinctive strength of this study is the good range of outcome measures, however we need to balance this against the relatively small sample size and lack of data about the long-term impact of the treatment.

Systematic desensitisation can be applied to dental phobia.

Apply it Methods: SD for DS

Jeff is conducting a naturalistic observation with DS airlines. When people book with DS they indicate whether they are willing to be observed at the airport on either their outbound or inbound flight, but are not told which. If they say yes, they are also given a questionnaire about attitudes to flying.

1. One question on the questionnaire asks participants to rate how nervous flying made them on a scale of 1–10.
   (a) State the type of data that this scale will produce. (1)
   (b) Explain **one** advantage of taking this type of measure of a fear of flying. (2)
2. Explain how Jeff could use event sampling to record the frequency of anxious behaviours, such as nail-biting and pacing. (3)
3. Explain **two** ethical problems with Jeff's study. (4)
4. Jeff decides he will also use interviews and conduct a thematic analysis on the transcripts produced.
   (a) Explain how Jeff would use thematic analysis. (4)
   (b) Explain **one** advantage for Jeff of using thematic analysis compared to observation. (3)

Apply it Concepts: Dental desensitisation

Katie is a dentist with new clients who are dental-phobic. She wants to help them to overcome their fears and has read about Capafóns *et al*.'s study. The psychology staff at her local university want to set up a study to see how effective systematic desensitisation would be for Katie's clients.

1. Write a leaflet to explain to clients how the therapy would work for them. (4)
2. Write a balanced assessment considering whether Capafóns *et al*. is a valid and reliable study. (4)
3. (a) Suggest **one** reason why Capafóns *et al*.'s findings would generalise to fear of the dentist. (2)
   (b) Suggest **one** reason why Capafóns *et al*.'s findings would *not* generalise to fear of the dentist. (2)

Study tip

When you are writing about strengths or weaknesses, don't just say *what* the strength or weakness is, say *why* it is one.

Check it

1. (a) Describe the procedure of **one** contemporary study that you have learned about in the learning theories topic. (2)
   (b) Explain **two** strengths of this procedure. (4)
2. Explain **one** control used in the contemporary study that you have learned about as part of the learning theories topic. (2)
3. **Standard:** Evaluate **one** contemporary study that you have learned about as part of the learning theories topic. (8)
4. **AS (Synoptic):** To what extent are your chosen contemporary studies from the learning theories and biological topics valid and reliable? (12)

Key questions for learning theories

The specification says…

4.4.1 One key question of relevance to today's society, discussed as a contemporary issue for society rather than an academic argument.

4.4.2 Concepts, theories and/or research (as appropriate to the chosen key question) drawn from learning theories as used in this specification.

Suitable examples

- Is the influence of role models and celebrities something that causes anorexia?
- Would it be a good idea for airline companies to offer treatment programmes for fear of flying?

(Note that these are examples and therefore no exam question will specifically ask you about one of these.)

The key to key questions

Key questions may be worth anything between 1 and 12 marks for AS level and up to 20 marks for A level. On this spread we focus on 8-mark questions – but you can add more paragraphs to turn this into a 12- or 16- or 20-mark answer.

A 'key question' essay needs to combine a *description* of the key question with application of concepts, theories and research evidence from the learning theories topic. We think the secret lies in using black/blue/green paragraphs.

When answering an 8-mark exam question, first state your key question and then write three paragraphs structured as follows:

- **Black:** Describe one aspect of your key question and explain why it is important in contemporary society.
- **Blue:** Link to relevant psychological concepts and theories.
- **Green:** Support your blue ideas with relevant research evidence or introduce competing arguments (from other research evidence or comparisons with other topics in psychology). Be sure to LINK BACK to the key question.

End with a balanced conclusion.

Each paragraph should be 100–140 words.

There is more advice on key questions on pages 9 and 17.

Photo-sharing apps have made many people more body-conscious than ever, in some cases leading to serious disorders like anorexia nervosa.

Example 1

Discuss the key question you have studied using concepts, theories and/or research from the learning theories. (8)

Key question: Is the influence of role models and celebrities something that causes anorexia nervosa?

The number of under-19s hospitalised for eating disorders (e.g. anorexia) has tripled in the last ten years. This has been blamed on increased exposure to celebrity culture through hand-held mobile devices (*Guardian* 2015). Social learning theory (Bandura) suggests that young women identify with models and actresses due to their status and success, and follow them on social media. If the celebrities are rewarded, e.g. through Instagram likes, young woman experience vicarious reinforcement, meaning they will be even more likely to imitate the celebrities. Becker *et al*. (2002) supports this, finding that dieting rocketed when TV was introduced to Fiji, where curviness was previously celebrated. This suggests that celebrity culture may be partly responsible for the increased prevalence of anorexia. (119 words)

Picture-sharing apps have made users more body-conscious than ever. Instagrammers who promote dieting and fitness are particularly popular and hashtags like #eatclean make inspiration easily accessible. Users often compliment each other but 'body-shaming' of celebrities who post more natural images is very common. When individuals upload photos post-weight loss, 'likes' act as rewards (positive reinforcement), and operant conditioning suggests these behaviours will be repeated. This could lead to excessive exercise and dieting. Body-shaming is punishing and ensures celebrities refrain from posting more natural images, giving a warped version of reality, which young people try to emulate. However, despite widespread exposure to celebrity culture, only a small percentage become anorexic. This suggests that genetic factors may also be involved. This is supported by studies of MZ and DZ twins with anorexia (e.g. Holland *et al*. 1984). (135 words)

Anorexia is a serious disorder, 8% of people with the disorder die within five years. The cost to families is immeasurable. Regulating media exposure should therefore be a top priority if there is believed to be a link with anorexia. However, if media is part of the problem, it could also be part of the solution. Bandura and Sabido have used telenovelas to tackle social problems using popular characters who become role models. This could help educate viewers about the dangers of overexposure to unrealistic models. Research has shown the Sabido method has been highly effective in increasing the use of contraception and encouraging take-up of literacy classes in countries round the world and this is a strength of the learning explanation for anorexia as it also provides suggestions for health promotion. (132 words)

In conclusion, although anorexia may also be determined by biological factors, the learning theories offer plausible reasons to explain excessive weight loss and suggest important interventions that could save lives. (30 words)

Total = 416 words

On this page we have presented a full answer to one of the key questions in the specification and added comments to draw your attention to specific features.

Identify the extent of the problem using terms from the key question posed.

Make it contemporary: The increase in children using mobile devices and recent statistics make this response relevant to today's society.

Integrating psychological theory: Notice how theoretical terminology is blended with ideas linked to the key question.

AO1 the sequel: This paragraph keeps the response relevant to today's society and provides the necessary opportunities to bring in a second learning theory.

Terminology from a second area of theory is used to explain the AO1 above.

Injecting a competing argument: A biological alternative explanation is presented before the response returns to AO1 to ensure enough points are made in the limited time available.

The big finish: A balanced judgement is always a useful way to end your response. See how we finish using terms from the original key question.

Example 2

Discuss the key question you have studied using concepts, theories and/or research from social psychology. (8)

State your key question: Would it be a good idea for airline companies to offer treatment programmes for fear of flying?

Paragraph 1

Describe: How many people have a fear of flying in the UK? What symptoms do they exhibit? What impact might this have on their lives? How might this affect their work and family?

Link: Use classical conditioning to explain how phobias are acquired. You could use a bad experience with turbulence as your UCS for example.

Support/challenge: Many people who fear flying have never been on a plane. If classical conditioning is not part of developing the phobia, would it be a helpful part of the solution?

Paragraph 2

Describe: How might people deal with their fear of flying? How is it treated? How effective are treatments?

Link: Outline systematic desensitisation or flooding in the context of fear of flying.

Support/challenge: Use a study such as Capafóns et al. (1998) to support your explanation. Think about why this therapy may be more effective if it was delivered in an airport as this fits with the key question proposal that therapy is delivered by the airline. Are there any practical issues with this?

Paragraph 3

Describe: People often cope with their anxiety by drinking alcohol but too much alcohol can lead to drunken behaviour on flights which poses a serious risk.

Link: Discuss anti-anxiety medication as an alternative treatment programme. Bring in your knowledge of neurotransmitters and how these might be linked to extreme anxiety of fear of flying thus suggesting drugs as a possible alternative treatment.

Support/challenge: Is there any evidence that anxiety might be biological and therefore biological treatments might be more effective than psychological ones? This might suggest that access to specialist pharmacists at airports might be more beneficial than treatment programmes which take time.

Finish with a balanced judgement. Could treatments based on the learning theories realistically be delivered by airlines at the airport, for example?

This is a useful article from the *Telegraph* newspaper that might help with your research for the key question above: tinyurl.com/ybcymuqy

On this page we have provided a scaffold to help you prepare your own answer.

Remember that these are simply suggested answers. Use such suggestions to help you think about how you could structure your own response.

Some airlines offer courses based on systematic desensitisation at major British airports to help people overcome their fear of flying.

Try your own

You don't have to do the key question in the specification. Here is a different one that you might try:

Should schools be doing more to educate parents and pupils about the negative effects of violent video games?

As televisions sets appeared in people's homes, the on-screen violence debate began. Bandura's studies of learned aggression paved the way for years of research. Nowadays, hyper-realistic graphics in video games mean anxiety is at fever-pitch yet psychologists are pretty split in their opinions. The following links should kick-start your research:

- *Violent crime, linked to playing violent video games* (see tinyurl.com/yd362jsx) These stories could help you make a case for why this area needs careful investigation.
- *Safer children in a digital world* (see tinyurl.com/y7kprvpw) In 2007, the government commissioned Tanya Byron to write a report about the risks of exposure to inappropriate material online or in video games.
- *What does research suggest?* (see tinyurl.com/ofzw9hm) This great documentary examines recent research regarding whether violent video games really do harm players.
- *A professional view* The American Psychological Association (APA) created a resolution on violent gaming in 2015 (see tinyurl.com/y9k5ylxf) but this prompted a backlash from numerous critics which you can investigate here: tinyurl.com/h8dcmtz

Study tip

If there is a classic or contemporary study that is relevant to your key question, you can use it as evidence, but make sure you use other evidence too so that you develop your answer fully.

Check it

1. State your key question and use **one** concept or theory to explain **one** aspect of your key question. (4)
2. Processes of learning are used in society for people's benefit, but equally learning is often the cause of society's problems.
3. **Standard:** Discuss the extent to which your key question suggests that learning is a help or a hindrance in modern society. Use relevant concepts, theories and/or research in your answer. (8)
4. **AL (Key Question/I&D/Synoptic):** Evaluate the usefulness to society of the psychological knowledge from your key questions in learning theories and cognitive psychology. (12)

Practical investigations for learning theories

Practical investigation example from the specification.

The specification says...

4.5.1 Two observations (one observation can be carried out if both qualitative and quantitative data are gathered in the same observation). In conducting the practical research exercise, students must:

- Ensure that observations relate to an aspect of learned behaviour, such as behaviour of different sexes, driving characteristics, age-related behaviour, politeness and helping behaviour.
- Ensure that observations enable the gathering of both qualitative and quantitative data (including the use of note-taking, tallying and thematic analysis). (See pages 174 and 206)
- Analyse the findings to produce results, including using a chi-squared test. (See page 212)
- Consider the strengths and weaknesses of the studies and possible improvements.
- Write up the results of the quantitative data, including appropriate graphs and tables. (See page 172)
- Write up the results of the qualitative analysis (thematic analysis). (See page 174 and 213)

Do men and women behave differently when listening?

Ethical principles

Ethical principles are discussed in detail in chapter 5, on pages 176–177. We strongly suggest that you complete this checklist before collecting data.

1. Participants know participation is voluntary.	☐
2. Participants know what to expect, i.e. the task(s) they will be doing.	☐
3. Participants know they can withdraw at any time.	☐
4. Participants' responses will be anonymous.	☐
5. I minimised the risk of distress to participants.	☐
6. I have avoided collecting any sensitive data.	☐
7. I considered all other ethical issues.	☐
8. I have not done anything that would bring my school/teacher/psychology into disrepute.	☐
9. My teacher has approved my plan.	☐

An observation of gender differences in listening behaviour

Both of the investigations on this spread are related to the observation of polite, helpful behaviour (one of the suggestions in the first bullet point of the specification on left). The investigations illustrate situations where we might choose to gather either quantitative or qualitative data. This first study gathers quantitative data only.

Design considerations

This study is looking at differences between males and females, so the independent variable (IV) is gender (male or female) and there has to be an independent groups design. The dependent variable (DV) is listening behaviour, which will be measured using an observation procedure. Controlled observation is the technique used to measure the DV.

Prepare materials

You will record listening behaviour and need to identify behavioural categories which you can then tally. You might want to focus on the extent to which your participants listen well, maintaining eye contact, nodding, imitating the expression and posture of the speaker, etc. You can also look for the frequency of unhelpful behaviours, for example interrupting and changing the subject.

It is worth conducting a small pilot study to see if these categories work well as a way of observing listening behaviour.

Sampling decisions

You do not need equal numbers of males and females (although you will need some/ enough of each gender to make a comparison). An opportunity sample is the easiest sampling method but least representative of the population.

A tally chart might look like this if you decide to do event sampling, or you could do time sampling.

Tally chart of listening behaviours observed in females.

Nods	Smiles	Matches expression	Matches position	Total
̄H̄H̄T̄ //	///	//	//	̄H̄H̄T̄ ̄H̄H̄T̄ ////

Special ethical concerns

You will be recording measures of individuals' listening skills. This is potentially quite sensitive, so confidentiality and (written) informed consent are important. Make sure participants are fully informed and under no social pressure to take part, and don't reveal individual results to anyone else. As always, remember no under-16s.

Analyse your data

You will need a table to display descriptive statistics to show the average frequency of each observed behaviour in males and females (use median for the average). This data should be represented in a bar chart showing average frequency of each behaviour or, if you time-sampled, a pie chart showing the percentage of the time this behaviour was observed.

Table showing median frequency for each listening behaviour.

	Nods	Smiles	Matches expression	Matches position	Total
Female	6	4	4	5	19
Male	4	3	2	1	10

You are required to carry out a chi-squared test to establish the significance of the results.

Consider an inter-observer reliability exercise to check whether the record of observations you produce is reliable.

Write the report

You should record the details of how you carried out this study, along with the rationale for doing so. You should include a summary table(s) like the one above and appropriate graphs. In the discussion section you must include comments on strengths and weaknesses of the study and any ideas you have for possible improvements.

A naturalistic observation of student politeness and considerate behaviour

Practical investigation example from the specification.

This second investigation involves gathering qualitative data. No hypothesis is being tested – the purpose of the study is purely investigatory.

Design considerations

This is a rather different study. Naturalistic observation lends itself to investigatory studies where, rather than comparing conditions or testing a hypothesis, you are interested in exploring what sort of behaviours take place in a group of people in a given situation. The aim of this suggested study is to investigate the range of ways in which students in school or college cafeterias display courtesy and consideration to their peers.

Preparing materials

For this kind of observation you don't need a tally chart because you do not know what behaviours you will be recording. The only materials you need to use to gather your data are a pen and notebook to record everything you see. We recommend leaving a column free in your notebook to start recording themes as soon as they emerge.

Sampling decisions

You want to observe a typical selection of behaviour for this study, but you have no way of knowing when or how frequently the kind of behaviour you are interested in will occur. Event sampling is therefore probably a better bet than time sampling.

Special ethical concerns

A naturalistic observation can be carried out overtly or covertly – you will need to make a decision here. There is nothing unethical *per se* about observing public behaviour covertly in a public space, as long as you can be sure of not upsetting observees or focusing on behaviour they may consider private. Remember that people behave more naturally when you observe covertly.

Analysing your data

As this is a qualitative analysis you will not be using tables or graphs to display your findings. Instead you need to produce a marked-up transcript of what you observed ('field notes') and summarise what it shows ('themes').

Field notes	Themes
In the queue for lunch as two wheelchair-users arrived another student handed them trays and all queuing students moved to let them in first. Most students while I was observing thanked staff serving them lunch. All students observed queued without pushing or pushing in. Moving to observe tables, all students observed moved along to let others sit down. On one table students who had finished moved completely so others could sit and eat. They were typically thanked for this.	Considerate behaviour Considering others' needs Verbal courtesies

Writing the report

You should record the details of how you carried out this study, along with the rationale for doing so. You won't need tables or graphs but include your themed field notes. You can also display findings in the form of a concept map if you wish.

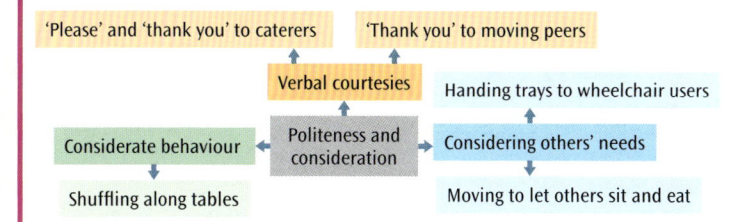

In the discussion section you must include comments on strengths and weaknesses of the procedure and any ideas you have for possible improvements.

Student cafeterias lend themselves to naturalistic observation.

Other ideas

Controlled observation of age differences in nonverbal communication. Do younger people differ from older people in the hand gestures and facial expressions they use when they discuss what they watch on TV?

Naturalistic observation of window shopping behaviours in a shopping centre. What do people do when they are window shopping, on their own or with friends? Are there gender differences?

Apply it Methods: Kim's codes

Kim's group are conducting an observation in a shopping centre. They are testing whether older or younger people are more helpful. They have created codes for behaviours such as helping with a pushchair and holding a door open and are going to note the code and age group of each person they see helping.

1. Explain whether the situation is naturalistic or controlled. (1)
2. Kim thought using their phones to record data would be less obvious than notes on paper.
   (a) Explain **one** practical advantage of this decision. (2)
   (b) Explain **one** ethical disadvantage of this decision. (2)
3. Kim needs operational definitions for each code.
   (a) Write an operational definition for **one** of the two behaviours Kim's group are recording. (1)
   (b) Explain **two** reasons why it is important for the group to have operational definitions. (2)

Study tip

If you want, you can conduct just one observation as long as you collect both qualitative and quantitative data. You need to be prepared for questions requiring detailed answers on either of these aspects.

Check it

1. For the 'learning theories' practical investigation you will have used a chi-squared test to analyse the results.
2. (a) Draw and fully label the contingency table you used to calculate chi-squared in your investigation. (3)
   (b) Explain how you calculated *df* (degrees of freedom) for your chi-squared test. (2)
3. **Standard:** Evaluate your practical investigation for the learning theories topic. (8)
4. **AL (Practicals/I&D/Synoptic):** Most psychologists believe that research should be scientific.
   To what extent were the procedures of your practical investigations for learning theories and cognitive psychology scientific? (12)

Revision summary

Chapter 4 Learning theories

Classical conditioning (CC)

The main features

The process of classical conditioning
Before: UCS produces UCR.
During: NS paired with UCS.
After: NS/CS now elicits CR.

Extinction
When CS is experienced repeatedly without UCS it ceases to elicit CR.

Spontaneous recovery
Sometimes extinct responses to CS reappear, usually in weakened form.

Stimulus generalisation
Stimulus similar to CS produces CR.

Pavlov (1927)

Aims
To explore role of conditioned reflexes in eating behaviour (salivation) of dogs.

Procedure
Dogs: NS (e.g. metronome) paired with UCS (food), salivation (UCR) measured.

Findings
After pairing NS with UCS (food), NS typically elicited salivation response (now CS).

Conclusion
Link made in brain between UCS and NS so both trigger same response (UCR and CR).

Evaluation

Research evidence
Studies (e.g. Watson and Rayner 1920, Brom et al. 2014).
However issues remain e.g. Pavlov's emphasis on contiguity between NS and UCS.

Incomplete explanation of learning
CC only explains acquisition of simple reflex behaviours.

Application to aversion therapy
CC used to condition new fear responses to previously undesirable conditioned stimuli.

EXTRA: Issues and debates
CC good science, falsifiable, e.g. Rescorla's (1968) research on contiguity.

Evaluation

Some good experimental controls
Internal validity enhanced by control of extraneous variables, e.g. soundproof room.

Generalisability to humans
Unclear how well findings generalise to humans, more complex brain.
However Watson and Rayner (1920) showed CC in humans.

Application to eating problems
Obesity explained by strong associations between food cues and salivation, leads to overeating (Jansen et al. 2003).

EXTRA: Issues and debates
Benefits for society – health promotion uses CC, e.g. images on cigarette packaging.

Operant conditioning (OC)

The main features

The Skinner box
Food pellets used as reinforcers for animals.

Reinforcement
When consequence of action increases probability of action being repeated.
Positive = something nice introduced.
Negative = something unpleasant removed.

Primary and secondary reinforcement
Primary (e.g. food) has biological significance.
Secondary (e.g. money) associated with primary reinforcers.

Punishment
When consequence of action means behaviour less likely to be repeated.
Positive = something unpleasant introduced.
Negative = something pleasant removed.

Schedules of reinforcement

Continuous and partial reinforcement
Continuous = behaviour always reinforced.
Partial = behaviour sometimes reinforced.

Fixed and variable *ratio* reinforcement
Fixed ratio = reinforcers given after fixed number of behaviours.
Variable ratio = reinforcers varied around a mean.

Fixed and variable *interval* reinforcement
Fixed = reinforcement always after same interval.
Variable = reinforcement varied around mean interval.

Behaviour modification

Modifying behaviour
Systematic use of operant conditioning to increase frequency of desired behaviour.

Shaping
Reinforce successive approximations.

Evaluation

Research evidence
OC demonstrated in humans and animals, neural correlates identified (Chase et al. 2015).

An incomplete explanation of learning
OC doesn't explain origins of novel behaviours, only how existing behaviours are strengthened.

Application to education and childcare
Understanding reinforcement helpful for children's behaviour in school, childcare settings.

EXTRA: Issues and debates
OC lends itself to social control.
However degree of social control necessary.

Evaluation

Research evidence
Many studies. e.g. Latham and Dossett (1978) beaver trappers' pay.

Fails to take account of intrinsic motivation
Can explain extrinsic motivation in humans, but ignores role of intrinsic rewards (powerful motivators in humans).

Application to treating inappropriate behaviour
Successfully used, e.g. Lovaas therapy for autism.

EXTRA: Issues and debates
Ethical issues, therapist's power.
However usually client and therapist agree on behaviours to change.

Social learning theory

The main features

Modelling
One individual displays social behaviour in presence of observer.

Observation and imitation
Observation = paying attention to behaviour of model.
Imitation = behaviour is copied.

Vicarious reinforcement
Observer sees model reinforced for their behaviour.

Stages of social learning
1. Attention to modelled behaviour.
2. Retention of event.
3. Reproduction of behaviour.
4. Motivation to repeat behaviour.

Evaluation

Research evidence for SLT
Social learning demonstrated in humans (Bandura's studies) and animals (Nicol and Pope 1999).

Research evidence against SLT
Other factors (e.g. genes) involved in aggression (Kendler et al. 2015).
However SLT does not ignore this. Urge to aggress is innate, manner of aggression is socially learned.

Application to violent behaviour
SLT can explain effect of media violence on behaviour.

EXTRA: Issues and debates
Fairly reductionist, emphasis on learning behaviour.
However SLT less reductionist than CC or OC.

Bandura et al. (1961)

Transmission of aggression through imitation

Aims
To see whether aggressive behaviour could be acquired by observing modelled aggression.

Procedure
72 children observed aggressive or non-aggressive model, or control, then opportunity to aggress.

Findings
Children who witnessed aggressiveness modelled specific behaviours, slightly more aggressive.

Conclusion
Behaviour can be acquired through observation.

Evaluation

Clever experimental design
Extraneous variables controlled (e.g. matching aggressiveness, children tested individually).

Artificial environment
Playing with doll is not typical situation where children might model aggression, may not generalise.

Application to learning aggressive behaviour
Helps psychologists understand acquisition of aggressive behaviour by observing adult models.

EXTRA: Issues and debates
Ethical issues, children deliberately frustrated.
However distress was mild and short-term.

Bandura et al. (1963, 1965)

Film-mediated aggressive models

Aims
To test whether filmed/cartoon model will have same effect on aggression as live model.

Procedure
96 children observed: filmed, cartoon or no aggression.

Findings
No difference between aggression of children in three conditions.

Conclusion
Exposure to any modelled aggression increases likelihood of aggression.

Influence of models' reinforcement

Aim
To test whether reinforcement and punishment of model affects acquisition of aggression.

Procedure
66 children saw aggressive model receive reinforcement, punishment or no response.

Findings
Punishment condition, less aggressive. Promise of reward, increased aggression for all.

Conclusion
Vicarious punishment reduces aggression. Promised rewards more important.

Evaluation

Control of extraneous variables
Extraneous variables controlled in both studies (e.g. matching aggression, children tested individually).
However Bandura only showed short-term effects, and aggression towards a doll.

Risk of demand characteristics
Elements of procedure (Bobo doll) may have cued participants to study aim (Noble 1975).

Application to the Sabido method
Bandura and Sabido (2017) developed telenovelas using SLT to tackle social problems.

EXTRA: Issues and debates
Socially sensitive research, suggests that parents who let children watch violent media affect their development.

Phobias

Acquisition — *Treatments based on learning theories*

Learning theory explanations

The two-process model
Mowrer (1960) identified two processes: phobias acquired by CC and maintained by OC.

Acquisition of phobias by classical conditioning
NS associated with fear stimulus and becomes CS provoking CR of fear.

Maintenance by operant conditioning
Avoidance of feared stimulus reinforced by fear reduction.

Social learning of phobias
Children may also acquire phobias by imitating adult fear responses.

Evaluation

Supporting evidence
Watson and Rayner (1920) and Cook and Mineka (1989) demonstrated how phobias are learned in terms of CC and social learning.

Does not explain all aspects of phobias
Some phobias are more easily learned e.g. dangerous things in our evolutionary past.

Application to treating phobias
Therapies like systematic desensitisation use CC.

EXTRA: Issues and debates
Alternative explanations for phobias, e.g. Freud's theory of displacement.
However more evidence for learning theory explanations.

Systematic desensitisation

What it is
New response learned (counterconditioning), new CR (relaxation) blocks anxiety (reciprocal inhibition).

The anxiety hierarchy
Fearful situations involving phobic stimulus are ranked.

Relaxation
Client taught relaxation techniques, e.g. breathing exercises, imagery.

Exposure
Client exposed to phobic stimulus, working up hierarchy whilst maintaining relaxation.

Evaluation

It is effective
Gilroy et al. (2003): SD reduced spider phobia compared to controls.

Not suitable for all cases
May not work for complex cases, e.g. multiple phobias, history of trauma.

EXTRA: Issues and debates
Developed over time, e.g. now using virtual reality.

Flooding

What it is
Immediate exposure to very frightening situation, may last 3 hours.

How flooding works
Fear response extinguished as experienced for extended period without UCS.

Ethical safeguards
Informed consent important, flooding is traumatic.

Evaluation

Cost effective
Quicker, cheaper and at least as effective as other therapies, e.g. cognitive ones (Ougrin 2011).

May not be effective for all phobias
Not effective for social phobias with cognitive elements (unpleasant thoughts).

EXTRA: Issues and debates
Ethical issues, involves trauma.
However flooding done with consent and trauma balanced by benefits.

Classic study

Watson and Rayner (1920)
Conditioned emotional reactions

Aim
To demonstrate the acquisition of fear response through CC.

Procedure
11-month-old boy presented with white rat paired with unexpected loud noise.

Findings
Albert showed fear of rat and similar white furry objects.

Conclusion
Fear can be acquired by CC and generalises.

Evaluation

Some good experimental controls
Control of participant and situational variables (e.g. emotional stability, well-controlled room) eliminated many extraneous variables.
However presentation of related stimuli not well-controlled.

Poor generalisability
n = 1 design, hard to generalise findings.

Application to acquiring phobias
Study shows how phobias may be acquired.

EXTRA: Issues and debates
Ethical issues, child was distressed.

Contemporary studies

Becker et al. (2002)
Eating behaviours following prolonged exposure to television

Aim
To investigate impact of Western style television on eating behaviour and body satisfaction in Fijian girls.

Procedure
63 girls questioned when TV introduced, different 65 girls after introduction, 3 years later.

Findings
Dysfunctional eating behaviour increased, body satisfaction decreased.

Conclusion
American TV characters became role models for Fijian girls, imitated body type.

Evaluation

Reliable measurements
Rivas et al. (2010) found +.9 internal reliability for EAT-26.
However problems with predictive validity of EAT-26 (Nunes et al. 2005).

Poor generalisability
Distinctive Fijian culture (high BMIs attractive), findings may not generalise to other countries.

Application to treating eating disorders
Suggests modelling can treat eating disorders.

EXTRA: Issues and debates
Reductionist, study only looks at role of media.

Bastian et al. (2011)
Cyber-dehumanisation

Aim
To investigate link between playing violent video games and dehumanisation.

Procedure
Study 1: 106 participants played *Mortal Kombat* or *Top Spin Tennis*, then assessed for humanness.
Study 2: 38 participants played *Call of Duty* against avatars, then assessed self and co-player for humanness, self-esteem and mood.

Findings
In both studies humanness ratings lower after playing violent games.
Study 2: Avatars rated low in humanness but not co-player.

Conclusion
Playing violent video games dehumanises gamers but not co-player.

Evaluation

Good internal validity
Tightly controlled conditions (e.g. temperature), therefore low risk of extraneous variables affecting findings.
However participant variables in independent groups design may have affected findings (though controlled in study 2).

Poor external validity
Artificial set-up and short-term effects assessed, may not predict real-life humanness.

Application to parenting
Suggests parents should limit violent gaming.

EXTRA: Issues and debates
Implications for nature-nurture debate because findings show humanness affected by environmental variable.

Capafóns et al. (1998)
Systematic desensitisation for fear of flying

Aims
To test the effectiveness of systematic desensitisation (SD) for fear of flying.

Procedure
41 adults with a fear of flying were treated by SD or put on waiting list (control).

Findings
Fear declined in 90% of treatment group but not in control group.

Conclusion
SD has high success rate for fear of flying.

Evaluation

Good range of anxiety measures
Reliable psychometric tests (e.g. *Fear of Flying Scale* with +.85 test-retest) and physiological measures (e.g. heart rate).

Short-term measures of improvement
Decline in fear only demonstrated immediately after treatment.
However other studies demonstrated long-term effectiveness (e.g. Botella et al. 2004).

Application to treating fear of flying
This study shows that using imagination and watching videos reduces phobias.

EXTRA: Issues and debates
Implications for use of knowledge in society, SD is evidence-based treatment and therefore recommended.

Practice questions, answers and feedback

On this spread we look at some typical student answers to exam style questions. The comments provided indicate what is good and bad in each answer.

Learning how to produce effective question answers is a SKILL. Read pages 6–19 for guidance.

Question 1: When Victor was in the army, he witnessed his friend's leg being blown off by a landmine. Victor is now living a civilian life but is now affected by post-traumatic stress from this event. One day a car backfired while he was shopping in town and there was a very loud bang. Victor had a severe panic attack, which left him housebound for many days.

Use classical conditioning to explain Victor's reaction. [4]

Sam's answer
Seeing someone get their leg blown off would be a ghastly experience for Victor, which he has found difficult to forget and this has been the cause of his problems. Now, when he hears a bang from the car or probably any bang it is enough to make him remember the fear and horror from his time in the army. This is why Victor is suffering from panic attacks and why he has become housebound as his house is a safe place.

Each of Sam's sentences is linked to the extract but he has not used any psychological concepts in his answer. In fact, he mentions the term 'remember' which is linked to cognitive psychology rather than learning theories. Therefore, no marks for this answer.

Ella's answer
Classical conditioning is when an unconditioned stimulus leads to an unconditioned response. If there is something else present at the time, then that thing can become associated with the unconditioned stimulus and can bring about the same response. This example about Victor is similar to Little Albert when he became scared by the rat because of the loud bang of the steel bar. Victor has learned to associate the loud bang with his friend being injured.

Ella's first two sentences give a basic explanation of classical conditioning but neither sentence is linked to the extract and therefore she is not answering the question which is about Victor's reaction. Sadly, sentence three is also not addressing the question – although she has brought in a useful study that could help explain Victor's reaction. Sentence three does mention Victor, but just using his name is not enough, as she is still failing to address the command term 'explain'. The last sentence is applied to the extract but is very limited, so possibly just 1 mark for this answer.

Larina's answer
The horrific scene of Victor's friend's leg being blown off is the unconditioned stimulus. This would have led to terror and feeling sick at the sight of the injury (the unconditioned response). The sound of the explosion would be the conditioned stimulus, which preceded the injury. It only required one pairing to lead to a conditioned fear response occurring when Victor hears similar sounds. Although extinction may have reduced the fear response over the years, it seems that the car backfiring led to spontaneous recovery, and then the loud bang led to the panic attack because of the association Victor learned when he was in the army.

Larina's answer is detailed and each sentence is linked to the extract but also includes a psychological concept (classical conditioning). She has used two psychological terms (spontaneous recovery and extinction) to good effect although these haven't been explained in full. Given the time available, she has created an excellent answer (full marks), combining extract information with her psychological knowledge and understanding.

Question 2: Explain what is meant by a 'variable ratio reinforcement schedule'. [3]

Sam's answer
Variable ratio reinforcement means that a reinforcer is given after an unpredictable number of behaviours that varies around a mean value. When a variable ratio schedule is used, it becomes very hard to extinguish the behaviour.

Sam gives an excellent description in his first sentence and elaborates this – the elaboration explains why variable reinforcement might be used, e.g. because behaviour becomes hard to extinguish. This said, Sam really needs to give an example to extend his answer and gain the final mark.

Ella's answer
Variable ratio means that the person is not rewarded every time they show the desired behaviour, but they are rewarded after an average number of times. The number of times is unpredictable and sometimes they need to do more behaviours before getting the reward and sometimes less. An example is when salespeople are trying to sell something on the phone, sometimes they get a sale and sometimes they don't.

Ella's answer is good in that she gives an accurate and detailed description and attempts to take this further with an example, turning simple description into something more explanatory. The trouble here is that her example is unclear – she hasn't linked the sales to reinforcement. Therefore, only 2 marks.

Larina's answer
Variable ratio means that sometimes the person will have to wait for longer before they get their reward and sometimes they will not have to wait so long. The example here would be that if you gain enough points in a video game sometimes you will be rewarded with an extra life, but every time you play the game, the number of points that you need to get the extra life changes and this is why people get addicted to playing the game as they know they will get an extra life if they keep playing longer.

Larina's answer sounds as though she is getting a bit muddled between variable ratio and variable interval as she talks about 'waiting longer'. She gives an interesting real-life example, maybe from trying to apply what she has learned in class to her own life. The example works but it's a bit longwinded, therefore just 1 mark because the example is reasonable but the knowledge is confused.

Question 3: In the learning theories topic you have learned about Watson and Rayner (1920) as your classic study. Evaluate the classic study from the learning theories topic. [8]

Sam's answer

Watson and Rayner (1920) aimed to classically condition an 11-month-old boy to be scared of a white rat. They wanted to see whether the fear would generalise and how long the fear would last before becoming extinct.

One problem from the outset is that the generalisability of this study could be judged to be weak as Albert may not be representative of other young children, and indeed Watson and Rayner suggested he may be unusual, i.e. he rarely cried and infants often cry and therefore may have a different reaction.

However, it could also be said that he was chosen for his normalcy. Yes, he seemed fearless but then reacting to loud noises and furry animals in the way he did could be seen as normal, and therefore not a unique response from an 'unusual' individual, so maybe it was more generalisable than first thought.

In the study Albert was shown a white rat and then a hammer struck a suspended steel bar to make a loud, startling noise. Next the rat was presented without the bang to see whether Albert became scared. It took many pairings before Albert started to cry and crawl away from the rat when presented without the noise.

A strength of this study is that the internal validity is strong because the researchers carefully controlled the environment using the same room, researchers, lighting and so on. They also checked Albert's 'normal' reactions to the rat and other items like building blocks before the conditioning trials. This allowed them to compare his reactions to the same stimuli after classical conditioning.

However, in the real world, the situation would not be this controlled – other people may be present, for example, if Albert's mother showed she was not afraid Albert might have modelled her. This is important because social factors probably also affect the development of phobias.

This study was useful as it showed classical conditioning could change phobic behaviour leading to therapies such as systematic desensitisation, which help people. However, it does not explain why phobias develop after just one trial. Given the questionable ethics, only using one infant was good, but this also reduced scientific merit as the findings lack generalisability.

365 words

Sam has taken the 'sandwich' approach (see page 16) and given a brief AO1 statement and then linked a chain of reasoning to this, and continued throughout the essay.

In the first chain of reasoning he discusses generalisability, clearly flagging the point at the start. Notice how he says 'could be judged to be weak' instead of claiming it is weak – it is better to avoid making definite claims.

In the third paragraph a competing argument is given. It is good to present this as a separate paragraph to flag this to the examiner.

We now return to a second chunk of description about the procedures of the study, and this is followed by a chain of reasoning, nicely flagged with 'A strength ..' which also alerts the examiner to the balance in this essay between weaknesses and strengths – there is no harm in making your answer more readable for the examiner.

In the penultimate paragraph another competing argument is given about the drawbacks of too much control.

Sam has all the elements of a good essay here including a balanced conclusion at the end.

One slight issue is that Sam brings up ethics in his conclusion but has not mentioned this anywhere else in the essay so we don't know why they were questionable. It is best to avoid bringing up anything new in the conclusion.

This is a level 4 response, possibly at the lower end. The evaluation has been explicitly linked to the description and there is quite a bit of knowledge of the study scattered throughout the answer. Two competent chains of reasoning and each with well thought out competing arguments. A little more description would have sealed top marks.

Larina's answer

Watson and Rayner (1920) aimed to condition a young child to be scared of a white rat.

One strength of this study is that it used a human and previous research, such as Pavlov's study, only used animals and therefore it was not clear whether classical conditioning was applicable to humans.

On the other hand, one problem with the study is that it only used one child and therefore the findings may not be representative as it is possible that this boy was easily scared for some reason. This means that the study is not generalisable.

Albert was shown a white rat and then the researchers made a loud bang. They wanted to know how many times they would need to do this before Albert was scared of the rat.

This is a weakness of the study, as in real life people often become phobic after one bad experience and sometimes people have phobias where they have never even had a bad experience. Another weakness with the study is that Albert was not protected from harm. Also sometimes there were up to four people in the room meaning Watson and Rayner were not using a standardised procedure.

This shows that the study has poor ethics, is not generalisable and is not reliable so overall it is a poor study although it does shows fears can be learned.

227 words

Larina, like Sam, has taken the 'sandwich' approach. She starts with the aim of the study and then goes into her first chain of reasoning, swiftly followed by a competing argument.

She then outlines the procedure and findings however she does not inject as much detailed knowledge as Sam, meaning her description is not thorough.

The penultimate paragraph contains two further weaknesses which means that the essay is becoming imbalanced. In addition she has forgotten to use the three part structure to ensure that the critical points are logical. Furthermore she is slipping into a rather generic approach by not always supporting the criticism with sufficient descriptive knowledge of the procedural details.

There is a conclusion of sorts but it is very superficial.

While the structure of this answer is good, it is far too short. The description lacks any depth of knowledge and the chains of reasoning have not been developed. The answer would probably be at the top of level 1.

Multiple-choice questions

Classical conditioning

1. A stimulus that produces a response without learning is called:
   (a) The unconditioned stimulus.
   (b) The conditioned stimulus.
   (c) The neutral stimulus.

2. The phenomenon in which we respond to a stimulus that is similar to an existing CS is called:
   (a) Extinction.
   (b) Generalisation.
   (c) Spontaneous recovery.

3. Commonly used as a UCS in aversion therapy:
   (a) A nice smell.
   (b) A painful shock.
   (c) An unfamiliar photograph.

4. Classical conditioning can explain:
   (a) Complex chains of behaviour.
   (b) Imitation of a role model.
   (c) Reflexes in new situations.

Classical conditioning: Pavlov (1927)

1. The dependent variable in Pavlov's experiments:
   (a) Metronome.
   (b) Meat powder.
   (c) Salivation.

2. An example of a NS used by Pavlov was:
   (a) A metronome.
   (b) Meat powder.
   (c) An electric shock.

3. An example of Pavlov's experimental controls:
   (a) The soundproofed chamber.
   (b) The same dog used in all experiments.
   (c) A different bell being rung.

4. A weakness of Pavlov's work:
   (a) Practical applications.
   (b) Generalisability to humans.
   (c) Experimental controls.

Operant conditioning

1. An operant chamber is better known as a:
   (a) Watson box.
   (b) Skinner box.
   (c) Pavlov box.

2. An example of a secondary reinforcer:
   (a) Cash.
   (b) Food.
   (c) Shelter.

3. An example of a negative punishment:
   (a) A smack.
   (b) A public flogging.
   (c) A fine.

4. An example of positive reinforcement used in a children's nursery:
   (a) Time out.
   (b) Relief from tidying up duty.
   (c) A star chart.

Operant conditioning: Reinforcement and behaviour modification

1. An example of continuous reinforcement is paying a child:
   (a) Every time they wash up.
   (b) Every third time they wash up.
   (c) Somewhere between every first and fifth time but every third time on average.

2. A therapy in which reinforcement is used to systematically increase the frequency of a desired behaviour is:
   (a) Aversion.
   (b) Behaviour modification.
   (c) Shaping.

3. An ethical issue with the use of behaviour modification:
   (a) Unpleasant side effects.
   (b) Lack of evidence for effectiveness.
   (c) Maintenance of individual liberty.

4. Variable ratio reinforcement schedules lead to:
   (a) Behaviour change that is hard to extinguish.
   (b) Very quick behaviour change.
   (c) Highly consistent behaviour.

Social learning theory

1. In SLT someone who demonstrates a behaviour is the:
   (a) Subject.
   (b) Model.
   (c) Poser.

2. Cognitive process that comes first in the social learning of a behaviour:
   (a) Retention.
   (b) Reproduction.
   (c) Attention.

3. An example of vicarious reinforcement, a child:
   (a) Is rewarded for hitting a classmate by getting to eat his lunch.
   (b) Sees a TV character get what they want by hitting a bad guy.
   (c) Imitates the behaviour of their local vicar.

4. Social learning provides a theoretical basis to understanding the effect of:
   (a) Media violence.
   (b) Social media use.
   (c) Internet addiction.

Social learning theory: Bandura et al. (1961)

1. Participants in this study were:
   (a) 72 adults.
   (b) 36 children.
   (c) 36 boys and 36 girls.

2. The design of this study involved:
   (a) Comparing younger children to older children.
   (b) Studying children over a long period of time.
   (c) Matching participants on aggressiveness.

3. The children were frustrated during the procedure because:
   (a) It was fun for the researchers.
   (b) It would make it more likely that they would display aggression later.
   (c) They saw an aggressive model.

4. Percentage of children in non-aggressive model condition who displayed any aggression:
   (a) 30%.
   (b) 50%.
   (c) 70%.

Social learning theory: Bandura et al. (1963, 1965)

1. The main independent variable in the 1963 study:
   (a) The amount of frustration.
   (b) The nature of the model.
   (c) The consequence of the modelled aggression.

2. The main independent variable in the 1965 study:
   (a) The amount of frustration.
   (b) The nature of the model.
   (c) The consequence of the modelled aggression.

3. Demand characteristics in Bandura et al.'s studies are a threat to:
   (a) Reliability.
   (b) Ethics.
   (c) Validity.

4. Results of the studies may *not* extend to real life because:
   (a) Aggression to a doll may not generalise to humans.
   (b) The experimental controls were very poor.
   (c) The situation was very lifelike.

Phobias: Learning theory explanations

1. In the two-process model, phobias are acquired through:
(a) Social learning.
(b) Operant conditioning.
(c) Classical conditioning.

2. In the two-process model, phobias are maintained through:
(a) Social learning.
(b) Operant conditioning.
(c) Classical conditioning.

3. UCS that might lead to the acquisition of a phobia:
(a) A nice cup of tea.
(b) Gentle music.
(c) A painful bite or sting.

4. Study that supports a social learning explanation of phobias:
(a) Mowrer's study of rats.
(b) Watson and Rayner's study of Little Albert.
(c) Cook and Mineka's study of monkeys.

Phobias: Treatments based on learning theories

1. The goal of systematic desensitisation:
(a) Exposure to phobic stimulus.
(b) Anxiety hierarchy for phobic stimulus.
(c) Relaxation in presence of phobic stimulus.

2. Advantage of systematic desensitisation compared to flooding:
(a) It is more effective.
(b) It is quicker.
(c) It is less traumatic.

3. Means we cannot have two conflicting states at the same time:
(a) Vicarious reinforcement.
(b) Reciprocal inhibition.
(c) Spontaneous recovery.

4. Example of flooding:
(a) Zemmiphobic looking at a picture of a mole rat.
(b) Arachnophobic watching a small spider through glass.
(c) Kinemortaphobic watching in the front row at a zombie film.

Classic study: Watson and Rayner (1920)

1. The stimulus that triggered the initial fear response in the child:
(a) Cotton wool.
(b) A loud noise.
(c) Wooden blocks.

2. Albert's age at the end of the study:
(a) 9 months, 2 weeks.
(b) 11 months, 1 week.
(c) 12 months, 3 weeks.

3. Findings at sessions 4 and 5 (the new environment):
(a) Less extreme fear reactions.
(b) More extreme fear reactions.
(c) No fear reaction.

4. A potential weakness of the Little Albert study.
(a) No practical applications.
(b) No experimental controls.
(c) Hard to generalise from a single participant.

Contemporary study: Becker et al. (2002)

1. The study is best described as:
(a) A community survey.
(b) A lab experiment.
(c) A field experiment.

2. Name of the questionnaire used:
(a) EAT-21.
(b) EAT-26.
(c) FAT-26.

3. The independent variable in this study:
(a) The introduction of Western TV.
(b) The interviews.
(c) Eating behaviour.

4. A strength of the Becker et al. study:
(a) Reliability of eating questionnaire.
(b) Participant variables well-controlled.
(c) Generalisability to other populations.

Contemporary study: Bastian et al. (2011)

1. The dependent variable measured in both studies:
(a) Mood.
(b) Aggression.
(c) Humanness.

2. One advantage of using *Call of duty* over *Mortal Kombat*:
(a) More violent.
(b) Uses human characters.
(c) Easier to play.

3. Variable not kept constant between conditions:
(a) The participants.
(b) The games console type.
(c) The location.

4. In study 2, not rated lower in humanness after playing a violent game:
(a) Self.
(b) Avatars.
(c) Co-players.

Contemporary study: Capafóns et al. (1998)

1. Variable not standardised well between participants in experimental and control conditions:
(a) Age.
(b) Anxiety.
(c) Sex.

2. How often did participants have therapy?
(a) Once a week.
(b) Twice a week.
(c) Twice a month.

3. Success rate for SD:
(a) 75%.
(b) 80%.
(c) 90%.

4. Likely weakness of the Capafóns et al. study:
(a) Unreliable measures of anxiety.
(b) Lack of practical applications.
(c) Lack of long-term improvement.

MCQ answers

Classical conditioning 1A 2B 3B 4C
Classical conditioning: Pavlov (1927) 1C 2A 3A 4B
Operant conditioning: 1B 2A 3C 4C
Operant conditioning: Reinforcement and behaviour modification 1A 2B 3C 4A
Social learning theory 1B 2C 3B 4A
Social learning theory: Bandura et al. (1961) 1C 2C 3B 4A
Social learning theory: Bandura et al. (1963, 1965) 1B 2C 3C 4A
Phobias: Learning theory explanations 1C 2B 3C 4C
Phobias: Treatments based on learning theories 1C 2C 3B 4C
Classic study: Watson and Rayner (1920) 1B 2C 3A 4C
Contemporary study: Becker et al. (2002) 1C 2B 3A 4A
Contemporary study: Bastian et al. (2011) 1C 2B 3A 4C
Contemporary study: Capafóns et al. (1998) 1A 2B 3C 4C

Chapter 5: Research methods

This chapter covers the methods and techniques that psychologists use when conducting research studies. The content is relevant to both AS and AL students.

In the AS exams (AS Papers 1 and 2) there are not separate sections on research methods – the questions on research methods appear within, and are related to, the other topics you are studying, such as social psychology or biological psychology.

In the AL exams the research methods questions again appear within the topics on Papers 1 and 2 but on Paper 3 there is a section just on research methods.

You are expected to study research methods in relation to each topic as you learn about that topic and therefore this chapter is organised to fit in with that.

Contents

Page	Topic
168	Self-reporting data: Questionnaire design
170	Sample selection and techniques
172	Quantitative data and its analysis
174	Qualitative data and thematic analysis
176	Ethical issues and guidelines
178	Self-reporting data: Interviews
179	Researcher effects
180	Validity and reliability of self-report
181	Writing a report

See Practical investigation ideas on page 58

PRACTICAL INVESTIGATION for Chapter 1 Social psychology

Design and conduct a questionnaire to gather both qualitative and quantitative data to look for a difference in the data.

Consider questionnaire construction, sampling decisions and ethical issues.

Collect and present an analysis of quantitative data using measures of central tendency, measures of dispersion, (including range and standard deviation as appropriate), bar graph and frequency table.

Collect and present an analysis of qualitative data using thematic analysis.

Consider strengths and weaknesses of the questionnaire and possible improvements.

Write up the procedure, results and discussion section of a report.

Page	Topic
182	Experiments
183	Hypotheses
184	Experimental design
186	Experiments: Internal validity
188	Experiments: Ecological validity
190	Inferential statistics: Tests of difference
192	Inferential statistics: Tests of difference (continued)
194	Type I and II errors
195	Normal and skewed distributions
196	Case studies and HM

See Practical investigation ideas on page 86

PRACTICAL INVESTIGATION for Chapter 2 Cognitive psychology

Design and conduct a laboratory experiment to gather quantitative data and include descriptive statistics as analysis and a non-parametric test of difference.

Make design decisions when planning and conducting their experiment, including experimental design, sampling decisions, operationalisation, control, ethical considerations, hypothesis construction, experimenter effects and demand characteristics.

Collect, present and comment on data gathered, including using measures of central tendency (mean, median, mode as appropriate); measures of dispersion (including range and standard deviation as appropriate); bar graph, histogram, frequency graph as relevant; normal distribution if appropriate and draw conclusions.

Use a Mann-Whitney U or Wilcoxon non-parametric test of difference to test significance (as appropriate), including level of significance and critical/observed values.

Consider strengths and weaknesses of the experiment, and possible improvements.

Write up the procedure, results and discussion section of a report.

Page	Topic
198	Correlation
200	Inferential statistics: Test of correlation
201	Levels of measurement
202	Other biological research methods
204	Twin and adoption studies

See Practical investigation ideas on page 120

PRACTICAL INVESTIGATION for Chapter 3 Biological psychology

Design and conduct a correlational study.

Link their research to aggression or attitudes to drug use.

Include inferential statistical testing (Spearman's rho) and explain the significance of the result and the use of levels of significance.

Use descriptive statistics (strength/direction) to explain the relationship.

Produce an abstract of the research method and a discussion section that includes conclusions.

Include research question/hypothesis, research method, sampling, ethical considerations, data-collection tools, data analysis, results, discussion.

Consider strengths and weaknesses of the correlational study and possible improvements.

Page	Topic
206	Observation and content analysis
208	Observation: Reliability and validity
210	Use of animals in laboratory experiments
212	Inferential statistics: Test of association
213	Return to qualitative data and thematic analysis
214	Scientific status of psychology

See Practical investigation ideas on page 158

PRACTICAL INVESTIGATION for Chapter 4 Learning theories

Ensure that observations relate to an aspect of learned behaviour, such as behaviour of different sexes, driving characteristics, age-related behaviour, politeness and helping behaviour.

Ensure that observations enable the gathering of both qualitative and quantitative data (including the use of note-taking, tallying and thematic analysis).

Analyse the findings to produce results, including using a chi-squared test.

Consider the strengths and weaknesses of the studies and possible improvements.

Write up the results of the quantitative data, including appropriate graphs and tables.

Write up the results of the qualitative analysis (thematic analysis).

Page	Topic
216	Mathematical skills
218	A few final things
220	Conventions of published research
221	The A level checklist

Page	Topic
222	Revision summary
226	Practice questions, answers and feedback
228	Multiple-choice questions

Self-reporting data: Questionnaire design

Chapter 5 Research methods

The specification says...
Self-reporting data

1.2.1 Designing and conducting questionnaires and interviews, considering researcher effects (interviews and research effects on pages 178 and 179).

1.2.2 Unstructured, semi-structured and structured interviews (page 178), open, closed (including ranked scale) questions.

1.2.3 Alternate hypotheses.

[AL Topic 9 includes: social desirability.]

The term *self-report* refers to any data collection method that involves asking people to report their thoughts, feelings or behaviour.

This data can be collected by giving people a fixed set of written questions (a *questionnaire*) or by an interviewer who asks face-to-face questions in an *interview* (see page 178).

On this first spread we start by looking at designing and conducting questionnaires.

Exam advice
You may be asked about a strength or weakness of a particular piece of research. The answers on the left provide you with the beginning of any answer – your task is then to link these to the actual context in the question to be answered.

For example, here is a possible exam question:

Jo is investigating obedience. Give **one** strength of using a questionnaire in her investigation. (2)

Answer: *Respondents may feel more willing to reveal personal/confidential information in a questionnaire than in an interview.* This would be especially true when investigating obedience because people don't like to say they disobey, so might be more honest than if Jo interviewed them.

(The underlined text above illustrates how the link is provided to the specific context.)

In a nutshell

Questionnaire

Respondents record their own answers. The questions are predetermined (i.e. structured). They are provided in written form and there is no face-to-face contact with another person.

+ Self-report methods are a means of finding out what people think and feel. That is not true of other methods you will study, such as *observation*.

+ Can be easily repeated so that data can be collected from large numbers of people relatively quickly because they can all do it at the same time.

+ Respondents may feel more willing to reveal personal/confidential information in a questionnaire than in an *interview* because they feel more anonymous.

− People don't always tell the truth! This may be because they simply don't know what they think about a particular topic or don't know how they would behave in a particular situation. Or their lack of truthfulness may be because they don't want to look foolish or unlikeable so they present themselves in a way that makes them 'look better' – this is called a *social desirability bias*.

− The group of people involved (called the *sample*) may be biased because only certain kinds of people fill in questionnaires – literate individuals who are willing to spend time filling them in.

Designing questionnaires (and interviews)

Closed question
Has a fixed number of possible answers.

Closed questions provide *quantitative data*, i.e. answers that can be counted. We will look at this in more detail later in this chapter.

+ Easy to analyse because data is in numbers (quantitative data) which can be summarised using averages as well as simple graphs. This generally makes it easier to draw conclusions, for example because you can make comparisons.

+ Answers are more objective because they are more likely to be interpreted in the same way by any researcher.

− May not permit people to express their precise feelings because the researcher determined the choice of answers. Therefore, data collected may be low in *validity* and tends not to uncover new insights.

− Oversimplifies reality and human experience because it suggests that there are simple answers – whereas people are likely to actually think several possible answers would reflect their views.

Open question
Invites respondents to provide their own answers.

Open questions tend to produce *qualitative data*, i.e. descriptive data which can't be immediately counted.

+ Provides rich details of how people behave because they are given free range to express themselves. Participants can express what they actually think rather than being restricted by preconceived categories. This increases the validity of the data collected.

+ The fact that participants can provide any answer means that researchers may collect unexpected findings. With closed questions the researcher makes decisions about likely answers and this closes off any unusual possibilities.

− More difficult to draw conclusions because there are likely to be a wide range of respondents' answers. Therefore, a researcher may look for patterns rather than using *descriptive statistics*.

− Interpreting what people mean is likely to be *subjective* – each researcher may have a slightly different view of what a participant actually meant.

Ranked scale
A kind of closed question where respondents are asked to give an assessment of their views using a scale, e.g. from 1 to 5 where 5 represents very positive and 1 represents very negative.

+ A reasonably objective way to represent feelings and attitudes related to the topic being researched.

+ Produces quantitative data which is easy to analyse or represent in graphs. It is also easy to draw straightforward conclusions.

− Participants may prefer to respond in the same way to all questions, regardless of context. For example, a tendency to select high values or to circle a middle value. In order to avoid a *response set* it is a good idea to switch the positive and negative sides of the scale.

− Social desirability bias may be an issue in terms of the validity of responses given.

Just do it

Doing research is really the only way to understand the content in this chapter. You will be asked exam questions which require you to apply your understanding of research methods concepts – and therefore you really do have to understand the concepts. For this reason we have provided **TRY THIS** activities and you have a **PRACTICAL INVESTIGATION** to work on in each topic you study.

Writing good questions

Questionnaires can be an objective and scientific way of conducting research but this involves more than just thinking up some questions.

The questions must be clear. If they are ambiguous then the answer given is likely to be meaningless. Here is an example of ambiguity: 'Did you see the girl with the binoculars?' which could mean 'Did you see the girl holding the binoculars?' or 'Did you see the girl through your binoculars?'.

Questions also must not be leading questions, i.e. the researcher should not state the question in a way that might lead to a particular answer. For example, 'Did you see the umbrella by the door?' suggests that there was an umbrella in the room and it was by the door, whereas 'Did you see an umbrella? If so, where was it located?' is less suggestive. This is an example of a *researcher effect* where the researcher's beliefs and expectations are unwittingly communicated to the participant and affect the validity of the answer given.

Open and closed questions

The form a question takes affects the kind of data that you will collect. Open questions invite respondents to provide their own answers. Such questions tend to produce qualitative data which we will discuss on page 174.

Examples of open questions
1. Describe what being in love feels like.
2. What things make you feel stressed?

Closed questions have limited choices and produce quantitative data. Most closed questions are fixed-choice, i.e. there is a fixed set of possible answers as in the questions below. Some closed questions have an 'other' category so the range of answers is limited but not fixed.

Examples of closed questions

3. Do you find work stressful? Yes / No / Not sure
4. Which of the following factors at work make you feel stressed?
   (You may tick as many answers as you like.)
   ☐ Noise at work   ☐ Lack of control
   ☐ Too much to do   ☐ Boredom
   ☐ Workmates   ☐ No job satisfaction
5. How much stress do you feel? (Circle the number that best describes how you feel.)
   At work
   A lot of stress   5   4   3   2   1   No stress at all
   At home
   A lot of stress   5   4   3   2   1   No stress at all
6. Work is stressful. How much do you agree with this statement?

Strongly disagree	Disagree	Neither agree nor disagree	Agree	Strongly Agree
☐	☐	☐	☐	☐

Question 5 is an example of a ranked scale where respondents are asked to give a number to represent their views or feelings. You can have 3-point ranked scales or 7 points or 9 points, etc. Odd numbers are best so there is a mid-point.

There are other kinds of ranked scale. For example, *Likert scales* allow people to indicate how much they agree or disagree with a statement, see question 6 above.

How does a plumber learn his or her skills? By doing it and practising a lot.

Writing good questionnaires

A good questionnaire should contain good questions (obviously). There are other considerations too such as the order of the questions. It is best to start with questions that will encourage respondents to keep going – for example, easy rather than difficult ones (e.g. simple, closed questions) and ones that don't make them feel anxious.

Hypothesis

It is the proper thing to do, when conducting a research study, to start with an aim and a hypothesis. For reasons to be explained later the research hypothesis is sometimes called the *alternate hypothesis*. This hypothesis is a statement of what you believe to be true, for example you might believe that women are more obedient than men. The aim of your study would be to investigate whether this is true – your hypothesis would state it as a fact to be tested: 'Women are more obedient than men'.

✓ Check it

1. Explain why the following question lacks clarity: 'How much do pyrotechnics scare you and what kind do you prefer?' (3)
2. Explain the difference between a closed and open question. (3)
3. Is this an open or a closed question: 'How old are you?' Explain your answer. (2)
4. Suggest an example of a ranked scale that could be used to assess obedience. (2)
5. A group of students conduct research on obedience to authority using a questionnaire.
   (a) One of the questions on the questionnaire is, 'Who is the person who you wouldn't dare disobey?' Explain **one** strength and **one** weakness of this question as a means of finding out about obedience. (4)
   (b) Write **one** closed question that the students could include in their questionnaire. (2)
   (c) Explain **one** strength and **one** weakness of using this closed question in this study. (4)
   (d) The students' teacher suggests they might use a ranked scale in their study. Write a suitable question using a Likert scale. (2)

Sample selection and techniques

The specification says...
Sample selection and techniques
1.2.4 Random, stratified, volunteer and opportunity techniques.
[AL Topic 9 includes: generalisability.]

Before you actually use your questionnaire, there are a few more design issues you need to learn about. First up is thinking about who it is that psychologists study – their sample.

When psychologists conduct research they can't test everyone in the world or even everyone in their own town. Therefore, when conducting research, psychologists select a small group of participants (called a *sample*) from a *target population* (this is the group of people they are interested in, such as adolescents in the UK).

Participants are drawn from a **target population** (the group of people the researcher is interested in).

This is a **sample** of the target population.

Sampling techniques methods used to select a sample.

Random sample A sample of participants produced using a random technique such that every member of the target population has an equal chance of being selected. How? Examples of random techniques include giving everyone in the target population a number, putting the numbers in a hat and drawing out the required number of participants, or using a random number generator (available on computers and smartphones). Random number generators are *pseudorandom* techniques.	+ Unbiased, all members of the target population have an equal chance of selection. However, the researcher may end up with a biased sample because not all of the participants who are identified agree to participate. + It is possible to choose a specific subgroup in the target population first, which makes it easier to randomly select participants.	− Takes more time and effort than other techniques because you need to obtain a list of all the members of your target population, then identify the sample and then contact the people identified and ask if they will take part. − Random samples are often not random because not all the participants identified can be accessed or agree to take part. Therefore, the final sample may be more like a volunteer or opportunity sample.
Stratified sample Participants are selected from different subgroups (*strata*) in the target population in proportion to the subgroup's frequency in that population. How? Subgroups, such as age groups, are identified and the number in each subgroup in the target population is identified. This is represented as a percentage total of the whole population. For example, 30% of the target population might be 10–12 years old. Then 30% of participants in the study should be in that age group. The researcher uses random selection to identify the right number of 10–12-year-olds.	+ This is the most representative of all the sampling techniques because all subgroups are represented *and* these subgroups are represented in proportion to the numbers in the target population. + Specific subgroups can be chosen according to the variables considered to be important by the researcher. This increases control over possible extraneous variables.	− However, the decision about which subgroups to use may be biased, thus reducing the representativeness of the sample. − This method involves a very lengthy process and those participants selected may not always agree to take part. This means that it is not a technique that is used much in psychological research. It is used when conducting opinion polls.
Volunteer sample A sample of participants produced by asking for people willing to take part. How? For example, advertise in a newspaper or on a noticeboard.	+ A convenient way to find willing participants. Researchers need committed participants for time-consuming studies and participants are less likely to drop out as they volunteered. + May be a good way to get a specialised group of participants. This is called *purposive sampling*. For example, if you wanted to study the behaviour of medical students it would make sense to put an ad on the noticeboard of a medical school rather than standing around in a shopping centre hoping to find some medical students.	− Sample is biased because volunteer participants are likely to be more highly motivated and/or with extra time on their hands than the population in general (= *volunteer bias*). − Volunteers may also be more willing to be helpful and thus may be more prone to guessing the aims of the study and responding to *demand characteristics*.
Opportunity sample A sample of participants produced by selecting people who are most easily available at the time of the study. How? For example, ask people walking by you in the street or in your common room at school, i.e. select those who are available.	+ The most convenient technique because it takes little preparation. You just use the first participants you can find. This means it takes less time to locate your sample than if using one of the other techniques. + It may be the only technique available because the whole target population cannot be listed (needed for random and stratified sampling).	− Inevitably biased because the sample is drawn from a small part of the target population and therefore is not likely to be representative. For example, shoppers in a city centre on a Monday morning form a small part of the population, e.g. they are largely not people at work. − Participants may refuse to take part so the final sample also has the weaknesses of a volunteer sample, such as being more likely to respond to demand characteristics.

Exam advice
Many students say that an opportunity sample means 'you just choose anyone at random', but 'just choosing anyone' is not random because there are aspects of some people that make it more likely that you would choose them.

Generalisability and representativeness

Once a research study is conducted the researcher hopes to be able to generalise from the study to the target population. For example, if a study looks at the dreams experienced by a sample of UK adolescents, then the results will be used to make statements about all UK adolescents.

This principle of *generalisability* is very important for research. Researchers want to be able to draw conclusions about *people* from the research they conduct with a small sample.

The problem is that it is only acceptable to make generalisations about 'people' (i.e. the target population) based on the sample *if* the sample is representative of the target population. The aim of all sampling techniques is to produce a representative sample.

How many participants should be in a sample?

The number of participants in any study varies enormously. When using questionnaires it is relatively easy to distribute them to hundreds if not thousands of people (your sample).

Experiments can use small samples, as few as 25 is acceptable (Coolican 1996). Larger samples are more representative, have less risk of bias and are more likely to identify minor patterns in results. However, finding general patterns creates a risk that the pattern detected is actually a minor one and relatively meaningless.

Consider a study about noise and memory. Noise may have no effect on most people's memory but it does affect those with sensitive hearing. If you have a very large sample with enough noise-sensitive participants it may appear that everyone is affected by noise. In a small sample, these individual differences have less overall effect so the sample may end up being more representative than if you use a large sample.

You're very special

Your parents have probably told you at some time or other that you are very special. And it's true, you are. In fact you are unique. There is no one quite like you (even if you are an identical twin).

However, when psychologists investigate human behaviour they end up making generalisations about people because they want to know about general trends. We have to be careful about making generalisations because, although we share common features with other people, we are all unique and quite unlike anyone else.

25%

For A level, knowledge about research methods is at least 25% of your overall mark.

For AS it may be as much as 45%!!!

Stratified sample – A worked example

Here is an example of using stratified sampling: A researcher plans to study students' food preferences in the school canteen. To do this he wants the sample to reflect the age range of students in the school and decides to use a stratified sample. 300 are 10–12 years old, 500 are 13–15 and 200 are 16–18.

Therefore, the frequency of the subgroups is 30%, 50% and 20% respectively.

If the researcher is going to recruit 50 participants to answer his questionnaire then:

30% should be aged 10–12 – 30% of 50 is 15.
50% should be aged 13–15 – 50% of 50 is 25.
20% should be aged 16–18 – 20% of 50 is 10.

The researcher then randomly selects the right number of participants from each age group.

Try this: A tube of Smarties

Your target population is 300 smarties. Count how many of each colour there are in the target population (the tube).

Try out the various sampling methods with your smarties, selecting a sample of 20 'participants'.

Keep a record of each sample.

Do any of the samples you produce offer a true representation of the characteristics of the sweets? (You determine this by comparing, for example, the percentage of yellow smarties in your sample with the percentage in the target population.)

Try this: Randomness

Randomness is not what you may think it is. It means every item has an equal chance of being selected. In a lottery draw, the numbers 1, 2, 3 and 4 are just as likely to come up as 5, 13, 26 and 48. Also if you replace those numbers you are just as likely to get 1, 2, 3 and 4 a second time as any other combination.

Try it, on a smaller scale. Put ten slips of paper in a hat, numbered 1–10. Make 20 draws, recording the number and replacing the slip in the hat each time.

What do you notice about the numbers you have drawn?

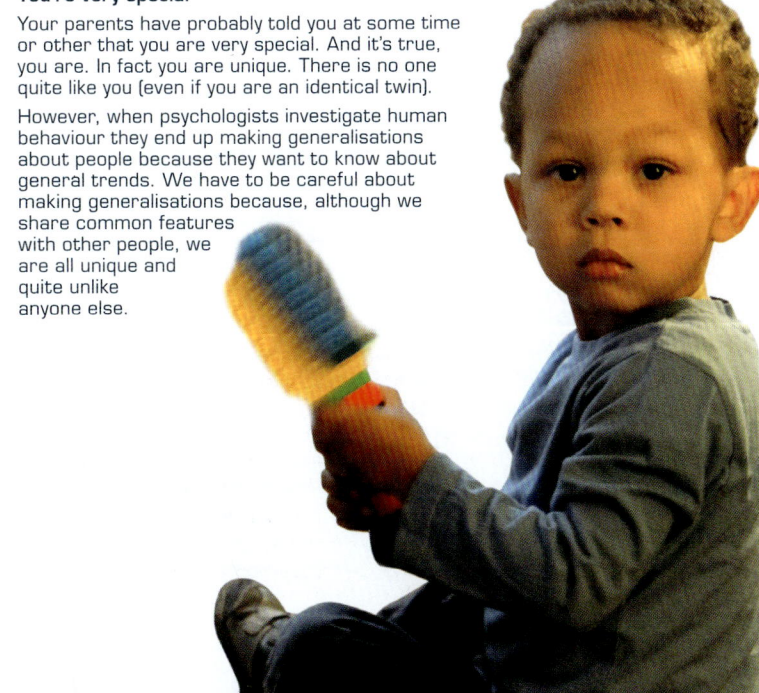

Exam advice

Most research methods questions are applied – they require you to use your knowledge in the CONTEXT of a particular study. There are examples of these throughout this chapter to help you practise this important skill.

In such questions you will not get full marks unless your answer refers to the context and sometimes you may get no marks at all.

However, sometimes the questions do not contain any context, they just ask for description or evaluation.

Check it

A college tutor asks a group of psychology students to produce a questionnaire to find out what students at the college like or dislike about their course.

1. Identify the target population in this study. (1)
2. Explain how you would use an opportunity sampling technique to obtain your participants in this study. (2)
3. What would be the benefit of using a volunteer sample rather than an opportunity sample in this study? (2)
4. The students thought about using stratified sampling. How would they do this? (3)

Quantitative data and its analysis

Chapter 5 Research methods

The specification says...

Qualitative and quantitative data

1.2.5 Analysis of quantitative data: calculating measures of central tendency, frequency tables, graphical presentation using a bar chart, measures of dispersion (range and standard deviation).

[AL Topic 9 includes: histogram, and produce, handle, interpret data - including drawing comparisons (e.g. between means of two sets of data.)]

The end result of any research is data – which is called raw data until it has been processed in some way. In order to make sense of raw data it needs to be described or summarised using descriptive statistics.

The methods on this spread apply to quantitative data.

- **Measures of central tendency** tell us about typical or average values for a data set.
- **Measures of dispersion** tell us about the spread of a set of data – are the items closely bunched together or spread out?
- **Tables and graphs** allow us to 'eyeball' our data and see the pattern in the results at a glance – as the saying goes, 'a picture is worth a thousand words'.

Measures of central tendency (averages)

Mean How? Add up all the values and divide by the number of values.	**+** A 'sensitive' measure because it reflects the values of all the data in the final calculation. Note, the use of the word 'values'. All measures of central tendency use all the data values. But only the mean uses all the values in the final calculation.	**−** Can be unrepresentative of the data set if there are extreme values. For example: Set A: 5, 7, 8, 11, 12, 16, 18 mean = 11.0 Set B: 5, 7, 10, 11, 14, 17, 41 mean = 15.0 (Note: In both data sets the median and mode are the same.)
Median How? Place all values in order and select the middle value. If there are two middle values calculate the mean of these two values.	**+** Not affected by extreme scores. For example, in the data sets above right, the median in both cases would be 11.	**−** Not as 'sensitive' as the mean because not all values are reflected in the final calculation of the median.
Mode How? Identify the group or groups which is/are most frequent or common.	**+** Useful when the data is in categories (*nominal data*). For example, asking people to vote for their favourite colour. The mode would be the colour that was most often chosen.	**−** Not a useful way of describing data when there are several modes. For example, if 12 people choose yellow and 12 people choose red and 10 people choose purple, the modal groups are yellow and red but this isn't very useful information.

Exam advice

If you are asked to explain whether you would use the mean or median with a particular data set, check whether the data set has extreme values (outliers), in which case it is better to use the median. The level of measurement used is also a deciding factor but you have yet to learn about levels of measurement (on page 201).

The same applies to choosing between the range and standard deviation. Range is more affected by extreme values.

Calculations

In the exam you may be required to calculate:
- The mean, median or mode of a data set.
- The range or standard deviation.

The formula for standard deviation is given in the exam paper (on page 2):

$$\sqrt{\left(\frac{\Sigma(x - \bar{x})^2}{n - 1}\right)}$$

You need to:
1. Calculate the mean ($\bar{x}$) of your data set.
2. For each data item (x), subtract the mean from the data item ($x - \bar{x}$).
3. Add up all the new values and square the result.
4. Divide by $n - 1$ (n = the number of values).
5. Work out the square root.

You MUST take a calculator into the exam.

Measures of dispersion (the spread of the data)

Range How? Arrange data in order from highest to lowest and subtract the lowest number from the highest number.	**+** A convenient way to express how spread out a data set is as highest and lowest value are used. **+** Easy to calculate.	**−** Affected by extreme values. **−** Fails to take account of the distribution of the data set, for example it doesn't indicate whether most numbers are closely grouped around the mean or spread out evenly. Using the example at the top right: Set A: 18 − 5 = 13 Set B: 41 − 5 = 36
Standard deviation (SD) How? See left.	**+** A precise measure of dispersion because all the exact values are taken into account. **+** It is not difficult to work out if you are using a calculator.	**−** May hide some of the characteristics of the data set (e.g. extreme values). **−** Cannot be immediately sensed from the data, whereas the range is fairly quick to identify.

Try this: Practise calculating measures of central tendency and dispersion at tinyurl.com/bhulvu

Raw data is data before it has been processed in any way (ed – apologies to vegetarians).

You need to be able to put raw data into a table, not onto a table.

And then you need to know how to process it. Various processing methods are discussed on this spread and the following spread.

In a nutshell

Key term	Definition	Example
Raw data table	A table is a means of arranging raw data in rows and columns.	See pages 191 and 192.
Frequency table	A table displaying a record of how often an event occurred. The example on the right uses *tally marks* to show the results when 50 people were asked to name their favourite colour.	Red $\cancel{||||}\ \cancel{||||}\ \cancel{||||}$ = 15 Yellow $\cancel{||||}\ \cancel{||||}$ = 10 Blue $\cancel{||||}\ ||||$ = 9 Green $||||$ = 4 Purple $\cancel{||||}\ \cancel{||||}\ ||$ = 12
Bar chart (graph)	The height of each bar represents the frequency of each item. Bar charts are especially suitable for data that has no particular order such as graph A on the right which represents categorical or nominal data. In a bar chart a space is left between each bar to indicate the lack of continuity.	Graph A: Bar chart to show favourite colour.
Histogram	A histogram is similar to a bar chart except it is for *continuous data* and the area within the bars must be proportional to the frequencies represented (see graph B). This means that the vertical axis (frequency) must start at zero, though a gap in the y-axis with two short horizontal lines can indicate missing numbers if all values are quite big. In addition the horizontal axis must be continuous. There should be no gaps between the bars.	Graph B: Histogram (with line graph superimposed) to show the ages of people who attended a concert.
Line graph	A line graph, like a histogram, has continuous data on the *x*-axis. There is a dot to mark the highest value in each category which is connected by a line (see graph B).	
Scatter diagram	A graph to display correlation data.	See page 199.

Exam advice
Always have a title for a graph and label the *x* and *y* axes fully.

Check it

1. A psychology class conducts a study comparing memory ability in boys and girls. Each member of the class has to test two children – one boy and one girl. The data they collected is given below. Put this data into a table. [4]

   This is the data they collected:
   Tom's scores: 4.3 (boy), 5.6 (girl),
   Alice's scores: 6.7 (boy), 6.3 (girl),
   Aziz's scores: 1.2 (girl), 3.9 (boy),
   Ruth's scores 7.2 (boy), 4.6 (girl),
   Guang's scores: 5.4 (boy), 5.4 (girl),
   Jack's scores: 4.0 (boy), 8.4 (girl),
   Rosa's scores: 2.5 (boy), 6.0 (girl),
   Rehana's scores: 4.9 (boy), 9.1 (girl),
   Rob's scores: 9.3 (girl), 8.4 (boy),
   Pip's scores: 4.7 (boy) 8.4 (girl),
   Sean's scores: 3.3 (girl), 4.4 (boy),
   Megan's scores: 5.6 (boy), 5.0 (girl),
   Jane's scores: 3.8 (girl), 7.1 (boy),
   Jason's scores: 4.6 (boy), 6.2 (girl),
   Sophie's scores: 3.5 (boy) 8.4 (girl),
   Max's scores: 7.4 (boy), 8.4 (girl),
   Amar's scores: 3.6 (girl), 3.9 (boy),
   India's scores: 5.7 (boy), 6.4 (girl),
   Kasim's scores: 3.0 (boy), 7.8 (girl),
   Alonzo's scores: 5.6 (boy), 4.8 (girl).

2. Draw a graph of the data in question 1. Label both axes and write a title. [3]

3. For each of the data sets below:

Set 1: 5, 9, 12, 15, 21, 22, 25, 29, 32
Set 2: 3, 8, 10, 11, 13, 13, 14, 14, 29, 32
Set 3: 2, 2, 4, 5, 5, 5, 7, 7, 8, 8, 8, 10
Set 4: cat, cat, dog, budgie, snake, gerbil

   (a) Estimate the mean. [1]
   (b) Calculate the mean. [1]
   (c) Calculate the median. [1]
   (d) Calculate the mode. [1]
   (e) State which of the three measures would be most suitable to use and why. [2]

4. For data sets 1, 2 and 3 above:
   (a) Calculate the range. [1]
   (b) Estimate the standard deviation. [1]
   (c) Use the formula on the facing page to calculate the standard deviation [2].

5. Compare the means for data sets 1 and 2. What can you conclude? [2]

Qualitative data and thematic analysis

Chapter 5 Research methods

The specification says...
Qualitative and quantitative data
1.2.6 Analysis of qualitative data using thematic analysis.
[AL Topic 9 includes: grounded theory.]

Your practical investigation for Chapter 1 Social psychology must involve both quantitative and qualitative data. On the previous spread we looked at quantitative data and its analysis. On this spread we compare both types of data, and look at qualitative data and its analysis.

Quantitative and qualitative data

Sometimes people define qualitative data as being about what people think and feel, but quantitative questions can also concern what people think and feel.

Qualitative data can't be counted or quantified though it can be turned into quantitative data by placing the data in categories and then counting frequency.

In a nutshell

Quantitative data	Qualitative data
Quantity.	Quality.
Focuses on numbers.	Focuses on descriptions.
Data that can be counted or measured.	Data that is described not counted or measured.
Psychologists develop measures of psychological variables.	Examining behaviour through the messages people produce.
Looking at averages and differences between groups.	Concerned with attitudes, beliefs, fears and emotions.

A psychology class

Quantitative data	Qualitative data
24 students.	Very enthusiastic about psychology.
18 girls, 6 boys.	Mixture of boys and girls.
72% gained grade A on mock exam.	Hardworking students.
10 plan to go on to study psychology at university.	School located in an inner city area.
Most psychology teachers are female.	Teacher's name is Mrs Jones.

***The Kiss* by Gustav Klimt**

Quantitative data	Qualitative data
Painted between 1907 and 1908, when the artist was 45 years old.	An example of Art Nouveau.
Measures 180 × 180 cm.	Shows how bright, beautiful and golden everything is when you first kiss someone.
First bought for 25,000 crowns.	Painted in oil and gold leaf on canvas.
33% of surface covered in gold leaf.	Probably his most famous painting.

Types of data

Quantitative data Information in numbers, i.e. quantities.

+ Easier to analyse because data is in numbers which can be summarised using descriptive statistics. This generally makes it easier to draw conclusions because, for example, you can see at a glance that men did better on a particular maths test than women, or that the average rating for a particular film was 7 out of 10.

+ Quantities are a more *objective* measure because measurements (height, test score) should be the same no matter who is doing the measuring, and therefore are *reliable*. This gives the measurements greater *credibility* because they are not biased by the person doing the measurements.

− May not express participants' precise thoughts/feelings because the answers provided are fixed – there may not be an answer to represent what they think. Therefore, the data collected may be low in *validity*.

− Oversimplifies reality and human experience because it suggests that there are simple answers. In other words it is a *reductionist* approach, reducing human experience to quantities.

Qualitative data Information in words or pictures, non-numerical.

+ Represents the true complexities of human behaviour because thoughts and behaviours are not reduced to numbers. Thus it is a *holistic* approach.

+ Provides rich details of how people think and behave because they are given a free range to express themselves. Therefore, higher in *validity* as the researcher is more likely to be measuring the variable of interest.

− More difficult to detect patterns and draw conclusions because of the large variety of information collected, and because words cannot easily be reduced to a few simple points.

− Interpreting what people mean is likely to be *subjective*, lowering credibility.

Try this Identify the quantitative and qualitative data in one of your studies, such as Milgram's (1963) study. Most studies produce both kinds of data rather than being just quantitative or just qualitative.

Painting in the style of *The Kiss* by Gustav Klimt. You can describe this qualitatively or quantitatively.

Thematic analysis

One problem with qualitative data is that it is difficult to summarise. Quantitative data can be readily summarised with measures of central tendency and dispersion, as well as graphs. None of these options is possible with qualitative data. For example, a researcher might wish to study the graffiti that people produce. They may spend many months recording graffiti from many different places. The researcher could count the number of items in each place or record the colours used – but such quantitative data would not tell us much about graffiti.

The analysis of qualitative data involves identifying themes. This is a very lengthy process because it is painstaking and iterative – every item is carefully considered and the data is gone through repeatedly to see if the themes identified do match the original data. The main intentions are:

- To impose some kind of order on the data.
- To ensure that the 'order' represents the participants' perspective (where it is based on what people have said).
- To summarise the data so that hundreds of pages of text or pictures, or hours of videotapes can be reduced to something more meaningful.
- To enable general conclusions to be drawn.

Doing a thematic analysis

General principles	Applied to the analysis of graffiti	Applied to the analysis of videotaped play
1. Read and reread the data transcript dispassionately, trying to understand the meaning communicated and the perspective of the participants. No notes should be made.	Study a photographic record of a wide range of graffiti, using *purposive sampling* where you select samples based on who/what would be appropriate for the study.	A play session can be transcribed to include details of what was said, and describe facial expressions and body movements.
2. Break the data into meaningful units – small bits of text that are independently able to convey meaning. This might be equivalent to sentences or phrases.	In the case of graffiti the 'unit' would be each item of graffiti or subcomponents of the graffiti.	Each verbal and nonverbal movement would constitute a unit.
3. Assign a name or code to each unit (on page 159 we show how you can use colours to identify units). Such names/codes are the initial themes that you are using. You will have developed some ideas when initially reading through the data in step 1.	Each unit of graffiti is given a name/code to describe its meaning, such as 'humour' or 'advice', 'love' or 'power domination'.	Each unit is coded, for example 'playing with toy', 'sadness expressed', 'request made'.
4. Themes identified by grouping together similar units.	Larger themes are developed, such as 'interpersonal concerns'.	Larger themes are developed, such as 'negative emotion'.
5. Data chunks may be given more than one name/code. (From here on the steps are the same for any thematic anaysis.)		
6. Reread the text to ensure themes are correctly allocated and that they include all important aspects of data. This is the iterative part of the process.		
7. The final report should discuss and use quotes or other material to illustrate these themes.		
8. Conclusions can be drawn, which may include new theories.	What do people represent in graffiti? Thematic analysis is one way to study this.	

Types of data

Thematic analysis	A technique used when analysing qualitative data. Data is produced, for example from the transcripts of an interview or interviews, and then themes or categories are identified. The researcher then goes back through the transcripts and notes where each theme/category is found and might draw out a few examples. Thus responses can be organised according to these themes, patterns identified and conclusions drawn.
Grounded theory	A bottom-up technique used when analysing qualitative data. It is an 'emergent' research process in which theoretical explanations emerge during the course of the investigation.

Grounded theory

Most qualitative analysis aims to be inductive or 'bottom-up' – the categories ('themes') that emerge are based or 'grounded' in the data (thus *grounded theory*). Subsequently, the categories/themes may lead to new explanations (called 'emergent theory').

A less common approach to the analysis of qualitative data is a deductive or 'top-down' one, where the researcher starts with preset categories/themes. Such categories are likely to be generated by previous theories/studies. The researcher would aim to see if the data is consistent with the previous theoretical viewpoint.

There is no one method used, but the table on the left gives a general picture of what is done when conducting a thematic analysis.

Qualitative to quantitative

Results that have been obtained through qualitative methods can be 'reduced' to a quantitative form. For example, *content analysis* involves counting the content of anything. Once you have created categories/themes you can then count instances within that category/theme and use graphs to represent the findings.

If you represent each category/theme with examples then it remains qualitative. Once you start counting instances the data becomes quantitative. This becomes a *content analysis*, which is discussed on page 207.

Try this Here's a fun bit. Look through the pictures people use for their Facebook profile photo. What categories would you use to classify them?

Check it

1. Explain the difference between quantitative and qualitative data. (4)
2. Explain why open questions collect qualitative data. (2)
3. How would you use grounded theory to investigate what people use Facebook for? (3)
4. Explain why thematic analysis is a lengthy process. (3)

Ethical issues and guidelines

Chapter 5 — Research methods

The specification says…

Ethical guidelines

1.2.7 British Psychological Society (BPS) code of ethics and conduct (2009) including risk management when carrying out research in psychology.

[AL Topic 9 includes: ethical issues in research using humans.]

You may be itching to get going with some real research but there is one more key element to consider before you begin – which is ethics. It might be nice to think of our participants as our 'subjects' to do with as you wish, but you can't.

For that reason psychologists have developed a set of rules about how to behave towards their participants. These 'rules' or guidelines are produced by their professional body. In the UK this is the British Psychological Society (BPS), in America it is the American Psychological Association (APA).

In order to understand the guidelines, you need to first understand the issues.

Couple kissing on a park bench. A public place but does that make it acceptable to observe them without their knowledge or consent?

In a nutshell

Ethical issues	An issue is a dilemma. An *ethical* issue is a dilemma about right and wrong. The dilemma arises because researchers wish to investigate behaviour to benefit our understanding of people and improve our world. But there are costs to participants. Ethical guidelines (or codes) try to work out how to get the balance right.	
	The participant's point of view	**The researcher's point of view**
Anonymity and confidentiality — A participant's right to have personal information protected through anonymity or by keeping information safe.	The General Data Protection Regulation (GDPR) makes confidentiality a legal right.	It may not be possible to keep information anonymous/confidential because some details of a study may lead to an individual's identification.
Deception — This occurs when a participant is not told the true research aims of a study and/or not told what they will be required to do.	This prevents being able to give truly informed consent (see below). However, there is a difference between withholding information and falsely informing participants about the aims of a research study. Both are deception, the first one more acceptable than the other.	If participants know the research aims this would spoil the study (*demand characteristics*). It might be argued that some deception is relatively harmless and/or can be compensated for by adequate *debriefing*.
Informed consent — Participants are given comprehensive information concerning the nature and purpose of a study and their role in it, so that they can make a decision about taking part.	This is necessary so that participants can make a decision about whether to participate. Without full information they cannot do this. Certain participants are unable to give informed consent (e.g. young children and vulnerable individuals who may not understand instructions).	Asking for informed consent may reduce the meaningfulness of the research because the researcher has to provide information that could reveal the study's aims. This might affect participants' behaviour because they would know what the researcher is investigating. This creates demand characteristics.
Privacy — Refers to a person's right to control the flow of information about themselves. Invasion of privacy is included as a form of psychological harm.	People expect to be observed by others in a public place, so this is acceptable. However, there isn't universal agreement on what constitutes a public place, for example listening to someone's conversation on a bus – is this public or private?	Researchers do not wish to alert participants to the fact that they are being observed because that is likely to affect the participants' behaviour.
Right to withdraw — Participants should be told that they can stop participating in a study if for any reason they are feeling uncomfortable.	Participants often do not fully understand what is involved and/or may simply not imagine how they would feel in certain situations. Thus it is important for them to be able to leave a study if things turn out to be different from what they expected.	The loss of participants may bias the study's findings because the ones that remain may be more highly motivated or less emotionally sensitive.
Protection from harm — Participants should not experience negative physical effects, such as physical injury, nor should they experience negative psychological effects, such as lowered self-esteem or embarrassment.	People are robust and can tolerate some anxiety. However, it is reasonable for a participant to expect, at the end of any study, to be in the same 'state' they were in at the beginning (e.g. not less happy or confident).	It may not be possible to estimate harm before conducting a study – however, any study should be stopped as soon as harm is apparent.

BPS code of ethics and conduct

The British Psychological Society (BPS) is the representative body for psychology and psychologists in the UK. All professionals (doctors, lawyers, etc) have a group that represents them and which ensures that the members 'police' themselves, i.e. check that fellow professionals are behaving in an ethically acceptable manner.

To do this the BPS prepares and regularly updates a *code of ethics and conduct*. This code is then used to guide psychologists in their research and also to guide psychologists who are treating individuals with psychological problems. Any psychologist who does not obey the code will lose their professional standing and their job. This is not a legal code so they are not sent to prison.

BPS code of ethics and conduct (2009)

The code published in 2009 is organised around four core principles. Within each of these core principles there are links to the ethical issues described in the table on the facing page and also below:

1. **Respect** – Includes informed consent, confidentiality, privacy and right to withdraw.
2. **Competence** – Includes awareness of professional ethics and making ethical decisions.
3. **Responsibility** – Includes protection from harm and debriefing.
4. **Integrity** – Includes honesty (avoiding deception) and addressing misconduct.

Ways of dealing with ethical issues

BPS code of ethics and conduct discusses a number of ways to deal with ethical issues. The three key ones are described here.

Risk assessment and management

Risk *assessment* refers to identifying the potential physical or psychological harm to participants during a research study (an ethical *issue*). As there are a large number of potential risks this means that risk *management* involves weighing up the balance of long-term gains versus short-term risks to participants. Such arguments are presented to an ethics committee (see below) who decides whether the risks are justified.

It is difficult to determine all risks at the outset of any study but researchers should develop a strategy for managing any risks that become apparent during the study. This strategy is also reviewed by the ethics committee.

Consent and debriefing

The issue of informed consent is dealt with by seeking freely given consent from participants who have been given sufficient information on which to make a decision.

In the case of studies where the true aims of the study are not revealed participants should still be clear about what participation will entail.

The participants should be debriefed after the study to inform them, where appropriate, about the true nature of a study. They should have the opportunity to ask questions and be reassured about any aspects of the study that concern them. The aim is to restore participants to the state they were in at the start of the study.

Participants should also have the right to refuse permission for the researcher to use any data they produced.

Research ethics committee (REC)

The REC is a group of people within a research institution who approve a study before it begins. The group may consist of both professional and lay people. The committee looks at all possible ethical issues and at how the researchers plan to deal with these, weighing up the value of the research against the possible costs in ethical terms.

In ethical terms they are concerned with the dignity, rights and welfare of research participants, the safety of the researcher(s) and also the legitimate interests of other stakeholders.

The British Psychological Society – promoting excellence in psychology.

Try this: Watch any Derren Brown *Trick or Treat* clip (for example tinyurl.com/y773c7j8) and decide which of the ethical issues discussed on this spread are relevant.

Sometimes researchers use *presumptive consent* to deal with a lack of informed consent. They ask a group of people who are similar to the participants whether they would agree to take part in a study. If this group of people consent to the procedures in the proposed study, it is presumed that the real participants would agree as well.

Try this: Try this for yourself. Divide your class into groups. Each group should devise a study that raises one of the ethical issues listed on this spread – but not a wild idea! Something that might be just acceptable.

Write a research proposal that identifies the ethical issues and how you intend to deal with them. You should also be clear about the aim of the research and why it is important.

Then present your proposal to a research ethics committee consisting of some of your class members, some playing the role of lay people and others as university staff.

Check it

1. A psychologist plans to conduct a study. Each participant will take a 30-minute memory test and also be asked to provide their GCSE grades. Some of the tasks on the test are quite challenging. The results will be used to consider whether GCSEs are really just a test of memory.

   What do you think would need to be included on an informed consent form in order for participants to make an informed decision about whether to participate? [4]

2. Milgram conducted a study on obedience (see page 32). Before he conducted the study he asked his students and colleagues how they thought people would behave.

   In what way could this be considered as an example of presumptive consent? [3]

3. Milgram has been accused of causing psychological harm to his participants as they were extremely stressed by the experience of taking part in the study, one even had a seizure. He argued that the stress experienced was no greater than that which people face in everyday life and therefore his study did not cause harm to participants. Furthermore, he debriefed participants afterwards.

   Assess whether Milgram's studies of obedience can be seen as ethical. [8]

Self-reporting data: Interviews

The specification says...
Self-reporting data

1.2.1 Designing and conducting questionnaires (see page 168) and interviews, considering researcher effects.

1.2.2 Unstructured, semi-structured and structured interviews, open, closed (including ranked scale) questions (page 168).

Questionnaires are not the only way to ask people questions that enable them to represent their thoughts, i.e. self-reporting. Interviews also involve asking people to answer questions, i.e. are self-report methods.

In a nutshell

Structured interview		
Predetermined questions delivered by an interviewer who does not probe beyond the answers received but may answer questions from the interviewee.	+ Can be easily repeated. + Easier to analyse than unstructured interviews because answers are more predictable. + Interviewer can provide extra information, for example explaining what a particular question means.	− The interviewer's expectations may influence the answers the interviewee gives (this is called *researcher/interviewer bias*). − Participants may feel reluctant to reveal personal information when face-to-face with an interviewer.
Semi-structured interview		
Some questions are predetermined but also new questions are developed as the interview proceeds.	+ More detailed information can be obtained from each respondent than in a structured interview because subsequent questions are specially shaped to the participant. + Can access information that may not be revealed by predetermined questions.	− More affected by interviewer bias than structured interviews because the interviewer is developing questions on the spot and may be prone to issues such as inadvertently asking leading questions. − Requires well-trained interviewers, which may be difficult to obtain and makes the research more expensive.
Unstructured interview		
No questions are decided in advance.		

Comparing questionnaires and interviews

Questionnaires	Interviews
Can be given out to lots of people and therefore the researcher can collect a large amount of data.	Numbers of participants are restricted because of the time it takes to conduct the interview and the expense of training and employing interviewers.
People may feel more willing to reveal confidential information on a questionnaire because the presence of an interviewer may make them feel they are being judged by someone else.	People may reveal more information because a skilled interviewer can encourage more thoughtful responses.

FIND the missing item

Some IQ tests have items like this.

The right answer 4

Psychological tests
Psychologists often need to measure psychological variables such as personality or intelligence or depression. They do this with psychological tests which are quite similar to self-report techniques.

On psychological tests the questions are usually called 'test items' instead of questions. Many of the same issues are important when evaluating psychological tests, such as researcher effects.

Interviews

A questionnaire is given in written form. This may be given to you on a piece of paper or you might fill in a questionnaire on the internet. When questions are delivered in real time it is called an interview. 'Real time' means that the respondent answers each question as it is presented by an interviewer. The interviewer may simply read a questionnaire out (a structured interview).

One advantage of the presence of an interviewer is that the respondent can ask the interviewer questions, such as asking for an explanation of a question. However, the great advantage is that questions can be adapted during the interview (if it is unstructured or semi-structured). In this case the interviewer is no longer just reading out a list of predetermined questions.

The interviewer may begin with some predetermined questions, in the same way that your GP interviews you when you are unwell. The answers you give lead the GP to think of new questions. This kind of interview is called semi-structured because it begins with some structure and then the questions develop from there.

Typically, the interviewer will take notes throughout the interview, or alternatively, the interview may be recorded (audio or video).

Quantitative and qualitative data
Interviewers may ask *closed questions* and thus collect *quantitative data* but the main point of an interview is to ask *open questions* which produce qualitative data. However, this data can be analysed in such a way that categories are identified and instances can then be counted (turning qualitative data into quantitative data).

(Note that open questions can also be asked in a questionnaire – questionnaires can collect quantitative and/or qualitative data, and the same is true of an interview.)

Check it

1. A group of students wishes to study the revision techniques used by people aged 14–18. Why might it be preferable to:
   (a) Conduct an interview rather than a questionnaire? (2)
   (b) Conduct a questionnaire rather than an interview? (2)
2. Imagine instead that the students wished to find out about sexual behaviour. Answer the same questions (a) and (b) above.
3. For each of the studies described in questions 1 and 2, suggest **two** different ethical issues that should concern the students and suggest how they might deal with these. (2 marks each)
4. Explain **two** differences between a questionnaire and an interview. (4)

Researcher effects

Researcher effect
A researcher's *expectations* (bias) may encourage certain behaviours in participants. The result is that the researcher's expectations/biases are fulfilled.
(Researcher effects and research bias are related – the bias produces the effect.)

In a nutshell
An experimenter might unconsciously be more encouraging to participants in group A than group B so this would explain why participants in group A do better on that task, rather than the IV being responsible.

The specification says...
Self-reporting data

1.2.1 Designing and conducting questionnaires (see page 168) and interviews, considering researcher effects.

[AL Topic 9 includes: researcher bias.]

Researcher effects

One of the classic examples of researcher effects comes from a study by Robert Rosenthal and Kermit Fode (1963) (ed – that's not a spelling error). The participants in this study were psychology students who were asked to train albino rats to learn to find food in a T-shaped maze.

The participants (believing they were experimenters) were told that there were two groups of rats: one group were 'fast learners' (maze bright) having been bred for this characteristic, whilst the other group of rats were described as 'slow learners' (maze dull). In fact there were no differences between the rats, they were all from the same litter and had been randomly allocated to the students.

The findings of the study showed that the supposedly brighter rats actually made more correct responses and were quicker in their maze running. When the students were asked about their rats afterwards those with maze-bright rats described them as smarter, more attractive and more likeable than the students with maze-dull rats. The only explanation can be that the students' expectations affected the rats' performance.

Research effects and interviews

A specific kind of researcher effect occurs in interviews because of the close interaction between interviewer and interviewee. The interviewer's nonverbal behaviours may express agreement/disagreement. For example, smiling, leaning forwards, nodding or saying uh-huh all indicate agreement and approval, whereas sitting with arms crossed, frowning and sighing indicates disapproval.

An interviewer may be quite unaware of what is called 'nonverbal leakage'. These signals are very powerful just because they are so difficult to control – and therefore communicate a powerful message. Customs officers are trained to detect them to spot people carrying contraband.

Therefore, interviewers are carefully trained to remain neutral and minimise biasing the answers an interviewee gives. Also interviews are standardised so there is a clear protocol for the interview and the same procedures are followed for every interviewer.

Researcher effects and questionnaires

Even when questionnaires are used there may be some interaction between the researcher and person doing the questionnaire, which may have an effect on their performance. For example, the way the researcher phrases a question is affected by the researcher's expectations and, without knowing it, the researcher may ask a slightly leading question. This influences the answers that are given.

Researcher effect with Clever Hans
Wilhelm Von-Osten claimed to have taught basic arithmetic to his horse, Clever Hans. Hans gave the answers to problems by tapping his hoof on the ground.

People were impressed by his abilities – however, Oskar Pfungst showed that his skills were indeed clever, but not arithmetical. He found that Hans only got the questions right when Von-Osten knew the answer, and could be seen by the horse. Pfungst's studies showed that when Hans was counting with his hoof Von-Osten inclined his head downwards. When the correct answer was reached he would either straighten up slightly or raise an eyebrow or even slightly flare his nostrils.

Pfungst himself was able to get the same level of performance out of Hans using these tricks.

Try this
You could test the effect of expectations. To do this you need to find a puzzle which is reasonably difficult (it could be, for example, a word search).

Now ask two friends to complete the word search. Tell friend A it is an easy puzzle and tell friend B it is a difficult puzzle.

Time how long it takes each of them to complete the puzzle.

Check it

1. Sukie is interviewing people on their beliefs about the supernatural. These are three of her questions:

   i. Do you believe in any form of afterlife? Yes / No
   ii. Describe how you would feel if you saw an inexplicable hazy light in a graveyard at night.
   iii. Do you think UFOs are people from a nearby solar system, people from much further away in the universe, people from the future, people from the past?

   (a) Identify **one** different problem with each of the three questions i, ii and iii. (3)
   (b) Rewrite question iii to improve it. (2)
   (c) Explain **one** possible cause of researcher effects in this study. (2)

Validity and reliability of self-report

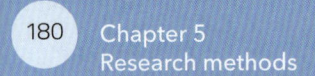

The specification says...
Issues of validity and reliability in studies using different research methods.

Probably the two most important concepts to consider, when evaluating a study, are *validity* and *reliability*.

You are going to be hearing a lot more about these terms so don't worry if you don't feel you have understood these key concepts straight away.

- **Validity** – The data collected in a questionnaire or interview should hopefully represent reality. What if a person does not give honest answers to a questionnaire or interview? Basically, the data collected is meaningless.

- **Reliability** – We would also expect a questionnaire or interview to work in a consistent way. So, if a person feels or thinks the same from one week to the next their scores would be the same both times.

In a nutshell

Validity	Refers to the 'trueness' or 'legitimacy' of the data collected.
Internal validity	Concerns whether a test (questionnaire) does assess what it intended to assess.
	In a questionnaire, if a respondent does not provide an answer that represents what they actually think or feel, then the researcher is not measuring what they intended to measure. This is internal validity, which can be affected by the issues discussed on pages 168–169, for example ambiguous questions, *social desirability bias* and *leading questions*.
Ecological validity	Concerns the extent to which the findings from a questionnaire or interview can be *generalised* beyond the particular study. This will depend to some extent on internal validity but also the extent to which the questions represent the actual experience that is being investigated.
	Furthermore the sample will affect ecological validity – if the sample is not representative then we cannot generalise the findings to the wider population – for example, if the sample consisted of female students only then the results might not apply to older adults who are male.

Reliability	Refers to consistency of measurements.
Inter-rater reliability	Often more than one interviewer is used to collect data for a research study. Low reliability may be caused if different interviewers behave differently.
	This can be assessed by comparing the results from two or more interviewers questioning the same person. The data from all raters should be similar.
Test-retest reliability	A measure of whether something varies from one time to another, i.e. is consistent over time. The same questionnaire or interview is given to the same participants on two occasions to see if the same result is obtained.
	The interval between test and retest must be long enough so that the participant can't remember their previous answers but not too long because their thoughts or feelings may have changed and then we would expect their scores/answers to be different.

The psychomeasure of intelligence

It has been suggested that the circumference of a person's head could be used as a measure of intelligence. This is likely to be a fairly RELIABLE measure of intelligence because using a tape measure to measure adult head size is likely to produce consistent results from one year to the next.

You may even feel this is a VALID measure of intelligence. After all, if you have a bigger brain then you might have more intelligence. However, research doesn't bear this out. Intelligence is not related to brain or head size. This means that this measure of intelligence lacks VALIDITY.

Understanding reliability

If you use a ruler to measure the height of a chair and the following day you find that the measurement is different, you might think the chair has changed magically overnight. You would expect the ruler to be reliable (consistent) so any change must be because the chair changed. If, in fact, the fluctuation was due to some change in the ruler it would be pretty useless as a measuring instrument – it wouldn't be dependable, consistent or reliable.

Try this

Take a psychological test yourself. For example:

- Intelligence: tinyurl.com/llvmfd
- Personality: tinyurl.com/lpwk828

Now try and establish whether your test result is reliable. Perhaps try test-retest and see what happens.

What about validity?

Reliable, but not valid  | Not reliable, not valid | Reliable and valid

It is easy to muddle validity and reliability. Being valid is being on target, in relation to what you are aiming to do (far right). Being reliable is being consistent (far left and far right).

Writing a report

Writing your report

Procedure

In this section of a report researchers aim to provide sufficient detail so that someone else could *exactly* repeat the study conducted. This is an important principle of science – the validity of the results can be checked by repeating the study but in order to do this the researcher needs to give the exact details.

The details that need to be included are:

- Participants – How many, what gender and age? Any other important details such as job?
- Sampling technique – How were the participants selected? Were any participants rejected?
- Apparatus/materials – Descriptions of any materials used such as a questionnaire, photographs or a stopwatch. Examples should be included in the report.
- Standardised instructions – What were participants told? This would include the instructions of what they had to do.
- Location – Details of where the research was conducted and any important features of the environment.
- What the researcher(s) actually did – This is the most critical part, a step-by-step set of instructions to repeat procedures.
- Ethical considerations – Mention any procedures related to dealing with ethical issues, such as a debrief.

You are required to conduct a practical investigation for each of the four topics in this book, and for each of them to write a report of what you did (the procedure you followed), the results of your study and a discussion of the results. This mirrors what psychologists actually do to report their own research.

Here is the first page of Alan Baddeley's classic study on memory (see page 76). It was published in an academic journal called the *Quarterly Journal of Experimental Psychology*. Scientists publish a report of their research in academic journals. Such reports start with a summary of the report (called the *abstract*) and an introduction discussing previous research. These two elements of a research report are discussed later in this chapter (see page 220). On other pages the procedure and results are described and issues related to the study are in the discussion.

> **The specification says…**
> 1.5 Practical investigation
> 1.5.1 Write up the procedure, results and discussion section of a report.

Results

Details are given about what the researcher found.

For quantitative data this might include:

- Measures of central tendency and dispersion.
- Tables and graphs showing overall trends.
- Inferential statistics (statistical tests, covered later in this chapter), including calculated values and significance level. (Note that inferential statistics are not required for the social psychology practical investigation.)

For qualitative research this might include:

- Thematic analysis – Themes identified and examples given.
- Content analysis – Count of instances within each theme/category (discussed on page 207).

Try this
Look up online some of the research studies you have covered and have a look at how the study was reported.

Discussion

In this section the researcher aims to interpret the results of the study and consider their implications for future research as well as suggesting real-world applications.

- State conclusions – Report what the results *show*. It is one thing to state a result but what can we say about what that actually tells us? There is an important difference between a result and a conclusion – you should state the result and then write '… this suggests that …' or ' … this means that …' or '… therefore I would conclude …'.
- Relationship to previous research – You might relate your results to theories or other studies you are familiar with. Your results may support or challenge other theories/studies.
- Criticise your research – What design decisions were flawed and how would you improve them? Don't say obvious things like the sample should have been larger but dig deep and just think of two major flaws.
- Possible real-world applications – Make some suggestions.

✓ Check it

1. Think about one of your practical investigations.
   (a) If you worked in a group, did the researchers collecting the data act in different ways? Explain whether this would be a threat to reliability or validity. [2]
   (b) (i) Was it possible that some of the participants worked out the aim of your study or thought they had? Explain whether this would be a threat to reliability or validity. [2]
       (ii) Describe **one** way that this problem could have been overcome in your investigation. [2]

2. Noah wrote up his investigation. He has included the following passages:

i.	The findings showed that colour produced better recall than black and white.
ii.	The stimuli were presented using an iPad with a 9.7" screen.
iii.	The mean recall for colour was 19.5 and the mean recall for black and white was 16.2.

   (a) For each passage, explain which section of the report it belongs in. [3]
   (b) Suggest **two** other pieces of information that Noah should include in both his procedure section and his results section. [2]

Experiments

Chapter 5 Research methods — 182

The specification says…
Experiments
2.2.1 Designing and conducting experiments, including field and laboratory experiments.
2.2.2 Independent and dependent variables.

When psychologists want to investigate *causal* relationships they use the *experimental method*. This method is the only way to determine whether, for example, studying for ten hours a day actually *causes* a student to do better in their exams or whether playing loud music while studying causes a person to remember their work less well.

We can *ask* people (*self-report*) if they think that more studying leads to better exam performance but only an experiment can determine whether there is a causal effect.

The secret lies in the *independent variable* (IV) – the experimenter deliberately controls the IV and can see if this affects the *dependent variable* (DV).

Always consider ethical issues when conducting any research.

In a nutshell

Experiment	A research method which demonstrates causal relationships. All experiments have an IV and a DV.	Baddeley's study of memory involves a number of experiments. Milgram's study of obedience is not an experiment. The increasing shock levels are used to measure obedience. This study is a *controlled observation*.
Variables	The independent variable (IV) is a factor that is directly manipulated by the experimenter in order to observe the effect of this variation on the DV. There are at least two levels of the IV in an experiment.	For example, let's consider an experiment looking at the effect of sleep on memory – the IV is how much sleep a participant has had. We can have two levels of the IV: in condition 1 participants sleep for eight hours the night before a memory test and in condition 2 participants sleep for five hours the night before the test.
	Dependent variable (DV) is measured by the experimenter to assess the effects of the IV.	The DV in this study would be memory.
Operationalisation Variables must be operationalised, i.e. defined in a way that they can easily be tested.	'Memory' needs to be assessed or measured. We could give all the students a test, so the DV would be memory test score. 'Sleep' also needs to be operationalised. We need to specify what counts as a lot of sleep and a little sleep – in the example above we have defined this as eight hours and five hours.	

Types of experiment

Laboratory experiment Experiment conducted in a very controlled environment. Participants go to experimenter.	For example, compare memory scores in participants who sleep eight hours with those who sleep five hours.	
	IV manipulated by experimenter – the experimenter might arrange for participants to sleep in a laboratory and can carefully control the number of hours they sleep.	DV measured in a laboratory, e.g. a test to measure memory.
Field experiment Experiment conducted in more everyday surroundings than a laboratory. Experimenter goes to participants.	For example, compare memory scores in participants who sleep eight hours with those who sleep five hours.	
	IV manipulated by experimenter – the experimenter tells some participants to wake up after eight hours and other participants to wake up after five hours. The procedure is conducted at home.	DV may be measured in a laboratory or the DV may be measured in the 'field', e.g. participants' own home – but still using a test to measure memory.

Try this

Headaches

Elizabeth Loftus (1975) investigated leading questions by asking people the following question: 'How often do you get headaches each week?' She asked other people 'Do you get headaches occasionally, and if so, how often each week?'

She found that people gave a different answer depending which question she asked them.

- What was the thing that she varied? (This is the IV.)
- What was the thing that she measured? (This is the DV.)

Try it yourself, with ten people for each question type.

Experimenting with nail varnish.

People use the word 'experiment' quite loosely. In fact it is a word you might use in an ordinary conversation, e.g. 'I thought I would experiment with a new nail varnish' or 'I experimented with a cheap phone but it was no good'.

In science the word 'experiment' has a specific meaning. It isn't just another word for an investigation. The experimenter alters the levels of one variable (the IV) and observes the effects of the IV on the DV. Only by doing this can the experimenter discover a causal relationship because any change in the DV must be due to the changes made to the IV – as long as all the other *extraneous* variables have been controlled (we will explain these extraneous variables soon …).

Hypotheses

The starting point of any study is an *aim* – deciding the general point of the study.

This is followed by a formal statement of what the researcher believes to be true – called a *hypothesis*.

Note that a hypothesis, strictly speaking, is a statement of what is 'true' – therefore it should be stated in the present tense.

It is also a statement about the whole population rather than just the sample and therefore it is about people not participants.

The specification says…

Experiments

2.2.3 Experimental and null hypotheses.

2.2.4 Directional (one-tailed) and non-directional (two-tailed) tests and hypotheses.

2.2.6 Operationalisation of variables.

Many people have the wrong image of an experiment. This is a chemistry experiment. Psychology experiments aren't like this. For a start people rather than chemicals are involved. Psychologists also rarely wear a white coat. Experiments may be conducted in a laboratory setting – but can be conducted outside a laboratory too, in the 'field'.

Experimental hypotheses Abbreviated as H_1	A hypothesis is not a question – it is a statement.	This is not a hypothesis: Do people who sleep more do better at school? That is a *research question*.
		This is a *research aim*: To investigate whether sleeping more means that your memory is better.
	It is a statement about the effect of the IV on the DV.	This is an experimental hypothesis: People who sleep more do better on a memory test.
	A hypothesis should include both levels of the IV.	People who sleep for eight hours do better **than those who sleep for five hours**.
	A hypothesis should be precise and testable, i.e. it must be operationalised.	People who sleep for eight hours have a **higher score on a memory test (with 20 words following a 10-minute interference task)** than those who sleep for five hours.
Direction of hypothesis	A directional (one-tailed) hypothesis states the direction of the hypothesis, for example one condition is more than another.	The hypothesis above is directional (one-tailed).
		This is the non-directional (two-tailed) version: People who sleep for eight hours perform *differently* on a memory test than those who sleep for five hours.
	A non-directional (two-tailed) hypothesis just states there is a difference.	
		When you look at a one-tailed cat you know which way it is going. A two-tailed cat could be going either way.
Null hypothesis Abbreviated as H_0	A statement of no difference. (Do not use the term 'relationship'.)	**There is no difference** between the memory test scores of people who sleep for eight hours than those who sleep for five hours.

Check it

1. A researcher wished to test the hypothesis, 'Blondes have more fun than brunettes'.
   (a) Suggest how you could measure (operationalise) the independent variable and dependent variable. (3)
   (b) Outline **one** strength and **one** weakness of the way you have operationalised the dependent variable. (4)

2. Rewrite the following as fully operationalised hypotheses (in some cases you will need to add a second level of the independent variable):
   (a) Are arts students less clever than science students? (2)
   (b) Does alcohol cause goldfish to have poor memories? (2)
   (c) Positive expectations lead to differences in performance. (2)

3. For each of the following, decide whether it is a directional (one-tailed) or non-directional (two-tailed) hypothesis.
   (a) Boys score differently on aggressiveness tests than girls. (1)
   (b) Participants remember words that are early in a list better than the words that appear later in the list. (1)

4. 'Students who have a computer at home do better in exams than those who don't.'
   (a) Identify the independent variable and dependent variable in this hypothesis. (2)
   (b) State a null hypothesis for this study. (2)
   (c) Rewrite the experimental hypothesis so that it is non-directional (two-tailed). (2)

Experimental design

The specification says...

Experiments

2.2.5 Experimental and research designs: repeated measures, independent groups and matched pairs.

2.2.7 Counterbalancing, randomisation and order effects.

The process of designing any research study is like designing a room – you have to decide what you would like the room to look like. When designing a questionnaire you decide, for example, what questions to include and how to ask them.

When designing an experiment you decide how to operationalise the independent and dependent variables (IV and DV).

However, there is one particular aspect of planning an experiment that gets the name *experimental design* – this is the decision about whether to have one group of participants who do all levels of the IV or have more than one group of participants, each of which does just one level of the IV.

Are people in a better mood on a sunny day?
- IV is the weather, sunny or cloudy.
- DV is mood, measured on a ranked scale.

Repeated measures

Condition A — Sunny day
Condition B — Cloudy day

The same people take part in condition A and B.

Independent groups

Group A — Sunny day
Group B — Cloudy day

Group A has 10 people and group B has 8 people – the groups don't have to be equal.

In a nutshell

Experimental design	Strengths	Weaknesses	Dealing with the weakness
Repeated measures design Each participant takes part in every condition being tested. Each condition represents one level of the independent variable (IV). There may be a control condition (see facing page).	+ Good control of *participant variables* (see next spread) because the same person is tested twice. In an independent groups design the people in group A may be happier and that's why they do better on a task than group B. In a repeated measures design such participant variables are the same across conditions. + Fewer participants are needed than with independent groups design because, if you have 20 participants, you end up with 20 rather than 10 results in the final analysis. This is important because more data makes the conclusion more dependable.	− Order effects are produced, for example a participant may be better on the second test because of getting better with experience (a *practice effect*) or may perform less well because of being bored or tired (*fatigue effect*). − Participants may guess the purpose of the experiment because they do both conditions and this may make the research aims obvious.	Can control order effects with counterbalancing (see facing page).
Independent groups design Different participants are allocated to two (or more) experimental groups representing different levels of the independent variable. There may be a control group.	+ Avoids order effects because each participant is only tested once. + Avoids participants guessing the aims of the experiment.	− There is no control of participant variables, for example the participants in group A may be more intelligent or younger and that is why group A has higher scores on a test. − Needs more participants than with a repeated measures design because, if you have 20 participants, there are 10 in each group and you end up with 10 items in the final analysis.	Lack of control over participant variables can be dealt with by using randomisation of participants to conditions, i.e. participants are allocated to groups using a random technique (see page 170). This means that participant variables should not cluster in one particular group.
Matched pairs design Participants who are similar on key variables (e.g. memory ability, age) are paired. One member of the pair is placed in group A and the other in group B. This means there are two groups of participants. Each group is given one level of the independent variable.	+ Controls for participant variables because of the matching (means that it is similar to repeated measures). + Avoids order effects because it is like an independent groups design.	− Very time-consuming to match participants on key variables. − May not control all participant variables because you can only match on variables known to be relevant, but it could be that other variables are important.	You should start with a large group of participants to ensure you can obtain matched pairs on key variables.

Conditions and groups

In all experiments there are at least two conditions, where each 'condition' is one level of the IV.

- In a repeated measures design each participant does both conditions.
- In an independent groups design each participant does one condition (and each group is doing one condition).
- In a matched pairs design each participant does one condition.

For example, in the classic study by Alan Baddeley (1966b) on acoustic and semantic similarity and long-term memory (see page 76) four of the conditions were: acoustically similar words, acoustically dissimilar words, semantically similar words, semantically dissimilar words.

Control conditions/groups

In some studies a distinction is made between the experimental condition/group where participants receive a 'treatment' and a *control condition/group* where they receive no treatment.

For example, on page 73 a study by Sylvie Belleville *et al*. (2006) is described. One group of participants undertook a training programme to improve their episodic memories. This group was compared with a control group who received no training.

There is another example of a control condition/group in chapter 4 (page 140) where Albert Bandura *et al*. (1961) studied aggression in children. Their aim was to see if children who watched someone behave aggressively would be more likely to then behave aggressively themselves.

- One group watched a person play aggressively.
- One group watched a person play non-aggressively.
- A control group did not watch a person playing.

The control group controls for the possible effects of just watching another person playing.

Counterbalancing

When using a repeated measures design there is the problem of order effects (see facing page). One way to deal with this is to change the order of conditions so that:

- Half the participants receive condition A first followed by condition B.
- Half the participants receive condition B first followed by condition A.

This acts as a counterbalance because people doing condition A last will benefit from a practice effect but an equal number of those doing condition B last will also benefit from a practice effect – so the effects cancel each other out.

Counterbalancing ensures that each condition is tested first or second in equal amounts.

Randomisation

When using an independent groups design there is a problem with participant variables. One way to control for differences between the two groups is to decide who goes in each group randomly so, in theory, the two groups should be pretty similar. We would expect characteristics such as intelligence, motivation, focus on the task and so on to be balanced across the two groups.

Try this

Thinking about experimental design

A psychologist is planning to test the effect of hunger on perception of food – past research has shown that people rate pictures of food as brighter if they are hungry.

There are two possible ways to do this:

A. Ask each participant to rate pictures of food just before lunch (having not eaten anything for four hours) and then do the same just after lunch.

B. Ask one group of participants to rate the food just before lunch (having not eaten anything for four hours) and then ask a different group of participants to rate the pictures after lunch.

Can you suggest why each of these designs might have problems?

It's a little known fact that the Swedish pop group ABBA took their name from a way of reducing order effects in a repeated measures design experiment. The ABBA design is a sophisticated form of counterbalancing – the two conditions are called A and B. Each participant does four trials, A, B, B then A, or half the participants do AB and the other half do BA.

Check it

1. For each of the following experiments state whether it is a repeated measures, independent groups or matched pairs design. When trying to decide it might help if you ask yourself, 'Would the findings be analysed by comparing the scores from the same person or by comparing the scores of two (or more) groups of people?' If it is two or more groups of people, then are the people in the different groups related (i.e. matched) or not?

    (a) Boys and girls are compared on their IQ test scores. [1]

    (b) Dogs are tested to see if one breed is better at finding food in a maze compared to another breed. [1]

    (c) Reaction time is tested before and after a reaction time training activity to see if test scores improve after training. [1]

    (d) Students are put in pairs based on their GCSE grades, and then one member of the pair is tested in the morning and one tested in the afternoon on a memory task. [1]

    (e) Three groups of participants are given different word lists to remember, to see whether nouns, verbs or adjectives are easier to recall. [1]

2. Some psychology students are interested in testing the effects of rewards on how well students do on a task.

    Explain how you would conduct this study. Include full details of your procedures including choice of sample, experimental design and ethical issues. Justify your decisions as part of your explanation. [6]

Experiments: Internal validity

Validity has already been discussed on page 180 and refers to whether a finding from any kind of study is a genuine one – does the data collected really represent people's everyday behaviour? When thinking about experiments a distinction is made between:

- *Internal validity* – Concerns what is going on inside an experiment.
- *Ecological validity* – Concerns the extent to which experimental results can be generalised to other people and settings. Ecological validity is considered on the next spread.

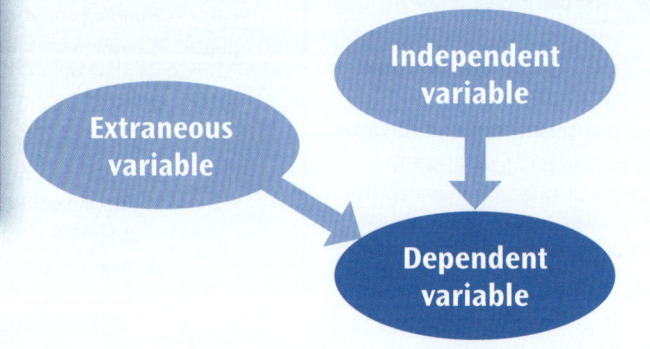

The specification says…

Experiments

2.2.6 Extraneous variables and confounding variables.

2.2.8 Situational and participant variables.

2.2.9 Objectivity, reliability and validity (internal, predictive and ecological).

2.2.10 Experimenter effects, demand characteristics and control issues.

2.2.11 Quantitative data analysis (see pages 172-173).

[AL Topic 9 includes: subjectivity.]

In a nutshell

Internal validity	The researcher is testing what they intended to test.

Term	Explanation	Examples	How to deal with it
Extraneous variable (EV)	In an experiment, any variable other than the independent variable (IV) that might potentially affect the dependent variable (DV) and thereby confuse the results. This includes both participant and situational variables.	A **participant variable** is a characteristic of the participants, such as age or intelligence. A **situational variable** is a feature of the environment that may affect performance, such as distracting noise or time of day.	Such variables should be held constant, for example all participants should be a similar age. Or the researcher must ensure that such variables are randomly spread across conditions.
Confounding variable	This is a special class of extraneous variable – where the extraneous variable changes *systematically* with the IV. This means that you cannot be sure that any change in the DV was due to the IV. In fact the confounding variable is acting as another IV.	A study on memory looks at whether people remember familiar or unfamiliar words better (familiarity is the IV). All participants are given five familiar words and five unfamiliar words. The familiar words are always first in the list. The findings are that the familiar words were recalled better – but we cannot be sure that these words were remembered better because they were familiar or because the first words in the list were remembered. Therefore, there were two variables affecting recall, the confounding variable of position in the list and the IV of familiarity.	Confounding variables should be identified and controlled before a study is conducted.
Predictive validity	Concerns the extent to which a test score actually is related to the behaviour you want to measure. Therefore, the test score can forecast performance on another measure of the same behaviour.	For example, the score on a memory test or an intelligence test should be positively related to performance in A level exams.	

Extraneous variables (EVs) are 'extra' to the IV and DV but they can be divided into confounding variables and random variables – random variables do not vary systematically with the IV so should not confound the results.

However, they may 'muddy the water' making it harder to detect differences and therefore should be controlled.

Assessing validity and reliability in experiments

We have looked at two research methods so far – self-report (questionnaires and interviews) and experiments. These methods may be combined, in fact they often are because the DV in an experiment has to be measured and a common way to do that is to give participants a test – a kind of questionnaire.

Therefore, if we want to assess the reliability of an experiment, we can consider the reliability of the test/questionnaire used to assess the DV. Test-retest (see page 180) is a common way to do this.

Predictive validity

One way to assess the validity of a test is in terms of predictive validity. To do this a researcher correlates the results of a test with some later example of the behaviour that is being tested. If the test result is positively correlated with the later behaviour this confirms the predictive validity of the test.

Standardisation

In any experiment it is important to have a set of procedures that will be identical for each participant. 'Standardisation' is the term used to describe identical procedures.

If the procedures differed between levels of the IV this could act as a confounding variable.

Also, if procedures were not consistent this would reduce the reliability of the experiment.

Objectivity and subjectivity

These are two themes that you should be thinking about all the time. Research methods techniques aim to make the research process as *objective* as possible, i.e. not influenced by the researcher's emotions, personal opinions or expectations, being free from bias. This concerns both designing a study and conducting it. The opposite of this is subjectivity.

Explanation	Examples	How to deal with it
Demand characteristics Cues in a research situation that communicate to participants what is expected of them and may then unconsciously affect a participant's behaviour.	Participants are given two memory tests, one in the morning and one in the afternoon. Participants might guess that the experimenter is trying to see if people do better in the morning or afternoon. This might lead participants to try to perform the same each time because they have guessed the research aims.	In the example on the left it might be better to use an *independent groups design*.

Demand characteristics

One way that situations affect us is by giving us cues on how we should behave. Depending on where we are we will behave differently. For example, if someone bumps into you in a shop you might feel cross and say something, but at a football match you probably wouldn't think anything of it.

Different situations *demand* different behaviours, so as a student you sit relatively quietly and listen, but as a member of the audience at a pantomime you shout 'Behind you!' endlessly at the actors. You are the same person but behaving as the situation *demands*.

Martin Orne (1962) described these cues to behaviour as *demand characteristics* and showed how powerful they can be in a number of studies. One of these involved a psychologist asking a few friends for a 'favour'. When they agreed they were asked to do five press-ups. Their reaction tended to be to ask *why*, with a degree of puzzlement. Another group of friends were asked if they would take part in an 'experiment'. When they agreed they were asked to do five press-ups. Their reaction tended to be to ask *where*. This suggests that people are prepared to do things as research participants that they would not normally be prepared to do in other social contexts.

The implication for psychology is that the experience of being a participant creates demand characteristics. If this is so then the behaviour we observe might be due to the participant being in a psychology study rather than solely due to the variable being tested.

Demand characteristics
People seek cues about how to behave. For example, watching a football game at home you sit relatively quietly, but on a football ground you chant and jump up and down. These different situations 'demand' different behaviours.

Try this

Design your own investigation into demand characteristics. First you need to decide on a task for people to do, like help colour in a picture or sign your petition. Then you need to decide on two conditions to compare how responsive they are. One possibility is to vary the reason for the task (for example, doing it as a favour, for a psychology study, or for charity) or you could vary where you ask them (for example, at home or in the classroom) or how you appear (for example, smart or scruffy).

Then you measure how many people comply with your request in the different situations. This will tell you something about the demand characteristics of each situation.

Remember that your question should be ethical – think about whether even being presented with the question would cause embarrassment.

Check it

1. An experiment is conducted to investigate whether students living in cities do better at school than those from rural communities.
   (a) Identify the independent variable and the dependent variable in this experiment, and state how each could be operationalised. [4]
   (b) Suggest **two** extraneous variables that should be controlled. [2]
   (c) Describe an appropriate standardised procedure that could be used in this study. [5]

2. Another psychological study looks at the effect of eating chocolate on mood.
   (a) Describe how you could investigate this by doing an experiment using a repeated measures design. [2]
   (b) How might researcher effects impact on the objectivity of this study? [2]
   (c) Describe how demand characteristics might affect the findings of this study. [2]

Experiments: Ecological validity

Chapter 5 — Research methods (188)

The specification says...
Experiments
2.2.9 Ecological validity.
[AL Topic 9 includes: generalisability.]

The obvious aim of conducting an experiment is to be able to make a statement about factors that cause human behaviour – psychologists want to be able to *generalise* from the particular *sample* used in their study to the *target population* (and maybe even to the wider population).

In order to do this:
- The sample should be representative (see page 171).
- Any measurement tools (such as a questionnaire to measure the dependent variable) must be valid and reliable (see page 180).
- The experiment must have internal validity (see previous spread).
- And finally we need this special ingredient, ecological validity.

Where is this 'field'?
An experiment may be conducted in a laboratory or in the field. The 'field' is anywhere that is not a highly controlled environment, but one that is more usual for your participants. One way to distinguish between the laboratory and the field is to ask whether the participants went to the experimenter (a laboratory) or whether the experimenter went to the participants (not a laboratory).

In a nutshell

Term	Explanation	How to deal with low ecological validity
Ecological validity	Concerns the ability to *generalise* a research finding beyond the particular setting in which it is demonstrated to other settings. In the case of an experiment the issue is whether the experimental experience represents the actual behaviour being investigated. There are key features of the experiment that should be considered, for example: • What task was used? Did it have *mundane realism*? • Were participants aware they were being studied? • What was the environment like?	Conduct research in everyday settings (low control, low internal validity) and compare to studies (with the same aims) that are highly controlled but lack ecological validity. This can confirm overall validity. This process is called *triangulation* – comparing the results from a number of studies, some of which are highly controlled (but more 'artificial') and some with low control (but more like everyday life). If the studies have similar findings this increases the likelihood that the conclusion represents something genuine (i.e. is valid).

Comparing the ecological validity of laboratory and field experiments

Laboratory experiment				
Experiment conducted in a very controlled environment.	For example: Students study in an experimenter's laboratory. One group are given two hours to study and another group are given one hour. The next day they are given a test in the experimenter's laboratory.		+ High level of control possible and therefore *confounding/extraneous variables* can be minimised (increasing validity). + Can be easily *replicated* because most aspects of the environment have been controlled (enhancing validity).	− A contrived situation where participants may not behave naturally (as they would in day-to-day life). Low ecological validity. − *Demand characteristics* and *researcher bias*/effects may reduce validity.
	IV manipulated by experimenter.	DV measured in a laboratory.		
Field experiment				
Experiment conducted in more everyday surroundings than a laboratory.	For example: Students study at home. One group of students are told by their teacher to study for two hours and another group is told by their teacher to study for one hour. The next day their class teacher gives them a test in their usual classroom.		+ Less contrived, the whole experience feels more like everyday life. Therefore, there is usually higher ecological validity. + Avoids demand characteristics and researcher bias/effects if participants are not aware of being studied (increases validity). This is true in some field experiments but not all field experiments.	− Less control of extraneous variables (reduces validity). − May be more time-consuming because the researcher has to set up the whole experiment at a distant location. Therefore, it may be more expensive. − There may be ethical issues if participants are not aware of being studied – *informed consent* and *debriefing* may not be possible.
	IV manipulated by experimenter.	DV measured in the field.		

Try this
Do keep a list of the laboratory and field studies in your course and discuss their ecological validity.
There are no clear-cut answers – every study is high in ecological validity in some respects and low in ecological validity in others.

Laboratory and field experiments differ in terms of where the dependent variable (DV) is tested. If these students are in their classroom it is a field experiment, if they have gone to the experimenter's office it is a laboratory experiment.

Some examples of ecological validity

Ecological validity is one of the favourite concepts for students to use when evaluating a study – but if you are to gain credit you must use it thoughtfully. It is not good enough to say, 'It was a laboratory study and therefore was artificial and we can't generalise to everyday life.'

You can't say that for several reasons.

1. It isn't always true

Some studies conducted in a laboratory actually have high ecological validity. For example, Milgram's (1963) study (which wasn't an experiment but was conducted in a well-controlled laboratory) is arguably high in ecological validity. Milgram was testing the effect of an authority figure on obedience. He used the laboratory setting as an everyday example of where you would find an authority relationship between researcher and participant.

2. What task was used?

Many studies of memory involve word lists which is fine if the researcher wants to know how well people remember word lists but less relevant if we are interested in the more everyday ways that we use our memories, such as investigating whether eyewitnesses to a crime are likely to be accurate or not. (This was one of Frederic Bartlett's (1932) criticisms – that testing memory with consonants did not reflect everyday memory, see page 74.)

We use the phrase *mundane realism* to describe the extent to which a task reflects what we ordinarily do. In a field study the task may be as low in mundane realism as in a laboratory study.

3. Were participants aware they were being studied?

If participants know their behaviour is being watched they may well act in a way that does not represent 'reality'. Furthermore, knowing they are in a psychology study may mean participants respond to demand characteristics.

In some laboratory studies participants are not actually aware that they are being studied. For example, in one study participants sat in a laboratory waiting to be called by the experimenter. While waiting, a man ran through the room holding a bloody knife or greasy pen and participants were later asked to identify the man (Johnson and Scott 1976).

It is more likely that participants are aware of being studied when in a laboratory but worth reflecting on how much this would or would not affect the naturalness of their behaviour.

4. What was the environment like?

In an everyday environment people are likely to feel more relaxed whereas if people have to report to a researcher's laboratory they may feel more anxious. In this sense field experiments may have higher ecological validity.

But the line between field and laboratory is not always clear-cut. Let's say your teacher is conducting a research study and uses your classroom as a laboratory because conditions can be carefully controlled. In one lesson the teacher doesn't tell you she is conducting an experiment. Is that a laboratory or field experiment? You can actually argue that both answers are correct.

And one more thing...

When we are talking about laboratory versus field experiments, it is important to remember that this doesn't have to be about experiments. All the same points apply to any study conducted in a laboratory or in the field. Experiments are not more artificial than non-experiments.

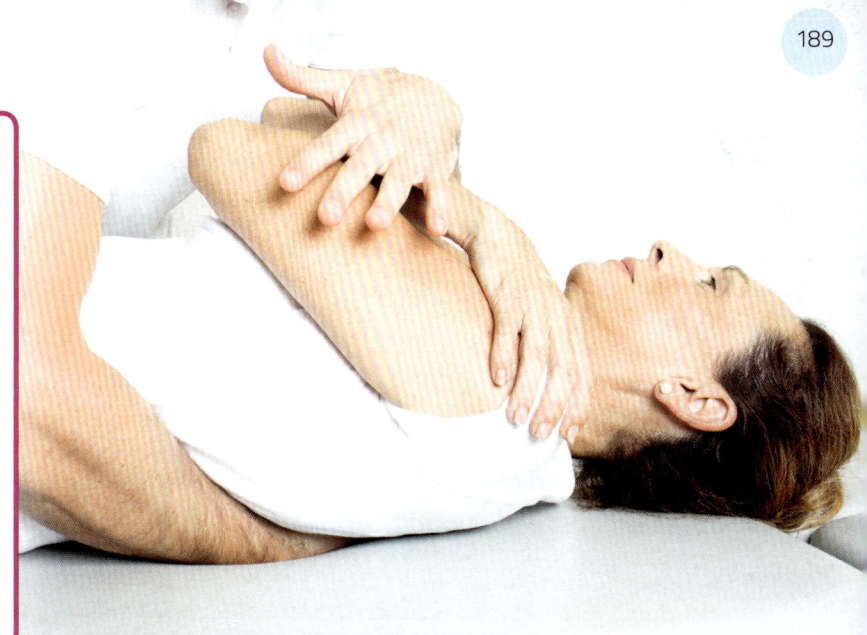

A bit of manipulation from a chiropractor.
When an experimenter 'manipulates the IV' he/she is causing a deliberate change.

Quasi-experiments

Manipulation is what makes a study a true experiment. In both laboratory and field experiments the independent variable is manipulated. There are other studies in psychology that are not 'true' experiments, often called *quasi-experiments* ('quasi' means 'almost') or difference studies.

For example, a researcher may compare the behaviour of men and women (as Sheridan and King did in the obedience study, see page 36). In such studies the IV is gender but this has not been manipulated by the researcher – the researcher is making use of an existing difference between participants.

Reliability and experiments

In an experiment you can consider the reliability of the way the DV was measured. For example, if a questionnaire was used to assess performance then the reliability of that questionnaire can be considered.

Check it

1. Assess the ecological validity of the following studies:
    (a) Sherif *et al.*'s (1961) Robber's Cave experiment (see page 48). (8)
    (b) Bartlett's (1932) 'War of the Ghosts' study (see page 74). (8)
    (c) Baddeley's (1966b) study of memory (see page 76). (8)

2. A group of psychology students decide they would like to assess the effects of temperature on aggression. They choose to conduct a repeated measures experiment.
    (a) Identify the independent variable in this experiment. (1)
    (b) Explain how you would measure the dependent variable in this experiment. (2)
    (c) Identify **three** potential confounding variables and say how you would deal with each of these. (6)
    (d) Explain how you could conduct this study as a laboratory experiment. (6)
    (e) Explain how you could conduct this study as a field experiment. (6)
    (f) Explain **one** strength and **one** weakness of your two designs in parts (d) and (e). (8)

Inferential statistics: Tests of difference

Chapter 5 Research methods — 190

The specification says...

2.2.12 Decision-making and interpretation of inferential statistics

- Non-parametric test of difference: Mann-Whitney U (next spread) and Wilcoxon.
- Probability and levels of significance ($p \leq 0.10$ $p \leq 0.05$ $p \leq 0.01$).
- Observed and critical values, use of critical values tables and sense-checking of data.
- One- or two-tailed regarding inferential testing.

Descriptive statistics describe data collected.

Inferential statistics allow researchers to draw inferences about the target population based on the *sample* of participants that were tested/observed.

Inferential tests are based on the mathematics of probability – so we can decide how likely a hypothesis is to be true given the results from a study.

In a nutshell

Inferential test	Procedures for drawing logical conclusions (inferences) about the *target population* from which samples are drawn.
Observed value	The number (value) produced after applying an inferential test formula. This is sometimes called the *calculated value* because the researcher calculates it.
Critical value	The number (value) which must be achieved in order for a result to be significant.
Probability (*p*)	A measure of the likelihood that an event may occur. Probability is given as a number between 0 and 1 (where 0 indicates impossibility and 1 indicates certainty).
Significance	A statistical term indicating that the research findings are sufficiently strong to enable a researcher to reject the *null hypothesis* under test and accept the *alternate hypothesis*.
Levels of significance	The level of probability at which it has been agreed to reject the null hypothesis. $p \leq 0.10$ means that there is less than or equal to a 10% possibility that the result was due to chance rather than the effect being 'real', i.e. representing what is actually 'out there'. A researcher must decide, before conducting a study, what level of significance will be acceptable.
Critical values table	A list of numbers that inform you whether an observed value is significant or not. There are different tables for each inferential test.

Probability

We all have a basic understanding of probability – if you toss a coin you know that the likelihood of whether you would get heads or tails is 1 out of 2 (1/2) or the likelihood of getting a particular number when you throw a die is 1 out of 6 (1/6).

If you test memory in 20 boys and 20 girls and the boys do better than the girls, how probable is it that the same is true of the target population? Statisticians have worked out the probabilities and produced inferential tests based on these probabilities.

Statisticians also produce critical values tables that indicate what value needs to be obtained in order to claim a certain level of probability.

Basically ...

- A researcher conducts a study and collects data.
- The data is processed using an inferential test. All inferential tests produce a final number, called the *observed value*.
- To determine if the results are significant the observed value is compared with a *critical value* in a critical values table. Each inferential test has its own critical values table.
- Before checking the critical values table the researcher needs four pieces of information:
  - The number of participants in the study (*n*) or sometimes degrees of freedom is used (*df*).
  - The direction of the hypothesis, so we know whether we need a one-tailed or two-tailed test.
  - The required level of significance, which is usually 5%.
  - Whether the observed (calculated) value has to be more than or less than the critical value for significance to be shown. This varies from test to test but is written below the critical values table (as you can see on the facing page, bottom right).
- The researcher finally decides whether to accept or reject the null hypothesis.

There is a simple rule for deciding whether the observed (calculated) value needs to be more than or less than the critical value – it's called the rule of R...

If the inferential test has an R in its name then the observed value has to be gReateR than the critical value for significance to be shown.

Check it

1. Explain how a researcher obtains the observed value of an inferential test. (1)
2. A researcher analysed data from a study with a repeated measures design. Each group had eight participants. The researcher calculated that the observed value for Wilcoxon (*T*) was 17. Should he reject the null hypothesis? (3)
3. Dave runs an experiment and finds a significant difference at $p \leq 0.05$. Bert wants to check Dave's findings and be more confident in his conclusion. Should Bert use a significance level of $p \leq 0.10$ or $p \leq 0.01$? (1)
4. Siobhan does a Mann-Whitney *U* test. She has ten participants in each condition and a non-directional (two-tailed) hypothesis. Her observed value is 18. Explain whether she would accept her null hypothesis at $p \leq 0.05$ or $p \leq 0.01$. (2)

Wilcoxon Signed Ranks test

This is your first inferential test. It is used when an experiment has a *repeated measures design* and we are comparing performance in two conditions. The level of measurement must be at least ordinal (level of measurement is discussed soon, page 201).

Here are step-by-step instructions for processing a set of results.

STEP 1: State the alternate hypothesis

Participants have a higher test score in the morning than when taking the same test in the afternoon.

This is a one-tailed (directional) hypothesis.

STEP 2: Place raw data in table

The raw data are the test scores – morning scores placed in column A and afternoon scores in column B (see right).

STEP 3: Find differences and rank

Calculate the difference between each score.

If the difference is zero, omit this from the ranking and reduce n accordingly.

Rank the differences from low to high ignoring the signs. The lowest number receives the rank of 1, the next lowest number is rank 2 and so on.

If there are two or more of the same number (tied ranks) calculate the rank by working out the mean of the ranks that would have been given. In our case 0.5 occurs twice and would have a rank of 3 and 4, so they each get a rank of 3.5.

(You may find it easier to write the numbers down somewhere else and place them in order and then rank them.)

STEP 4: Calculate observed (calculated) value of T

Add up the ranks for positive differences:

In our example this is $3.5 + 11 + 8 + 6 + 9 + 10 + 1 + 7 = 55.5$

Add up the ranks for negative differences:

In our example this is $5 + 3.5 + 2 = 10.5$

T is the figure that is the smallest when the ranks are added up (may be positive or negative).

In our example T is 10.5

STEP 5: Is the result in the right direction?

The predicted direction was that morning scores would be higher and the result is in this direction (morning scores are generally higher).

STEP 6: Find critical value of T

You need to know:

- Level of significance: 5% (0.05)
- Kind of hypothesis: One-tailed
- n value (total number of scores ignoring zero values). In our case $n = 11$ (1 score omitted). In the critical values table on the right locate the intersection of the column for one-tailed test at 5% and the row that begins with our n value. The critical value of $T = 13$

STEP 7: Report the conclusion

The observed (calculated) value of T (10.5) is equal to or less than the critical value (13) shown in the table for $n = 11$ for a 5% level of significance and a one-tailed test.

This means there is a significant difference between morning and afternoon performance on the test.

Sense-checking

It is very easy to make arithmetic errors when calculating the mean or range or even when using a calculator to work out the standard deviation. Therefore, it is good practice to always have an approximate idea of what the answer is likely to be. That is 'sense-checking'.

The same is even more true when calculating an inferential statistic – so you should always 'eyeball' the data. One way to do this is to look at a graphical representation of the data. Another way is to do a rough calculation.

Then when you do the actual calculation you can say TLAR (That Looks About Right).

Try this with the data below – do the scores in column A look bigger than column B? What would you estimate the mean of each column to be?

Table with scores, difference between scores and rank of differences.

Condition A Morning score	Condition B Afternoon score	Difference	Rank
12.6	13.3	–0.7	5
10.9	10.4	0.5	3.5
14.0	11.4	2.6	11
7.4	7.4	0	omit
10.8	9.2	1.6	8
12.5	11.1	1.4	6
12.8	10.8	2.0	9
13.9	14.4	–0.5	3.5
11.6	9.2	2.4	10
11.2	11.1	0.1	1
10.1	8.6	1.5	7
9.9	9.5	–0.4	2

Critical values for the Wilcoxon Signed Ranks test

	Level of significance for a one-tailed test		
	0.05	0.025	0.01
	Level of significance for a two-tailed test		
n	0.1	0.05	0.02
$n = 5$	0	–	–
6	2	0	–
7	3	2	0
8	5	3	1
9	8	5	3
10	11	8	5
11	13	10	7
12	17	13	9

The calculated value must be equal to or less than the critical value in this table for significance to be shown.

Inferential statistics: Tests of difference (continued)

The specification says...

2.2.12 Decision-making and interpretation of inferential statistics

- Non-parametric test of difference: Mann-Whitney U.

On the previous spread we introduced inferential statistics and worked through one of the non-parametric tests you are required to be able to use.

On this spread we work through a second test, the Mann-Whitney U test which is used when you have two sets of data and an independent groups design was used.

In a nutshell

Tests of difference	Inferential statistics enable us to compare two data sets. We want to know whether the distribution of one set of data is significantly *different* from the other set. When comparing two distributions both the *mean* value and the distribution of the values around the mean *(standard deviation)* are taken into account. The question is whether this difference is significant. If it is significant we can reject the *null hypothesis* (which states there is no difference) and accept the *alternate hypothesis*.
Alternate hypothesis	In an experiment this can be called the experimental hypothesis, but in non-experimental research it is called the alternate hypothesis because it is alternative to the null hypothesis.
Wilcoxon Signed Ranks test	Test of difference between two sets of data.	Data must be ordinal or interval (i.e. not nominal). These 'levels of measurement' are explained on page 201.	*Repeated measures* or *matched pairs design*.	Test statistic is *T*
Mann-Whitney *U* test			*Independent groups design*.	Test statistic is *U*

Non-parametric

The specification refers to 'non-parametric tests of difference'. Inferential tests are classed as parametric or non-parametric. Edexcel only requires you to use non-parametric tests. Parametric tests are more powerful, which means that if a non-parametric test does not find a significant effect, a parametric test may do so because it has increased power (like a magnifying glass).

Data distributions

In the study on friendliness scores on the right, two sets of data were collected – one from girls (condition A) and one from boys (condition B). A histogram has been drawn for each data set showing the distribution of the data. They are clearly different but is the difference significant? We need an inferential test to answer that.

Distribution of girls' scores in condition A (left) and boys' scores in condition B (right).

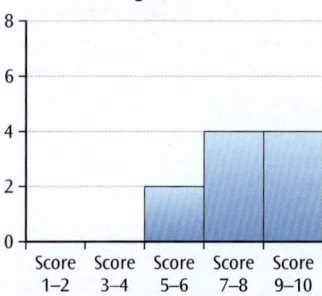

Mean for condition A = 7.9
Standard deviation for condition A = 1.66

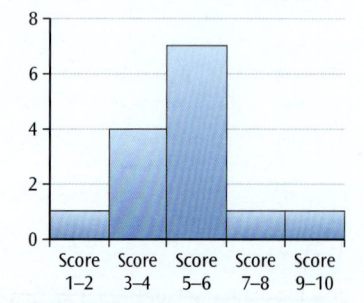

Mean for condition B = 5.0
Standard deviation for condition B = 1.80

Mann-Whitney

This is your second inferential test. It is used when an experiment uses an *independent groups design* and we are comparing performance in two conditions. The level of measurement must be at least ordinal.

Here are step-by-step instructions for processing a set of results.

STEP 1: State the alternate hypothesis

Girls' friendliness score (measured using a ranked scale) is different from boys' friendliness score.

This is a two-tailed (non-directional) hypothesis.

STEP 2: Place raw data in table

The raw data are friendliness scores – place in a table with additional columns for rank scores (see table in step 4).

STEP 3: Rank each data set

Rank all data items jointly, following the steps on the previous spread for ranking. As there are so many tied ranks it may be best to work out a frequency count as shown below:

Score	Frequency	Ranks	Final rank
2	/	1	1
3	//	2 and 3	2.5
4	//	4 and 5	4.5
5	////	6, 7, 8, 9 and 10	8
6	////	11, 12, 13 and 14	12.5
7	///	15, 16 and 17	16
8	//	18 and 19	18.5
9	///	20, 21 and 22	21
10	//	23 and 24	23.5

STEP 4: Add each set of ranks

Place ranks in table below and then add ranks for A and B.
Total for condition A is ΣR_a and for condition B is ΣR_b

Condition A girls' score	Rank	Condition B boys' score	Rank
7	16	4	4.5
10	23.5	6	12.5
8	18.5	2	1
6	12.5	5	8
5	8	3	2.5
8	18.5	5	8
9	21	6	12.5
7	16	4	4.5
10	23.5	5	8
9	21	7	16
		9	21
		3	2.5
		5	8
		6	12.5
$n_a = 10$	$\Sigma R_a = 178.5$	$n_b = 14$	$\Sigma R_b = 121.5$

STEP 5: Calculate observed (calculated) value of U

The formula for calculating U is shown below for both conditions A and B:

$$U_a = n_a n_b + \frac{n_a(n_a + 1)}{2} - \Sigma R_a$$

$$U_b = n_a n_b + \frac{n_b(n_b + 1)}{2} - \Sigma R_b$$

The value of U that we will use is the smaller of the two.

$$U_a = 10 \times 14 + \frac{10(10+1)}{2} - 178.5$$

$$= 140 + 55 - 178.5 = 16.5$$

$$U_b = 10 \times 14 + \frac{14(14+1)}{2} - 121.5$$

$$= 140 + 105 - 121.5 = 123.5$$

STEP 6: Is the result in the right direction?

No direction was stated in the alternate hypothesis.

STEP 7: Find critical value of U

You need to know:
- Level of significance: 5% (0.05)
- Kind of hypothesis: Two-tailed
- n_a = Number in condition A = 10
- n_b = Number in condition B = 14

In the critical values table on the right locate the square where our n_a and n_b value intersect.

The critical value of U = 36

STEP 8: Report the conclusion

The observed (calculated) value of U (16.5) is equal to or less than the critical value (36) shown in the table for n_a = 10 and n_b = 14 for a 5% level of significance and a two-tailed test.

This means there is a significant difference between girls' and boys' friendliness scores.

In the exam the first pages of the exam paper contain all the formulae you need.

The Mann-Whitney formulae are given on page 4.

You may be required to substitute values into this formula.

Make sure you have a calculator for the exam.

Mr and Mrs Wilcoxon are one couple – in repeated measures the two values are related.

Ms Mann and Mr Whitney are independent.

UNLESS they have met through a dating agency and were matched – and, even though they are not married, the matching means they are related.

Critical values for the Mann-Whitney U test

$p \leq 0.025$ (one-tailed), $p \leq 0.05$ (two-tailed)

n_a \ n_b	5	6	7	8	9	10	11	12	13	14	15	16	17	18	19	20
5	2	3	5	6	7	8	9	11	12	13	14	15	17	18	19	20
6	3	5	6	8	10	11	13	14	16	17	19	21	22	24	25	27
7	5	6	8	10	12	14	16	18	20	22	24	26	28	30	32	34
8	6	8	10	13	15	17	19	22	24	26	29	31	34	36	38	41
9	7	10	12	15	17	20	23	26	28	31	34	37	39	42	45	48
10	8	11	14	17	20	23	26	29	33	36	39	42	45	48	52	55
11	9	13	16	19	23	26	30	33	37	40	44	47	51	55	58	62
12	11	14	18	22	26	29	33	37	41	45	49	53	57	61	65	69
13	12	16	20	24	28	33	37	41	45	50	54	59	63	67	72	76
14	13	17	22	26	31	36	40	45	50	55	59	64	67	74	78	83
15	14	19	24	29	34	39	44	49	54	59	64	70	75	80	85	90
16	15	21	26	31	37	42	47	53	59	64	70	75	81	86	92	98
17	17	22	28	34	39	45	51	57	63	67	75	81	87	93	99	105
18	18	24	30	36	42	48	55	61	67	74	80	86	93	99	106	112
19	19	25	32	38	45	52	58	65	72	78	85	92	99	106	113	119
20	20	27	34	41	48	55	62	69	76	83	90	98	105	112	119	127

The calculated value must be equal to or less than the critical value in this table for significance to be shown.

On the formula pages of your exam paper there are also critical values tables.

For the Mann-Whitney these are on pages 4–6.

There are four of them:
- Table 1
  $p \leq 0.05$ (one-tailed)
  $p \leq 0.10$ (two-tailed)
- Table 2
  $p \leq 0.01$ (one-tailed)
  $p \leq 0.02$ (two-tailed)
- Table 3
  $p \leq 0.025$ (one-tailed)
  $p \leq 0.05$ (two-tailed)
- Table 4
  $p \leq 0.005$ (one-tailed)
  $p \leq 0.01$ (two-tailed)

Check it

1. A researcher tests students before and during the exam period to compare how stressed they feel. State an appropriate statistical test to analyse the data you would collect. Give reasons for your choice. (3)

2. Create a set of 'dummy' data for the study described in question 1 and follow the steps for the appropriate statistical test. Are your results significant? (6)

3. A researcher conducts the same study using an independent groups design. Explain **one** strength and **one** weakness with using independent groups instead of repeated measures. (4)

4. The researcher decided to turn this into a matched pairs design study.
   (a) Explain what he would do with the sample of participants to turn this into a matched pairs design. (2)
   (b) What test should the researcher use to analyse the data? (1)

5. The hypothesis for a study was, 'Young people and older people differ in their ability to remember a list of 50 words.'
   (a) Explain why a Mann-Whitney U test would be used in this study. (2)
   (b) If there were ten participants in each condition and the observed value of U was 26 explain whether we can accept the alternate hypothesis ($p \leq 0.05$). (2)

Type I and II errors

Chapter 5 Research methods — 194

The specification says…
2.2.12 Decision-making and interpretation of inferential statistics
- Type I and Type II errors.

In a nutshell
- A **Type I** error occurs when a researcher *rejects* a null hypothesis that is true.
- A **Type II** error occurs when a researcher *accepts* a null hypothesis that was not true.

Psychologists generally use the 5% probability level because this is a good compromise between being too strict or too lenient about accepting the null hypothesis – or, more formally, a good compromise between a Type I and a Type II error.

		Truth (which we will never know)	
		Alternate hypothesis H_1 true	Null hypothesis H_0 true
Test result	Reject null hypothesis	True positive	False positive **TYPE I ERROR**
	Accept null hypothesis	False negative **TYPE II ERROR**	True negative

5% level of significance
An inferential test only gives the *probability* that a particular set of data did not occur by chance. The level of significance psychologists tend to use is 0.05. This means that there is a 0.05 or 5% probability that the distribution of results would have occurred by chance.

1% level of significance
Sometimes researchers wish to be more certain and use 0.01 (1%), for example if testing the effect of a drug on treating a disease.

In general 1% is avoided because it is too stringent and increases the chance of accepting a null hypothesis which was in fact false (Type II error).

10% level of significance
Sometimes researchers are content to be less certain and use 0.10 (10%), for example when conducting an initial investigation.

In general 10% is avoided because it is too lenient and increases the chance of rejecting a null hypothesis which was in fact true (Type I error).

TTFN
… means
Ta ta for now
or
TYPE TWO FALSE NEGATIVE

Trial by jury
You have been selected to be a member of a jury and have listened to all the evidence in a particularly gruesome murder trial. Now you have to decide – is the accused innocent or guilty? There are four possibilities:

- **Possibility 1** You decide the accused is guilty and in actual truth he is, so you are correct and the accused certainly deserves to be behind bars.
- **Possibility 2** You decide the accused is guilty and in actual truth he is not guilty, and you have just put an innocent man in prison for 20 years minimum.
- **Possibility 3** You decide the accused is not guilty and in actual truth he is not guilty, so you have made a correct judgement.
- **Possibility 4** You decide the accused is not guilty and in actual truth he is guilty, and you have freed a dangerous criminal.

Two of the possible outcomes are errors – neither of which is desirable. You have to weigh one against the other.

The grid below summarises the possibilities in terms of Type I and Type II errors.

		Truth (which we will never know)	
		Guilty	Not guilty
Jury verdict	Guilty verdict	True positive	False positive (Guilt reported, i.e. positive.) **TYPE I ERROR**
	Not guilty verdict	False negative (Guilt not detected, i.e. negative.) **TYPE II ERROR**	True negative

Check it

1. A psychologist found a significant difference at the 5% level for a one-tailed test ($p \leq 0.05$). What is the likelihood of the psychologist having made a Type I error in this study? Explain your answer. (2)

2. Bella is testing whether people who are competitive are more or less prejudiced than people who are non-competitive. Her results lead her to accept her null hypothesis at $p \leq 0.05$, but she has reason to believe this is a mistake.
   (a) Does Bella believe she has made a Type I or a Type II error? (1)
   (b) To reduce the likelihood of making this type of error, Bella replicates her study and uses a different significance level. What significance level should she choose? Justify your answer. (2)

Normal and skewed distributions

On page 173 we looked at *bar charts* and *histograms*. These graphs allow us to display frequency data (frequency on one axis). These graphs show the distribution of the data.

On this page we look at three types of *frequency distribution*.

The specification says...

2.2.12 Decision-making and interpretation of inferential statistics
- Normal and skewed distribution.

[AL Topic 9 includes: standard deviation related to normal distribution.]

Data distributions

When we plot frequency data the *y*-axis usually represents frequency and the *x*-axis is the item of interest, as in a histogram. When plotting this we can see an overall pattern of the data, especially with a large data set. This pattern is called a distribution.

Normal distribution	The normal distribution occurs when certain variables are measured, such as IQ or the life of a light bulb. Variables such as these are distributed so that most of the scores are clustered around the mean, median and mode. All measures of central tendency are at the mid-point. 68.26% of the scores should lie within one standard deviation of the mid-point, as shown on the right. 95.44% lie within two standard deviations – leaving less than 5% which are at a greater distance from the mean. The curve has a characteristic symmetrical bell-shape.	The percentage of people in each part of the normal distribution curve is shown below. 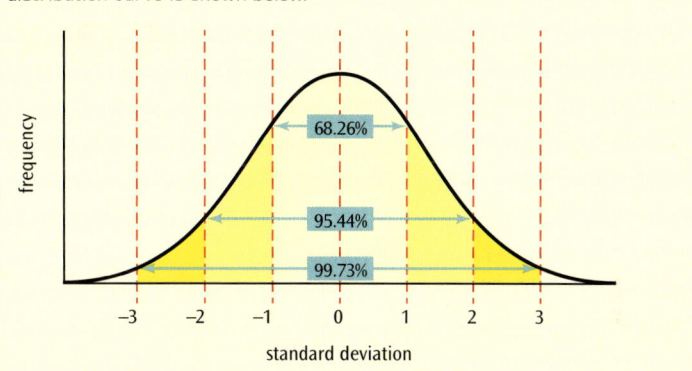
Skewed distribution	In a skewed distribution the mean, median and mode do not all share the same value (as they do in a normal distribution). In a positive skew most of the scores are bunched towards the left. The mode is to the left of the mean because the mean is dragged to the right by the extreme scores tailing in a *positive* direction (tail to the right). In a negative skew most of the scores are bunched to the right and some tail off in a *negative* direction (to the left). 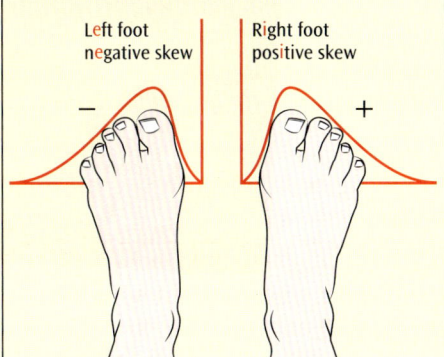 Left foot negative skew. Right foot positive skew.	Positive skew (tail is right, in a positive direction, mode to left). 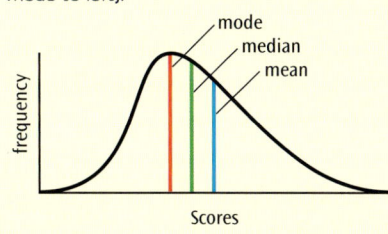 Negative skew (tail is a negative direction, mode to right). 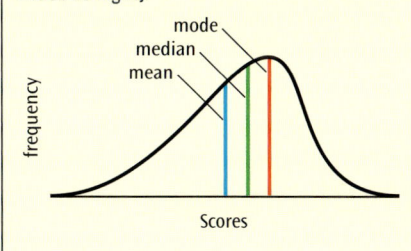

Left or right skew?

Check it

1. How would you describe the distribution of data in the two graphs on the previous spread? (2)
2. The term 'ceiling effect' is used to describe a test that is too easy so most people get really high marks. If you plotted the scores from such a test would you get a positive or negative skew? (1)
3. IQ is believed to be normally distributed. One standard deviation is 15 IQ points and the mean is 100. What percentage of the population should have an IQ in the range 85 to 115 IQ points? (2)

Case studies and HM

The specification says...

2.2.13 Case study of brain-damaged patients, including Henry Molaison (HM) and the use of qualitative data, including the strengths and weaknesses of the case study.

A *case study* is what it says on the tin – a study of one case. Case studies are usually about one person (but not always) and are usually conducted over a lengthy amount of time (but not always). Perhaps most significantly case studies are 'in-depth' involving large amounts of detailed, *qualitative* information.

More on case studies

A case study may be conducted within a short space of time (e.g. one day) or may follow the case over many years.

The key feature of a case study is that a lot of information is collected about the case and this is likely to involve a variety of techniques – interviews, psychological tests, observations and even experiments to test what an individual can or can't do.

Data collected

The information might be collected from the case being studied or from other people involved, such as family and friends. It is likely to be mainly qualitative data, for example interview answers or observations of behaviour.

Quantitative data may also be collected, such as scores on psychological tests for depression or IQ test scores.

A case study may be about unusual individual(s) or events, such as a person with brain damage, or may be about 'normal' people or events, such as a day in the life of a typical teenager.

Case history

A case history (often confused with a case study) is a record of a person's previous experiences or behaviours. A doctor often records a patient's case history in order to make a diagnosis. Case studies often include recording a case history.

In a nutshell

Case study

The detailed study of one case – but the case could be one person, one group of people (such as a family or a football team or a school) or an event.

+ Can be used to investigate instances of human behaviour and experience that are rare (for example mental illness) or cases which could not possibly be created in research labs (for example cases of damage to specific areas of the brain).

+ The method produces rich, in-depth data because the complex interaction of many factors can be studied, in contrast with experiments where variables are held constant. This means that information that may be overlooked using other research methods can be researched. The case study method is important for psychologists who adopt a holistic approach.

− It is difficult to generalise from individual cases as each one has unique characteristics and/or because we can't make before-and-after comparisons. For example, in the case of Phineas Gage (below) we only have anecdotal evidence of what he was like before the accident.

− It is often necessary to use recollection of past events as part of a case study. Such evidence may be unreliable because people's memories are inaccurate.

− Researchers may lack objectivity as they get to know the case, or because their theoretical biases may lead them to interpret the data less objectively.

− There are important ethical issues such as confidentiality and anonymity. Many cases are easily identifiable because of their unique characteristics, even when real names are not given.

Case study of Phineas Gage

In 1848 Phineas Gage was working on the construction of the American railway. An explosion of dynamite drove a tamping iron (a metre long and 7 kg in weight) right through his skull. The artist's impression below shows how the iron passed through his head – it landed 25 metres away from him.

Remarkably he survived and was able to function fairly normally, showing that people can live despite the loss of large amounts of brain matter.

However, the accident did appear to affect Phineas' personality. Before the accident he was hard-working, responsible and popular, whereas afterwards he became restless and indecisive and swore a lot. His friends said he was no longer the same man.

This case was important in the development of brain surgery to remove tumours because it showed that parts of the brain could be removed without having a fatal effect. It also indicated that the frontal lobe is important in aspects of behaviour such as conscientiousness.

However, there is some doubt about the validity of the reports about his behaviour. In truth it appears that he eventually returned to a normal life and a responsible job. It is possible that the personality changes were just temporary.

Case study of an event: London riots 2011

Psychologists have always been interested in mob behaviour, so this case provided an opportunity to re-examine some of the explanations for the apparently unruly behaviour of 'mobs'.

For example, Steve Reicher and Cliff Stott (2011) studied the events and argued that the 'mob' did not behave in an unruly manner. 'They don't simply go wild but actually tend to target particular shops and particular types of people. The patterns of what they attack and don't attack reveals something about the way they see the world and their grievances about the world.' (Furlong 2011)

Check it

1. One case study in chapter 2 is about a man referred to as KF (see page 69).
   (a) Why is he referred to as KF? (1)
   (b) Explain the importance of this case study. (2)
   (c) Describe problems with using the evidence from this case study. (6)

2. On the right the case of HM is discussed. Describe **three** key findings from this study. (6)

Case study of Henry Molaison (HM)

Early life
Henry Gustav Molaison was born in 1926 in Connecticut, USA. He was referred to as HM for most of his life to preserve his anonymity but, when he died in 2008 (aged 82) his full identity was revealed.

Henry had an average childhood but all that was to change when, on his 16th birthday, he had his first major epileptic fit. He had experienced mild epileptic seizures from the age of 7 as the result of a bicycle accident but now, despite strong medication, his fits became progressively more debilitating and uncontrollable. By the age of 27 his fits had become so severe that he was no longer able to work.

Psychosurgery
In the 1940s the medical profession began performing operations on the brain to treat psychological disorders – psychosurgery. For example, *prefrontal lobotomies* were performed where connections between the *prefrontal lobe* and the rest of the brain were cut to reduce violent behaviour.

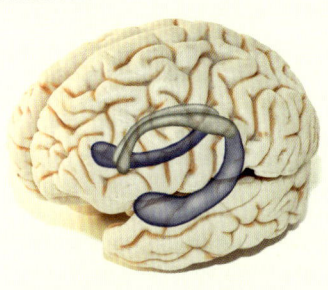

The hippocampus is located in the temporal lobe deep inside the brain as shown in the diagram above. There is one hippocampus on each side of the brain, i.e. one in the left hemisphere and one in the right hemisphere.

HM was referred to Dr William Scoville for such surgery to relieve his epilepsy. At the time no one knew what the purpose of the *hippocampus* was but it was thought it might be the source of some epileptic seizures, therefore this was what Scoville decide to remove. On a summer day in 1953 he bored two holes into HM's skull, each 1½ inches wide. He inserted a spatula into each one to push the frontal lobes aside and then inserted a silver straw deep inside the brain and sucked out most of both hippocampi in HM's brain. Officially this was a 'bilateral medial temporal lobe resection'.

Effect of the surgery
HM's epilepsy appeared to have got slightly better, but this was now overshadowed by a much greater problem – significant memory loss. His personality and intellect remained intact, but he had lost some of his memories from the ten years prior to the operation (*anterograde amnesia*). More importantly, he lost the ability to form new long-term memories (*retrograde amnesia*).

This outcome of the operation was clearly a disaster for HM, although he only vaguely understood it. He did have a memory that there had been an operation and was aware that he couldn't remember things but, as he formed no new memories he couldn't remember that he couldn't remember! For many years, he reported that his age was 27 and the year was 1953. After a while, he realised that this was absurd and tried guessing the answer. He watched the news every night, yet had no recall for major events. He happily reread magazines with no loss of interest. He couldn't recall the faces of people he met. He didn't remember that his father had died, and every time they told him, he mourned all over again.

However, his loss was psychology's gain. HM was intensively studied for about 50 years by more than 100 researchers. Suzanne Corkin (2016), the primary researcher of HM, claimed that HM's case study brought about 'an epiphany in the science of memory'.

In fact he continues to be studied because his brain was preserved and sliced into 2,401 sections to create an atlas of his brain which is available on the internet so that anyone can study the structures of his brain (tinyurl.com/ya2ymldz).

Henry in 1953.

Specific assessments
- HM's intelligence was unimpaired and his personality seemed unchanged, according to reports from childhood friends.
- His short-term (working) memory was about the same as control participants but only up to 20 seconds. After 20 seconds he had no idea how much time had passed (Richards 1973).
- His procedural memory also appeared to be intact, for example he could learn new motor skills such as drawing a figure by looking at its reflection in a mirror. However, he could not remember he had learned these new skills.
- He appeared largely unable to form new episodic memories, though this was not entirely true. For example, he never did recognise Suzanne Corkin even though she tested him regularly over five decades. However, if she said her name was Suzanne he answered with 'Corkin' (Corkin 2002).
- His semantic memory was also severely affected though again there were occasional successes, such as cued retrieval of celebrities' names.

Analysis of the brain damage
During his lifetime it was possible to use *MRI scans* to determine the exact nature of his brain damage and this understanding was further refined in post-mortem studies. It became apparent that some of the hippocampus had not been damaged (which might explain some of the new episodic and semantic memories). The investigations also showed that there were other areas of damage (e.g. structures near the hippocampus and also parts of the frontal lobes), which means that some of the deficits may not be related to the hippocampus.

However, it should be remembered that some of HM's behavioural deficits may have been due to damage caused by his severe epilepsy rather than removal of specific parts of the brain.

Conclusion
This case study clearly demonstrated the localised nature of different brain functions and the role of the hippocampus in episodic/semantic memory, which has been confirmed in many other studies.

Ethical issues
One of the key issues is one of consent. As HM had no memory he was not in a position to provide *informed consent* for any of the tests carried out on him. Furthermore he never consented to his brain being preserved nor were any of his closest relatives approached. Ethics is about a balance between costs and benefits. It seems that the infringement of the personal rights of a vulnerable individual were balanced against the benefits to society in gaining a deeper understanding of memory.

A second key issue is the operation itself. HM's operation was not the first time the temporal lobe resection had been carried out. Scoville had some idea of the possible consequences. The ethical issue here concerns the monitoring of professionals by their colleagues – no one should be allowed to make such decisions alone and, had he discussed it with others, he might not have operated.

(Note that the operation was *not* done for the purposes of psychological research, so when you are talking about ethical issues, focus on those surrounding the testing of HM, not his general welfare.)

Correlation

Chapter 5 Research methods

The specification says...

3.2.1 Correlational research

- The use of the correlational research method in psychology, including co-variables.
- Types of correlation: positive, negative and including the use of scatter diagrams.
- Issues surrounding the use of correlations in psychology; issues with cause and effect, other variables.

A *correlation* is a way of measuring the relationship between two variables – instead of looking at the difference (which is what we do in an experiment).

Age and beauty co-vary. As people get older they become more beautiful. This is a *positive correlation* because the two variables increase together.

You may disagree and think that as people get older they become less attractive. You think age and beauty are correlated but it is a *negative correlation*. As one variable increases the other one decreases.

Or you may simply feel that there is no correlation between age and beauty.

A scatter diagram is a graph that shows the correlation between two co-variables by plotting dots to represent each pair of scores. The scores must be *continuous data*, i.e. data that has a linear order and can take any value within a range.

For each individual we obtain a score for each co-variable, in our case the co-variables are age and beauty.

- The top graph on the facing page illustrates a positive correlation.
- The middle graph shows a negative correlation.
- The bottom graph is an example of no correlation.

The extent of a correlation is described using a *correlation coefficient*. This is a number between +1 and −1. +1 is a perfect positive correlation and −1 is a perfect negative correlation.

The correlation coefficients for the graphs on the facing page are +.76, −.76 and +.002

The plus or minus sign shows whether it is a positive or negative correlation. The coefficient (number) tells us how closely the co-variables are related. −.76 is just as closely correlated as +.76. It's just that −.76 means that as one variable increases the other decreases (negative correlation) and +.76 means that both variables increase together (positive correlation).

In a nutshell

Correlation

A correlation is a method used to assess the degree to which two co-variables are related.

The term 'correlation' is used to refer to a study that uses a correlational analysis.

+ Correlational analysis provides a means of looking at relationships between *continuous* variables and determining whether the relationship is significant. The alternative is to look at differences as in experimental research.

+ Correlation is a useful way to conduct a preliminary analysis on data. If a correlation is not strong then we can rule out a causal relationship. We can't demonstrate a causal relationship using a correlation but if there is no correlation between co-variables then there can't be a causal relationship.

If the correlation is strong then further investigation is justified because there may be a causal link.

− Cannot show a cause-and-effect relationship because there is no independent variable that has been deliberately altered. People often misinterpret correlations and assume that a cause and effect have been found whereas this is not possible. The graphs at the bottom of the page illustrate this.

− If co-variables are correlated one may be causing the changes in the other but we do not know the direction of the possible effect. For example, research studies have shown a positive correlation between amount of violent videos watched and aggressiveness. It might be that watching violent videos is increasing aggressiveness, or it could be that more aggressive people choose to watch violent videos.

− There may be *intervening variables* that can explain why the co-variables being studied are linked. For example, research studies have shown a positive correlation between amount of TV watched and aggressiveness. However, it is wrong to conclude that watching TV is directly related to aggressiveness because it could be that a low boredom threshold was the cause of both of them, an intervening factor.

− The method used to measure either co-variable may lack *reliability* or *validity*. For example, one co-variable may be measured using a questionnaire (such as when measuring aggressiveness). The reliability and validity of the questionnaire would affect the reliability and validity of the research using a correlation.

The scatter diagram below shows a strong negative correlation between global warming and piracy. What could be the explanation?

If you don't have an explanation for an apparent correlation then there is likely to be an intervening variable.

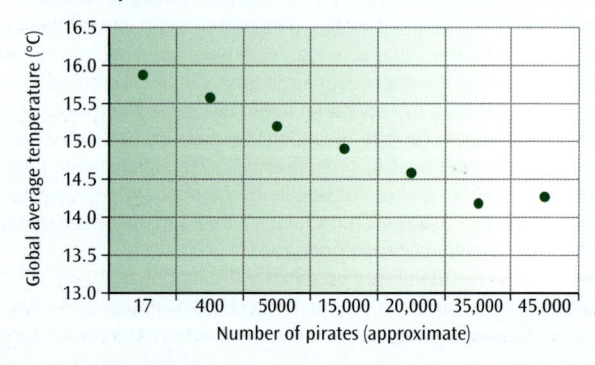

It is relatively obvious that global warming isn't likely to cause decreased piracy (scatter diagram on left) but people are often fooled by correlations. For example, the graph below shows a positive correlation between autism (number of diagnosed cases) and year of birth. Year of birth is related to vaccinations because each year more children are vaccinated – but in 1975 the MMR vaccine was introduced and, it is argued, the sharp rise in autism from that date suggests the disorder is caused by the vaccine. However, the link is a only a correlation so we should not conclude that an increase in MMR vaccinations is the cause of the increase in the number of autism cases.

Scatter diagram showing the global average temperature vs. number of pirates.

Scatter diagram showing relationship between diagnoses of autism and year of birth/number of MMR vaccinations.

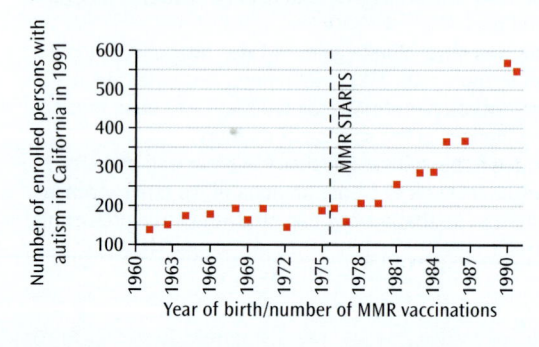

Note that a line can be drawn through the points (a 'line of best fit'). The strength of the correlation is not indicated by the angle of the slope of this line, it's how well the points hug the line that matters.

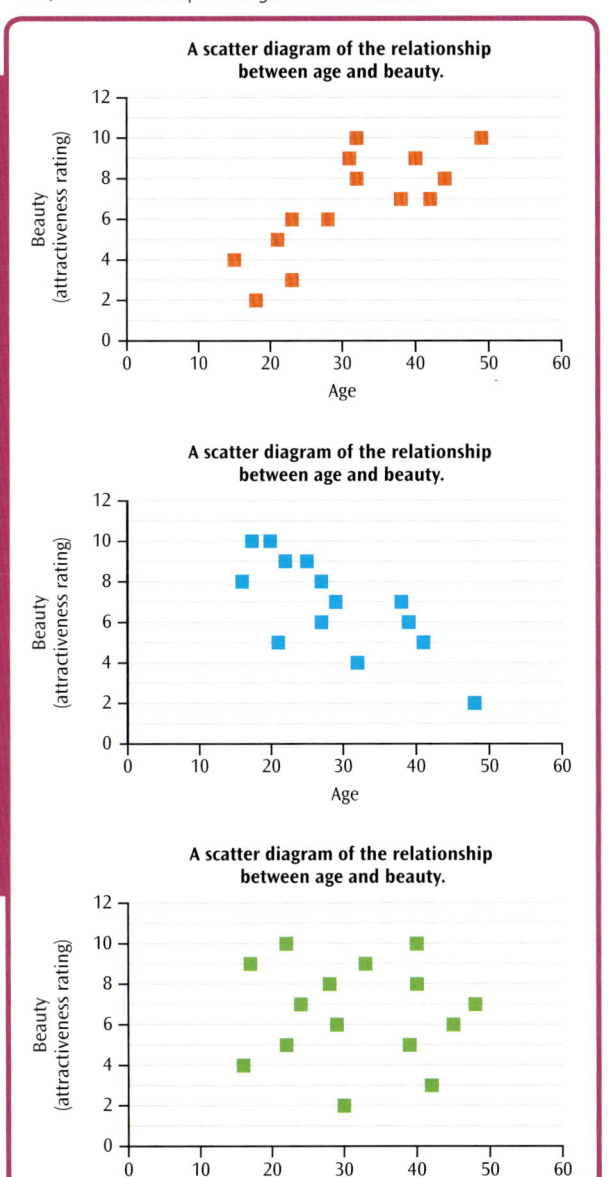

A scatter diagram of the relationship between age and beauty.

A scatter diagram of the relationship between age and beauty.

A scatter diagram of the relationship between age and beauty.

Interpreting a correlation coefficient

The benefit of using graphs to represent data is that you can 'eyeball' the results – in this case you can see at a glance whether there is a strong or a weak correlation between co-variables. You may be asked, in an exam, to comment on the kind of relationship shown in a scatter diagram and you can use the table below to help you.

In order to get a 'feel' for scatter diagrams and correlation coefficients you might have a go at constructing scatter diagrams and seeing what correlation coefficients are produced. Try the Excel method above right.

The closer a correlation is to 1 the stronger it is (remember the sign doesn't matter, +1.0 is as strong as –1.0).

Correlation coefficient	Type of correlation
1.0	perfect
.80	strong
.50	moderate
.30	weak

Try this

Playing with scatter diagrams

It will help you understand correlations if you 'play around' with them – enter different data sets and see what the scatter diagram looks like and what size the correlation coefficient is.

There are a number of websites where you can enter data and a scatter diagram will be produced with the correlation coefficient for you, for example tinyurl.com/yccdpbk2

Or you can use Microsoft Excel:

- On an Excel sheet enter your data in two columns.
- To see a scatter diagram click and drag your cursor from the top left to the bottom right of the two columns. From the toolbar menu select 'chart' and select 'XY scatter'.
- To obtain the correlation coefficient, place the cursor in an empty box and type '=correl(' . Then select with your cursor one column of your data and type a comma in the box and then select your other column of data and finish with a closing bracket. The formula should look something like: =correl(a6:a13,b6:b13). When you press return the correlation coefficient should appear in this box.
- Alter one of the values and see how this affects the scatter diagram and correlation coefficient.
- Produce a scatter diagram with the following correlation coefficients: –.10, +.10, –.90, +.90

Check it

1. A psychological study investigates whether there is a relationship between how well students do in exams and how highly motivated the students are, in order to see if motivation and performance are related. Motivation is measured by assessing how much the students participate in class (for example, counting how often they answer a question in class or how much of class time is spent working).
   (a) Suggest **one** problem that might arise with the way class participation has been operationalised. (2)
   (b) Describe and evaluate **one** way to assess motivation. (2)
   (c) At the end the researchers plot a scatter diagram of average exam scores and level of motivation. Their graph looks like the third graph on the left. What would you conclude from this? (3)

2. A class of psychology students want to investigate whether there is any relationship between how hungry you feel and how good the food you are about to eat looks!
   (a) In order to assess hunger and how good the food looks the students devise two ranked scales. Give an example of what these ranked scales might look like. (2)
   (b) Describe **one** problem with measuring hunger in this way. (2)
   (c) The students find a strong positive correlation between the co-variables. Sketch a graph to show what this should look like. (3)
   (d) One of the students concludes that hunger must have caused the food to look better. What is wrong with this conclusion? (2)
   (e) Describe **one** ethical issue that might arise in conducting this study and say how it could be dealt with. (3)

3. Tara thinks that tidy people are less stubborn. Megan thinks that the more stubborn people are the tidier they will be. Geoff doesn't believe there will be any relationship.
   (a) Describe the type of relationship each friend is predicting. (3)
   (b) The results show that Megan was right. Draw a scatter diagram to illustrate the general pattern of their results. Label the axes of your graph. (2)
   (c) Geoff accepts that there is a relationship, and is convinced that being stubborn must be causing people to be more tidy. Explain why this conclusion is incorrect. (2)
   (d) Tara only collected data on how stubborn people were, Megan only collected data on tidiness and Geoff collected some of each. Suggest why lack of reliability may have been a problem in their study. (2)

Inferential statistics: Test of correlation

The specification says...

3.2.2 Analysis of correlational data

- Analysis of, use of, and drawing conclusions from correlational studies, including scatter diagrams, using inferential statistical testing (use of Spearman's rho) and issues of statistical significance; levels of measurement; critical and observed values.
- The use of alternate, experimental and null hypotheses. The use of IV and DV in experiments and co-variables in correlations.

On the previous spread we looked at scatter diagrams and considered how you can do a rough analysis of data in such a diagram. Now we are going to look at an inferential test which will give us a precise value for the correlation between two co-variables.

Spearman's rho

STEP 1: State the alternate hypothesis

There is a positive relationship between a person's age (in years) and their attractiveness rating (on a ranked scale of 1 to 20).

This is a one-tailed (directional) hypothesis.

STEP 2: Place raw data in table and perform calculations

Place the raw scores in columns A and B.

Rank A and B separately, from low to high (i.e. the lowest number receives the rank of 1). As before, if there are two or more of the same number (tied ranks) calculate the rank by working out the mean of the ranks that would have been given.

Calculate the difference (d) between rank A and rank B.

Square each difference (d^2).

Add up all the squared differences.

In a nutshell

Tests of correlation	Inferential tests that enable us to study the relationship between two sets of data. In an experiment we are comparing two conditions of the independent variable (IV) to see if they had a different effect on the dependent variable (DV). In a correlation we are looking at the relationship between co-variables, not the difference.
Correlational hypothesis	Therefore, the hypothesis states a relationship instead of a difference. A one-tailed (directional) alternate hypothesis would be, 'There is a positive relationship between age and beauty.' A two-tailed (non-directional) alternate hypothesis would be, 'There is a relationship between age and beauty.' The null hypothesis would be, 'There is no relationship between age and beauty.'
Spearman's rho	Test of relationship between co-variables.	Data must be ordinal or interval (i.e. not nominal).	Test statistic is rho

Exam advice

Never use the word 'association' in a hypothesis – it is 'relationship' for a correlation, 'difference' for an experiment.

Participant number	Column A Age	Column B Attractiveness score	Rank A	Rank B	Difference between rank A and rank B (d)	d^2
1	52	5	10	2.5	7.5	56.25
2	36	16	5.5	9	–3.5	12.25
3	47	8	9	5	4.0	16.0
4	32	6	4	4	0	0
5	30	15	3	8	–5.0	25.0
6	21	11	1	7	–6.0	36.0
7	40	9	7	6	1	1.0
8	41	5	8	2.5	5.5	30.25
9	25	17	2	10	–8.0	64.0
10	36	3	5.5	1	4.5	20.25
n = 10					Σd^2 (add up all the squared differences) = 261.0	

STEP 3: Find the observed (calculated) value of rho

$$rho = 1 - \frac{6\Sigma d^2}{n(n^2 - 1)} = 1 - \frac{6 \times 261.0}{10 \times (100 - 1)} = 1 - 1566/990 = 1 - 1.58 = -.58$$

STEP 5: Is the result in the right direction?

The predicted direction was a positive correlation and the result is negative.

STEP 6: Find critical value of rho

You need to know:
- Level of significance: 5% (0.05)
- Kind of hypothesis: One-tailed
- n value = 10

In the critical values table on the left locate the intersection of the column for one-tailed test at 5% and the row that begins with our n value.

The critical value of rho = 0.564

STEP 7: State the conclusion

The observed (calculated) value of rho (–.58) taken as a value without the sign is greater than the critical value (0.564) shown in the table for n = 10 for a 5% level of significance and a one-tailed test. However, it is not in the predicted direction (it is negative whereas the predicted direction was positive).

This means we must accept the null hypothesis that there is no correlation between age and beauty.

Critical values for Spearman's rank

	Level of significance for a one-tailed test				
	0.05	0.025	0.01	0.005	0.0025
	Level of significance for a two-tailed test				
n	0.10	0.05	0.025	0.01	0.005
5	0.900	1.000	1.000	1.000	1.000
6	0.829	0.886	0.943	1.000	1.000
7	0.714	0.786	0.893	0.929	0.964
8	0.643	0.738	0.833	0.881	0.905
9	0.600	0.700	0.783	0.833	0.867
10	0.564	0.648	0.745	0.794	0.830
11	0.536	0.618	0.709	0.755	0.800
12	0.503	0.587	0.678	0.727	0.769
13	0.484	0.560	0.648	0.703	0.747
14	0.464	0.538	0.626	0.679	0.723
15	0.446	0.521	0.604	0.654	0.700
16	0.429	0.503	0.582	0.635	0.679
17	0.414	0.485	0.566	0.615	0.662
18	0.401	0.472	0.550	0.600	0.643
19	0.391	0.460	0.535	0.584	0.628
20	0.380	0.447	0.520	0.570	0.612
21	0.370	0.435	0.508	0.556	0.599
22	0.361	0.425	0.496	0.544	0.586

The calculated value must be equal to or exceed the critical value in this table for significance to be shown.

The critical values table in your exam paper goes up to n = 30 but we ran out of space!

Levels of measurement

One of the factors involved in deciding which inferential test to select is the level of measurement used with the variables in the study – some inferential statistical tests are restricted to certain levels of measurement (as you have seen). 'Level of measurement' refers to the different ways of measuring items or psychological variables, the lower levels are less precise – higher levels are 'better' because they are more precise.

In a nutshell

Nominal data	Data is in separate categories, such as grouping people in your class according to their height – one group might be tall, another group would be medium and the final group is small. Within each category we have a count of how many people or items are in that category (= frequency data). In this case measurement is not very detailed.
Ordinal data	Data is ordered in some way, for example each person in your class lines up in order of size. The 'difference' between each person is not necessarily the same. Data from a ranked scale is considered ordinal, for example if participants are asked to rate how much they like school on a scale of 1 to 5. The intervals between the numbers 1, 2, 3, etc. are equal but they may not represent equal differences in liking. Data from psychological tests (such as IQ tests) are also considered to be ordinal because such tests use standardised scores which are not a simple reflection of the actual items scored correct.
Interval data	Data is measured using units of equal intervals, such as measuring everyone's height in centimetres. Since the units have equal intervals between them, the level of measurement is more precise.

NOIR An acronym to help remember the four levels of measurement of data: nominal, ordinal, interval and ratio – though the last one is not required in your specification.

Don't give up on the statistics

The inferential statistics questions are very easy marks, for example:

- State an appropriate inferential statistical test to analyse the data you would collect. Give reasons for your choice. (3)
- Using the critical values table provided, explain whether the psychologist has found a significant difference. (2)
- Rank the data. (3)
- Determine the degrees of freedom. (1)

Giving reasons for your choice

If asked to select a suitable inferential test, you need to decide:

1. Test of DIFFERENCE (an experiment) or CORRELATION?

   If it is a test of difference then you need to consider whether it was repeated measures or independent groups.

2. Is the data NOMINAL or ORDINAL/INTERVAL level?

   If it is nominal then you will use a test that we have not covered yet.

BUT...

When making these choices you must EXPLAIN, for example:

A test of correlation is required because there are two sets of data and we want to know if pairs of data increase together.

The Spearman test is suitable because the data is ordinal – the data is numerical but equal intervals cannot be assumed.

The Wilcoxon test is chosen because we are looking at the difference between two sets of data which are related.

A test of difference is needed because we are comparing two sets of scores.

Check it

1. A researcher conducted a correlational study with 20 participants. She has calculated the difference between each pair of scores and the square of each difference. The sum of the differences squared is 700.
   (a) Estimate what the observed value of *rho* is likely to be using the formula on the left. (2)
   (b) Calculate the observed value of *rho*. (2)
   (c) For a two-tailed hypothesis, would the observed value you calculated be significant at $p \leq 0.05$? (2)

2. A researcher tests students before and during the exam period to compare how stressed they feel.
   (a) State an appropriate inferential statistical test to analyse the data you would collect. (1)
   (b) Give reasons for your choice. (2)

3. Create a set of 'dummy' data for the study described in question 2 and follow the steps for the appropriate inferential statistical test. Is the pattern of your results significant? (3)

4. In a psychological study data is collected for each participant about their age (in months) and their heart rate. The researcher wants to know if older people have a faster heart rate.
   (a) State an appropriate inferential statistical test to analyse the data you would collect. (1)
   (b) Give reasons for your choice. (2)

5. Create a set of 'dummy' data for the study described in question 4 and follow the steps for the appropriate inferential statistical test. Is the pattern of your results significant? (3)

6. A researcher analysed data from a study with an independent groups design. Each group had eight participants. The researcher calculated that *T* was 17. Should he reject the null hypothesis? (3)

7. A psychologist found a significant difference at the 5% level for a one-tailed test. What is the likelihood of the psychologist having made a Type I error in this study? Explain your answer. (2)

Other biological research methods

Chapter 5 Research methods

The specification says...

3.2.3 Other biological research methods

- *Brain-scanning techniques (CAT, PET, and fMRI).*
- *The use of brain-scanning techniques to investigate human behaviour, e.g. aggression.*

Nothing is more important to psychologists than the brain, so from the very beginning researchers wanted to find ways to look inside the brain – at the structures and processes.

The field of cognitive neuroscience (scientific study of the influence of brain structures on mental processes) has grown considerably in the last 20 years or so because of advances in brain scanning.

But remember these techniques are used as part of, for example, experiments and correlations. They provide ways to measure the brain.

In a nutshell

CAT scan Computerised tomography (CT or CAT)	Uses X-rays and a computer to create detailed structural images of the inside of the body, including the brain. The person lies inside a large doughnut-shaped scanner and the scanner is slowly rotated around them. Images of the brain (or body) are taken from different angles. Each image is a cross-section of the person's brain (or body). When all the 'slices' are put together this can build up a very detailed picture.	+ CAT scans are useful for revealing abnormal structures in the brain such as tumours or structural damage. The quality of the images provided by the CAT scan is much higher than that of traditional X-rays.	− CAT scans require more radiation than traditional X-rays, and the more detailed and complex the CAT scan is, the more radiation exposure the patient receives. This means that CAT scans cannot be used often. − CAT scans only provide structural information. Unlike other scans, such as PET scans, they do not give information about activity of the 'live' brain, they just produce still images. This means they have a limited use in research linking brain areas to particular behaviours.
PET scan Positron emission tomography	Measures metabolic activity in the brain, i.e. the areas that are most active. A person is injected with a small amount of a radioactive substance such as glucose (the *radiotracer*). Brain areas that are most active will use more of it and this can be detected by the scanner. This information is sent to a computer. The most active areas are coloured red or yellow and the least active areas are represented as blue.	+ PET scans show the brain in action, which is useful for psychological research. For example, Nora Volkow et al. (see page 101) used PET scans to correlate the activity of dopamine transporters during a cocaine-induced 'high' to a participant's subjective experience of the drug. This means that biological activity could be linked to behaviour (the participant's experience). + PET scans indicate the specific areas of the brain that are involved in experience, i.e. they provide evidence of localisation of function. For example, the person can be asked to look at a picture, solve a jigsaw puzzle, or think about family holidays they went on as a child, and the linked brain area can be identified.	− Sometimes the results are not easy to interpret. For example, PET scans on people doing the same task have shown different brain activity in different people. This makes it difficult to draw conclusions about which brain areas are linked to which behaviours. − The precise location of active areas in relation to brain structure is difficult to pinpoint. − There are ethical issues to do with the injection of radioactive glucose as used in PET scans. Radioactive substances cause damage to the tissues of the body, they may kill cells or cause mutations in the DNA code in cells. This means the technique can only be carried out once every six months with any one individual and some people may refuse to participate. This further limits the use of PET scans for psychological research.
fMRI scan Functional magnetic resonance imaging	Uses radio waves to measure blood oxygen levels in the brain. Those areas of the brain that are most active use most oxygen and therefore blood is directed to the active area. This is a *haemodynamic response*. This activity/response is picked up through radio signals and these signals produce a series of images of successive 'slices' which are then turned into a 3D image by a computer.	+ As with PET scans, fMRI shows important information about which areas of the brain are being used at any one time. For example, Dustin Pardini et al. (see page 103) used fMRI brain scans to measure the volume of participants' amygdalas and relate this to observed levels of aggression. + Unlike PET and CAT scanning, fMRI does not use radiation and so it is a very safe method of studying the brain. + The images produced by fMRI are extremely clear and can show brain activity to the millimetre.	− Like PET scans, fMRI is expensive to use. − The technique is only effective if the person whose brain is being investigated stays perfectly still and this may be a problem for some people, such as children. This limits the use of fMRI with some kinds of research. − There is around a 5-second time lag between the brain activity and the image appearing on the screen. This can cause problems when trying to interpret the information received.

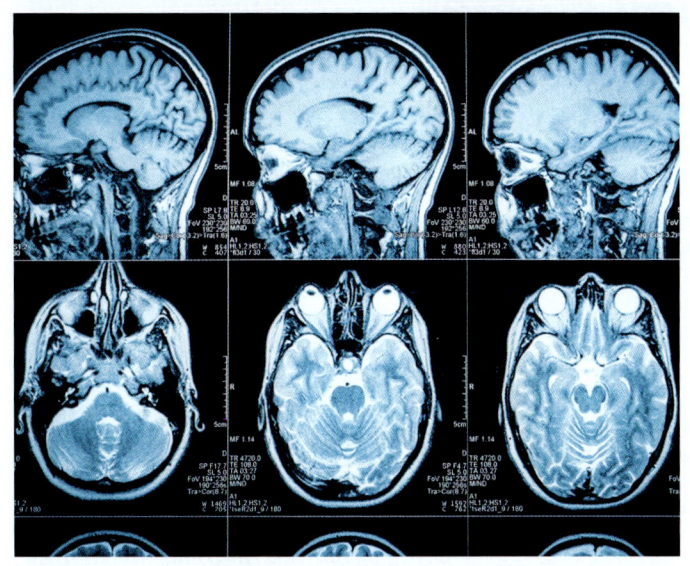

Images produced by a CAT scan of the brain.
This is a bit like looking into a loaf of bread by cutting it into many very thin slices!

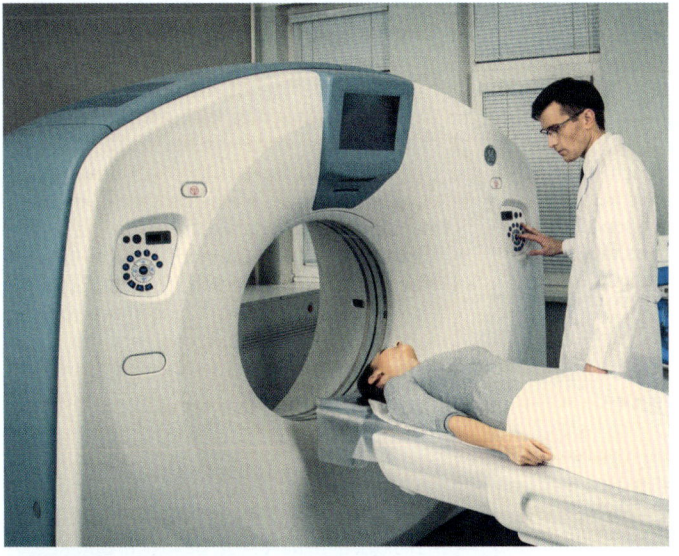

CAT scanner

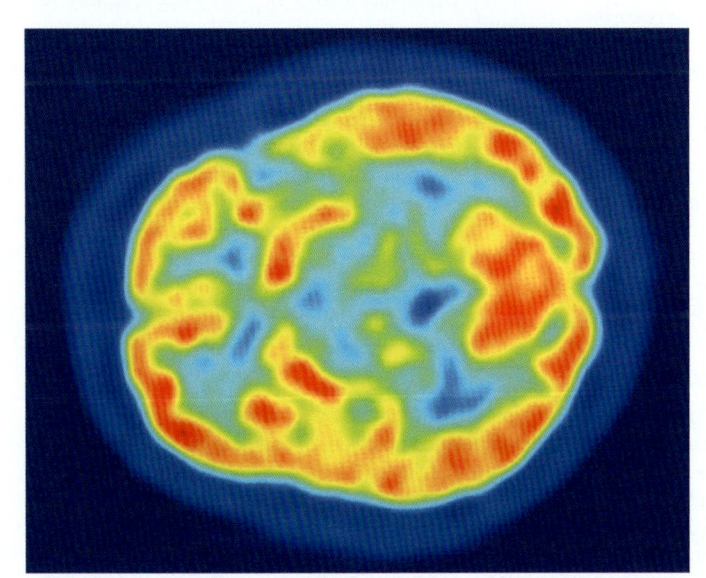

A PET scan reveals the areas of the brain that are active while a participant is engaged in a particular task.

It's enough to put you off omelette and tomato ketchup for life.

fMRI works in a similar way to PET scans. However, rather than tracking a radiotracer, the researcher measures changes in blood oxygen levels in the brain.

More biological methods

The scanning techniques named on the specification are not the only methods used for studying the brain. A few others are described below.

MRI scans

fMRI scans developed from the early use of MRI scans. The difference is that MRI scans do not provide information on function however they do provide higher resolution of images than fMRI. A further difference is that MRI uses water molecules' hydrogen nuclei and reads radio signals emitted from them.

EEG

Electroencephalography (EEG) is another scanning technique, where overall brain activity is measured by recording brainwaves. This has proved very useful in diagnosing rare conditions such as epilepsy. It has also been used to show how activity in our brain changes during sleep and particularly when we are dreaming.

Post-mortem

An old-fashioned but still used method of studying the brain is a post-mortem. This is the analysis of a person's brain after they have died (*post-mortem* means 'after death'). Often a person who has suffered an unusual condition in life is the subject of a post-mortem. Their brain is compared to a 'normal' brain to see if there are any unusual areas of damage. This is how Paul Broca (referred to on page 97) was able to identify the source of language difficulties in his patients – he examined their brains after they died.

Lesioning

Researchers deliberately cut (lesion) areas of the brain in animals to observe behavioural effects. This method was used by David Weinshenker and Jason Schroeder (see page 101) to study the mesocorticolimbic reward circuit of mice brains and draw conclusions about the role of dopamine.

Measuring hormones

Hormones such as testosterone are tested using blood samples or analysing saliva. For example, James Dabbs and Marian Hargrove (see page 109) measured testosterone in the saliva of female criminals and looked at the correlation between testosterone and levels of violence.

Identifying genes

Research on genetic influences on behaviour requires analysis of genes. We will look at this on the next spread.

Check it

1. The classic study by Raine *et al.* (1997) used positron emission tomography (PET scans) to study brain abnormalities in murderers.

   Explain **one** strength and **one** weakness of using PET scans in this study. (4)

2. A researcher wished to investigate structural differences in the brain that are related to aggression. He studied two families: one with many aggressive family members and one with no aggressive family members.

   (a) Describe **two** techniques that could be used to study living people. (4)

   (b) Select **one** of the techniques in (a) and explain **two** advantages of this technique. (4)

   (c) Describe **one** technique that could be used after the individuals had died. (2)

   (d) Suggest **one** advantage of the technique in (c) over either of your answers to (b). (1)

3. Some studies use both MRI and PET. Suggest **one** reason why this combination may be necessary. (2)

Twin and adoption studies

The specification says...

3.2.3 Other biological research methods
- One twin study and one adoption study, e.g. Gottesman and Shields (1966); Ludeke et al. (2013).

One of the big questions in psychology is whether any particular behaviour is better explained by nature or nurture – the genes you were born with or the social and physical environment that surrounds you.

The main ways to study nature versus nurture has been to use twin or adoption studies. More recently techniques have been developed to look directly at genes and we look at this briefly on the facing page.

In a nutshell

The logic of twin studies

The logic is that the more genes two people share, the more similar their behaviour/characteristics should be – if the behaviour/characteristic has a genetic basis.

There are two kinds of twins:

- *Identical twins* whose genes are the same, also called monozygotic (MZ) because they develop from one fertilised egg (zygote).
- *Non-identical twins*, also called dizygotic (DZ) twins because they develop from two fertilised eggs. DZ twins share, on average, about 50% of their genes. They are as similar as any pair of siblings.

There is an assumption that both kinds of twin pairs grow up in the same environment so the only difference between the twin pair types is how genetically related the twins are.

Similarity is measured by correlation or concordance between any two individuals. If we are looking at a behaviour measured numerically (e.g. IQ) we can calculate a *correlation coefficient* to measure similarity. If we are studying a behaviour which is all-or-nothing (e.g. whether a person has been diagnosed with depression or not) then we use *concordance* – the percentage of those studied are concordant (similar).

In order to conduct twin research a researcher might advertise for twins. But if the topic to-be-studied is not found in everyone, such as research on schizophrenia, the researcher finds twins by locating one twin with a disorder (called a *proband*) and then assessing the co-twin of the proband.

The logic of adoption studies

Adopted children are compared with:
- Biological relative, e.g. biological parent.
- Adoptive relative, e.g. adoptive parent or adoptive sibling.

The non-shared environment

Researchers have recognised that it is wrong to assume that twins grow up in the same environment. There are small differences between even identical twins, for example one twin may be more sporty or one twin may break a leg. All these differences mean that there are two different environmental influences – a shared one and a non-shared one.

Twin study

A study where twins are compared on a specific trait to see how similar they are.

If a particular behaviour is *entirely* genetic then we expect MZ twins to show 100% concordance.

If a particular behaviour is more genetic than environmental then we would expect MZ twins to show a higher concordance rate than DZ twins.

+ Enables researchers to investigate the influence of genes because it is assumed that both MZ and DZ co-twins share the same environments. The only difference between the two groups of participants is genetic. Therefore, if a trait is genetic then MZ twins should show higher concordance than DZ twins.

+ Although twins are unusual, information for twin studies is often taken from twin registries (such as the MTFS used in Ludeke et al's study on facing page). These hold data on thousands of twins and also contain information about many variables. This means that the sample is large and the data is likely to be representative.

− Twin studies may overestimate genetic influence. MZ twins have more similar environments than same-sex DZ twins – they are treated more similarly, spend more time with each other and tend to share friends. The environmental experience of one MZ twin is to a large extent the same as the environmental experience of the other – much more so than for DZ twins. Therefore, some of the estimated similarity is actually due to a shared environment.

− Twins studies provide a very broad indication that a behaviour/characteristic has a genetic origin, but they cannot identify the specific genes involved. A twin study is therefore a useful starting point for research, but more recent technologies (see 'association studies' on facing page) are required to help us uncover specific genetic influences.

Adoption studies

Genetic factors are implicated if children are more similar to their biological parents with whom they share genes (but not environment) than to their adoptive parents with whom they share environment (but not genes).

Environmental factors are implicated if the reverse is true.

+ Adoption studies have the advantage of removing the extraneous variable of environment – if MZ twins are similar it is not clear whether the similarity is due to the same environment or the same genes. In adoption studies, environment is not shared or biology is not shared.

+ Adoption studies have been useful in showing that twin studies overestimate genetic factors. For example, a study by Eley et al. (1998) using adoption studies to research depression found that environmental factors are more important, whereas twin studies have detected a greater role for genetics. This may be one area in which the assumption of equal environments is clearly untrue.

− Children may be adopted to families similar to their biological families (called 'selective placement') and therefore environmental influences may be similar. For example, a child whose biological parents are well-educated is placed with a similar family. This means that apparent similarities with biological relatives may be due to environmental similarities rather than genes.

− People who adopt other people's biological offspring are unusual, so are unlikely to be representative of the population. They tend to be better educated, have lower rates of mental illness and come from higher socioeconomic groups. This means any conclusions we draw from adoption studies about the effects of genes (versus environment) on traits such as intelligence may not be generalisable to the population as a whole.

Twin dancing girls – researchers in the 20th century did not have access to techniques for checking whether twins were actually identical genetically. Therefore, not all MZ twins were actually genetically identical – they just looked very similar.

Concordance and heritability

The degree to which two people are similar on a particular trait can be represented by a correlation coefficient and is called *concordance*. Such concordance can provide an estimate about the extent to which a trait is inherited – this is called *heritability*. Heritability is the proportion of differences between individuals in a population, with regards to a particular trait, that is due to genetic variation. A figure of 0.0 (or 0%) means genes do not contribute at all to individual differences and 1.0 (or 100%) means genes are the only reason for individual differences.

One way to calculate heritability is to compare MZ and DZ concordance rates. For example, let's say the concordance rate for IQ is +.86 for MZs and +.60 for DZs. Subtracting +.60 from +.86 gives us +.26 (or 26%). But this figure only represents the half-genome shared by DZ twins (i.e. 50% of their genes). To calculate the effect of sharing a full genome (as MZ twins do), we have to multiply our figure by two. So the real estimate for the heritability of IQ in the population is +.26 × 2 = +.52, or 52%.

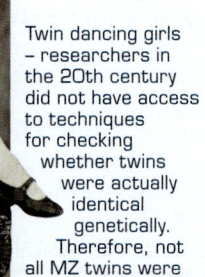

Examples of twin studies

Gottesman and Shields (1966) – Schizophrenia
Irving Gottesman and James Shields investigated the genetic basis of schizophrenia. A search through the records of about 45,000 psychiatric patients at the Maudsley and Bethlem hospital in London, found 57 pairs of twins where at least one had a diagnosis of schizophrenia. This was an opportunity sample.

In order to establish concordance they contacted co-twins. Zygosity was determined by looking at, for example, blood type. Therefore, the researchers could identify MZ and DZ twin pairs.

An analysis of this data and data from other studies, suggested that if one MZ twin had schizophrenia, their co-twin was at least 42 times more likely to have schizophrenia than a person from the general population. A DZ twin of the same sex was at least nine times as likely to have schizophrenia if their co-twin had been diagnosed.

Ludeke et al. (2013) – Parent–child relationships
Steven Ludeke and colleagues considered parent–child relationships, questioning the extent to which genetic factors might contribute to conflict in adolescence and how such an influence changes over time.

The participants were drawn from an ongoing longitudinal study of reared-together, same-sex twin pairs and their parents (the *Minnesota Twin Family Study*, MTFS).

At the start of the study there were 563 MZ and 439 DZ twins aged 11 years. At the end (age 17 years) this reduced to 375 MZ and 379 DZ twins, with fairly equal numbers of male and female twins. At age 11, 14 and 17 years, self-report measures were used to assess levels of warmth and conflict in parent–child relationships.

The self-report data was analysed using a statistical model to identify changes in genetic and environmental influences – environmental influences were separated into shared and non-shared factors.

The analysis showed that genetic influence on the parent–child relationship increased over time, while the quality of the relationship deteriorated. This can be explained in terms of genetically-determined traits in the child having an increasing effect on the parent–child relationship, gradually displacing the effects of parental (environmental) influences.

Brendgen et al. (2005) – Aggression
This is one of the optional contemporary studies in chapter 3 (see page 114). Mara Brendgen et al. investigated aggression in MZ and DZ twins to assess the contributions of genetic and environmental factors.

They used a twin study to compare concordance rates for 234 pairs of MZ and DZ twins. Each twin was rated for his or her level of social and physical aggression by peers (other children) and teachers.

Physical aggression was mostly explained by genetic factors, but social aggression was much more influenced by environmental factors. They concluded that heritable characteristics (such as poor self-control) predisposes some children to aggression. But the form the aggression takes (social or physical) depends more on the environment.

DZ twins – being different genders would create many dissimilarities when compared to same-sex DZ twins.

Examples of adoption studies

Tienari et al. (1994) – Schizophrenia
Pekka Tienari et al. conducted the *Finnish Adoptive Family Study* also looking at schizophrenia.

They found that the lifetime schizophrenia risk for adopted children of biological mothers who had schizophrenia was 9.4%. The corresponding figure for adopted-away children of unaffected biological parents was 1.2%. This difference strongly suggests that genetic influences have an important role in schizophrenia.

Horn et al. (1979) – Intelligence
Joseph Horn et al. initiated the *Texas Adoption Project* which aimed to show the extent to which intelligence is inherited.

The participants in the study were 300 Texan families who had adopted children within a few days of birth from a church-related home for unwed mothers. The children and their parents were first assessed when the children were aged between 3 and 14 years. They found higher correlations between the children's IQs and those of their adoptive mothers than with their biological mothers.

In a follow-up study about ten years later, the children (now adolescents or young adults) were retested. The only IQ correlations that remained above +.20 were between the children and their biological relatives (Horn 1983).

This finding has been evident in many other studies (including Ludeke et al.'s study on the left). The impact of family influences tends to decrease with age, while genetic influences tend to increase. This has been explained in terms of *niche-picking*. Genetic factors influence preferences (such as for risky behaviours or quiet contemplation) and these preferences shape your environment, which in turn affects development. Therefore, adopted children may initially be more similar to adoptive relatives but as they get older they come to more closely resemble their biological parents, i.e. biological influences become more important.

> **Exam advice**
> All of the studies on this page look at genetic influences and therefore are examples of investigations in *biological psychology* – which is the focus of the exam-style questions, below right.

Association studies
Psychological traits such as mental disorder or intelligence are not caused by single genes. Instead it is likely that a range of genes are involved that have additive effects – the more of those genes that are present, the more likely a particular condition will be.

There are two approaches in use to study multiple gene effects. *Candidate-gene association studies* (CGAS) focus on specific 'candidate' genes that individually create a vulnerability for a disorder. *Genome-wide association studies* (GWAS) look at the entire human genome for candidate genes of interest rather than focusing on specific genes.

For example, Stephan Ripke et al. (2014) conducted a GWAS study comparing genes of 36,989 people with schizophrenia and 113,075 non-affected control participants. They found that 108 separate genetic variations were associated with increased risk of schizophrenia.

✓ Check it

1. You have covered one twin study as an example of a research method to investigate human behaviour in biological psychology.
   (a) Describe the method of the twin study you have covered. [4]
   (b) Explain **two** weaknesses of this study as a way to investigate biological psychology. [4]

2. Twin and adoption studies are two methods used to investigate human behaviour in biological psychology.
   (a) Describe what **both** methods aim to test. [2]
   (b) Explain **one** difference between the methods. [2]
   (c) Explain **one** way in which adoption studies are more useful than twin studies. [2]

3. Adoption studies are used as a research method to investigate human behaviour in biological psychology.
   Evaluate **one** adoption study you have covered in biological psychology. [8]

Observation and content analysis

Chapter 5 Research methods

The specification says...
4.2.1 Human research
- The use of the observational research method in psychology, including the gathering of both qualitative and quantitative data (including tallying, event and time sampling).
- Use of content analysis as a research method.

We observe behaviour, record it, look for patterns in the behaviour and then try and make sense of it. The first task is to devise ways of categorising behaviour and recording it.

It's more difficult than you think – try one of the activities on the right.

(Note that observations can involve listening as well as watching.)

Try this

Work with a partner and take turns observing each other. Perhaps observe one partner working on a difficult task while the other person just reads a magazine.

OR ... you know you want to do this one (you probably do it anyway for fun). Take a seat in a public space such as a shopping centre or near a bus queue and watch people go by. Try to describe what they are doing.

Devise some categories (thematic analysis) to capture most of the behaviour you observe.

In a nutshell

Observational research		
Watch or listen to what participants do.	**+** What people say they do is often different from what they actually do, so observations give a different take on behaviour than other research methods, such as self-report. Possibly greater *validity*.	**−** Observers may 'see' what they expect to see (*observer bias*). **−** Observations cannot provide information about what people think.

Collecting qualitative data

Observer records everything – in a lab or naturalistic environment.	**+** A first step in creating a structured, quantitative system for classifying observations. *Thematic analysis* can be used to create *behavioural categories*.	**−** Behaviours recorded may be those most visible or eye-catching to the observer but these may not necessarily be the most relevant behaviours.

Collecting quantitative data

Behavioural categories		
Objective methods to separate continuous stream of action into components. Behaviours are counted.	**+** Enables systematic observations to be made so important information is not overlooked, enhances validity. **+** Categories can be tallied and conclusions drawn.	**−** Categories may not cover all possibilities, some behaviours not recorded (low validity). **−** Poor design of categories may also reduce reliability.

Event sampling		
Draw up a list of behavioural categories. Then count (tally) every time each of the behaviours occurs in a specified time period.	**+** Both methods make observing behaviour more manageable by taking a sample. **+** Event sampling is useful when behaviour to-be-recorded only happens occasionally. Missing events would reduce validity. **+** Time sampling allows for tracking of time-related changes in behaviour.	**−** Observations may not be representative if list of events is not comprehensive, reduces validity. **−** Time sampling may decrease validity because some behaviours are missed if important behaviour occurs outside of the observation interval.
Time sampling Count behaviours at regular intervals (such as every 5 seconds or 8 minutes), or take a sample at different times of day or month.		

Making observations

If you tried the activity above, you should now realise that observing behaviour is difficult.

It is difficult to identify different and separate behaviours.

This is because our perception of behaviour is often seamless; when we watch somebody perform a particular action we see a continuous stream of action rather than a series of separate behavioural components.

In order to conduct systematic observations we need to break up this stream of behaviour into a set of components, called behavioural categories.

The behavioural categories should:

- *Be objective*. The observer should not have to make inferences about the behaviour. For example, a category such as 'Target person looks happy' means the observer has to think about whether the target person looks happy. The categories must relate to explicit actions such as smiling or laughing.
- *Cover all possible component behaviours* and avoid a 'waste basket' category (i.e. a category where you can include anything that isn't already covered).

An example of event sampling

Robert Jordan and Gordon Burghardt (1986) devised a list of behavioural categories and used them to record bears' behaviour in two different zoos. Part of their list is shown on the right.

Sometimes behavioural categories are given a code, as shown here – this is then called a 'coding frame'.

Code	Activity level 1: Reclining postures	Tally
P6	Lying on back	
P7	Lying on front	
P8	Lying on side	
P28	Lying/sitting in a tree	
	Activity level 2: Sitting or standing	
P3	Standing on all fours	
P29	Standing on two feet	
P4	Sitting erect or semi-erect	
	Activity level 3: Bipedal standing and slow locomotion	
P1	Standing on two feet while touching an object	
P11	Walking on all fours	
P18	Rolling over	

Sampling people and sampling behaviour

On page 170 we explained sampling. If you conduct an observational study you need a group of participants (or, in the case of content analysis, a pile of books or selection of TV programmes). You would select these using a sampling technique such as opportunity sampling.

Once you have this sample, you observe the behaviour of the participants/items using an observational sampling method – event or time sampling.

So you have two forms of sampling in one study. A little confusing, we know.

In a nutshell

Content analysis

A kind of observational study in which behaviour is seen indirectly in written or verbal material such as books, diaries or TV programmes. Categories (themes) are identified (possibly using thematic analysis) and then instances in each category can be counted so that *quantitative data* is produced.

+ Tends to have high *ecological validity* because it is based on observations of what people actually do – real communications that are current and relevant, such as recent newspapers or the books that people read.

+ When sources can be retained or accessed by others (e.g. back copies of magazines or videos of people giving speeches) the content analysis can be exactly replicated and therefore the observations can be tested for *reliability*.

− Observer bias reduces the objectivity and validity of findings because different observers may interpret the meaning of the categories differently.

− Likely to be culture-biased because source material is rooted in a culture and behavioural categories are likely to be determined by culture of the observer.

It is difficult to record *everything* that is happening.

An observer can try to record every instance of behaviour. This works if the behaviours of interest do not occur very often. However, usually continuous observation is not possible because there would be too much to record. Therefore, observers use a systematic method such as:

- *Event sampling*, for example, counting how many times a person smiles in a one-hour period or counting how many times a bear walks upright when observed once a day for an hour on 20 separate days. Alternatively a list of behavioural categories may be selected and a count is kept of every time they occur within the observation period.

- *Time sampling*, for example, observing a child playing in their backyard for an hour and making a note of their behaviours every 30 seconds, or asking students to record what they are doing at 11 am and 5 pm every day over a period of one month.

Content analysis

The concept of content analysis was discussed on page 175 as it is linked to thematic analysis. In thematic analysis the aim is to identify recurrent themes in the behaviour being observed. The results are then presented in terms of the themes identified. The data produced is *qualitative*. Content analysis differs because it represents the themes (categories) *quantitatively* by counting instances.

In fact both thematic and content analysis are forms of observation but indirect rather than direct. In an observation the researcher identifies behavioural categories in order to record, for example, children playing in a playground or bears in a zoo. In a content analysis the researcher also identifies categories but uses these to 'observe' the artefacts produced by people such as graffiti or books.

Both observation and content analysis may be used in an experiment as the way to measure the *dependent variable*.

Doing a content analysis

A researcher might analyse the ways men and women are portrayed in TV ads.

Step 1: Select suitable ads, for example record two ads per day and randomly choose the time of day.

Step 2: Create a set of *operationalised* behavioural categories. This might be done by looking at ads and deciding categories such as those listed on the right.

Step 3: Watch ads and tally frequency in each category.

Step 4: Draw conclusions. Inferential statistics can be used such as *chi-squared*, which we will look at on page 212.

	Category	Tally
Main character	Male	
	Female	
	Male and female	
Food advertised	Male focus	
	Female focus	
Drink advertised	Male focus	
	Female focus	
Body products advertised	Male focus	
	Female focus	
Time of day	After 9 pm	
	Before 9 pm	

Check it

1. In each of the following observations state which sampling procedure (time or event sampling) would be most appropriate and explain how you would do it.
   (a) Observing the different activities young children engage in at a nursery school. (3)
   (b) Observing what dog owners do when walking their dogs in a park. (3)
   (c) Observing what people say when talking on their mobile phones. (3)

2. Dan conducts an observational study of football fans at a live game.
   (a) List **three** specific behavioural categories Dan might use. (3)
   (b) Identify a suitable sampling procedure for selecting the participants and explain the advantage of using this method. (3)
   (c) Explain a suitable method for sampling the behaviours. (3)
   (d) How could Dan observe target individuals so that they were not aware that they were being observed? (3)
   (e) Identify **two** ethical issues that might arise and explain how Dan would deal with them. (4)

3. A university department was given funding to investigate the coverage of crime in different newspapers.
   (a) Suggest **three** operationalised categories that could be used in this study. (3)
   (b) Explain how you would do this content analysis. (4)

Observation: Reliability and validity

Chapter 5 Research methods

The specification says...

4.2.1 Human research
- Types of observation: participant, non-participant, structured, naturalistic, overt and covert.

On this spread we continue to explain how *observational methods* are used in research.

Thus far you have discovered why it helps to use observational techniques such as *behavioural categories* and methods of sampling (*time* and *event sampling*). You might even have tried some out for yourself.

You can observe with your ears.

In a nutshell

Type	+	−
Participant observation Observer is a participant in the behaviour being observed, for example being in a bus stop queue and observing behaviour in the queue.	+ Likely to provide special insights into behaviour, from the 'inside'. The participant has greater familiarity with what is likely to happen and therefore may 'see' greater detail that would be missed by someone new to the situation. + Being on the inside means the observer may see more. For example, being in the bus queue means you are closer to the action and may actually see/hear more of what is going on than an observer at a distance.	− *Objectivity* is reduced (*observer bias*). Because the observer is familiar with what is going on they are looking at the situation more *subjectively*. − More difficult to record and monitor behaviour unobtrusively if the observer is part of the group being observed. Therefore, the observation is likely to be *overt* and participants are aware they are being studied, which may alter their behaviour.
Non-participant observation Observer is not a participant in the behaviour being observed.	+ Increased objectivity because of a psychological and also possibly a physical distance. + Can observe unobtrusively. Therefore, participants will not be self-conscious about being observed. This may increase *validity* because participants behave more naturally.	− The observer may misinterpret the communications within the group because they are an outsider. This could reduce the validity of the observations. − Observer may see less.
Structured observation Some variables are changed (manipulated) by the researcher, e.g. in a laboratory.	+ Controlled environment allows focus on particular aspects of behaviour, for example children playing with 'feminine' toys to observe how boys and girls react. This means that specific conclusions can be drawn about gender responses – if everything was natural the children might not encounter different types of toys. + It may be possible to draw some tentative causal conclusions. If variables are deliberately changed by the researcher and different effects are observed then it suggests that one caused the other. For a true experiment there would need to be a *control condition* to make comparisons.	− Environment may feel unnatural and then participants may not behave as they would in everyday life. This means that the observations may lack *ecological validity*. − Participants may know they are being observed, for example if the observation takes place in a laboratory so that the researcher can control aspects of the situation. This awareness means that participants may try to guess what the study is about which alters their behaviour (i.e. *demand characteristics* are present).
Naturalistic observation Everything is left as usual. Environment unstructured but may use 'structured' techniques, e.g. behavioural categories.	+ A realistic picture of natural, spontaneous behaviour. The observation takes place in a person's (or animal's) natural environment and so they are likely to behave as they normally do. This means the results are likely to be high in ecological validity. + Useful method to use when investigating a new area of research. Gives the researcher ideas of what further investigations may be planned, for example using certain behavioural categories or experimental methods.	− The observation is more likely to be *covert*, which raises ethical issues (see below). − It is difficult to draw conclusions if the focus is too wide. If behavioural categories and event/time sampling have been used that may restrict the amount of data collected which makes it easier to see patterns of behaviour.

Note that both structured and naturalistic observations may use systems to record data such as event/time sampling and behavioural categories. Or both may simply involve recording everything that happens.

Type	+	−
Overt observation Participant is aware of being observed.	+ Avoids lack of *informed consent* because participants can decide whether to participate. + It is easier to see everything that is going on because the observer doesn't have to hide.	− If participants know they are being observed they are likely to alter their behaviour (see demand characteristics above).
Covert observation Observations made without a participant's knowledge.	+ Participants behave more naturally because they are not aware of being observed.	− Raises ethical issues about observing people without their knowledge. Participants may be able to give informed consent if asked afterwards (and can withhold their data) but in practice this is difficult. − The second issue is invasion of privacy. Even for observations in a public place, such as a bus queue, people might regard it as unethical to record what they are doing.

Reliability and validity

Reliability

When making observations of a person (or animal or event) we require the observations to be something we can depend on. If they are *reliable* we would expect to end up with the same data when the observations were made a second time.

For example, you could compare the observations made by two people of the same event. Both sets of observations should be the same, in the same way as using two tape measures to measure a table should produce the same result if they are reliable. When comparing scores from two raters this is called *inter-rater reliability*. Just doing this doesn't make the observations reliable but calculating inter-rater reliability enables us to evaluate how reliable the observations are. To calculate inter-rater reliability the scores from one observer are correlated with the scores from a second observer.

Reliability can be improved by making sure that observers are trained in the use of the selected behavioural categories. It might also be necessary to review the categories and see if any are unclear or need subdividing to make for more accurate recording. Note that simply having more observers does not increase reliability.

Validity

When an observer records what they see or hear their observations may be influenced by their expectations. For example, if an observer believes that boys are more aggressive in their play than girls, this may mean they pay different attention to aggression in the boys. If a little boy puts his hand on a friend the observer may say he was 'hitting' his friend whereas the same action may be interpreted differently when a little girl does it. Such *observer bias* reduces the *objectivity* and *validity* of observations.

In an overt observation the presence of an observer may lead participants to behave in a way that is not typical. This reduces the validity of what is observed. Using more than one observer can reduce observer bias by averaging data across observers (balances out any biases).

An example of evaluating the reliability of an observation

The University of Bern had a nursery unit where people could be trained to use observational techniques (BEO 2004). They provided a coding system (see far right) so that observers could count individual behaviours. Observations were made through a one-way mirror.

The two scatter diagrams show the inter-rater reliabilities for two observers and their obervations of two children. Each dot represents the scores from two observers for one behavioural category.

Scatter diagram showing inter-rater reliability for Child 1 (correlation = +.843)

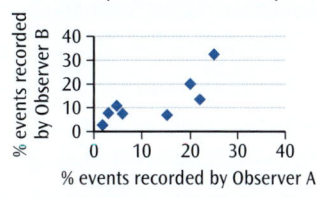

Scatter diagram showing inter-rater reliability for Child 2 (correlation = +.954)

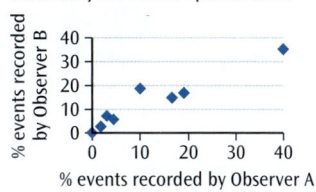

Coding system used by observers in the nursery unit.

	No social participation
1	Occupied alone participation
2	Hanging around alone
3	Alone – onlooker
4	Alone – unclear
	Solid participation
5	Parallel behaviour 1
6	Parallel behaviour 2
7	Loosely associated but interactive
8	Role play – identifiable
9	Social participation unclear
	Not identifiable
10	Child not in view, generally unclear

Examples of observational studies

Study A An example of a naturalistic, non-participant, overt observation

One study observed boys and girls aged 3–5 years during their free-play periods at nursery school. The researchers classified activities as male, female or neutral and recorded whether playmates responded to each other positively (e.g. praise and imitation) or negatively (e.g. criticism and stopping play). The researchers found that children behaved positively towards peers if they showed sex-appropriate play and were quick to criticise sex-inappropriate play (Lamb and Roopnarine 1979).

Study B An example of a controlled, non-participant, covert observation

The same research as described above could be conducted by controlling some of the variables. For example, particular toys may be made available to see how participants respond to them (as in Bandura *et al.*'s study of aggression, page 140). The researchers might have set up a special playroom in their laboratory with certain types of toys available (male, female and neutral). They could have observed the children through a one-way mirror so the children would be unaware of being observed.

Study C An example of a naturalistic, participant, covert observation

In the 1950s the social psychologist Leon Festinger read a newspaper report about a religious cult that claimed to have received messages from outer space predicting a great flood would lead to the end of the world on a certain date. The cult members were going to be rescued by a flying saucer so they all gathered with their leader, Mrs Keech. In order to observe how the followers would respond, Festinger and some colleagues posed as cult followers and were present on the expected eve of destruction. When it was apparent that there would be no flood, the group initially became disheartened but Mrs Keech announced that she had received a new message from the aliens saying that the group's efforts had saved the day (Festinger *et al.* 1956).

Try this

Inter-rater reliability

The table below shows the observations from two observers who were watching while one student spoke for five minutes. The observers used event sampling.

Calculate a correlation coefficient for this data using the Excel method (see page 199).

What can you conclude about the inter-rater reliability? (+.80 is usually considered to be acceptable for high inter-rater reliability.)

Table showing observations of a student speaking to class.

Behaviour	Observer 1	Observer 2
Says 'um' or similar	20	15
Puts hand on face	2	4
Scratches head	3	3
Giggles	7	1
Changes feet	5	3
Stutters	11	7
Licks lips	2	3
Puts hand on hip	2	1

Check it

1. At the top of the page there are two graphs showing the observations of two children made by two observers. Do you think that the graphs indicate an acceptable level of inter-rater reliability? Explain your answer. (3)

2. In the column above three studies are described. For each study give **one** advantage and **one** disadvantage of the observational design in this study. (12)

3. Jed is going to observe aggression amongst skateboarders. He has two possible ideas: (i) to conduct a naturalistic, covert, participant observation or (ii) to conduct a naturalistic, overt, non-participant observation.
   (a) Describe how Jed would conduct the study using method (i) and using method (ii). (4)
   (b) Explain **one** advantage of method (i) and **one** advantage of method (ii). (4)

Use of animals in laboratory experiments

The specification says...
4.2.2 Animal research
- The use of animals in laboratory experiments where results can be related to humans.
- Ethical issues regarding the use of animals in laboratory experiments, including Scientific Procedures Act (1986) and Home Office Regulations.

Many people have strong views about the use of animals in laboratory experiments. There are two important points to bear in mind when thinking about such research:

1. We are only concerned with the use of animals in psychological research in laboratories. We do not need to consider, for example, the ethics of testing cosmetics on animals nor naturalistic observations of animals in the wild.
2. It is important to put images of cuddly kittens out of mind. Our arguments must be objective.

In a nutshell

Arguments for and against the use of animals in laboratory experiments.

+ Behaviourists argue that conditioning processes (discussed in chapter 4) are the same in all animals. This means we can conduct experiments with animals and *generalise* the results to human behaviour.

+ It is preferable to use animals because there are fewer ethical issues – *informed consent* is not required and *psychological/physical harm* is more acceptable. It would simply not be possible to keep humans in a laboratory for lengthy research studies (though there have been one or two examples of this, such as studies of sensory deprivation).

+ More complex behaviours can be studied in mammals and generalised to humans, for example studying aggression over successive generations, because their brains are similar to human brains. Again there are fewer ethical issues and, on the plus side, animals have shorter breeding cycles and this means we can study effects over generations more easily. We can also test the effects of drugs on mammals (see below).

− It may not be justifiable to generalise from animals to humans, especially when complex behaviours, such as addiction, are being studied. In some cases, such as conditioned reflexes, the basic process in lower animals and humans are the same. When more complex behaviours are studied it may not even be appropriate to generalise from apes to humans as human behaviour is more controlled by higher cognitive thinking.

− Animal experimentation may be unethical. Pain and suffering are unavoidable in most animal experiments. This ranges from being caged in a laboratory to surgery and death. It can be argued that, in many cases the benefits do not outweigh the harm caused, for example in Harlow's experiments on attachment on the right. In other cases the benefits may outweigh the harm, for example testing antidepressant medications that alleviate the suffering of millions of people with depression worldwide.

− Guidelines that regulate the use of animals in research may not be effective. Joan Dunayer (2002) argues that animal legislation simply sets standards for the imprisonment, enslavement, hurting and killing of animals. Carol Kilkenny *et al.* (2009) reviewed animal studies (not all psychological ones) and reported that over half of them had failed to accurately report how many animals were used and many studies were poorly designed. This suggests that regulations have not had the desired effect.

Examples

Experiments on conditioning
Both Pavlov and Skinner used animals in their experiments to demonstrate conditioning (see pages 132 and 134). This research is experimental because there are before and after conditions.

In Pavlov's research dogs were used. A small operation was performed so he could collect saliva. This intervention caused little harm or distress but he subsequently did conduct experiments on involuntary reactions to stress and pain.

Skinner used rats and pigeons in his experiments on operant conditioning. Some operant chambers also contained electrified floors which could be used to punish behaviour.

Experiments on attachment
Harry Harlow (1959) placed infant rhesus monkeys in a cage with two wire mothers – one with a feeding bottle and one wrapped in soft cloth. The monkeys spent most time with the cloth-covered mother demonstrating the importance of contact comfort.

So where's the harm? The monkeys developed into emotionally maladjusted adults despite their contact comfort – they couldn't socialise with other monkeys and rejected their own infants (psychological harm). However, the research had an important influence on our understanding of infant emotional development.

Experiments on recreational drugs
Animals are used in experiments on addiction (see page 100). In one study, Bruce Alexander *et al.* (1978) showed that morphine addiction in rats was not just due to the drug but also related to the social environment. Prior to Alexander's study rats were placed in Skinner boxes and hooked up to intravenous drugs. They could choose whether or not to press a lever to self-administer drugs and did so increasingly often. This led to the conclusion that drugs were irresistibly addictive.

Alexander created a 'rat park' where about 20 rats lived together and had access to water or a morphine solution. He found that rats in solitary confinement showed a preference for morphine but, once placed with others, sought the water. This showed that social environments have a profound effect on addiction.

Experiments on sensory deprivation
Colin Blakemore and Grahame Cooper (1970) demonstrated how the visual system develops by using kittens reared in a visually-restricted environment. One kitten spent its waking hours in a cylinder with only vertical stripes while the other kitten had only horizontal stripes. Aged five months they were moved to an ordinary environment but showed no response to lines of the opposite orientation. This meant, for example, that the vertically-deprived kitten could not see a black rod held vertically.

The kittens' visual cortex was tested by anaesthetising and paralysing them so that individual cells could be assessed for responsiveness. This showed that the brain cells for the deprived orientation had ceased to exist.

This research had benefits for treating children with visual problems. Children who are born with squint eyesight (eyes turn in different directions) can have this corrected with surgery but if the surgery is left too late the brain is permanently damaged by the abnormal input which is explained by Blakemore and Cooper's research.

Pie chart showing experimental procedures by species (2016)
- Other 6% (114,000)
- Specially protected species 1% (18,000)
- Birds 7% (150,000)
- Rats 12% (239,000)
- Fish 14% (287,000)
- Mice 60% (1.22 million)

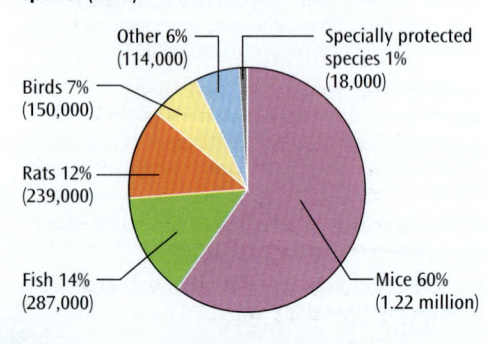

The facts
British law requires that any new drug (e.g. antidepressants) must be tested on at least two different species of live mammal. This means, if we wish to have these treatments available, we must accept the need for such research.

The graph on the left shows that 'specially protected species' such as mammals other than rats and mice actually account for a very small amount of the total research. Data is not kept separately for psychological research so the data shown here is for all scientific research.

Ethical issues regarding the use of animals in laboratory experiments

Ethical controls

Scientific Procedures Act (1986) and Home Office Regulations in the UK requires that animal research only takes place at licensed laboratories with licensed researchers on licensed projects.

- *Protected animals* The act relates only to vertebrate animals and only to those more than halfway through their gestation period. One invertebrate class (cephalopods, e.g. octopus) was added in 1993.

- *Replacement, reduction and refinement* (the 3Rs) Where possible animals should be *replaced* with suitable alternatives. If this is not possible, then the *number* of protected animals used must be reduced to a minimum. Finally, methods used in breeding, accommodation and care of protected animals must be *refined* to reduce any possible pain, suffering, distress or lasting harm to those animals.

BPS guidelines The British Psychological Society (BPS) produce their own guidelines about what is acceptable, such as:

- Confinement, restraint, stress and harm – should be minimised to reduce trauma to the animal.
- Different species should be considered to minimise pain and discomfort.
- Optimise research design to minimise numbers of animals used.
- Caging and social environment should be appropriate to the needs of the species to avoid distress caused by overcrowding or isolation.
- Deprivation (of food and water) should be considered in the light of the needs of the species and the individual.

Other controls

A different approach is to develop principles which can guide decisions about the use of animals, such as Patrick Bateson's decision cube (see below).

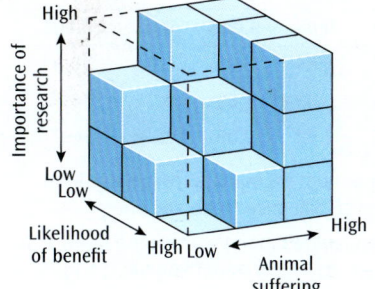

Ethical arguments

The main ethical issue is about pain and distress experienced by laboratory animals. This is considered below, followed by two important arguments – speciesism and the rights of animals.

1. Pain and distress Do animals experience pain in the same way that humans do? One study (Sneddon *et al.* 2003) injected rainbow trout with bee venom and found that the fish started rocking from side to side, indicating distress and pain.

However, just responding to noxious stimuli may not mean animals *feel* pain, i.e. have self-awareness.

Self-awareness may be the key question. Do animals have self-awareness and feelings, i.e. are they *sentient* beings? They do form lasting relationships and they do demonstrate psychological capacities. In addition the Treaty of Lisbon (2009) declared that all animals are sentient.

We might also remember that some human beings (e.g. those with brain damage) lack sentience. This suggests that even if we think animals lack sentience this does not provide moral justification for the use of animals.

2. Speciesism Peter Singer (1990) argues that discrimination on the basis of membership of a species (speciesism) is no different from racial or gender discrimination (racism or sexism).

However, Jeffrey Gray (1991) argues that we have a special duty of care to humans, and therefore speciesism is not equivalent to, for example, racism.

Gray asks, 'If you see two creatures fighting and you have a gun, who would you shoot if (1) it was your son and a stranger, (2) both are strangers, (3) it was your son and a lion, (4) it was a stranger and a lion?' He predicted that most people would save the humans rather than the lion.

Singer's response is that there is a difference between questions about life and questions about inflicting pain. He also points out that human behaviour is not always determined by principles of natural selection (the duty of care to your own species). For example, we can and do overcome our natural instincts of aggression in some situations.

Patrick Bateson (1986) suggested that decisions about the rights and wrongs of animal research could be resolved by considering costs versus benefits. He proposed three main criteria:

- The degree of animal suffering.
- The quality/importance of the research.
- The likelihood of benefit.

Mirror test

When an animal looks in a mirror do they see a reflection of themselves or do they think what they see is another animal? The 'mirror test' involves placing a red mark on an animal. If an animal is self-aware they'll turn and adjust their body to get a better view and touch the coloured spot or try to remove it. This proves that the animal understands the reflection is its own.

Using this test it has been shown that humans first show self-awareness around the age of two. Self-recognition/self-awareness has also been observed using this test in a number of animals including apes (orangutans, chimpanzees, gorillas), monkeys (macaques), dolphins, whales and possibly some birds (magpies, parrots, pigeons).

3. Rights of animals Singer's view is a *utilitarian* one, i.e. whatever produces the greater good for the greater number of individuals is ethically acceptable. This means that if animal research can alleviate pain and suffering, it is justifiable.

Tom Regan (1984), on the other hand, argues that there are no circumstances under which animal research is acceptable (an *absolutist* position). Regan claims that animals have a right to be treated with respect and should never be used in research.

The 'animal rights' argument can be challenged by examining the concept of *rights* – having rights is dependent on having responsibilities in society, i.e. as citizens we all have responsibilities. It can therefore be said that as animals do not have any responsibilities, they do not have any rights.

It may be better to distinguish between rights and obligations. Obligations are owed by humans to animals (e.g. acting humanely, being aware of animals' sentience).

Check it

1. Eira is planning an experiment in which animals respond to light by moving away. She can use large insects (locusts) or mice. She needs 100 animals for her study but only has a small lab to keep them in.
   - (a) Choose **one** species and use the Home Office Regulations to explain **two** reasons for making this choice. (4)
   - (b) Explain **one** ethical decision that Eira would need to make about the caging and environment of the species that you have chosen. (2)
   - (c) Eira's study ultimately causes little pain or distress to the animals. Explain the impact of this on the **two** other factors in Bateson's decision cube. (2)
2. Assess the use of animals in studies in biological psychology. (8)

Inferential statistics: Test of association

Chapter 5 Research methods

The specification says...
4.2.3 Analysis of data
- With regard to inferential statistics: levels of measurement (see page 201); reasons for choosing a chi-squared test; comparing observed and critical values to judge significance; the chi-squared test.

You have learned about three inferential tests so far and this is the fourth and final one you have to study.

Chi-squared is an unusual test for two reasons: it deals with *nominal data* and can be used for data looking at either a difference or an association.

In a nutshell

| Chi-squared | Test of difference or association. | Frequency, nominal data. | Independent items. | Test statistic is χ^2 pronounced 'ki' (to rhyme with sky). |

Chi-squared

STEP 1: State the alternate hypothesis

There is an association between age (over and under 40) and intelligence (high or low score on an IQ test) OR There is a difference in the intelligence test scores of people under the age of 40 years and those over the age of 40.

Both are two-tailed (non-directional) hypotheses.

STEP 2: Place frequency data in a contingency table

Below is a 2 × 2 contingency table which means two rows (*r*) and two columns (*c*). The number of people in each cell is recorded and then totals for *r* and *c* calculated.

	Young (under 40)	Old (over 40)	Totals
High IQ	5 (cell **A**)	12 (cell **B**)	17
Low IQ	10 (cell **C**)	9 (cell **D**)	19
Totals	15	21	36

This is a 2 × 2 contingency table but you can have any number of rows and columns if you have other variables. A 3 × 2 contingency table has 3 rows and 2 columns – the number of rows is stated first.

For a 3 × 2 table, *df* = 2 (see formula at STEP 4) below.

STEP 3: Find observed (calculated) value of χ^2

The observed value of chi-squared is calculated using the formula

$$\chi^2 = \Sigma \frac{(o-e)^2}{e}$$

This may look complicated but it isn't if you follow the steps in the table below.

	row total X column total / overall total = expected frequency (*e*)	Subtract expected frequency (*e*) from observed frequency (*o*) (*o* – *e*)	Square previous value (*o* – *e*)²	Divide previous value by expected frequency (*o* – *e*)² / *e*
Cell A	17 * 15 / 36 = 7.08	7.08 – 5 = 2.08	4.3264	0.6111
Cell B	17 * 21 / 36 = 9.92	9.92 – 12 = –2.08	4.3264	0.4361
Cell C	19 * 15 / 36 = 7.92	7.92 – 10 = –2.08	4.3264	0.5463
Cell D	19 * 21 / 36 = 11.08	11.08 – 9 = 2.08	4.3264	0.3905

$\Sigma(o-e)^2 / e$ (means add up all the values in the final column of $(o-e)^2 / e$) = 1.984

STEP 4: Find critical value of χ^2

You need to know:
- Level of significance: 5% (0.05)
- Kind of hypothesis: Two-tailed
- *df* (degrees of freedom) = (*r* – 1)(*c* – 1) = 1

In the critical values table on the right locate the intersection of the column for two-tailed test at 5% and the row that begins with our *df* value.

The critical value of χ^2 = 3.84

STEP 5: State the conclusion

The observed (calculated) value of chi-squared (1.984) is less than the critical value (3.84) shown in the table for *df* = 1 for a 5% level of significance and a two-tailed test.

This means there is no significant difference between people below and above the age of 40 in their IQ test scores.

Frequency data

You can only use chi-squared with *frequency data*. This means you count how many people belong to each group.

For example, imagine we wish to find out whether age is associated with intelligence. We divide our group of participants into people over the age of 40 and under the age of 40. We divide them again into people who scored high on an intelligence test and people who scored low.

Note that intelligence test data is classified as *ordinal* but here we are counting how many got high or low scores and therefore the data is frequency and *nominal* (it is in categories).

Independent data

You can also only use chi-squared with independent data. Below is a 2 × 2 *contingency table* which has four cells:

(cell **A**)	(cell **B**)
(cell **C**)	(cell **D**)

The data in each cell must be independent – imagine having to physically place each person in one of the four squares of the contingency table. Each person is only allowed to stand in one square.

Note that the observed frequency (*o*) in the formula is different from the observed value of the statistic!

Critical values for chi-squared distribution

	Level of significance for a one-tailed test					
	0.10	0.05	0.025	0.01	0.005	0.0005
	Level of significance for a two-tailed test					
df	0.20	0.10	0.05	0.025	0.01	0.001
1	1.64	2.71	3.84	5.02	6.64	10.83
2	3.22	4.61	5.99	7.38	9.21	13.82
3	4.64	6.25	7.82	9.35	11.35	16.27

The calculated value must be equal to or greater than the critical value for significance to be shown.

Note that the table provided in the exam goes up to a *df* value of 70 which would mean something like 11 rows and 8 columns in the contingency table (unlikely!).

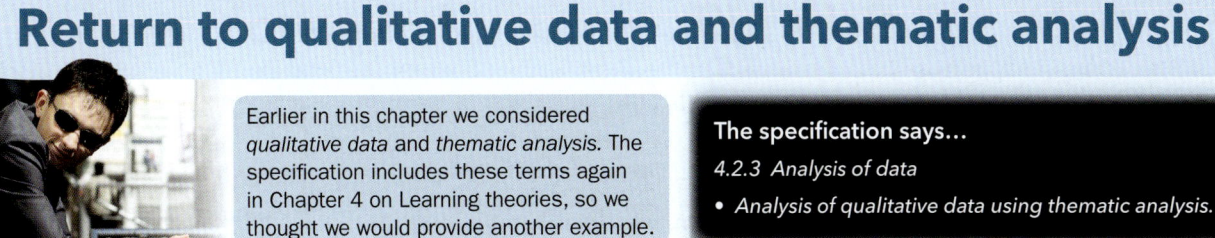

Return to qualitative data and thematic analysis

Earlier in this chapter we considered *qualitative data* and *thematic analysis*. The specification includes these terms again in Chapter 4 on Learning theories, so we thought we would provide another example.

The specification says...
4.2.3 Analysis of data
- Analysis of qualitative data using thematic analysis.

Men managing their body image

Aim
Hannah Frith and Kate Gleeson (2004) considered how changing cultural values might mean that men are feeling more dissatisfied with their appearance.

Procedure
A total of 75 men aged between 17 and 75 took part. This was initially an *opportunity sample* but members of the first sample then recruited further participants (called *snowball sampling*).

Questionnaire Each participant was asked to write answers to the following four questions on a questionnaire entitled 'Clothing and body questionnaire':

1. How much does the way you feel about your body influence the kinds of clothing you buy or wear?
2. Do you dress in a way that hides aspects of your body?
3. Do you dress in a way that emphasises aspects of your body?
4. Is there anything else you think we should know, or are there any questions we should have asked but didn't?

Respondents were instructed to answer questions fully, giving specific examples and spending some time thinking about their answers before they wrote.

Analysis A thematic analysis was conducted by:

1. Reading all the answers carefully to identify meaningful units of text relevant to the research topic.
2. Units of text dealing with the same issue were grouped together in categories and given provisional definitions. The same unit of text could be included in more than one category.
3. The data was systematically reviewed to ensure that there was a name, definition and exhaustive set of data to support each category identified.

86.6% of the data was allocated to at least one category.

The coherence and replicability of the themes (i.e. likelihood that the same set of data would be reproduced) were established by a second researcher who recoded the first question (61.5% of the data) with a high level of inter-rater reliability (correlation = +.9089, SD = 0.1382). Levels of agreement for individual categories were also calculated.

Results and conclusions
Fifty categories were identified and grouped into four key themes and one miscellaneous, as shown in the table on the left.

The authors concluded that the data shows the 'pervasive and mundane role of clothing in men's self-surveillance and self-presentation and the range and complexity of the processes involved in clothing the body.'

Theme	Categories
Men are very practical in choosing their clothes.	Comfort is a priority. Clothes must fit well. Clothes must be functional. Cost of clothes is important. Physical size imposes limitations. Clothes are used to communicate about roles.
Real men shouldn't care about how they look.	Body shape does matter. We shouldn't care too much about appearance. The shape of my body is irrelevant. I want to look good. I want clothes that flatter the body. I respond to fashion. I am not a fashion victim. I don't want to appear vain. Using clothes to look attractive is not an issue for men. My personal style is important. I want to look tidy. Clothes affect people's judgements. I want my clothes to reflect my images.
Clothes are used to conceal or reveal.	Clothing is used to hide the body. Men have nothing to hide. I have mixed feelings about displaying the body. I want to display the body. I use clothes to emphasise particular features of the body. Clothing choices are linked to confidence. Age affects clothing choice. Clothing is used to reflect a desire to blend in. Clothing can reflect shyness.
Clothes are used to fit a cultural ideal.	Clothing reflects acceptance of the body. I want to appear taller. I want to look muscular. I want to appear slim. I am concerned with not appearing too thin. I want to look masculine. I want to appear heterosexual. Continuity in appearance is valued. I like labels. I hate labels. I use smaller clothes to motivate weight loss. I want to be attractive to women. Clothing can reflect not being smart. There is pressure from others about appearance.
Miscellaneous	Overlapping and specificity of the questions. Shoes and accessories. Style and colour. Cross-dressing. Cultural aspects of clothing. Is it the body or the clothes that make the difference? Male image as holistic.

Check it

1. Put the following data into a 2 × 2 contingency table. [3]
   A psychologist investigated whether first-born children were more likely to be creative or logical thinkers and found:
   - 20 out of the 50 artists were first-born.
   - 35 out of 65 lawyers were first-born.

2. A group of students plan their own qualitative research on the experience of owning pets.
   (a) Write **three** questions they might use in a questionnaire. [3]
   (b) Describe how they could collect their data. Include details of the target population, sampling technique, instructions to participants and ethical issues that should be mentioned. [6]
   (c) Outline how the students would analyse their results. [4]

Scientific status of psychology

Chapter 5 — Research methods

The specification says...

4.2.4 Scientific status of psychology, including:
- Replicability, reliability, validity (internal, predictive and ecological), reductionism, falsification, empiricism, hypothesis testing, and use of controls.

[AL Topic 9 includes: credibility.]

This chapter has been about the research methods and techniques that psychologists (and scientists generally) use to gather data. These methods and techniques aim to make the subject of psychology scientific.

In a nutshell

Replicability	If a finding from a research study is true (*valid*) then it should be possible to obtain the same finding if the study is repeated. Repeating a study confirms the 'trueness' of the original finding.
Reliability	Ensuring that all procedures are the same for every participant so that their performances are comparable.
Validity (internal, predictive, ecological)	*Internal validity* concerns the extent to which a research study is testing what was intended. If there are confounding variables then the findings may be due to these rather than the independent variable. *Predictive validity* concerns the extent to which a test actually is related to the behaviour you want to measure, and therefore is able to forecast performance on some other measure. *Ecological validity* concerns whether the findings of a study can be generalised beyond the research setting to other people and situations.
Reductionism	Experimental research requires identifying individual variables that may contribute to a complex behaviour – the *independent* and *dependent variable*.
Falsification	The attempt to prove something wrong. This involves the use of the null hypothesis which we seek to disprove within set bounds of certainty.
Empiricism	The view that knowledge can only come through direct observation or experiment rather than by reasoned argument or beliefs.
Hypothesis testing	A hypothesis is a statement of what a researcher believes to be true. In order to test such a statement, it must be clearly operationalised.
Use of controls	Refers to the extent to which any variable is held constant or regulated by a researcher.
Credibility	Believability. In order to be believable something must also be valid – and all the other features expected in scientific research (replicable, reliable, falsifiable as well as objective and generalisable).

Scientific status of psychology

Psychology is often defined as the 'science of behaviour and experience'. Science aims to discover natural laws in order to predict and control the world (e.g. build dams, create vaccines, treat schizophrenia).

The use of a scientific approach in psychology is important because people might claim, for example, that men are more aggressive than women or that a certain drug cures depression – but people quite rightly demand evidence to support such claims. The term 'science' refers to knowledge based on systematic and objective methods of data collection:

Science is empirical People can make claims about the truth of a theory or the benefits of a treatment but the only way we know such things to be true is through empirical evidence. It is not enough to collect some anecdotal support for a set of beliefs. A systematic and objective method must be used.

Hypotheses must be falsifiable A belief that cannot be falsified can never be tested.

Science is controlled Any confounding or extraneous variables reduce internal validity so must be controlled to obtain generalisable findings (high ecological validity).

Science permits replication Because the methods used are objective and reliable, they can be repeated. By repeating a study and getting the same results we can be more confident of the validity of the conclusions. In psychology, replications often involve small changes to the procedures or participants to see if we get the same results, thus confirming the original explanation.

Science is reductionist The ultimate aim is to demonstrate causal relationships and the ideal way to discover such relationships is in lab experiments where an independent variable can be manipulated to observe its causal effect on a dependent variable. This involves the reduction of complex behaviours to individual variables.

Falsification

Until the 1930s scientists believed that their task was to find examples that would confirm their theories. Karl Popper, a philosopher of science, brought about a revolution in the way scientists thought about proof (confirming their theories). He pointed out, 'No matter how many instances of white swans we may have observed, this does not justify the conclusion that all swans are white' (Popper 1934).

No number of sightings of white swans can prove the hypothesis that all swans are white, whereas the sighting of just one black swan will disprove it. This proposition led to the realisation that the only way to prove a theory correct was actually to seek disproof (falsification) – i.e. look for those black swans.

Therefore, we start research with a null hypothesis: 'Not all swans in the world are white, i.e. there are black swans.' We then go looking for swans and record many sightings but if we see no black swans this leads us to be reasonably certain (we can never be absolutely certain) that the null hypothesis is false.

We therefore can reject the null hypothesis (with reasonable certainty). If the null hypothesis isn't true this means we can accept the alternate hypothesis ('All swans are white') with reasonable certainty.

This is, in the present state of knowledge, the best approximation to the truth.

The scientific method

The process used to gain scientific knowledge is called the *scientific method*.

The human mind does not naturally think in an objective way. We are prone to all sorts of biases in the way we think about the world. If we want to discover 'truths' about the world we need a process to follow to ensure that what we are 'seeing' is free from bias.

For example, you may believe that women are more helpful than men. This is called 'armchair psychology'. We do it all the time.

In order to test the truth of such observations a scientist follows a series of well-defined steps, called the scientific method.

1. **Make observations**

   Women are more helpful than men.

2. **Produce an explanation or theory**

   Women being more helpful might be due to differences in hormones. The female hormone oestrogen may make people more willing to help strangers.

3. **Produce a testable hypothesis**

   Men who are given a dose of oestrogen are more prepared to help a confederate pick up some dropped objects than men not given the hormone.

4. **Design a well-controlled study to test the hypothesis**

   This could be an experiment – but observation, self-report and correlation are all methods that can be objective and controlled.

   Design: Participants are recruited for a study on the effect of hormones. Some men are given oestrogen and some are given a placebo and they all do a memory test.

   After they leave the laboratory they are observed as they pass another man who has just dropped a pile of books.

5. **Draw conclusions, publish research, receive positive criticisms from peers** (see peer review on page 220)

   Go back to step 2 – develop new explanations/hypotheses. The scientific method is an iterative process – we repeat it over and over again, to get closer to what is 'true'.

An empirical test

The picture above is of a burger from a well-known fast-food outlet. Or at least this is what you are led to expect you will get, but what about in reality? You may think you know something but unless you test this empirically you cannot know if it is true.

Where is the evidence?

My friend went into a restaurant that used the picture above to advertise its burgers. On the right is a picture that represents the *empirical* evidence of what the burger was really like.

'Empirical' refers to information gained through direct experience. Science uses empirical methods to separate unfounded beliefs from real truths.

[Thanks to Professor Sergio della Sala for this example of empiricism.]

Is psychology a science?

Psychology is a science insofar as it seeks to put into practice all the principles outlined on the facing page. However, psychology struggles to maintain objectivity and internal validity. For example, human participants respond readily to demand characteristics which reduces the validity of many studies. However, Werner Heisenberg (1927) argued that it is not even possible to measure a subatomic particle without altering its 'behaviour' in doing the measurement (called the *uncertainty principle*). Thus validity and objectivity are problematic for all sciences.

Furthermore complex human behaviours may simply not be possible to study using the reductionist methods of science and require more holistic qualitative approaches. Though such methods also seek to be systematic and objective, i.e. scientific.

Finally, there is the question of whether simply using the scientific method turns psychology into a science. Jonathan Miller (1983) suggests that psychologists who attempt to be scientists are doing no more than 'dressing up'. They may take on the tools of sciences such as quantified measurements and statistical analysis, but the essence of science is missing.

Check it

1. Which feature of science refers to the importance of being able to refute a psychologist's claim? [1]
2. What method can be used to help make decisions about scientific research? [1]
3. How do psychologists standardise their research? [2]
4. Explain how an independent variable can be used to demonstrate a cause-and-effect relationship. [2]
5. Name a method used by psychologists to demonstrate the reliability of their findings. [1]
6. Select **one** study you are familiar with and name two variables that would be controlled. Explain your answer. [4]
7. What term is used to describe measurements that do not lead to bias? [1]
8. Use **one** of the classic/contemporary studies and find as many examples as you can in the study of each of the nine concepts defined on the facing page. [5]

Mathematical skills

Are you someone who feels your muscles tense up at the mere mention of the word *mathematics*? Or do you actually enjoy the challenge?

Either way maths skills are part of your psychology exam and it isn't as bad as it sounds. If you look at the list of what is included as 'maths skills' (table on right) you will see that you have actually covered many of these maths skills already.

It's time to feel the fear and do it anyway.

Live a little – enjoy some maths challenges. Here is a selection of websites to practise your skills:

tinyurl.com/ycf3erea
tinyurl.com/y973m3yz
tinyurl.com/ycczyqoq
tinyurl.com/yc9xfjsg

The specification says…

Students are required to apply the mathematical skills listed in Appendix 3 to relevant psychological contexts. Appendix 3 is listed below and can be found in the A level Edexcel specification (pages 67–69). The same table appears in all Psychology specifications.

Category	Concepts	Page
Arithmetic and numerical computation	Recognise and use expressions in decimal and standard form.	Facing page
	Use ratios, fractions and percentages.	
	Estimate results.	
Handling data	Use an appropriate number of significant figures.	
	Find arithmetic means.	172
	Construct and interpret frequency tables and diagrams, bar charts and histograms.	173 and 195
	Understand simple probability.	190
	Understand the principles of sampling as applied to scientific data.	170
	Understand the terms mean, median and mode.	172
	Use a scatter diagram to identify a correlation between two variables.	199
	Use a statistical (inferential) test.	191, 192, 200 and 212
	Make order of magnitude calculations.	Facing page
	Distinguish between levels of measurement.	201
	Know the characteristics of normal and skewed distributions.	195
	Select an appropriate statistical test.	191, 192, 200 and 212
	Use statistical tables to determine significance.	
	Understand measures of dispersion, including standard deviation and range.	172
	Understand the differences between qualitative and quantitative data.	174
	Understand the difference between primary and secondary data.	218
Algebra	Understand and use the symbols: =, <, <<, >>, >, ∝, ~	Below
	Substitute numerical values into algebraic equations using appropriate units for physical quantities.	193, 200 and 212
	Solve simple algebraic equations.	193
Graphs	Translate information between graphical, numerical and algebraic forms.	192 and 199
	Plot two variables from experimental or other data.	192 and 199

In a nutshell

Decimals, fractions, percentages and ratios	Methods used to express numbers that are a part of a whole.						
Order of magnitude	Working out approximately how much larger one number is than another.						
Significant figures (sf)	The number of interesting or important digits. Zeros are just place holders.						
Standard form	Expressing a number mainly in terms of its size. A method to write very small or very large numbers, e.g. 7×10^{-6} or 5×10^5						
Symbols	=	<	<<	>>	>	∝	~
	Equals	Less than	Much less than	Much greater than	Greater than	Proportional to	Approximately equal

Decimals

These numbers all contain decimals: 1.34, 0.45809, 131.416 (the number of decimal places is 2, 5 and 3 respectively).

The digits to the left of the decimal point are whole numbers: 1s, 10s, 100s and so on. The digits to the right of the decimal point are fractions out of 10, 100, 1000 and so on.

0.5 means 5 out of 10, 0.05 means 5 out of 100.

Decimal places

If you are calculating an inferential test statistic you may end up with a number such as 2.38592. There is no need for all the digits after the decimal point, the answer 2.38 would be sufficient precision.

Therefore, we say, 'Give your answer to 2 decimal places', which means only report two digits to the right of the decimal point.

However, in the example above 2.38 would be incorrect – because when you remove the remaining digits you have to decide whether you need to round up. The rule is if the remaining digits are greater than 5 round up, otherwise just remove the remaining digits. Therefore, in our example of 2.38592, you should round the answer up to 2.39

Consider the following example:

- 2.39592
- This number, to 2 decimal places, is 2.40

Why? Because rounding 2.39 up means we get 2.4 but we have to show two decimal places.

Fractions

0.5 can be expressed as a fraction = 5/10 (because one decimal place is one tenth, two decimals places is one hundredth and so on).

Fractions can be reduced if there is a number that divides evenly into the top (numerator) and bottom (denominator). The number 5 divides into both 5 and 10 reducing our fraction to 1/2.

If we want to convert a fraction to a decimal then we divide the numerator by the denominator, often best done with a calculator. For example, 5/39 = 5 divided by 39 = 0.12820513

Percentages

Percentages are another way to express a fraction because 'per cent' means 'out of 100'.

- So 65% means 65 out of 100 or 65/100
- We can reduce this fraction by dividing the top and bottom by 5 = 13/20

Percentages can be expressed as a decimal quite easily because 65 out of 100 is clearly 0.65.

To work out the percentage of another quantity, multiply the quantity by the percentage and divide by 100. For example, 65% of 20 is 20 × 65 (= 1300) and then divide by 100 = 13

Ratios

Ratios are written with a colon, such as 2:5 or 3:10

Such ratios would be read as 'a ratio of two to five' or 'a ratio of three to ten'.

Ratios can be part-to-part, where 3:5 means that altogether the whole is split into 8 parts and, for example, one person gets 3 parts and the other person gets 5.

Ratios may alternatively be part-to-whole, where 3:5 means, for example, one person gets 3 parts out of a total of 5.

Reduce ratios following the same steps as used with fractions. A ratio of 6:10 could be reduced to 3:5 by dividing both numbers by 2.

Exam advice
It is important to keep to the order of the parts given, e.g. if the question asks about the ratio of men to women, don't answer with the ratio of women to men.

Make estimations from data collected

When making calculations it is helpful to estimate the answer, for example estimating 428 × 6529

We do this by working out an approximate value for each number: 428 can be rounded down to 400 and 6529 rounded up to 7000 (closer to 7000 than 6000). 4 × 7 = 28 and we add 5 zeros = 2,800,000

Order of magnitude

Making order of magnitude calculations means making an approximate comparison of one number with another, larger number. For example, comparing 327 with 40,262,030. We first work out an approximate value for each number: 400 and 40,000,000. The second number has 5 more zeros and is therefore 100,000 times bigger.

Standard form

This method is a way of simplifying very small or very large numbers.

The form used is: [number between 1 and 10] × [10 to the power of x] where x is the number of zeros. For example:

- 0.00000682456 is first rounded up if required, so we just have one digit besides the zeros: 0.000007
- The decimal point must be moved so it is immediately to the right of the 7, i.e. moves 6 places to right (negative).
- So the standard form is 7×10^{-6} (or you can include decimal places and use 6.8×10^{-6}).

If our original number was 56,732,127 we could round this to 57,000,000. The number part will be 5.7 (it must be a number between 1 and 10). To get 5.7 we have moved the decimal point 7 places to the left (positive) and so the standard form is 5.7×10^7 (or it could be 5.67×10^7).

Significant figures (sf)

Another way to comprehend a number is remove some of the digits.

For example, 0.00000682456 is easier to comprehend if we write 0.0000068. This is two significant figures, i.e. the number of digits aside from the zeros. 0.00000682 would be three significant figures and 0.000007 would be one significant figure (we rounded up when we dropped the 8).

The number 56,732,127 to two significant figures is 57,000,000 (rounded up).

Check it

1. Express the following decimals as fractions reduced to their lowest form. (1 mark each)
   (a) 0.175 (b) 0.32 (c) 0.9 (d) 0.79

2. Express the following percentages as fractions reduced to their lowest form. (1 mark each)
   (a) 33.33% (b) 25% (c) 61% (d) 15%

3. Convert the following fractions to percentages. (1 mark each)
   (a) 3/4 (b) 5/6 (c) 17/20 (d) 1/10

4. If we wish to distribute 32 participants to two groups in a ratio 3:5 (part-to-part), how many would be in each part? (2)

5. Estimate the answers for the following. (1 mark each)
   (a) 93 × 1652 (b) 430 divided by 27 (c) 63% of 178,379

6. Make order of magnitude calculations for the following. (1 mark each)
   (a) 452 and 40,345 (b) 15 and 210,320

7. Express the following numbers in standard form. (1 mark each)
   (a) 34,530,000 (b) 6,700 (c) 0.0000561 (d) 0.0091023

8. Convert the following. (1 mark each)
   (a) 43,600 to 2 sf (b) 423 to 1 sf (c) 0.01673 to 2 sf
   (d) 0.032 to 1 sf

9. Convert 8(c) and 8(d) above to 2 decimal places. (1 mark each)

A few final things

The specification says...

In Topic 9 the following further methods are listed:

9.1.1 Types of data: Primary and secondary data.

9.1.8 Additional research methods and techniques: Longitudinal and cross-sectional, cross-cultural and meta-analysis.

As this chapter draws to a close (about time) we pick up a few topics that are included in the full A level specification that are not mentioned in topics 1–4.

You may wonder why this chapter is so long – it is because it underpins the whole of your course. Psychology would be nothing without the methods used to collect data. Without research methods there would be no study of human (and animal) behaviour.

In a nutshell

Primary data		
Information collected by a researcher specifically for the purpose of the current study.	+ Primary data suits the aims of the study. Because the researcher knows the type of data they need for their investigation, they can identify specifically the kind of information required. + Primary data is authentic, as it comes first-hand from the participants themselves. This means the data may be more useful.	− It takes more time and effort to collect primary compared with secondary data. Designing and piloting data collection methods and then collecting data is time-consuming and therefore costly. − A researcher may spend time collecting primary data only to discover that the methods used were flawed. It might have been a better use of time and money to adjust the research aims and use existing data.
Secondary data		
Data used in a research study that was collected previously for another study or a researcher uses government statistics. Basically such data is 'second-hand'.	+ This approach means access to large data sets, for example, records kept by psychiatric hospitals provide information on diagnosis rates in close relatives. + Using secondary data saves time in designing data collection methods and also validating the methods. If someone has carried out a very similar study before, the data is already checked. This means the research involves less time and expense.	− Previously collected secondary data may not quite fit the needs of the current study or may be out-of-date, not quite complete or of poor quality. − Using secondary data may waste valuable time because, if it turns out not to be directly relevant to the aims of the current study, that time could have been better spent designing a primary data investigation.

SECOND HAND

Triangulation

Observational study

Synthesis and evaluation of evidence

Laboratory experiment   Field experiment

In mathematics this term refers to a method of determining the exact location of a point (such as on a map) by taking measurements from various positions. In both quantitative and qualitative research one is not seeking a perfect fit but using multiple and diverse perspectives to provide a fuller picture of a phenomenon.

The multi-method approach

In reality very few studies simply use one method. Many studies reported in this book use the multi-method approach – a combination of all sorts of different techniques and methods to investigate the target behaviour. For example, Milgram (1963) conducted a controlled observation in a lab. But he also extensively interviewed his participants after the study to find out their views on why they did or didn't obey.

In addition our understanding of human behaviour increases by looking at a variety of studies using different techniques. For example, many memory studies are very controlled and use highly artificial tasks (such as the simple word lists used by Baddeley, page 76). We criticise such studies for having low *ecological validity* – but they are part of the process. We need to compare the results with other studies that may be more realistic but less controlled. Jointly the results tell us something about human behaviour. We also might think of everyday experiences to confirm the data. This process is called *triangulation* (also discussed on page 188), whereby the results of many studies (providing quantitative and qualitative data) as well as anecdotal observations are considered and, if they all point in the same direction support the validity of the conclusions.

Primary and secondary data

Most of the studies in your course have involved primary data collection. For example, Milgram (page 32) might have looked at a historical record of obedience in certain situations. However, he had very specific requirements so primary data was the obvious choice.

On the other hand there are other studies, especially correlational ones that partly or wholly use secondary data. For example, research on crime rates uses statistics collected by the government.

Longitudinal and cross-sectional research

The case study of HM (page 197) is an example of longitudinal research. Other examples include a study of TV and aggression where over 500 children were studied aged 6–10 years and 25 years later more than 300 of them were revisited. At Time 1, data was collected about violence watched on TV. At Time 2, aggressive behaviour was again measured. The study found a link between early and later aggression (Huesmann *et al.* 2003).

Cross-sectional research is often used to study the effects of ageing, for example on intelligence. One way to study this would be to test a group of 20-years-olds and then wait 40 years and retest them (a repeated measures design). It is quicker to test a group of 20-year-olds and 60-year-olds (independent groups design). The problem is that as diet and living conditions improve so does intelligence, on average. This means that the older cohort are likely to perform less well not because of the effects of ageing but because of the environment in their early childhood when their brains were developing.

Cross-cultural research

One memorable study looked at mate preferences in people from 33 countries. According to natural selection, all men should prefer to mate with younger women because that is a better guarantee of fertility and successful reproduction. All women should show a preference for a mate who has good financial prospects because that enhances their reproductive success of having someone to look after them during the years of child-rearing. David Buss (1989) found support for this in all cultures – men sought good looks and women sought ambition and industriousness. This suggests that such preferences are innate and related to sexual selection.

Meta-analysis

Peter Ditto *et al.* (page 54) looked at 41 experiments on partisan bias and found that all of them supported the view that right and left wing supporters are equally prone to remembering facts that support rather than challenge their beliefs.

Some meta-analyses report an effect size (see facing page). For example, one study looked at the relationship between serotonin levels and antisocial behaviour in 20 studies and found an overall effect size of −.45 (45%), meaning that low levels of serotonin were related to antisocial behaviour (Moore *et al.* 2002).

Cohort effects – Roman soldiers

The term 'cohort' comes from groups of Roman soldiers. The term is now used for a group of people who share certain common features. A cohort might be one of the year groups in your school or it might refer to people born in certain decades such as Generation Z. Economic and social conditions during childhood affect the attitudes of any group of young people which acts as a confounding variable in longitudinal studies.

Ethnocentrism in psychology

Ethnocentrism leads us to believe that everyone else is like 'us' and we assume that the behaviours observed in our group are the way everyone behaves (or ought to behave).

An analysis of top psychology journals (Arnett 2008) found that 96% of the participants were from Western industrialised countries which actually represent only 12%.

Joseph Henrich et al. (2010) use the acronym WEIRD (Western, educated, industrialised, rich and democratic) to describe the populations studied by psychologists. They noted that not only were the participants from Western, rich, industrialised countries but the participants were mainly students (i.e. educated).

Effect size – weight loss

We use effect sizes in our everyday lives, for example a weight-loss programme may boast that it leads to an average weight loss of 30 pounds. This is the size of the effect.

Longitudinal research Any study that takes place over months and years so that the effects of time (age) can be studied.	+ This enables psychologists to study the effects of age on, for example, intelligence, mental health attitudes and so on. One group of participants are tested at Time 1 and then tested again at Time 2 and maybe a number of other times. + Participant variables are controlled in longitudinal experiments because a repeated measures design is used – the same person is studied over time.	– *Cohort effects* occur because the group (or cohort) of people studied may all be of the same age and share certain experiences, such as children born just before the Second World War having poor diets in infancy due to rationing. This means the findings may not be generalisable because of the unique characteristics of the cohort. – When research takes place over time some participants are no longer available. This is called *attrition*. The issue is that some kinds of people are more likely to drop out than others (e.g. people who have personal problems). This means the remaining sample is biased.
Cross-sectional research Compares behaviours of different cross-sections of the population – people of differing ages, professional groups (teachers, doctors, solicitors, etc).	+ This may be a better way to study the effects of age than a longitudinal study because the data collection can be conducted in a shorter space of time – each participant only needs to be tested once and scores from two groups (younger and older) are compared. + Aside from the effects of age this method is also useful in comparing other groups of people.	– Participant variables are not controlled (see longitudinal research). – Cohort effects may occur because of differences between the two groups studied. See example on facing page under 'Longitudinal and cross-sectional research'.
Cross-cultural research Compares behaviours in different cultures. 'Culture' refers to the different beliefs and norms shared by a particular group of people. Cultural beliefs and norms are learned through interactions with other group members.	+ This technique enables psychologists to investigate the effects of nature versus nurture. If a behaviour is mainly due to innate factors (nurture) then we would expect people from different cultural environments to still show similar behaviours, such as aggressiveness. However, if aggression is significantly moderated by culture (nurture) then this would be indicated by cultural differences. + Psychology has been dominated by data collected in the Western world (mainly America), using white middle-class male college students. Thus our knowledge about human behaviour is actually very biased. Conducting research in different cultures provides contrasting information which seeks to address the current imbalance.	– Until fairly recently most cross-cultural studies have been conducted by Western psychologists. This can be a problem because researchers have expectations about how they anticipate other cultural groups will behave and this may affect their measurements. The use of indigenous (local) researchers can help overcome this. – Furthermore researchers may use tests or procedures that have been developed by Western psychologists, such as IQ tests or scales for assessing depression. The items on such tests may not be valid in another culture, which makes individuals in the other culture appear 'abnormal' or inferior. The term used to describe this is an *imposed etic*.
Meta-analysis The results of several studies that have addressed similar aims are combined. Statistical methods are used to produce an effect size to express overall trends.	+ A meta-analysis is a useful way to increase the validity of conclusions by increasing the size of the sample. + In a meta-analysis the selection of samples included may cover a large range of different cultures, gender, age groups, etc. This makes the results more generalisable. Note that in some research papers a number of studies are reviewed but no effect size is calculated. Such studies are simply called 'reviews' rather than a meta-analysis.	– The decision about which studies to include or exclude may be affected by a selection bias. For example, researchers may select those studies with more positive results. – The studies that comprise the meta-analysis may use rather different methods and therefore it is not appropriate to combine their data. This means that the final effect size is likely to be meaningless.

Check it

1. Molly and Kat are debating how it would be best to investigate whether older people and younger people are equally respectful of authority figures. Molly thinks a longitudinal study would be more effective and Kat believes a cross-sectional study would be better.
   Explain **two** reasons in favour of each girl's idea. You must refer to the context in your answers. [8]

2. Sven discovers differences in aggression between infants in Swedish and British nursery schools.
   Describe **one** conclusion he could draw from this cross-cultural study. [3]

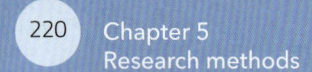

Conventions of published research

The specification says...

9.1.14 *Conventions of published psychological research: abstract, introduction, aims and hypotheses, method, results, discussion; the process of peer review.*

During your studies you may have had the opportunity to read one or more of the classic or contemporary studies in their original form. Such research reports are published in academic journals. We have already looked at some sections of published reports (page 181). These are described again below in the full list of typical content.

We also look at the process of peer review.

In a nutshell

Abstract	A summary of the study covering the aims, hypothesis, method (procedures), results and conclusions (including implications). Usually about 150–200 words.
Introduction	Outlines what a researcher intends to investigate. The introduction is a review of related research (theories and studies), providing the background to the study to be conducted.
Aims and hypotheses	The focus of the research review should lead logically to the aims and hypotheses so the reader is convinced of the reasons for this particular research.
Method	The overall method, e.g. laboratory experiment. This includes information about the: • *Research design* – The particular variation of the method, e.g. repeated measures or covert observation. • *Sample* – How many participants took part, details of age, gender and any other important characteristics plus the sampling technique. • *Materials/apparatus* – Brief details of any psychological tests, questionnaires, equipment or other materials used. • *Procedure* – A step-by-step account of what the researchers did. This must be detailed enough to enable other researchers to replicate the study exactly. Significant ethical issues may be mentioned, as well as how they were dealt with.
Results	This section contains what the researcher(s) found, which includes descriptive statistics (tables and graphs showing frequencies, measures of central tendency and measures of dispersion) and inferential statistics (observed value and significance level).
Discussion	This section may include: • A summary of the results. • A consideration of the relationship to previous research. • Comments on possible methodological problems that arose and improvements suggested. • Implications for psychological theory and possible real-world applications. • Suggestions for future research.
References	A list of other articles, books and/or websites referred to.
Appendices	Contains examples of materials (e.g. questionnaire, standardised instructions, diagrams of research set up), raw data, calculations.

The process of peer review

Peer review is the assessment of scientific work by others who are experts in the same field (i.e. 'peers'). The intention of peer review is to ensure that any research that is conducted and published is of high quality. Peer reviewers are largely unpaid.

The decision about whether to publish a research article depends on:

- The article being seen to make a significant contribution to the body of knowledge in the area.
- The strength of the methodology and results analysis.
- The usefulness of the conclusions that are drawn.
- Whether the study has followed ethical guidelines. Failure to reach publication is a powerful pressure on researchers to follow ethical guidelines (and to explain that they have done so).

The value of peer review

Publication is an important part of the *scientific process* – through publication, other researchers may criticise the methodology so the original researchers may revise their procedures and enhance the validity of their results.

In addition the publication of methodological details allows for replication by other researchers and thus the potential for *falsification*, thus strengthening of conclusions.

This cycle of testing, revising and retesting is critical to scientific progress.

Peer review and the internet

The sheer volume and pace of information available on the internet means that new solutions are needed in order to maintain the quality of information. Scientific information is available in numerous online blogs, online journals and, of course, Wikipedia. To a large extent such sources of information are policed by the 'wisdom of crowds' approach – readers decide whether it is valid or not, and post comments and/or edit entries accordingly. Several online journals (such as ArXiv and Philica) ask readers to rate articles. On Philica papers are ranked on the basis of peer reviews. On the internet 'peer' is coming to mean 'everyone' – perhaps a more egalitarian system.

Criticisms

There have been criticisms of the peer review process.

Reviewing is usually done anonymously so reviewers can be honest and objective. However, it may have the opposite effect if reviewers use the veil of anonymity to settle old scores or bury rival research. Research is conducted in a social world where people compete for research grants and jobs.

Editors tend to prefer to publish positive results on headline-catching topics (called *publication bias*), to increase the standing of their journal. This results in a bias in published research that in turn leads to a misperception of the true facts.

A different, but related problem is called the *file-drawer effect*. Researchers tend not to report research with non-significant results or results that challenge their preferred hypothesis. This results in a biased view of research in a given area because only significant, positive results are published.

Peer review results in a preference for research that goes with existing theory rather than dissenting or unconventional work. Richard Horton (2000), a former editor of the medical journal *The Lancet*, made the following comment: 'The mistake, of course, is to have thought that peer review was any more than a crude means of discovering the acceptability – not the validity – of a new finding'.

The A level checklist

Research methods are examined throughout all the AS and A level papers. For those studying A level, Paper 3 Section A assesses research methods. The specification contents for A level are listed below along with the page numbers of where we have covered this material in this chapter. The contents of topic 9 are almost identical to the methods listed throughout topics 1–4.

For revision you can tick when you have covered each element: use the red, amber and green columns to monitor the level of your understanding: red = needs more work, amber = improving and green = ready for the exam.

		Page
9.1.1	Types of data: qualitative and quantitative data; primary and secondary data.	174, 218
9.1.2	Sampling techniques: random, stratified, volunteer and opportunity.	170–171
9.1.3	Experimental/research designs: independent groups, repeated measures and matched pairs.	184–185
9.1.4	Hypotheses: null, alternate, experimental; directional and non-directional.	183, 200
9.1.5	Questionnaires and interviews: open, closed (including ranked scale questions); structured, semi-structured and unstructured interviews; self-report data.	168–169, 178
9.1.6	Experiments: laboratory and field; independent and dependent variables.	182
9.1.7	Observations: tallying; event and time sampling; covert, overt, participant, non-participant; structured observations; naturalistic observations.	206–207, 208–209
9.1.8	Additional research methods and techniques: twin and adoption studies, animal experiments, case studies as used in different areas of psychology, scanning (CAT, PET, fMRI), content analysis, correlational research, longitudinal and cross-sectional, cross-cultural and meta-analysis.	196, 198–199, 202–203, 204–205, 207, 210–211, 218–219
9.1.9	Control issues: counterbalancing, order effects, experimenter effects, social desirability, demand characteristics, participant variables, situational variables, extraneous variables, confounding variables, operationalisation of variables.	182, 185, 186–187
9.1.10	Descriptive statistics • Measures of central tendency, frequency tables, graphs (bar chart, histogram, scatter diagram), normal distribution (including standard deviation), skewed distribution, sense-checking data, measures of dispersion (range, standard deviation). • Produce, handle, interpret data – including drawing comparisons (e.g. between means of two sets of data). Students do not need to know formulae but are expected to be competent in simple mathematical steps.	172–173, 191, 195

		Page
9.1.11	Inferential statistics Decision-making and interpretation • Levels of measurement. Appropriate choice of statistical test. The criteria for and use of Mann-Whitney U, Wilcoxon, Spearman's, chi-squared (for difference) tests. Directional and non-directional testing. • Use of critical values tables, one- and two-tailed testing. • Levels of significance, including knowledge of standard statistical terminology such as p equal to or smaller than (e.g. $p \leq 0.05$). Rejecting hypotheses. Type I and Type II errors. The relationship between significance levels and p values. • Observed and critical values.	190–191, 192–193, 200, 201, 212 194
9.1.12	Methodological issues: validity (internal, predictive, ecological), reliability, generalisability, objectivity, subjectivity (researcher bias), credibility.	179, 180, 186–187, 188–189, 209
9.1.13	Analysis of qualitative data (thematic analysis and grounded theory).	175, 213
9.1.14	Conventions of published psychological research: abstract, introduction, aims and hypotheses, method, results, discussion; the process of peer review.	181, 220
9.1.15	Ethical issues in research using humans (BPS Code of Ethics and Conduct 2009), including risk assessment when carrying out research in psychology.	176–177
9.1.16	Ethical issues in research using animals (Scientific Procedures Act 1986 and Home Office regulations).	211
Appendix	Mathematical skills	216–217

THE END

Revision summary

Self-reporting data

Questionnaires

Questions in written form, predetermined.	+ Reveal thoughts/feelings. + Easy data collection – repeatable, include many participants. + Respondents feel more anonymous than in interview.	− Social desirability bias, affects validity. − Sample may be biased (e.g. literate people with time).
Closed question Fixed number of possible answers. Quantitative data.	+ Easy to analyse. + More objective (requires less interpretation).	− Restricts self-expression. − Oversimplifies reality.
Open question Provide own answer. Tends to produce qualitative data.	+ Free range for self-expression, increases validity. + Unexpected answers.	− Difficult to draw conclusions. − Subjective interpretation of answers.
Ranked scale Closed question, rate feelings, views, etc., e.g. from 1 to 5.	+ Objective way to express views. + Easy to draw conclusions.	− Response set. − Social desirability bias.

Interviews

Structured Predetermined questions.	+ Easily repeated. + Easy to analyse. + Can answer respondent's questions.	− Interviewer bias. − Respondents may not reveal information face-to-face.
Semi-structured Some questions predetermined, others develop.	+ More detailed information collected. + Can reveal unexpected information.	− More affected by interviewer bias. − Needs well-trained interviewers.
Unstructured No questions are decided in advance.		

Validity and reliability of self-reporting data

Validity — Legitimacy of data collected

- **Internal validity**: Whether a test/study does measure what it intended to measure. May be extraneous/confounding variables.
- **Ecological validity**: Concerns the extent to which findings can be generalised beyond a particular study. Affected by task, sample, setting.
- **Predictive validity**: A test score should forecast performance on some other measure of the same behaviour.

Reliability — Consistency of measurements

- **Inter-rater reliability**: Compare data from more than one interviewer/observer.
- **Test-retest reliability**: Compare test scores over time.

Experiments

Demonstrates causal relationships.
IV directly manipulated by experimenter.
DV is measured.

Types of experiment

Laboratory experiment Very controlled environment.	+ High control, minimises extraneous/confounding variables. + Easy replication.	− Contrived situation, behaviour may not be natural. − Demand characteristics, researcher bias reduces validity.
Field experiment More everyday surroundings.	+ Feels more natural. + Participants not always aware of being studied, avoids demand characteristics.	− Less control, reduces validity. − More time-consuming. − May be ethical issues.

Experimental design

Repeated measures Each participant takes part in every condition being tested.	+ Controls participant variables. + Fewer participants needed.	− Order effects (dealt with using counterbalancing e.g. ABBA). − May guess aims.
Independent groups Different participants in two (or more) experimental groups representing different levels of the IV.	+ Avoids order effects. + Avoids guessing aims.	− Participant variables not controlled (dealt with using randomisation). − Needs more participants.
Matched pairs Participants paired on key variables, and one placed in group A and the other in group B.	+ Controls participant variables. + Avoids order effects.	− Time-consuming. − May not control all participant variables.

Internal validity in experiments

Extraneous variable (EV): Any variable other than the IV that affects the DV. Can be:
- Participant variable, e.g. intelligence.
- Situational variable, e.g. time of day.

Confounding variable: An EV that varies systematically with the IV, and confounds findings.

Sampling

Group selected from target population, aims to be representative and generalisable.

Sampling methods

Random sample Each person has equal chance of selection.	+ Unbiased. + Can use a subgroup of population.	− Takes time. − May be biased if some decline to take part.
Stratified sample Participants selected from subgroups in proportion to frequency in population.	+ Most representative. + Select subgroups, reduces EVs.	− Selection of subgroups may be biased. − Lengthy process and some may decline.
Volunteer sample Advertise for willing participants.	+ Committed participants. + Specialised group (purposive sampling).	− Volunteer bias, e.g. highly motivated. − More likely to respond to demand characteristics.
Opportunity sample Most easily available.	+ Convenient and quick. + Only option if can't list whole population.	− Biased because only drawn from part of target population. − Refusal means we end up with volunteer sample.

Other research methods

Observation

Watching or listening to people or animals.	+ Shows what people do instead of saying what they do, higher validity.	− Observer bias. − Understanding what people think may be important.
Collecting qualitative data Observer records everything.	+ Basis of quantitative analysis by identifying themes (categories).	− The most relevant behaviours may be missed.
Collecting quantitative data Count behaviours in each behavioural category.	+ Systematic observations. + Draw conclusions.	− Categories may not include all behaviours. − Poor design reduces reliability.
Event sampling Count behaviours in a specified time period.	+ Sampling in general makes observations more manageable. + Good for occasional behaviours which might be missed.	− List of events may not be comprehensive.
Time sampling Count behaviours at regular intervals.	+ Tracks time-related changes.	− Some behaviours may be missed.
Participant observation Observer is part of observation.	+ Special insights. + May see more from inside.	− Observer bias. − Difficult to record behaviour unobtrusively.
Non-participant observation Observer is separate from group being observed.	+ Objectivity. + Unobtrusive.	− Misinterpretation. − May see less.
Structured observation Controlled environment, e.g. laboratory.	+ Focus on specific behaviours and test hypotheses. + Tentative causal conclusions.	− May feel contrived, low ecological validity. − Demand characteristics.
Naturalistic observation Everything is left as usual, but may use 'structured' techniques.	+ Realistic, high ecological validity. + Useful for new areas of research.	− Likely to be covert, ethical issues. − Difficult to draw conclusions.
Overt observation Participants aware of being observed.	+ Participants can give consent. + Observer freer because doesn't have to hide.	− Demand characteristics.
Covert observation Participants unaware.	+ More natural behaviour.	− Lack of consent. − Invasion of privacy.

Content analysis

Indirect observation in artefacts (e.g. books). Categories (themes) identified, instances then counted.	+ High ecological validity because based on what people do/say. + Exact replication possible, enhances reliability.	− Observer bias. − Culture bias of source material and categories used.

Case study

Detailed study of one person, group or event. Involves psychological tests, experiments, interviews, observation etc.	+ Rare cases. + In-depth data, complex interactions.	− Poor generalisability. − Recollection from the past. − Low objectivity. − Ethical issues, e.g. confidentiality.

Correlation

Positive correlation – Bottom left to top right, perfect coefficient = +1.00 Negative correlation – Top left to bottom right, perfect coefficient = −1.00 No correlation = 0	+ View relationship between two continuous co-variables. + Permits preliminary analysis.	− No cause-and-effect. − Intervening variables lead to false conclusions. − Reliability/validity of one of the co-variables may be poor.

Biological methods

CAT scan Detailed picture built up from X-ray slices.	+ Reveals structural features.	− High radiation. − No information about activity.
PET scan Radioactive substance injected, taken up by active brain areas.	+ Shows brain in action. + Can identify specific areas of brain linked to behaviour.	− Interpretation difficulties. − Can't pinpoint locations. − May damage tissues.
fMRI scan Radio waves measure blood oxygen levels.	+ Shows brain in action. + No radiation, so safer. + Clear picture, to the millimetre.	− Expensive. − Person has to stay very still. − Time lag may cause interpretation difficulties.

Twin and adoption studies

Twin studies MZ and DZ twins, e.g. Gottesman and Shields (1966) schizophrenia, Ludeke et al. (2013) parent–child relationships, Brendgen et al. (2005) aggression.	+ Shows genetic influences if MZs more similar than DZs, assuming equal environments. + Twin registries can provide large data sets.	− MZs treated more similarly, may overestimate genetic influence. − Can't identify specific genes.
Adoption studies Compare adopted children to biological and adoptive relatives, e.g. Tienari et al. (1994) schizophrenia, Horn et al. (1979) niche-picking.	+ Controls extraneous variable of environment. + Twin studies have been shown to overestimate genetics.	− Selective placement. − Adoptive parents tend to be better educated, etc.
Longitudinal research Takes place over time.	+ Study effects of age. + Participant variables controlled.	− Cohort effects. − Attrition effects.
Cross-sectional research Compares sections of population.	+ Takes less time to study age effects. + Enables comparison between groups.	− Participant variables not controlled. − Cohort effects.
Cross-cultural research Compares behaviour of cultures.	+ Can study nature versus nurture. + Takes psychology beyond white middle-class behaviour.	− Researchers often Westerners. − Use imposed etics (Western tests/methods).
Meta-analysis Data from many studies combined, report effect size.	+ Increases sample size. + Variety of samples.	− Sample bias, e.g. those with positive results. − Studies may not be comparable.

Use of animals in laboratory experiments

e.g. Pavlov and Skinner, Harlow (attachment), Alexander (rat park), Blakemore and Cooper (visual cortex).	+ Conditioning processes same in all animals. + Fewer ethical issues. + Easier to study complex behaviours over generations.	− Generalisation may not be justified. − Pain may not be justified. − Guidelines may not be effective.

Ethical controls
- Scientific Procedures Act (1986) and Home Office Regulations (protected animals only, e.g. vertebrates, 3Rs)
- BPS guidelines (e.g. minimise confinement, optimise research design).
- Bateson's cube.

Ethical arguments
- Pain and distress – Self-awareness necessary to actually feel pain.
- Speciesism (Singer 1990), idea challenged because we have a duty of care to humans (Gray 1991).
- Rights (Regan 1984), challenged because animals have no responsibilities.

Summary continued on next spread

Revision summary (continued)

Research issues

Researcher effects
A researcher's expectations (bias) may encourage certain behaviours in participants.

Hypotheses
- Alternate hypothesis – States the relationship between variables.
- Null hypothesis – Statement of no relationship.
- Experimental hypothesis – Statement about the effect of the IV on the DV.
- Directional (one-tailed) hypothesis – States direction of difference/correlation.
- Non-directional (two-tailed) – No direction stated.
- Operationalisation – State variables in a form that is testable.

Demand characteristics
Cues in a research situation that communicate to participants what is expected of them and may then unconsciously affect their behaviour.

Objectivity and subjectivity
Objectivity – Research process should not be influenced by the researcher's emotions, personal opinions or expectations (= subjectivity).

Scientific status of psychology
- Replicability – Repeat study, demonstrates validity of results.
- Reliability – Consistency of measurements.
- Validity (internal, predictive and ecological), hypothesis testing, use of controls.
- Reductionism – Identify variables that contribute to complex behaviours.
- Falsification – Need to be able to reject null hypothesis.
- Empiricism – Knowledge through direct observation.
- Credibility – Believability, as a result of all the above.

Peer review
Assessment of scientific work by others who are experts in same field.

- + Ensures only high quality work was published.
- + Part of scientific process, enables criticism.
- − Reviewers may not be impartial.
- − Publication bias.
- − File-drawer effect.

Ethical issues and guidelines

Ethical issues

The issue	Participants' rights	Researchers' wish to collect meaningful data
Anonymity and confidentiality	Personal information protected.	May be difficult.
Deception	Prevents informed consent, though sometimes just involves withholding information.	Knowing aims leads to demand characteristics.
Informed consent	Need to know nature of study and their role in the study.	
Privacy	Covert observation in a public place is OK.	
Right to withdraw	Protects from harm.	Loss of participants reduces validity.
Protection from harm	Psychological and physical.	Hard to predict.

BPS code of ethics and conduct
- Respect.
- Competence.
- Responsibility.
- Integrity.

Ways of dealing with ethical issues

Risk assessment and management
Weighing up long-term gains versus short-term risks to participants.

Consent and debriefing
Report true aims and give opportunity to withdraw data.

Research ethics committee (REC)
Concerned with interests of research participants, the researcher(s) and other stakeholders.

Writing your report

Journal articles include ...

At start
Abstract
Introduction
Aims and hypotheses

Procedure
- Details of what you did.
- Participants, sampling technique, apparatus/materials, standardised instructions, location, ethics.

Results
- Quantitative data – Descriptive and inferential statistics.
- Qualitative data – Thematic and content analysis.

Discussion
- Conclusions, relationship to previous research, criticisms, real-world applications.

At end
References
Appendices

Mathematical content

The arithmetic content

Decimals, fractions, percentages, ratios
Ways to express parts of a whole.
Reduce to lowest form.

Decimal places
Number of digits to right of decimal point.

Significant figures
Number of figures aside from zeros.

Standard form
[number between 1 and 10] x [10 to the power of x]

Estimation and order of magnitude
Approximations.

Symbols
$= < \ll \gg > \propto \sim$

Types of data

Quantitative and qualitative data

Quantitative data Data in numbers.	+ Easier to analyse. + More objective.	− May restrict expression of precise feelings. − Reductionist.
Qualitative data Data in words/pictures.	+ Holistic approach. + Free range for expression, increases validity.	− More difficult to detect patterns. − Subjective.

Primary and secondary data

Primary data Collected for the specific study.	+ Suits aims of study. + First-hand from participants, authentic.	− Takes time, money. − May end up with flawed data.
Secondary data Data already collected for a different purpose.	+ Large data sets. + Saves time in design and checking.	− May not exactly fit current aims. − May waste time on inappropriate data.

Data analysis

Quantitative data analysis

Descriptive statistics

Measures of central tendency (averages)

Mean Add up and divide by n.	+ Most sensitive, uses all values.	− Affected by extreme values.
Median Middle value in ordered list.	+ Not affected by extreme values.	− Not as sensitive as mean.
Mode Most frequent score(s).	+ Useful for nominal data.	− Not useful where there are many modes.

Measures of dispersion (spread)

Range Subtract lowest from highest number.	+ Convenient. + Easy to calculate.	− Affected by extreme values. − Doesn't reflect distribution.
Standard deviation Mean distance of values from the mean.	+ Most precise, uses all values. + Just use calculator.	− May hide extreme values. − Not immediately sensed.

Tables and graphs

Raw data table Data in rows and columns.	Frequency table How often each event occurred.
Bar chart Height of each bar represents frequency of each item. Nominal data.	Histogram Continuous data, frequency axis must start at 0.
Line graph Line linking highest values on histogram.	Scatter diagram Correlation data, dot for x and y values. Positive correlation, scatter from bottom left to top right. Negative correlation, scatter from top left to bottom right.

Distributions

Normal distribution Mean, median and mode at mid-point. 68.26% of scores lie within one standard deviation of the mean. 95.44% lie within two standard deviations.	Skewed distributions Positive skew – Mode to left of mean, tail to right. Negative skew – Mode to right of mean, tail to left.

Inferential statistics

Determine significance
- n = number of participants/data values.
- One- or two-tailed hypothesis.
- Level of probability, e.g. $p \leq 0.05$
- Calculate observed value.
- Compare to critical value in critical values table.
- Accept or reject null hypothesis.

Levels of measurement
- Nominal – Categories.
- Ordinal – Ordered but not equal intervals, e.g. ranked scale.
- Interval – Equal intervals on scale.

Inferential tests
- Wilcoxon T test of difference, repeated measures/matched pairs, ordinal data or better.
- Mann-Whitney U test of difference, independent groups, ordinal data or better.
- Spearman's rho test of correlation, ordinal data or better.
- Chi-squared χ^2 test of difference/association, independent items, frequency/nominal data. Uses a contingency table.

Type I and II errors
Type I false positive, true null hypothesis rejected, likely when significance is too lenient (e.g. $p = 0.10$).
Type II false negative, false null hypothesis accepted, likely when significance is too stringent (e.g. $p = 0.01$).

Qualitative data analysis

Thematic analysis
Categories identified and then used to organise data.
1. Read/reread transcript.
2. Identify meaningful units.
3. Give name/code to each unit.
4. Themes identified.
5. Data chunks may have more than one name.
6. Reread (iterative process).
7. Final report uses quotes to illustrate units.
8. Conclusions drawn.

Grounded theory
Categories emerge from data (bottom-up).

Practice questions, answers and feedback

On this spread we look at some typical student answers to questions. The comments provided indicate what is good and bad in each answer. Learning how to produce effective question answers is a SKILL. Read pages 6–19 for guidance.

Jemma is conducting some research with a group of people, all of whom have a phobia of dogs, i.e. they scored more than 7/10 on a checklist of questions about fear of dogs. She asked them about whether they can remember ever having a bad experience with a dog. Some said yes and others said no. She also interviewed a matched group of people who scored less than 5/10 on the 'fear of dogs' checklist and found out how many of them could recall a bad experience with a dog. Her results are shown in the table on the right.

A frequency table to show Jemma's findings regarding the number of people who have a phobia of dogs and the number who recall a bad experience with a dog.

	Phobia of dogs	No phobia of dogs
Bad experience with a dog	13	28
No bad experience with a dog	7	35

Question 1: State a suitable directional alternate hypothesis for this study. [3]

Ella's answer
People who score 7/10 or more on a fear of dogs checklist are more likely to remember having had a bad experience with a dog compared with those people who scored less than 5/10 on the fear of dogs checklist.

Ella has given a directional hypothesis and she has identified and operationalised both the IV and DV very well using the information from the scenario, full marks.

Larina's answer
People with a fear of dogs are more likely to remember having had a bad experience with a dog.

Larina has not operationalised her variables fully and she has also failed to give both levels of the IV in her answer. 1 mark for this answer.

Question 2: State **two** reasons why Jemma would use a chi-squared test to analyse her data. [2]

Sam's answer
She has used a repeated measures design because she asks people about how scared they are of dogs and whether they can remember a bad experience with dogs. She also has ordinal data because the people were given a score about how scared they were of dogs out of 10.

Oh dear, this answer couldn't be more wrong! Sam needs to revisit the meaning of repeated measures design. Also he has misunderstood the design of the study – the fear checklist was used to sort the people into two categories and therefore the data is not ordinal. No marks.

Larina's answer
Jemma is using an independent measures design where people either have a phobia of dogs or they don't and also she has nominal data, meaning the people have been put into one of two categories, either they can remember a bad experience with a dog or they can't remember a bad experience with a dog.

Great answer from Larina, both reasons are correct and contextualised well with information from the scenario, full marks.

Question 3: Using the data in the table above, calculate the observed value of chi-squared. Show your workings. [4]

Sam's answer
Working out the expected frequencies

A: 41 × 20 = 820/83 = 9.88, B: 41 × 63 = 2583/83 = 31.12

C: 42 × 20 = 840/83 = 10.12, D: 42 × 63 = 2646/83 = 31.88

$(o - e)^2/e$

13 − 9.88 = 3.12^2 = 9.7344/9.88 = 0.985

28 − 31.12 = $−3.12^2$ = 9.7344/31.12 = 0.313

7 − 10.12 = $−3.12^2$ = 9.7344/10.12 = 0.962

35 − 31.88 = 3.12^2 = 9.7344/31.88 = 0.305

Calculating X^2

0.985 + 0.313 + 0.962 + 0.305 = 2.565

Sam's calculations are laid out meticulously so that each step can be checked and credited. The underlining will have helped him to keep track of what he was doing. This answer obviously gets the full 4 marks.

Ella's answer
A: 9.88 B: 31.12 C: 10.12 D: 31.88

13 − 9.88 = 3.12^2 = 9.7344/13 = 0.7488

28 − 31.12 = $−3.12^2$ = 9.7344/28 = 0.348

7 − 10.12 = $−3.12^2$ = 9.7344/7 = 1.391

35 − 31.88 = 3.12^2 = 9.7344/35 = 0.278

X^2 = 2.77

Ella has not laid her expected frequency calculation out as effectively as Sam but they are accurate. She has made an error in her calculations though in the next stage. She has divided her totals by the observed (o) values instead of by the expected (e) values each time and this means that when she adds the four figures together she gets the wrong value for chi-squared. Because she showed her working she will gain partial credit up until the point that she went wrong. And her error will not be carried over into the next question as it would not be fair to penalise her twice. She would be given 2 marks for her answer here as the expected frequencies are right.

Question 4: Explain whether Jemma should reject her null hypothesis. (3)

Sam's answer

No, Jemma should not reject the null hypothesis, she must accept the null. This is because her observed value is less than the critical value.

Sam is correct, Jemma will have to accept her null and he will gain credit for knowing this. However, he has not used any figures in his answer or explained how he knew which critical value to use. He has not made any effort to contextualise his answer using details of Jemma's study and does not state the p value. Just 1 mark for the correct identification.

Ella's answer

No, Jemma should not reject the null hypothesis. The observed value (2.565) is less than the critical value (2.71) for a one-tailed test, when degrees of freedom are equal to one and at the 5% level of significance ($p > 0.05$).

This means that people with a fear of dogs are not more likely to remember a bad experience with a dog in the past than people with no fear of dogs.

Ella gives a 'textbook' answer, using all the figures correctly and explaining every detail of her decision. She contextualises well to the scenario and would gain full marks.

Issie and Florence conducted a field experiment on a Monday to see whether the way a request is presented affects whether people sign a petition to improve the rights of local workers. In condition 1 passers-by in the crowded shopping area were asked, 'Would you sign our petition?' Later in the day, in condition 2, the experimenters use a megaphone and shouted, 'Sign the petition!' They tally how many signatures they achieved in the two conditions of the experiment and also how many people walked by without signing.

Question 5: Describe the sampling method that has been used in this study. (2)

Ella's answer

This study uses opportunity sampling which is an easy and convenient way to get the participants for the study. Basically Issie and Florence are just sampling whoever happens to be at the shops on the day they do the study.

Ella gives a correct answer and explains why she has opted for opportunity sampling with reference to the scenario, 2 marks.

Larina's answer

The study uses opportunity sampling which is a problem for the girls as their data may not be representative as different types of people go to the shops on different days. People who are at work can't go on a weekday but people who work weekends can go in the week and this is important because the study is about workers' rights.

Larina also states the correct sampling method but has given a weakness of the method as her elaboration and this is not what the question is asking. She has done more than she is being asked for and this sadly does not mean she will necessarily get more marks. Always try to do exactly what you are asked for. This answer only gains 1 mark.

Question 6: Explain **one** confounding variable that might have affected this study. (3)

Ella's answer

The street might have been a lot busier in the morning than the afternoon, as more shoppers come out earlier in the day and this means that it's not just the strength of the message that is different in the morning and afternoon, it's also the busyness of the street.

This means that more people might sign the petition in the morning, simply because there are more people available. Or the higher volume of people on the street in the morning might make shoppers feel harassed or distracted by others which might make them less inclined to stop and sign a petition.

So it is impossible to know whether it was the strength of the message or the presence of more people that caused the difference in signatures and this decreases the internal validity due to lack of control.

Ella understands the term confounding variables. She has thought carefully about the study and come up with a sound example which she explains fully in relation to the findings of the study described in the scenario. Breaking her answer into three sections is helpful to her and the examiner in showing where the points may be found – she has identified a confounding variable (paragraph 1), explained why it might have an effect on participants (paragraph 2) and then explained how this would confound the results (paragraph 3). Full marks for this answer.

Larina's answer

The girls might have found it hard to record the number of people walking past and not signing the petition because the people are hurrying along in a big crowd and this means their data might not have been accurate and therefore it is not valid either.

If they had CCTV that would have helped because they could have watched it back and counted the number of people more carefully.

Larina seems to realise that the question has links with validity and her answer looks at a problem with recording results accurately. However, this is not an example of a confounding variable. She also recognises the need to write enough to meet the mark allocation but in order to do this she has provided an improvement to the study. This is not what she is being asked to do and therefore will not gain any credit. No marks for this response.

Multiple-choice questions

Self-reporting data: Questionnaire design

1. Open questions:
   (a) Are easily analysed.
   (b) Have a fixed range of answers.
   (c) Produce qualitative data.

2. A strength of questionnaires is that they:
   (a) Are cheap.
   (b) Can be given to many people at the same time.
   (c) Have a fixed range of answers.

3. Ranked scales are a kind of:
   (a) Closed question.
   (b) Qualitative question.
   (c) Open question.

4. A question that suggests what answer is required is:
   (a) An open question.
   (b) A leading question.
   (c) A qualitative question.

Sample selection and techniques

1. Choosing whoever happens to be there best describes:
   (a) A random sample.
   (b) A volunteer sample.
   (c) An opportunity sample.

2. A strength of random sampling is that it:
   (a) Is unbiased.
   (b) Is easy and convenient.
   (c) Identifies subgroups.

3. The group the researcher is interested in is called the:
   (a) Sampling.
   (b) Target population.
   (c) Stratified sample.

4. The most representative sampling technique is:
   (a) A volunteer sample.
   (b) A stratified sample.
   (c) An opportunity sample.

Quantitative data and its analysis

1. The middle value in a list arranged in numerical order is the:
   (a) Mean.
   (b) Median.
   (c) Mode.

2. A weakness of standard deviation:
   (a) Not all values used in final calculation.
   (b) Very hard to calculate.
   (c) May hide extreme values.

3. In a histogram the data must be:
   (a) Continuous.
   (b) Nominal.
   (c) Qualitative.

4. The most sensitive measure of central tendency is the:
   (a) Mean.
   (b) Median.
   (c) Mode.

Qualitative data and thematic analysis

1. Data that represents thoughts and feelings:
   (a) Quantitative.
   (b) Qualitative.
   (c) Both quantitative and qualitative.

2. *Not* used to analyse qualitative data:
   (a) Interviews.
   (b) Thematic analysis.
   (c) Grounded theory.

3. Represents true complexities of human behaviour:
   (a) Quantitative data.
   (b) Qualitative data.
   (c) Both quantitative and qualitative data.

4. Qualitative analysis is:
   (a) Reductionist.
   (b) Easy to analyse.
   (c) Prone to being subjective.

Ethical issues and guidelines

1. Deception can be dealt with by:
   (a) Changing names to numbers.
   (b) Debriefing participants.
   (c) Confidentiality.

2. Making participants feel anxious is an example of:
   (a) Psychological harm.
   (b) Breach of confidentiality.
   (c) Lack of informed consent.

3. Anonymity is a way to deal with:
   (a) Lack of informed consent.
   (b) Invasion of privacy.
   (c) Right to withdraw.

4. Ethical issues are:
   (a) Guaranteed to be resolved by ethical guidelines.
   (b) Monitored in all countries by the BPS.
   (c) Dilemmas over costs to participants and benefits for science.

Self-reporting data: Interviews

1. An interview where no questions are decided in advance:
   (a) Structured.
   (b) Semi-structured.
   (c) Unstructured.

2. Interviewer bias is a bigger problem in:
   (a) Structured interviews.
   (b) Semi-structured interviews.
   (c) Questionnaires.

3. More detailed information is likely to be produced in:
   (a) Structured interviews.
   (b) Semi-structured interviews.
   (c) Questionnaires.

4. The effect of an interviewer's expectations is called:
   (a) Interviewer bias.
   (b) Social desirability bias.
   (c) Observer bias.

Researcher effects

1. Rosenthal and Fode (1963) demonstrated researcher effects in an experiment with:
   (a) Teachers and rats.
   (b) Students and rats.
   (c) Students and cats.

2. Which of the following is an example of a researcher effect?
   (a) Interviewer smiles at participant.
   (b) Interviewer tells the participant what to say.
   (c) Interviewer deceives the participant.

3. There are never researcher effects in:
   (a) An interview.
   (b) A questionnaire.
   (c) A bar chart.

4. Which is true?
   (a) Researcher bias causes researcher effects.
   (b) Researcher effects cause researcher bias.
   (c) Researcher effects are the same as researcher bias.

Validity and reliability of self-report

1. A way to assess reliability in a questionnaire:
   (a) Inter-participant reliability.
   (b) Inter-rater reliability.
   (c) Intra-participant reliability.

2. Social desirability bias affects:
   (a) Validity.
   (b) Reliability.
   (c) Validity and reliability.

3. Reliability is defined as:
   (a) Consistency.
   (b) Trueness of data collected.
   (c) Dependability.

4. Ecological validity is best defined as:
   (a) Being able to generalise findings beyond a particular study.
   (b) The naturalness of a study.
   (c) Being true.

Writing a report

1. Which of the following should *not* be part of the procedure?
   (a) The aims of the study.
   (b) How many participants.
   (c) What the researcher(s) actually did.

2. The discussion includes:
   (a) Standardised instructions.
   (b) Inferential statistics.
   (c) Criticisms of the research.

3. You would find measures of central tendency in the:
(a) Procedure section.
(b) Results section.
(c) Discussion section.

4. If you were reporting qualitative data, you would use:
(a) Thematic analysis.
(b) Measures of central tendency.
(c) Tally charts.

Experiments

1. Which would *not* be a useful way to operationalise aggression?
(a) Number of punches thrown.
(b) Distance between the people.
(c) Feeling angry.

2. Which of the following is *not* true of all experiments?
(a) All have an IV and DV.
(b) All are artificial.
(c) All demonstrate causal relationships.

3. Which variable is measured by the experimenter:
(a) DV.
(b) IV.
(c) EV.

4. The key difference between a laboratory and field experiment is:
(a) The kind of location.
(b) The way the DV is measured.
(c) The kind of IV that is tested.

Hypotheses

1. A directional hypothesis is:
(a) One-tailed.
(b) Two-tailed.
(c) Three-tailed.

2. A hypothesis is:
(a) The aim of the study.
(b) A question.
(c) A statement.

3. A hypothesis should be written in the:
(a) Past tense
(b) Present tense.
(c) Future tense.

4. The null hypothesis is a statement of:
(a) No difference/relationship.
(b) The opposite to the alternate.
(c) No association.

Experimental design

1. Which is *not* an example of experimental design:
(a) Repeated measures.
(b) Independent groups.
(c) Participant measures.

2. Order effects are a problem in:
(a) Repeated measures.
(b) Independent groups.
(c) Participant measures.

3. Counterbalancing is used to deal with:
(a) Participant variables.
(b) Random allocation.
(c) Order effects.

4. Participant variables are a problem in:
(a) Matched pairs.
(b) Repeated measures.
(c) Independent groups.

Experiments: Internal validity

1. Variable that changes systematically with the IV:
(a) Extraneous variable.
(b) Confounding variable.
(c) Dependent variable.

2. Predictive validity:
(a) A test measures what it intended to measure.
(b) A test generalises to other situations.
(c) A test that has the ability to forecast performance somewhere else.

3. Demand characteristics:
(a) Affect the reliability of a study.
(b) Change the IV in a study.
(c) Communicate the aims of a study.

4. If procedures are not standardised there might be a:
(a) Confounding variable.
(b) Demand characteristic.
(c) Participant variable.

Experiments: Ecological validity

1. Mundane realism is used to describe a:
(a) Boring task.
(b) Task that reflects ordinary life.
(c) Household task.

2. Conducting a number of studies on the same topic and comparing the results is called:
(a) Triangulation.
(b) Comparative research.
(c) Trigonometry.

3. Laboratory experiments may have high validity because:
(a) Variables can be carefully controlled.
(b) Participants generally don't know they are being studied.
(c) It is easy to measure the IV.

4. Field experiments may have high validity because:
(a) Variables can be carefully controlled.
(b) Participants generally don't know they are being studied.
(c) It is easy to measure the IV.

Inferential statistics: Tests of difference

1. The information needed to find the critical value for a Wilcoxon test is:
(a) p, n and df.
(b) p, n and 1- or 2-tailed.
(c) p, df and 1- or 2-tailed.

2. The observed value of an inferential test:
(a) Indicates probability.
(b) Is also called the critical value.
(c) Is calculated.

3. A probability value of 10% is:
(a) 0.01
(b) 0.10
(c) 1.00

4. The most commonly used level of significance is:
(a) 1%
(b) 5%
(c) 10%

Inferential statistics: Tests of difference (continued)

1. The Mann-Whitney U test is used for:
(a) Repeated measures.
(b) Independent groups.
(c) Matched pairs.

2. The test statistic for the Wilcoxon test is
(a) U
(b) T
(c) B

3. When calculating the Mann-Whitney U test you rank:
(a) All data items together.
(b) Only one set of scores.
(c) Sets A and B separately.

4. Wilcoxon and Mann-Whitney U are used with:
(a) Nominal data only.
(b) Interval data only.
(c) Ordinal and interval data.

Type I and II errors

1. A Type I error occurs when a researcher:
(a) Rejects a true H_0.
(b) Accepts a false H_0.
(c) Rejects a false H_0.

2. The 5% level of significance is generally used because it:
(a) Avoids accepting a false H0.
(b) Avoids rejecting a true H0.
(c) Is a good compromise between Type I and II errors.

3. A Type I error is a:
(a) False negative.
(b) True negative.
(c) False positive.

4. The 1% level of significance is generally avoided because it is too:
(a) Lenient.
(b) Stringent.
(c) High.

Normal and skewed distributions

1. In a normal distribution the shape of the curve is:
(a) Cup-shaped.
(b) Triangle-shaped.
(c) Bell-shaped.

2. In a normal distribution, 95.44% of the population lies within:
(a) One standard deviation of the mean.
(b) Two standard deviations of the mean.
(c) Three standard deviations of the mean.

Continued on next spread

Multiple-choice questions (continued)

3. In a positive skew the mean is:
   (a) To the right of the mode.
   (b) To the left of the mode.
   (c) In the same position as the mode.

4. Most of the scores are bunched to the right in a:
   (a) Positively skewed distribution.
   (b) Negatively skewed distribution.
   (c) Normal distribution.

Case studies and HM

1. Case studies can be:
   (a) Longitudinal.
   (b) Conducted in a short space of time.
   (c) Both (a) and (b).

2. A strength of a case study:
   (a) In-depth information.
   (b) Objective.
   (c) Generalisable.

3. HM was studied mainly because:
   (a) He had epilepsy.
   (b) He had brain surgery.
   (c) He was unique.

4. The part of HM's brain that was removed from both hemispheres was:
   (a) The hypothalamus.
   (b) The hippopotamus.
   (c) The hippocampus.

Correlation

1. All correlations fall between:
   (a) −1.0 and +1.0
   (b) 0 and +1
   (c) −10 and +10

2. As the number of people in a room increase the temperature rises. This is:
   (a) A positive correlation.
   (b) A negative correlation.
   (c) No correlation.

3. The kind of graph used to plot a correlation is a:
   (a) Bar chart.
   (b) Histogram.
   (c) Scatter diagram.

4. In a correlation the apparent link between co-variables may be due to:
   (a) Irrational variables.
   (b) Intersecting variables.
   (c) Intervening variables.

Inferential statistics: Test of correlation

1. The test statistic for Spearman's test is:
   (a) rho.
   (b) who.
   (c) rhi.

2. When looking up the critical value required you need to know the n value, the significance level and the:
   (a) Type of experiment.
   (b) Null hypothesis.
   (c) Direction of the hypothesis.

3. $\sum d^2$ means
   (a) Add up all the squared differences.
   (b) Find all of the differences.
   (c) Square all the differences.

4. If the observed value calculated is −.781 this means:
   (a) A negative correlation.
   (b) A positive correlation.
   (c) It is probably not significant.

Levels of measurement

1. Data that is in categories is:
   (a) Nominal data.
   (b) Ordinal data.
   (c) Interval data.

2. Data from a ranked scale is considered to be:
   (a) Nominal data.
   (b) Ordinal data.
   (c) Interval data.

3. Data that has equal interval units is:
   (a) Nominal data.
   (b) Ordinal data.
   (c) Interval data.

4. Data from psychological tests use standardised scores and may be considered to be:
   (a) Nominal data.
   (b) Ordinal data.
   (c) Interval data.

Other biological research methods

1. Which scanning method measures metabolic activity?
   (a) CAT scan.
   (b) PET scan.
   (c) fMRI scan.

2. Which technique is potentially harmful if used repeatedly?
   (a) DOG scan.
   (b) PET scan.
   (c) fMRI scan.

3. fMRI scans measure:
   (a) Heart rate.
   (b) Blood carbon dioxide levels.
   (c) Blood oxygen levels.

4. Which scanning technique does *not* provide information about the activity of the 'live' brain?
   (a) CAT scan.
   (b) PET scan.
   (c) fMRI scan.

Twin and adoption studies

1. DZ twins:
   (a) Have identical genes.
   (b) Share about 50% of the same genes.
   (c) Share exactly 50% of the same genes.

2. High concordance rates on a particular trait between MZ twins suggests:
   (a) Genetic factors are important.
   (b) Environmental factors are important.
   (c) It is not possible to draw a conclusion.

3. A proband is:
   (a) A biological relative of the twin first identified for a study.
   (b) A co-twin.
   (c) The person who is the starting point for a study of genetically-related people.

4. Adoption studies have the advantage of:
   (a) Being much easier because there are more adopted children than twins.
   (b) Participants are reared in similar environments.
   (c) Not having the environment as an extraneous variable.

Observation and content analysis

1. Event sampling is when you:
   (a) Record behaviours at regular intervals.
   (b) Take a sample at set times each day.
   (c) Count each time a behaviour occurs in a specified time period.

2. An observer's expectations influence what they observe. This is called:
   (a) Observer strain.
   (b) Observer bias.
   (c) Observer effect.

3. Content analysis produces:
   (a) Qualitative data.
   (b) Quantitative data.
   (c) Secondary data.

4. Behavioural categories are used:
   (a) To reduce the amount of data to be observed.
   (b) To produce systematic observations.
   (c) To increase event sampling.

Observation: Reliability and validity

1. In naturalistic observations:
   (a) The environment is very structured.
   (b) Some small changes are made to the environment to see what effect this has on behaviour.
   (c) Everything is left as it usually is.

2. Which kind of observation raises the greatest ethical concerns?
   (a) Overt observations.
   (b) Covert observations.
   (c) Naturalistic observations.

3. One weakness of participant observation is:
   (a) It cannot be used in some places.
   (b) It is difficult to observe participants covertly.
   (c) Ecological validity is low.

4. The reliability of observations can be checked using:
(a) Inter-rater reliability.
(b) Ranked reliability.
(c) Predictive reliability.

Use of animals in laboratory experiments

1. The date of the Scientific Procedures Act was:
(a) 1968.
(b) 1986.
(c) 1988.

2. Which of the following is *not* one of the 3 Rs?
(a) Replace.
(b) Refine.
(c) Renew.

3. The class of invertebrate animals covered by the act is:
(a) Cephalopods.
(b) Crustaceans.
(c) Coelacanths.

4. Sentience refers to:
(a) Being able to read.
(b) Having rights and responsibilities.
(c) Having self-awareness and feelings.

Inferential statistics: Test of association

1. The chi-squared test requires data to be:
(a) Nominal and interval.
(b) Nominal and independent.
(c) Interval and independent.

2. *df* is calculated in order to:
(a) Know how many rows there are.
(b) Calculate the observed value.
(c) Look up the critical value.

3. A 2 × 2 contingency table has two rows and:
(a) One column.
(b) Two columns.
(c) Three columns.

4. In the formula used to calculate chi-squared are the letters *o* and *e*, which stand for:
(a) Observed and expected.
(b) Ordered and ended.
(c) Ordered and expected.

Return to qualitative data and thematic analysis

1. Firth and Gleeson used a combination of two kinds of sampling:
(a) Opportunity and snowball.
(b) Opportunity and random.
(c) Random and snowball.

2. Data was collected using:
(a) A structured interview.
(b) An unstructured interview.
(c) A questionnaire.

3. The final step of the thematic analysis involved:
(a) Identifying meaningful units.
(b) Reviewing the data to check that each category was well supported.
(c) Grouping the units into categories.

4. Replicability of the themes was calculated using:
(a) Significant reliability.
(b) Inter-rater reliability.
(c) Predictive validity.

Scientific status of psychology

1. Standardising procedures is about:
(a) Reliability.
(b) Reductionism.
(c) Empiricism.

2. The null hypothesis is used for:
(a) Replication.
(b) Credibility.
(c) Falsification.

3. 'Empirical' refers to:
(a) Evidence from reasoned arguments.
(b) Anecdotal support.
(c) Through direct observation.

4. A good hypothesis is:
(a) Reliable.
(b) Valid.
(c) Operationalised.

Mathematical skills

1. The number 2306.34 has
(a) One decimal place.
(b) Two decimal places.
(c) Four decimal figures.

2. The number 26,478,000 can be written as:
(a) 2.64×10^7
(b) 2.6×10^8
(c) 2.65×10^7

3. The fraction 26/50 can be written as:
(a) 26%
(b) 52%
(c) 13%

4. The number 21.304 to 2 significant figures is:
(a) 21
(b) 21.30
(c) 20.30

A few final things

1. Primary data is best described as data collected:
(a) By a researcher.
(b) For the purpose of a particular study.
(c) By someone else and is already existing.

2. A weakness of cross-sectional studies is:
(a) Order effects.
(b) Participant variables are not controlled.
(c) Attrition.

3. An imposed etic is:
(a) A type of cross-cultural study using foreign researchers.
(b) Observer bias.
(c) A test designed by one cultural group and used to measure others.

4. In a meta-analysis the studies that are included may be affected by:
(a) A selection bias.
(b) Demand characteristics.
(c) Cohort effect.

Conventions of published research

1. An abstract should be about:
(a) 200 words.
(b) 300 words.
(c) 500 words.

2. The introduction should:
(a) Lead logically to the aims.
(b) Come after the method section.
(c) Come before the abstract.

3. A key feature of the method section is:
(a) It is kept quite short.
(b) Ethics are unimportant.
(c) Others should be able to repeat the study exactly.

4. In peer review, 'peers' refer to:
(a) Experts in the same academic area.
(b) Experts in a different academic area
(c) Teenagers.

MCQ answers

Self-reporting data: Questionnaire design 1C 2B 3A 4B
Sample selection and techniques 1C 2A 3B 4B
Quantitative data and its analysis 1B 2C 3A 4A
Qualitative data and thematic analysis 1C 2A 3B 4C
Ethical issues and guidelines 1B 2A 3B 4C
Self-reporting data: Interviews 1C 2B 3B 4A
Researcher effects 1B 2A 3C 4A
Validity and reliability of self-report 1B 2A 3A 4A
Writing a report 1A 2C 3B 4A
Experiments 1C 2B 3A 4A
Hypotheses 1A 2C 3B 4A
Experimental design 1C 2A 3C 4C
Experiments: Internal validity 1B 2C 3C 4A
Experiments: Ecological validity 1B 2A 3A 4B
Inferential statistics: Tests of difference 1B 2C 3B 4B
Inferential statistics: Tests of difference (continued) 1B 2B 3A 4C
Type I and II errors 1A 2C 3C 4B
Normal and skewed distributions 1C 2B 3A 4B
Case studies and HM 1C 2A 3B 4C
Correlation 1A 2A 3C 4C
Inferential statistics: Test of correlation 1A 2C 3A 4A
Levels of measurement 1A 2B 3C 4B
Other biological research methods 1B 2B 3C 4A
Twin and adoption studies 1B 2A 3C 4C
Observation and content analysis 1C 2B 3B 4B
Observation: Reliability and validity 1C 2B 3B 4A
Use of animals in laboratory experiments 1B 2C 3A 4C
Inferential statistics: Test of association 1B 2C 3B 4A
Return to qualitative data and thematic analysis 1A 2C 3B 4B
Scientific status of psychology 1A 2C 3C 4C
Mathematical skills 1B 2C 3B 4A
A few final things 1B 2B 3C 4A
Conventions of published research 1A 2A 3C 4A

Index/Glossary

acetylcholine A neurotransmitter that plays a role in attention and arousal in the central nervous system. In the peripheral nervous system, it works by causing muscles to contract. 99–100, 122

acquisition The process of *acquiring* (getting or developing) something, in this case a phobia. We tend to use the term 'acquisition' in psychology because it is theoretically neutral. This is preferable to saying 'learning' because learning is actually an explanation for acquisition, not a synonym. 4–5, 131, 135, 138–140, 143–145, 160–161, 165

adoption studies Genetic factors are implicated if children are more similar to their biological parents with whom they share genes (but not environment) than to their adoptive parents with whom they share environment (but not genes). Environmental factors are implicated if the reverse is true. 119, 167, 204–205, 221, 223, 230–231

adrenaline A hormone produced by the adrenal glands which is part of the human body's immediate stress response system. Adrenaline has a strong effect on the cells of the cardiovascular system – stimulating the heart rate, contracting blood vessels and dilating air passages. 108, 125, 127

agentic shift The switch between the autonomous and agentic state that occurs when we perceive someone to be a legitimate source of authority and allow them to control our behaviour. 16, 28–29, 57, 60, 64

agentic state A mindset which allows us to carry out orders from an authority figure, even if they conflict with our personal sense of right and wrong. We absolve ourselves of responsibility, believing that as we are acting on someone else's behalf, blame for any negative consequences ultimately lies with them. 16, 28–29, 64

aggression Behaviour that is intended to cause injury. In humans this could be psychological as well as physical injury. In animals (including humans), aggression is often directed at establishing and maintaining dominance, or acquiring resources (e.g. food). Aggression is often expressed in ritualised form to prevent actual physical harm (e.g. raising your arm as a threat, or making a loud noise). 11, 23, 44, 95–96, 99, 102–111, 114–115, 118–127, 138–143, 157, 160, 164–165, 167, 185, 189, 202–203, 205, 209–211, 218–219, 223, 229

agonist A drug that has the same effect as a naturally produced neurotransmitter. 100–101, 103, 122, 126

alternate hypothesis In an experiment this can be called the experimental hypothesis, but in non-experimental research it is called the alternate hypothesis because it is alternative to the null hypothesis. 'Alternate hypothesis' can be used instead of 'experimental hypothesis'. 36, 86–87, 120–121, 131, 149, 169, 190–194, 200, 212, 214, 224, 226

Alzheimer's disease See dementia

amnesia A loss of memory due to brain damage, disease, or psychological trauma. 69–71, 73, 75, 78–79, 88, 90–91, 197

amygdala A small region located in the temporal lobe of the cerebral cortex. It is part of the limbic system and is responsible for detecting fear and preparing for emergency events. It is associated with memory, emotion, sleep, arousal and the fight or flight response. 96, 102–103, 110, 122–123, 126, 202

androcentric Male-centred, when 'normal' behaviour is judged according to a male standard (meaning that female behaviour is often judged to be 'abnormal' or 'deficient' in comparison). 37, 50, 60–61

angular gyrus A region of the brain in the parietal lobe. It is involved in a number of processes related to language, number processing and spatial cognition. 110

anonymity An important aspect of confidentiality. A participant remains anonymous, i.e. their name is withheld or simply not recorded. 54, 58, 176, 196–197, 220, 224, 228

antagonist A drug that prevents the effects of a naturally produced neurotransmitter. 42, 65, 100–101, 122, 126

attention The cognitive process of focusing on a stimulus. In SLT the stimulus is the modelled behaviour. 10, 15, 61, 68–70, 80, 88, 91–92, 112, 136, 138–139, 160, 164, 209

auditory cortex Located in the temporal lobe and concerned with the analysis of speech-based information. 97, 122

authoritarian personality A type of personality that is especially susceptible to obeying people in authority and being submissive to those of higher status. Such individuals also are likely to be prejudiced because they displace feelings of inadequacy on to their inferiors. Inadequacy arises because their authoritarian parents gave conditional love. 36–37, 44, 60–61

autism More correctly known as autism spectrum disorder (ASD). This is an umbrella term for a wide range of symptoms. All disorders on the spectrum share impairments to two main areas: social communication and repetitive behaviours. 136–137, 160, 198

autonomous state A mindset where we behave independently, make our own decisions about how to behave and take responsibility for the consequences of our actions. 16, 28–29, 57, 60, 64

average See measures of central tendency.

backward conditioning A conditioning method in which the unconditioned stimulus (UCS) is presented before a neutral stimulus (NS). 132

bar chart A type of graph in which the frequency of each variable is represented by the height of the bars. In contrast to a histogram, the data in a bar chart is in discrete categories. There are spaces between the bars. 34, 39, 58, 111, 140, 153, 158, 172–173, 216, 221, 225, 228, 230

behaviour modification The use of operant conditioning techniques to change the frequency of desired behaviours, for example in therapeutic settings. 136–137, 160, 164

behavioural categories Objective methods to separate continuous stream of action into components. Behaviours are counted. pages 158, 206–209, 230

behaviourist An approach to explaining behaviour in terms of what is observable and in terms of learning. 3, 56, 149, 210

binding factors Being in a social situation involves a commitment to others. It is seen as rude to break off once involved, and this 'binds' us to the situation. 28–29

brain scans A technique used to investigate the structure or functioning of the brain by taking images of the living brain. This makes it possible to match regions of the brain to behaviour by asking participants to engage in particular activities while the scan is done. Brain scans are also used to detect brain abnormalities such as tumours. Examples: CAT scan, PET scan, MRI scan, fMRI scan. 103, 110, 112, 118, 127, 202

British Psychological Society (BPS) code of ethics and conduct A set of core principles (respect, competence, responsibility and integrity) to guide psychologists' professional behaviour, linked to key ethical issues, e.g. informed consent, privacy, etc. 22–23, 176–177, 211, 221, 223, 224, 228

Broca's area An area of the frontal lobe of the brain in the left hemisphere (in most people), responsible for speech production. 97, 122

candidate-gene association studies (CGAS) Focus on specific 'candidate' genes that individually create a vulnerability for a disorder. 205

capacity The amount of information that can be held in a memory store. 9, 68, 70, 71, 82, 83, 87, 88, 89, 91, 92

case study The detailed study of one case – but the case could be one person, one group of people (such as a family or a football team or a school) or an event. 7, 52, 69, 73, 78, 90, 148, 196, 197, 218, 223, 230

CAT (or CT) scan (Computerised tomography) Uses X-rays and a computer to create detailed structural images of the inside of the body, including the brain. 202, 223, 230

catharsis The process of releasing pent-up psychic energy. 106, 107, 123

CBT See cognitive-behavioural treatment

central executive (CE) The component of the working memory model that coordinates the activities of the subsystems in working memory. It also allocates processing resources to those activities. 68, 84

central nervous system (CNS) Consists of the brain and the spinal cord and is the origin of all complex commands and decisions. 96–98, 100, 116, 122

cerebellum A large structure at the back of the hindbrain, which has many deep folds. It is involved with motor control. 96, 122, 126

cerebral cortex The surface layer of the forebrain (the two hemispheres of the brain). It is grey in colour and it is highly folded to make it possible to fit the massive amount of material inside the skull. 96–98, 100, 122, 130, 132–133

chi-squared Test of difference or association between two sets of data. Data must be nominal or frequency and must be independent. Test statistic is χ 131, 141, 143, 147, 158–159, 167, 207, 212, 221, 225, 226, 231

classical conditioning Learning by association. It occurs when a neutral stimulus is repeatedly paired with an unconditioned stimulus. The neutral stimulus eventually produces the same response as the unconditioned stimulus. 4–5, 10–11, 17, 72, 129–135, 144–146, 148–149, 157, 160–165

closed question Has a fixed number of possible answers and provides quantitative data, i.e. answers that can be counted. 11, 37, 55, 58–59, 61, 73, 105, 120, 151, 168–169, 178, 222, 228

co-variables The variables investigated within a correlation, for example looking at how height and weight vary in association with each other. They are not referred to as the independent and dependent variables because a correlation investigates the association between the variables, rather than trying to show a cause-and-effect relationship where one variable 'depends' on the other. 103, 120, 198–200, 223, 230

cocaine A strong stimulant mostly used as a recreational drug. It alters synaptic transmission involving several neurotransmitters, most particularly dopamine. 19, 100–101, 116, 118, 122, 124, 202

cognitive Refers to 'mental processes' (e.g. thoughts, perceptions, attention) and how they affect behaviour. 4–8, 17–18, 22, 28, 40–41, 43–45, 47, 51, 52–53, 55–57, 61, 64, 66–90, 92, 97–98, 102–103, 113, 115, 117–119, 122, 125, 133, 137–139, 145, 147, 152, 157, 159, 161–162, 164, 167, 202, 210

cognitive-behavioural treatment A method for treating mental disorders based on both cognitive and behavioural techniques. From the cognitive viewpoint the therapy aims to deal with thinking, such as challenging negative thoughts. The therapy also includes behavioural techniques, such as behavioural activation. 154

cohort effect An effect caused because one group of participants has unique characteristics due to time-specific experiences during their development, such as growing up during the Second World War. This can affect both cross-sectional studies (because one group is not comparable with another) and longitudinal studies (because the group studied is not typical). 219, 223, 231

collectivist People who place more value on the 'collective' (i.e. the other group members) rather than each individual being most focused on themselves. Collectivist cultures also value interdependence rather than independence. The opposite is true of individualist cultures. 38–39, 41, 46–47, 55, 60–61, 63–64

concordance A measure of similarity (usually expressed as a percentage) between two individuals or sets of individuals on a given trait. 204, 205, 230

conditioned response (CR) The response elicited by the CS, i.e. a new association has been learned so that the NS/CS produces the UCR which is now called the CR. 4, 130, 144

conditioned stimulus (CS) A stimulus that only produces the target response *after* it has been paired with the UCS. 4, 130, 132, 144

confederate An individual in a research study who is not a real participant and has been instructed how to behave by the researcher. 16, 29, 31, 33–34, 38–39, 47, 51, 64–65, 107, 215

confidentiality A participant's right to have personal information protected through anonymity or by keeping information safe. 176

confounding variable A special class of extraneous variable where the extraneous variable changes *systematically* with the independent variable (IV). This means that you cannot be sure that any change in the dependent variable was due to the IV. In fact the confounding variable is acting as another IV. 31, 47, 77, 83, 86–87, 89, 103, 111–113, 117, 120–121, 123, 127, 140, 149, 152, 186, 189, 214, 219, 221–222, 227, 229

consent See informed consent.

content analysis A kind of observational study in which behaviour is seen indirectly in written or verbal material such as books, diaries or TV programmes. Categories (themes) are identified (possibly using thematic analysis) and then instances in each category can be counted so that quantitative data is produced. 5, 145, 175, 181, 206–207, 221, 223–224, 230–231

contiguity A series of things in contact or in proximity with each other. 131, 160

contingency table A matrix of rows and columns that displays the frequency distribution of variables. 141, 159, 212–213, 225, 231

continuous data Data that has a linear order and is not in categories, can take any value within a range. 173, 198, 225

continuous reinforcement A reinforcement (e.g. a reward) is delivered after every single target behaviour. 136, 164

control condition In an experiment with a repeated measures design, the procedure that provides a baseline measure of behaviour without the independent variable (IV). 140, 142, 149, 165, 184–185, 208

control group In an experiment with an independent groups design, a group of participants who receive no treatment. Their behaviour acts as a baseline against which the effect of the independent variable (IV) may be measured. 47, 73, 76, 81, 92, 110–113, 116, 140–143, 147, 152, 154, 161, 184–185

controlled observation Watching and recording behaviour within a structured environment, i.e. one where some variables are managed. 158–159, 182, 218

corpus callosum A bundle of nerve fibres that are part of the cerebral commissures and connect the left and right cerebral hemispheres, enabling communication between the two halves of the brain. 96–97, 110–111, 122–123, 126

correlation A research method used to assess the degree to which two co-variables are related. 32, 37, 47, 50, 54–55, 61, 68, 78, 103, 107, 108, 112, 114–115, 120–123, 125, 151, 167, 173, 198–205, 209, 212–213, 215, 216, 218, 221, 223–225, 230–231

correlation coefficient A number between −1.0 and +1.0 that represents the direction and strength of a relationship between co-variables. 151, 198

cortex The outer part of an organ. The cerebral cortex is the surface layer of the forebrain. 19, 41, 78–79, 89, 92, 96–98, 100, 102, 110, 112, 116, 118, 122, 126–127, 130, 132–133, 210, 223

cortisol An important hormone produced by the adrenal cortex. It helps the body to cope with stressors by controlling how the body uses energy. Cortisol suppresses immune system activity. 52, 65, 108–109, 123, 125, 127

counterbalancing An attempt to control for the effects of order in a repeated measures design: half the participants experience the conditions in one order, and the other half in the opposite order. 184, 185, 221–222, 229

covert observation Observations made without a participant's knowledge. 48, 135, 208–209, 220, 223–224, 230

credibility Believability. In order to be believable something must also be valid – and all the other features expected in scientific research (replicable, reliable, falsifiable as well as objective and generalisable). 214

critical value The number (value) which must be achieved in order for a result to be significant. 11, 77, 87, 103, 121, 147, 190–191, 193, 200–201, 212, 221, 225, 227, 229–231

critical values table List of numbers that inform you whether an observed value is significant or not. There are different tables for each inferential test. 147, 190–191, 193, 200–201, 212, 221, 225

cross-cultural research Compares behaviours in different cultures. 'Culture' refers to the different beliefs and norms shared by a particular group of people. Cultural beliefs and norms are learned through interactions with other group members. 47, 57, 218–219, 223

cross-sectional research Compares behaviours of different cross-sections of the population – people of differing ages, professional groups (teachers, doctors, solicitors, etc). 218–219, 223

cultural norms Behaviours and attitudes that are typical of a community of people. A 'cultural group' is larger than a 'social group'. 38–39, 46–47, 105, 151

culture The ideas, customs and social behaviour of a particular group of people or society. Note that the term 'culture' does not describe the group of people – it refers to their shared practices and beliefs. 23–24, 27, 38–39, 45–47, 49, 55, 60–61, 63–65, 74, 81, 83, 89, 105, 150–151, 156, 161, 207, 218–219, 223

culture bias Refers to a tendency to ignore cultural differences and interpret all phenomena through the 'lens' of one's own culture. 223, 207

debrief A post-research interview designed to inform the participants of the true nature of the study and to restore them to the state they were in at the start of the study. 71, 181

deception This occurs when a participant is not told the true research aims of a study and/or not told what they will be required to do. 29, 33, 60, 176–177, 224, 228

degrees of freedom (df) The number of values in the final calculation of a statistic that are free to vary. 212, 227, 131, 141, 159, 190, 201

demand characteristics Cues in a research situation that communicate to participants what is expected of them and may then unconsciously affect a participant's behaviour. 51, 59, 86, 143, 160, 164, 167, 170, 176, 186–189, 208, 215, 221–224, 229, 231

dementia A set of symptoms caused by a number of diseases. The symptoms include memory loss, confusion and personality change. 72–73, 78–79, 82–85, 89, 92

dependent variable (DV) Measured by the experimenter to assess the effects of the independent variable(s). 59, 109, 112, 152, 158, 182, 186, 188, 200

descriptive statistics The use of graphs, tables and summary statistics (measures of central tendency and dispersion) to identify trends and analyse sets of data. 86–87, 120, 158, 167–168, 172, 190, 220–221, 225

direction of hypothesis See directional hypothesis and non-directional hypothesis.

directional (one-tailed) hypothesis States the direction of the hypothesis, for example one condition is more than another. 87, 183, 224

discrimination Literally means 'to distinguish between two things'. It is the behaviour that results from prejudiced attitudes so that a person behaves differently towards a particular group of people because of their negative attitudes. 13, 27, 40–47, 49, 61, 65, 211

displacement A form of ego defense where the individual unconsciously redirects the threatening emotion from the person or thing that has caused it onto a third party. For example, you might kick your door after having a row with your boyfriend. 5, 106–107, 123, 145, 161

dissent Having opinions that differ from those held by others. In relation to obedience it means refusing to carry out orders (disobedience). 27, 34, 36–39, 43, 60, 64–65

dizygotic twins See DZ twins.

dopamine A neurotransmitter that generally has an excitatory effect and is associated with the sensation of pleasure. Unusually high levels are associated with schizophrenia and unusually low levels are associated with Parkinson's disease. 19, 99–102, 118, 122, 124, 126–127, 202–203

double dissociation A method used to demonstrate for instance that two functions are localised in different parts of the brain. A single dissociation demonstrates that a behaviour disappears if part A of the brain is damaged but part B is intact. But this, on its own, is not enough to show part A controls the behaviour so researchers look for a second dissociation, for example the behaviour is present if part A is intact but part B is damaged. 110

downregulation The process of reducing or suppressing a response to a stimulus, specifically the cellular response to a molecule is reduced because of a decrease in the number of receptors for that molecule. 99–100, 116, 123, 126

dual task performance A method used to test working memory where a person is required to perform two tasks simultaneously and separately. If their performance on either task is impaired when performed simultaneously that suggests they both involve the same region of the brain. 69, 86, 88

duration The length of time information can be held in memory. 9, 34, 49, 70–71, 80, 87–88, 91, 112

DV See dependent variable.

DZ twins Develop from two fertilised eggs. DZ twins share, on average, about 50% of their genes. They are as similar as any pair of siblings. 114–115, 123, 156, 204–205, 223, 230

ecological validity Concerns the extent to which the findings from a questionnaire/interview/research study can be generalised beyond the particular study. This will depend to some extent on internal validity but also the extent to which the questions/procedures represent the actual experience that is being investigated. 13, 39, 41, 43, 62–63, 80–81, 89, 92, 147, 167, 180, 186, 188–189, 207–208, 214, 218, 222–223, 228–231

EEG (electroencephalogram) Electrodes are attached to a person's scalp to record the tiny electrical impulses produced by the brain's activity. By measuring characteristic wave patterns, the EEG can help diagnose certain conditions of the brain. 21

ego The 'reality check' that balances the conflicting demands of the id and the superego. 21, 106–107, 123, 126

empiricism The view that knowledge can only come through direct observation or experiment rather than by reasoned argument or beliefs. 214–215, 224, 231

encoding The format in which information is stored in the various memory stores. 68–71, 75–77, 88–89, 91–92, 117

endocrine system One of the body's major information systems that instructs glands to release hormones directly into the bloodstream. These hormones are carried towards target organs in the body. 96, 108, 122, 125, 127

episodic buffer The component of the working memory model that brings together material from the other subsystems into a single memory rather than separate strands. It also provides a bridge between working memory and long-term memory. 68, 88, 92

episodic memory A long-term memory system for personal events. It includes memory of when the events occurred (time-stamped) and of the people, objects, places and behaviours involved. Memories from this store have to be retrieved consciously and with effort. 8, 72–73, 80, 88–92, 112

ethical guidelines (or codes) A set of principles designed to help professionals behave honestly and with integrity. 176

ethical issue A dilemma about right and wrong. The dilemma arises because researchers wish to investigate behaviour to benefit our understanding of people and improve our world, but there are costs to participants. 20, 22, 33, 41, 43, 48, 50–51, 58, 60–61, 69, 75, 86, 88, 103, 111, 120, 133, 136–137, 141, 147, 149, 158, 160–161, 164, 167, 176, 177, 178, 181–182, 185, 188, 196–197, 199, 202, 207–208, 210–211, 213, 220–224, 228, 231

ethics committee See research ethics committee

ethnocentrism Judging other cultures by the standards and values of one's own culture. In its extreme form it is the belief in the superiority of one's own culture which may lead to prejudice and discrimination towards other cultures. 23, 41, 44, 47, 61, 219

event sampling Draw up a list of behavioural categories. Then count (tally) every time each of the behaviours occurs in a specified time period. 135, 155, 158–159, 206–209, 223, 230

evolution The changes in inherited characteristics in a biological population over successive generations. 9, 95, 104–105, 109, 119, 122, 126–127

experiment A research method which demonstrates causal relationships. All experiments have an independent variable (IV) and a dependent variable (DV). 8, 10–11, 13, 16, 18–19, 25, 28–29, 31, 32, 34–35, 38–39, 41, 43, 46–48, 50, 52–53, 60–62, 64, 69, 71, 75–78, 80–82, 86–90, 92, 103, 109–110, 112, 125–126, 132–133, 135, 137, 140–143, 148–152, 164–165, 167, 171, 182–192, 196, 198, 200–202, 207–211, 214–215, 218–223, 227–231

experimental hypothesis The statement about the effect of the independent variable on the dependent variable in an experiment. 151, 183, 192, 224

external validity The degree to which a research finding can be generalised to, for example, other settings (ecological validity), other groups of people (population validity) and over time (temporal validity). 35, 60, 77, 81, 89, 92, 141, 153, 161

extinction When the CS and UCS have not been paired for a while and the CS ceases to elicit the CR. 4–5, 116–117, 127, 130–133, 144–146, 160, 162, 164

extraneous variable (EV) In an experiment, any variable other than the independent variable that might potentially affect the dependent variable and thereby confuse the results. This includes both participant and situational variables. 186, 222

F-scale A test of tendencies towards fascism, used to assess the authoritarian personality. 32, 36–37, 47, 60, 64

falsifiable/falsification The attempt to prove something wrong. This involves the use of the null hypothesis which we seek to disprove within set bounds of certainty. 25, 43, 131, 214, 220, 231

fatigue effect A problem caused when participants repeat a test or task and their performance falls, e.g. as a consequence of boredom or tiredness. A type of order effect. 184

field experiment Study with independent and dependent variables conducted in more everyday surroundings than a laboratory. Experimenter goes to participants. 89, 182, 188, 218, 222, 229

file-drawer effect Bias created because the results of some studies are not published (filed away), for example studies with negative results. 224

fitness In evolutionary theory, fitness is a measure of reproductive success, i.e. the likelihood that an individual will be represented in the next generation. 104

flooding A behavioural therapy in which a phobic client is exposed to an extreme form of a phobic stimulus in order to reduce anxiety triggered by that stimulus. This takes place across a small number of long therapy sessions. 146–147, 161

fMRI scan (functional magnetic resonance imaging) Uses radio waves to measure blood oxygen levels in the brain. Those areas of the brain that are most active use most oxygen and therefore blood is directed to the active area. 103, 112–113, 123, 202–203, 223, 230

forward conditioning A conditioning method in which the unconditioned stimulus (UCS) is presented after a neutral stimulus (NS). 132

frequency data Numbers representing how often a particular event occurs. 195, 201, 212

frequency distribution A graph displaying how often events occur in a particular sample. 80, 195

frequency table A table organising information in rows and columns, displaying a record of how often an event occurred. 58, 167, 172–173, 216, 221, 225–226

GABA Gamma-aminobutyric acid, a neurotransmitter that inhibits the activity of neurons in most areas of the brain. 99–101, 127

gender A person's sense of their maleness or femaleness, including attitudes and behaviour of that gender. 4, 11, 20, 23–24, 27, 36–38, 44, 47, 49–50, 54, 58, 60–61, 77, 92, 105, 108, 120–122, 126, 140, 144, 158–159, 181, 189, 205, 208, 211, 219–220

generalisability/generalise The extent to which findings and conclusions from a particular investigation can be broadly applied to the population. This is made possible if the sample of participants is representative of the population. It also depends on good internal and external validity. 22–23, 35, 51, 53, 55, 59, 61, 77, 79, 81, 83, 89–90, 111, 133, 141, 149, 151, 153, 155, 160–161, 163–165, 170–171, 180, 188–189, 196, 210, 221, 223, 228

genes Genes consist of DNA strands. DNA holds 'instructions' for general physical features of an organism (such as eye colour, height) and also specific physical features (such as neurotransmitter levels and size of brain structures). These may impact on psychological features (such as intelligence and mental disorder). Genes are transmitted from parents to offspring, i.e. inherited. 3, 25, 39, 100, 104–105, 114–116, 122–123, 127, 151, 160, 203–205, 223, 230

genome-wide association studies (GWAS) Look at the entire human genome for candidate genes of interest rather than focusing on specific genes. 205

glutamate The principal excitatory neurotransmitter in the brain, involved in most aspects of normal brain function including cognition, memory and learning. 99, 116, 127

grounded theory A bottom-up technique used when analysing qualitative data. It is an 'emergent' research process in which theoretical explanations emerge during the course of the investigation. 174–175, 221, 225, 228

hemispheres The forebrain (largest part of the brain) is divided into two halves or hemispheres. 78, 94, 96–97, 111, 122, 126, 230

heritability The ratio between (a) genetic variability of the particular trait and (b) total variability in the whole population. 204

heroin A drug that can act as a painkiller and is highly addictive. 100–101, 112–113, 116–118, 122–123, 126

hippocampus A structure in the subcortical area of each hemisphere of the forebrain, associated with memory. It is part of the limbic system, and is therefore also involved in motivation, emotion and learning. 72, 78, 85, 97, 102, 110, 126, 197, 230

histogram A type of graph where the frequency of each category of continuous data is represented by the height of the bar. In contrast to a bar chart, the data in a histogram has a true zero and a logical sequence. There are also no spaces between the bars. 86, 167, 172–173, 192, 195, 216, 221, 225, 228, 230

hormones Chemical substances that circulate in the bloodstream and only affect target organs. They are produced by glands in large quantities but disappear quickly. Their effects are very powerful and widespread in the body. 95–96, 108–109, 119, 122–123, 125, 127, 203, 215

hypothalamus A small subcortical brain structure which plays a major role in the body's stress response and maintaining a state of balance (homeostasis) by regulating many of its key processes such as heart rate and body temperature. 96–97, 100, 102, 108, 122, 126–127, 230

hypothesis/hypothesis testing A hypothesis is a statement of what a researcher believes to be true. In order to test such a statement, it must be clearly operationalised. 8, 11, 37, 43, 71, 73, 77, 83, 86, 87, 92, 147, 149, 151, 159, 167, 183, 190, 191, 192, 193, 194, 169, 200, 201, 212, 214, 215, 220, 224, 225, 226, 227, 229, 230, 231

id The part of the personality driven by the pleasure principle, which functions only in the unconscious and is made up of selfish aggressive instincts that demand immediate gratification. 21, 106–107, 123, 126

imitation Copying behaviour previously observed in others. In SLT imitation is a selective process and only models with key characteristics are likely to be imitated. 138–143, 160, 164, 209

imposed etic A technique or psychological test is used in (i.e. imposed upon) one culture even though it was designed for use in another culture. 219, 223, 231

independent groups design Different participants are allocated to two (or more) experimental groups representing different levels of the independent variable. 58, 71, 76, 80, 86, 142, 152–154, 158, 161, 184, 185, 187, 192–193, 201, 218

independent variable (IV) A factor that is directly manipulated by the experimenter in order to observe the effect of this variation on the dependent variable(s). 58–59, 109, 158, 182, 184, 186, 200

individual differences The characteristics that vary from one person to another. People vary in terms of their intelligence, emotional type, resilience and so on – two key individual differences are personality and gender. 4, 5, 11, 23, 27–28, 30, 32, 36–37, 39, 44–45, 47, 48, 52, 54, 57, 61, 64, 65, 71, 77, 78, 79, 80, 81, 97, 99, 103, 106, 110, 111, 115, 116, 117, 131, 136, 138–139, 141–146, 152–153, 171, 204

individualist People who value the rights and interests of the individual. This results in a concern for independence and self-assertiveness. People tend to live in small families unlike collectivist societies. This is typical of Western cultures, in contrast to many non-Western cultures that tend to be collectivist. 38, 46–47, 49, 60, 63–64

inferential test Procedures for drawing logical conclusions (inferences) about the target population from which samples are drawn. 11, 25, 83, 87, 190–192, 194, 200–201, 212, 216–217, 225, 229

information processing The mind works like a computer in that it processes (manages) information in terms of input, storage and retrieval. 70, 84, 88

informed consent Participants are given comprehensive information concerning the nature and purpose of a study and their role in it, so that they can make a decision about taking part. 11, 48, 146, 158, 161, 176–177, 188, 197, 208, 210, 224, 228

ingroup Any social group to which you belong, as distinct from the outgroup. 10–11, 13, 40–41, 43–44, 46, 48–49, 56, 59, 61–62, 64–65

ingroup favouritism The preference for people who belong to a group you identify with, such as your football team or your college or your family. This preference results in giving advantage to ingroup members, such as allocation of resources or rating them more highly. 13, 40–41, 48, 59, 61

intelligence test A set of tasks designed to measure a person's cognitive abilities such as reasoning, problem solving, comprehension. 41, 68, 186, 212

inter-observer reliability The extent to which there is agreement between two or more observers involved in observations of a behaviour. This is measured by correlating the observations of two observers. A general rule is that if (total number of agreements)/(total number of observations) > +.80, the data has high inter-observer reliability. 158

inter-rater reliability Assessed by comparing the results from two or more raters (e.g. interviewers or observers) questioning/observing/rating the same person. The data from all raters should be similar. 140, 180, 209, 213, 222, 228, 231

internal validity Concerns whether a test/questionnaire/research study does assess what it intended to assess. 16, 29, 31, 33, 35, 47, 49, 51, 60–61, 77, 83, 89, 92, 111, 113, 117, 123, 133, 141, 143, 149, 151, 153, 160–161, 163, 167, 180, 186, 188, 214–215, 222, 227, 229, 231

interval data Data is measured using units of equal intervals, such as measuring people's height in centimetres. 201, 229–230

intervening variable A variable that comes between two other variables and can be used to explain the relationship between two variables. For example, if a positive correlation is found between ice cream sales and violence this may be explained by an intervening variable – heat – which causes both the increase in ice cream sales and the increase in violence. 198, 223, 230

interview A 'live' encounter (face-to-face or on the phone) where one person (the interviewer) asks a set of questions to assess an interviewee's thoughts and/or experiences. The questions may be pre-set (as in a structured interview) or may develop as the interview goes along (unstructured interview). 11, 17, 25, 32, 34–35, 39, 49, 53, 55, 90, 110, 121, 150, 155, 165, 167–168, 175, 178–180, 186, 196, 218, 221–222, 228, 231

interviewer bias A form of researcher bias, in this case the researcher is an interviewer. 178, 222, 228

IV See independent variable.

laboratory Any setting (room or other environment) specially fitted out for conducting research. A lab is not the only place where scientific experiments can be conducted. It is, however, the ideal place for scientific experiments because it permits maximum control. Labs are not used exclusively for experimental research, for example controlled observations are also conducted in labs. 18, 25, 32, 34–35, 50, 69, 71, 76–77, 80–81, 86, 88, 90, 101, 109, 126, 130, 132, 135, 137, 140–143, 152–153, 167, 182–183, 188–189, 208–211, 215, 218, 220–223, 229, 231

laboratory experiment Study with independent and dependent variables conducted in a very controlled environment. Participants go to experimenter. 18, 50, 69, 71, 76–77, 80–81, 86, 88, 90, 109, 126, 135, 140–142, 152–153, 167, 182, 188–189, 210–211, 218, 220, 222–223, 229, 231

lateralisation The idea that the two halves (hemispheres) of the brain are functionally different and that certain mental processes and behaviours are mainly controlled by one hemisphere rather than the other, as in the example of language (which is localised as well as lateralised). 96–97, 112, 122, 126

leading question A question (or statement) which, because of the way it is phrased, suggests a certain answer. For example: 'Did you see the knife in the accused's hand?' (when there was no knife). 169, 178–180, 182, 228

learning theories A collective term for explanations based on conditioning (classical and operant). This also includes social learning theory. 3–6, 11, 15, 17–19, 25, 35, 44, 59, 97, 105, 109, 129, 130–132, 134–165, 167, 213

lesioning Destroying or cutting through neural areas or pathways, using surgery, heat, radiation etc. 19, 101, 203

level of measurement The different ways of measuring items or psychological variables, the lower levels are less precise (such as nominal and ordinal). Higher levels (such as interval) are 'better' because they are more precise. 31, 75, 99, 172, 191–192, 201

level of significance The level of probability at which it has been agreed to reject the null hypothesis. 86, 167, 190–191, 193, 194, 200, 212, 227, 229

Likert scale Respondents can indicate the extent to which they agree or disagree with a statement. There are usually five levels ranging from 'strongly agree' through 'neutral' to 'strongly disagree'. 169

limbic system Subcortical structures in the brain (including the hypothalamus and amygdala) thought to be closely involved in regulating emotional behaviour including aggression. 92, 96–97, 100, 102, 118, 122, 126

line graph Has continuous data on the x-axis, like a histogram. There is a dot to mark the highest value in each category which is connected by a line. 173, 225

localisation The theory that different areas of the brain are responsible for different behaviours, processes or activities. 97, 122, 126, 202

locus of control (LOC) Refers to the sense we each have about what directs events in our lives. Internals believe they are mostly responsible for what happens to them (internal locus of control). Externals believe it is mainly a matter of luck or due to other outside forces (external locus of control). 36–37, 60

long-term memory (LTM) The permanent memory store. Coding is mainly semantic (meaning), it has unlimited capacity and can store memories for up to a lifetime. 70, 72, 76, 88

longitudinal research Any study that takes place over months and years so that the effects of time (age) can be studied. 103, 122, 218–219, 223

maintenance The processing of maintaining something (keeping it going). If a phobia is acquired by classical conditioning we would expect it to decline over time unless some other process maintains it. 4, 5, 68, 70, 88, 131, 144–145, 161, 164

maintenance rehearsal Vocally (or sub-vocally) repeating an item to keep it in memory. 68, 70, 88

Mann-Whitney U test Test of difference between two sets of data. Data must be ordinal or interval (i.e. not nominal). Used for independent groups design. Test statistic is U. 76–77, 86, 167, 190, 192–193, 221, 225, 229

matched pairs design Participants who are similar on key variables (e.g. memory ability, age) are paired. One member of the pair is placed in group A and the other in group B. This means there are two groups of participants. Each group is given one level of the independent variable. 110, 123, 140, 184–185, 192–193

mean The arithmetic average. Add up all the values and divide by the number of values. 8, 29, 50, 54, 58, 69, 76, 78–80, 82, 86, 105, 111–112, 121, 136, 140, 142, 150, 154, 160, 162, 167, 172–173, 181, 191–192, 195, 216, 225, 228–230

measures of central tendency The general term for any calculation of the average value in a set of data. 59, 86–87, 167, 172, 175, 181, 195, 220–221, 225, 229

measures of dispersion The general term for any calculation of the spread or variation in a set of scores. 55, 58, 86, 167, 172, 216, 220–221, 225

median The central value in a set of data when values are arranged from lowest to highest. 69, 121, 153, 158, 167, 172–173, 195, 216, 225, 228

mesocorticolimbic pathway Sometimes called the 'reward pathway', it involves several regions of the brain. When activated by a rewarding stimulus (e.g. food, sex), information travels from the ventral tegmental area to the nucleus accumbens and then up to the prefrontal cortex. 100–101, 122

meta-analysis The results of several studies that have addressed similar aims are combined. Statistical methods are used to produce an effect size to express overall trends. 54, 218–219, 221, 223, 231

metabolite Any substance produced by chemical processes in the body. 102

mode The most frequently occurring value in a set of data. 86, 121, 167, 172–173, 195, 216, 225, 228, 230

modelling From the observer's perspective modelling is imitating the behaviour of a role model. From the role model's perspective, modelling is the demonstration of a specific behaviour that may be imitated by an observer. 4–5, 44, 114–115, 138–140, 144, 145, 151, 160–161

monozygotic twins See MZ twins.

moral strain A state of mental discomfort or anxiety experienced in the agentic state when a person's actions conflict with their personal morality. 16, 28–29, 60, 64–65

motivation The force that drives a person to enact the behaviour. In SLT this is the result of vicarious reinforcement. 19, 21, 40, 44, 96, 100, 116–117, 119, 122, 137–139, 160, 185, 199

motor cortex A region of the frontal lobe involved in regulating movement. 96–97, 122, 126

MRI scans The difference between fMRI and MRI scans is the latter do not provide information on function however they do provide higher resolution of images than fMRI. A further difference is that MRI uses water molecules' hydrogen nuclei and reads radio signals emitted from them. 197, 203

multi-store model A representation of how memory works in terms of three stores. It also describes how information is transferred from one store to another, how it is remembered and how it is forgotten. 9, 17, 67–68, 70–72, 85, 87–88, 91–93

mundane realism Refers to how an experiment mirrors the real world. The simulated task environment is realistic to the extent to which experiences encountered in the simulated environment will occur in the real world. 13, 41, 61, 188, 189, 229

MZ twins Develop from one fertilised egg (zygote) and are genetically identical. 114–115, 123, 204, 230

natural selection The major process that explains evolution whereby inherited traits that enhance an animal's reproductive success are passed on to the next generation and thus 'selected', whereas animals without such traits are less successful at reproduction and their traits are not selected. 9, 95, 104–105, 119, 122, 126–127, 211, 218

naturalistic observation Everything is left as usual. Environment unstructured but may use 'structured' techniques, e.g. behavioural categories. 155, 159, 208, 210, 221, 223, 230

negative correlation As one co-variable increases, the other decreases. For example, the following two co-variables: the number of people in a room and amount of personal space are negatively correlated. 50, 61, 103, 122, 198, 223, 225, 230

negative punishment Occurs when something nice is removed from an individual following a behaviour, decreasing the probability of that behaviour being repeated. 134, 164

negative reinforcement Occurs when something unpleasant is removed from the individual following a behaviour, increasing the probability of that behaviour being repeated. 4, 19, 134, 144

negative skew Most of the scores in a distribution are bunched towards the right. The mode is to the right of the mean because the mean is dragged to the left by the extreme scores tailing in a negative direction (tail to the left). 195, 225

neuron The basic building block of the nervous system. Neurons are nerve cells that process and transmit messages through electrical and chemical signals. 22, 95–102, 116, 122, 124, 126–127

neurotransmitters Brain chemicals released from synaptic vesicles. Neurotransmitters relay signals from one neuron to another across a synapse. Neurotransmitters can be broadly divided into those that perform an excitatory function and those that perform an inhibitory function. 25, 95, 98–101, 118–119, 122, 126–127, 157

neutral stimulus (NS) A stimulus that does not produce the target response. It becomes a conditioned stimulus after being paired with the unconditioned stimulus. 130–133, 144, 148–149, 160–161, 164

nominal data Data is in separate categories, such as grouping people in your class according to their height. One group might be tall, another group would be medium and the final group is small. 172–173, 201, 212, 225–226, 229–230

non-directional (two-tailed) hypothesis States there is a difference or correlation, and does not give the direction of that difference. 71, 109, 147, 183, 190

non-participant observation Observer is not a participant in the behaviour being observed. 208–209, 223

noradrenaline A hormone and a neurotransmitter that generally has an excitatory effect, similar to the hormone adrenaline. The hormone is produced by the adrenal gland. 100–101, 108

normal distribution Occurs when certain variables are measured, such as IQ or the life of a light bulb. Variables such as these are distributed so that most of the scores are clustered around the mean, median and mode. 68.26% of the scores should lie within one standard deviation of the mid-point. 86, 167, 195, 221, 225, 229–230

nucleus accumbens A part of the mesolimbic pathway, the reward pathway of the brain. 100

null hypothesis A statement of no difference. (Do not use the term 'relationship'.) 73, 77, 83, 87, 103, 107, 183, 190, 192, 194, 200–201, 214, 224–225, 227, 229–231

obedience A form of social influence in which an individual follows a direct order. The person issuing the order is usually a figure of authority who has the power to punish when obedient behaviour is not forthcoming. There is usually the assumption that the person receiving the order is made to respond in a way they would not otherwise have done. 8, 11, 16, 23, 27–39, 44, 50–51, 58, 60, 63–65, 168–169, 177, 182, 189, 218

objectivity The research process should not be influenced by the researcher's emotions, personal opinions or expectations. It should be free from bias. This concerns both designing a study and conducting it. The opposite is subjectivity. 25, 75, 79, 81, 83, 88, 186–187, 196, 207–209, 215, 221, 223–224

observation To observe is to watch or listen to behaviour in others. 48, 52, 62, 81, 108, 125, 131–133, 135, 138–140, 143, 155, 158–160, 167–168, 182, 196, 206–210, 214, 215, 218, 220–221, 223–224, 230–231

observational learning Learning through imitation, a key concept in social learning theory. 4, 140, 144

observational research Watch or listen to what participants do. 206

observed value The number (value) produced after applying an inferential test formula. This is sometimes called the calculated value because the researcher calculates it. 11, 77, 86, 103, 131, 167, 190, 193, 200–201, 212, 220, 225–227, 229–231

observer bias In observational studies there is a danger that observers' expectations affect what they see or hear. This reduces the validity of the observations. 206–209, 223, 228, 230–231

occipital lobe One of four major regions of the cerebral cortex. There are two occipital lobes, one in each hemisphere. The occipital lobes are at the back of the brain and contain the visual area. 97, 110, 122, 126

one-tailed hypothesis See directional hypothesis.

open question Invites respondents to provide their own answers, and tends to produce qualitative data, i.e. descriptive data which can't be immediately counted. 25, 37, 45, 58–59, 73, 121, 168–169, 175, 178, 222, 228

operant conditioning Learning that occurs when a behaviour is followed by an event, and the nature of this event increases or decreases the probability of the behaviour being repeated. 4–5, 11, 19, 25, 116, 129, 134–137, 139, 144–145, 156, 160–161, 164–165, 210

operationalisation Variables must be operationalised, i.e. defined in a way that they can easily be tested. 86, 167, 182–183, 221, 224

opportunity sample A sample of participants produced by selecting people who are most easily available at the time of the study. 54, 158, 170–171, 205, 213, 222, 228

order effects In an experiment with a repeated measures design, a participant may be better on the second test because of getting better with experience (a *practice effect*) or may perform less well because of being bored or tired (a *fatigue effect*). 87, 184–185, 221–222, 229, 231

order of magnitude Working out approximately how much larger one number is than another. 216–217, 224

ordinal data Data is ordered in some way, for example each person in your class lines up in order of size. The 'difference' between each person is not necessarily the same. 201, 225–226, 230

outgroup Any social group to which you do not belong, as distinct from the ingroup. 9–10, 13, 40–44, 46–49, 53, 55–57, 59, 61–62, 64–65

overt observation Participant is aware of being observed. 48, 133, 135, 208–209, 220, 223–224, 230

oxytocin A hormone with the main function of causing contraction of the uterus during labour and stimulates lactation. 108

partial reinforcement When a behaviour is reinforced only some of the time it occurs (e.g. every tenth time or at variable intervals). 136–137, 160

participant observation Observer is a participant in the behaviour being observed, for example being in a bus stop queue and observing behaviour in the queue. 139, 208–209, 223, 230

participant variable A characteristic of the participants, such as age or intelligence. 109, 141, 143, 149, 153, 161, 165, 184–186, 219, 221–223, 229, 231

peer review The assessment of scientific work by others who are experts in the same field (i.e. 'peers'). 215, 220–221, 224, 231

peripheral nervous system (PNS) Sends information to the central nervous system (CNS) from the outside world, and transmits messages from the CNS to muscles and glands in the body. 96, 98, 122

personality An individual's characteristic, coherent and relatively stable set of behaviours, attitudes, interests and capabilities. These characteristics are useful for predicting future behaviour, e.g. we have expectations that a kind person will behave in a kind fashion. Personality is a means of distinguishing between people. It is an individual difference. 11, 16, 32, 34, 36, 37, 38, 39, 44, 45, 47, 50, 52, 54, 55, 57, 60, 61, 65, 100, 101, 106, 107, 108, 123, 138, 144, 146, 178, 180, 196, 197

personality disorder A class of mental disorders where an individual's enduring pattern of behaviour (i.e. their personality) is maladaptive. 108

personality test A psychological assessment of personality. 37, 55, 60

PET scan (positron emission tomography) Measures metabolic activity in the brain, i.e. the areas that are most active. A person is injected with a small amount of a radioactive substance such as glucose (the radiotracer). Brain areas that are most active will use more of it and this can be detected by the scanner. 21, 101, 102, 111, 123, 127, 202, 203, 221, 223, 230

phonological loop (PL) The component of the working memory model that processes information in terms of sound. This includes both written and spoken material. It's divided into the phonological store and the articulatory process. 68, 69, 82, 83, 84, 86, 88, 89, 92

pie chart A circular descriptive statistic where frequency is represented by the proportion of each slice. 118, 158, 210

pituitary gland Called the master gland of the body's hormone system because it directs much of the hormone activity. 96, 108, 127

pleasure principle In psychoanalytic theory, the drive to do things which produce pleasure or gratification, and to avoid pain. 106, 123

population People of differing ages, professional groups (teachers, doctors, solicitors, etc). 42, 45, 46, 51, 63, 69, 79, 82, 84, 88, 96, 104, 108, 149, 150, 151, 158, 165, 170, 171, 180, 183, 188, 190, 195, 204, 205, 213, 219, 222, 223, 228, 229

positive correlation As one co-variable increases so does the other. For example, the number of people in a room and noise are positively correlated. 32, 68, 78, 108, 112, 121, 125, 198, 199, 200, 223, 225, 230

positive punishment Occurs when something unpleasant is introduced to the individual following a behaviour, decreasing the probability of that behaviour being repeated. 134

positive reinforcement Occurs when something nice is introduced to the individual following a behaviour, increasing the probability of that behaviour being repeated. 19, 134, 156, 164

positive skew Most of the scores in a distribution are bunched towards the left. The mode is to the left of the mean because the mean is dragged to the right by the extreme scores tailing in a positive direction (tail to the right). 195, 225, 230

post-mortem studies The brain is analysed after death to determine whether certain observed behaviours during the patient's lifetime can be linked to abnormalities in the brain. 197, 203

postsynaptic neuron The neuron that is receiving the information at the synapse. 99, 100, 116, 124

power distance index (PDI) A measure of the extent to which the lower ranking individuals of a society accept and expect that power is distributed unequally. 38, 60, 63, 64

practice effect A type of order effect in a repeated measures design where performance is improved as a result of doing a task on earlier trials. 184, 185,

predictive validity Concerns the extent to which a test score actually is related to the behaviour you want to measure, and therefore is able to forecast performance on another measure of the same behaviour. 103, 161, 186, 214, 222, 229, 231

prefrontal cortex A region in the frontal lobe which is involved with highest-order cognitive activities, such as working memory. 92, 102, 110, 116, 118, 122, 127

prejudice Literally, a pre-judgement. There are three key components. A for affect as it is experienced as an emotion. B for the resulting behaviour, which is discrimination. C for cognitive because prejudice is a biased belief held about an individual or group prior to direct experience of that person/people. Such attitudes are often based on stereotypes and/or group characteristics. Individual attributes are ignored. 11, 24, 36, 40–49, 54, 55, 56, 59, 61, 62, 64, 65, 75, 137, 194

presumptive consent A way of dealing with a lack of informed consent. A group of people similar to prospective participants are asked whether they would agree to take part in a study. If this group of people consent to the procedures in the proposed study, it is presumed that the real participants would agree as well. 177

presynaptic neuron The transmitting neuron, before the synaptic cleft. 99, 100

primary data Information collected by a researcher specifically for the purpose of the current study. 90, 218, 225, 231

primary reinforcement Takes place when the thing that acts as a reinforcer has biological significance, such as food. 134

privacy Refers to a person's right to control the flow of information about themselves. Invasion of privacy is included as a form of psychological harm. 22, 120, 121, 176, 177, 208, 223, 224, 228

probability A measure of the likelihood that an event may occur. Probability is given as a number between 0 and 1 (where 0 indicates impossibility and 1 indicates certainty). 80, 134, 138, 160, 190, 194, 216, 225, 229

procedural memory Our knowledge of how to do things. This includes our memories of learned skills. We usually recall these memories without making a conscious or deliberate effort. 72, 90, 197

protection from harm Participants should not experience negative physical effects, such as physical injury, nor should they experience negative psychological effects, such as lowered self-esteem or embarrassment. 176, 177, 224

pseudorandom order Not truly random, for example numbers generated by a computer program rather than a truly random method such as using atmospheric noise to generate random numbers. 112

psychological test A set of questions or tasks that assess some aspect of psychological functioning, such as intelligence or personality. 178, 180, 196, 201, 220, 223, 230

psychopathy Lacking a conscience and empathy for others, making it more likely that an individual will commit crimes and have difficulty forming relationships. 108,

publication bias The tendency for academic journals to publish only positive results, or results that agree with existing theories. 45, 220, 224

punishment Takes place when an event follows a behaviour and this decreases the probability that the behaviour will be repeated. 22, 29, 44, 111, 129, 134–136, 142, 160, 164

purposive sampling A non-random means of selecting research participants where the researcher deliberately selects people to suit the needs of the study. For example, if you wanted to study the behaviour of medical students it would make sense to put an ad on the noticeboard of a medical school rather than standing around in a shopping centre hoping to find some. 170, 175, 222

qualitative data Information in words or pictures, non-numerical. It can be turned into quantitative data by placing the data in categories and then counting frequency. 7, 17, 29, 31, 32, 35, 53, 58, 59, 60, 90, 121, 139, 141, 150, 158, 159, 168, 174–175, 178, 196, 204, 213, 218, 221–225, 228–231

quantitative data Information in numbers, i.e. quantities. 7, 8, 17, 29, 35, 48, 53, 55, 58, 59, 61, 73, 90, 120, 121, 150, 151, 158, 159, 168, 169, 172, 174–175, 178, 181, 196, 206, 207, 216, 221–225, 228–230

quasi-experiment A study that is almost an experiment but lacks key ingredients, for example the independent variable has not been manipulated by the researcher and therefore participants cannot be randomly allocated to conditions. 78, 189

questionnaire Respondents record their own answers. The questions are predetermined (i.e. structured). They are provided in written form and there is no face-to-face contact with another person. 37, 39, 45, 48, 50, 54, 55, 58, 59, 62, 73, 105, 120, 121, 124, 125, 150, 151, 155, 165, 168–171, 178–181, 184, 186, 188, 189, 198, 213, 220, 221, 222, 228, 231

random allocation An attempt to control for participant variables in an independent groups design which ensures that each participant has the same chance of being in one condition as any other. 47, 52, 111, 123, 140, 142, 152, 153, 179, 229

random sample A sample of participants produced using a random technique such that every member of the target population has an equal chance of being selected. 49, 170, 222, 228

randomisation/random techniques Ensures that every member of the target population has an equal chance of being selected. Examples include giving everyone in the target population a number, putting the numbers in a hat and drawing out the required number of participants, or using a random number generator (available on computers and smartphones). Random number generators are pseudorandom techniques. 170, 184, 185, 222

range A simple calculation of the dispersion in a set of scores which is worked out by subtracting the lowest score from the highest score. 172, 173, 191, 216, 221, 225

ranked scale A kind of closed question where respondents are asked to give an assessment of their views using a scale, e.g. from 1 to 5 where 5 represents very positive and 1 represents very negative. 45, 48, 52, 53, 54, 65, 120, 121, 168, 169, 184, 192, 199, 200, 201, 221, 222, 225, 228, 230

realistic conflict theory (RCT) An explanation of prejudice which sees competition for limited resources as a key determinant of intergroup relations. 42–43, 46, 48, 61, 62, 64

reality principle In psychoanalytic theory, the drive to accommodate to the demands of the environment in a realistic way. 106, 123

reconstructive memory Fragments of stored information are reassembled during recall. The gaps are filled in by our expectations and beliefs so that we can produce a 'story' that makes sense. 74–75, 85, 88, 91, 92

recreational drugs Drugs are biochemicals that have specific effects on the functioning of the body's systems. Drugs may be used for physiological purposes (e.g. antibiotics used to kill viruses) or for psychological purposes (e.g. antidepressants). Drugs for psychological treatments are called 'psychoactive' and affect transmission at the central nervous system (CNS), altering an individual's mental processes. A distinction is made between using such drugs for medical purposes (as in the case of antidepressants used to treat depression) and using drugs for enjoyment or leisure purposes (i.e. recreation). 100–101, 116, 119, 121, 122, 124, 126, 210

reductionism Experimental research requires identifying individual variables that may contribute to a complex behaviour – the independent and dependent variable. 20, 25, 29, 31, 60, 77, 79, 89, 103, 109, 117, 122, 123, 139, 151, 160, 161, 174, 214, 215, 224, 225, 228, 231

reinforcement Takes place when a behaviour is followed by an event and this increases the probability of that behaviour being repeated. 7, 19, 134–139, 142, 144, 151, 156, 160, 162, 164–165

reinforcement schedule A plan of how often and when reinforcement will be provided, i.e. vary or keep constant the ratio of behaviour to reinforcer and the time interval between reinforcements. 19, 136–137, 162, 164

reliability Ensuring that all procedures are the same for every participant so that their performances are comparable. Refers to consistency of measurements. 22, 25, 51, 53, 55, 59, 65, 75, 77, 83, 88, 90, 103, 111, 115, 133, 139, 151, 153, 164, 165, 180, 181, 186, 198, 189, 199, 206, 207, 209 214, 215, 221, 222, 223, 224, 228–231

repeated measures design Each participant takes part in every condition being tested. Each condition represents one level of the independent variable. 87, 92, 112, 127, 184, 185, 187, 189–193, 201, 218–222, 225, 226, 229

replicability If a finding from a research study is true (valid) then it should be possible to obtain the same finding if the study is repeated. Repeating a study confirms the 'trueness' of the original finding. 33, 35, 36, 38, 39, 41, 46, 49, 50, 51, 52, 55, 60, 61, 63, 64, 69, 83, 87, 90, 109, 113, 188, 194, 207, 213, 214, 220, 222, 223, 224, 231

reproduction The recall and enactment of the modelled behaviour in response to appropriate circumstances. 138, 139, 160, 164

research aims A general statement of what the researcher intends to investigate; the purpose of the study. 176, 183, 184, 187, 218

research ethics committee (REC) Group of people within a research institution who approve a study before it begins. The group may consist of both professional and lay people. 177, 224

researcher bias A researcher's expectations or beliefs which may encourage certain behaviours in participants. Leads to a researcher effect. 179, 188, 221, 222, 228

researcher effect A researcher's expectations (bias) may encourage certain behaviours in participants. The result is that the researcher's expectations/biases are fulfilled. 49, 169, 178, 179, 187, 224, 228

resistance The ability of people to withstand the social pressure to conform to the majority or to obey authority. This ability to withstand social pressure is influenced by both situational and dispositional (personality) factors. 35, 36, 37, 38, 53, 61

response set A tendency for interviewees to respond in the same way to all questions, regardless of context. This would bias their answers. 168, 222

retention The cognitive process of storing the modelled behaviour in memory. 138, 139, 160, 164

retrieval The process of transferring information from LTM to STM, recalling information. 70, 71, 75, 88, 91, 197

right to withdraw Participants should be told that they can stop participating in a study if for any reason they are feeling uncomfortable. 50, 59, 176, 177, 224, 228

right wing authoritarianism (RWA) Three behavioural clusters which correlate together – high submissiveness to legitimate authority, hostility/aggressiveness and adherence to social conventions. 44, 52, 54, 61, 65

risk management Involves weighing up the balance of long-term gains in a research study versus short-term risks to participants. Such arguments are presented to an ethics committee who decides whether the risks are justified. 49, 177

role models See 'modelling'.

scapegoating A means of dealing with negative feelings such as anger, frustration or unhappiness by transferring them onto other, less powerful people or objects (the scapegoat) rather than being turned onto oneself. The transferring (or projection) is a form of ego defence because you are protecting your ego from self-aggression. 44

scatter diagram A type of graph that represents the strength and direction of a relationship between co-variables in a correlational analysis. 97, 120, 173, 198, 199, 200, 209, 216, 221, 225, 230

schema A mental framework of beliefs and expectations that influence cognitive processing. We are born with some schemas but they develop in complexity with experience of the world. 74, 75, 87, 88, 92

scientific method An objective means of testing hypotheses in order to develop empirically based explanations/theories. 25, 215

secondary data Data used in a research study that was collected previously for another research study or, for example, a researcher uses government statistics. Basically such data is 'second-hand'. 90, 216, 218, 221, 225, 230

secondary reinforcement Takes place when the thing that acts as a reinforcer has become associated with something of biological significance, such as money which is associated with being able to buy food. 134, 160

self-esteem The feelings that a person has about their self-concept. 40, 41, 46, 58, 61, 64, 120, 121, 150, 152, 161, 176

semantic memory A long-term memory system for our knowledge of the world. This includes facts and our knowledge of what words and concepts mean. These memories usually need to be recalled deliberately. 8, 72–73, 78, 79, 80, 88–91, 197

semi-structured interview Some questions are predetermined but also new questions are developed as the interview proceeds. 11, 53, 90, 178, 228

serotonin A neurotransmitter with widespread inhibitory effects throughout the brain. It has a key role in aggressive behaviour. 19, 25, 99–101, 122, 126, 218

sexual selection An evolutionary explanation of partner preference. Attributes or behaviours that increase reproductive success are passed on and may become exaggerated over succeeding generations of offspring. 104, 105, 122, 126, 218

shaping A process of modifying behaviour by reinforcing successive approximations to a desired behaviour. 136, 137, 160, 164

short-term memory (STM) The limited-capacity memory store. Encoding is mainly acoustic (sounds), capacity is between 5 and 9 items, duration is between about 18 and 30 seconds. 9, 68–71, 76, 87, 88, 90, 91, 92

significance A statistical term indicating that the research findings are sufficiently strong to enable a researcher to reject the null hypothesis under test and accept the alternate hypothesis. 86, 167, 190–191, 193, 194, 200, 212, 227, 229

significant figures (sf) The number of interesting or important digits. Zeros are just place holders. 216, 217, 224, 231

situation Features of the immediate physical and social environment which may influence a person's behaviour. The alternative is dispositional factors where behaviour is explained in terms of personality. 10, 24, 25, 28, 29, 31, 32, 35, 37, 38, 42, 43, 44, 46, 49, 52, 56, 60, 61, 62, 63, 64, 65, 74, 75, 80, 81, 88, 89, 104, 120, 138, 141, 145, 146, 153, 154, 159, 160, 161, 168, 187, 188, 208, 214, 218, 222, 224

situational factors Features of the immediate physical and social environment which may influence a person's behaviour. The alternative is dispositional factors where behaviour is explained in terms of personality. 34, 35, 36, 39, 40, 45, 46, 47

situational variable A feature of the environment that may affect performance, such as distracting noise or time of day. 161, 186, 221

skewed distribution The mean, median and mode do not all share the same value (as they do in a normal distribution). See positive skew, negative skew. 195, 221, 225, 229, 230

Skinner box An operant conditioning chamber, laboratory apparatus used to study the effects of rewards and punishments on animals using food pellets (as rewards) or electrified floor (as punishment). 116, 117, 134, 135, 137, 160, 164, 210

snowball sampling A method of obtaining participants for a study that relies on referrals from initial participants to generate additional participants. 213, 231

social desirability bias A tendency for respondents to answer questions in such a way so as to present themselves in a 'better light'. 54, 168, 180, 222, 228

social dominance orientation (SDO) The extent to which people are motivated to seek out ingroup power, dominance and superiority. People with high SDO prefer hierarchical versus equal distribution of power. 44, 47, 52, 54, 61

social identity theory (SIT) The view that your behaviour is motivated by your social identity. A person's self-image has two components: personal identity and social identity. Personal identity is based on your characteristics and achievements. Social identity is determined by the various groups of people to which you belong, your 'ingroups'. 10, 29, 40, 41, 46, 52, 56, 57, 61, 62, 64

social impact theory An explanation of the extent to which other people's real or imagined presence can alter the way an individual thinks, feels or acts. The impact is determined by strength, immediacy and number of sources during any interaction. 12, 30, 31, 38, 56, 57, 60, 64

social learning theory (SLT) A way of explaining behaviour that includes both direct and indirect reinforcement, combining learning theory with the role of cognitive factors. 9, 36, 44, 138–139, 140, 142, 144, 152, 156, 160, 164

social norms Refers to a behaviour or belief that is standard, usual or typical of a group of people. 23, 34, 45–48, 61, 62, 64

socialisation The process by which individuals learn the social behaviours of their culture. The 'social behaviours' include morals, values, social skills, norms, language and so on. 28, 34, 35, 38, 44, 46

socioeconomic status A measure of a person's economic and social position in relation to others, based on theirs or their family's income, education, and occupation. 30

somatosensory cortex An area of the parietal lobe that processes sensory information, such as touch. 97, 122, 126

Spearman's *rho* Test of relationship between co-variables. Data must be ordinal or interval (i.e. not nominal). Test statistic is *rho*. 103, 121, 200–201, 225, 230

spontaneous recovery An extinct response activates again so that the CS once again elicits the CR. 130–133, 154, 160, 162, 164, 165

standard deviation A measure of dispersion. It tells us how much values deviate from the mean by calculating the difference between the mean and each value, and then squaring this. All the squared differences are added up and divided by $n - 1$ (where n = number of values). This gives the variance. The standard deviation is the square root of the variance. 58, 111, 172, 173, 191, 192, 195, 216, 221, 225, 228, 229

standard form Expressing a number mainly in terms of its size. 216, 217, 224

standardisation The procedures used in any study should be the same for each participant. If the procedures differ between participants this would act as a confounding variable, affecting the validity of the study. Also, if procedures were not consistent this would reduce the reliability of the study. 25, 33, 34, 50, 60, 83, 87, 88, 89, 90, 111, 113, 117, 123, 127, 163, 179, 186, 187, 201, 215, 229, 231

standardised instructions A set of instructions that are the same for all participants so as to avoid investigator effects caused by different instructions. 58, 75, 181, 220, 224, 228

stereotyping A perception of an individual in terms of some readily available feature, such as their group membership or physical attractiveness, rather than their individual attributes. Stereotypes summarise large amounts of information and provide an instant picture from meagre data. We are 'cognitive misers' and stereotypes allow us to conserve cognitive energy. 40, 48, 56, 59, 75

stimulus generalisation When an individual who has acquired a conditioned response to one stimulus begins to respond to similar stimuli in the same way. 130, 148, 160

storage The process of holding information in memory. 8, 68, 70–74, 76, 82, 85, 88, 91, 138

stratified sample Participants are selected from different subgroups (strata) in the target population in proportion to the subgroup's frequency in that population. 45, 58, 65, 103, 120, 121, 170, 171, 221, 228

structured interview Predetermined questions delivered by an interviewer who does not probe beyond the answers received but may answer questions from the interviewee. 55, 178, 221, 222, 228, 229

structured observation Some variables are changed (manipulated) by the researcher, e.g. in a laboratory. 143, 206, 208, 221, 223, 228

subjectivity See objectivity.

superego The moralistic part of the personality which represents the ideal self – how we ought to be. 106, 107, 121, 123

superordinate goal An aim which is shared by all group members. This serves to unite a group and encourage cooperation, rather than emphasising individual goals and competition. 42, 43, 48, 49, 56, 61, 64

synapse The junction between two neurons. This includes the presynaptic terminal, the synaptic cleft and the postsynaptic receptor site. 98–101, 122, 124

synaptic cleft The space between the pre- and postsynaptic neuron. 99, 122

synaptic transmission The process by which neighbouring neurons communicate with each other by sending chemical messages across the tiny gap (the synapse) that separates neurons. 8, 98–100, 122, 124, 126

systematic desensitisation (SD) A behavioural therapy designed to reduce an unwanted response, such as anxiety, to a stimulus. SD involves drawing up a hierarchy of anxiety-provoking situations related to a phobic stimulus, teaching a client to relax, and then exposing them to phobic situations. The client works their way through the hierarchy whilst maintaining relaxation. 10, 17, 131, 133, 145, 146–147, 154–155, 157, 161, 163, 165

tally chart A table with tally marks, each mark represents one case and together shows the frequency of each category in the table. 158, 159, 229

temporal cortex/lobe One of four major regions of the cerebral cortex. There are two temporal lobes, one in each hemisphere. The temporal lobes are at the side of the brain and contain the auditory area and some of the language area (e.g. Wernicke's area). 78, 79, 89, 90, 92, 97, 110, 122, 126, 197

test-retest reliability A measure of whether something varies from one time to another, i.e. is consistent over time. The same questionnaire or interview is given to the same participants on two occasions to see if the same result is obtained. 155, 161, 180, 186, 222

testosterone A hormone from the androgen group that is produced mainly in the male testes (and in smaller amounts in the female ovaries). Associated with aggressiveness. 108–109, 119, 123, 125, 127, 203

thalamus A structure in the centre of the subcortical area of the forebrain, one in each hemisphere. It has been described as the great relay station of the brain because most sensory information first goes to the thalamus, where it is processed and sent on to the cerebral cortex. 96, 102, 110, 122

thematic analysis A technique used when analysing qualitative data. Data is produced, for example from the transcripts of an interview or interviews, and then themes or categories are identified. 25, 35, 47, 58, 121, 151, 155, 158, 167, 175, 181, 206, 207, 213, 221, 225, 228, 229, 231

time sampling Count behaviours at regular intervals (such as every 5 seconds or 8 minutes), or take a sample at different times of day or month. 135, 158–159, 206–207, 208, 221, 223

triangulation Comparing the results from a number of studies, some of which are highly controlled (but more 'artificial') and some with low control (but more like everyday life). If the studies have similar findings this increases the likelihood that the conclusion represents something genuine (i.e. is valid). 188, 218, 229

twin study A study where twins are compared on a specific trait to see how similar they are. If a particular behaviour is entirely genetic then we expect MZ twins to show 100% concordance. If a particular behaviour is more genetic than environmental then we would expect MZ twins to show a higher concordance rate than DZ twins. 114–115, 123, 204–205

two-tailed hypothesis See non-directional hypothesis.

Type I error Occurs when a researcher *rejects* a null hypothesis that is true. 83, 89, 92, 105, 113, 123, 127, 149, 194, 201, 221, 225, 229

Type II error Occurs when a researcher *accepts* a null hypothesis that was not true. 83, 92, 105, 194, 221, 225, 229

unconditioned response (UCR) An unlearned response to an unconditioned stimulus. 8, 130–132, 148, 162

unconditioned stimulus (UCS) A stimulus that produces a response without any learning taking place. 130–132, 144, 146, 148, 162, 164

unconscious The part of the mind that we are unaware of but which continues to direct much of our behaviour. 21, 22, 23, 106–107, 123, 126, 145

unstructured interview No questions are decided in advance. 25, 53, 121, 178, 221, 231

use of controls Refers to the extent to which any variable is held constant or regulated by a researcher. 214, 224

validity Refers to the 'trueness' or 'legitimacy' of the data collected. 12, 22, 25, 35, 50, 51, 53, 55, 59, 61, 63, 65, 73, 75, 77, 83, 88, 89, 101, 103, 105, 107, 109, 115, 117, 122, 125, 133, 143, 149, 151, 153, 164, 168, 174, 180–181, 186, 188, 196, 198, 206–209, 214–215, 218–221, 222–225, 227, 228–230

vicarious reinforcement 'Reinforcement' refers to a consequence of behaviour that increases the likelihood of that behaviour being repeated. In the case of *vicarious* reinforcement, it is not directly experienced but occurs through observing someone else being reinforced for a behaviour. This is a key factor in imitation. 138–139, 142, 151, 156, 160, 165

virtual reality A computer-generated immersive environment that creates a lifelike experience. 146–147, 161

visual cortex A part of the occipital lobe that receives and processes visual information. 97, 122, 210, 223

visuo-spatial sketchpad (VSS) The component of the WMM that processes visual and spatial information in a mental space, often called our 'inner eye'. 68–69, 84, 88, 92

volunteer bias A form of sampling bias because volunteer participants are usually more highly motivated/have more time on their hands than randomly selected participants. This may mean, for example, that they respond more readily to demand characteristics. 170, 222

volunteer sample A sample of participants produced by asking for people willing to take part. 32, 50, 52, 170–171, 222, 228

wait list/waiting control group In an independent groups design one group acts as a control while the other receives treatment. The control group are on a waiting list and are given treatment at the end. 154, 161

Wernicke's area An area of the temporal lobe (encircling the auditory cortex) in the left hemisphere (in most people) responsible for language comprehension. 97, 122

Wilcoxon Signed Ranks test Test of difference between two sets of data. Data must be ordinal or interval (i.e. not nominal). Used for repeated measures or matched pairs design. Test statistic is T. 86–87, 167, 190–194, 201, 221, 225, 229

working memory model A representation of short-term memory (STM). It suggests that STM is a dynamic processor of different types of information using different subunits coordinated by a central decision-making system. 68–69, 71, 76–77, 84–85, 88, 91, 92

Acknowledgements

p6 Covers of Edexcel AS and A Level Psychology specifications, with kind permission of Pearson Edexcel; p32 Photo of Stanley Milgram by Eric Kroll. Reproduced with permission from Alexandra Milgram; p32 Milgram advert, Granger, NYC/ TopFoto.co.uk; p48 Image of Carolyn and Muzafer Sherif, reproduced with kind permission of Joan, Sue and Ann Sherif; p50 Photo of Jerry Burger, reproduced with kind permission of Jerry Burger; p51 Image of 'Death Game' © YAMI 2; p52 Photo of Alex Haslam and Steve Reicher, reproduced with kind permission of Alex Haslam and Steve Reicher; p52 Image of plan of the prison, reproduced with kind permission of Alex Haslam and Steve Reicher; p53 Image of BBC experiment, reproduced with kind permission of Alex Haslam and Steve Reicher; p76 Photo of Alan Baddeley, reproduced with kind permission of Alan Baddeley; p79 Photo of Heike Schmolck, reproduced with kind permission of Heike Schmolck; p80 Photo of Mark Steyvers, reproduced with kind permission of Mark Steyvers; p80 Data in graph, reproduced with kind permission of Mark Steyvers and Pernille Hemmer; p82 Photo of Maria Victoria Sebastián, reproduced with kind permission of Maria Victoria Sebastián; p110 Photo of Adrian Raine, reproduced with kind permission of Adrian Raine; p112 Graphs, Creative Commons BY-NC-SA; p115 Photo of Dr Mara Brendgen, reproduced with kind permission of Mara Brendgen; p117 Photo of Michel Van den Oever, reproduced with kind permission of Michel Van den Oever; p140–141 Two images of the Bobo doll and photo of Albert Bandura, reproduced with kind permission of Professor Albert Bandura; p151 Photo of Anne Becker, reproduced with kind permission of Anne Becker; p152 Photo of Brock Bastian, reproduced with kind permission of Brock Bastian; p154 Photo of Juan Capafóns, reproduced with kind permission of Juan Capafóns; p171 Photo of child, reproduced with kind permission of Philip Banyard; p177 The British Psychological Society logo and code of conduct text © 2018 British Psychological Society www.bps.org.uk; p181 Front page of study: Baddeley, A. D. (1966b) The influence of acoustic and semantic similarity on long-term memory for word sequences. *Quarterly Journal of Experimental Psychology*, 18(4), 302–309, copyright © 1966 SAGE Publications Ltd, reprinted by Permission of SAGE Publications, Ltd; p196 Phineas Gage artist impression, courtesy of Barking Dog Art; p197 Photo of Henry Molaison from PERMANENT PRESENT TENSE by Suzanne Corkin, copyright © Suzanne Corkin, 2013, used by permission of The Wylie Agency (UK) Limited.

Picture credits

Cover © Shutterstock / FotoAndalucia, Sebastian Kaulitzki

Shutterstock ©
p5 zandyz; p8 Valery121283, Alextype; p9 Daniela Staerk; p10 Nejron Photo; p12 Anneka, Artyzan; p13 Julien Tromeur, Studiostoks; p15 Lightwavemedia; p17 KlaraBstock, Kurhan; p18 Vladimir Gjorgiev; p19 Rus Limon; p20 studiostoks; p21 Fisher Photostudio, air009, Benny Marty; p22 Annykos; p23 nito; p24 ambrozinio, pzAxe; p25 Joe Gough; p29 Khakimullin Aleksandr; p34 Stokkete; p35 Nejron Photo; p41 Everett Art; p42 Clive Chilvers; p43 Ollyy; p48 RAphoto77; p49 Pavel Ilyukhin; p54 Iakov Filimonov; p55 The World in HDR; p56 azure1, 1000 Words; p57 Jane Rix; p58 Sergey Nivens; p66 Realstock; p71 Alex Mit; p72 Ruth Black; p73 Alex Zabusik; p74 Ammit Jack; p75 Alexander_P; p78 Sebastian Kaulitzki; p83 Rawpixel.com; p84 azure1, Rawpixel.com; p85 Cartoon Resource; p86 Gino Santa Maria; p87 ShandArt; p93 Realstock; p94 Oksana Telesheva; p96 Sebastian Kaulitzki; p97 Alex Mit; p99 Alena Ozerova; p101 ChameleonsEye; p102 Sebastian Kaulitzki; p103 Wavebreakmedia; p105 Nejron Photo; p106 vkilikov; p107 Click49; p109 Billion Photos; p111 sirtravelalot; p113 Pic2frames; p114 Gelpi; p116 Sebastian Kaulitzki; p118 azure1; p119 majivecka; p120 ruigsantos; p121 ALPA PROD; p128 Neil Lockhart; p130 chrisdorney; p137 charles taylor; p138 Bukhanovskyy; p139 Tinseltown; p143 agusyonok; p144 Bruno Passigatti; p145 SpeedKingz; p146 Halfpoint; p147 fizkes; p150 Indira's work; p152 Paul Stringer; p153 Everett Historical; p154 Fasttailwind; p155 Netor Rizhniak; p156 azure1, sakkmesterke; p157 Syda Productions; p158 Look Studio; p159 WAYHOME studio; p166 muratart; p168 Galushko Sergey; p169 Phovoir; p170 jan kranendonk; p173 eZeePics; p174 Stuart Miles, Liliya Kulianionak; p175 EQRoy; p176 Aleksandar Mijatovic; p178 rodnikovay; p180 lanych, kirbyedy; p182 marigo20; p183 Edward Fielding, kuroksta; p184 glyph ; p185 Simon Booth, catwalker; p187 mangostock; p188 Monkey Business Images; p189 Adam Gregor; p190 Denphumi, Bluezace; p191 pathdoc; p193 hase4Studios, Javier Brosch; p194 sirtravelalot, Michaelpuche; p195 Eder; p196 Bumble De; p197 rozbeh; p198 cobalt88; p201 PathDoc; p203 Triff, Nejron Photo; p204 Everett Collection; p205 Donna Ellen Coleman; p206 Lori Labrecque; p207 Rob Hyrons; p208 Javier Brosch; p209 phoelix; p211 Rocket Photos; p213 hurricanehank; p214 Potapov Alexander; p215 MaraZe, Vladimir Gjorgiev; p216 JRP Studio; p218 Arcady; p219 kurhan; p221 durantelallera; p222 rodnikovay; p224 Stuart Miles; p225 Stuart Miles, JRP Studio

Alamy ©
p26 Lorna Roberts/Alamy Stock Photo; p28 Everett Collection Inc / Alamy Stock Photo; p38 PhotosIndia.com RM19 / Alamy Stock Photo; p40 David Bagnall / Alamy Stock Photo; p41 World History Archive / Alamy Stock Photo; 47 Frans Lemmens / Alamy Stock Photo

Cartoonstock ©
p31 jmp090615; p36 bstn894; p37 mkan26_hi; p45 Mbcn3877; p46 Mban4748; p127 aban879; p202 wwe0732

Creative Commons licence
p133 photo of Pavlov; p148 photo of John Watson; p203 PET scan

Other illustrations © Illuminate Publishing